KNIVES 2009

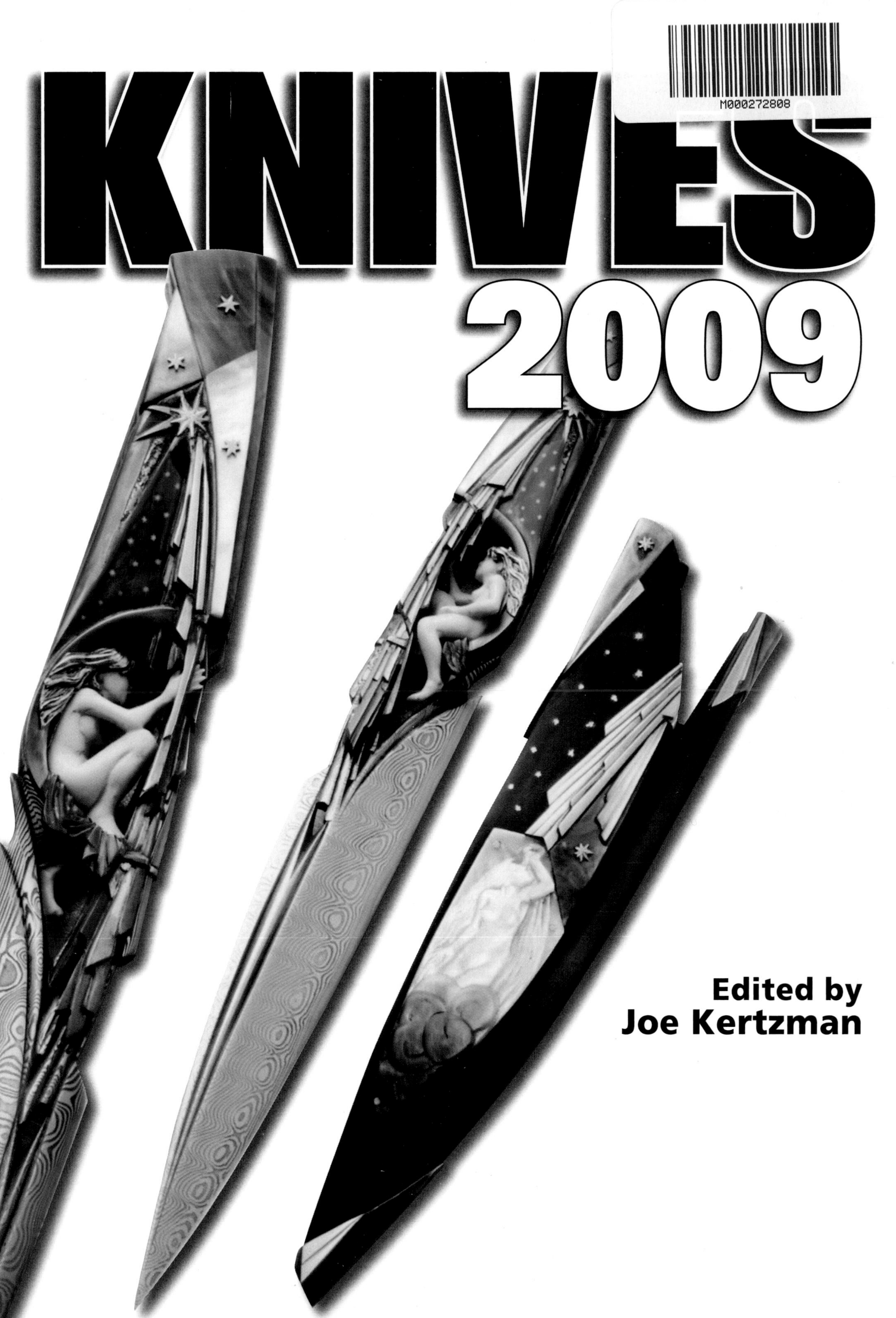

Edited by
Joe Kertzman

Published by

700 East State Street • Iola, WI 54990-0001
715-445-2214 • 888-457-2873
www.krausebooks.com

Our toll-free number to place an order or obtain a free catalog is (800) 258-0929.

ISSN 0277-0725

ISBN 13-digit: 978-0-89689-675-8
ISBN 10-digit: 0-89689-675-7

Designed by Kara Grundman
Edited by Derrek Sigler

Printed in the United States of America

Dedication and Acknowledgments

I've never dedicated the *Knives* annual book. No one has ever asked me to do so, and I didn't look upon it as my right as an author. Perhaps it is, and I feel honored. I'm honored mostly because I know who to dedicate it to—my wife, Tricia, who moved from Milwaukee, Wis., to Iola, a town of 1,300 people, so I could become associate editor of *BLADE Magazine*. I also dedicate this book to Steve Shackleford, editor of *BLADE*, who taught me the ropes and has an abundance of patience and talent. I dedicate the *Knives* annual to all of the editors and publishers who have given me a chance to hone my skills, including my current boss, who's more friend than supervisor, Paul Kennedy.

I dedicate this to my children, Danny and Cora, who would be lucky to meet as many fantastic people and be given as many opportunities in their lifetimes as I have in mine. Be good kids, and Dad loves you.

Acknowledgments are an equally painless process. Recognition and gratitude are extended to the knifemakers themselves, those who spend unimaginable, inhuman hours wrestling steel, forging it, pounding it, polishing alloys, carving knife grips, sanding, engraving and inlaying. They work for themselves but also for collectors and knife enthusiasts. Most knifemakers aspire to great art. They work to improve themselves and to build better tools. The results, and a reader needs only flip a few pages of this book to agree, are inspirational. The art shines through the utility of the edged objects.

The knives embody the American spirit, showcasing such traits as ingenuity, quality, greatness, worth and integrity. They represent people who are dedicated to improving the world, who wish to make quality products, but also those who appreciate the finer things in life, who have taste and hold high standards. These are knives that will undoubtedly make their owners proud, pieces of cutlery that take their place among display cases, shelves and art museums.

The photographers deserve recognition for their role in photographing the shiny steel, sans reflections and shadows, and holding them up to the light they deserve. Thank you one and all for allowing your art to be shared.

Joe Kertzman

On the Cover

Prettier than a sow's ear and more dangerous than a polecat are the cover knives chosen for this edition of the greatest book of blades in existence, *Knives 2009*. Starting, from left to right, with Wade Colter's locking-liner folder, it showcases a niter-blued damascus blade and bolsters with "fade away" coloring, and a carved ancient-walrus-ivory handle. Propped up against the pool cue beside it stands a .22-caliber, black powder, muzzle-loading pistol knife from the hands and mind of Bruce D. Bump. Features include a twist-pattern damascus blade, a preban ivory handle, Jere Davidson engraving on the bolsters, grip and spine, and a ramrod stored in the pommel. Doug Turnbull is credited for the charcoal bluing and the color case hardening of the pistol knife.

To its right leans the Ken Steigerwalt "Supreme Custom Dagger" sculpted from one solid slab of 440C steel and sporting a pin-shell handle with 18k-gold wire inlay, gold pins on the blade and handle, and a thin strip of stainless damascus following the curved bolsters. At far right remains Scot Matsuoka's colorful flipper folder parading a hollow-ground CPM-154 blade, a box elder handle, titanium bolsters engraved by C.J. Cai, and an anodized-titanium back strap in a vine file-work pattern.

Contents

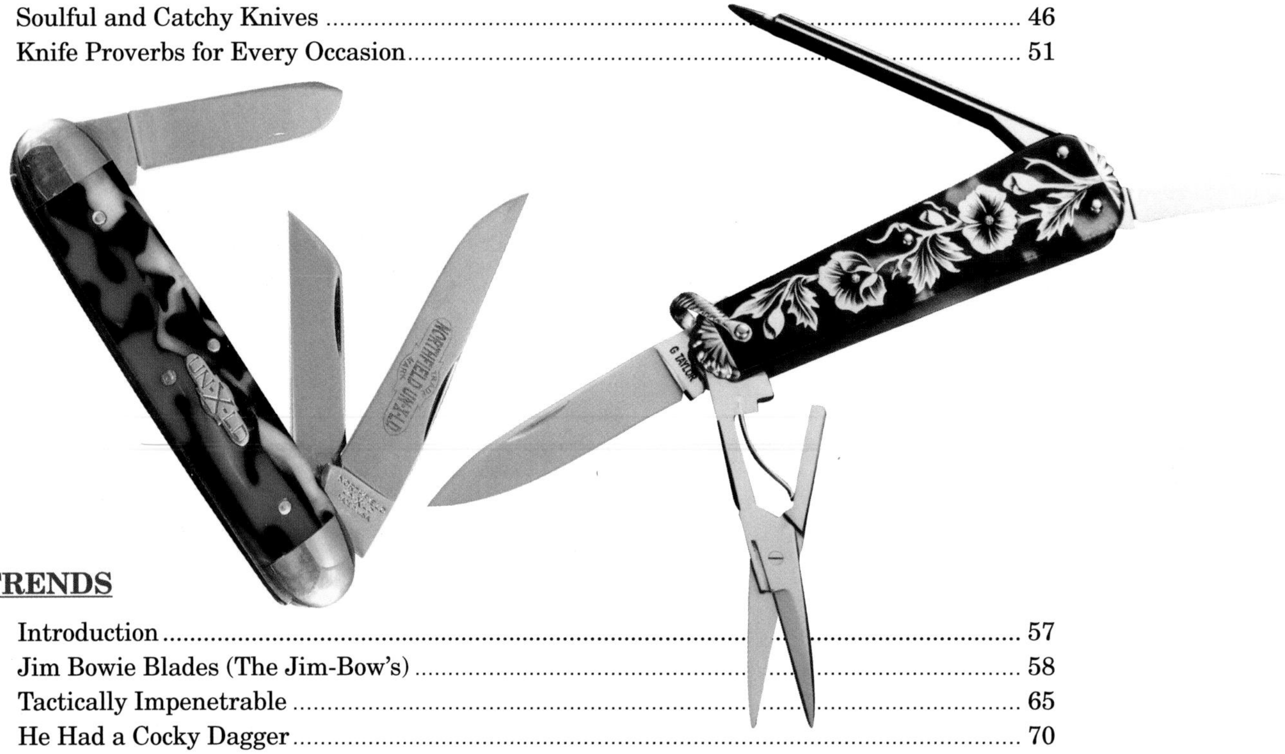

STATE OF THE ART

FACTORY TRENDS

DIRECTORY

Introduction

The knife industry is a welcome respite from a frenetic, fast-paced world. While automation, technology, the Internet, microcomputers, iPods and streaming video creep into ever facet of human existence, and the rest of the upload, download, crash and burn planet spins wildly out of control in an attempt to keep pace, a segment of society still polishes knife blades by hand.

A group of custom artisans tans, stitches and stamps leather sheaths, pins custom-made bolsters onto sanded wood knife handles, files liners and frames, engraves metal with handheld tools, scrimshaws ivory with needles and ink, and uses grinding wheels and belts to shape steel before rubbing it with incrementally decreasing grits of sandpaper until a sheen so bright winks back at them.

There are those who adorn their works of edged art with pearl and ivory, cutting gemstones into cabochon-shaped facets, setting them in gold and silver, inlaying wire, engraving precious metal and adding embellishments previously saved for the likes of kings, queens, masters and commanders.

While the world goes green, the prices of gas skyrocket, the polar icecaps melt, the politicians jockey for position and insurance companies, oil companies and drug companies report record profits, custom knifemakers buy more equipment, pay for show tables, research new materials and better steels, and, yes, some even take pictures and set up websites where they can exhibit their wares.

Even the knifemaker is affected by technology, mostly in a good way, through self-promotion, better tools and materials, steel that cuts longer and remains flexible enough to chop with, handles that withstand the elements yet parade arrays of colors only dreamed of a century ago, and Internet shopping that allows a craftsmen in Idaho to market his edged creations to an appreciative collector in Japan, New Zealand, Hong Kong or Columbia.

Rest assured, few knifemakers download Justin Timberlake songs onto their iPods for a few hours' work in the shop. And not many custom craftsmen use camera phones to share pictures amongst each other while forging mosaic-damascus sword blades. Only a select few text message their buddies in the middle of heat treating and quenching.

It seems they've found other secrets to societal living besides instant gratification and exotic vacations. They prefer historical perspectives, proven designs, exotic materials, creative thinking, individualism, craftsmanship, finely finished products and pride in ownership. Don't those seem like rare qualities today? Welcome to the world of knives, it's a fine land in which to live, a refuge from the brutality of modernism and a peaceful place to stop and rest, admire the surroundings and clear your head. There are too many things demanding our attention these days, and so few of them are as worthwhile as a handmade knife.

Now that the mood is set, the editor of *Knives 2009* encourages you to enjoy the feature articles penned by some of the world's most talented knife writers. Read about Murray Carter's Samurai-style blade-making school; hunting knives that are a notch above; the leanest, meanest tactical folders; why knife proverbs are ingrained in our very souls; how Mongolian dining knives deliver history lessons; about a magical unicorn knife; other edged creations that are millions of years in the making; and why Jim Schmidt remains such an influence more than a half-dozen years after his death.

In the "Trends" section of the book eager readers will find "Pristine Pocketknife Patterns;" "Stag-Handle Hotties;" a "Ti-Dyed Crowd;" "Points Encased;" "Furious Fighters;" "Blades of the Behemoths;" and the "Tortoise and the Ware." All lead to the "State of the Art" section where "Stone-Cold Cutters;" "Sharp Deco;" "Bountiful Blades;" a "Color Guard;" and a "Crazed Knife Carvers Convention" convene in one location, a simple setting, within the four-color pages of a classy knife book.

The book wraps up with a short section on "Factory Trends" and a directory of custom knifemakers, suppliers, photographers, dealers, wholesalers, clubs and organizations, their contact information, websites, email addresses and specialties.

Turn off the computer, mute the television, let the answering machine pick up the calls and slow down the heart rate long enough to enjoy a book about the best damn artistic hobby in the universe.

2009 WOODEN SWORD AWARD

It is 27 inches overall and is made completely of solid 14k gold, 22k gold, 24k yellow gold, oxidized sterling silver and fine silver. To be exact, the art dagger sports 4.175 pounds of solid 14k yellow gold and 3.62 pounds of sterling silver.

Fashioned by the renowned knifemaking team of Van Barnett and his beautiful wife, Dellana, the dagger showcases more than a thousand diamonds weighing in at 25 carats, and over 80 carats of natural, brilliant-cut rubies and cabochons. Dellana and Van say everything that appears black on the knife is nothing less than textured and anodized sterling silver.

The blade is 14k spring gold, stretches 19 inches overall, is hollow ground by hand and inset with diamonds and rubies. The guard and wings are solid 14k yellow gold. The entire piece can be disassembled by hand.

Yet that says nothing of the design. The design is breathtaking with a nearly heart-shaped, carved guard, a crown-shaped pommel, and diamond-shaped handle and sheath overlays. Everywhere there are jewels, gold and diamonds. This is an art dagger like no other before it. It is the piece de resistance, the coup de grace, the crème de la crème. It is the finest piece in a book filled with high art knives. It is the 2009 Wooden Sword Award winner, and there's no better candidate in the kingdom of knives.

To see photographs taken of the dagger at other angles, see the "Bountiful Blades" chapter in the "State of the Art" section of this book, *Knives 2009*.

Photo by Eric Eggly, PointSeven Studios

He Was The Master

Jim Schmidt was a peerless bladesmith—but that was just a part of what he meant to those whose lives he touched

By Steve Shackleford

For those unfamiliar with Jim Schmidt, he was one of the first master smiths of the American Bladesmith Society. For about a quarter century until his death in 2000, he crafted and sold some of the most impeccable handforged folders and fixed blades ever built. But this gentle giant of a man was much more than one of the best knifemakers who ever lived.

He was a loving husband to his soul mate and business partner, Linda. Together they built their home in Ballston Lake, N.Y., where they worked the land and raised their own farm animals.

In addition to making meticulous knives, he shared his ample knowledge with such contemporary knifemaking stars as Steve Schwarzer, Dellana, Barry Davis and others. He was instrumental in establishing the Ashokan bladesmithing seminar, perhaps the granddaddy of all knifemaking seminars, in Ashokan, N.Y.

Most important of all, he was a teacher of life and how to live it, how to interact with others and be a friend when a friend was needed, and to be a critic when a critic was needed.

Three Musketeers

Together with bladesmiths Jimmy Fikes and Don Fogg, Schmidt completes a legendary trio in the world of bladesmithing. "In the [1970s and early '80s] I was very fortunate to be included in monthly meetings at

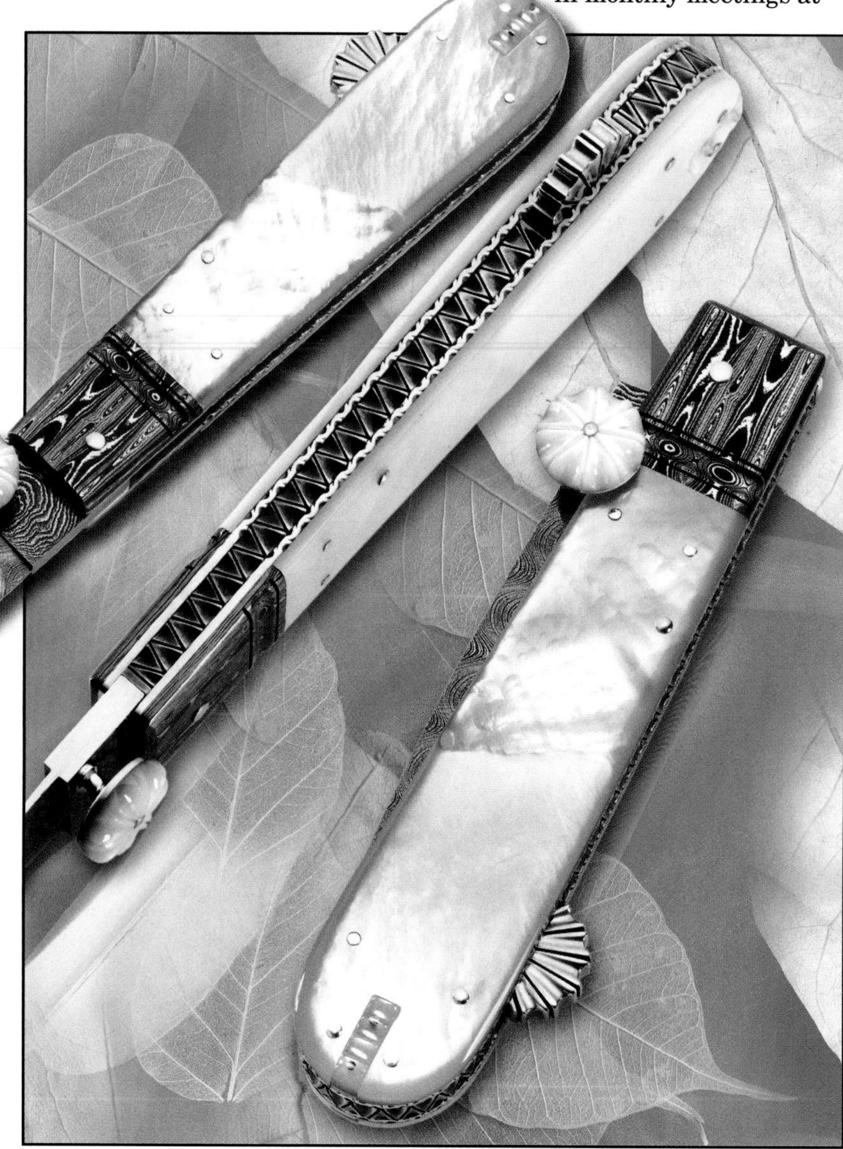

Collector Larry Marton says Schmidt's damascus had a kind of "iridescent ghost pattern" to it that few could reproduce. Though that iridescence may not stand out so much here, his Rainbow folder is an excellent example of what Dellana calls Schmidt's "flawless" damascus. *(from the Pierluigi Peroni collection; Peroni photo)*

The Goblin folder was one of the designs for which Schmidt was best known. The carved faces in the crown stag butt—some even had wagging "tongues"—served as a showcase for his playful side. He also named each of them. This one is "Cricket." *(from the Pierluigi Peroni collection; Peroni photo)*

Jimmy Fikes' house with Jim Schmidt," Fogg recalls. "I was the junior maker and often just sat and watched them tease each other. They were very competitive and each would do their best to outdo the other."

"Those three guys pushed each other along. The quality of their damascus, pattern welds and blade geometries set those guys ahead," Davis adds.

Fikes was more into how well his knives would perform, while Schmidt was more interested in seeing how great a knife he could create. "[Fikes] wanted to make a knife and test it," Davis explains, "while [Schmidt] wanted to make a knife and finish it. [Schmidt] was a renaissance man. He was an artist and one of his talents was making knives."

"Before Jim made knives he made flintlock guns, entire locking mechanisms, the butt plates, everything from scratch [and] with an eye toward design, Davis notes. "He had an extensive library of antique arms from all genres. He drew a lot of inspiration from historic designs. He did the research and tried to incorporate it in his work."

The decision to have a seminar at Ashokan came from one of the monthly meetings at Fikes'. "We felt that the only way bladesmithing was going to gain momentum was if we taught each other and demonstrated to the public," Fogg recalls. "In the early days [Ashokan] was a premier event and attracted everyone who was interested in the craft.

"It was the place to go to learn the craft," Fogg says.

It was at an Ashokan seminar in the early '80s that collector Larry Marton met Schmidt. "He was giving a seminar on filework," Marton remembers, "and I asked him about forging damascus and he said, 'It's not just a science, it's an art. You've got to do it.' He said next time you're here we'll make a knife together, and we eventually did."

"He was absolutely genuine," Marton says. "What you saw is what you got with him."

Marton tells of one show where a very famous person who collected knives approached Schmidt's table. The person told Schmidt he had "really wanted" one of his knives for a long time, and they talked about what the knife would be. The fellow wanted to know if Schmidt could have the knife ready in six months.

Schmidt looked down and in his slow, deliberate way, admitted that, due to his waiting list, it would be more like a few years. "The guy said, 'Money is no object.' Jim paused, looked down again and said, 'Money's no object to me either. I have a list and I have to go by it,'" Marton recalls. "I don't think that guy ever got his knife. That kind of captured who Jim was."

Schmidt was a big fan of premier makers and had no compunction about telling people at shows of the outstanding knives on other makers' tables, at the expense of his own work. "At a Solvang Show he said, 'Did you see that knife on Kaj Embretsen's table? You've got to go look at it. I'd like to think I could make it.' He was really excited about the skills of other makers," Marton stresses.

Perhaps at the top of the list of Schmidt's pupils is Dellana. A member of the Art Knife Invitational—an exclusive show that includes 25 of the world's elite knifemakers held every two years in San Diego—Dellana remembers Schmidt affectionately. In the early '90s, when she expressed an interest in making knives, he not only taught her how but he eventually opened his shop to her.

"He was really wonderful to me. It never seemed like he was too busy to teach me about folder mechanisms, to forge damascus and a lot about life, too. He was there during some difficult times for me. I always knew I had a place to go if I needed to," Dellana says.

Striving for Perfection

When it came to making knives, Schmidt strove for perfection in each and every one.

"He was fond of saying there was no such thing as close enough," Fogg relates. "Every year I would stop by to visit him at the New York show and I always took a close look at his work. Every year there was a noticeable improvement in the knives. He was fond of hiding details that could only be

Jim Schmidt

Don Fogg ***(left)*** **and, from right, Jimmy Fikes and Jim Schmidt at the 1981 Ashokan Seminar, are a legendary trio in the history of modern bladesmithing. The decision to have a seminar at Ashokan came from one of the monthly meetings at Fikes' house, meetings that included Schmidt and Fogg.** *(photo courtesy of Don Fogg)*

found on close examination."

"He got satisfaction out of making something interesting," Dellana says. "One time he made a Viking sword and added a small dagger to the pommel and waited three days before the collector discovered the dagger. Jim got a big kick out of that."

Schmidt's best-known knives are his Goblin folders, snake-handle Mediterranean dirks and his damascus folders. "The damascus folders were really his forte," Davis opines. "When I first met him, there were only two or three guys making them. Now you see them everywhere."

The Goblin folder got its name from the crown stag of the butt end, which Schmidt carved into the face of a goblin.

"I was there [at one of Fikes' monthly meetings] when the first Goblin 'peeked out' of its silk bag. Schmidt introduced the knife like it was a pet creature. It was marvelous," Fogg says.

"The Goblin folders were wonderful and really let Jim be playful. He had a real playful streak to him," Dellana says. "He would make their 'tongues' move. He got a kick out of making these toy-like things."

Schmidt did not forge elaborate damascus patterns but the damascus he created was always unblemished. "If there was any flaw in it he would throw it away," Dellana recalls.

Of all Schmidt's contributions to modern custom knives, perhaps the greatest was his reintroduction of the filework reminiscent of that on the late-19th-century knives of Sheffield, England.

"Jim was one of the first [modern] knifemakers to use filework to embellish his knives, and he developed hundreds of [filework] patterns," Fogg notes.

"He worked methodically, with precision, polishing the bottoms of every cut to enhance the drama in the design," Fogg adds.

Today, Schmidt's knives are highly valued by collectors worldwide. Since he made what by estimates were only about 300-400 knives, their limited number adds to the dollar amounts they fetch.

The values mentioned by informed sources include $15,000-$20,000 for one of his two-blade damascus folders and $25,000-$30,000 for one of his Viking daggers. "Last year at a show in Milan, Italy, I heard one of his pieces went for $19,000," one source observes. "In talking with dealers, I hear that if you can find one of his pieces for less than $15,000 you're lucky."

Hall-Of-Fame Bound? It is the feeling here that Jim Schmidt should be in the Blade Magazine Cutlery Hall Of Fame©.

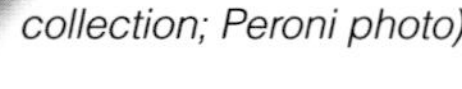

According to Barry Davis, damascus folders were Schmidt's forte. Early on, Schmidt did not use a surface grinder but rather handfiled the blades to make them fit just so in the handles of his folders. The fact that he went to such trouble is a fete in itself. The fact that the folders were the epitome of the genre is testimony to his brilliance. This is Schmidt's "Touch of Midas." *(from the Pierluigi Peroni collection; Peroni photo)*

The Startling Clean, Steely Icicle

Generations of gifted knifemakers have attached names to custom cutlery

By Amanda Anderson Sullivan

When my friend John Jensen asked me to help him with an article about how artists name their knives, it immediately piqued my interest—not only as a writer, but also on a very personal level.

Throughout my life I have always been deathly afraid of knives, but from the moment I was first introduced to John's work, I felt an entirely new reaction that both startled and thrilled me.

I wanted to handle and experience his knives, turn them over in my hand and examine every detail.

And there it is—John's knives aren't tools or weapons, they are beings, they have stories, they have names.

Turns out, my reaction to his work is just what John is going for as an artist—to dance down the line between danger and beauty, to juxtapose people's preconceptions about what a "knife" is with the concept of a knife as high art. John pushes boundaries.

He writes on his website, "For most people, however, it seems that knives symbolically represent war and violence, which often brings forth fearful emotions. This reaction makes the knife such an interesting platform of art to explore. One of the objectives of art is to challenge people's views. The art knife conceptually does just that."

A major theme in John's work is the ideology of dualism. "With every knife I make," he says, "I consciously work to infuse a balance between violence/aggression and beauty/harmony. I do this with the hopes of changing the way knives are perceived by the general public."

The author says she wanted to handle and experience John Lewis Jensen's knives, turn them over in her hand and examine every detail. It's a feeling she got from even the smallest yet still potentially-finger-removing switchblade, such as John's "Cello Ghost" model.

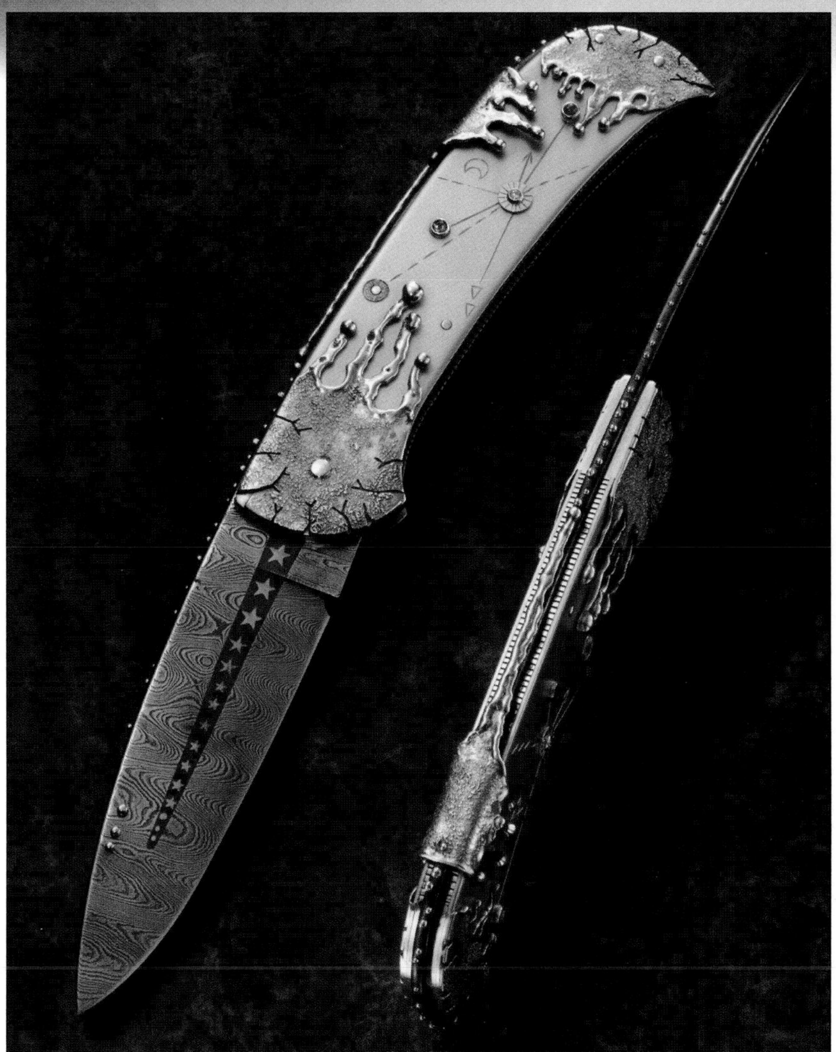

Dellana says her "Big Magic" lock-back folder is "fused, fabricated, bead blasted, engraved, textured, file worked and forged." It features a 324-layer, ladder-pattern damascus blade and a solid-14k-gold handle inset with diamonds, emeralds and Tanzanite. *(PointSeven photo)*

Knife Personalities

Every knife John crafts has not only its own characteristics, but its own personality.

It is easy to see why his "Icicle" model, a fixed blade stiletto, is so named. It is slick, with startlingly clean lines.

Icicle was created at a time when John was just beginning to work with asymmetrical designs. Originally, he was drawing up what he thought would become a dagger. His process is to draw one half of a piece along a center line, then hold the sketch to a mirror to see what it would look like as a whole symmetrical dagger.

With this piece, however, while he liked the shape he had rendered, it simply didn't work for him as a dagger. The piece wanted to be what John referred to as a "half dagger," a sleek, glacial blade tapered out from its simple handle—an Icicle.

To follow were a set of knives called "Stalactite Tears," a pair of fixed blade daggers commissioned by the collector who'd purchased Icicle. So enamored was the collector of the piece, he now wanted John to create an identical copy of Icicle so that he could display them side by side as a mirrored pair, a symmetrical entity.

Instead, he offered to make him a pair that that was intended to be one overall two-piece work, and look great together or individually. And they do. And it is easy to see how they merit their name, for stalactites are icicle-shaped, formed from the slow and steady dripping of mineral-rich water.

Last in this series, and one of John's favorite pieces to date, is "Krystallos." In creating this piece, John wanted to "max out" the ice/mineral theme of the series, making the design even more complicated and embellished.

Creating the bolsters of Krystallos required a highly specialized technique in which the actual grain structure of the titanium becomes visible to the naked eye through a complex heating process conducted in an oxygen-free environment.

The Mineral Moniker

What once was hidden from the naked eye becomes "crystal" clear. In another nod to the mineral, John mimicked the appearance of rutilant quartz in the mother-of-pearl handle scales. Rutile is a lustrous, dark-red titanium-oxide mineral that often forms needle-like crystal inclusions inside quartz that look like small bars of imbedded gold.

These shimmering shocks of light are alternately referred to as "Cupid's Darts," "Venus' Hair" or "Flèches d'amour." John recreated this veined look in what he calls "Rutilated Mother-of-Pearl." While many artists do find the naming of their pieces to be an integral part of the creation process, others place greater emphasis on the stories behind

Knifemaker Larry Fuegen crafted a gold and ivory forged scroll folder inspired by Hernan Cortes who sailed to the Mexican mainland in 1519 to conquer the Aztec empire in less than three years. The blade is hand-carved, ladder-pattern damascus with a heavy 18k-gold-plate finish. The handle is composed of carved mammoth ivory with walrus-ivory inlay. All fittings are hand formed from solid 18k gold.

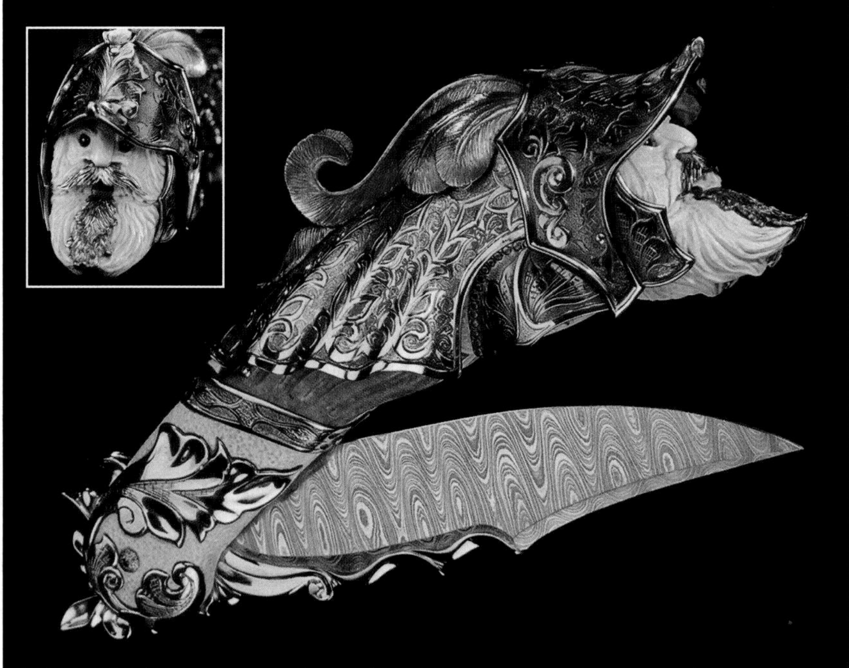

them. Vince Evans' pieces, for example, are inspired by originals and are then re-created while simultaneously following strict historical guidelines and maintaining his own identity as a smith in the 21st century.

Some of Evans' work is inspired by reading about great heroes of the past. He is currently working on an early British Celtic sword of the style that could have been carried during the era of Queen Boadicea.

"The antique swords inspire the work," he says; "the *stories* bring it to life."

To this point, knifemaker Larry Fuegan says, "I don't name all of my knives, only the ones that have a story to tell." He often names his mythology-inspired pieces.

"Sometimes names help create a mood or impression of the piece," Fuegan says. For example, Larry crafted a forged scroll folder from deer antler that became white from all the carving he did. He added ruby eyes to the piece and named the knife "Albino."

Recently, he has started to create a series of forged scroll folders that are inspired by ancient leaders and warriors. One of them, "Alaric, King of the Visigoths," is in the permanent display of the Smithsonian's Luce Center and Renwick Gallery.

Knifemaker Dellana says she started naming her pieces for two reasons. First, "It was something my late, great mentor, Jim Schmidt, did. He would think up interesting names as he worked and then write them on a cabinet he had next to his finishing area," she says. "This cabinet was covered with really interesting names.

"I don't name all of my knives, only the ones that have a story to tell." –Larry Fuegen

"When he'd finish a knife, if he didn't have a name thought up already, he would look through the names on the cabinet and find the perfect one for the knife and then cross that one off so he would know not to use it again," Dellana remembers. (For more on Jim Schmidt and Dellana, see the story by Steve Shackleford on Schmidt in this edition of *Knives*.)

Name That Series

Dellana had been a jewelry artist before becoming a knifemaker, and as such, she was used to working on a series of pieces. In these cases, it was the series that always had a name and a concept or story behind it. Each jewelry piece was not given a separate name, but was known as part of its family, one of a series.

She names her knives differently. "I don't have a name thought up ahead of time," she says. "The name comes to me as I work on the knife, usually toward the time it is finished. I feel like the knives name themselves, since it's rarely a struggle finding the right name—it just pops into my head and that's that!"

Dellana then engraves the name of the knife on the inside of the liner so that people will always know what it has been named. "It's hidden," Dellana notes, "but it is still a part of the knife."

Like Dellana's mentor, John keeps a list of potential names for his pieces.

My favorite knife-naming story is that of John's piece in progress, "Skinwalker." Perhaps I should say, "Skinwalker, The Haunted Knife," or, as John referred to it, "Oh, that devious little thing."

In Native American legend, a skinwalker is someone who posesses the supernatural ability to turn into any animal he or she feels like at any given moment.

Navajo tradition held that skinwalkers had the ability to steal the "skin" or body of another and that if you locked eyes with a skinwalker they could absorb themselves into your body.

Stuck with the Name "Skinwalker"

John pondered with me whether or not in naming this fighter Skinwalker he was, in a sense, opening a can of worms. Was he playing with fire, bestowing such a moniker on this knife?

"Skinwalker is definitely an opinionated knife," John tells me. Countless bizarre "tests" occurred in the building of him.

While John does keep a storehouse of fossilized beast teeth and antlers, rare gems, finely wrought metals and treasures from under the sea on hand, if the right piece isn't in his trove, he will invariably go out in search of precisely what each individual piece demands.

In the case of Skinwalker, John started with fossilized mastodon ivory for the handle. At first, it came out beautifully. But then, ever so slowly, it started to warp. It soon became so misshapen that the piece wouldn't stay on the handle at all.

Next, John tried composite black-lip pearl. But it, too, fought him. While one side of the handle came out beautifully, the other underwent a strange color shift from a lovely iridescent black to an ugly whitish hue.

John then turned to fossilized mastodon tooth. Everything seemed to be at last going to plan, up until when John was about 95 percent through with the work, and the piece suddenly snapped in half. Now, John finds he can only work on Skinwalker intermittently.

John's personal philosophy is that the spiritual goal of humanity is to find balance within all aspects of life. For him, this is what constitutes enlightenment.

"One-way to achieve this balance," he believes, "is to take opposing ideas and bring them into a place of union"—to tell the story of how great beauty and harmony can be embodied in what is all too commonly thought of as merely a potentially violent object. Part of how this is accomplished is by framing each piece with its own story, its own, unique name.

Indeed, it was Shakespeare's legendary Juliet who, in taking her own life by thrusting her beloved's "happy" dagger into her breast, asked Romeo (and us all) to consider, "What's in a name? That which we call a rose by any other name would smell as sweet."

Though I hate to argue with The Bard, I can't help but think that it just wouldn't be the same.

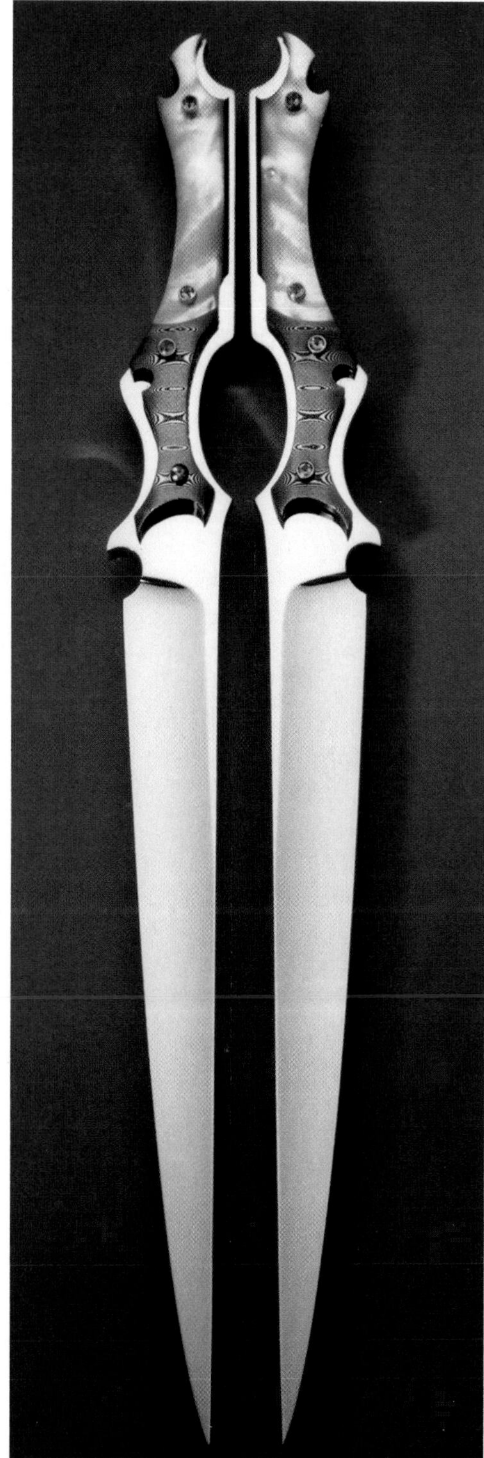

John Lewis Jensen's"Stalactite Tears" is a pair of daggers commissioned by a collector who'd purchased "Icicle." So enamored was the collector of the Icicle model, he wanted John to create an identical copy so that he could display the two knives side by side as a mirrored pair, a symmetrical entity. As all of John's pieces are strictly one-of-a-kind, he would not re-make an old knife. Instead, he offered to make him a pair that that was intended to be one overall two-piece work, and look great together or individually. And they do.

Dining Knives In Folds of Sashes

Knife sets offer a small glimpse into Mongolia's rich nomadic history and culture

By Leslie Jordan Clary
Photographs by Bob Clary

The coral-inlaid Mongolian knife and dining sets were discovered by the author while browsing in the Ulaan Bataar Antique Shop. Most such sets are each comprised of a sharp knife, a flint and steel, a set of ivory chopsticks and often a snuff box.

When I was young, the very name Mongolia conjured up images of a country about as far away from any place as you could possibly get. For that reason alone, I always wanted to visit. Last summer, I finally made it.

Mongolia is a great place to explore and almost all expeditions are outfitted from Ulaa Bataar, the capital city. While waiting for arrangements to be finalized for travel into the countryside, I spent my time visiting local museums and shops. Browsing through antique shops, I encountered some intriguing, utilitarian nomadic knife sets.

The knife sets are comprised of a sharp knife, a flint and steel, a set of ivory chopsticks, and often, a snuff bottle.

As I began to ask questions about the intricately-designed sets, I discovered that they were not only functional, but each one offered a small glimpse into Mongolia's rich nomadic history and culture.

Mongolians don't use pockets in their clothing, so all necessary utensils hang from their sashes.

The clothing accessories, called dells, are silk sashes several yards long and tied like belts. Any essentials, such as rope, tools or money pouches, are attached to the sashes by toggles or pins.

The eating sets hang from two silver chains with hooks.

Artistic Form and Skilled Craftsmanship

As a nomadic culture, Mongolians didn't build palaces or cathedrals. However, as an artistic and resourceful society, virtually everything they own shows a high degree of artistic form and skilled craftsmanship. This is especially true of the dining sets. Much of the craftsmanship has been absorbed from other cultures, especially China and Tibet.

At one time, both men and women carried the knife sets, but they were most often given as "coming of age" gifts when boys entered manhood.

Coral, turquoise, gold, silver and ivory were especially prized for decorating knife sets, which indicates the importance of trade in the land-locked country. The extent and quality of decoration was an important symbol of wealth and power.

Some knife sets are embellished with the "four literary pursuits" of the Chinese scholar: the seven-stringed *qin*, a musical instrument, the chessboard, a case of books and painting scrolls.

One set residing in the Museum of Mongolian History was made in 1918 for Ondor Gongor, a government bodyguard. The handle of his knife is decorated with the 12 animals of the Chinese zodiac shown against a background of lotus, mountains and waves.

Most of the decorative work on the knife sets uses one of the five following Mongolian motifs: geometric, zoomorphic, botanical, natural phenomena or symbols.

Nose-Like Knife Scrolls

Some of the zoomorphic depictions on the knife sets are slightly abstract, such as horn-like and nose-like scrolls inspired by animals like the yak, ram or bull. Others may include the "four friendly animals," which are the rabbit, elephant, monkey and dove; or the "four strong animals," the lion, tiger, dragon, and the mythical bird, the Garuda. The twelve animals that make

The Mongolian people live a nomadic life that is much the same today as it was a thousand years ago, with the possible addition of satellite dishes and motorcycles outside their yurts.

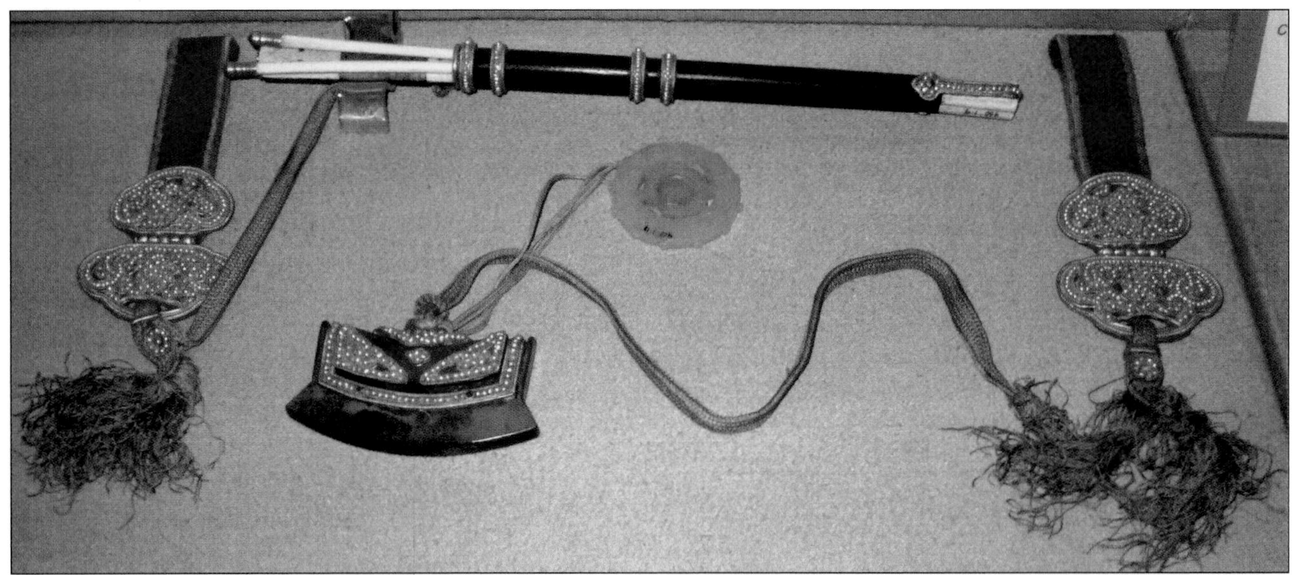

The elaborately beaded knife and dining set resides at the Mongolia National Museum.

The knife and ivory-chopstick set is from the National Museum of Ulaan.

up the Asian zodiac signs are also extremely popular.

Another symbol strongly inspired by Chinese philosophy is a circle made up of two fish that represent yin and yang, or balance, in the Taoist religion. One design commonly found on the knife handles is two dragons facing each other as an emblem of protection of the hearth.

In a country that is cold and dry with harsh storms for much of the year, botanical motifs are an important reminder of new growth and of coming spring. The lotus is one of the more commonly used plant motifs and represents purity. The lotus is also an important element in the artistic works in Tibetan Buddhism, which is Mongolia's major religion. A lotus is often depicted as a throne for the Buddha. Other plants have different representations: peaches mean longevity and the peony is for prosperity.

Motifs using natural phenomena are among the most prevalent depictions in Mongolian art and are commonly found engraved on the dining sets. These may be of water, flames, clouds, mountains, sun or moon. Figures from nature represent the cyclical nature of life and are considered to have mystical meanings. Natural phenomena are of great magnitude in Mongolian art and are often personified as gods.

Fire is a particularly popular motif, probably because of its importance in surviving the cold winters. A rising flame is used to represent cleansing, wealth and power. Three flames are used to signify the "eternal three" –past, present and future.

A symbol is probably the most abstract of the Mongolian ornamentations as all of the other four motifs may also be considered symbols. However, there are some symbols that are uniquely Mongolian, especially the one known as the Soyombo.

The Soyombo represents freedom and independence for the Mongolian people and has often been used on their national flags. It also incorporates parts of the other four motifs. The upper part of the Soyombo is the natural phenomena's three flames. Below that is the sun and moon, which represent the sky.

In Mongolia, the greatest deity of all is known as the Sky God and is interchangeable with the wide blue sky. Next come two triangles to represent the spear and arrow. They are pointed down to indicate defeat of enemies. Two horizontal rectangles are used to give stability to the round shape inside them. The rectangles stand for the honesty and justice of the Mongolian people.

The Chinese yin yang symbol mentioned under the zoomorphic heading sits between the rectangles. Finally, are two vertical rectangles that may be decoded as the walls of a fort. They represent unity and strength and are based on a Mongolian proverb: the friendship of two is stronger than stone walls.

Buddha Blades

Other patterns that draw strongly from the Tibetan and Chinese traditions come from Buddhism. One or more of the "Eight Auspicious Symbols" representing the eight attitudes of Buddha are frequently found on various objects of the dining sets. These are a conch shell, a lotus, a parasol or umbrella, a wheel, an endless knot, a pair of golden fish, a banner proclaiming victory and a treasure vase. Each of these symbols is imbued with meaning dates back to India and the rise of the Buddhist religion.

The Seven Jewels of the Monarch are also associated with Buddhism. The seven jewels are not actually jewels but rather the accessories of power that a king needs to stay in power. In Buddhism, the jewels are the tools of the Buddha and are often found in *mandalas*.

Three of the jewels are human: the queen, general and minister. Two are animals: the horse and elephant. One is a wheel, and another a jewel that is said to provide clairvoyance. While these images may have their origins in Tibet or China, in Mongolia they've merged with their own motifs to become uniquely Mongolian.

Probably the most famous Mongolian in history began his life as the son of an obscure village chief. He was named Temujin, and after his father was killed by Tartars, he was shunned and deserted by his people. As he struggled to survive, he grew skilled and strong, eventually emerging into a powerful warrior.

By the time he was a young man, Temujiin not only avenged those who disgraced him as a child but restored his position as head of his clan. At 28 years old, he earned the official title of "Genghis." Seventeen years later, he began to merge other powerful Mongolian tribes with his own and the unparalleled reign of Genghis Khan emerged.

Non-Mongolians sometimes

Mongolia's modern-day herders carry the knife and dining sets in dells, or silk sashes worn like belts.

think of Genghis Khan as a villainous warlord, a barbarian who mercilessly slaughtered hundreds of thousands of innocent civilians. In Mongolia, however, Genghis Khan is a national hero. He's seen as the man who united the disparate tribes, instituted a climate of religious tolerance that exists to this day and was, in fact, the precursor to democracy.

His image adorns the national currency. "Everywhere the Mongols rode, the present is haunted by the shade of Genghis," John Man wrote in his biography, *Genghis Khan: Life, Death, and Resurrection.*

Regardless of whether Genghis Khan was a hero or villain, there is no doubt that he had a profound impact on world history. While his conquests were violent and bloody, the aftermath of them resulted in a rise in trade—of goods, culture and communication. He built more bridges than any other world ruler in history.

While the pattern of most conquerors is to impose their own ideas and beliefs on the vanquished nation, in the case of Genghis Khan and the Mongolians, the defeated cultures were absorbed into their own. This is especially evident in Mongolian art and crafts. In the case of the Mongolian knife sets, unquestionably advanced jewelry techniques learned from other cultures were used to decorate knives, as well as flint and steel pouches.

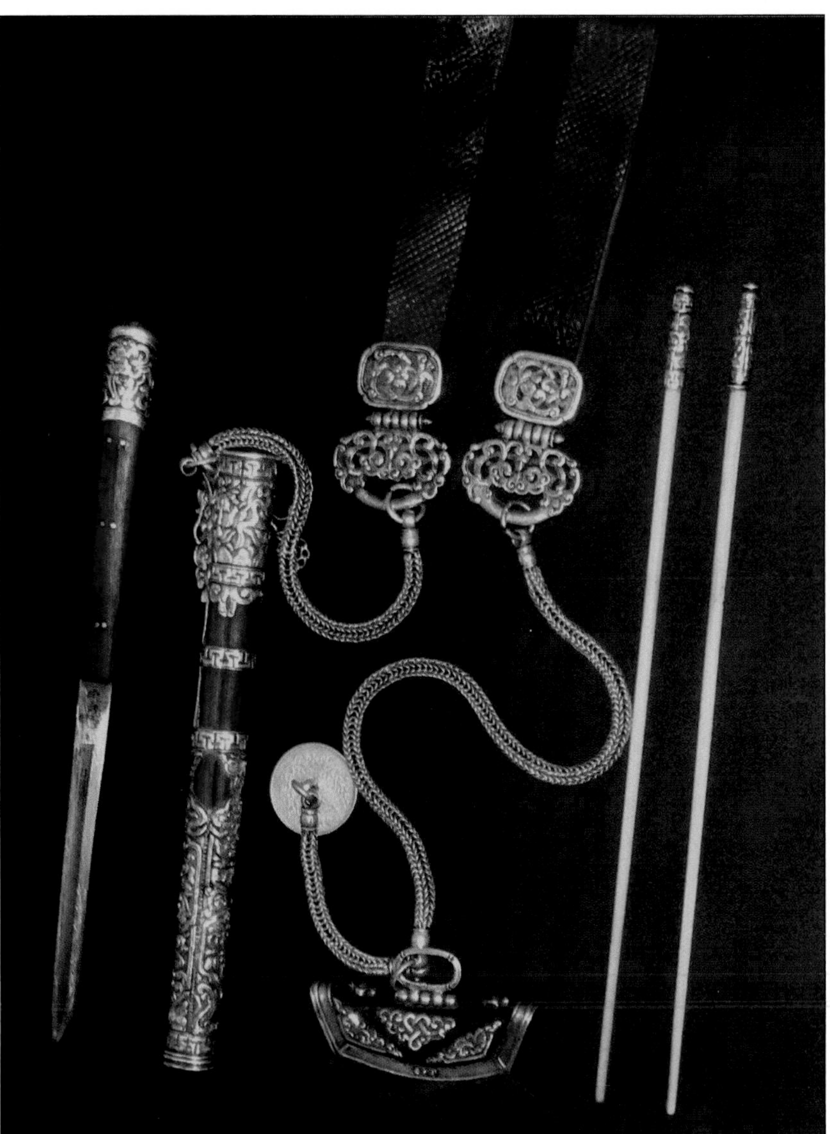

All the essential elements are accounted for in this impressive Mongolian knife and dining set.

Blades Burst Into Flame

Legends and folklore are intrinsically woven into the culture and daily life of Mongolia, so it's no surprise that, when asking local people about the history of their knives, one hears about ancient blades that burst into flame, glowed in the dark or put a curse on their enemies.

There are stories of magicians who forged blades from gold in the depths of the Khangai Mountains. Some claim that very special swords could sing songs that struck fear into their enemies. It is a fact that some depictions represent past events and are a form of written history from a people with no written language of their own.

A trip through Ulaan Baatar's National Museum provides a fascinating glimpse of the evolution from early crude bronze knives to the exquisitely decorated specimens that I encountered in Ulaan Bataar's antique shops. What I found most amazing is that there are still museum-quality examples of the art for sale in these shops. They range in price from about $200 up to several thousand dollars for the most elaborate. If one ventures into the countryside, it is still possible to find these knives and chopstick sets in use in remote areas of the country.

The Magical Unicorn Knife

Larry Fuegen's art knife is inspired by the sword of Charles the Bold

By Don Guild

One million dollars for a tusk? Yes, throughout history, monarchs and royalty paid just that. Here is the truth about a historical fairytale. And knifemaker Larry Fuegen, in his contemporary dissertation of an extravagantly expensive edged weapon, expresses composite evidence.

For many years the unicorn and the myths surrounding it

The Unicorn Dagger built by Larry Fuegen for Don Guild is built in the likeness of Charles the Bold's sword, but is not an exact replica. Among its many features are a narwhal-tusk handle (the closest one comes to unicorn horn) made in two sections with six individual panels, all held in place by an engraved and heavily gold-plated frame. The blade is hand-forged carbon steel, and the carved and engraved steel guard is heavily gold plated. *(SharpByCoop.com photo)*

Larry Fuegen copied engravings found throughout Charles the Bold's original sword scabbard and hilt that represent a flint-striker from which sparks and flames leap.

Knifemaker Larry Fuegen engraved an image of a unicorn beneath the amber window of the dagger handle, unlike the original sword that had an image of baby Jesus with his mother.

fascinated me. I enjoyed accumulating its lore and memorabilia and currently have three unicorn horns (OK, so they're actually narwhal tusks) from the fabled animal. Each time I cast my eye on one of them, I'm thrilled by their elegance, texture and ivory-like, spirally tapered shapes. In my pursuit of things unicorn, I uncovered tales, both strange and fantastic, and often thought of how sublime it would be to have an art knife made in the spirit of the unicorn.

A few years ago I looked for a knifemaker that could create one using the horn of the mystical unicorn. My thoughts turned to Larry Fuegen, a superb artist as well as a history buff, whose exacting approach to his art knives has landed his work in the permanent collection of the Smithsonian Institution.

I see Larry Fuegen as the Ralph Lauren of couture knifemakers. He grew up on a ranch and, somewhere along the line, acquired impeccable taste. Being a history nut since childhood didn't hurt. His lifetime fascination with the arms and armor of antiquity helped develop his sense of appropriateness in design.

His work reflects his favorite art style, Art Nouveau, exemplified in his trademark of organically rendered carvings in steel and ivory. Sole authorship has been his creed and banner since his first knife in 1975. He does it all, including engraving, forging, carving, heat treating—the whole tamale. Larry is the best. He's in such demand a collector must wait three years for one of his knives. Few makers research a theme as he does, and his knives have integrity of expression from design to fineness of finish.

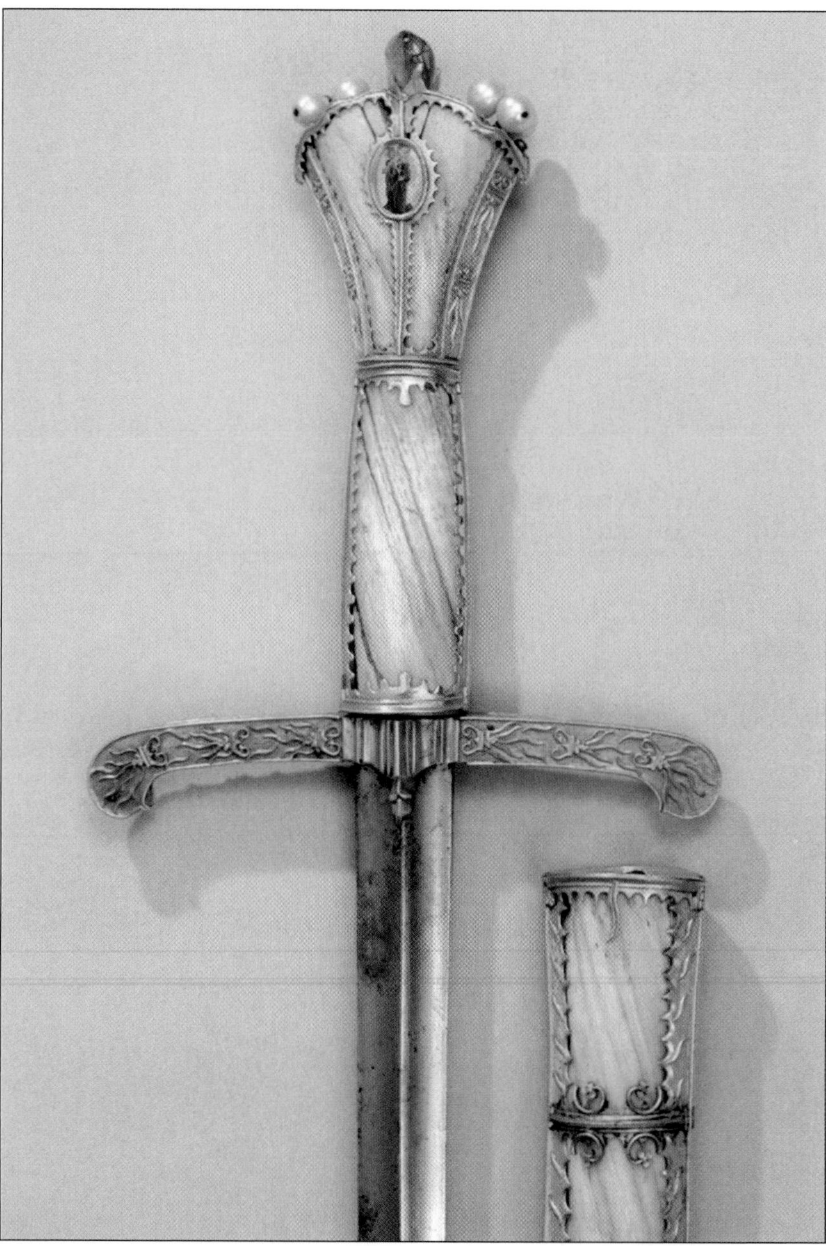

When the author of this article, collector Don Guild, commissioned knifemaker Larry Fuegen to build him a unicorn-themed art knife, Fuegen began researching unicorns and unicorn-based weaponry and art knives. His research uncovered a sword—the original shown here—built for Charles the Bold and currently housed in the Kunstverlag Museum of Vienna. It is purported to have a hilt made from unicorn tusk (undoubtedly narwhal tusk).

I knew he would be the right man for the job, so I contacted Larry to see if he'd be interested in making a knife with a unicorn theme. He responded with such enthusiasm, I said, "Go for it," and sent him several books about the unicorn along with gleanings from my files.

After searching and digging in archives, Larry unearthed the existence of a large sword created for The Duke of Burgundy, and found that it is currently owned by the Kunstverlag Museum of Vienna. He collected photographs along with historical records and learned that the sword's handle

The Duke of Burgundy, also known as Charles the Bold, Europe's most powerful ruler during the Middle Ages, was sitting around thinking how he could cook up a little immortality, when the idea popped into his head to commission the world's finest sword. It had to be the best the world had ever seen, because in the year 1449, a monarch's personal weapon was a symbol of power and wealth. Gold or elephant ivory was commonly used, but Charles wanted the world's grandest and most expensive material for his sword's handle and scabbard. To use unicorn horn that commanded a price at least 10 times its weight in gold was a slam dunk!

and scabbard were purportedly made from a unicorn's horn.

As the story goes, The Duke of Burgundy, also known as Charles the Bold, Europe's most powerful ruler during the Middle Ages, was sitting around thinking how he could cook up a little immortality, when the idea popped into his head to commission the world's finest sword. It had to be the best the world had ever seen, because in the year 1449, a monarch's personal weapon was a symbol of power and wealth.

The sword had to be impressive, not like the stuff of the other power-guys who ruled huge hunks of Europe. Gold or elephant ivory was commonly used, but Charles wanted the world's grandest and most expensive material for his sword's handle and scabbard. To use unicorn horn that commanded a price at least 10 times its weight in gold was a slam dunk!

The Illusive One-Horned Beast

A number of legends circulated about the magnificent, mystical and illusive one-horned beast, including the belief that powdered unicorn horn was the most powerful poison antidote available. To catch a unicorn was tricky business.

Artists throughout medieval and renaissance times, like Albrecht Durer, Raphael Santi and Leonardo da Vinci, depicted the unicorn in religious tones. Perhaps the most famous works are the seven Belgian tapestries woven in the late 1400s, measuring 12-by-14 feet each, hanging in The Cloisters of the New York Metropolitan Museum of Art and bequeathed by the wealthy John D. Rockefeller Jr.

The tapestries illustrate how to capture a unicorn: Seat a virgin in a meadow to attract a unicorn; when the beast appears, it circles the meadow until it comes to rest with its head in the virgin's lap, and finally falls asleep. Then the hunters come forth with their dogs and spears to capture the unicorn and sever its magical horn. Virgins, unlike today, must have been plentiful in the 15th century.

The earliest records of a one-horned beast appeared in Chinese art and literature about 2800 BC, and by 1000 AD, spirally-fluted horns made their way to Europe through China and India and spread the legend of the unicorn's horn with its healing powers. The unicorn symbolized purity, chastity and the embodiment of Christ Jesus.

Because of these qualities, a poisonous lake or stream was reputedly rendered pure when a unicorn dipped his horn into it.

After building the Unicorn Dagger, Larry Fuegen felt that a forged scroll folder offered unique opportunities to incorporate the symbolism that was involved with the sword and dagger and bring Charles the Bold's personality to light.

The engraved sterling silver helmet of Larry Fuegen's scroll folder, with the moveable visor and gold trim, were patterned after armor that would have been available to Charles the Bold.

Since poisonings were frequently perpetrated by relatives to speed up gaining their inheritance, personages of royalty and wealth kept powdered unicorn horn close by at all times.

The healing and purifying image of the unicorn horn prevailed for many centuries, and even today one can find pharmacies in Germany and England that display a unicorn image on their storefronts.

The famous Unicorn Tapestries were woven half a century before Queen Elizabeth the First, who also paid today's equivalent of a million dollars for a unicorn horn, and thereafter she lived a long and poison-less life. Today, the unicorn and the lion are represented on the British Coat of Arms, and one finds them on official buildings, documents, currency and stationery.

In 1587, not to be outdone by former monarchs, Christian V of Denmark nearly broke his royal treasury when he commissioned the most expensive throne ever made—one that incorporated 200 pounds of pure gold and ten unicorn horns. Did it top Charles the Bold's sword? No way!

The Unicorns of the Sea

A few horns made their way to Europe over the centuries, giving rise to the belief they came from the fabled unicorn. So, what about this fabled unicorn? Was it? Or wasn't it? Norsemen and Vikings, the only ones bouncing around in the frigid north seas in the Middle Ages, found horns protruding from the heads of certain whales (narwhals) that plied the waters of Greenland and the Baffin Bay.

When word of unicorn horns reached the Norsemen, the entrepreneurial explorers reasoned, "These things might be worth something," and once they realized the tusks of the whales had value, they whisked them off to Europe and developed a brisk trade, representing them as horns of the fabled and mysterious unicorn.

Narwhal horns sold like hot cakes for 600 years at huge profits. Considering that the tusks had first been acquired from the natives for a few iron nails, the scam goes down in history as one of the world's largest and longest swindles. "Mum's the word," they said to their fellow entrepreneurs, "and if you tell our secret that they're actually the horn of a 15-foot whale, you'll be stretched and drawn until dismembered." By the mid-1700s the magic had blown off because the scam was exposed, and the value of a unicorn horn dropped precipitously.

For Fuegen's proposed Unicorn Horn Dagger, inspired by the Sword of Charles the Bold, I sent a large piece of narwhal tusk to Larry, who said, "It's perfect for this project." After we conferred on several of his drawings, he was off on a venture to make a dagger in the likeness of the original large sword, but not as an exact copy.

For instance, he engraved an image of a unicorn beneath the amber window of the dagger handle, unlike the original sword that had an image of baby Jesus with his mother. The resulting dagger and sheath are beyond compare—with the spiral-horn as their main focus.

Larry described his work for my knife: "The dagger used a construction method similar to the original sword. Due to the diameter and the natural spiral of the narwhal tusk, the handle is made in two sections with six individual panels, all held in place by an engraved and heavily gold-plated frame.

"The blade is hand-forged carbon steel," Fuegen continued, "and the carved and engraved steel guard is heavily gold plated. The fittings on the original sword appear to be gilded. This process is not used today because of environmental hazards. Gold plating is a close alternative."

And a River-Washed Ruby Pommel

For authenticity, all materials used in the original sword were duplicated as closely as possible. Larry used gold, amber, natural pearls, narwhal tusk and carbon steel, and he found a natural river-washed ruby that he mounted on the pommel (like the one used in the original sword).

He also copied engravings found throughout the original sword scabbard and hilt, based on Charles the Bold's Order of the Golden Fleece [still an order of honor], that represent a flint-striker from which sparks and flames leap.

According to Fred Bruemmer's description of the narwhal in his book *The Narwhal—Unicorn of the Sea,* it is a small whale found in the Baffin Bay of northeast Canada. The tusk, actually the male's left tooth, pierces the lip, and grows to an average length of six feet.

By Canadian law, the Inuit Indians are allowed to take up to 500 narwhals a year (40 or so per village) to provide themselves with food. The Inuits utilize the tusks and bones as structural materials due to their lack of wood. Since 1976, it has been illegal to import narwhal tusks into the United States, even though narwhal numbers have gained to approximately 40,000 in the last few decades.

"After doing research for the dagger project," Larry said, "I felt that a forged scroll folder offered unique opportunities to incorporate the symbolism that was involved with the sword and dagger and bring Charles the Bold's personality to light. I had been doing a series of forged scroll folders that revolved around historical figures from the 1300's onward—Barbarosa, Alaric [the folder accepted into the Smithsonian's permanent collection], Timur the Lame and Hernan Cortez for example."

Larry continued: "The ruby, pearls and engraved designs, such as the engraved imagery of flint/striker/sparks, were used on the original sword, and were symbols associated with the Order of the Golden Fleece, a Medieval order of Knights. The engraved sterling silver helmet of my scroll folder, with the moveable visor and gold trim, were patterned after armor that would have been available in that period of history to Charles the Bold.

"The carved, white-mammoth-ivory horsehair accent of the folder represents the magical unicorn's tail. The unicorn figured prominently in medieval society, and narwhal ivory was believed to be the fabled horn of a unicorn, possessing magical powers. The copper cape is stipple engraved to represent a heavily brocaded fabric common to the times."

Fuegen's research and artistry have resulted in a beautiful folding knife and a splendid 16-inch dagger that would have made Charles the Bold proud. Larry's creations are a harmonious complement to the monarch's majestic sword.

I keep Fuegen's classical dagger close at hand, so it's reassuring to know that if my third cousin's nephew adds hemlock to my cocoa, I can take a bite out of my Unicorn Dagger's handle and live.

Hunting Knives a Notch Above

The world's finest custom craftsmen lend their design expertise to factory hunting knives

By Durwood Hollis

Known for his sleek, graceful and well-balanced knife designs, Tom Mayo's artistic ability and his attention to detail are clearly manifest in his design collaborations with Buck Knives. Featuring a skeletonized-titanium handle, an incredibly strong frame-lock mechanism, a CPM S30V stainless steel blade and ergonomic contours, the Buck Knives "TNT" is based off of Mayo's most popular folder.

If you're a knife enthusiast, then you've probably had the desire at some point in time to own a custom knife. The problem is, unless you have more funds than good sense, most custom knives are beyond the means of an average working man.

Caught between the desire for a custom cutter and any reasonable way justifying such an expense, the dream of obtaining that "special" knife can slip away.

Rest assured there is a way out of the dilemma. For some time, production knife manufacturers and importers have been collaborating with custom knifemakers. This provides the factory the opportunity to include a custom-designed knife in its product line, as well as exposing the work of handmade knifemakers to a wide audience.

Looking at the product lines of prominent knife manufacturers quickly demonstrates just how advantageous it is for knife buyers to look closely at custom collaborations. Rather than paying a high price for a custom knife, it is possible to purchase a knife designed by a well-known maker for far less than an original, handmade piece would cost.

Benchmade keeps an entire stable of custom knifemakers, including Mel Pardue; Ken Steigerwalt; Neil Blackwood; Mike Snody; Armin Stuetz; Steve Fecas; Warren Osborne; Bill McHenry; Jason Williams; and Bob Lum. While each has contributed his own expertise to Benchmade knives, it was Lum's

"Dejavoo" folder that garnered the 2006 Knife of the Year® Award at the BLADE Show.

Growing up in Astoria, Ore., Lum hunted and fished the Pacific Northwest from an early age, giving him a real appreciation for fine knives.

"Designing knives is one of the best parts of knifemaking to me. I enjoy using my creative ideas to make a high-quality product," Lum says.

The Dejavoo folder, available in two versions, is certainly a unique design that has its own elegance. At its core is a marvelously tapered CPM S30V stainless steel blade, ground all the way to the top for enhanced slicing. This knife can further boast a phosphor bronze washer at the main pivot pin, titanium locking liners incorporated into the ergonomic G-10 handle scales and a simplicity of design combined with peerless execution.

Benchmade is able to produce the Dejavoo for far less than what is would cost to order a similar knife from Lum.

Hunt with a Lightfoot

While BladeTech is probably best known for its extensive line of Kydex® pistol holsters and other law enforcement and military accessories, the company also makes some fine hunting knives. BladeTech has collaborated with custom knifemaker Greg Lightfoot to produce one of his designs.

This compact Spyderco fixed blade (Model FB01), designed by the late Bill Moran, features a slightly upswept trailing-point blade of VG-10 stainless steel and a synthetic handle with non-slip Kraton inlays.

BladeTech President Tim Wenger has hunted all over the world, and he was quick to recognize that Lightfoot's folding hunter was a great, edged game-care tool. The result is the "Rijbak" model.

The new folder features a 3 ¾-inch, CPM S30V stainless steel blade with a V-hole for ease of one-hand opening. An integral titanium locking mechanism is situated within the black G-10 handle scales, and a carbon fiber handle overlay provides enhanced gripping.

Without the BladeTech collaboration, Lightfoot would only be able to produce enough knives to service the needs of a select few, but the large-scale manufacturing capabilities of the company make his fine lock-blade folder available for everyone.

Tom Mayo's distinctively designed knives have been coveted by collectors and knife users alike for many years, so when Buck Knives first gave thought to a collaborative effort with a custom knifemaker, Mayo's name quickly rose to the top of a very short list.

Inspired by the work of famed knifemakers like Bob Loveless, Bo Randall and others, Mayo developed his own distinctive knife designs. And in time those creations garnered international attention and acclaim.

The knife that came from the initial joint venture with Buck Knives is one of Mayo's most popular designs, a frame-lock folder with a titanium handle and a CPM S30V stainless steel blade. If that knife was purchased directly from the maker, it would cost $550. However, Buck Knives was able make a production version to Mayo's specifications that has a suggested retail price of $320.

Two other Buck/Mayo collaborative knives are even more affordable. The Buck/Mayo "Cutback," with a 420HC stainless steel blade and titanium-coated handle, is priced at a surprisingly low $47. The slightly larger "Hilo," with similar features, carries a retail price of $54.

Northwest Knife Territory

Based in the Pacific Northwest, Columbia River Knife & Tool (CRKT) has a bevy of custom knifemakers with which to collaborate, including Jim Hammond; Ed Van Hoy; Ed Halligan; Brian Tighe; Allen Elishewitz; Lightfoot; Pat Crawford; Kit Carson; Mike Franklin; and Russ Kommer.

Kommer, a former Alaska resident, now lives in Fargo, N.D. He has held a commercial hunting guide's license since 1980, spending most of his time guiding in Alaska. When one of his clients showed up in camp with a custom hunting knife and field-dressed a moose without ever sharpening the blade, Russ decided to learn how to make knives.

In 1997, Kommer began making his own line of knives. His goal was "to make a quality knife that would perform and be comfortable to handle." He quickly garnered the attention of the folks at CRKT, who liked his designs for one reason—they work. More than a dozen of Kommer's knife designs can be found in the latest CRKT catalog, and every single one priced well within a working man's budget.

A new player in the cutlery game, DiamondBlade introduces a unique Friction Forging blade edge process, as well as a new knife model designed by American Bladesmith Society master smith Wayne Goddard.

Capitalizing on his field experience, Greg Lightfoot (shown here with a trophy wild boar) designs knives that are both functional and comfortable to use. The BladeTech/Lightfoot "Rijbak" is a lock-blade folder that's the perfect tool for field dressing and skinning game, as well as all-around hard use.

While Goddard has years of experience as a knifemaker, his only previous collaboration was with Spyderco.

"I've only participated in a collaborative project once. While discussions have taken place over the years about other involvements, there wasn't anything new in the cutlery industry that interested me," Goddard explains. "That is, until I tested one of the DiamondBlade Friction Forged knives. The results of that process were so remarkable I wanted to be part of the new technology. Subsequently, the folks at DiamondBlade produced a traditional fixed-blade hunting knife that I designed for them."

Goddard's Friction Forged Traditional Hunting Knife not only features a simplistic design, it also combines tradition with a peerlessly performing edge. Featuring a clip-point D-2 blade with a full tang, the knife is offered with a choice of a stag, desert ironwood, Micarta® or G-10 handle. The Friction Forged knife is all you could ever ask for in a fixed-blade hunter. It starts out sharper and stays sharp longer than any competitive edged product.

"In the hands of an average deer hunter that takes one or two deer a year, the edge on my new Friction Forged Traditional Hunting Knife probably won't need to be re-sharpened for up to 25 years." Goddard said.

Sidewalk Sharp

One of the most respected custom knifemakers in the industry is Ken Onion. Ken received his first knife when he was only five years old. His dad ground off the point

World-renowned knifemaker R.W. "Bob" Loveless partnered with Lone Wolf Knives to produce several of his designs at affordable prices. Currently, Lone Wolf catalogs two of Loveless's classic fixed-blade designs, the "Classic Utility" (shown) and the "Semi-Skinner." Both pieces are priced below $200.

and made the knife as dull as possible. When Ken restored the point and the edge by countless hours of hard work on a concrete sidewalk, he dad had to confiscate the knife and make it dull again. That was all it took to get Ken interested in making knives.

In 1991, Ken met Stan Fujisaka, a talented knifemaker, who taught him how to make fixed-blade knives. From that point on, Onion has been deeply involved in knifemaking and knife design. Onion's knives can be found in several prestigious cutlery collections. However, his collaboration with the folks at Kershaw Knives has made many of those designs available at factory prices.

Most notable among his many innovative creations is the SpeedSafe® assisted-opening system built into several of Kershaw's best-selling folding knives. The system employs a torsion bar to keep the knife blade closed. The user simply has to apply pressure to the thumb stud situated on the blade to overcome the torsion bar resistance and instantly deploy the blade.

Without a doubt, R. W. Loveless is the most famous knifemaker alive today. A southern California resident, Loveless has been making knives for over 50 years. Recently, one of his knives was sold for more than $200,000. And there is a line of collectors ready to purchase every knife that comes out of his Riverside, Calif., shop.

Affordable Loveless Knives

Recently, Loveless partnered with Lone Wolf Knives to produce several of his designs at affordable prices. This led to the development of proprietary high-carbon knife steel, enhanced with molybdenum and vanadium for flexibility and added edge retention, to be incorporated exclusively on Lone Wolf, Loveless-designed, fixed-blade knife models.

The new partnership places actual Loveless-authorized knives, in the hands of customers at an affordable price point.

"Now you can get a knife that I have authorized to be built because the design, materials and overall quality is something I am proud of," Loveless said.

Currently, Lone Wolf catalogs two of Loveless's classic fixed-blade designs, the "Utility" and the "Semi-Skinner." Both pieces are priced below $200, and that's a real bargain in my book. In Loveless's own words, "I want my knives in someone's hands, not in a museum." Certainly, the folks at Lone Wolf have made that a reality.

When it comes to collaborative efforts, Spyderco has been a leading force within the knife industry. Among its many knife designs are those that originated with such custom makers as Ed Schempp; Chad Los Banos; Jason Breeden; Ralph Turnbull; Fred Perrin; R.J. Martin; Jerry Hossom; and famed knifemaker Bill Moran.

Like all boys, knives fascinated young Moran. While it occasionally occurred to him to attempt to make his own knife, it wasn't until he was in his mid-teens that he first experimented with knifemaking. As an adult, Moran's knife work brought both artistry and character to the steel forge. Moreover, he was instrumental in opening the first blade school in the world for knifemakers.

Sadly, in 2006, the cutlery industry lost a trendsetting pioneer with Moran's passing. During his lifetime, many of his knives sold for multiple thousands of dollars. Since his passing, the price of those remaining knives has continued to increase. However, Spyderco produces two of his most outstanding designs, the Moran "Upswept Fixed Blade" and the Moran "Drop-Point Fixed Blade," at an incredibly affordable price point.

The knives feature VG-10 stainless steel blades, molded ergonomic handles with Kraton® inlays and Kydex sheaths with a five-position Tek-Lock® fasteners. Either of the knives is an outstanding, edged game care tool that any big game hunter will treasure.

In recent years, many custom-built knives have become works of art, rather than something an individual would actually use in the field. In most instances, that wasn't the intent of the knifemaker. Even so, you now have a choice.

You can either order a custom knife directly from the maker, or you can simply purchase one of the many readily available custom/production collaborative knives at a far lower cost. I don't know about you, but my wife has already made that choice for me.

Wayne Goddard, shown here with a couple of his own custom-made knives, has recently collaborated with a new player in the cutlery game, DiamondBlade, on the "Friction Forged Traditional Hunting Knife" (not shown). The new DiamondBlade piece features a clip-point D-2 blade with a full tang, and a choice of a stag, desert ironwood, Micarta® or G-10 handle.

Designed by Ken Onion, the Kershaw Tyrade features the SpeedSafe® assisted-opening mechanism, employing a torsion bar to keep the knife blade closed. The user simply has to apply pressure to the extended tang of the blade, when the knife is in the closed position, to overcome the torsion bar resistance and instantly deploy the blade. Designed for use where one-handed folding knife opening is safe and preferable, the Onion design is a benchmark accomplishment in the cutlery industry.

Confederate Edged Weapons: Rare and Valuable

A mostly non-industrial South did a remarkable job of putting fighting blades in the hands of its men

By Edward Crews

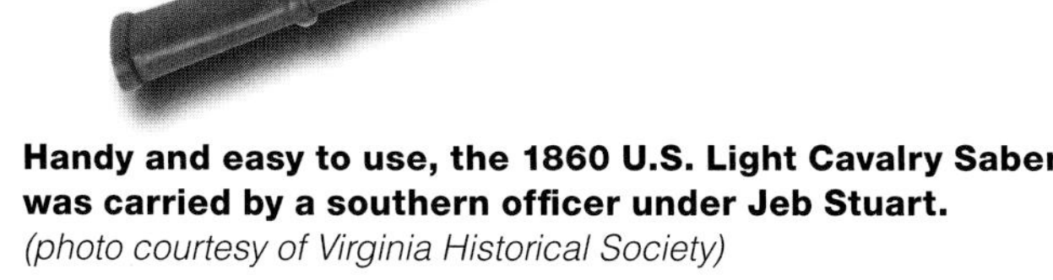

Handy and easy to use, the 1860 U.S. Light Cavalry Saber was carried by a southern officer under Jeb Stuart. *(photo courtesy of Virginia Historical Society)*

The vintage photo shows Robert E. Lee in his best uniform and wearing a dress sword, a symbol of his rank as commander of the Army of Northern Virginia, at his side. *(J. Vannerson photo courtesy of the Virginia Historical Society)*

Gen. Robert E. Lee knew that the Union assault launched against his lines at Petersburg, Va., eventually would break through. After a nine-month siege of this city by Ulysses S. Grant, he didn't have enough men to stop the enemy. The troops he did have were tired, hungry, sick and short of every kind of supply. Yet, they still had fight in them, and he could deploy them skillfully.

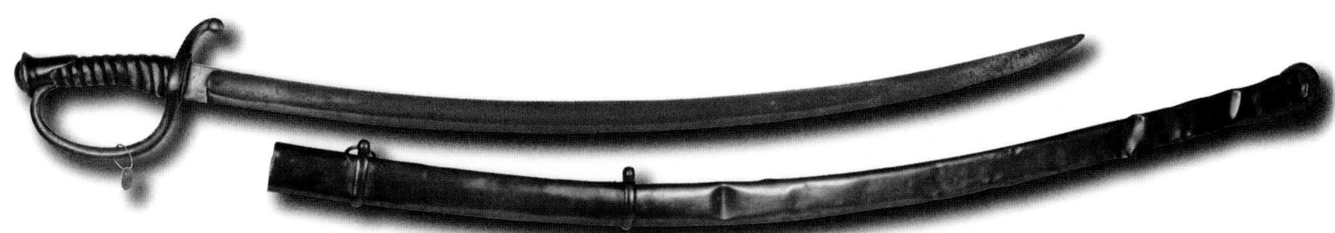

Shown is an example of a Confederated artillery saber, made by a small enterprise headed by Thomas Griswold. Southern edged weapons were effective, but tended to be more utilitarian, even crude, compared to northern blades. *(photo courtesy of Virginia Historical Society)*

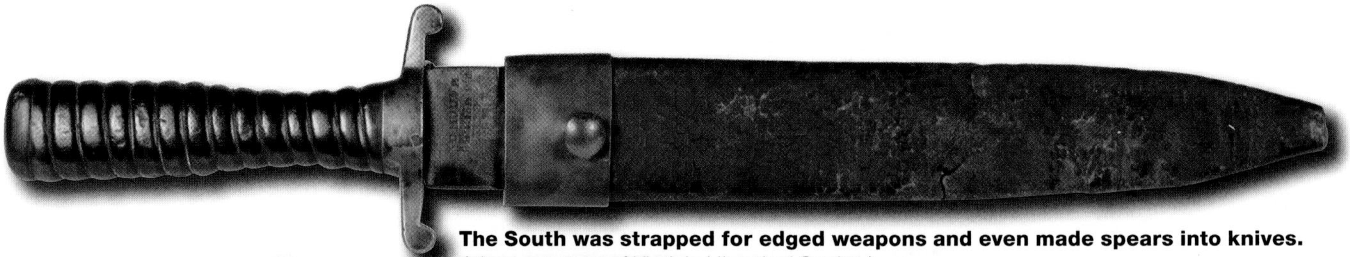

The South was strapped for edged weapons and even made spears into knives. *(photo courtesy of Virginia Historical Society)*

An example of a Confederate sword bayonet, the Cook & Brother blade slid onto the muzzle of a rifle and was locked into place by a spring on the handle of the bayonet. *(photo courtesy of Virginia Historical Society)*

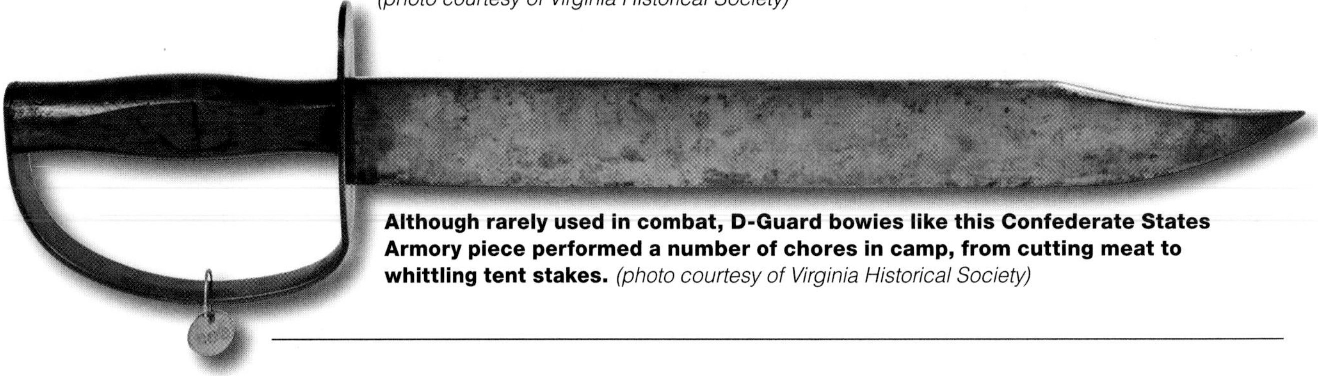

Although rarely used in combat, D-Guard bowies like this Confederate States Armory piece performed a number of chores in camp, from cutting meat to whittling tent stakes. *(photo courtesy of Virginia Historical Society)*

He needed time to reinforce defensive lines closer to the city to avoid disaster. Of course, holding those positions was only a stopgap measure. The odds against standing and fighting for a protracted time were too great. If Lee's luck held, he could fight until dark and then escape to North Carolina to continue the war.

The southern general needed time. So, on April 2, 1865, he ordered the men stationed at Fort Gregg, a small earthen outpost, to delay a Union attack headed their way until he could reposition his army. It was a suicide mission. Fort Gregg had 300 men. The attacking force numbered 5,000.

The fighting was fierce. Despite artillery fire, the Federals eventually clambered up the parapets of Fort Gregg. A southern officer described the fury of the Union soldiers as they clawed their way into the fort, saying, "'Tis true that when they rushed into the fort upon us, they were yelling, cursing, shooting with all the frenzy and rage of a horde of barbarians."

The Confederate Army fought with everything they had. Musket fire cut into federal ranks. When men ran out of ammunition, they threw bricks and even dirt clods at the federals. Several artillerymen began using shells that lay around.

"I was down behind the breastworks and lit the fuse of the shells and these men (other southerners) rolled them to the Yankees," one soldier wrote. Continuing, he noted, after lighting one round, "The sulfur burned blue, the powder s-s-s-s'd and away she went."

In the desperate fighting, the bayonet played a central role. Soldiers from both armies slashed, hacked and stabbed. Bare blades wielded by brave men determined individual fates and, ultimately, the future of a nation.

Confederate soldier Marshall McCandish holds a saber. Cavalry engagements in the Civil War's eastern theater were, from time to time, resolved using edged weapons. *(photo courtesy of Virginia Historical Society)*

When the fighting ended, Fort Gregg was in Union hands and the site was filled with dead and dying men. The Confederate losses added up to 56 dead and 200 wounded. Federal casualties amounted to about 122 dead and 592 wounded. Yet, the brave garrison had bought Lee valuable time for the evacuation that would end days later in surrender at Appomattox.

The Battle of Fort Gregg was a small, short engagement in a long, bloody conflict. However, it reveals that during the Civil War soldiers North and South relied on bayonets during close-quarter fighting. Likewise, cavalrymen readily turned to their sabers in desperate, hand-to-hand encounters, like those on the battlefield at Brandy Station.

Blades at Hand

In many ways, one of the war's most interesting stories is how the South was able to provide its armies and navies with edged weapons. When the conflict began, the Confederacy had scant industrial resources. The region depended on agriculture. Not only did it lack factories, but it also had relatively few engineers or artisans who understood the demands and techniques required for mass production. Yet, the Confederate government did a remarkable job in putting fighting blades in the hands of its men.

Today, original Confederate edged weapons, especially those made in the South, are extremely rare and valuable. The finest collection of these on view to the public can be seen at the Virginia Historical Society in Richmond. Years of collection and preservation have allowed the society to assemble a large number of rare pieces and to display them in a meaningful way.

Visitors to the society's galleries will find that the Confederacy had three sources of supply for edged weapons—battlefield capture from the U.S. Army, domestic production and imports.

The Confederacy received a huge amount of supplies, from overcoats to artillery pieces, by capturing federal items. A favorite wartime anecdote, perhaps apocryphal, made this clear. A southern prisoner of war reportedly marched past a huge northern artillery park where hundreds of cannons were positioned hub to hub. Glancing over them, he noticed the "U.S." stamped on each barrel for "United States."

"Us" Guns

The soldier obviously didn't know what the abbreviation stood for because he remarked to one of his guards, "You have as many of these 'us' guns as we do."

Regardless of which side used them in combat, Federal bayonets came in two basic forms—socket and sword. Socket bayonets typically had triangular blades and were stabbing weapons. When first developed, they represented a huge advancement over the first plug bayonets.

The small Confederate Navy was well-equipped with one of the most traditional of naval edged weapons—the cutlass. This is a Robert Mole & Son cutlass. *(photo courtesy of Virginia Historical Society)*

Plug bayonets were knives with butts that fit snuggly into musket barrels, thus turning long arms into pikes. However, firing and reloading were impossible as most military weapons were muzzleloaders.

Socket bayonets, on the other hand, allowed soldiers to continue to load and to fire, and to fight with an edged weapon. They consisted of knives attached to hollow tubes that fit over and locked onto musket barrels. Many standard-issue American firearms took socket bayonets, including the U.S. Model 1855 .58 caliber rifled musket, the U.S. Model 1842 .69 caliber rifled musket and the imported Austrian Lorenz .54 caliber musket, which had a quadrangular bayonet.

Some federal muskets took saber bayonets. These looked like swords or sabers and had flat blades, typically sharp on one side and pointed at the end. Saber bayonets could be used as stabbing and slashing weapons. They attached to muskets by means of rings in the hand guards and slots in the handles that engaged lugs on the sides of rifle barrels. Federal troops carried saber bayonets for a variety of muskets, including the imported and widely used British Model 1853 Enfield .577 caliber rifled musket.

While every infantryman got a bayonet, the U.S. Army issued comparatively few swords to troops, typically only to musicians and some artillerymen. Officers also carried swords but rarely employed the edged weapons in combat and, more often, the long blades were symbols of rank.

The military used French patterns for almost all regulation swords. Swords had straight blades sharpened on one side. They could be used for stabbing and slashing. Perhaps the most common sword in active service was the 1850 Foot Officer's Sword, authorized for all commissioned ranks. This weapon ranged from a simple government-issue type to ornate ones made by private firms.

Federal cavalrymen of all ranks carried sabers, which were curved and designed mainly for slashing. When the Civil War began, horsemen typically carried two types. One was the Ames Contract of 1833 saber, which had a 34-inch blade. The other was the Heavy Cavalry (Dragoon) Saber, Model 1840. Troops referred to it as "Old Wristbreaker," which suggests it was not the handiest of weapons.

The Model 1840 had a blade that was almost three feet long. The ordnance department quickly realized that something lighter was needed. So, it adopted the 34-inch Light Cavalry Saber, Model 1860.

A Bevy of British Blades

In addition to using captured federal items, the Confederacy imported edged weapons from abroad. When it came to bayonets, many were coupled with Enfield rifles brought through the blockade from Great Britain. Britain became a source of sabers, swords and cutlasses of diverse types.

The Confederacy also made many of its own blades. This required a lot of ingenuity and adaptation because the South lacked much in the way of heavy industry. Some manufacturers fashioned saber bayonets using the Fayetteville rifle bayonet as a model.

The Richmond Armory was likely the most productive source for southern bayonets. It created a bevy of simple, triangular weapons.

With steel being scarce, the Richmond Armory employed iron for blades and a small amount of steel for the tips. Interestingly enough, the South also produced thousands of bayonets for shotguns.

Many homeowners had shotguns handy for hunting when the war began. Officials thought they might work as a stopgap measure until enough rifled muskets could be found or made. So, early on, the Richmond government ordered thousands of shotgun bayonets.

In addition to bayonets, the Confederacy also made swords and sabers. Manufacturers often copied federal models. Though crude, the swords and sabers were serviceable for the most part, with their crudeness reflecting the low state of southern production capabilities.

Southern soldiers felt a deep attachment to another homemade blade—the bowie knife. Named for legendary Indian fighter and defender of the Alamo, Col. James Bowie, the weapon did not come in a standard size. In fact, Confederates tended to refer to any large knife they carried as a bowie.

Bowies were large knives with wide blades, usually ranging from 6 to 18 inches in length. Of all southern weapons, bowies have the crudest and most utilitarian appearance. That's because local blacksmiths often made them. While bayonets and sabers saw a lot of service, soldiers rarely used knives in combat.

Regardless, historians note that Confederates were deeply attached to bowies and lugged them around for a long time, although they usually did nothing more military than skin an animal or slice a piece of meat. The affection for bowies is reflected in dozens of surviving photos that show young men sitting stiffly with the large knives displayed prominently in their hands.

Not All Were Pikers

Early in the war, Confederate leaders became fascinated with pikes, one of the most ancient weapons known to man. A pike is basically a long spear that usually wasn't thrown but thrust. Even in 1861, the pike had obvious shortcomings. No unit armed with them could have fought successfully against enemies carrying muskets.

Infantrymen used bayonets in hand-to-hand fighting. Pictured is a southern-made musket and triangular bayonet manufactured by the Palmetto Armory in South Carolina. *(photo courtesy of Virginia Historical Society)*

Some southerners saw the pike as a cheap, quick fix to the lack of firearms. The Confederate Congress recommended arming troops with them in 1862. Some normally rational generals, like Robert E. Lee and Joseph E. Johnston, seriously considered their use.

Georgia politicians particularly adored pikes. Private manufacturers made hundreds of them. However, the pike was such an obviously bad idea that only one reported incident refers to them even being carried onto a battlefield.

For some reason, civilian inventors tinkered with pikes occasionally, trying to perfect a weapon that was utterly useless on the Civil War battlefield. One of the most remarkable variants came before Confederate ordnance Chief Josiah Gorgas for approval.

"I remember a formidable weapon that was invented at that time in the shape of a stout wooden sheath, containing a two-edged straight sword some two feet long," wrote Gorgas after the conflict. "The sheath or truncheon would be leveled and the sword liberated from the compression of a strong spring by touching a trigger, when it leaped out with sufficient force to transfix an opponent."

While such odd creations played no role in the war, the truth is that swords, sabers and bayonets did. In fact, the Civil War was the last major conflict in which edged weapons figured prominently. It was the end of a long era that began before the ancient Greeks and stretched across European and American history for centuries.

The use of swords and bayonets by Confederates and Federals proves conclusively that the Civil War was not only the first modern conflict, but also, truly, the last ancient one as well.

Schooled in the Ways of the Samurai

Murray Carter has learned the secrets of Japanese smiths and is willing to share them

By William Hovey Smith

The students of Murray Carter's knifemaking school learned to forge knife blades using a 150-year-old power hammer.

Lives based on love and learning are fulfilling, and the participants in Murray Carter's first Japanese knifemaking school experienced such fulfillment. An American Bladesmith Society master smith, Carter took five neophytes through the intricacies of Japanese blade-forging techniques while making three knives each at his five-day school in Vernonia, Oregon.

All of the participants had known Carter prior to the school. Two, known as "uncles" to his four children, drove from Louisiana; another of Japanese-American descent came from California; one lived in Oregon; and a local apprentice, along with the aforementioned students, made his first knives. I had met Carter at BLADE Show events and flew from Georgia to attend.

Since Carter's move from Japan to Oregon two years ago, his home and shop are works in progress.

The house was up, roofed and habitable, and the adjacent shop was covered and enclosed. The shop provided space to house the power-hammer, grinders and other equipment—altogether weighing tons—that he brought from Japan, although some pieces were temporarily located outdoors to make more room for people in the shop. Hundreds of years before Commodore Matthew Perry led his squadron of "black ships" into Tokyo Bay in 1853, Japanese smiths had been forging steel in open-air furnaces. They smelted black sand (magnetic iron ore) with charcoal to produce the equivalent of carbonized steel mixed with impurities.

The chunks of steel into high- and low-carbon batches. They heated the baseball-size masses and beat them into flat plates.

The smiths then stacked the plates together and forged them into rectangular billets, pounding them flat, folding them and re-forging them. With each reworking, they forged together layers of comparatively lower and higher carbon steels, eventually achieving steel bars that exhibited uniform characteristics.

Often the smiths would insert

This is an array of antique Japanese knifemaking tools.

a layer of mild steel between two layers of hard steel to produce a blade that would be tough yet easily re-sharpened.

Conversely, the forging of a layer of hard steel between two layers of soft steel resulted in an extremely hard edge with a soft exterior and spine for flexibility. By sandwiching hard, high-carbon steel between soft layers, more brittle steel could be used as a cutting edge than would otherwise be possible in a homogenous blade.

Hallmarks of Japanese Swords

Such multi-steel blades were able to absorb the impact of an opponent's blow. A laminated blade combined strength, flexibility and sharpness—three qualities that were to become hallmarks of Japanese knives and swords.

Modern Japanese bladesmiths have access to more uniform steels, but still achieve some of their best results by laminating a very pure Hitachi high carbon White Steel between two layers of softer steels to produce laminated knives with superior edge retention and strength.

Carter's knifemaking is an operation done by eye and feel. He finds that the look of white-hot steel in the forge, the dance of water droplets on a blade and the sound of a file rasping on hard metal are truer to Japanese traditional practices than modern computer controlled measuring equipment.

Five Day, Five Students, 15 Knives

The challenge that Carter faced with was to welcome five people, and me as a reporter, into his small shop, and in five days, teach the students to make three knives apiece. This task was complicated because some of the participants had little experience with grinders, band saws, forges, sanding belts and the hand tools necessary to work steel, wood and brass into functional knives.

Not only were the five participants to make three knives each, and me one, there would also be lectures and a running commentary covering more than a dozen topics, such as selecting knife steels, knife design and sharpening techniques, any of which could have been the subject of an all-day seminar.

Although the group ranged in ages from 18 to 65, they worked well together, and all contributed to making the first class at Carter's new school a success.

I brought 38 pounds of deer, wild hog and shark meat as well as my version of hog's head Brunswick stew. Stephen Payer did a one-man clean up of the shop. Bert

The students were allowed to strike patterns on the blades.

A blade is heated in the forge.

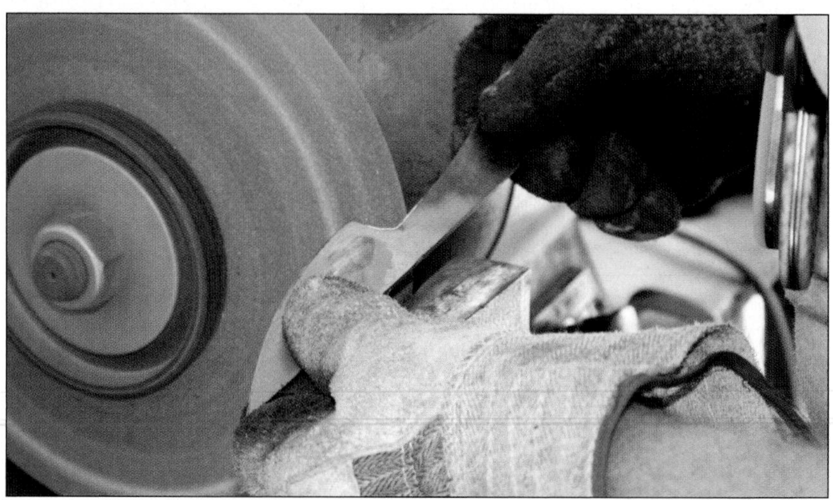

A student does some final shaping of a kitchen knife blade on a grinder.

Seal and George O'Brien offered transportation and years of experience in machine shop and quality control programs.

Ronald Yamaguchi, a third generation Japanese-American, had an interesting Southern California perspective to the proceedings as he partly reconnected with his Japanese roots. Shamus Dotsch, Carter's apprentice, helped us find needed items around the shop.

After a safety orientation, work began with each student making a neck knife and sheath. The blade steel was factory-laminated stock with high-alloy Blue Super Steel cores and stainless steel exteriors. The steel was chosen because fewer fabrication steps would be required and heat-treating was somewhat less critical. While the forge was heating, each student had the chance to practice with Carter's 150-year-old Japanese power hammer.

All watched intently as Carter explained how to use differing heat zones within the forge to achieve the proper temperature of the steel for shaping it on the power hammer. He also stressed the necessity for rapidly transferring the steel to the hammer and correct tong handling techniques to ensure that the red-hot metal was in flat contact with the hammer's anvil and striker.

Annealing Blade Blanks

Thinning the metal using the power hammer resulted in rectangular plates that were allowed to cool. Each student annealed a blade blank in rice straw ash, sandblasted the scale away, cold forged it to final thickness and scribed the outline of the blade and tang on the blank prior to cutting it out with a cutting wheel or band saw.

Each student employed a grinding wheel to rough out the blade shapes, and for the first time, it was obvious that we were making knives and not door hinges.

The students straightened the blades for the first time using brass hammers and working the steel on wooden blocks. They stamped their initials or other marks on the steel while it was still soft, and coated the blades with mud, heated them in the forge to white-hot temperatures and quenched the blades in tepid oxygen-depleted water. They then reheated the blades, and when they reached proper tempering temperature, allowed them to air cool.

Murray Carter poses wearing one of his neck knives.

The author checks the edge angle during blade polishing.

Tempering was done after dark so that the precise heat color of each blade could be properly judged. At the end of the first day and evening, everyone's blades were shaped and tempered.

The next morning, each student held their blades by hand while shaping them and grinding edges on a 4-foot concrete grinding wheel. Care had to be taken that each side of the blade was ground at a uniform angle and the grind extended to the end of the blade to establish the point.

Once the blades were shaped, it was time to select wood blanks for the handles, grind them into shape, epoxy them to the blades, attach them with brass rivets, contour the wood and metal together on belt sanders and do the final buffing and polishing. The final buffing brought out the beauty of the wood handles and the knives became transformed from utilitarian in appearance to something approaching art.

The students finished their knives on the afternoon of the second day. They fashioned neck sheaths by cutting and heating sheets of Kydex to plasticity, and pressure molded the plastic around each blade using a padded vise. Once cool, they drilled the Kydex sheaths, riveted them and attached thongs, thus completing the 61 steps it took to make each neck knife.

A real challenge came on day three because the kitchen knives would be made from split bars of mild steel into which hard steel cores would be forged and worked into broad, thin blades without de-laminating the steels.

First Carter cut and fluxed the hard steel inserts. They initially appeared to be too small as they were each only about two inches long, a half inch wide and a quarter inch thick. He coated them with flux and allowed the steel to cool on the anvil.

Among Sparks and Flying Flux

He heated the mild steel bar to a red heat, split it about halfway down with a hot chisel propelled by the power hammer, installing the hard steel core into the groove and tapping it into place. Carter reheated the steel in the forge, refluxed it, and forge-welded the two pieces together under the power hammer amid sparks and flying jets of liquefied flux.

After initial welding, the students heated each bar and cut off their billets, which would ultimately become kitchen knives. Each pupil forged a long rat-tailed tang and bent it over the horn of the anvil

Shown are camp knives the students made at Murray Carter's school, all lying alongside their original patterns.

Represented are all the kitchen and neck knives the class made.

to provide a grasping point for further work. Following this began the delicate job of hammer forging the blades into a uniform thickness without pounding through the steel.

One new step was to cut the kitchen knife blades out of the blanks using floor-mounted shears.

We heated the tang of each kitchen knife to red hot and "burnt in" the handles by pounding on the rear of the grips, seating and searing the wood along the way. Despite the additional technical challenges, by the morning of the fourth day the kitchen knives had been completed.

"Sometimes," Carter said, "describing something to someone beforehand is not nearly as meaningful as delivering this information after he has some hands-on experience."

During the final two days, the students had the opportunity to design and make their own camp knives using one of Carter's patterns or those of their own creation. These knives had the added complication of featuring brass bolsters that had to be shaped and silver soldered into place.

Novices and Knives

Each of the five students came with different expectations of what they would receive for their $5,000 fee and five days spent with Carter. Could a novice take this course and leave expecting to start pounding out salable knives? Eventually. But it would not be realistic to assume that one five-day course could pass on all the knowledge Carter has gained through nearly two decades of making over 10,000 knives.

Carter's course is suitable for anyone who wants to learn about knifemaking by getting some hands-on experience rather than participating vicariously through reading and videos. The master bladesmith's teaching incorporates modern machinery and steels to make world-class blades that still retain the flavor, utility and skills developed over 1,200 years of Japanese blade making.

For additional information, visit www.cartercutlery.com, email him at carter.cutlery@verizon.net, or send a letter to POB 307, Vernonia, OR 97064.

The Leanest, Meanest Tactical Folders

Ergonomics combine with aesthetics to raise the bar on factory tactical folders today

Text and photos by Dexter Ewing

Timberline's Greg Lightfoot-designed 18-Delta folders are available in three blade shapes.

Tactical folders have been popular for more than 15 years. In that time, the trend has taken on a life of its own within the knife industry, as factories have picked up on collaborations with custom knifemakers, those who fashion, lean, mean tactical folders.

The custom collaborations, in turn, have resulted in new designs, materials and mechanisms. By the time the new millennium rolled around, the tactical folder market was solidified not only by its popularity in the consumer market but in the military, with tactical folding knives deployed all over the world. The knives were being used—and still are—as tools and backup weapons.

In the past few years, a concentration on tactical folder design has become imminent. The knives are more stylish and sleek, looking less "blocky" and less "military" but still strong enough to get down and dirty when the situation calls for it. This goes well with the prevailing attitude among savvy knife consumers that knives are personal accessories that express styles and tastes.

A close look at tactical folders from leading knife companies makes evident a copious abundance of curves and streamlining in handle and blade designs.

Custom knifemaker Ken Onion is one of those responsible for making tactical folders sleek and more refined in appearance, for his designs have "flow" to them, meaning when the folder is opened, there is a seamless transition in the design lines from the blade to the handle. It all looks like it should be one piece.

Kershaw's Ener-G 2 and Benchmade's Skirmish are two popular tactical folders resulting from collaborations with custom knifemakers.

The all-business Folding Hissatsu from Columbia River Knife & Tool was designed by martial arts expert James Williams.

Onion's collaborations with Kershaw Knives brought the maker's design influence to the masses, and other companies began to take notice. Tactical folders have not only become more stylish in appearance but ergonomically friendly as well. A knife without a comfortable handle will not be used, period.

Manufacturers place emphasis on user ergonomics, with a secondary objective toward a unique look or style resulting from the ergonomic design. The two go handle in hand, so to speak. Rarely do modern knife companies design tactical folder handles to primarily look cool. They are designed for user comfort and safety, a fact revealed by examining some of the newest tactical folder designs and what makes them popular today.

Kershaw Knives recently paired up with knifemaker Lee Williams from Texas City, Texas, to produce the Ener-G 2 folder. The stylishly sleek folder features a 3 ½-inch, hollow-ground, drop-point Sandvik 13C26 stainless steel blade and dual steel liners.

No Hand-Edge Contact

A G-10 handle with textured-rubber inlays enhances its grip, and an integral hand guard is built into the design to prevent the user's hand from sliding onto the blade edge. The handle tapers toward the back for comfort.

The Ener-G 2's opening mechanism is rather unique among manual folders. What appears to be a "flipper" mechanism, or an extended blade tang that protrudes through the handle when the folder is in the closed position, serves as more than a standard flipper.

Jeff Goddard of Kershaw explains, "The flipper is called 'Kick Stop,' and it is not really part of the blade; it is a separate part."

Goddard says the Kick Stop pushes the blade out 90 degrees and then disappears into the spine of the handle. By giving the Kick Stop a swift tug with the index finger, the blade is propelled open and into the locked position, similar to how a standard flipper works.

"The Kick Stop also stays in the handle after it's used to actuate the blade," Goddard summarizes. "This really cleans up the profile of the knife when it's open without losing any of the characteristics of a flipper knife."

Kershaw also offers a smaller Ener-G with a 3-inch blade. It's a

The Boker Automat Kalashnikov folders can be had in two versions—with a plain-edge, bead-blasted blade (the K101), or a partially serrated, black blade (K102), as shown here.

compact folder that still has the Kick Stop opener but in an easier-to-carry size.

"Big" is just one word to describe the Benchmade 630SBK Skirmish frame-lock folder. It instantly commands attention via its 4 ¼-inch, re-curved, S30V drop-point blade, and ergonomically curved titanium handle. Custom knifemaker Neil Blackwood designed the Skirmish to be a scaled-down version of one of his original custom knife designs.

"When you handle the 630, you really notice the ergonomics and weight-to-size ratio," says Vance Collver of Benchmade. "No matter your hand size, this knife will fit because of the high thumb and finger guard. It's like shaking hands."

With its stylish curves, no-nonsense build and easy one-handed opening, the 630 Skirmish represents the epitome of forward-thinking tactical folder design. Because of the handle's flat profile, and a pocket clip that allows it to disappear in a front pants pocket, the large Skirmish carries as well or better than a small knife.

The Tapered-Butt-End Tactical

"The tapered butt end of the handle adds many tactical defenses," Collver says, "and the re-curve on the back end of the blade is designed to enable trapping [trapping the cutting medium in the curve of the blade]."

For those who find the 630 Skirmish to be too big for daily carry, Benchmade offers the 635 Mini Skirmish, a scaled down, more pocket-friendly version of its bigger brother.

Columbia River Knife & Tool's (CRKT's) Folding Hissatsu may not win any awards for beauty, but it is designed perfectly for its intended purpose. Designed by martial arts expert James Williams, the Folding Hissatsu is about as lean and mean as they come. Sporting a modified tanto blade measuring 3.875 inches in length, it takes the concept of a tanto blade a few steps further.

Williams explains, "The curve of the blade allows it to spend a long time in the cut, and the longer the blade spends in the cut, the deeper the cut. The point is extremely aggressive in penetration."

The knife was designed with "personnel engagement" in mind and, as Williams says, it is a purpose driven design. "The Folding Hissatsu was primarily designed for United States Military Special Operators, either as a concealable backup weapon, or for those special circumstances where they cannot carry a higher level of force," he notes.

"It is a focus-driven knife that can be used for things other than personal defense, however everything that went into the design is for personal defense with no compromise for multi-purpose use," Williams adds.

The handle sports two stainless steel liners to give the knife solidity, and a reversible pocket clip is also incorporated to facilitate ease of right- or left-side carry. The Folding Hissatsu looks lean and mean, but does its performance match its looks? To ensure top performance, Williams subjected the knife to rigorous testing.

The Plywood Stabber

"One of the things I do is repeated stabbing through half-inch plywood," he illustrates. "With one of the prototypes I did this 50 times with no damage or degradation of performance."

Williams points out that the pivot bolt of the knife is three times bigger than that of normal folding knives, thus one reason why the knife has withstood downright abusive field testing. The Folding Hissatsu is equipped with CRKT's AutoLAWKS safety, which automatically engages when the blade is open and, therefore, prevents unwanted closure of the blade.

"It basically makes a folder, with proper design function, as strong as a fixed-blade knife," Williams says of the AutoLAWKS. The knife also comes with CRKT's OutBurst assisted-opening mechanism that propels the blade out with authority, ready for use.

"From the beginning, the team at Boker wanted, obviously, a large knife," states Dan Weidner, president of Boker USA. "We were looking for such a knife that would be mechanically strong and reliable, would fill the needs of the tactical field and would provide a blade shape that would allow for everyday use from shaping a tent pole, to carving an apple."

Thus, out of these requirements Boker brought forth the Automat Kalashnikov 101 and 102 tactical folders. "We are the only authorized company sanctioned my Mikhail Kalashnikov to use his name on cutlery," states Weidner.

The K101 and K102 folders are offered under the Boker Plus banner, made in Taiwan out of the best material for the money. The folders showcase 4-inch, re-curved, drop-point blades of 440C, dual stainless steel liners and Zytel handles.

"The re-curve shape of the blade allows for effective cutting using a pulling motion," Weidner explains. "While this is a large knife, it really carries a low profile and just molds into the hand. It really is not bulky at all, for the size."

The ergonomic handle features finger grooves, traction notches that keep your hand in place, a reversible pocket clip for left- and right-hand carry, along with a glass breaker point in the butt end of the handle. A flipper provides speedy opening. The Kalashnikov 101 offers remarkable bang for the buck in terms of fit and finish.

Blade Shape Choices

For its latest, heavy duty tactical folder, Timberline Knives has paired up with custom knifemaker Greg Lightfoot to bring out the 18 Delta series. The Delta series features blade lengths of 3 ¾ inches and three distinct blade shapes—a partially serrated, modified spear point; a plain-edge, chisel-ground tanto; and a fully serrated sheepsfoot rescue-style blade. Regardless of blade style, the handle construction is the same—an ergonomic and contoured handle with dual titanium liners and black G-10 scales.

The blade steel of choice is 440C stainless because of its ease of resharpening in the field, states John Anthon, president of Timberline Knives. The 440C blade steel provides a good balance of edge holding power, superior corrosion resistance and ease of maintenance.

Another feature of the 18 Delta series is the recessed, reversible pocket clip. "Clips are notorious for coming loose," says Anthon. "We recess our pocket clips into the handle, making for a stronger clip-to-handle fastening." As an added touch, a metal plate and extra screws are provided to cover up the cavity of the non-clip side, to make it look more "finished," if you will.

Anthon says, "We live in a right-hand-dominated society. However, many police, military and EMTs are left-handed."

So Timberline made a reversible clip as a standard feature on the 18 Deltas, and Anthon praises

Blade-Tech's MLEK Magnum is a high-end tactical folder made with premium materials.

Greg Lightfoot both as a premier designer and knifemaker. "Greg makes good, simple, hard-use cutting tools," he begins. "They are not overly complicated, but are very well constructed. Greg is easy to work with, and all his designs are driven with the end-user in mind."

Blade-Tech Industries has garnered a loyal fan base with the Pro Hunter series of folding hunters. So much so that the company began to receive requests to bring out a tactical version of the Pro Hunter, and thus, the MLEK was born.

MLEK is an acronym that stands for "Military and Law Enforcement Knife, As Mikey Vellekamp, Blade-Tech's cutlery production manager, explains it, "The MLEK is designed to accommodate military and law enforcement cutting needs, as well as civilian utility applications. The sleek, clip-point blade is ideal for thrusting and piercing."

The MLEK sports a 3 5/8-inch, flat-ground blade. "We kept the same S30V blade steel and ergonomic handle design as on the Pro Hunter, but added a clip point with a swedge and a re-curve," Vellekamp notes.

The Blade Has Backbone

Blade-Tech retained the same handle design that made the Pro Hunter famous, an ergonomic handle with an integral, lower finger guard to prevent the user's hand from slipping forward. Handle scales are of black G-10 with a pair of stainless liners nested into each scale that gives the knife a strong backbone without the extra thickness. What you get is a strong folder that carries well in the pocket.

Blade-Tech gave the MLEK a boost for 2008 by increasing the thickness of the liners from .04 inches each to .05 inches, and blade stock thickness from 1/8-inch stock to 5/32-inch stock. The new name is the MLEK Magnum.

The overall thickness of the knife increased over the original but remains easy to carry in the pocket, and the extra width makes the knife feel even more comfortable in the grip.

The MLEK Magnum is a fashionable folder due to its handsome, re-curved, clip-point blade, but looks aren't everything, as it is a workhorse folder. .

A sampling of the latest production tactical folders available on the market today reveals those ready for professional or civilian duty. They all offer good looks with sturdy construction and premium materials throughout. The knives represent some of the best, leanest and meanest tactical folders manufactured today.

Soulful and Catchy Knives

Brian Chovanec builds carefully conceived blades, difficult to describe, yet skillfully presented

By Keith Spencer

Back in 1867, a fellow named James Nash discovered gold 120 miles north of Brisbane, Australia, at a place called Gympie, which these days is embodied in the vast Murgon Shire Council that stretches from the Great Dividing range to the fabulous Queensland coastline and Fraser Island.

Known as "the wine and leisure shire of the South Burnett," the region is the fastest developing wine area in the state. Tucked away on Redgate Road near Murgon, not far from the Redgate Winery, lives an extraordinary knifemaker named Brian Chovanec.

Encouraged and inspired by his dad, Brian set about making bladeware only four years ago to help pay the bills. A mechanic by trade, Brian turned his hand to a variety of things in the past.

"To keep the bills at bay, hands-on was my favorite way," says Brian. He drifted onto the Australian knifemaking scene, immediately grabbing the attention of discerning collectors with his one-of-a-kind works of blade artistry, thematic in old European style.

Along with the first knives Brian mailed to my office for examination came a homemade demo disc entitled "of BEAT: BASS-iks at Random," containing 12 songs and two instrumentals. It features Brian on bass guitar, guitar, keyboard and drum machine, accompanied by Catya, a female vocalist friend.

The disc cover itself features unusual (Chovanec) art and the musical experience is strangely different—kind of soulful and catchy, difficult to describe, yet carefully conceived and skillfully presented with a message embodied therein. That probably also describes Chovanec custom-crafted knives!

Since then I've seen several examples of exotic Chovanec blade artistry, each knife having a distinctly unique theme designed to arouse the curiosity of collectors, who forever have an eye out for something special.

Brian Chovanec's Celtic dagger features a Vladimir Pulis damascus blade, a ruby-inlaid, carved brass guard, a tulipwood handle embellished in a classic motif using buffalo horn and antler, and a matching tulipwood sheath.

Brian is multi-skilled, which reflects in his highly embellished knife-sheath combinations. What he doesn't already know he learns along the way—he seeks sole authorship in knifemaking—and Brian picks things up very quickly, which reflects in his driven aptitude for handmade knife concepts.

Knifemaker Brian Chovanec is hard at work.

Fertile Mind, Trained Hands

His fertile mind sees clearly what he feels compelled to create, which his sure, trained hands then bring to life in the workshop. It's this clarity of vision, coupled with determination, he maintains for the duration of the production process, establishing the uniqueness of Brian's finished knives. He doesn't plagiarize patterns or adornments made popular by others. His buyers get Chovanec absolute originals!

Brian's obsession for perfection in what he does comes from his father, Igor Chovanec, a toolmaker by trade, restorer of antique weaponry, custom knifemaker and perfectionist. For the past 16 years, he has been mainly restoring front-loading rifles and flint locks, some dating back to the 16th century.

Using authentic blueprints and traditional techniques wherever possible, Igor restores them to their original glory. Amongst his many acquired skills, he carves, engraves and inlays gold, silver, bone and other materials.

I asked Brian about his work at the Redgate workshop and it is best described in the knifemaker's own words to me.

"As far as my work goes, I've been running a little engineering-mechanical workshop here—a bit of a 'jack of all trades thingy,'" he quips. "You know, it's all farms around here, so everything that needs fixing, welding, building, modifying or fabricating, well, I'm the local Mr. Fixit, repairing motorbikes, lawn mowers, farm machinery, plus small (and big) engines and so on.

"Also, just out of interest, from time to time I've employed my artistic side and among other things, built out of scrap or recycled materials a number of small statues and stick-men for people's gardens and driveways," Brian adds.

"Gradually though, I've been trying to stay away from all the other things to concentrate exclusively on making knives. So far knifemaking takes up about 80 percent of the time," he concludes, "but I'm hoping to end up doing only knives eventually, fingers crossed."

For all intents and purposes, Brian can be legitimately classified as a full-time custom knifemaker with extra duties. The primary function of his workshop is to produce knives, but he undertakes other tasks in between. He is one of an elite group of knifemaking artisans in Australia who earns a living entirely off his own hand and with no incoming funds from a working spouse or government benefit. Brian Chovanec is a full-timer—it's his livelihood.

By the sheer quality and innovativeness of his exceptional knives, along with modest marketing endeavours, Brian has, in his words, "managed to get my work out there a bit."

Quiet Achiever Plying His Craft

His stylish, exquisitely-adorned bladeware has found its way into some of the finest private collections around the globe, in the United States, United Kingdom, Portugal, the Netherlands, Slovakia, and into

The "Spiky Skinner" showcases a hand-forged damascus blade, a leopard-burl and hand-checkered buffalo horn handle, and 416 stainless steel and nickel silver fittings.

every state and territory of Australia. He accomplished all of this in a few short years as a knifemaker, not bad for a quiet achiever plying his newfound craft in a place that's off the pace in the shade of the Bunya Mountains.

It was his dad that triggered Brian's interest in knifemaking. While displaying his wares at a Slovak gun show, Igor studied knives on display by custom knifemakers and decided that he, too, would make a knife to see, as he said to Brian later, "what all the fuss was about." He entered that knife in a show and won an award and, as they say, the rest is history. Igor became hooked on knifemaking ala Czech style!

Early in 2005, Igor urged his son to get started. "He has been helping me along the way with advice, new materials and techniques," Brian explains, "but mainly with his uncompromising criticism, for he is a perfectionist."

Regardless of Igor's uncompromising nature, Brian nevertheless dearly loves his dad and respects him greatly, so he painstakingly made a nice knife for his dad's birthday. "I was a bit stressed," admits Brian, "about what Igor's reaction to my creation was going to be."

Evidently, Igor was so taken by his son's gift that, without telling him, he entered it into a competition at a prestigious international knife show, Knives Bratislava, held annually in the Slovak Republic. "You can imagine my shock and surprise when I discovered it actually won an award," declares Brian, "third place in the 'Best Embellished Knife' category."

While Brian is an approachable person and great to chat with, he has nevertheless factored a few strong personal disciplines into his knifemaking that provide some insight into the character of the man. Brian is inspired by the work of Arpad Bojtos who is of Slovakian descent and whose magnificent hand-carved bladeware appears in David Darom's *Art & Design in Modern Custom Fixed-Blade Knives* (2005).

Brian's knives reflect the style of Bojtos' incredibly sculpted grips and blades. "When I grow up, I wannabe just like him," Brian admits humbly. "So, following that path I also make my knives 100 percent by hand. I don't use machinery other than a few handheld power tools for 'roughing-out' the knife and blade profiles.

"Doing it all by hand allows a better 'connection' with the piece I'm working on," he adds. "I want my knives to be different, and if I start using machinery, such as milling machines, lathes and so on, there would be no difference between my knife and any other knife that's been manufactured in a factory somewhere, perhaps by the thousands.

"Besides, if I went down that road I couldn't compete with the 'big boys' price-wise, due to the huge quantity of factory-made knives produced," he says. "And some of them are pretty damn-good quality as well, selling at prices that I can't even buy my material for. Trying to compete would turn my passion for knifemaking into a repetitive job that I would quickly get sick of doing. I would rather work at McDonalds."

No Repeats

"I potter along slowly, doing it all by hand, never making two knives the same and selling them with guaranteed 'no repeats,'" Brian explains. "This is why I use the logo 'A Knife Like No Other,'

Among other amenities, Brian Chovanec's "Snake Hunter 2" sports a snakewood grip with a hand-carved brass pommel, and citrine and ruby inlays. The forged damascus blade comes from the hands of Vladimir Pulis.

Vladimir Pulis and Brian Chovanec collaborated on "Odin," a large damascus dagger with a carved buffalo horn grip, bone spacers and inlays, a damascus pommel and nickel-silver fittings.

which sometimes works against me when collectors ask for a knife 'just like that one.' I have to say sorry, no can do."

He also has a mindset about limited-edition knives, like one of only 1,000 made, and questions their collectable value. Brian finds it difficult to get excited about owning a knife that 999 other collectors also own.

Brian goes on to say, "So I'd rather do everything myself, and if it turns out badly, I only have myself to blame. You live and learn, and I'll try harder to do better next time. But if the knife turns out OK, I can put my hand up and honestly say 'I've made this' and that means a lot to me."

To keep from getting over-excited with his results, Brian looks at the pictures of bladeware made by the great makers, which, he says, "very quickly puts me back in my place. There's a long path ahead of me yet, which makes it all the more exciting when I think of the unexplored ground there is to cover."

Brian is keen to assemble the necessary equipment and find the time to learn about forging his own damascene (damascus-type) blade steel. For the time being, he uses the pattern-welded blade steel produced by master smith Vladimir Pulis, a friend of his father in the Slovak Republic.

A letter to the editor of *Knives Australia* magazine put Brian's "nose out of joint" and he subsequently wrote to me (the editor) strongly advancing his viewpoint.

The Vladimir Pulis hand-forged damascus blade reveals a distinct hamon (temper line), and is complemented by Brian Chovanec's fine silver inlay. The composite handle includes 10 individually hand-carved pieces of ebony, amboyna burl and nickel silver, as well as gold pins and bone and paua-shell inlays.

The Brian Chovanec "Birdie" model is a quality broad-blade skinner of hand-forged damascus, a comfort-contoured timber grip with inlay and a fancy-chiseled solid brass guard.

The grip of Brian Chovanec's knife with Vladimir Pulis damascus blade is fashioned from Mulga burl, buffalo horn and carved stag. The piece also sports a 416 stainless steel guard with nickel silver and forest green tourmaline spacers.

I didn't publish Brian's letter in the magazine, opting to save it for *Knives 2009*.

The original letter outlined how the reader was fed up with seeing useless and overpriced art knives featured and that much cheaper knives (presumably working knives) are far more interesting to read about. Brian's letter and the analogy that he chooses to use provide considerable insight into the man and his work.

Brian writes, "Speaking for myself, and maybe also on behalf of those readers and collectors who are interested and buy this kind of work, I bet you that the bloke in question would very quickly change his mind and opinion about collectable art knives if he actually came to have one. It's like the person who's got a print hanging on the wall saying they wouldn't rather have the original oil painting if they could... yeah, right!

"And as for the art knife being useless or non-functional, well I beg to differ," he continues. "It's a matter of common sense. Technically, one could use an art knife in the bush in the same way that one could hang an expensive original oil painting in a dirty workshop, but it is hardly likely one would do so. Just because it isn't the done thing doesn't mean the original painting is overpriced and useless and that the print is more interesting.

"True, perfectly good factory knives can be bought for a fraction of the price tag on some art knives. I buy them too, when I'm looking for a serviceable all-round knife, one that I won't feel bad about 'taking bush' with me or using in the shed and possibly scratching or damaging it," Brian writes. "But I won't put a working knife in the display cabinet, nor would I display my steak knife in the cabinet either.

"An art knife, however, is a completely different ballgame, even though it will perform as efficiently as the work knife, perhaps even better."

Brian tells me that his dad doesn't pick on him any more and even murmurs a few nice remarks about some of his knives. "So he's either given up criticizing my work or I'm on the right track," he surmises.

I think it's the latter.

Brian Chovanec can be contacted by email: bccustomknives@westnet.com.au.

Knife Proverbs for Every Occasion

The following quotations prove that the tongue may actually be mightier than the sword

By Dr. Louis P. Nappen

As one knife proverb goes, "He who lives by the sword dies by sword." Knifemakers Don Hanson III and Anders Hogstrom teamed up on the Khyber/yataghan featuring a damascus blade forged by Hanson, a bronze and copper guard and jet inlays. *(SharpByCoop.com photo)*

Have you ever felt tension *so thick you could cut it with a knife?; taken a stab in the dark?;* lived life to *the hilt or on the razor's edge?* Symbolic blade comparisons are so engrained in our collective psyche that we take for granted their literal foundations.

Due to their word-of-mouth nature, many proverbs are impossible to attribute. For example, the *on the razor's edge* expression could have originated in Native North American culture with the saying, "The world is as sharp as the edge

Perhaps keeping the proverb, "A razor may be sharper than an ax, but it cannot cut wood," in mind, Greg Lightfoot built the "Katanaxe." The piece features a 20-CV steel head and haft, and a cord-wrapped, stingray-skin grip with a shark's tooth menuki (handle charm). *(Mitch Lum photo)*

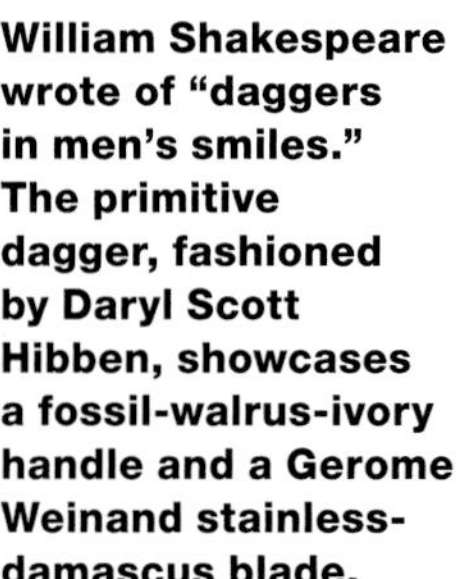

William Shakespeare wrote of "daggers in men's smiles." The primitive dagger, fashioned by Daryl Scott Hibben, showcases a fossil-walrus-ivory handle and a Gerome Weinand stainless-damascus blade.

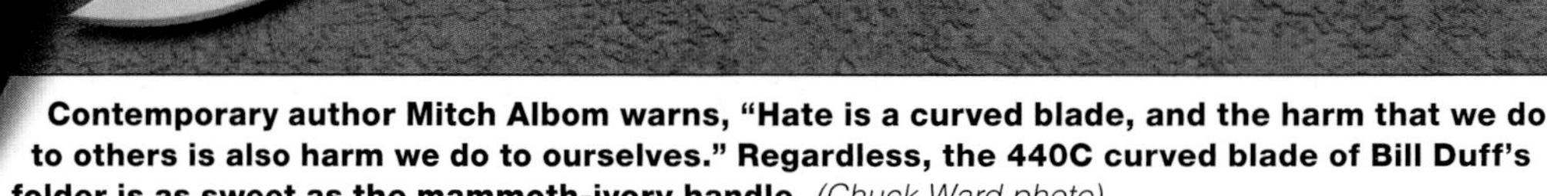

Contemporary author Mitch Albom warns, "Hate is a curved blade, and the harm that we do to others is also harm we do to ourselves." Regardless, the 440C curved blade of Bill Duff's folder is as sweet as the mammoth-ivory handle. *(Chuck Ward photo)*

of a knife;" or in Asia via, "The sharp edge of a razor is difficult to pass over; thus the wise say the path to Salvation is hard." (Katha-Upanishad)

Arguably, the most famous blade analogies of all time compare "pen" and "sword." Versions date back over two millennia: "The sword the body wounds, sharp words the mind." (Menander, 342-292 B.C.)

In 1839, English novelist Edward Bulwer-Lytton coined the version with which most people are familiar. Few people, however, are familiar with the full quote from his play *Richelieu; Or the Conspiracy,* which promotes at least two noteworthy sword proverbs:

Beneath the rule of
men entirely great,
The pen is mightier than
the sword. Behold
The arch-enchanters wand!
— itself a nothing! —
But taking sorcery from the
master-hand
To paralyse the Cæsars,
and to strike
The loud earth breathless!
— Take away the sword —
States can be saved without it!

If words are mightier than blades, then every warrior is well-advised to carry an arsenal of wit. Consider modeling yourself after the beloved Cyrano de Bergerac. This large-nosed swordsman, as presented by French author Edmond Rostand (1868-1918), is equally renowned for defeating enemies with his blade as for persuading hearts with words. As Cyrano duels, he comically composes verse, such as:

Hark, how the steel
rings musical!
Mark how my point floats,
light as the foam,
Ready to drive you back
to the wall,
Then, as I end the refrain,
thrust home!

Yet, be forewarned, satire cuts both ways:

- Sharp wits, like sharp knives, do often cut their owner's fingers.
- If your mouth turns into a knife, it will cut off your lips. (African)
- Wit without discretion is a sword in the hand of a fool. (Spanish)

Practical Advice

Another hugely famous blade proverb is, "He who lives by the sword dies by sword." As with many popular aphorisms, this one has Biblical origins. Matthew 26:52 reads: "Then said Jesus unto him, Put up again thy sword

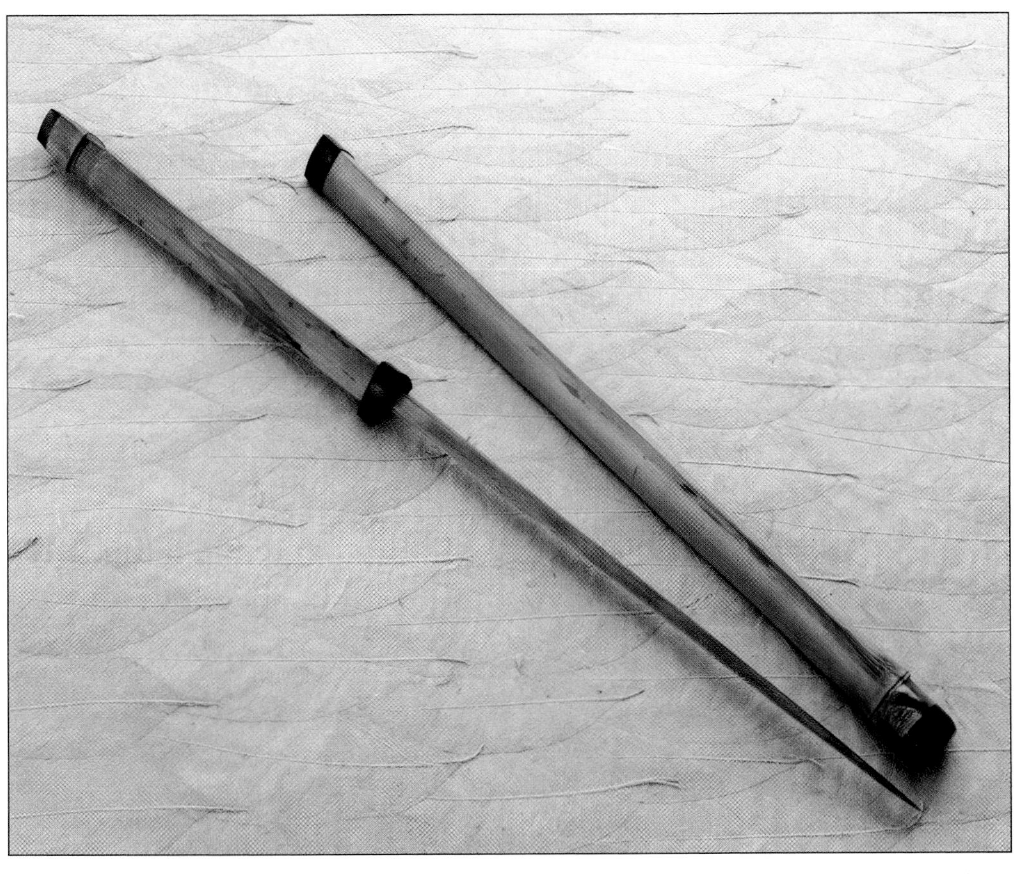

Several European cultures recognize, "One knife keeps another in its sheath," because, once unsheathed, "One knife whets another." Daniel Stephan's unsheathed knife sports a 9 ¾-inch damascus blade, a bamboo handle and buffalo horn inlays. *(PointSeven photo)*

into his place: for all they that take the sword shall perish with the sword."

Tao philosopher Lao Tzu similarly cautions, "Fill your bowl to the brim and it will spill, keep sharpening your knife and it will blunt."

In Africa they warn, "The knife that has been lent never comes back alone;" and in Tibet, "Do not buy the knife that will cut your own throat."

An old European-American proverb states, "Whether the stone hits the jug or the jug hits the stone, it's going to be bad for the jug." Likewise, an African knife proverb furthers, "Whether the knife falls on the melon or the melon on the knife, the melon suffers."

Regarding safety, "If a child holds both fire and a knife, if the fire does not burn him, the knife will cut him." Roman dramatist Plautus (254-184 BC) advised, "Leave not a sword in the hand of an idiot." Other similar admonitions include the Portuguese saying, "A bad knife cuts one's finger instead of the stick;" and the French proverb, "A fool cuts himself with his own knife."

Whatever the mission, one should always use the right tool for a job and avoid overkill, as in the saying, "Never cut with a knife what you can cut with a spoon." Likewise, "A razor may be sharper than an ax, but it cannot cut wood." And finally, "Why use an ox-knife to kill a fowl?" (Confucius 551-479 B.C.)

An ancient Turkish saying advises, "Measure a thousand times and cut once." Contemporarily expressed, that saying equates to, "Measure twice, cut once."

Since knives are also used as utensils, numerous blade-related proverbs have been forwarded regarding the dangers of gluttony. King Solomon counseled, "Put a knife to your throat, if you are a man given to appetite." (Proverbs 23:2)

Bishop of Gaeta, Franciscus Patricius Senensis (1413-1494), noted, "Gluttony kills more than the sword, and is the kindler of all evils." Other cultures likewise caution:

- Most suicides are committed with a knife and fork. (Swedish)
- Don't dig your grave with your own knife and fork. (English)
- Whoever has thirst for everything risks swallowing a knife. (African)

Overeaters beware, "It is the fat bull that feels the butcher's knife;" or alternatively stated, "For a lean ox, there is no knife." (Turkish)

As the Filipino proverb goes, "Never catch at a falling knife or a falling friend," for, "A desperate person will even hold on to a knife edge." Someone would have to be desperate to hold onto the edge of Dan Piergallini's long dirk, which features a Jerry Rados Turkish damascus blade, including saw teeth at its base, incredible filework, a pretty fossil-ivory handle and a pointed pommel. *(SharpByCoop.com photo)*

Combat Wisdom

The importance of knives for survival is perhaps best stated in the Nordic rhyme, A knifeless man is a lifeless man; also expressed, "A man without a knife is a man without a life." To those who risk being unprepared, a West African proverb warns, "He who is pierced with a thorn must limp off to him who has a knife."

A Kalabari proverb states, "War comes before the knife is whetted." Besides promoting preparedness, this proverb is also uttered after victory to imply there was never any concern for failure.

During WWII, a popular song endorsed: *Praise the Lord, and pass the ammunition.* Nepal's analogous mantra advises: *The God's name in the mouth, but in the pocket a knife.*

Probably no knife proverb is more endearing than the classic, "Unlike a gun, a knife never runs out of ammo." Comparably, an Islamic proverb teaches, "A lone runner with a sharp knife can cut a hundred throats before dawn."

Proverbs regarding blades and battle are plentiful. Highlights include: Shakespeare's: *The peace of heaven is theirs that lift their swords, in such a just and charitable war;* (King John) Mussolini's, *Let us have a dagger between our teeth, a bomb in our hands, and an infinite scorn in our hearts;* De Rivera's, *The sword of justice has no scabbard;* and, Bismarck's comic, *You can do everything with bayonets, except sit on them.*

As for fighting against one's country, Thomas Fuller (1608-1661) noted, "Rebellion must be managed with many swords; treason to his prince's person may be with one." Unfortunately, "Whoever draws his sword against the prince must throw the scabbard away." (European)

Regarding unchivalrous behavior, Shakespeare wrote of *daggers in mens' smiles*, and Chaucer warned of *the smiler with the knife under his cloak.* Be careful whom you trust because:

- The stranger's knife is the sharpest. (African)
- The bigger the smile, the sharper the knife. (Ferengi Rule of Acquisition #48, "Star Trek: Deep Space Nine")
- Not everyone with a long knife is a cook. (Russian/German/Dutch)
- A knife dressed as a sandwich is more likely to reach the stomach.

A century ago, Justice Oliver Wendell Holmes (1841-1935) promoted responsible self-defense when he pronounced in a Supreme Court decision, Detached reflection cannot be demanded in the presence of an uplifted knife. Nigerians further question, "If you fail to take away a strong man's sword when he is on the ground, will you do it when he gets up?"

"The chicken frowns at the cooking pot, ignoring the knife that killed it." (African) In Croatia they mock, "Someone with a knife in his back is not considered a brave man." Simply put, "To die with one's sword still sheathed is most regrettable." (Miyamoto Musashi 1584-1645)

"Before you can defend against a knife, you must learn to fight with a knife." As every street-fighter knows, "Don't pull a knife unless you are prepared to use it." Regarding such training, "If you want to understand your knife, you must first learn to follow your left hand."

Practice with real opponents. "Knife sharpens on stone, man sharpens on man." (Chinese) The same sentiment is similarly promoted in the religious saying, "As steel sharpens steel, so one friend sharpens another."

Allegedly, according to an Ethiopian saying, "A blade won't cut another blade; a cheat won't cheat another cheat." Yet, as the Filipino proverb goes, "Never catch at a falling knife or a falling friend," for "A desperate person will even hold on to a knife edge."

Christian Bovee (1820-1904) stated, "The [coward], like the scabbard, is an encumbrance when once the sword is drawn." Meanwhile, Irish dramatist Brinsley Sheridan (1751-1816) heartens, "Let your courage be as keen, but, at the same time, as polished as your sword."

U.S. Marines promote: "In a knife fight, he who brings the gun wins." Or, as the Spanish recognize, "An inch in a sword, or a palm in a lance, is a great advantage."

Pacifistic Expressions

As knives have long been the symbol of war, it is not surprising that they are also in proverbs promoting peace. The Bible famously advises, *And they shall beat their swords into plough-shares, and their spears into pruning-hooks.* (Micah 4:3; Isaiah 2:4) In the same vein, Buddism promotes, "The butcher who lays down his knife, at once becomes a Buddha." Even Napoleon recognized, "There are only two forces in the world, the sword and the spirit. In the long run the sword will always be conquered by the spirit."

"The heavy sword will not cut soft silk; by using sweet words and gentleness you may lead an elephant with a hair." (Moslih Eddin Saadi, 1184-1291)

At some point, every mother cautions, "If you play with a knife, you will cut yourself." Perhaps that is because, "He who plays with a sword plays with the Devil." (Galician) A Spanish proverb observes, "A child who fears beating would never admit that he played with a missing knife." A Kenyan saying promotes, "If a child cries for a knife, he should be given a stick instead."

In India, it is known, "Great anger is more destructive than the sword." And, in Italy, "Love rules his kingdom without a sword."

On the other hand, regarding vengeful planning, Thomas Moore (1779-1852) noted, "Who sleeps with head upon the sword/His fever'd hand must grasp in waking." A century ago, Peter Pan author James Barrie cautioned, "Temper is a weapon that we hold by the blade." Contemporary author Mitch Albom similarly warns, "Hate is a curved blade, and the harm that we do to others is also harm we do to ourselves."

In Zambia, a proverb promotes, "To start a fight, one does not bring a knife that cuts, but a needle that sews." This coincides with the Ugandan, "Before you throw the knife, look for the needle."

A few proverbs strike a workable balance between belligerence and pacifism. Several European cultures recognize, "One knife keeps another in its sheath," because, once unsheathed, "One knife whets another." (European) Consider the Polish prayer, "God grant me a good sword and no use for it," or the non-attributed, "Let the blade of the knife cut the one who sharpened it."

Nowhere is cautious moderation better promoted than in Massachusetts' motto: *Ense petit placidam sub libertate quietem* (By the sword we seek peace, but peace only under liberty.)

Insults

The word "word" hides within "sword," and when it comes to insults, nothing cuts like a knife proverb.

Cultures from around the world have particularly incorporated blade references to promote misogynistic attitudes, for instance:

- Educating a woman is like handing a knife to a monkey. (Hindu)
- Being but a woman, raise not the sword. (Latin)
- Stone keeps a knife in good form and beating keeps a woman in good form. (Indian)
- A blunt knife is an enemy to the hand, a bad woman is an enemy to the man. (Eastern Yugur)
- It fares ill with the house when the spinning-wheel commands the sword. (Portuguese/Spanish)
- Give your wife the short knife, and keep the long one for yourself. (Danish)

Given the above attitudes, women may be advised to "Choose a husband as you would choose a knife, look to its temper." Similarly, consider George Herbert's (1593-1633) recommendation, "In choosing a wife, and buying a sword, we ought not to trust another."

As for male criticism, consider the Italian, "Big knife, little man," or its French variant, "A short sword for a brave man."

Sexist remarks are not the only type of knife-related insults, however. Consider the ageist, "A man of sixty is only good for the knife" (Lebanese), meaning that old people should be slaughtered as worthless.

Several professions are also maligned with blade proverbs:

- Lawyers: A man may as well open an oyster without a knife, as a lawyer's mouth without a fee. (Barton Holyday, 1593-1661)
- Scientists: Science is an edged tool, with which men play like children and cut their own fingers. (Arthur Eddington, 1882-1944)
- Educators: Education is like a double-edged sword. It may be turned to dangerous uses if it is not properly handled. (Wu Ting-Fang, 1842-1922)
- Physicians: A quack doctor can kill you without a knife. (Chinese)

In traditional American culture, "Someone who eats peas with a knife" is considered uncouth, yet Polish author Stanislaw Lem (1921-2006) contrarily queried, "Is it progress if a cannibal uses a knife and fork?"

Lastly, if you are ever in a position to twist a person's words (or sword) against him, consider quoting Ancient Roman Terence: *Suo sibi gladio hunc jugulo!* (With his own sword do I stab this man!) (circa 185-159 B.C.)

A Falling Knife Has No Handle (Japanese)

From ancient philosophical foundations to contemporary fortune cookie wisdom, deep concepts have long entertained the human mind.

Several Eastern Zen cultures recognize, "A knife cannot whittle its own handle." Regarding handles, "If fate throws a knife at you, there are two ways of catching it: by the blade or by the handle." (Moroccan)

Nineteenth-century "Fireside Poet" James Russell Lowell noted, *Mishaps are like knives, that either serve us or cut us, as we grasp them by the blade or the handle.* And, Henry Ward Beecher (1813-1887) recognized, *The worst lies are those whose blade is false, but whose handle is true.*

In addition to handles, several of the most thought-provoking knife proverbs concern sheaths, such as "Do not go between the knife and the sheath," and, "The blade wears out the sheath." (French). A French remark curt recognizes, "Like sheath, like knife."

Outward appearances can be deceiving, however. Consider the Italian, "In a golden sheath, a leaden knife," or its ancient variant, "A sword of lead in a scabbard of ivory." (Latin)

As seen regarding handles and sheaths, wisdom is often found in simple observances. Consider: "You can't cut water with a knife," and "The knife doesn't open the mouth."

In his play *Revenge,* Edward Young (1683-1765) wrote, "The blood will follow where the knife is driven." Other deceptively simple proverbs include, "A knife is the tooth of the old, the tooth is the oldest knife," (Finnish), and, "Fingers were made before forks, and hands before knives." (Jonathan Swift, 1667–1745)

Conversely, some blade proverbs are not simply understood or are lost in translation. They are, nonetheless, worth pondering.

- The best time to sleep is the early morning, the best thing to do with a knife is to cut betel nut. (Assamese) (Betel nuts are chewed like gum as a mild stimulant, and this saying basically promotes leisurely living.)
- Only a knife knows what the inside of a coco-yam looks like. (African) (Only the person who experiences something knows what it was like.)
- He strikes with a leaden sword. (Ancient Latin) (He presents a useless argument.)
- When Oxford draws knife, England's soon at strife. (Old English) (Collegiate issues foreshadow national agendas.)
- Don't break the handle of a knife with your knee. (Promoting the benefits of discipline and order.)

Go forth and incorporate the wisdom of the centuries into your life. Promote blade proverbs in lectures, add them to your emails, and etch them onto your blades!

TRENDS

An uninspired speaker could theoretically remark that if a person has lived through one autumn—seen the changing of the seasons—that he or she has experienced them all. Or if someone has gazed at one snowflake, there's no need to look at another.

Or perhaps, that same shortsighted orator would presume that if an islander has been awake to witness one sunrise over the ocean, that person can rest assured he's seen all there is to see. The hole in the logic, of course, is that every snowflake is unique, no two trees transform or change colors at the same rate, and each sunrise is its own brilliant spectacle.

And no two handmade knives are alike. They are each individually handcrafted pieces of utilitarian art exhibiting their own characteristics, their own qualities and taking advantage of their own features. Inevitably, knifemaking inspiration is not only borrowed from an artisan's surroundings, but also from other craftsmen's edged creations. There is a bit of copying, whether consciously or subconsciously, that occurs in the world of handmade knives. That borrowing of inspiration results in trends—trends in knives.

When a modern resurgence in custom knives began in the first half of the last century, not too many craftsmen were building tiger-coral- or antique-tortoise-shell-handled knives, and no one was forging mosaic damascus blades or using anodized-titanium bolsters and frames, but they are today.

Some of those practices have become trendy and even evolutionary. The trends change from year to year, decade to decade and century to century. Some trends are revisited, and others last a short while never to reemerge. It makes being a knife enthusiast interesting. It keeps collectors buying, knifemakers making and book readers reading. So forget the uninspired speaker, ignore the shortsighted orator and delve into a chapter of wonderfully diverse, even trendy, knives.

LERCH

Jim Bowie Blades

(The Jim-Bow's)

Here's a phrase that doesn't sit well with North Americans—"a siege and massacre of Texans by Mexican troops." That's how Webster's New World Dictionary, Second College Edition, describes the events that took place at a Franciscan mission in San Antonio, Texas, in 1836. You may remember—the Alamo.

Col. James Bowie played a significant role in the Texas Revolution, culminating in the Battle of the Alamo, where he died along with other defenders. He was known as a fighter, soldier and frontiersman, and largely due to real and fictitious stories that surround Bowie, he has since become an American legend.

A famous duel between Samuel Levi Wells III and Dr. Thomas Harris Maddox—the Sandbar Fight—cemented Bowie's reputation of possessing a sort of prowess with a knife. The duel deteriorated into a melee in which Bowie, having been shot and stabbed, killed the sheriff of Rapides Parish, La., using a large knife.

One knife fight, albeit one in which guns were involved, not only gave rise to an American legend, but also a genre of knife. Known as the bowie knife, the style endures to this day. Modern knifemakers have interpreted the style, tweaked it, studied it and copied it. Some fashion exact replicas of famous bowie-style knives dating back more than a hundred years. Others prefer to vary the style.

All bowie knives have certain elements in common—long, curved blades with single edges and slight "false edges," or clip points, double guards and hefty handles. Some of the blades are thinner than others, and a good many resemble old kitchen knives. The fancier models today incorporate stabilized wood grips, damascus blades and even gold or pearl inlays. All were made possible by one man—Jim Bowie.

His brother Rezin may have designed the first bowie knife, or maybe it was Rezin's personal blacksmith. Yet if it wasn't for Jim's use of the knife in a legendary fight, it would have never become a symbol of America's hard-fought freedom. A debt of gratitude is owed to Jim Bowie and the knife that shares his name, the Jim Bowie blade, the bowie knife, the old "Jim-Bow."

▲ LIN RHEA: A thought-out and executed design includes an exacting blade shape and a sheep-horn handle with grooves just ripe for the grippin'. *(Chuck Ward Photography)*

◀ BOB CROWDER: The heft starts in the fill-your-grip, fossil-walrus-ivory handle and ends at the clip point of the ATS-34 blade. *(PointSeven photo)*

◀ TIM HANCOCK: She sashays her S-guard, wags her damascus blade and parades her African blackwood handle, inlaid with black lip pearl, in front of an appreciative audience. *(SharpByCoop.com photo)*

▶ **RUSS ANDREWS II: The damascus, clamshell-style C-guard waves from its perch above the fossil mammoth ivory grip and 14-inch W-2 blade of the custom bowie.** *(SharpByCoop.com photo)*

▶ **WESLEY DAVIS: A damascus blade and a giraffe-bone coffin in which to lay.** *(Ward photo)*

▶ **MIKE MOONEY: The blade shape is so exacting. Look at the slight rise in the center of the false edge that eventually tapers and disappears into the point. The steel is Alabama forge damascus, the handle ironwood, and the look all bowie.**

▶ **JOHN WHITE: Here's a sight for sore eyes—a spear-point bowie—handsome and fine enough to win the American Bladesmith Society Bill Moran Award in 2007. The bark-mammoth-ivory handle and silicon bronze guard further the cause.** *(PointSeven photo)*

▲ **TOM GANN: Where to start—the damascus with lines that actually shimmer down the blade, the singular character of that dog-bone grip, the domed pins, file work, or gorgeous guard? Poets had it easier describing a desert sunrise.** *(PointSeven photo)*

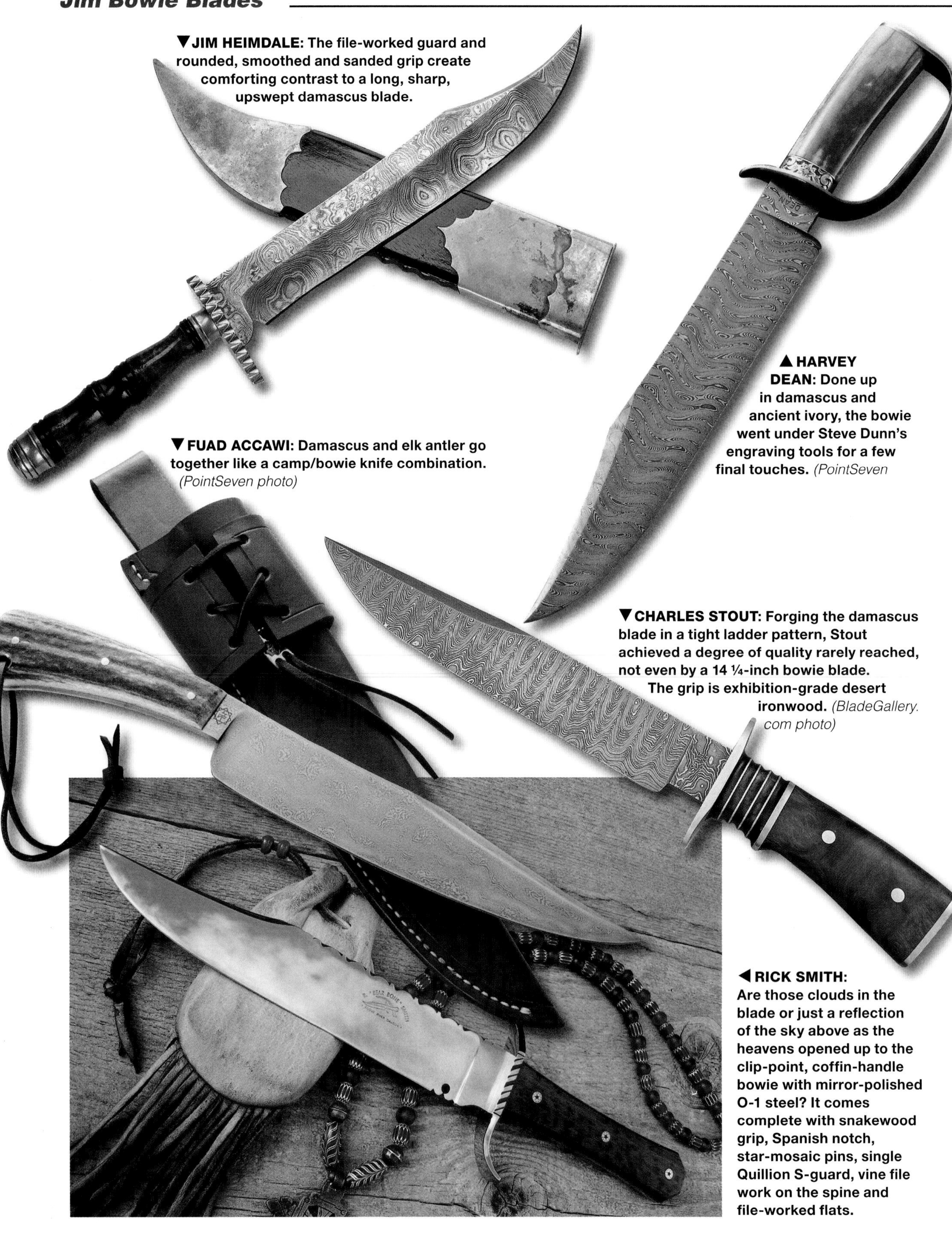

▼**JIM HEIMDALE:** The file-worked guard and rounded, smoothed and sanded grip create comforting contrast to a long, sharp, upswept damascus blade.

▲**HARVEY DEAN:** Done up in damascus and ancient ivory, the bowie went under Steve Dunn's engraving tools for a few final touches. *(PointSeven*

▼**FUAD ACCAWI:** Damascus and elk antler go together like a camp/bowie knife combination. *(PointSeven photo)*

▼**CHARLES STOUT:** Forging the damascus blade in a tight ladder pattern, Stout achieved a degree of quality rarely reached, not even by a 14 ¼-inch bowie blade. The grip is exhibition-grade desert ironwood. *(BladeGallery.com photo)*

◀**RICK SMITH:** Are those clouds in the blade or just a reflection of the sky above as the heavens opened up to the clip-point, coffin-handle bowie with mirror-polished O-1 steel? It comes complete with snakewood grip, Spanish notch, star-mosaic pins, single Quillion S-guard, vine file work on the spine and file-worked flats.

▶ **MIKE RUTH:** A Southwest bowie in stag. **'Nuff said.** *(Ward photo)*

◀ **TIM TABOR:** Named Maria for the wind that always blows in Texas calling for "My Maria," this Spanish Mona Lisa features a hand-forged "Texas Wind"-damascus blade, a file-worked, blued-damascus guard and a premium fossil-walrus-ivory handle. *(SharpByCoop.com photo)*

▶ **JAMES BATSON:** Even a sterling-silver-wrapped walnut handle with domed pins and a rectangular shield can't detract from the seamless shape of the 11 3/8-inch 1095 bowie blade. Give that dawg a bone! *(Ward photo)*

◀ **NICK WHEELER:** Wheeler sends a Southwest bowie to market donned in a silky-smooth, stabilized African-blackwood handle, a 416 stainless steel oval guard and a 10 ½-inch 52100 blade. *(SharpByCoop.com photo)*

▶ **DON HANSON III:** The wispy temper line stretches for nearly the entire length of the foot-long 1065 blade, while a single gold pin helps secure the fossil-walrus-ivory grip, all protected by a damascus S-guard. *(Mitch Lum photo)*

▲ **JAMES R. SHAVER II:** The three-bar damascus blade is outfitted with a one-bar cutting edge, hot blued, as are the steel and nickel silver fittings, all anchored by a Sambar-stag handle.

▶ **TERRY RODGERS:** The bowie knife pattern is established enough to embellish it only with a highly-patterned maple blade and a 5160 steel blade. *(Ward photo)*

◀ **JIM WALKER:** The blued-damascus blade is a perfect bedfellow to the blue-mammoth-ivory grip. *(Chuck Ward Photography)*

▶ **JON CHRISTENSEN:** The blade of the straight, steel bowie is clean, the blued-mild-steel guard left plain and the Bubinga wood handle smooth and unblemished. *(Mitch Lum photo)*

▲ **TERRY VANDEVENTER:** He forged wrought iron for the guard and 1084 steel for the blade, adding an antler and calling it a day.

▲ **MATT DISKIN:** The winsome walrus-ivory grip is decked out in domed pins, book-ended by mokumé and delivered to a damascus blade. *(PointSeven photo)*

▶ **JOSEPH KEESLAR:** The Southwestern bowie shows a little silver engraving n its ferrule, some stag in its grip and steel where it counts. *(PointSeven photo)*

◀ **JOHN WADE WALKER III:** The amber and walrus grip graciously allows the carved guard and gushing damascus blade to steal the limelight. *(PointSeven photo)*

▶ **J.R. COOK:** Damascus adorns and surrounds the mammoth-ivory grip and etched-iron fittings of this tasty Texas Toothpick. *(Ward photo)*

▶ **JASON KNIGHT:** Ebbs and flows. Rises and falls. Crests and crashes. Ups and downs. There are many ways to say the blade steel remains in constant motion. *(SharpByCoop.com photo)*

▲ **GARY MULKEY:** Silver-wire inlay acts as a couple clean fractures along the giraffe-bone handle, and the 1095 blade cuts its own swath. *(Ward photo)*

▶ **STEVE RAPP:** **The bow-tie-like handle and shield mimic the curvature of the clipped point. Notice how the center line along the length of the blade takes the bottom half of the clipped curve in stride and ends it beautifully at the point.** *(Eric Eggly, PointSeven photo)*

▶ **DENNIS FRIEDLY:** **It wasn't a bad idea to enlist the engraving talents of Gil Rudolph, something that goes nicely with a stunning mammoth-ivory grip and flawless 440C blade.** *(PointSeven photo)*

▲ **DAVID LISCH:** **The Broken-Heart-pattern damascus is ingeniously forged and matched up with a wrought-iron S-guard and a slim stag handle.** *(BladeGallery.com photo)*

▶ **J. NEILSON:** **The maker claims the oval guard of the swept-tip bowie is "jail bar" wrought iron, and the publisher opted not inquire as to where or how it was obtained.**

Tactically Impenetrable

◀ **KEN ONION:** Consisting of titanium, G-10 and CPM steel, the "Dead Sexy" folder is dead serious. *(Mitch Lum photo)*

◀ **GREG LIGHTFOOT:** The full-tang blades sport steel inner cores sandwiched between carbon fiber and complemented by leather cord wraps over python skin. *(SharpByCoop.com photo)*

▶ **PETER STEYN:** The Sandvik 12C27 blade features the maker's own "Crator" finish.

▲ **DAVID BOYE:** Though tactical in looks and handling, the Dendritic cobalt cutter is a basic utility sheath knife featuring a cord-wrapped handle and a 4-inch blade. *(Weyer photo)*

▶ **TIM GALYEAN:** The incredible blade shape and look, the geometric properties, cool handle overlays and the fact that it's a "flipper"-style, locking-liner folder with a pocket clip make it stand out from a crowd of tactical folders. *(SharpByCoop.com photo)*

▼ **NORMAN SANDOW:** Clean as a whistle is the ATS-34 gent's tactical with a textured-titanium handle.

▶ **KEITH OUYE:** The skull with the tentacle tongue eyes treasure lying before the CPM S30V blade, a blade that was heat treated by Paul Bos. *(SharpByCoop.com photo)*

▶ **LEE WILLIAMS:** Dig the black damascus tactical with the skeletonized blade and clip. *(SharpByCoop.com photo)*

▶ **RICK FRIGAULT:** The integral Karambit-style fixed blade parades a multi-ground blade reminiscent of a cobra hood, a G-10 handle scored in a rectangle pattern, and a pointy pommel perfect for tactical applications.

▲ **R.J. MARTIN:** The maker builds a solid flipper with positive lockup, a clean carbon fiber handle and re-curved, hollow-ground blade. *(SharpByCoop.com photo)*

▲ **MATT LERCH:** The titanium handle of the CPM S30V fighter is engraved by Mary Jo Lerch in an almost-thorn-branch-style pattern that is quite fitting. *(SharpByCoop.com photo)*

◀ **KIRBY LAMBERT:** Considering it's fashioned from CPM 154CM steel, carbon fiber, titanium and black G-10, not even fire would destroy the "Incinerator." *(SharpByCoop.com photo)*

▲ **THINKING BLADE KNIVES:** The upper frame of the titanium handle locks the blade open in what the maker calls a Xross Lock. *(Mitch Lum photo)*

▲ **DEAN BOSWORTH:** The mini-survival package includes an ATS-34 blade, and a signal mirror, sharpener, fire starter, fish hooks and line secured and hidden by a cord-wrapped handle. *(Hoffman photo)*

▲ **ROSS MITSUYUKI:** Such blade shapes have been referred to as "hawksbill," and orange and blue hue combinations as colorful plumage.

▶ PAT CRAWFORD: Hmm, do I wear the all-grey one, or the damascus and jeweled titanium piece? Honey, is the restaurant fancy? *(SharpByCoop.com photo)*

◀ JIMMIE BUCKNER: The re-curved 1075 steel blade bends down and drops at the pint, taking its cue from a curved and textured G-10 handle. *(PointSeven photo)*

◀ BRIAN FELLHOELTER: Green anodized liners match the lanyard and help highlight the steel and carbon fiber folder. *(Mitch Lum photo)*

◀ GARY LEBLANC: The "Air Assault" fixed blade is one solid piece of ATS-34 made even more tactically impenetrable with a canvas-Micarta® grip. *(SharpByCoop.com photo)*

▶ MATT CALDWELL: The stout, field-grade knife called for 154CM and canvas Micarta, and it got it. *(BladeGallery.com photo)*

▼**TODD BEGG:** If you ever find yourself in a situation where you need a combat cleaver with an A-2 blade, desert-ironwood handle and gold screws, then you're owed a "thank you" for your service. *(BladeGallery.com photo)*

◀**MICK STRIDER and DUANE DWYER:** Dwyer's "RC Tanto Trisula" is offered up in two versions of mega-machined S30V, "Striderized" titanium and G-10. *(Mitch Lum photo)*

◀**JEFF HALL:** With one semi-serrated and the other plain, and both with false edges, textured G-10 handles and integral finger guards, it's fun to hold a knife in each hand. *(PointSeven photo)*

◀**DEAN LANER:** The bead-blasted 154CM rescue knife sports a black-canvas-Micarta handle, a screw-driver blade tip, glass breaker on the handle butt, and serrated and plain edges. *(PointSeven photo)*

▲**JEREMY KRAMMES:** At close inspection, one realizes, while the blade is a homogenous S30V steel, the bolsters are Damasteel with a pattern that leads nicely into the carbon fiber handle scales. *(SharpByCoop.com photo)*

He Had a Cocky Dagger

The dagger is the very definition of cockiness. It breaks from the utilitarian, politically correct mold and basks in its individualism. Like a self-assured, strapping young lad, with chest out, gut in and fists clenched, daring schoolmates to make fun of his pa's profession, the dagger flares along its double edges and terminates at a sharp, stinging point.

Makers of daggers embrace the mystique surrounding the knife with dark, film-noir-style characteristics and features. Just like Wakizashis and Tantos that bring forth imagery of Samurais in darkened doorways, the dagger resurrects scenes straight from dime novels and Western movies, of gamblers on trains, cowboys in saloons and robbers leaping from horses onto covered wagons.

There's at least one writer and likely many others who will go into great detail about how a dagger is a utilitarian blade shape useful for all kinds of cutting chores, how it should not be considered sinister, evil or cuttingly cunning. The tip is a tried-and-true tool, after all, for fine cutting work and leather punching, while the long, curved blade excels at slashing rope or shaving wood.

Yet isn't the tarnished image all part of the allure of the dagger, the romance of the steel, the aura of the unsavory character? Shouldn't the dagger cling tightly to its rebellious side, capitalize on its bad rap and revel in its reputation? Not to worry. Any dagger worth its steel will take a stand, make a statement and cling everlastingly to its cold, calculating cockiness.

Joe Kertzman

▲ **VINCE EVANS: An inspired, classic design, the engraving gives way but isn't diminished by the splendid, carved desert-ironwood handle.** *(PointSeven photo)*

▶ **MIKE J. O'BRIEN: The maker rubbed the leaf-shaped dagger blade to a 1,000-grit finish, created a curved guard and gave it a snakewood grip.** *(Johnny Stout photo)*

◀ **CHRIS REEVE: The all-integral dagger is one solid piece of steel with only a braided-rayon grip, titanium fittings and 22k-gold spacers to embellish the gorgeously grooved blade.** *(Mitch Lum photo)*

▲ **JIM and JOYCE MINNICK: The Robert Eggerling damascus blade folds sweetly and silently into the antique-tortoise-shell handle with mild-steel overlays and 24k-gold inlays.** *(Mitch Lum photo)*

▶ **J.D. SMITH:** No, that's not a leather-wrapped handle, but an African blackwood grip cleverly carved, a sculpted pommel and Quillion guard, and a damascus blade forged by the maker. *(SharpByCoop.com photo)*

▶ **PAUL COOPER:** Shaping a blade like this damascus beauty takes more than a few files and a couple minutes, and the carved ebony handle was no menial task, either. *(PointSeven photo)*

▲ **DON HANSON III:** All the goodies in one blade, including damascus, fluted fossil ivory, twisted-gold-wire inlay and a bowtie-like guard, not that it needed dressing up. *(SharpByCoop.com photo)*

◀ **TIM HANCOCK:** Domed pins dot the ancient ivory handle, and roaming lines crisscross the damascus dagger blade. *(SharpByCoop.com photo)*

◀ **STEPHEN MACKRILL:** The carbon damascus pattern is near perfect, and the cape buffalo handle is a nice touch, but neither outshines the 12 emeralds, six diamonds and 18k-gold inlays. *(PointSeven photo)*

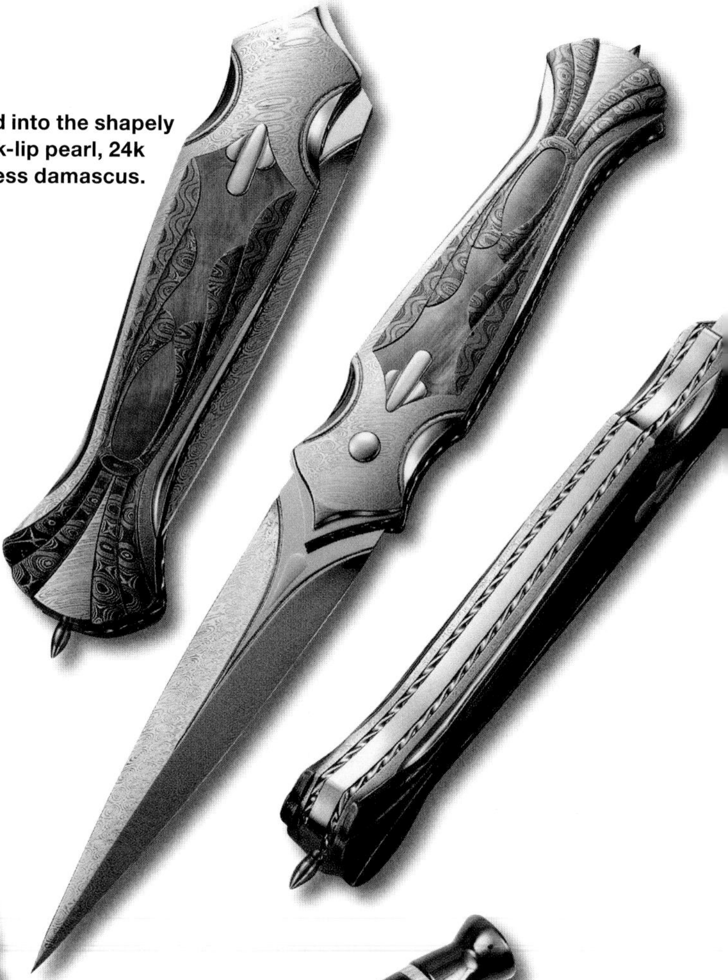

▶ **MATTHEW LERCH:** Inlaid into the shapely Damasteel dagger are black-lip pearl, 24k gold and Mike Norris stainless damascus. *(SharpByCoop.com photo)*

▲ **RONALD BEST:** If there was ever any doubt you could dress up a dagger then dissect this ivory and D-2 short sword featuring Jere Davidson engraving. *(PointSeven photo)*

◀ **JAMES SHAVER II:** The master damascus pattern makers forge the steel so it flows around the center line and leads straight to the pint. Other amenities include a curly maple handle and a hot-blued, mild-steel guard.

▶ **DON MAXWELL:** The pinks of the black lip pearl resurface in the Robert Eggerling damascus blade. She's a shapely little lass, too. *(Mitch Lum photo)*

▶ **STEVE CULVER:** The milky mammoth ivory with the gold wire inlays, the gray, mild-steel guard and the ladder-pattern-damascus blade converge in one great knife. *(Ward photo)*

▼ **ANDERS HOGSTROM:** Gold highlights the copper ferrule and pommel of the Salt Lake Ceremonial dagger, also done up in clay-tempered 1050 steel and walrus ivory.

▲ **LEE FERGUSON:** It's a mini dagger and made from steel, stone, gold wire and good-ol' ingenuity. *(Ward photo)*

▶ **JOSH SMITH:** The damascus push dagger feels so good in the hand, it might never see duty. *(PointSeven photo)*

▲ **RON WELLING:** Look closely and you'll see a diamond planted in the pommel of the walrus-ivory handle, a few colored spacers and a lot of damascus dagger blade. *(PointSeven photo)*

◀ **JIM SCHMIDT:** Phil Lobred shared this dazzling dagger from the hands of deceased, legendary knifemaker Jim Schmidt. The damascus is dripping with excitement, the file work fine, and the carved and gold-overlaid guard and pommel from the hands of a master. *(PointSeven photo)*

▲ **STEVEN RAPP:** Only rich dogs get ivory bones, and the elite would also appreciate gold inlay, engraving, a hand-finished blade and blood groove, and golden scroll across a silver sheath. *(PointSeven photo)*

▲ **DAN GRAVES:** The Quillions at the ends of the cross guard, as well as the pointed pommel, or skull crusher, of the dagger can be exchanged with shorter ones, also provided, while the elephant ivory handle, nickel silver guard and damascus blade stay put. *(SharpByCoop.com photo)*

Edges Of The Wood

▶ **RAY PIEPER:** The maple burl has more character than an inspired preacher at a pulpit. *(Chuck Ward photo)*

◀ **MARVIN SOLOMON:** The up-and-down strokes of Devin Thomas ladder-pattern damascus contrast with, yet somehow don't diminish the effects of, the California buckeye-burl handle. The water buffalo horn spacer is a nice reprieve. *(Chuck Ward photo)*

◀ **SCOT MATSUOKA:** The engraved bolsters, curly-Koa-wood handle and file work along the inner frame are equally easy on the eye. *(Mitch Lum photo)*

▲ **COLTEN TIPPETTS:** The leaf-shaped BG-42 blade practically begged for a bulbous Koa-wood grip. *(PointSeven photo)*

▲ **RICK BARRETT:** The graininess of the lace-wood grip is echoed in theW-2 blade, the latter complete with a hamon, or temper line. *(Cory Martin Imaging)*

▶ RICHARD HEHN: Alternating inserts of light and dark desert ironwood, all masterfully sanded and inserted, highlight the spotless and spot-on integral, drop-point hunting knife. *(Francesco Pachi photo)*

▶ BILL KENNEDY JR.: Just imagine the guys' faces when you slowly slide the green-curly-maple handle, then the shimmering D-2 blade, out of the ostrich-skin sheath. *(Chuck Ward photo)*

▶ ERIK FRITZ: The 1084 bowie and hunting knife measure about 10 inches each, including the lengths of African blackwood and spalted oak, respectively. *(PointSeven photo)*

◀ ANDERS HOGSTROM: If Masur birch were gold, which, in a way, it is, this 1050 Persian fighter would be one expensive sheath knife. The guard is antiqued and textured bronze. *(SharpByCoop.com photo)*

▶ **GORDON GRAHAM: A little filed bronze spacer furthers the impact of the handsome bowie's ironwood grip.** *(Ward photo)*

◀ **EMMANUEL ESPOSITO: Premium snakewood is the only non-steel element of the integral knife, but what a slab of wood it is.** *(Francesco Pachi photo)*

▶ **AL TRUJILLO: Ironwood and maple burl are the pretty little pulps of the file-worked D-2 fixed blades.** *(PointSeven photo)*

▶ **DICK FAUST: Dick broke out the good buckeye burl for the heavy-duty, sub-hilt fighter in 154-CM steel.** *(SharpByCoop.com photo)*

◀ **J. NEILSON:** The name given to the knife—"Dark Rider—Second Night"—implies a dark, mysterious character, like the murky damascus blade, a spectacular dresser, as in the ironwood handle and turquoise spacers, and a wicked side comparable to the pointed pommel and prone guard. *(Chuck Ward photo)*

◀ **DEREK FRALEY:** The curly Koa handle draws attention away from the 4-inch S30V edge, but it's only a temporary distraction. *(Mitch Lum photo)*

▲ **DERYK MUNROE:** Curly Koa wood slow dances with chocolate-brown titanium bolsters and an S30V blade. *(Mitch Lum photo)*

▶ **GARY MULKEY:** There's an Osage wood cross on the cocobolo handle and an upswept curve on the O-1 blade. *(Ward photo)*

▶ **RALPH RICHARDS:** Ringed and lined is the maple handle of the handsome hunter. *(Chuck Ward photo)*

▶ **MICHAEL TYRE:** The patterns never end, from the vine-pattern cable damascus blade by Marks Forge to the random-pattern-damascus bolsters, the rainbow-anodized-titanium frame, and finally to the black palm handle with 24k-gold screws. *(PointSeven photo)*

◀ **DAN FARR:** Grasses blow across the wood handle and the stainless steel finger guard, but nothing disturbs the steely stare of the blade. *(PointSeven photo)*

◀ **JON CHRISTENSEN:** It's called "flame maple" for a reason, and the fire licks the handle like a toddler's tongue on a twist cone. *(SharpByCoop.com)*

◀ **BEN VOSS:** African blackwood frames maple burl and preserves the natural art. *(PointSeven photo)*

▶ **HENRY TORRES:** The spike-head tomahawk is cloaked in curly maple. *(PointSeven photo)*

▶ **DON MCINTOSH:** The hues of the box elder handle complement the forest's fall colors. *(Ward photo)*

▶ **GEOFF KEYES:** **It took only a stabilized buckeye burl handle and a lot of hand sanding to dress up the ABS journeyman smith test knife.** *(Mitch Lum photo)*

◀ **MIKE WILLIAMS:** **The Hawaiian Koa wood handle of "Big Foot," combined with the 13-inch 1084 blade, would have impressed even the likes of Sasquatch himself.** *(PointSeven photo)*

▶ **MICHAEL RUTH:** **Maple wood is a syrupy sweet choice for a long 5160 bowie.** *(Ward photo)*

▶ **TOM FERRY:** **The she-oak handle is married to a dashing damascus blade and their children are destined to be sharp looking.** *(Mitch Lum photo)*

▲ **TIM TELLANDER:** **The rich brown and black hues of the maple handle dress up a 5160 hunting knife.** *(Johnny Stout photo)*

◀ **GARTH HINDMARCH:** So the hand doesn't slip off the smooth maple burl handle, Garth textured the bolsters and built the blade with an integral finger guard.

▲ **TRACY MICKLEY:** The 8-inch, hollow-ground CPM-154 blade sprouts forth from an Amboyna wood base. *(SharpByCoop.com photo)*

◀ **BRION TOMBERLIN:** The "Little River Camp Knife" features whirling ironwood grains along its grip. *(Ward photo)*

◀ **ROBERT BEATY:** With the stabilized and dyed birch in hand, the forefinger resting on the sheep horn spacer and the blade shimmering in the sunlight, the hunt heats up. *(BladeGallery.com photo)*

▲ **DANA HACKNEY:** The hunter emerged from the woods carrying a trophy-sized slab of spalted fiddle-back maple, and mounted it next to a 1084 blade. *(BladeGallery.com photo)*

Pristine Pocketknife Patterns

▶ **RICHARD ROGERS:** Call it a sowbelly if you will, but the three-blade ATS-34 folder with integral, grooved and pinned bolsters, and a checkered mother-of-pearl handle, is cuter than a sow's ear. *(Mitch Lum photo)*

▶ **T.R. OVEREYNDER:** When you have rose-gold bolsters, pins and a shield, and a black-lip-pearl body to boot, you flash your blades to the admiring crowd and go about your business. *(Terrill Hoffman photo)*

▶ **KIRK REXROAT:** The mosaic-damascus hues pay homage to the gripping mammoth ivory. *(PointSeven photo)*

▼ **BILL RUPLE:** Even more amazing than the fine fit and finish of the amber-jigged-bone handle, stainless bolsters and CPM-154 blade are the tapering, file-worked liners. *(Mitch Lum photo)*

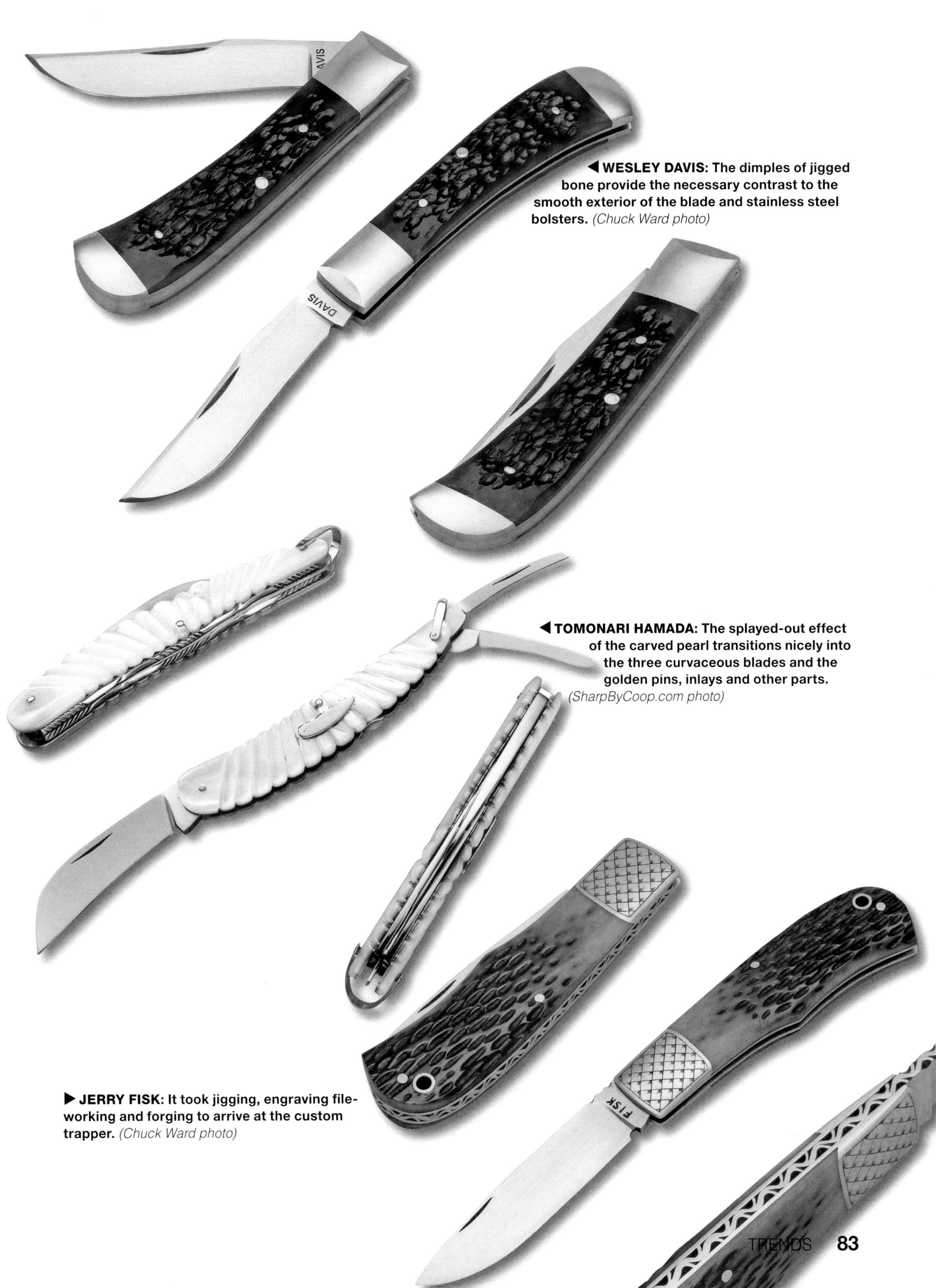

◀ **WESLEY DAVIS: The dimples of jigged bone provide the necessary contrast to the smooth exterior of the blade and stainless steel bolsters.** *(Chuck Ward photo)*

◀ **TOMONARI HAMADA: The splayed-out effect of the carved pearl transitions nicely into the three curvaceous blades and the golden pins, inlays and other parts.** *(SharpByCoop.com photo)*

▶ **JERRY FISK: It took jigging, engraving file-working and forging to arrive at the custom trapper.** *(Chuck Ward photo)*

◀ **C. GRAY TAYLOR:** Tim George's "shaded flowers" adorn the antique tortoise-shell handle of the smoker's knife, yet the 14k-gold liners, pins and inlays, not to mention the hand finished and fitted implements, help take this one to the market. *(PointSeven photo)*

▲ **HARVEY DEAN:** The feathery pattern of the forged damascus is definitely a focal point of the saddle horn trapper with India stag grip. *(Chuck Ward photo)*

◀ **JOHN HOWSER:** The engraved bolsters, short, sharp blades and jigged-bone and ancient-ivory grips of the Al Mar-style "SLB" knives are ingenious. Jim Small is the engraving talent. *(SharpByCoop.com photo)*

▲ **REESE BOSE:** The swayback jack is done up in D-2, stainless steel and stag. *(SharpByCoop.com photo)*

▶ **KELLY CARLSON:** The "Gold Chariot" awaits, driven by a Damasteel blade, assisted open by 14k-gold pins, adorned with gold discs and gold-lip-pearl scales, and inset with sapphires.

▶ **HARVEY DEAN:** The ancient ivory, damascus and engraving by Steve Dunn are equally spectacular. *(PointSeven photo)*

◀ **RUSTY PRESTON:** File work definitely fancies up a giraffe-bone-handled trapper. *(Johnny Stout photo)*

▲ **BILL RUPLE:** Even more amazing than the fine fit and finish of the amber-jigged-bone handle, stainless bolsters and CPM-154 blade are the tapering, file-worked liners. *(Mitch Lum photo)*

◀ **RYUICHI KAWAMURA: Whether you need a tweezers, a pick, a long edge or a short one, the stag-handle pocketknife with sterling-silver shield serves well.** *(PointSeven photo)*

▲ **DOC HAGEN: Is that what they mean by amber feels of neat?** *(Custom Knife Gallery of Colorado photo)*

▲ **TONY BOSE: Fitting and finishing five blades so they nest into their liners without friction is a practice saved for a skilled set of knifemakers. The sowbelly showcases a Remington bone handle.** *(SharpByCoop.com photo)*

The Tortoise and the Ware

▶ **REINHARD TSCHAGER:** The checkering and piqué work of the tortoise-shell handle, not to mention the gold pins and pendant, elevate the small pocket dagger to an art form. *(Francesco Pachi photo)*

▶ **PETER MARTIN:** One combination for a collector-grade knife might be a 376-layer damascus blade, mosaic-damascus bolsters forged by Doug Ponzio and inlaid with an 18k-gold spider, and a tortoise shell handle. *(Cory Martin Imaging)*

▶ **W.D. PEASE:** The gold-lip-pearl handle insert is carved to show a tortoise-shell inlay, and all is surrounded by Robert Eggerling damascus. *(SharpByCoop.com photo)*

▲ **DAN BURKE:** The stunning array of pocketknives parade tortoise-shell handles and pearl inlays. *(SharpByCoop.com photo)*

◀ **CLIFF PARKER:** Cliff likes to forge the animals into the blade and bolsters so that folks realize from what type of shell the handle is made. *(PointSeven photo)*

Classic Inclinations

Some opportunities are lost forever. It's impossible to recapture your youth, relive the past or go back in time. Strangers pass in the night without exchanging courtesies. Hard workers are passed over for promotions or let go during budget cuts. People make mistakes. They let things slide or time pass, and then they wake up one day and say, "If I had it to do over again, I'd ..."

Other opportunities are not lost to time. One can always revisit the classics. Whether movies, cars, hairdos, clothes, music or television programs, the classics are available today to be experienced over again, often as many times as one wishes.

Take knives for example. Does your heart desire a Samuel Bell-style bowie, a fighter of the Bill Moran ilk, a Bob Loveless-type chute knife or a San Francisco dress knife? Custom knifemakers with an eye toward the past are fashioning pristine examples of classic knives, often for a fraction of the cost of originals. The materials are the same or better, the styles exacting, the steels superior and the gestures of making the pieces a tribute to those who came before them.

The knives boast historic roots, proven designs, retro looks, old-school lines, refined materials and classic inclinations.

Joe Kertzman

◀ **T. KURAMOTO: The Marbles-style safety folder benefits from a pearl handle and fine English scroll engraving by Simon Lytton.** *(PointSeven photo)*

▶ **JERRY VAN EIZENGA: The late William Scagel called this type of dagger a "bowie," and no one in his right mind argued with Scagel. The master made them with stacked-leather and stag handles, brass guards and 5160 blades.** *(Ward photo)*

▲ **DR. JIM LUCIE: Not only does Jim hand forge his William Scagel-style hunters, but he also uses original parts, like the spacers and leather inherited from Scagel himself. A crown-stag butt completes the piece.** *(PointSeven photo)*

▶ **VICTOR ODOM:** In a nod to the George Herron style of knifemaking, Victor builds a couple drop-point, ATS-34 fixed blades with ivory and kudu-horn handles. *(PointSeven photo)*

▲ **BILL HERNDON:** The Samuel Bell bowie reproduction showcases a 440 stainless steel blade, guard and pommel, and an ivory handle. The velvet-lined sheath boasts grained leather and a sandblasted stainless steel throat and tip.

▶ **VINCE EVANS:** The reproduction of a 2nd-century-B.C. Iberian Falcata features a 20-inch damascus blade, a carved, antiqued-bronze guard and pommel, and a fossil-ivory hilt. The little knife below it follows the same classic lines. *(PointSeven photo)*

▶ **J.P. JONES:** The Bob Loveless-style fighter sports a 7-inch, ATS-34 blade, red liners and a black-Micarta® grip. *(Ward photo)*

◀ **A.G. BARNES:** There are few knifemakers who wouldn't recognize the Bill Moran ST-24 and even fewer who could actually build it. *(PointSeven photo)*

▶ **ROBERT PARKER:** The Bob Loveless-style chute knives remain true to the style, with Micarta® handles, tapered tangs and long, clip-point ATS-34 blades.

Our Fold Fathers

◀ **RON APPLETON: Like that of most fold fathers, Ron's style is recognizable but never predictable, and that includes this sculpted, curved and comely folder.** *(PointSeven photo)*

▶ **MICHAEL WALKER: Fold father Michael Walker works Damasteel, gold and titanium together into a clever cutter.** *(PointSeven photo)*

◀ **RON LAKE: It might be another inter-frame folder for Ron, but the gold, stag and stainless beauty is anything but ordinary.** *(PointSeven photo)*

▶ **JURGEN STEINAU: The small folder packs big punch, featuring a geometric LWL 34 blade, an 18k-gold handle and pearl, black pearl and Bakelite stone inlays.** *(Hoffman photo)*

▲ **DES HORN: The gold-lip-pearl handle of the Ball Release Lock Knife isn't nearly as gold as the 24k-gold-inlaid bolsters, as fashioned by Armin Winkler.** *(Hoffman photo)*

The Alloyed Nations

Are you friend or foe, communist or ally, or in modern times, terrorist or freedom fighter? Such questions matter when flying over international waters or visiting foreign lands, but not so much when studying the styles, heritage and customs of a people. There are occasions when war is put aside, when historical differences are overlooked, when politics are shelved. That sounds good right now, doesn't it?

The world of art, culture, ethnic diversity and national pride emerge in the tools and weapons of people throughout the planet. It is an opening of the minds, hearts and hands, a creative outpouring that erases borders and brings traditions alive, makes them palpable, presents new experiences and creates an environment of learning and sharing. This is not an inspirational speech; there are no pundits at the pulpit, no hidden agendas.

Knifemakers have opened their smithies, stopped selling wares and invited countries from around the world into their homes and workshops. Each brings his or her own tools of the trade and demonstrates their uses and attributes. No one is left out, no matter their political slants or world views. It is a sharing of ideas, a blending of styles and coalescence of cultures. Here people learn from others' mistakes. They teach new methods and share experiences openly, without ulterior motives.

The alloyed nations have congregated regardless of what the leaders of their countries think of the company they keep. Let the talking heads have their war of words, the brass clash and the politicians squabble. These are knives. They are the culture clashers, national treasures, ethnic edges and status symbols of the alloyed nations. Today they stand united before the fiery forge.

Joe Kertzman

◀ **STEVE SCHWARZER: The 1084 blade is clay tempered and forged using traditional Japanese methods. The tanto comes complete with a wrapped stingray-skin handle and carved gold pommel and menuki *(handle charm).*** *(PointSeven photo)*

▶ **KAJ EMBRETSEN: The Scandinavia fighter is as fierce as the mastodon that left the tusk, the forge that fired the damascus steel and the file that worked the thick spine.** *(PointSeven photo)*

◀ **FRED OTT: The double-edged takedown dagger, in a Japanese tanto style, includes a copper blade collar and ferrule, a cast-bronze guard and a desert-ironwood handle.**

▼**SCOTT SLOBODIAN:** Autumnal winds blow across the carbon steel blade of the Tanto, leaving marks on the silver fittings, and breezing across the silk-wrapped, stingray-skin handle. Barbara Slobodian is the real deal in engraving.

▶**DAVID GOLDBERG:** Following the wave of the hamon *(temper line)* is almost as fun as following the curve of the blade. *(PointSeven photo)*

▲**TOM FERRY:** The steel edge is welded to a mosaic-damascus blade, allowing the pattern to leaf its way toward a curly Koa handle, engraved tsuba *(guard)* and a gold-inlaid, koi-fish handle decoration. *(Mitch Lum photo)*

◀**RICHARD WRIGHT:** With cross-guards formed in a Celtic knot design, the origins of the dagger are revealed. The piece showcases Jerry Rados and Robert Eggerling damascus, pre-ban elephant ivory, rubies, and a spine carved in rope and vine patterns.

◀ **VINCE EVANS:** **The 18th-century Turkish yataghan is decked out in fossil ivory, silver and Turkish ribbon damascus, the latter a blade that stretches a full 20 inches.** *(PointSeven photo)*

◀ **GEOFF KEYES:** **The elk-handle camp knife comes to us in a scimitar style and dons brass bolsters and a 1084 blade.** *(BladeGallery.com photo)*

▲ **ED BRANDSEY:** **An expanded copy of an original Tlingit shaman's dagger, the blade is cold-blued O-1 tool steel with five graduated, round, gold-lip mother-of-pearl inlays, a stellar-sea-cow-bone handle, diamonds set in 14k-gold tube mountings and water-buffalo-horn inlays.** *(PointSeven photo)*

◀ **RICK BARRETT:** **Like traditional Japanese knives, the W-2 blade is forged with a distinct hamon *(temper line)*, and outfitted with a cord-wrapped bamboo handle.** *(Cory Martin Imaging)*

▶ **MICHAEL RADER:** **The curly maple handle with Peruvian walnut accents is only the beginning of the hand-forged damascus San-Mai sword that reaches a full four feet in length.** *(BladeGallery.com photo)*

▶ **RICK EATON:** The Mediterranean dirk features Arabesque engraving, 24k gold inlay, a mosaic damascus blade and a fossil-walrus-ivory handle. *(PointSeven photo)*

▼ **HANFORD MILLER:** The Italian Cinquedea, modeled after an exquisite Venetian specimen in the Wallace Museum of England, parades a forged-to-shape, leaf-spring-steel blade and a 43-part hilt, guard and pommel with ivory panels, and bronze roundels and rosettes. The handle is see-through at the middle and rear, fluted roundels. *(Buddy Thomason photo)*

◀ **DON HANSON III:** All a Mediterranean dirk really needs is a 1084 blade with mild hamon ***(temper line)***, an elephant-ivory handle, damascus bolsters and a willing participant. *(SharpByCoop.com photo)*

▶ **MARDI MESHEJIAN:** Mardi did some carving and shaping before he got to the point of the 20-inch 1095-and-4130-damascus poniard. *(SharpByCoop.com photo)*

▲ **RICHARD WRIGHT:** Master wood turner Spencer Cone crafted the African blackwood, mammoth-ivory and buffalo-horn handle with nickel-silver spacers. The random-pattern Jerry Rados damascus blade was forged to shape and hollow ground. Annette Wright is credited for the design.

◀ **FUAD ACCAWI:** The elk-handle Persian fighting knife even has forged furniture, but don't sit on it. *(PointSeven photo)*

◀ **WILLIAM LLOYD:** Credit metal smith R.C. Lund for the three-bar damascus blade, but the knifemaker for the rest of the 200 A.D.-period Celtic sword, including a carved warthog-tusk and carnelian handle, and a lignum vitae and bloodwood scabbard. *(PointSeven photo)*

▶ **ANDERS HOGSTROM:** Here's a Nessmuk fighter with a double hamon *(two temper lines)* along its exaggerated, sloped and curved blade, a carved-bronze guard and a red-walrus-tusk handle, all equally curvaceous.

▶ **STEVEN R. JOHNSON:** The tapered tang of the ATS-34 Mediterranean dirk is sandwiched by red liners and Indian Sambar-stag handle slabs. *(SharpByCoop.com photo)*

▶ RON WELLING: The damascus pattern of the Persian blade follows the swoop of the edge, and the walrus handle imitates the cradle, or palm, of the human hand. *(PointSeven photo)*

▲ WALLY HAYES: The damascus wakizashi stretches 19 inches overall and sports a leather-wrapped, stingray-skin grip. *(SharpByCoop.com photo)*

▶ ANDERS HOGSTROM: The toothy damascus blade of the fixed-blade Italian stiletto is just as handsome as the mammoth tooth grip. *(SharpByCoop.com photo)*

▲ ERIC ELSON: He wrapped the beaver-tail underlay in leather, gave it a black-bear-claw menuki handle charm and made a blade so grainy, so textured, forged and true, even though it's an Americanized tanto, the Japanese bow graciously. *(SharpByCoop.com photo)*

Furious Fighters

Hell hath no fury, and if these knives weren't furious they wouldn't be fighters. Or at least they wouldn't excel as fighters. Those wizened with years of experience in a testosterone-fueled world warn, "Never start a fight. Avoid it at all cost. But if you are forced to fight, if you have to, then fight as if your life depended on it."

If there is no passion behind a project, no fuel behind the fire, no fury in the fight, then the result will be disastrous. The passion behind the fighters on this and the following four pages is intense. Have you ever met a dull knifemaker? Sorry, but if you have, the blades are likely dull, too, and there is not a dull blade in the book. The passion bleeds from the surface of the steel and the pores of the ivory. The knifemakers are lively, excited and enthused. And the knives reflect their makers' intensity.

Those who fashion fine edges delve into the projects headlong, they lay it on the line, open themselves up to criticism and critique. They live and breathe knives, protect patterns, recognize beauty and utility, understand the science behind the steel and are inspired by use and abuse. They strive for perfection, aim for artistic freedom and achieve ultimate utility.

A fighter has a certain look and feel, a pointed purpose, a swedge along the spine, a good guard, sometimes a sub-hilt, a squared-off pommel or dagger-like demeanor. The purpose is protection, the aim to avoid conflict and the option to face it head-on. It is no game, but a serious undertaking with potentially dangerous consequences. Furious fighters have taken a stand and made their presence known.

Joe Kertzman

▼TODD BEGG: "Peacebreaker" stretches 13 ½ inches overall, passes itself off as a "straddle tang integral," and uses a D-2 frame and re-curved blade to complement a curly-Koa-wood grip. *(Mitch Lum photo)*

▼GEORGE HERRON: A trio of fighters features 154CM blades, stainless guards and walrus-ivory handles. *(SharpByCoop.com photo)*

▶THAD BUCHANAN: The 6 3/8-inch CPM-154 blade tapers at the tang to reduce the weight of the mammoth-ivory handle and make the fighter more fit for flailing. *(SharpByCoop.com photo)*

▶ **JOHN WHITE:** The damascus pattern is so tight and true, the file work so fancy and the silver so shiny, even the bowtie-shaped guard is nearly overlooked. *(PointSeven photo)*

◀ **CHUCK SCHUETTE:** Even the guard of the 16 ½-inch fighter is pointed and primed, while the foot-long 1084-and-15N20 blade is curvaceous, and the ironwood handle hot and handy. *(SharpByCoop.com photo)*

◀ **STEVEN R. JOHNSON and DIETMAR KRESSLER:** The asymmetrical boot knife is the only existing full-integral blade made in cooperation between the two knifemakers. Note the differing blade shape from one side of the knife to the other. *(Francesco Pachi photo)*

▲ **DON MCINTOSH:** The swedge along the 52100 spine tapers toward the point and meets the edge in a strategic location. *(Ward photo)*

◀ **JAY HARRIS:** Adding a folding factor to a stag-handle-sub-hilt fighter is akin to spiking the punch. *(Mitch Lum photo)*

▶ **NICK WHEELER:** The flat-ground W-1 blade showcases a temper line so squiggly it challenges the pattern of the stabilized maidou-burl handle. *(SharpByCoop.com photo)*

▼ **DIETMAR KRESSLER:** The sub-hilt fighter won "Best Fixed Blade" at the 2006 Knifemakers' Guild Show, a prize worth fighting for. Do you think the mammoth-tooth grip had anything to do with it, or the tapered, integral tang, sub-hilt and pommel? Wow. *(PointSeven photo)*

▶ **EDMUND DAVIDSON:** Another student of the fight, Edmund builds a big 440C integral with a cocobolo grip. *(PointSeven photo)*

◀ **RICARDO VELARDE:** Ricardo has become so good at creating the pattern we almost take his ancient-ivory-handle sub-hilt fighters for granted... almost. *(PointSeven photo)*

▶ **JOHN YOUNG:** Another integral in which the hilt, sub-hilt and tapered tang are one piece, it seems being a prize fighter is nearly becoming common place, but the ironwood grip also helps take this one beyond the ordinary.

▶ **MICHAEL MCCLURE: The mammoth ivory of the sub-hilt fighter is milky in caramel-colored and as sticky sweet as the hollow-ground blade.** *(BladeGallery.com photo)*

◀ **DAN GRAVES: Damascus is part of what makes the knife a gentleman's presentation fighter. The pre-ban-ivory grip is a second factor.** *(SharpByCoop.com photo)*

◀ **GIL HIBBEN: Gil has always been good at tweaking popular patterns to give them a look all his own. The handle is ebony, the damascus blade is black and the pommel is pointed.** *(SharpByCoop.com photo)*

▶ **RUSS ANDREWS II: Forging damascus is one thing, outfitting a knife with a stag handle relatively common, dying the stag an extra step and carving the damascus pommel so it recreates the grooves of the stag going above and beyond the call of duty.** *(SharpByCoop.com photo)*

▲ **JIM HAMMOND: The maker studied what he considers the four most popular fighting knife designs and created this 440C and stag composite from them.** *(SharpByCoop.com photo)*

▶ **CURT ERICKSON:** The furious fighter is armed with a stag grip and an engraved guard. *(SharpByCoop.com photo)*

▶ **COLTEN TIPPETTS:** For some reason coffin-handle fighters just call out for African blackwood handles and plain, smooth 52100 blades. *(PointSeven photo)*

▶ **J.D. SMITH:** The knifemaker eased the ebony handle into the 1095 blade by forging a damascus guard for the pretty piece. *(SharpByCoop.com photo)*

▲ **MICHAEL LOVETT:** The Bob Loveless-style chute knives sport ATS-34 blades, 416 stainless steel fittings and elephant-ivory handles. *(SharpByCoop.com photo)*

▶ **THINUS HERBST:** The bead-blasted blade complements the damascus bolster, while the desert ironwood handle tries to anchor the far-out fantasy fighter. Check out the humps and bumps and imagine the bruises. *(Dewald Reiners photo)*

Stag-Handle Hotties

Staples—those are things that have worked for so long and done such a good job that they become regular parts of a whole. Stag is a staple handle material of handmade and factory knives for several reasons. It is textured and aids in hand purchase.

Stag, particularly Sambar stag from India, is colorful, with black, brown, beige, yellow and red hues. It is stable—it does not shrink or expand as much as other materials like ivory, wood or pearl. At one time, before regulations prohibited the harvesting of Sambar stag, it was plentiful. And it is making a comeback again now that regulations are periodically eased.

Stag is relatively inexpensive compared to other handle materials. It is easy to work, to drill through, taper, shape and sand. You can dye and buff stag. It's beautiful and it complements other materials, like wood and steel. There's not much stag doesn't excel at doing for handmade knives. It is a staple.

What is harder to put into words is the way stag makes knives look like knives. There is something about a stag-handle hunter or a stag pocketknife that screams, "Use me, cut with me and hold me." It is a nice all-around source for knife grips. And in some people's eyes, it is gorgeous. So let's go stag, have a little stag party and look at some stag-handle hotties.

Joe Kertzman

▶ **LORA SUE BETHKE: The handle of the damascus fixed blade includes silver, fiber, leather and stag.** *(PointSeven photo)*

▶ **DAN FARR: A little stag and a lotta love.** *(PointSeven photo)*

▲ **DENNIS FRIEDLY: Leaves and vines separate stag from steel.** *(PointSeven photo)*

◀ **TIM HANCOCK: The eye-popping damascus pattern extends from the blade to the frame, spacer and guard, and is highlighted by file-worked spacers and an amber-stag handle.** *(PointSeven photo)*

▶ **JOHN PERRY:** It never ceases to amaze how knifemakers remember every detail, like the nickel-silver guard and butt cap, the blued steel spacer and pommel nut, and the way the butt cap is file worked to emulate the grooves of the stag. *(SharpByCoop.com photo)*

◀ **TIM TABOR:** The Sheffield-style bowie begins with a 7-inch damascus blade, and moves into a damascus guard, a bronze spacer and a sweet stag grip. *(SharpByCoop.com photo)*

◀ **THAD BUCHANAN:** The CPM-154 boot knife has the advantage of a stag handle that is easy to grab onto and pull it from the old footwear. *(Photo by Coop)*

▶ **SHAWN ELLIS:** The hot-blued "Backdraft"-damascus blade of the small bowie almost steals the show, but then along comes the stag handle and filed butt cap that matches the texture of the grip. *(Ward photo)*

▲ **RUSTY POLK:** Are there copper colors in the "lightning"-pattern damascus blade that complement the stag grip, or is it just an illusion?

▶ **HENRY TORRES: You have to like the way the 52100 blade stretches into a slightly tapered clip point, the way the stag grip is bold and beautiful, and the way the copper spacer is understated.** *(PointSeven photo)*

▶ **GREG NEELY: The little extra touch of engraving the spacer and butt cap of the stag-handle bowie brings it to a new level. The 5160 blade stretches 11 ¼ inches in length.** *(PointSeven photo)*

◀ **JERRY FISK: The master smith knows that polishing the stag at the ends and letting an engraved guard and pin heads do the talking is one way to accomplish a hot little W-2 fixed blade.** *(Ward photo)*

▶ **LIN RHEA: Bronze highlights and brings out the hues of the Southwest bowie's stag handle.** *(Ward photo)*

◀ **RON REEVES: Stag, nickel silver and 5160 is all the knifemaker felt necessary for a hot little hunter, and who's to argue?** *(Ward photo)*

◀ **DICK FAUST: Dick calls it his "heavy-duty hunter," and there's little doubt the stag-handle 154-CM hunting knife can field dress with the rest of them.**

▶ **WESLEY DAVIS: One nature created—the stag handle; and one comes from man—the impressive 1084-and-15N20 damascus blade.** *(Ward photo)*

▶ **J.W. RANDALL: The big-belly skinner benefits from a 15N20-and-1084-damascus blade** *(the big belly)*, **a stag handle and nickel silver guard.**

▶ **FRANK GAMBLE: The deer-antler handle is held by a copper sleeve and attached to an A-6 blade left rough in places for effect.** *(BladeGallery.com photo)*

▶ **ED BRANDSEY: Turquoise inlays grace the butt cap and sheath, and red liners and a wood spacer complement the dyed-stag grip.** *(Cory Martin Imaging)*

▶ **R.W. LOVELESS:** Mr. Loveless knows a little about stag, buffing pins and polishing perfect blades. Reportedly, this is Loveless's only New York Special with a utility blade. *(Francesco Pachi photo)*

◀ **MIKE HOUSTON:** Climb the ladder-pattern damascus blade up to the nickel silver guard and look over the stag horn harvest. *(Mitch Lum photo)*

▲ **BENONI BULLARD:** The red spacers and file-worked guard remind one of a bowtie on a well-dressed gent going stag to a party. *(Ward photo)*

▲ **MIKE RUTH:** The "Buckaroo" is a stag-handle damascus fixed blade itching for a ride in the saddle bag. *(Ward photo)*

▶ **BRION TOMBERLIN:** The stag-handle 1084 skinner won the Clyde Fischer Award at the Old Washington, Ark., School of Bladesmithing.

▶ RON LAKE: Lake might be known for inter-frame folders, but he's also partial to stag. *(Francesco Pachi photo)*

◀ RICARDO VELARDE: No matter whether a sub-hilt fighter or a drop-point hunter, Ricardo goes stag in either case. *(PointSeven photo)*

▶ J. NEILSON: In Jay's "Generations Series" of trailing-point skinners are four sizes of 1084 fixed blades with mustard patinas, ironwood spacers and stag handles. *(Ward photo)*

▶ **MITCH EDWARDS: The crown-stag handle isn't the only thing that defines it as a rifleman's bowie—the S-curved guard and 1065 blade with an aged patina help in that respect.** *(SharpByCoop.com photo)*

▶ **WES BYRD: The Joe Keeslar-style knife sports a 1084 blade, a stag grip and an integral guard.** *(PointSeven photo)*

◀ **RICK DUNKERLEY: It doesn't get much better than heat-colored Dunkerley damascus, unless you consider dyed stag, file-worked back spacers or anodized-titanium thumb discs and liners.** *(PointSeven photo)*

◀ **CHARLES STOUT: The trailing-point hunter showcases a convex-ground, ladder-pattern-damascus blade, a nickel-silver guard, red fiber spacer and a Sambar stag handle.** *(BladeGallery.com photo)*

▶ **ROB HUDSON: The bird's-eye maple spacer is a nice way to accessorize a stag grip.** *(BladeGallery.com photo)*

Fowl, Fur and Fish Knives

Some tools are specialized, others purpose driven. They are built for specific tasks or needs, and they are designed, altered and tweaked until they serve their purposes well. Such could be said for modern hand-made and factory hunting, fishing and bird-and-trout knives.

It's no coincidence that, when visiting the BLADE Show in Atlanta each year, or the S.H.O.T. Show in Las Vegas, when one happens upon a fine fillet knife, a nice bird-and-trout knife or a neat, drop-point hunter, it is inevitably designed by someone who claims to be a hunting or fishing fanatic. It is just such folks who spend every spare moment, every waking hour in the field or on a lake.

They don waders and cast into the best trout streams in the land. They drive hundreds of miles, hike into the high country, carry packs, sleeping bags and tents, and brave freezing temperatures just for a chance to land a brown trout in a mountain lake or down a deer in a wooded dell.

These are not folks who bring along a steak knife to field dress a deer. They aren't toting bowies for filleting fish (at least not most of them), and they aren't carrying daggers for cleaning birds. They bring hunting knives, skinners, fishing knives, bird-and-trout knives, and they know what they are, how to use them and how they work best. They aren't hiking through the Adirondacks just to fumble around with a dull blade or one built for the wrong purpose.

Such is the case with the knives on this and the following six pages. The blades, bevels and edges are a feast for the eyes. These are knives designed to perform specific duties. They are made with care, passion and purpose. Each is fashioned for one reason and one reason only, and together they excel at their given tasks. Featured herein are the fowl, fur and fish knives, and they aren't your average box cutters.

Joe Kertzman

◀ **MARVIN SOLOMON:** Once you've seen a skinner, you recognize a skinner. And this is a skinner, a beautiful damascus skinner, with mosaic pins, a mammoth-ivory grip and a red, leather thong. *(Ward photo)*

▶ **MIKE YOUNT:** Purpose designed as a bird-and-trout knife, every element is coordinated—the caramel color of the mokumé bolsters, the copper hues of the mosaic pins, the brown tones of mammoth ivory and the David Wilson damascus blade. *(Ward photo)*

◀ **JOHN BARTLOW:** The whitetail hunter wears not a stag grip, but a mastodon-ivory handle, and an ATS-34 blade. *(PointSeven photo)*

▶ **DON HANSON III:** The random damascus blade is as subtle as the mammoth ivory handle is spectacular. *(Mitch Lum photo)*

▶ **CURT ERICKSON:** Aside from having the ability to fashion sweet stag-handle hunting knives, Curt has a distinct advantage over other knifemakers. He's married to Julie Warenski-Erickson who engraves the sharp objects like there's no tomorrow. *(SharpByCoop.com photo)*

▶ **J.R. REEVES:** Once the stag handle was dyed just so, it sent shivers down the spine and face of the damascus blade. *(Ward photo)*

◀ **HARVEY KING:** There's something about walking around with a giraffe-bone-handle hunting knife, particularly one engraved by Jody Muller, that makes you feel taller. *(Hoffman photo)*

▲ **GARTH HINDMARCH:** It might not be able to cut down a redwood, but the burl handle comes from just such a giant tree. And the Vladimir Vancura engraving could bring Paul Bunyon to his knees.

◀ **SEAN O'HARE:** The S30V "Sparrow" sports a stabilized-wood grip and a black-polyester spacer. *(SharpByCoop.com photo)*

▶ **DEAN BOSWORTH:** Mike Norris "Gatorskin" damascus is gladdened by ironwood handle scales, framed mosaic bolsters and mosaic pins. *(Hoffman photo)*

▶ **LIN RHEA:** The bird-and-trout is damascus, blackwood and bronze, and those should be the materials the medals are made from at the next Olympics. *(Ward photo)*

◀ **JERRY LAIRSON:** Honed is the giraffe-bone hunter and skilled is the maker. *(Ward photo)*

◀ **THAD BUCHANAN:** The semi-skinner in amber stag is sweet and solid. The tang tapers and the handle swells. *(SharpByCoop.com photo)*

▶ JERRY HOSSOM: Some guys study bird-and-trout knives before attempting to fashion one, and others memorize every aspect of them, then improve upon them, add madroña-burl grips and CPM-154 blades. They hollow-ground the steel until it will cut through a walrus, let alone a pheasant or fish. *(SharpByCoop.com photo)*

◀ DON PARRISH: Pink ivory won't get lost in the woods, but any hunter worth his weight would hold on tightly to this D-2 skinner. *(Ward photo)*

▶ STEVE JOHNSON: The blade of the hunter was designed in collaboration with collector Pierluigi Peroni, but the snakewood handle is the way the tree left it, only sanded and buffed a bit. *(Francesco Pachi photo)*

▶ R.W. LOVELESS: The semi-skinner and drop-point hunter set is a rare example of the very few knives Loveless made with stacked-leather handles. *(Francesco Pachi photo)*

◀ BILL DUFF: In case one needs a small caping or bird-and-trout knife, there's one in the ironwood handle of the hunter, and both pieces are file worked to perfection. *(Ward photo)*

▶ **JIM FERGUSON:** The semi-skinner is treated to a Maidou-burl handle, a flat-ground ATS-34 blade and a nickel-silver guard that accepts the thumb when choking up to use the fine knife. *(Johnny Stout image)*

▶ **MARK KNAPP:** It isn't often one sees a damascus fillet knife with a fossil-walrus-ivory grip, and one should be glad for the opportunity. *(BladeGallery.com photo)*

▼ **C.R. MILES, JR.:** The bulbous curly maple handle tapers into a slim water-buffalo-horn guard, which in turn leads to a wide 440C blade. *(Hoffman photo)*

▶ **ERIK FRITZ:** The oak handle is formed just so, and the damascus "W's"-pattern blade forged in a fiery furnace indeed. *(BladeGallery.com photo)*

▲ **KEVIN HARVEY:** Calling it a "warthog hunter" just doesn't do it justice, especially considering the engraved, integral O-1 carbon steel bolsters, the buffalo horn spacers and the differentially-heat-treated blade. *(BladeGallery.com photo)*

▶ **DEAN LANER:** Ironwood and stag make for are a nice combination on a D-2 hunting knife. *(PointSeven photo)*

◀ **BILL MORAN:** Phil Lobred is the lucky owner of this damascus hunter with engraved guard and smiling-moon-embellished leather sheath. *(PointSeven photo)*

▲ **DAVE LISCH:** He is the sole author of the giraffe-bone hunter with the mosaic-damascus blade and damascus pins. *(Mitch Lum photo)*

▼ **STEVE KELLY:** More of a fighter than a hunter, the "fossil hunter" would suffice for either, but is really called such because it would take care of business when hunting fossils like the walrus ivory that graces the grip. The ironwood spacer is a nice touch, and the damascus blade a beauty. *(BladeGallery.com photo)*

▶ **DICK FAUST:** It may be a small 154-CM drop-point hunter, but the buffalo-horn handle is big time.

▶ **GORDON CHARD:** The 4-inch hunter boasts a hollow-ground, hand-finished VascoWear blade and a stabilized-maple-burl handle. Russ Green fashioned the leather sheath. *(David Hopkins photo)*

◀ **CHARLIE MAJORS:** It's hard to know where to look first, at the stabilized-mesquite-burl handle, the leather sheath or the engraved guard. *(Johnny Stout photo)*

▲ **BILL LEVENGOOD:** The leather washers bring out the brown in the Sambar-stag butt cap, while the ATS-34 blade complements the nickel silver fittings.

◀ **JOHN WHITE:** The South African black-ivory handle of the hunter is shaped to hold in several advantageous positions, and the damascus blade to cut in more than one way. *(Ward photo)*

◀ **JERRY MCCLURE:** The cleaver/hunter set is stunning in twist-Damasteel blades and mammoth-ivory grips.

Hand Me the Flipper

▲ **KEN ONION: Not only does the mid-tech folder have a stud lock, it's a stud of a knife, including a one-hand-opening "flipper" mechanism** *(extended tang)*, **a CPM-154 blade and blue-twill G-10 handle inlays.** *(Mitch Lum photo)*

▼ **D.B. FRALEY: The full-dress knife is a flipper folder in Gerome Weinand damascus, mother-of-pearl and fully file-worked titanium.** *(Mitch Lum photo)*

▶ **TODD BEGG: Don't expect a straight line on the "Front Line" flipper folder, but curves throughout the CPM-154 blade, green-Micarta® handle and zigzag titanium frame.** *(PointSeven photo)*

Blades of the Behemoths

The editor of Knives 2009 has been at this for more than a decade. Yet, when appreciating mammoth-tooth, mastodon-ivory or other fossilized knife handles, awe eventually sets in—astonishment, really, over the fact that the animals from which the bones came lived in prehistoric times. They roamed the planet millions of years ago. They tread the earth before and during caveman times.

The wooly beasts existed on an undisturbed planet, eating fresh grasses, tearing limbs from trees, under the blazing sun, the moonlit sky and the open heavens. None of human history had happened yet.

Today, in the first decade of the 21st century B.C., knifemakers offer the bones, tusks and teeth of such otherworldly beasts—behemoths, to be exact—on their handmade knives, and knives that are otherwise made from modern alloys, steels, damascus, titanium, gold, silver, G-10 and carbon fiber.

The prehistoric meets the post, post-modern era. It's a conundrum, an anomaly, a twist of fate that has brought evolution to the present. That's a good way to describe it, as "evolutionary art." The fossilized ivory is so full of character, so colorful, there are no other words to describe it but as breathtakingly beautiful. The mammoth tooth is like a dental rainbow. These are the "ivory-league" knives, the "tooth cutters"—the blades of the behemoths.

Joe Kertzman

◀ **LEON TREIBER: Remarkable are the green of the mammoth tooth, the copper of the mokumé and the Spirograph of the blade.** *(Ward photo)*

▲ **MIKE RUTH: The mammoth-ivory hunter is 5160 steel and style.** *(Ward photo)*

▲ **ALLEN ELISHEWITZ: The "Scarab" knife wears mammoth-tooth handle scales, a Mike Norris damascus blade, titanium liners, and front and rear damascus bolsters.** *(V. Elishewitz photo)*

▶ **KIRK REXROAT:** Mammoth tooth, damascus and mosaic damascus provide pattern, pattern and more pattern. *(PointSeven photo)*

◀ **DAN FARR:** Ancient ivory lends the lines that the engraving mimics and the knife carries forth. *(PointSeven photo)*

▶ **DON HANSON:** Blue this blue could only be premium Siberian mammoth ivory ... or an ocean or sky. The mosaic damascus is forged by Hanson himself. *(SharpByCoop.com photo)*

◀ **RUSTY POLK:** Damascus, mokumé and mammoth ivory are the mixed media of a drop-point skinner.

▶ **JERRY MCCLURE:** The lines are mammoth ivory, the circles rose-colored Damasteel and the squiggles Jody Muller engraving. *(Hoffman photo)*

◀ **JOHN WHITE:** Brown, green, beige and blue is the mammoth-ivory handle of the damascus fixed blade. *(SharpByCoop.com photo)*

▲ **GAYLE BRADLEY:** The mammoth had the most colossal teeth in the valley. *(Ward photo)*

▶ **HARVEY DEAN:** The veins of the mammoth ivory greet the gold inlays like long lost brothers, and the Steve Dunn engraving is a fine friend to the feathery damascus. *(PointSeven photo)*

◀ **BILL RUPLE:** If the mammoth ivory was a roadmap, we'd be lost, and if the Wes Davis damascus was a crossroads, there'd be countless ways to go. *(PointSeven photo)*

◀ **DOC HAGEN:** Even the untrained eye picks out brown, green, orange, blue, beige and black in the mammoth-bark-ivory handle of the four-line, ATS-34 trapper, a reproduction of a Camillus model. *(Custom Knife Gallery of Colorado photo)*

▶ **PAT CRAWFORD:** It's not overkill to marry damascus, jewels and mammoth tooth, it's just killer. *(PointSeven photo)*

▶ **CLIFF POLK:** Even the color red rears its handsome head on the mammoth ivory grip of the ATS-34 auto. *(Ward photo)*

◀ **JIM KRAUSE:** The mammoth ivory gives color to the Damasteel folder. *(Ward photo)*

▲ **GREG LIGHTFOOT:** The mammoth tusk crackles with excitement, while the lively stainless damascus blade carries on the enthusiasm. *(SharpByCoop.com photo)*

▶ **TIM HANCOCK:** The pattern of the damascus is concentric in places, and the ancient ivory on somewhat of a parallel plane. *(SharpByCoop.com photo)*

◀ **KEN ONION:** Under normal knife circumstances, gold-anodized titanium would be the most colorful part of a knife. Not so on the damascus Zero Tolerance knife with the mammoth-ivory grip. *(Mitch Lum photo)*

◀ **MICHAEL TYRE:** Blue mammoth ivory brings out the blues of the titanium frame, the pattern of the Devin Thomas raindrop damascus, the gold of the screws and even the white of the pearl. *(PointSeven photo)*

▶ **DAVID MIRABILE:** Ancient walrus ivory is as striped as the damascus blade is swirled. *(PointSeven photo)*

▲ **RAY RYBAR:** The damascus bowie showcases a copper-colored edge, a curly guard and an ancient ivory grip. *(PointSeven photo)*

◀ **MARK KNAPP:** The 1095 damascus hunter gives two for one in the extinct behemoth department—mammoth tooth and fossil walrus ivory. The bolster, guard and spacer are mokumé. *(BladeGallery.com photo)*

▶ **MACE VITALE:** The mammoth tooth had some tartar buildup but no cavities. *(SharpByCoop.com photo)*

◀ **DAN WESTLIND:** The fighter with the mammoth-tooth handle and damascus blade and bolsters is so highly patterned it would camouflage itself against a zebra. *(BladeGallery.com)*

▶ **JOHN YOUNG:** The bark mammoth ivory really does resemble tree bark, and the mosaic pins and engraved bolsters true art. *(SharpByCoop.com photo)*

▶ **JOSH SMITH:** For the grip of a damascus folder, the mammoth ivory adds a little hand purchase and a lot of class. *(PointSeven photo)*

◀ **CHARLES SAUER:** The mammoth-ivory handle anchors a 5160 hunting knife, including the cable damascus bolsters. *(PointSeven photo)*

◀ **MICHAEL TYRE:** Blue mammoth ivory brings out the blues of the titanium frame, the pattern of the Devin Thomas raindrop damascus, the gold of the screws and even the white of the pearl. *(PointSeven photo)*

◀ **BOB CROWDER:** Side effects of mixing mokumé and mammoth ivory may include dizziness, nausea and uncontrollable drooling. *(PointSeven photo)*

◀ **JIM CROWELL:** Mammoth ivory is the saccharine that makes the damascus bowie so sweet. *(Ward photo)*

▲ **BARRY GALLAGHER:** The slip joint folder with the 15N20 blades dons a mammoth-bark-ivory handle.

▶ **SCOT MATSUOKA:** The tooth of the beast was so big it could be cut to fit the human hand. *(Mitch Lum photo)*

◀ **SERGIO RAMONDETTI:** The fossil walrus ivory gives depth to an already powerfully patterned damascus folder. The blade spine is file worked, and the titanium liners oxidized. *(Francesco Pachi photo)*

◀ **THOMAS HASLINGER:** The "Suave" knife is debonair in mammoth ivory, gold, diamond and Robert Eggerling damascus.

◀ **TERRY VENDEVENTER:** The hunter/utility knife is the proud recipient of a W's-pattern-damascus blade and wooly-mammoth-ivory handle scales.

Cloaked in Tiger Coral

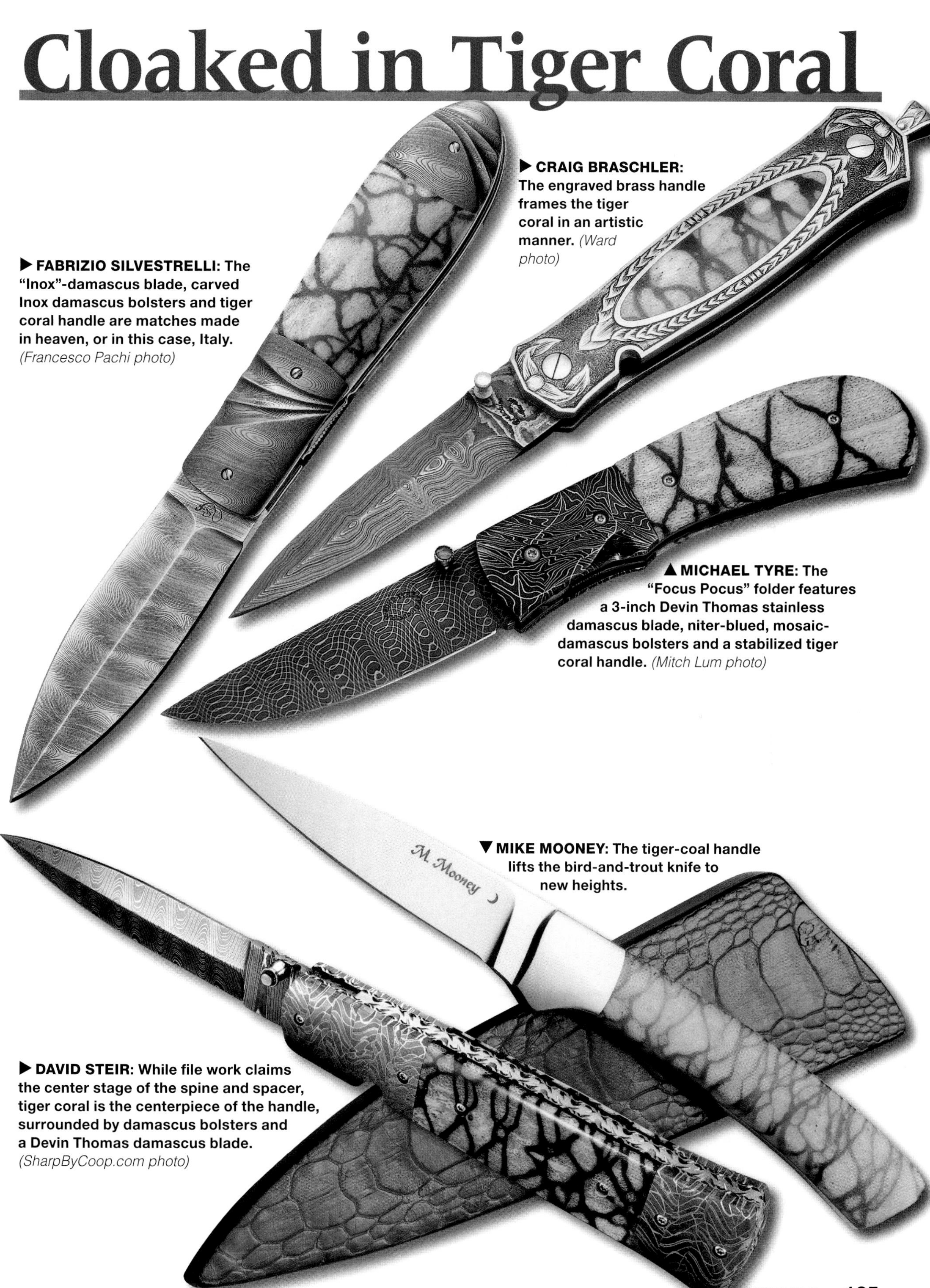

▶ **CRAIG BRASCHLER: The engraved brass handle frames the tiger coral in an artistic manner.** *(Ward photo)*

▶ **FABRIZIO SILVESTRELLI: The "Inox"-damascus blade, carved Inox damascus bolsters and tiger coral handle are matches made in heaven, or in this case, Italy.** *(Francesco Pachi photo)*

▲ **MICHAEL TYRE: The "Focus Pocus" folder features a 3-inch Devin Thomas stainless damascus blade, niter-blued, mosaic-damascus bolsters and a stabilized tiger coral handle.** *(Mitch Lum photo)*

▼ **MIKE MOONEY: The tiger-coal handle lifts the bird-and-trout knife to new heights.**

▶ **DAVID STEIR: While file work claims the center stage of the spine and spacer, tiger coral is the centerpiece of the handle, surrounded by damascus bolsters and a Devin Thomas damascus blade.** *(SharpByCoop.com photo)*

The Ti-Dyed Crowd

▶ **RON APPLETON:** For those of you who are red/blue colorblind, you're just going to have to trust us on this one. Not only is it a hot handle but also sculpted like the little dagger-shaped blade it holds. The opening mechanism is tricky, too. *(PointSeven photo)*

▼ **LOURENS PRINSLOO:** The mammoth tooth grip is brilliantly outlined by blue-anodized, file-worked titanium and butted up against a Damasteel blade. There's also a blue sapphire set into the thumb stud. *(SharpByCoop.com photo)*

▲ **DON MAXWELL:** The Barracuda flipper folder dons a chocolaty silver-vine handle and an anodized titanium bolster of the brass-looking variety. *(Mitch Lum photo)*

▲ **TIM GALYEAN:** It's called a "Bio-Mechanical Scorpion JYD," and you'd need a degree to create it, but Tim explains that it's a hand-carved, anodized-titanium handle with a CPM S30V blade. *(Mitch Lum photo)*

▶ **PAUL FOX:** Pink and purple aren't colors that immediately come to mind when knives are mentioned, but then not many knifemakers can pull off what Paul consistently manages—beautiful anodized-titanium blade spines with damascus or single-steel cutting edges, and canvas Micarta® or carbon fiber grips. *(PointSeven photo)*

◀ **BRIAN TIGHE:** There's gold in that there titanium handle, and a little pearl to go with the blade swirl. *(PointSeven photo)*

▶ **JOHN KUBASEK:** The entire knife, including the pivot and pivot screw, is titanium, some parts grey and another part golden. *(PointSeven photo)*

◀ **PETER CAREY:** The raindrop-Timascus handle whirlpools here, ebbs and flows there, and ingratiates everywhere.

▲ **KELLY CARLSON:** If you broke open a rock and saw crystals that color you'd be jumping for joy. It's heat-colored Timascus complemented by anodized-titanium liners, a D-2 blade and a sapphire-inlaid thumb stud.

Cuts for the Kitchen

▶ **LEIF HEDBLOM:** The Damasteel chef's knife and fork set sports stabilized-wood handles the color of gourmet food.
(Jan Carlsson photo)

▶ **MATT DISKIN:** Knives such as this pearl-handle, mosaic-damascus piece are purpose built for physically challenged people with one arm, enabling them to cut and eat using the same utensil.
(PointSeven photo)

▲ **STEVE SCHWARZER:** Gnarly stag handles are book-ended by carved-silver guards and pommels, and the utensils feature a damascus blade and tines.
(Eric Eggly photo, PointSeven Studios)

STATE OF THE ART

What a spectacular tool, the art barometer. It forecasts changes in creativity, or lack thereof, within the art community. You could say the mercury rises or falls along with innovative, groundbreaking art movements. When the creative juices flow, the pressure increases and mercury rises, yet when ingenuity dries up, the pressure decreases and the mercury falls. How fun to keep the pressure on, to tap into the creative genius, find inspiration, blend mediums, explore the unknown and induce innovation.

Poking into the pores of ivory with needles, leaving microscopic droplets of ink in each tiny pin prick and painting masterpieces under the ivory's surface one color-filled pore at a time could be called creative. If your barometric art meter tends to agree, see the "Scrimming with Excitement" section in the pages to follow.

Splashing a spectrum of color across a knife handle, bolster or blade is inspirational. Or blending hues to achieve a dye outside the spectrum is an even better use of artistic talent. If the mercury in your art barometer just rose, see "The Color Guard" in the pages to follow.

Holding a "Crazed Knife Carvers Convention" is different. "Stacking the Deck" of a knife is unique. Practicing "Sharp Deco" is out of the ordinary, and studying to become a "Mosaic Steel Layer" or a "Steel Sculptor" is not part of the everyday curriculum. If your art barometer is red to the very top, you'll enjoy all the pages that combine to form the "State Of The Art" chapter of *Knives 2009*. The pressure builds.

Joe Kertzman

Bountiful Blades

Bountiful does not always equate to beautiful. A bountiful harvest cov uld be a harvest of seaweed, and then beauty doesn't readily come to mind. Or a bountiful meal might consist of asparagus, liver and onions and squash, and though some would consider that beautiful, others might hold a different opinion.

Bountiful blades, on the other hand equate directly to beauty. They are beautiful. In regards to edged tools, the word "bountiful," in this instance, means full of riches and glory, made from precious metals and inlaid with jewels, gemstones and pearl. A girl might say that is like having a bountiful birthday, anniversary, Mother's Day or Valentines Day. Another classy lady might declare it the perfect date.

Knifemakers who fashion bountiful blades are first-rate artisans. They have not only learned to forge, buff, hone and grind steel, but inlay gold or silver, texture titanium, and set stones like diamonds, opals and garnets. They have taken up engraving, jewelry making, carving, sculpting and stone faceting.

These are not second-rate hacks plying their steel trade and pretending to be jewelers at the same time. They are often jewelers first and knifemakers second, or have incorporated jewelry skills into their first love—knifemaking. They build knives for collectors. They cater to a classy clientele. They build fine cutlery, collector-grade knives, and believeth thou me, bountiful blades.

Joe Kertzman

▲ C. GRAY TAYLOR: The insiders will recognize it as a sleeve-board lobster pocketknife with a tortoise shell handle. The rest will be in awe of the 14k-gold flowers with Tim George shading, and the gold liners and pins that make this multi-blade a masterpiece. *(PointSeven photo)*

▶ DWIGHT TOWELL: The gold leaf inlay not only elevates the dagger to an art form, but helps it levitate to an enlightened state. *(PointSeven photo)*

◀ DELLANA: It's just like Dellana to fashion one for the discerning taste, using three types of gold, diamonds, rubies, 324-layer damascus and Australian opal, all forged, fabricated, textured, set and finished. *(PointSeven photo)*

◀ JERRY MCCLURE: He calls it "Baby Sister," and any sister would squirm in her shoes to be gifted the 22k-gold handle, the TNT Damasteel blade, the knife with the imperial jade stone inlays. The gold work is by the sister named Elizabeth McDevitt. *(Ward photo)*

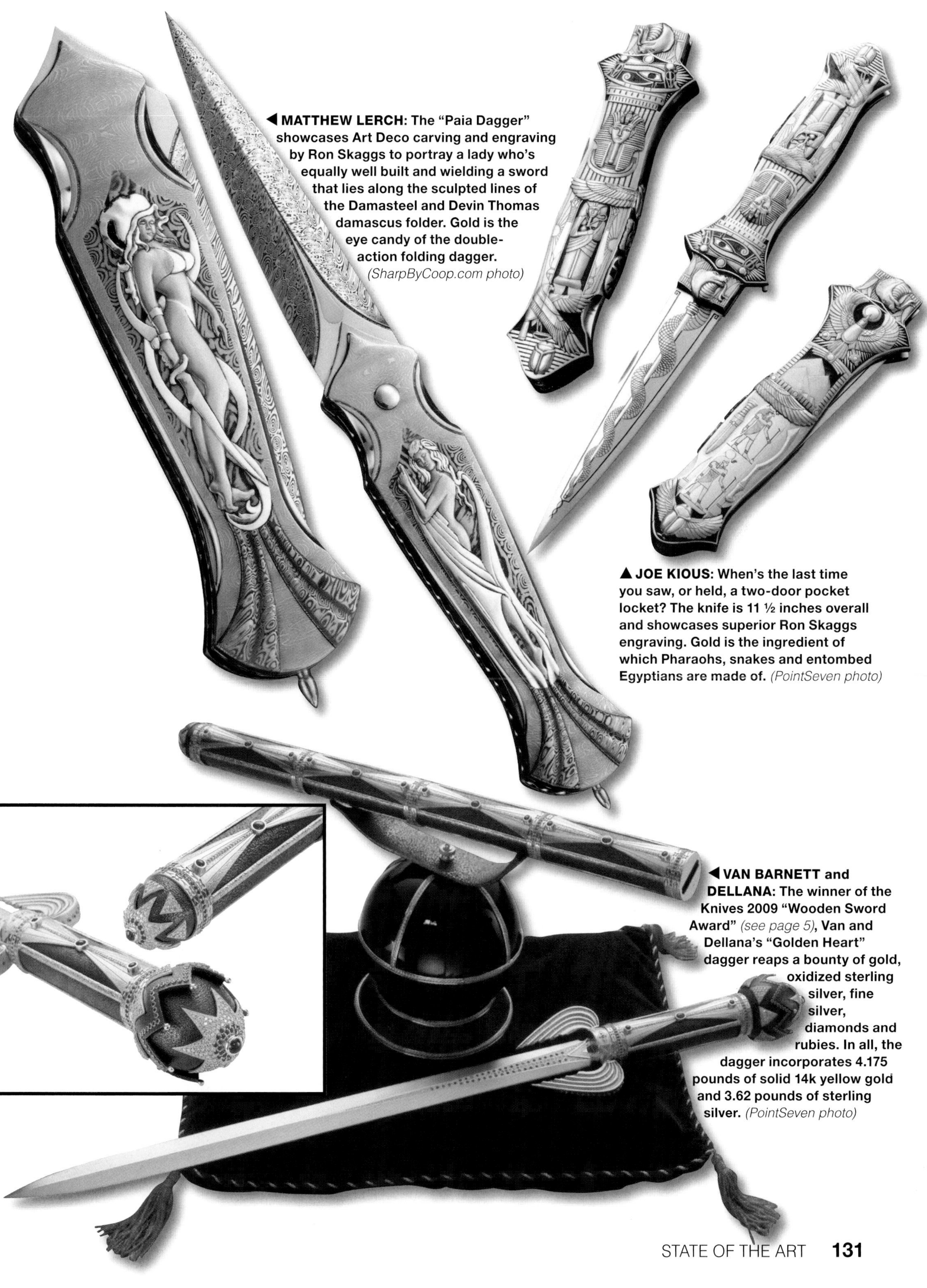

◀ **MATTHEW LERCH:** The "Paia Dagger" showcases Art Deco carving and engraving by Ron Skaggs to portray a lady who's equally well built and wielding a sword that lies along the sculpted lines of the Damasteel and Devin Thomas damascus folder. Gold is the eye candy of the double-action folding dagger. *(SharpByCoop.com photo)*

▲ **JOE KIOUS:** When's the last time you saw, or held, a two-door pocket locket? The knife is 11 ½ inches overall and showcases superior Ron Skaggs engraving. Gold is the ingredient of which Pharaohs, snakes and entombed Egyptians are made of. *(PointSeven photo)*

◀ **VAN BARNETT and DELLANA:** The winner of the Knives 2009 "Wooden Sword Award" *(see page 5)*, Van and Dellana's "Golden Heart" dagger reaps a bounty of gold, oxidized sterling silver, fine silver, diamonds and rubies. In all, the dagger incorporates 4.175 pounds of solid 14k yellow gold and 3.62 pounds of sterling silver. *(PointSeven photo)*

Engraved in our Souls

▶ **NORIMI: The titanium handle of Scot Matsuoka's flipper folder is engraved by Norimi in a saltwater scene of swimming ulua** *(Hawaiian fish)*. *(Mitch Lum photo)*

▶ **JERE DAVIDSON: Magnificently engraved are the bolsters, spine and blade of Edmund Davidson's all-integral, 440C "Von Karls Viper" trailing-point fixed blade with a desert-ironwood grip.** *(Hoffman photo)*

▶ **TIM GEORGE: Howard Hitchmough's knifemaking style has become recognizable, and Tim's engraving equally so.** *(PointSeven photo)*

▶ **JON ROBYN: Knifemaker Matthew Lerch commissioned Jon to engrave and gold inlay the handle of his latest double-action folding dagger, a piece that features Mike Norris stainless damascus. When Matt got the knife back, he fell in love.** *(PointSeven photo)*

▶ **GIL RUDOLPH:** Knifemaker Loyd McConnell demonstrates how best to complement the sheep-horn handle of a CPM-S30Vfolder—with Gil's engraving and gold inlay. *(PointSeven photo)*

▼ **JIM SMALL:** Jim may have performed the gold inlay and engraving work on the folding twosome, but knifemaker Johnny Stout provided the high-art damascus and titanium platforms. *(SharpByCoop.com photo)*

▶ **JODY MULLER:** Gold and copper inlays dress up the engraved bolsters of the mammoth-ivory-handle damascus folder.

◀ **JIM SMALL:** The Seraphinite stone from Eastern Europe might be the centerpiece of the Bailey Bradshaw Persian folder, but the engraving and gold inlay is what surrounds the glorious knife with freshness and, well, flowers. *(Custom Knife Gallery of Colorado photo)*

▲ **BRUCE SHAW:** A gold eagle head is the centerpiece of the all-engraved pommel of D'Alton Holder's fine fixed blade. Leaves and checks are the order of the day for the guard, and charcoal-colored spalted alder, oosic and black palm equate to the handle materials of choice. *(SharpByCoop.com photo)*

◀ **BRUCE SHAW:** The "Toothpick" by Jay Harris showcases engraved titanium bolsters, a mother-of-pearl handle and a stainless damascus blade. *(Mitch Lum photo)*

▶ **TIM GEORGE:** She thinks Owen Wood's engraved folder with a damascus blade and black-lip-pearl handle is hot, too. *(PointSeven photo)*

◀ **BOB SWARTLEY:** Let's put it this way, after knifemaker John Perry built the fully file-worked, mammoth-ivory-handle folder, he commissioned Swartley to engrave the piece in a bighorn sheep and cougar theme, with some scrolls, and then fellow knifemaker Ron Newton liked it so much, he bought it. That's like Picasso buying a Rembrandt. *(PointSeven photo)*

▲ **JULIE WARENSKI-ERICKSON:** What do you get when you combine the talents of knifemaker George Daily and engraver Julie Warenski-Erickson? Art speaks for itself. *(SharpByCoop.com photo)*

▶ **TOM FERRY:** First he forged the spectacular damascus—check out the exploding stars on the blade—and then he engraved the piece, making it all his own. *(Mitch Lum photo)*

▶ **C.J. CAI:** The "Dead Sexy" folder by Ken Onion features a wavy Mike Norris damascus blade and a titanium handle in a mermaid scene. *(Jeff Park, Bernie Pang and Mitch Lum photo)*

▶ **CHRIS MEYER:** The mane of the lion turns into the scrolls that surround his image, just as the clip-point blade of Dennis Friedly's knife turns into the bolster and full tang of the piece. *(PointSeven photo)*

◀ **RON APPLETON:** It's not often a folder reveals an entire fantasy world within its blade and handle. *(PointSeven photo)*

▶ **RAY COVER:** The engraving wraps itself around David Broadwell's sub-hilt fighter like a snake on a staff. The handle is carved walnut. *(Mitch Lum photo)*

▶ **LEE GRIFFITHS:** In knifemaker John Young's mind, he wanted a couple lions engraved on the guards of his stag handle hunter. In Lee's mind, he wanted a couple kings of the jungle engraved there. *(Photo by Coop)*

▶ RICHARD SEXSTONE: **The "Upwind Downwind" folder sports a wavy damascus blade, and a sailboat race engraved on the handle. A ruby marks the port side and an emerald stands for starboard.** *(SharpByCoop.com photo)*

▶ SIMON LYTTON and JOHN ROBYN: **These are no ordinary Japanese mythical characters, but disturbed and determined beasts beautifully engraved on the 416 stainless steel grips of two Warren Osborne damascus folding daggers.** *(PointSeven photo)*

◀ SALAN PRAYURAVONGSE: **The small, silver handle parades more engraving than a general's sword.** *(PointSeven photo)*

◀ **C.J. CAI:** The S30V and titanium folder benefits from engraving of a Chinese dragon-like fish. *(SharpBy Coop.com photo)*

◀ **RICK EATON:** Mythology may be magical, but the Bulino-style engraving is miraculous, and the mosaic damascus just as divine. *(PointSeven photo)*

▶ **JON ROBYN:** With little gremlins popping out of golden eggs, Owen Wood had to hurry up and finish the "herringbone"-damascus folding dagger with a mother-of-pearl grip. *(PointSeven photo)*

▶ **SHAUN and SHARLA HANSEN:** Bulino-style engraving and 24k-gold inlays not only highlight but enrich the stainless folding dagger. *(PointSeven photo)*

Sharp Deco

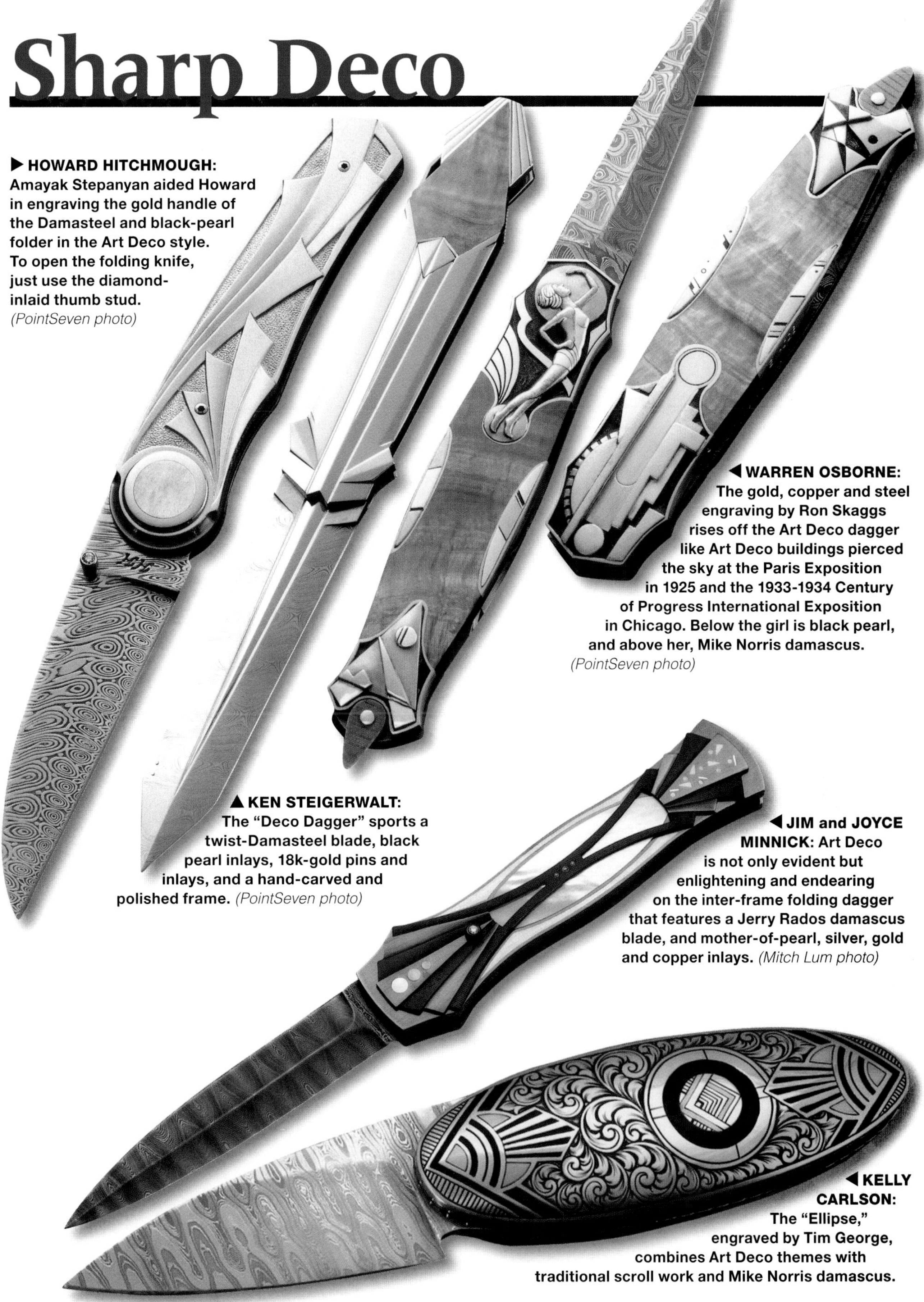

▶ **HOWARD HITCHMOUGH:** Amayak Stepanyan aided Howard in engraving the gold handle of the Damasteel and black-pearl folder in the Art Deco style. To open the folding knife, just use the diamond-inlaid thumb stud. *(PointSeven photo)*

◀ **WARREN OSBORNE:** The gold, copper and steel engraving by Ron Skaggs rises off the Art Deco dagger like Art Deco buildings pierced the sky at the Paris Exposition in 1925 and the 1933-1934 Century of Progress International Exposition in Chicago. Below the girl is black pearl, and above her, Mike Norris damascus. *(PointSeven photo)*

▲ **KEN STEIGERWALT:** The "Deco Dagger" sports a twist-Damasteel blade, black pearl inlays, 18k-gold pins and inlays, and a hand-carved and polished frame. *(PointSeven photo)*

◀ **JIM and JOYCE MINNICK:** Art Deco is not only evident but enlightening and endearing on the inter-frame folding dagger that features a Jerry Rados damascus blade, and mother-of-pearl, silver, gold and copper inlays. *(Mitch Lum photo)*

◀ **KELLY CARLSON:** The "Ellipse," engraved by Tim George, combines Art Deco themes with traditional scroll work and Mike Norris damascus.

The Crazed Knife Carvers Convention

The reason no one will take offense to this headline is that knifemakers, in general, have the best senses of humor of any industry professionals known to man. They are passionate and serious about their work. They live and breathe their art, and therefore, when the work is done, when the knives are made, when the customer is pleased and the family is fed, they need to blow off steam. And they blow it off, most of them, in good-natured ways. Some are jokesters. Others just like to have fun.

The ones who have an even more artistic slant than the rest—the carvers, etchers, engravers, scrimshanders and jewelers—become so lost in their art, they have to surface for air once in awhile. And it is then that you get to know the true folks behind the handcraft.

When they blow off steam, when they have a little fun, joke around, act jovially, maybe even tip a few back in a casual setting, it's like a fun family reunion. If you've ever been in "The Pit" at the BLADE Show in Atlanta after a day of buying and selling knives, you've heard the hum of people having fun. It's comparable to a party, a celebration, a place of entertainment, an event, or, by the stretch of imagination, a crazed knife carver's convention. Yeah, it gets a little kooky at times, but all in good fun.

Joe Kertzman

▶ **PETER MASON: The carved three-bar, composite-damascus blade is fitted with a carved bronze guard and a handle carved to bloom like the rest of the art dagger.**

◀ **VLADIMIR PULIS: Carved deer bone reveals horsemen of the plains, some skeletal, others with headdress and purpose in the buffalo hunting scene. The equine theme is carried on in the mosaic-damascus blade steel and the hazel-wood box.** *(Ivan Cillik photos)*

▶ **DENNIS FRIEDLY: The combination of carving and engraving, as well as jewelling, gold inlaying and all-around embellishing, busts this bowie wide open.** *(PointSeven photo)*

▲ **mystical lady serves as the handle of the damascus desk knife in the copper stand.** *(SharpByCoop.com photo)*

▼ **JAMES SCROGGS: The tiger-tail curly maple handles are carved with twists by Bill Scroggs.**

◀ **LARRY FUEGEN:** The fossil-walrus ivory handle, damascus blade and 14k-gold overlays are painstakingly carved to create a sculpted push dagger. *(PointSeven photo)*

◀ **JULIE WARENSKI-ERICKSON:** Carved ivory gives the appearance of a stem and draping leaf, and the gold inlay and engraving are equally enlivening on the art dagger. *(PointSeven photo)*

▲ **WILLIAM LLOYD:** What do you get when you carve moose antler, bull horn and bloodwood? Well, when you're Lloyd, you get a gorgeous damascus sword, one with a blade forged by Norm Schenk. *(PointSeven photo)*

▶ **JOSEPH SZILASKI:** It's the rare rifleman's belt axe and accompanying knife that exhibit such fine checkering, piqué and engraving work. Even the sheath is spectacular. *(SharpByCoop.com photo)*

◀ **STEVE SCHWARZER:** When Guy Shaw carved the snakewood, he went batty, in a good way. Damascus and gold round out the piece. *(PointSeven photo)*

▼ **GEORGE YOUNG:** It's not that eagle-head pommels are unusual, it's that high art eagle heads carved into sperm whale tooth and given realistic eyes and stag bodies are way above average. *(PointSeven photo)*

◀ **J.R. COOK:** The ironwood handle shows a skilled carving hand, and the damascus blade a forger to be reckoned with. *(Ward photo)*

▶ **TOMMY MCNABB:** The Indian, bear and wolf came to life through Tommy's carving tool. The blade is a nice tight-pattern damascus. *(Hoffman photo)*

◀ **ARPAD BOJTOS:** Luna, the comet and the southern wind settle into the titanium, ivory, gold, silver and pearl handle like a baby in the womb, or a child on a rocket ride to the golden stars above. All is fantastical and masterfully delicious. *(PointSeven photo)*

◀ **GENE BASKETT:** The white ivory, pistol-grip handle is a stark contrast compared to most knives, and carved by Willy B. with a scary skull. *(PointSeven photo)*

▶ **TIM HANCOCK:** Tim didn't need the fanciest pattern in the universe, just a good, clean, carved ebony handle and a smooth 52100 blade. *(PointSeven photo)*

▶ **KAJ EMBRETSEN:** After the damascus steel was forged and the supersonic bolster in place, the ivory was left to the carving skills of Isak Bergh, and what a smart decision that turned out to be. *(PointSeven photo)*

◀ **PIERRE REVERDY:** Pierre has never been able to stop carving once he gets started on a sperm whale tooth, but then his poetic damascus is a good way to further the flow. The silver is cast and the steel carved. *(PointSeven photo)*

◀ **DANIEL STEPHAN:** It's amazing what an artist can do with a little folder, some mammoth ivory and a carving tool. The damascus is by Jerry Rados. *(SharpByCoop.com photo)*

▶ **PETER MARTIN:** The body of the centipede double-action folder is carved Shokudo with a walrus ivory belly. The bug also showcases a three-bar "serpentine"-damascus blade, a 24k-gold and ruby thumb stud, and a twist-damascus head with black-onyx eyes and 14k-gold settings. More rubies complete the insect. *(Cory Martin Imaging)*

Why Go Wireless?

The wire has gotten a bad rap as of late. It seems no one wants wire around. Its status in the telephone industry has been greatly diminished, and similarly it has been relegated as an unwanted accessory in computer circles. Communication in general has gone wireless. Even stereo sound has shunned the once-popular wire. Where's a self-respecting wire to go?

Look no further than knives. Never ones to exclude newcomers, or make them feel unwelcome, the world of knives has embraced the wire, welcomed it into their homes and made it feel comfortable. The knife world has even given the wire an important dual role of embellishment and hand purchase, aesthetics and utilitarianism.

Wire that was once world-renowned might have a diminished role, but it is no less important than the other sectors it serviced. On knives, wire is often the first thing you see, the first to touch your skin and the last to leave an impression. What an impression it is, too. A skillfully inlaid wire can be formed into the most marvelous of patterns, figures and shapes, and when wrapped around a fluted handle, and even twisted a little, the wire is a looker bested by few others. It makes knife enthusiasts stand up indignantly and ask, "Why go wireless?" Now that's a good question.

Joe Kertzman

◀ **JASON KNIGHT:** The damascus dagger features a fluted African-blackwood handle, twisted-silver-wire overlay and a jade ***(Luna stone)*** pommel. *(SharpByCoop.com photo)*

▲ **JOSEPH KEESLAR:** Wispy, pinwheel-like wire inlay, file work and engraving embellish the curly-maple- and walnut-handle knives, complete with 1084 blades. *(PointSeven photo)*

▶ **E. JAY HENDRICKSON:** Fine vine-like silver wire inlay eventually leads to a nickel-silver flower escutcheon, all on a curly maple handle that butts up against an ivory ferrule, and a 1095-and-203E-damascus blade.
(PointSeven photo)

▶ **RICK EATON:** Gold wire wends its way along the mosaic-damascus handle and crisscrosses the black-lip-pearl inlay like a meandering bridge over a sea-green lake.
(PointSeven photo)

◀ **JOHN SMITH:** Gold wire partitions the gold quartz, frames the blued damascus grip and segues into the mosaic-damascus blade.
(PointSeven photo)

◀ **LARRY NEWTON:** The dark, black-pearl-handle, raindrop-damascus folding dagger is enlivened by gold wire inlay in a most appealing pattern. Devin Thomas is credited for the damascus.

Steel Sculptors

You walk into a room with little to no expectations, and then you spot this fantastic sculpture in the middle of the floor, like a gallery centerpiece, standing alone in all its elegance, stately yet grandeur. You want to touch it but are vaguely aware of etiquette in such situations, so you stand back and admire the artwork, making an attempt at an intellectual assessment.

Such a sculpture has admirably performed it sole duty, and the interior decorator of the room strategically placed the conversation piece. Art is to be taken in like a good lecture, dissected as if it is a laboratory animal and experienced like a natural hot spring in a green valley. Life is the little things too often missed while making other plans. Sculpture is the capturing of those little things never to be overlooked again.

Steel sculpture is an especially intricate undertaking, requiring skill, steady hand and focused attention. The grease of the elbow meets the sweat of the brow, and a small steel file works back and forth to the beat of a redundant rhythm. Yet creativity flows from the pores in droplets while hands manipulate steel as if it's malleable clay.

There are no softies in the world of steel sculpting, only headstrong individuals with the willpower of ill-tempered mules. Sanding steel is akin to blowing a hole in a glacier through pursed lips. It's no easy task, being a steel sculptor, and not an occupation for the faint of heart, yet the rewards are worth every ounce of energy burned while filing metal into pleasing formations. Knife enthusiasts rejoice in the steely knives that enliven a room like a well-placed sculpture, one that's visible, per se, from the vestibule of your favorite host's summer mansion.

Joe Kertzman

◄ **STEVEN RAPP: The carving and casting of the two-headed dragon guard is the handiwork of Mark DeGraffenreid, the damascus forging by Devin Thomas and the knifemaking by Steven himself.** *(PointSeven photo)*

◄ **JULIE WARENSKI-ERICKSON: Not only sculpted but pierced and engraved is the 440C blade and ferrule of the dagger, which comes complete with a black jade handle and 24k-gold inlays.** *(PointSeven photo)*

▶ **MARK LARAMIE:** Until you hear the name "Hummingbird," you might not even realize the form. Yet sculpture is sometimes mistaken. This bird has an angel-hair-damascus beak, a roots-pattern damascus body, 24k-gold veins, Peridot eyes and an abalone belly. The damascus is by Larry Donnelly. *(SharpByCoop.com photo)*

▶ **PETER MASON:** The mosaic-damascus blade, blackened-bronze guard and walrus-ivory grip were given equal carving treatment, yet each stands as an artistic entity, together making up the whole.

▲▶ **LARRY FUEGEN:** It doesn't seem to matter whether the medium is damascus, gold or pearl, Larry sculpts all with equal aplomb. *(PointSeven photo)*

▶ **RON LAKE and WOLFGANG LOERCHNER:** Ron made the two stainless steel knives and folding mechanisms, and Wolf sculpted the handles. *(Francesco Pachi photo)*

◀ **LLOYD HALE:** The "Khubla Khan" dagger is given the royal sculpting treatment, even overlays of twisted wire on a fluted wood handle, yet the guard and pommel are the crowning glories. *(SharpByCoop.com photo)*

◀ **KEN STEIGERWALT:** The sculpted handle and integral bolsters flow into a hollow-ground Damasteel blade. *(SharpByCoop.com photo)*

▶ **ALEXANDR POSPISIL:** Carbon damascus, Damasteel and ATS-34 were sculpted, pierced and carved until the jungle was immortalized. All grips are mammoth ivory. *(PointSeven photo)*

▼**STEPHEN OLSZEWSKI:** The tusks of the elephant-head auto are 14k white gold, while the blade is carved Jerry Rados ladder-pattern damascus. Don't overlook the sapphire eyes of the brute.

▲**RON BEST:** One knife so smooth, layered, engraved, sculpted and sensuous, it caresses black-lip pearl as if it's silk, not steel. *(PointSeven photo)*

▲**ARPAD BOJTOS:** Someone has to save the man of steel from the four-headed serpent, and perhaps the savior is atop the mammoth-ivory hill overhead. *(SharpByCoop.com photo)*

Mosaic Steel Layers

▶ **SHANE TAYLOR:** Shane didn't try to hide the naked nymph in the blade nearly as hard as he tried to hide the abalone beneath the carved-ancient-ivory grip. *(PointSeven photo)*

◀ **ED SCHEMPP:** The matching bees and hives in blade and handle equate to a mosaic marvel. *(PointSeven photo)*

▼ **LOURENS PRINSLOO:** Lourens allowed Ettore Gianfari to forge the mosaic damascus, and the wooly mammoth to provide the handle material. A diamond thumb stud and button are nice touches. *(SharpByCoop.com photo)*

▶ **RICK DUNKERLEY:** The spider-web-pattern mosaic damascus of the blade, forged complete with creepy crawlies, shows up again via inlays under the carved ladder-pattern-damascus handle. There's a diamond set in the 18k-gold thumb stud. *(PointSeven photo)*

◀ **RICK EATON:** Rick is most proud of the leaf engraving, gold inlay and directional shadowing, but the "Roman" mosaic damascus is reminiscent of traditional tile layers whose handcraft was world renowned. *(PointSeven photo)*

▲**TED MOORE:** Stars and other patterns are part of the square mosaics, and the blued rear bolsters, black-lip pearl and file work combine to create a brilliantly themed folder. *(SharpByCoop.com photo)*

◀**PETER MASON:** The Persian-style fighter features a carved mosaic-damascus blade, a sculpted, heat-colored and textured stainless-steel guard, and a carved California buckeye-burl handle.

▲**JOE OLSON:** Guitar junkies will love the mosaic-damascus theme, the engraved guitar and the overall rhythm of the piece. *(BladeGallery.com photo)*

▶ **PETER MARTIN:** **The "fire starter" hunter showcases a red-hot mosaic-damascus blade, a mosaic guard, and an Eskimo artifact fire starter and gold nugget inlay within a walrus-ivory handle.** *(Cory Martin Imaging)*

◀ **J.W. RANDALL:** **Horses high-tail it away from the wrought iron guard and ferrule—forged from a mid-1800s wagon wheel—and a mammoth ivory handle.** *(T. Randall photo)*

▼ **ANDERS HEDLUND:** **The floral pattern of the blade and bolters are readily apparent, but subtle touches include black-lip-pearl back spacer inlays, amethysts set in 14k gold, 18k-gold dots in the blade and 24k-gold pins in the brown-mammoth-ivory handle.** *(PointSeven photo)*

▶ **JOSH SMITH:** **The blued-damascus blade swarms with molecular mosaics, while the mammoth-ivory grip grounds the piece.** *(PointSeven photo)*

◀ **CLIFF PARKER:** **The walrus on the mosaic bolster is a fancy way of saying the handle is fossil walrus ivory.** *(PointSeven photo)*

▶ **ALLEN ELISHEWITZ:** The devilish Gary House damascus is grooved with vents for effect, matching up against a machined-titanium frame with titanium inlay.

▶ **TOM FERRY:** Koi fish and water lilies are engraved over the mosaic damascus handle of the fine folder. *(PointSeven photo)*

◀ **STEVE FREY:** The multi-bar damascus steel is forged to shape from 1080 and 15N20 blade steels, and combined with cold-blued 1080 carbon steel bolsters, a desert-ironwood grip and buffalo horn spacers. *(BladeGallery.com photo)*

▶ **FRANCESCO PACHI:** The locking-liner folder parades a Conny Persson mosaic-damascus blade and a black-lip-pearl handle with gold bail and fittings.

▲ **JOHN DAVIS:** The blued mosaic damascus is forged from 1084 and 15N20 carbon steels, and pure nickel. The grip is all mammoth ivory. *(BladeGallery.com photo)*

▶ **PAOLO SCORDIA:** There's just as much grain structure in the mosaic damascus as in the wood grip.

◀ **GARY ROOT:** Robert Eggerling might have done the damascus honors, but Gary gave the reddish hues to the knife, including the guard and wood handle that complement the red lines around the mosaic damascus. *(SharpByCoop.com photo)*

◀ **ALBERTO SYMONDS:** It took three handle materials to compete with the Mattias Styrefors mosaic damascus, including mammoth molar, black palm and axis stag.

◀ **JOHAN GUSTAFSSON:** The dinosaur damascus is a mosaic of reds, greens, purples, oranges and whites. The knifemaker chose a 150-million-year-old amber handle to make the dinosaurs feel at home. *(SharpByCoop.com photo)*

Damascus: It's Not Just a Place

It is a time, a tradition and a heritage. If all knifemakers fashioned and forged blades using modern methods, patterns and alloys, or even parts and mechanisms, with no eye to the past, the handcraft would be lost. Without looking back, damascus would have never experienced a resurgence, nor would it have developed to the extent of allowing quality damascus blades to look better, cut better and stay stronger than many single-steel alloys.

It's an art. Layering steel, then forging it through pounding, heating and quenching, and finally cross-cutting, finishing, buffing and etching the steel, achieves patterns. That is the art. Achieving the patterns you set out to forge into the steel is masterful.

It's a passion. Spending hours at the hot forge, and then using large, heavy handheld hammers on an anvil, or employing a power hammer, is work. And cutting and bending steel is not for the weak or meek. It is hot, exhausting work that some find exhilarating. It is a passion, a love and even a desire.

It's a skill. Not everyone who sets out to forge damascus will end up with beautiful, functional blades. Few will achieve workable blades. Fewer yet will stick with it long enough to find out.

It's not just a place.

Joe Kertzman

▶ **LIN RHEA: The sheephorn and damascus bowie is patterned plenty.** *(Ward photo)*

◀ **HARVEY DEAN: Superior forging skills aren't even sufficient to accomplish this high-quality damascus pattern, but only the study of steel and long-term commitment and experience allow a person to forge a blade billet such as this. The handle is mammoth ivory.** *(Ward photo)*

◀ **RUSTY POLK: A damascus pattern dances along the spine, edge and center line of the mammoth-ivory-handle dagger.** *(Ward photo)*

◀ **JOHN PERRY: Delbert Ealy's "fish"-pattern damascus swims up the blade and around the sea-green black-lip pearl.** *(SharpByCoop.com photo)*

▶ **DANIEL WINKLER:** The Daryl Meier damascus on the bowie and hunter features a tight yet alluring pattern that measures up to the natural qualities of the stag-handle grips. *(SharpByCoop.com photo)*

▼ **DAVID LISCH:** It's a 15N20, 1084 and 4800 damascus blade, and it has as much pattern as parts, all anchored by a giraffe-bone grip with a big damascus pin. *(BaldeGallery.com photo)*

◀ **FRANK GAMBLE:** A damascus pattern that tight should cut like the dickens. A similar blade was probably used to texture and carve the ebony grip of the gelding knife. *(BaldeGallery.com photo)*

▶ **MITCH EDWARDS:** Hippo ivory is the calming element that allows the damascus to get wild. *(SharpByCoop.com photo)*

▶ **MICHAEL MILLER: Flowers etched into the high-carbon damascus raise the bar once again on custom knives. The handle is stabilized juniper burl, also not a common denominator.** *(SharpByCoop.com photo)*

▶ **JERRY MCCLURE: Here's a "poker room fighter" in a "low-tide"-pattern damascus blade and a fossil-walrus-ivory grip.**

◀ **DAVID MIRABILE: The pitted oosic has that fossilized look, and the damascus a shockwave feel that electrifies.** *(SharpByCoop.com photo)*

▶ **DANNY NORDFELDT: The "Dama Axe" features a "Vinland"-pattern Damasteel blade and a hickory haft.** *(Jan Carlsson photo)*

▶ **GARY HOUSE:** Gary does his own damascus forging, this time using 1084 and 15N20 steels, and gives the piece an oval guard and a mammoth-ivory and African-blackwood grip. *(PointSeven photo)*

◀ **JOYCE and JIM MINNICK:** Robert Eggerling forged the damascus, but it takes the right eye and knifemaking skills to marry the patterns with the correct handle materials, knife shapes, carved bolsters and fine-art handles, the latter in black-lip pearl and mastodon ivory. *(PointSeven photo)*

▶ **REINHARD TSCHAGER:** A blued-"dragonskin"-pattern damascus blade is speckled with droplets and butted up against a checked-ivory grip with piqued pins and a gold pendant. *(Francesco Pachi photo)*

▲ **STAN WILSON:** The Devin Thomas damascus directs traffic along the edge, bolster and pointed pommel of the fine art folder, while the black-lip pearl provides some color to contrast the black, grey and silver. *(SharpByCoop.com photo)*

▶ **DANIEL CHINNOCK:** The maker carved the hummingbird scene in mother-of-pearl, inlaid it on a blued-giraffe-bone grip, gave the thumb stud a blue-sapphire inlay and then commissioned Craig Barr to forge a "jungle-stripe"-pattern damascus blade. *(SharpByCoop.com photo)*

▶ **BRIAN TIGHE:** Brian strategically placed the patterned portions in relation to the lines of the knife *(check out the bolster or guard area and the swirling pattern there)*, and did an equally tremendous job with carving the black-lip pearl just so. *(PointSeven photo)*

◀ **SHAWN ELLIS:** Shawn's "Back Draft Fighter" is on fire. *(Ward photo)*

◀ **CAL GANSHORN:** The damascus blade is all "smiles" pattern, and the handle Manitoba maple burl.

▶ **MARK NEVLING:** The drop-point folder features a feather-pattern blade, heat-colored "flower"-pattern mosaic-damascus bolsters, and a mammoth-ivory handle with gold-plated screws.

▶ **KEN ONION:** The gold-anodized-titanium handle accepts the Mike Norris damascus like a pit in the concrete allows water to puddle. *(Mitch Lum photo)*

▶ **ALLEN ELISHEWITZ:** The Mike Norris damascus blade features a groove and floating pins, while the machined and grooved titanium frame showcases meteorite and damascus inlays. Other amenities include guilloche work, an opal in the pivot area and an E-Lock. *(V. Elishewitz photo)*

◀ **DANIEL ZVONEK:** A small hunter boasts big materials—an Afzelia-lay handle and a 4 ¼-inch Robert Eggerling damascus blade. *(Hoffman photo)*

◀ **JERRY FISK:** The damascus pattern splays toward the edge of the blade as if jockeying for cutting position. *(Ward photo)*

▶ **BERTIE RIETVELD: He calls the small utility knives a pair of "Twiggy" pieces, featuring heat-colored, ladder-pattern damascus blades married to white mammoth-ivory grips. A Stanhope lens in each knife contains the maker's logo.**

◀ **TOMMY LEE: The Robert Eggerling damascus blades are twin ironies, considering one handle is pearl with a damascus inlay and the other is mammoth ivory with a pearl inlay.** *(PointSeven photo)*

◀ **JOHN WHITE: The Southwest bowie benefits from "W's"-pattern damascus and a bird's-eye African-blackwood grip, not to mention the file work and nickel-silver collar and finial.** *(PointSeven photo)*

◀ **ERIK FRITZ: The coffin-handle cowboy boot knife dons a 1084-and-15N20 damascus blade.** *(PointSeven photo)*

Stone-Cold Cutters

▼ **WARREN OSBORNE:** The Brian Hochstrat engraving and stone inlay complement rather than compete. *(SharpByCoop.com photo)*

▶ **LEE FERGUSEN:** The dagger might be miniature, but the green malachite with gold-wire overlay is a big selling point. *(Ward photo)*

◀ **JOT SINGH KHALSA:** In the knifemaker's signature style, he takes Robert Eggerling damascus, 18k gold, natural lapis lazuli and diamonds, and turns them into a curvaceous concert of cut. Julie Warenski provided the engraving touches. *(SharpByCoop.com photo)*

◀ **CURT ERICKSON:** Only Julie Warenski could engrave an art dagger so that the art not only matches but highlights the dendrite agate rock of the handle and the blued steel fittings. It's an all-around gorgeous piece. *(SharpByCoop.com photo)*

◀ **STEVEN RAPP:** Whether the engraving and gold inlay by Julie Warenski trips your trigger, or the gold-quartz and precious stone inlays, there's a lot to like about the ATS-34 art dagger. *(PointSeven photo)*

Stacking the Deck

Knifemakers offer variety in handle materials, with several stacked together in single grips

▶ **BILL DUFF:** Stag and leather alternate positions along the handle of the damascus hunter. *(Ward photo)*

◀ **DANIEL CHINNOCK:** Elephant ivory and baked black enamel create the black and white stripes, interrupted only by gold screws, of the damascus folding dagger. *(SharpByCoop.com photo)*

▲ **DENNIS FREIDLY:** Dennis likes his handle materials to be of the caramel, beige and brown variety. The engraved bolsters make for nice end caps. *(PointSeven photo)*

◀ **MARK KNAPP:** Not only is there variety in the handle, but with the colors chosen, congruity. The handle is stacked fossil walrus ivory, musk ox horn, ebony and cocobolo with swan inlays. *(BladeGallery.com photo)*

▶ **D'ALTON HOLDER:** The "Mountain Man" model sports a burl, whale rib and white amber handle, as well as Bruce Shaw's quality guard and pommel engraving. *(SharpByCoop.com photo)*

Points Encased

▶ **ANDERS HOGSTROM: Some knifemakers build the knife and sheath together, as one unit, in this case from clay-tempered 1050 steel, antiqued and textured bronze and beautiful Bocote wood.** *(PointSeven photo)*

▲ **KAREN SHOOK and DANIEL WINKLER: What a team—the knifemaker who can build the walrus-ivory-handle, damascus fixed blade with copper forged into the steel and a patterned-copper ferrule, and the sheath maker who matches the leather to the knife materials and gives it a Native American look and feel.** *(PointSeven photo)*

▲ **ED BRANDSEY: The buffalo-head nickels are shiny beacons on the leather sheath with the silver tip. The 440C bowie blends a stag grip with a stainless steel guard.** *(Cory Martin Imaging)*

▶ **CRAIG BRASCHLER:** The stingray-skin, silver and garnet-adorned sheath won the Best Sheath award at the Arkansas Custom Knife Show. *(Chuck Ward Photography)*

▲ **LARRY PARSONS:** There's a little more to it than tooled leather, some nice inlay and a little stitching. Craftsmanship plays a small role. *(Chuck Ward photography)*

◀ **JO ANN KELLEY:** Jo Ann says the smooth-leather sheath, with the silver cabochon and gold studs, is for a really big bowie.

◀ **MARK NEVLING:** The elk-overlay pouch sheath features fringe, silver beads and horse hair.

The Color Guard

▶ **BARRY GALLAGHER:** If you already have a pink and green pearl handle, why not go all out and marry it with a purple and blue blade and bolsters?

◀ **GAYLE BRADLEY:** The titanium bolsters are anodized gold, but the mammoth-ivory handle came about its color naturally. The blade is Damasteel. *(Ward photo)*

▶ **RUSTY POLK:** Rusty thought that hot-bluing a blade meant waiting until it turned the color of fire, and he was right. The mammoth ivory grip is a nice touch, too.

▶ **DAVID SEATON:** Robert Eggerling's "snakeskin"-pattern damascus bolster steel butts up against a Devin Thomas ladder-pattern damascus blade on one side and an elephant ivory grip on the other. *(PointSeven photo)*

◀ **MIKE TAMBOLI:** The green and brown hues of the stabilized maple burl handle are furthered by a mosaic handle pin and the stark contrast of the nickel silver guard and clean ATS-34 blade. *(PointSeven photo)*

▶ **WADE COLTER:** The carved-walrus-ivory handle counterbalances the blue-as-blue, mosaic-damascus blade and bolsters. *(PointSeven photo)*

▶ **DWIGHT TOWELL:** The gold leaf inlay not only elevates the dagger to an art form, but helps it levitate to an enlightened state. *(PointSeven photo)*

▶ **JOSH SMITH:** It's all damascus—some golden but most blue—and a citrine thumb stud for kicks. *(PointSeven photo)*

▶ **JOHN DAVIS:** The blue and violet flowers bloom where the mammoth ivory leaves off. *(BladeGallery.com photo)*

Scrimming with Excitement

You can't scrimshaw ivory lackadaisically. Uninspired scrimshaw artists work double shifts at Denny's restaurants. The most languid and listless of scrimshanders meet for coffee each month after the unemployment checks arrive. They fail to prick a hole in ivory for weeks, months and years at a time. Their dyes dry up, their wrists go weak, their eyes get lazy and the needles are literally pointless.

In high demand are the motivated, enthusiastic, excited scrimshaw artists. Theirs is an entirely different world of studios, creative genius, exhibitions, receptions and social gatherings. They turn common, everyday ivory into colorful paintings that will never tear, fade or need framing.

To accomplish such works of art, they steady their hands, adjust their magnifiers, dip their needles in ink, and poke one hole at a time into the pores of ivory, leaving miniscule dots of ink under the surface, creating brilliant scenes, subjects and sun splashes as they go along. It's tedious, time consuming, tireless work.

When inspiration runs dry, they turn to other forms of entertainment, taking walks, strolling through the woods or open meadows, or heading for the city to take in a show, dine at a fine restaurant or meander through a museum.

It can be no other way. Art critics blow the covers of aimless scrimshaw artists like foxhounds on a hunt. Revealed are the identities of the frauds, the pretenders, the complacent practitioners of scrimshaw. The true artists, the elite, the chosen ones continue their quest, ever raising the bar, reaching for higher goals and scrimming with excitement.

Joe Kertzman

◀ LINDA KARST STONE: Imagine hunting the woods nearest your house with this incredible Edmund Davidson knife at your side. The engraving is the handiwork of Jere Davidson. *(PointSeven photo)*

◀ LAURIA TROUT: The lifelike bass is about to strike a tempting lure, all within the pores of the mammoth-ivory handle of a Schuyler Lovestrand fillet knife. *(SharpByCoop.com photo)*

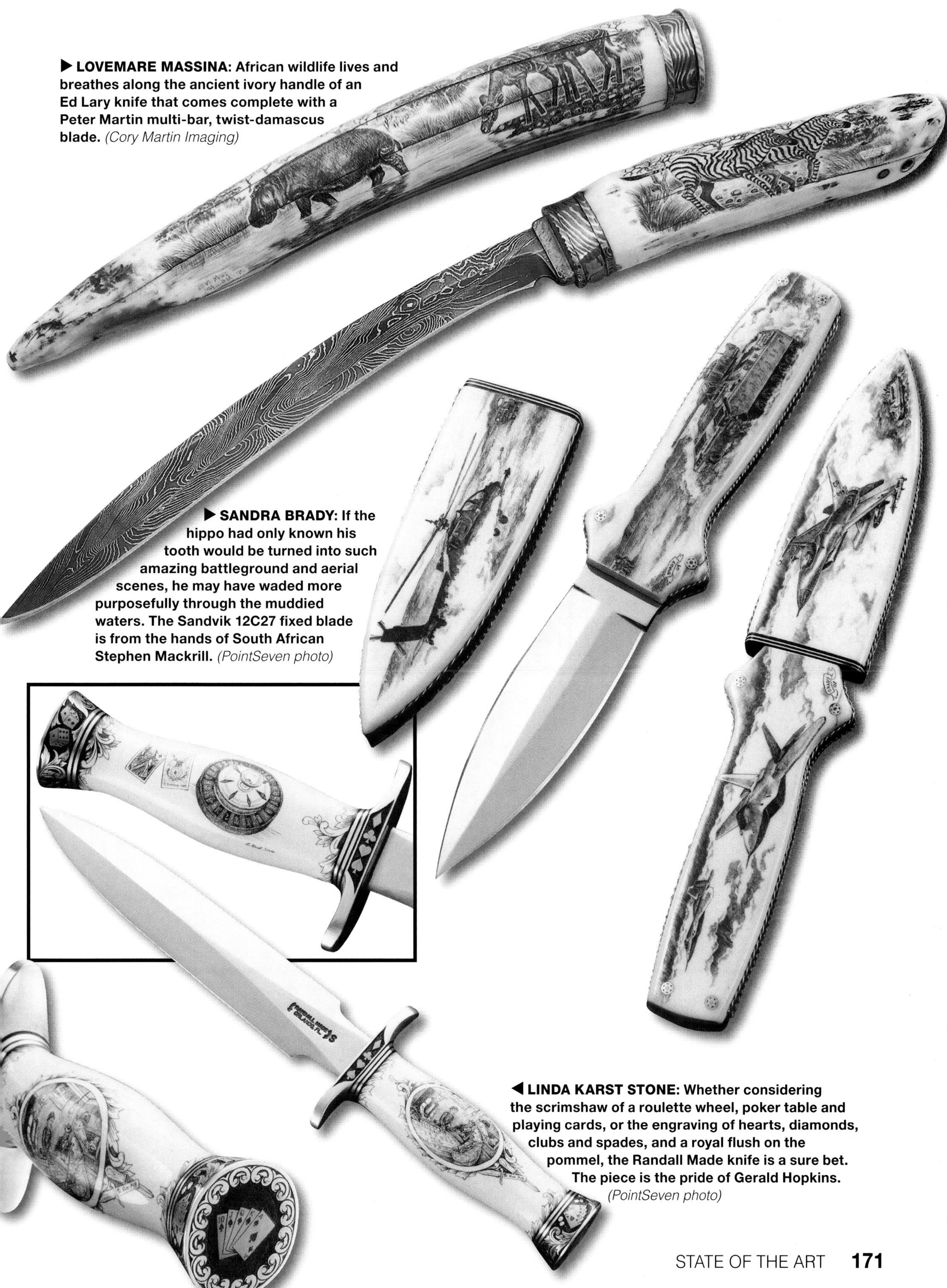

▶ **LOVEMARE MASSINA: African wildlife lives and breathes along the ancient ivory handle of an Ed Lary knife that comes complete with a Peter Martin multi-bar, twist-damascus blade.** *(Cory Martin Imaging)*

▶ **SANDRA BRADY: If the hippo had only known his tooth would be turned into such amazing battleground and aerial scenes, he may have waded more purposefully through the muddied waters. The Sandvik 12C27 fixed blade is from the hands of South African Stephen Mackrill.** *(PointSeven photo)*

◀ **LINDA KARST STONE: Whether considering the scrimshaw of a roulette wheel, poker table and playing cards, or the engraving of hearts, diamonds, clubs and spades, and a royal flush on the pommel, the Randall Made knife is a sure bet. The piece is the pride of Gerald Hopkins.** *(PointSeven photo)*

FACTORY TRENDS

In today's society, there's little room for corporate innovation, and a whole lot of cost saving measures, tightening of the belts, sending jobs overseas, watching jobs disappear, seeing factories close and standing by as towns and people suffer. It's not all bleak. The knife industry might not be thriving but it's surviving.

There's good reason for the good fortune experienced in the world of manufactured knives. Few knife factories have rested on their laurels. Keeping pace with technological advances, knife company R&D (Research and Development) teams constantly test new blade steels, manufacture bank-vault-tight locks for folding knives, invent practically indestructible handles and make knives work so well, so smoothly, so effortlessly, blade enthusiasts can't help but keep coming back.

Sure, some knife factories have closed their doors, but the majority have adapted to an ever-changing world with increasing expectations. Knife collectors have taken notice. Even some gun collectors have decided that the knife industry is a more hassle-free, innovative and fun industry in which to spend their money.

Custom knifemakers have helped keep the innovation coming, teaming with factories to bring the best of collaborative efforts to as many people as possible. It's all about building the best knife, and readers will agree, after looking at the following 12 pages, the knife industry is alive and kicking!

Joe Kertzman

Million-Year-Old Knives?

Millions of years of existence give character to just about anything, including knife handle materials

By Wm. Hovey Smith

A selection of fossilized teeth, bone and ivory from which to choose would constitute a knifemaker's dream.

The Santa Fe Stoneworks "Dinosaur Bone Collection" features dinosaur-bone-handle Spyderco and Camillus lock-back folders (top left) a two-blade money clip knife, and two letter openers.

Wm. Hovey Smith is a professional geologist and writer with degrees from the Universities of Georgia and Alaska. He also did postgraduate work at the Universities of Arizona and Arkansas. His most recent books are Practical Bowfishing (Stoeger, 2004) and Crossbow Hunting (Stackpole, 2006). He writes a column on crossbows for Whitetail Journal, and is Gun Digest's corresponding editor for features on black-powder guns.

Knife enthusiasts have the opportunity to purchase knives millions of years in the making, those that incorporate, in their very being, elements that have been on earth for many moons. They have seen the seasons change, so to speak.

Such knives aren't millions of years old themselves, but their natural stone and fossil-ivory or fossil-bone handles are, and as modern-day teenagers would say, "That's sweet!"

Such ancient knife handle materials range in appearance from the brilliant white of fossil ivory, through an entire spectrum of blues and greens common to copper minerals, to the lustrous black of polished obsidian.

As such raw materials are rare, costly and difficult to manipulate in a knife shop, they are only used on knives featuring the finest workmanship.

The tradition of incorporating stone and even gems into knife grips is thousands of years old.

Mammoth teeth make for handsome knife handles, as evidenced by the pair of William Henry Fine Knives "Catalina" folders.

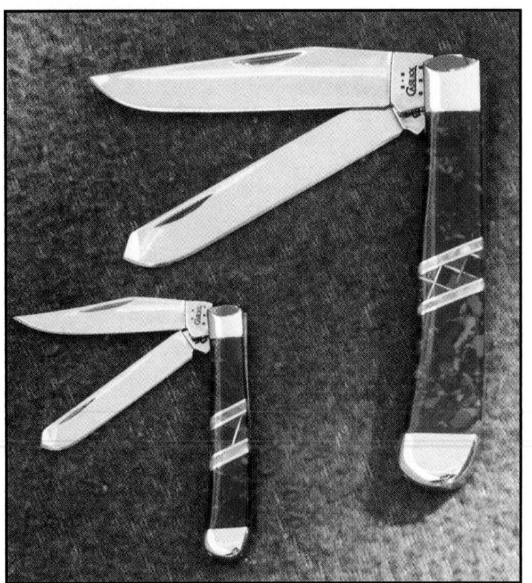

The W.R. Case & Sons Cutlery Co. folding trappers feature azurite grips.

The Case Texas toothpick and congress folders exhibit obsidian-inlaid grips.

Some of the surviving copper knives of ancient Egypt feature alabaster grips because the soft white material was cool and smooth to the touch, in addition to being attractive and easily worked.

As abrasives became more sophisticated in Roman times, it was possible to fashion even the very hard members of the quartz family into knife grips. Recent discoveries confirm the Chinese employed diamond dust to polish the lustrous but extremely hard jade knife handles for which they have become known.

To suffice as a folding-knife handle, the raw material must be stable, insoluble, non reactive to metallic components, able to take a good polish, not easily broken and hard enough to resist scratching.

One characteristic not mentioned is that the material must be easy to work. This is often not the case, and thin slices of some of the most attractive grips from rocks and fossils are devilishly difficult to cut and polish.

As Hard as Cave Onyx

Among the first discriminator to be considered is the hardness of the material. Minerals are ranked according to the Mohs' scale of hardness. Number one is talc, which feels greasy or slippery when touched. Number two is gypsum, also known as alabaster, which takes a lustrous polish but is easily scratched.

Most carbonate minerals, like calcite, have a hardness of three. In massive forms like cave onyx, carbonate minerals are readily scratched by steel objects.

The Bear & Sons Cutlery folder and fixed blade showcase turquoise inlays by David Yellowhorse.

A group of colorful mineral salts, like fluorite, have a hardness of four. This family of minerals is known to be yellow, blue, green or transparent, but break very easily along cleavage lines.

Moving up to five, the mineral apatite may be smoothed and shaped by a hard file, but not by the usual steel found in key rings or nail clips. Apatite is a phosphate mineral and its cousin turquoise has sufficient copper to give it a blue-green color.

Turquoise is also typically found in massive form, making it more useful for shaped objects such as jewelry. In thin pieces it is unfortunately brittle. Unless used as natural nuggets in a necklace, turquoise is almost invariably set in metal to protect the stone.

Feldspars, number six, give much of the luster to some polished "granite" sinks and countertops. The darker, more calcium-rich feldspars show iridescent blue colors, but it is rare to find these lustrous minerals in masses large enough for knife scales. White, almost glowing, feldspar is known as moonstone.

Members of the quartz family with a hardness of seven include quartz crystals in various colors, agates, true onyx and the very colorful jaspers that are red, yellow, green or in variegated colors. Jasper is a massive material, may be cut into thin slabs, polishes very well and is highly scratch resistant.

Although hard and tuff, jasper often contains hidden cracks that cause the material to break during polishing. Some members of the quarts family, like agate, are porous enough to be stained to enhance their natural colors.

Jade, although technically a rock rather than a mineral, exhibits a hardness of between six and seven along with a texture that gives it both toughness and luster when polished. This is the reason that it was prized by ancient cultures as far apart as China, New Zealand and Mexico.

Real Knife Handle Gems

Harder materials move into the classification of true gems and include topaz as number eight, corundum minerals like sapphire as number nine and diamonds as number ten.

Presently the most common fossil-ivory knife handle materials include mastodon ivory, mammoth ivory, walrus ivory and mammoth tooth. The ivories are mostly derived from the Arctic regions of the world and were once frozen in the tundra.

Formerly some of the best fossil ivory was found in placer goldmines in places like Chicken, Alaska, where a group of tusks was uncovered by a gold dredge and sold to Buck Knives. Some fossil-walrus and elephant ivories still come from Alaska, but more is derived from the Russian Arctic.

An additional source is from dredged material of the North Sea. The ivory from this source is not as fresh, but may showcase variety of colors ranging from black to shades of blue and green.

Mammoths had huge sets of grinding molars that acted like rasps to masticate woody material into digestible pulp. The teeth consisted of alternating hard and softer materials, resulting in sub-parallel, razor-sharp sets of crushing, grinding and shredding molars powered by huge jaw muscles.

The vertical tooth structure held together very well while the animal was living, but must be stabilized with resin before it can be cut into thin slabs and polished.

Bones, like dinosaur bones, are much older than the frozen mammoth and mastodon remains, and although the porous bone structure may remain, boney materials are commonly replaced by silica. Silicified wood, complete with growth rings, may also be polished and used for knife grips. It responds much like agate and has similar characteristics.

Azurite, malachite and turquoise are all secondary copper minerals most frequently found in the oxidized portions of copper deposits in arid parts of the world. For millennia, copper minerals have been recovered and worked into jewelry from sources in Arizona, Iran, Russia, Egypt and Tibet.

Material from the upper parts of these deposits may be too soft and bleached to make good gems. It is sometimes crushed, died and mixed with clear resin to make a reconstituted turquoise.

Rich Veins

Excavations of large, open-pit copper mines regularly expose fresh material and sub-contractors gather these minerals for resale. For safety and environmental reasons, the mines and dumps are closed to the public. Some of the best turquoise and azurite comes from Arizona and is exported worldwide.

Colorful jaspers are also associated with many pyrite-rich mineral veins that may not contain sufficient gold or other metals to be worth mining. The mineral veins, though not sufficient for gold or precious-metal mining, often generate sufficient mineral acids to remobilize quartz and make jasper.

Jasper was often employed by cultures worldwide to knap into arrow points and cutting blades. Particular deposits may yield red-toned jasper (bloodstone), although yellow and green-tinted jasper is not uncommon. Often jasper is quite colorful, but because the deposits are not actively mined the available amount of any particular color is small.

"Jasper was often employed by cultures worldwide to knap into arrow points and cutting blades." – the author

Obsidian is quite different in origin. Rather than being a crystalline mineral, it is a glass formed by the rapid cooling of silica-rich lavas. Very-very slowly it oxidizes on the surface forming a rind, and the age of a chipped obsidian arrowhead may be estimated by the amount of weathering.

If you own an obsidian-handle or obsidian-blade knife, don't worry as the weathering process requires exposures to rain and soils and takes thousands of years. Obsidian is most often black in color, but can be red and is known to exhibit white flakes.

Waste, breakage and disappointment are all too common results when attempting to make knife handles from these hard, but often brittle, materials. Fossil ivories are more like natural ivories, but as Matthew Conable of William Henry Fine Knives remarked, "They move all over the place unless they are stabilized."

Stabilization is accomplished by imbedding the material in a clear resin, fixing metal or fiberglass backings to add strength, or inletting steel knife frames to provide both side and bottom support for the grip materials.

Hopi-Style Handles?

Anyone who has visited the American Southwest has seen examples of the Hopi-style jewelry in which thin slices of turquoise, jet, coral and other stones are set in silver to form a thunderbird or other design. This work is similar to a mosaic, except that the chips are set in silver rather than in adhesives.

The style of work was transferred to knife handles by David Yellowhorse who made a long-running series of stone-inlayed, lock-back folders for Buck Knives. Today, David's sons carry on the tradition.

Although some companies manufacture their own grips using stone or fossil bones, most find it more practical to sub-contract the work out to artisans who specialize in the delicate inlaying and polishing work.

The efforts of the miner, knifemaker and jeweler combine to achieve edged objects that simultaneously possess beauty, value and utility.

Flat, Blunt, Talon and Tanto Tips

▼Here's a folding neck and jewelry knife from Mantis—the "MU-05 Jyro I"—that features a talon-style, flat-ground M-VX tool steel blade and a T-6 6061 aircraft aluminum handle.

▲The Waffentechnik SARD not only features a tanto blade, but also a lanyard hole, pocket clip, wire cutter/crimper, plastic handcuff cutter and a

▶The two cutting implements integral to Remington's "Escape II" rescue knife are a partially serrated sheepsfoot blade and a seatbelt/web cutter.

▶ Spyderco's "Caspian2" all-purpose knife is designed so a blade enthusiasts fingers remain free for other tasks when holding the handle. There is a line cutter mounted on the blade spine, a sharpened chisel tip and partial serrations along the edge.

▲ Al Mar Knives presents the "Payara" VG-10 stainless steel utility folder with a triple-ground blade tip designed for superior penetration and cutting power.

◀ The Blackhawk "Hawkhook" rescue tool features a serrated AUS-8A edge for cutting seatbelts, a glass breaker, bottle opener, wire stripper and a screwdriver/pry tip.

▲ Meyerco's newest auto-opening tactical folder—the "18-XRAY"—parades a tanto-style 154CM blade and an anodized-aluminum handle.

▲ Columbia River Knife & Tool's "Razel" is a multi-purpose fixed blade showcasing a sharpened chisel tip, serrations on the spine of the blade, a bottle-opener pommel and a Micarta handle.

Classic Folders

▲Case's "Seahorse Whittler" shows off three beautiful Devin and Rob Thomas raindrop-damascus blades—wharncliffe, pen and coping blades—along with an India stag handle and nickel silver bolsters. and re-curved blade to complement a curly-Koa-wood grip. *(Mitch Lum photo)*

▲The "#53 Northfield UN-X-LD" is a Cuban cigar-pattern pocketknife employing clip, sheepsfoot and spay blades, an acrylic "Dead Skunk"-pattern handle and nickel-silver bolsters.

▶ Cold Steel's classic Euro folder—the extra large "Espada"—boasts a 7 ½-inch, AUS-8A, clip-point blade and a finger-grooved, polished G-10 handle.

▼The Hallmark "Chief Muskrat" makes use of 440A stainless steel blades and a jigged-chestnut-bone handle.

▼Lone Wolf's "Paul Executive" is a classically styled gent's knife made of 400 series stainless steel, "marble" cocobolo and an Axiel lock.

Hot Little Hunters

▲ Browning's "Escalade" hunter incorporates a 3.25-inch 440C stainless steel blade, hollow ground and mirror polished, and a box-elder-burl handle.

▲ The Columbia River Knife & Tool "Brow Tine Hunter" is designed by Russ Kommer to include a hollow-ground 9Cr18 stainless steel blade for top skinning performance.

See-Through Knives

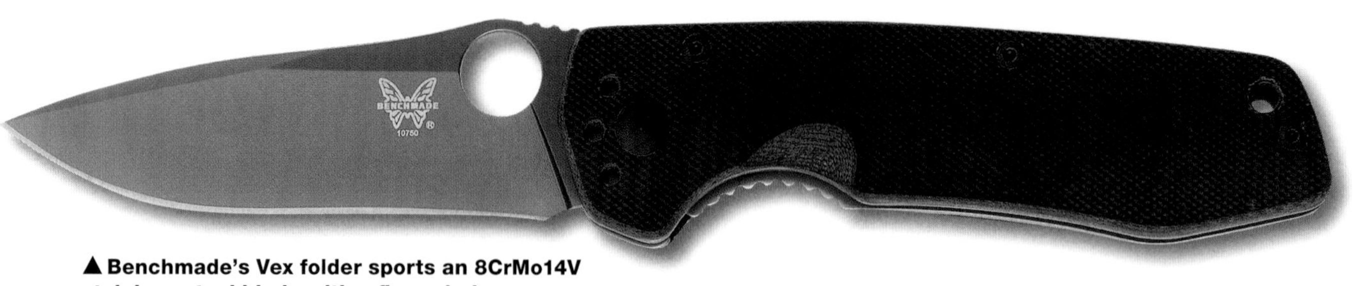

▲ Benchmade's Vex folder sports an 8CrMo14V stainless steel blade with a finger hole.

▶ The see-through part of the Buck "Redpoint" utility folder is the carabineer/bottle opener on the butt of the thermoplastic rubber-overlaid handle. The knife features a partially serrated 420HC stainless steel blade.

▶ The Buck Metro is a keychain knife with a hole in the blade for ease of one-hand opening, a large hole in the grip for choking up with the fingers or for lashing it to a vest or other gear, and a small thong hole.

▶ Complete with one-hand-opening hole in the blade, the Benchmade Pika II sports high-cobalt steel to give a fine cutting edge.

▲ Designed by Tom Krein, the Columbia River Knife & Tool Dogfish are 3Cr13 steel fish-like cutters.

▶ **Spyderco includes four holes in the VG-10 stainless steel blade of the Howard Viele-designed "Phoenix," as well as a Micarta-overlaid stainless steel handle and a ball bearing lock.**

▶ **The Chris Reeve Knives "Professional Soldier" is a collaborative effort with knifemaker Bill Harsey and features a CPM S30V stainless steel blade, an integral handle and a cutaway in the grip to reduce weight.**

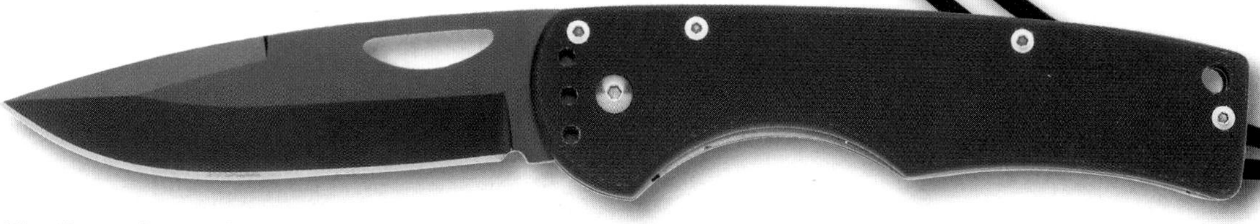

▶ **The Sovereign series of folding knives is designed by Blackie Collins for Meyerco, complete with slots in the blades for ease of one-hand opening.**

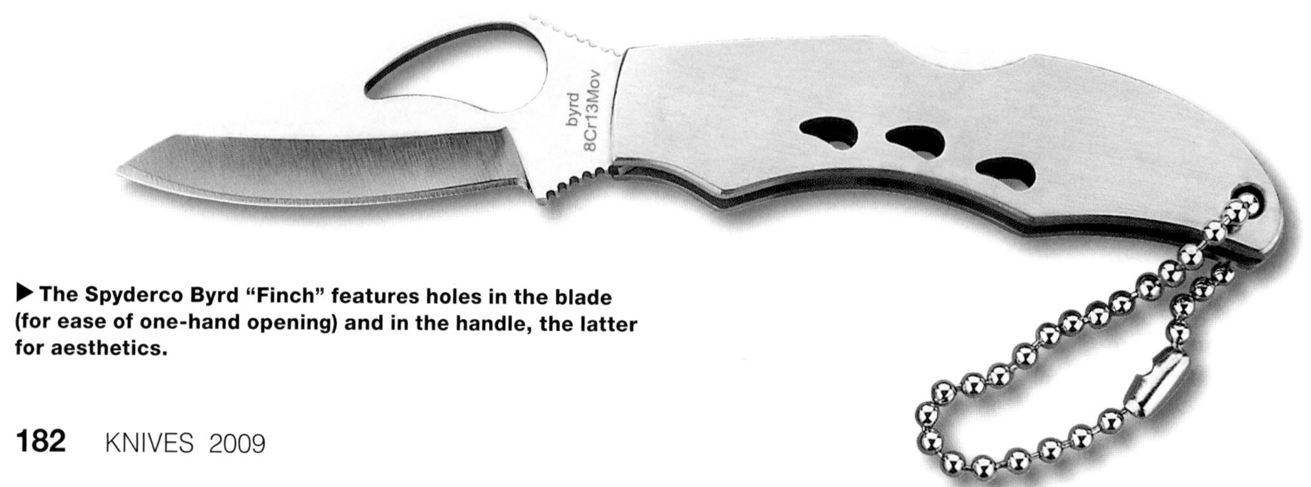

▶ **The Spyderco Byrd "Finch" features holes in the blade (for ease of one-hand opening) and in the handle, the latter for aesthetics.**

Utility Tools

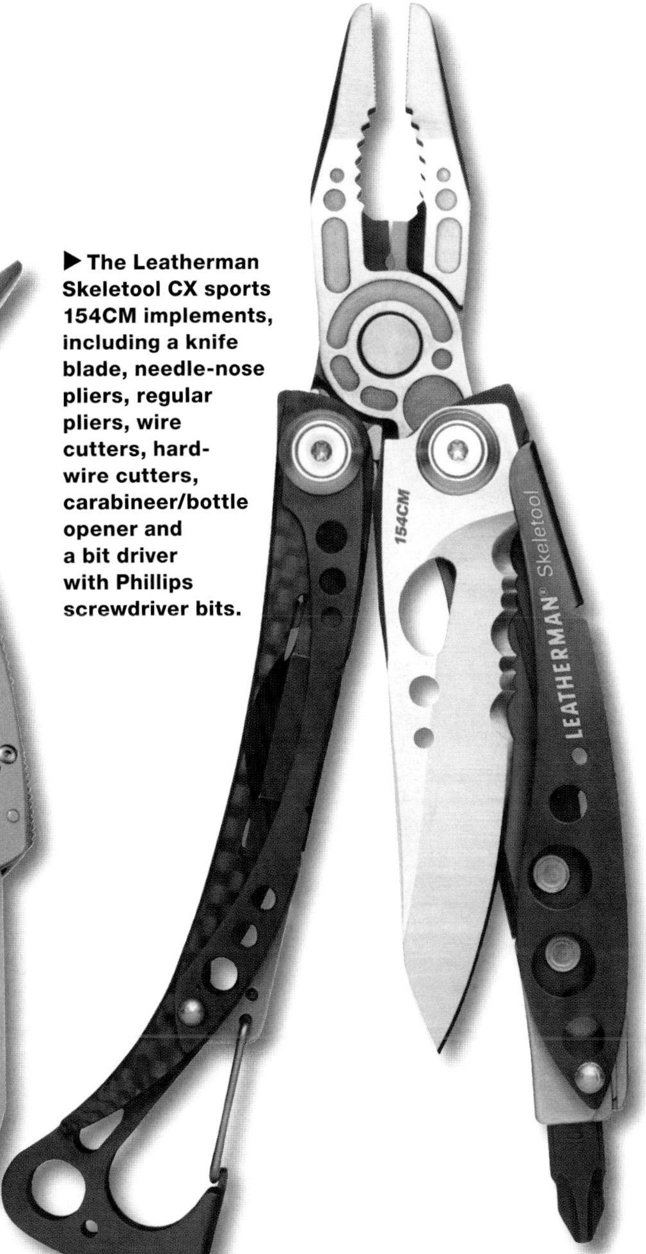

▶ The Leatherman Skeletool CX sports 154CM implements, including a knife blade, needle-nose pliers, regular pliers, wire cutters, hard-wire cutters, carabineer/bottle opener and a bit driver with Phillips screwdriver bits.

▶ Implements splay out from each handle of the Lansky MultiTool, specifically a blade, needle-nose pliers, wire cutter, small and medium screwdrivers, a file/rule, awl, magnetic bit holder, can/bottle opener and a socket drive with bits.

Tactical & Utility Folders

▲ Designed by Dietmar Pohl, the Eickhorn Pohl One Damascus flipper folder showcases a Markus Balbach damascus, re-curved blade, and a hard-anodized-aluminum handle with a wood inlay.

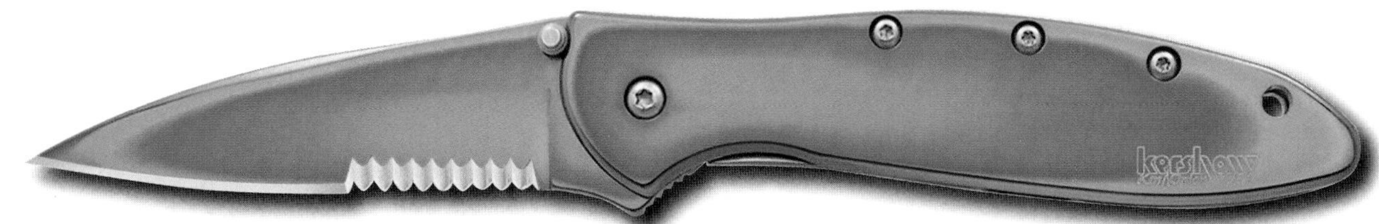

▲The rainbow-anodized, assisted-opening Rainbow Leek from Kershaw is an eyeful.

▲SOG's "Visionary" tactical folder parades a black-powder-coated VG-10 stainless steel blade, an Arc-Lock and a Zytel handle.

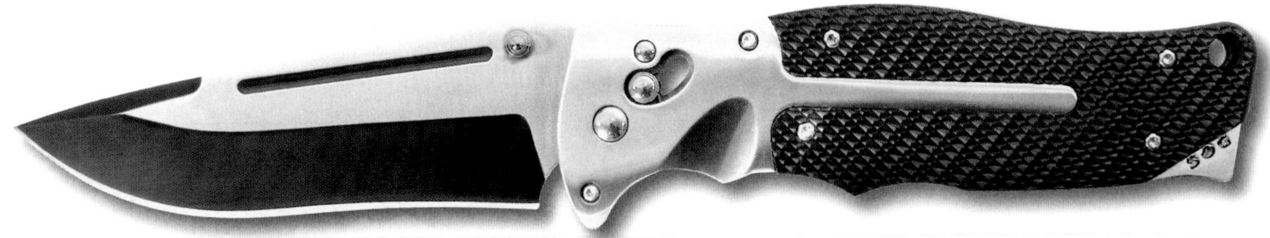

▲The SOG "Fatcat" is a fat cat indeed, boasting a 4 ½-inch VG-10 stainless steel blade with a titanium-nitride bevel, a Zytel handle, titanium bolsters, finger grooves and an Arc-Lock.

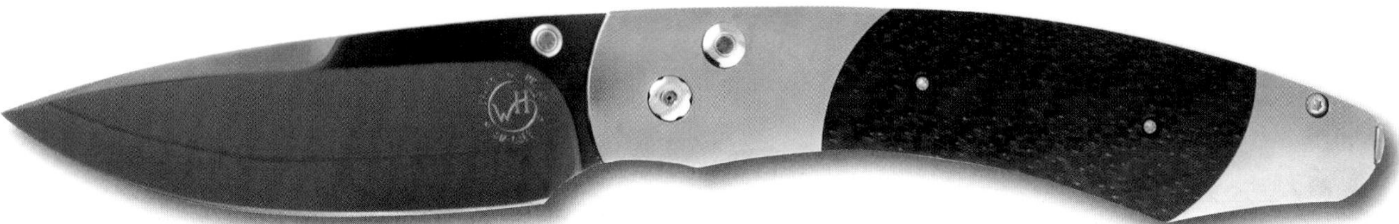

▲William Henry's latest offering, the "B12" fancy utility folder parades a ZDP-189 laminate, spear-point blade with a Tungsten DLC coating, a titanium handle and a palm wood grip.

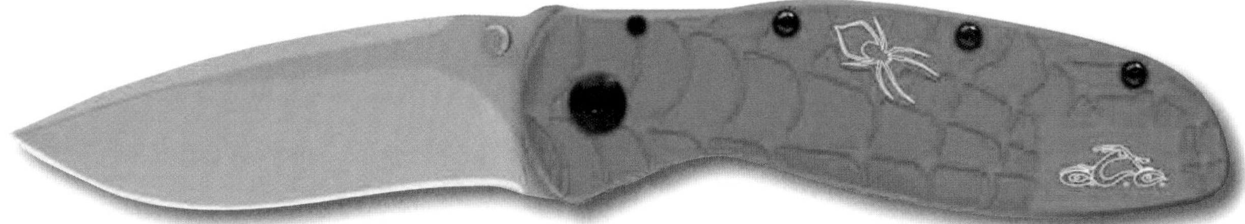

▲Kershaw debuts the "OCC Blur," a Sandvik 14C28N utility folder with an orange-anodized aluminum handle that displays a 3-D-machined spider web and an Orange County Choppers logo.

KNIVES MARKETPLACE

INTERESTING PRODUCT NEWS FOR BOTH THE CUTLER AND THE KNIFE ENTHUSIAST

The companies and individuals represented on the following pages will be happy to provide additional information — feel free to contact them.

Knives Marketplace

Custom Grips and Knives
305-613-2990
Ivory 1911 Grips
Custom Knives
www.gripsandknives.com

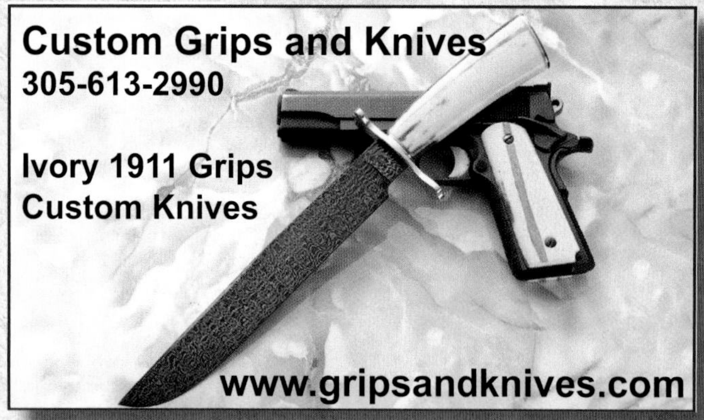

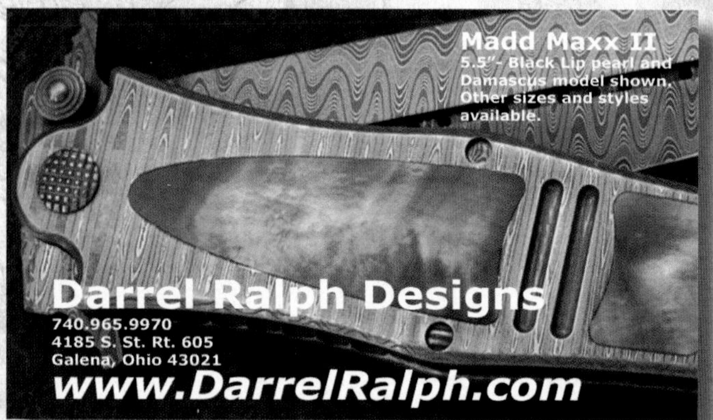

An edge above the rest
LANSKY®
SHARPENERS
World's largest and finest selection
of knife and tool sharpeners.
See them at better stores everywhere,
or visit us online at: lansky.com.
PO Box 50830, Henderson, NV 89016 • Phone: 716-877-7511

Madd Maxx II
5.5" - Black Lip pearl and Damascus model shown. Other sizes and styles available.
Darrel Ralph Designs
740.965.9970
4185 S. St. Rt. 605
Galena, Ohio 43021
www.DarrelRalph.com

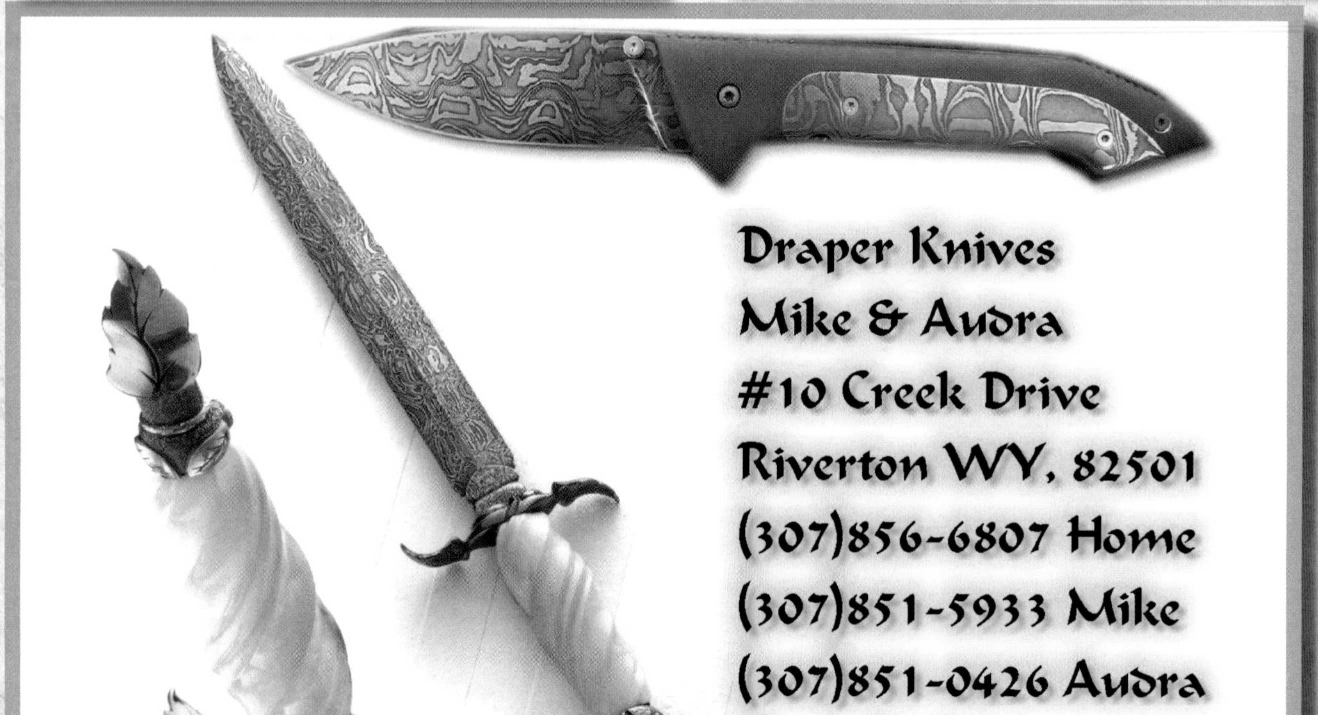
Draper Knives
Mike & Audra
#10 Creek Drive
Riverton WY, 82501
(307)856-6807 Home
(307)851-5933 Mike
(307)851-0426 Audra
One of a kind custom
knives since 1992.

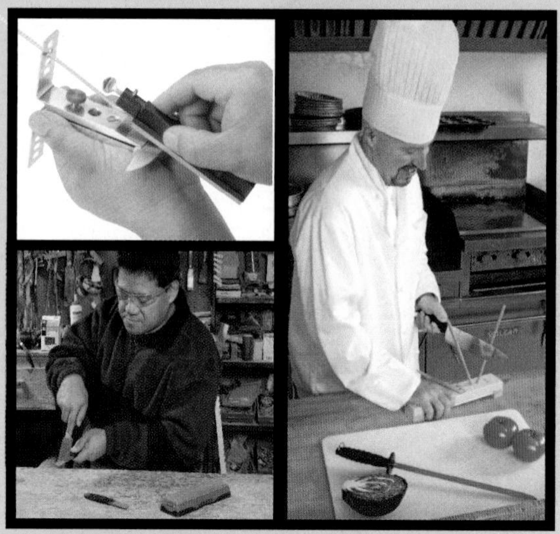

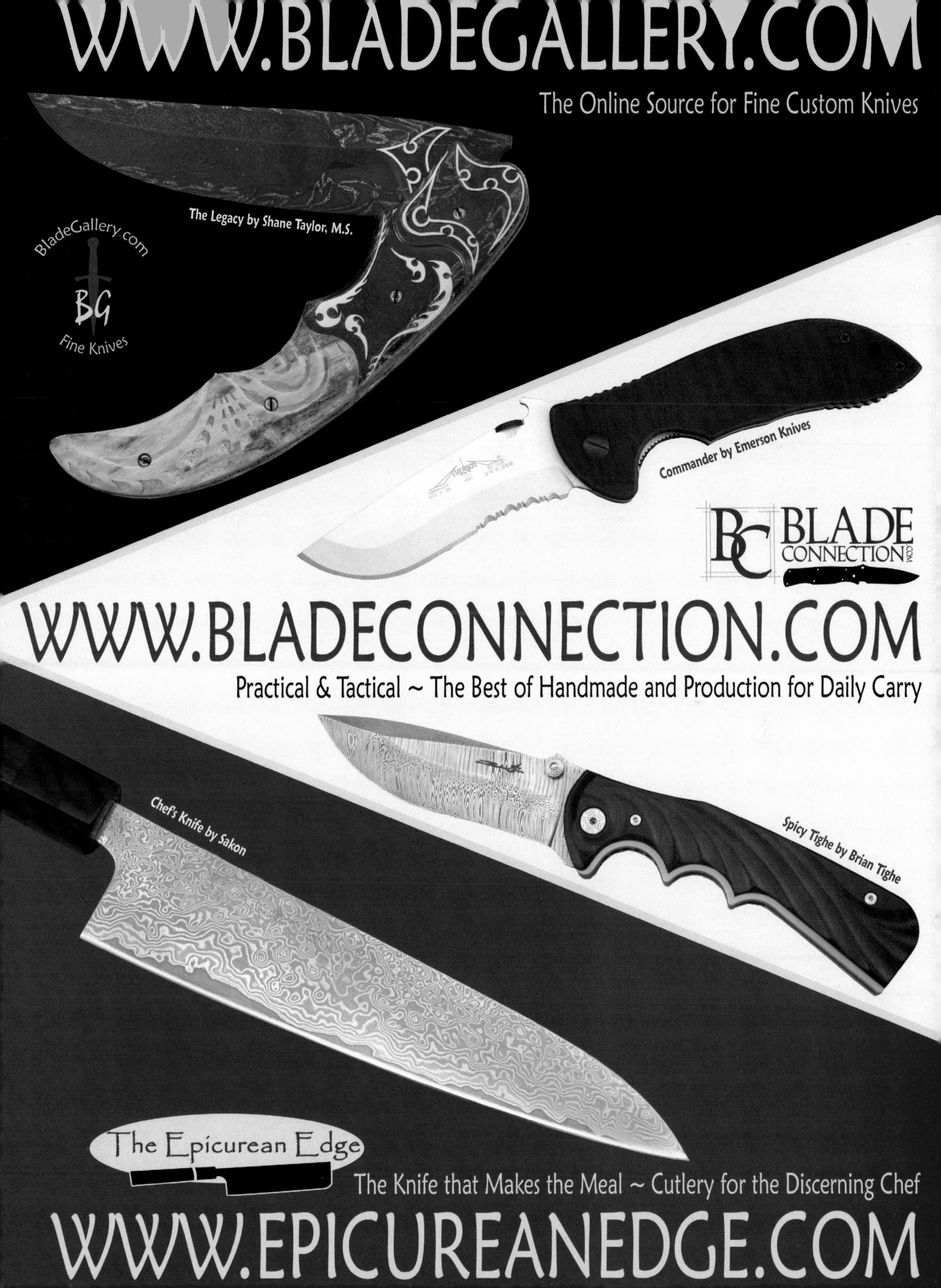
WWW.BLADEGALLERY.COM
The Online Source for Fine Custom Knives
The Legacy by Shane Taylor, M.S.
BladeGallery.com
BG
Fine Knives
Commander by Emerson Knives
BC BLADE CONNECTION.COM
WWW.BLADECONNECTION.COM
Practical & Tactical ~ The Best of Handmade and Production for Daily Carry
Chef's Knife by Sakon
Spicy Tighe by Brian Tighe
The Epicurean Edge
The Knife that Makes the Meal ~ Cutlery for the Discerning Chef
WWW.EPICUREANEDGE.COM

Knives Marketplace

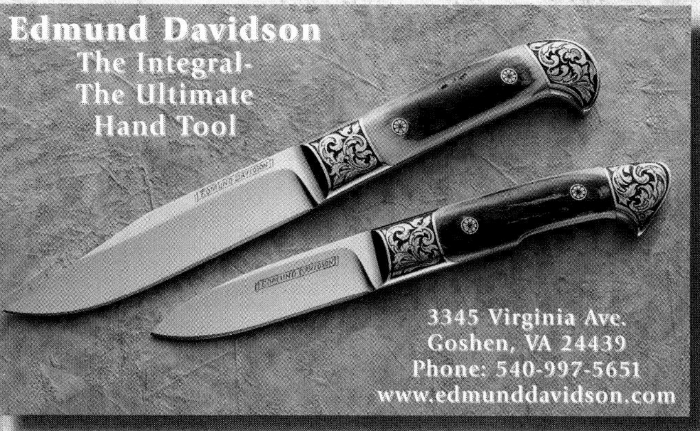

WARTHOG SHARPENERS - USA

Featuring the Warthog V-Sharp, a user friendly, empowering tool which allows a person to sharpen their straight edge knife blades to factory sharp condition with no special skill required. Ideal for hunting, fishing, kitchen, or working blades. Diamond rods, adjustable angles, and spring tension, all work together to put the perfect edge on each side of the blade simultaneously.

Warthog Multi-Sharpener Systems, are designed to sharpen scissors, chisels, planer blades, serrated edges, as well as fine collectible and working knives.

Dealer Inquiries Invited: Retailers, Gun & Knife Show Dealers, Outdoor Show Exhibitors & Dealers.

Call John Ring @ 954-275-6872
or visit our web site at http://www.warthogsharp.com
for more information or to locate the dealer nearest you.

Knives Marketplace

Gary Levine Fine Knives
A Dealer of Handmade Knives

Gary's goal is to offer the collector the best custom knives available, in stock and ready for delivery. He has the best makers as well as the rising stars at fair prices. Gary enjoys working with collectors who want to enhance their collections, as well as someone who just wants a great knife to carry. Gary is also always on the lookout for collections, as well as single custom knives to purchase. Please stop by his Web site.

GARY LEVINE FINE KNIVES
P.O. Box 416, Ridgefield, CT 06877
Phone: 203-438-5294
Web: http://www.levineknives.com
E-mail: gary@levineknives.com

More Titles Worth Wielding!

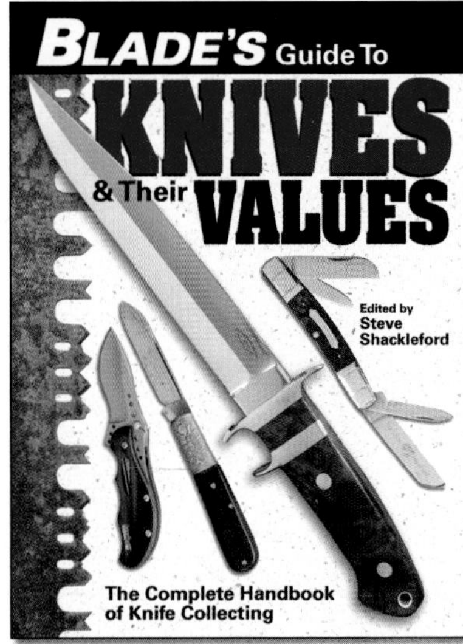

Covers most all knives made around the world, mostly from the 19th century through to the present, with up-to-date values, 2,000+ photos, and feature articles covering trends in the industry. Plus, detailed histories of knife companies, and contact information.
Softcover • 8-1/2 x 11 • 576 pages
2,000 b&w photos
Item# LGK6 • $29.99

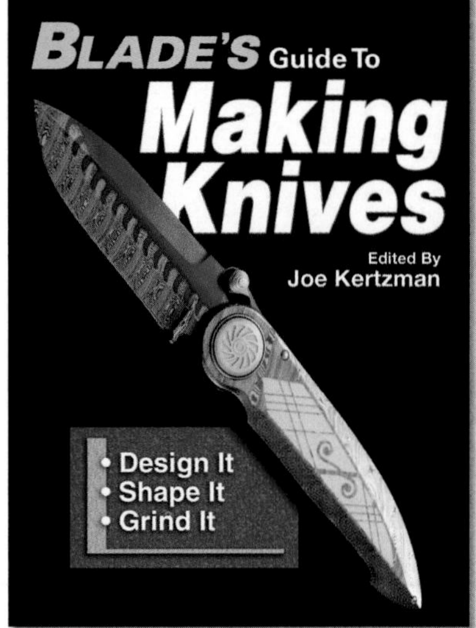

Gain professional technique tips and instruction for grinding blades, crafting hunting knives, forging pattern-welded steel into intricate designs, making folding knives, and fashioning the important bolster between knife and blade.
Softcover • 8-1/4 x 10-7/8 • 160 pages
250 color photos
Item# BGKFM • $24.99

Explore the creativity and craftsmanship of knifemaking in 350 brilliant color photos of highly engraved folders, engraved fixed blades, wire-wrapped knifes and more, with a basic explanation of materials.
Hardcover • 8-1/4 x 10-7/8 • 256 pages
350 color photos
Item# Z0733 • $35.00

Explore Wayne Goddard's trusted techniques through detailed instructions, demonstrated in 250 color photos and outlined in cost-saving hints for building your own workshop.
Softcover • 8-1/4 x 10-7/8 • 160 pages
250 color photos
Item# WGBWR • $19.99

Learn how with "the bible of knifemaking." Gives complete instructions on making high quality handmade knives—forging and stock removal, mirror polishing, sheath making, safety techniques, required tools and supplies, and
Softcover • 8-1/2 x 11 • 182 pages
448 b&w photos
Item# KHM01 • $13.95

Features current values and identification for thousands of Case, Crandall, Queen and Schatt & Morgan pocket knives, sheath knives and straight razors, as well as company histories. Plus, you'll discover a stunning color photo section.
Softcover • 8-1/2 x 11 • 504 pages
2,500+ b&w photos • 32-page color section
Item# Z2189 • $27.99

Order directly from the publisher at **www.krausebooks.com**

Krause Publications, Offer **KNB8**
P.O. Box 5009
Iola, WI 54945-5009
www.krausebooks.com

Call **800-258-0929** M-F 8 a.m. - 5 p.m. to order direct from the publisher, or shop booksellers nationwide.
Please reference offer **KNB8** with all direct-to-publisher orders

News to Forge Ahead in Your Hobby at www.blademag.com

DIRECTORY

A

ABEGG, ARNIE,
5992 Kenwick Cr, Huntington Beach, CA 92648, Phone: 714-848-5697

ABERNATHY, PAUL J,
3033 Park St., Eureka, CA 95501, Phone: 707-442-3593
Specialties: Period pieces and traditional straight knives of his design and in standard patterns. **Patterns:** Miniature daggers, fighters and swords. **Technical:** Forges and files SS, brass and sterling silver. **Prices:** $100 to $250; some to $500. **Remarks:** Part-time maker. Doing business as Abernathy's Miniatures. **Mark:** Stylized initials.

ACCAWI, FUAD,
131 Bethel Rd, Clinton, TN 37716, Phone: 865-414-4836, gaccawi@com azcast.net; Web: www.acremetalworks.com
Specialties: I create one of a kind pieces from small working knives to performance blades and swords. **Patterns:** Styles include, and not limited to hunters, Bowies, daggers, swords, folders and camp knives. **Technical:** I forge primarily 5160, produces own Damascus and does own heat treating. **Prices:** $150 to $3000. **Remarks:** I am a full-time bladesmith. I enjoy producing Persian and historically influenced work. **Mark:** My mark is an eight sided Middle Eastern star with initials in the center.

ACKERSON, ROBIN E,
119 W Smith St, Buchanan, MI 49107, Phone: 616-695-2911

ADAMS, LES,
6413 NW 200 St, Hialeah, FL 33015, Phone: 305-625-1699
Specialties: Working straight knives of his design. **Patterns:** Fighters, tactical folders, law enforcing autos. **Technical:** Grinds ATS-34, 440C and D2. **Prices:** $100 to $500. **Remarks:** Part-time maker; first knife sold in 1989. **Mark:** First initial, last name, Custom Knives.

ADAMS, WILLIAM D,
PO Box 439, Burton, TX 77835, Phone: 713-855-5643, Fax: 713-855-5638
Specialties: Hunter scalpels and utility knives of his design. **Patterns:** Hunters and utility/camp knives. **Technical:** Grinds 1095, 440C and 440V. Uses stabilized wood and other stabilized materials. **Prices:** $100 to $200. **Remarks:** Part-time maker; first knife sold in 1994. **Mark:** Last name in script.

ADDISON, KYLE A,
809 N. 20th St, Murray, KY 42071, Phone: 270-759-1564, kylest2@yahoo.com
Specialties: Hand forged blades including Bowies, fighters and hunters. **Patterns:** Custom leather sheaths. **Technical:** Forges 5160, 1084, and his own Damascus. **Prices:** $175 to $1500. **Remarks:** Part-time maker, first knife sold in 1996. ABS member. **Mark:** First and middle initial, last name under "Trident" with knife and hammer.

ADKINS, LARRY,
10714 East County Rd. 100S, Indianapolis, IN 46231, Phone: 317-838-7292
Specialties: Single blade slip joint folders. Bear Jaw Damascus hunters, Bowies, and fighters. Handles from stag, ossic, pearl, bone, mastodon-mammoth elephant. **Technical:** Forges own Damascus and all high carbon steels. Grinds 5160, 52100, 1095, O1 and L6. **Prices:** $150 and up. **Remarks:** Part-time maker, first knife sold in 2001. **Mark:** L. Adkins.

ADKINS, RICHARD L,
138 California Ct, Mission Viejo, CA 92692-4079

ADREWS, RUSS,
PO Box 7732, Sugar Creek, MO 64054, Phone: 816-252-3344, russandrews@sbcglobal.net; Web:wwwrussandrewsknives.com
Specialties: Hand forged bowies & hunters. **Mark:** E. R. Andrews II. ERAII.

AIDA, YOSHIHITO,
26-7 Narimasu 2-chome, Itabashi-ku, Tokyo 175-0094, JAPAN, Phone: 81-3-3939-0052, Fax: 81-3-3939-0058
Specialties: High-tech working straight knives and folders of his design. **Patterns:** Bowies, lockbacks, hunters, fighters, fishing knives, boots. **Technical:** Grinds CV-134, ATS-34; buys Damascus; works in traditional Japanese fashion for some handles and sheaths. **Prices:** $700 to $1200; some higher. **Remarks:** Full-time maker; first knife sold in 1978. **Mark:** Initial logo and Riverside West.

ALBERICCI, EMILIO,
19 Via Masone, 24100, Bergamo, ITALY, Phone: 01139-35-215120
Specialties: Folders and Bowies. **Patterns:** Collector knives. **Technical:** Uses stock removal with extreme accuracy; offers exotic and high-tech materials. **Prices:** Not currently selling. **Remarks:** Part-time maker. **Mark:** None.

ALBERT, STEFAN,
U Lucenecka 434/4, Filakovo 98604, SLOVAK REPUBLIC, stefan.albert@post.sk; Web: www.albertknives.com
Specialties: Art Knives, miniatures, Scrimshaw. **Prices:** From USD $300 to USD $2000. **Mark:** A.

ALDERMAN, ROBERT,
2655 Jewel Lake Rd., Sagle, ID 83860, Phone: 208-263-5996
Specialties: Classic and traditional working straight knives in standard patterns or to customer specs and his design; period pieces. **Patterns:** Bowies, fighters, hunters and utility/camp knives. **Technical:** Casts, forges and grinds 1084; forges and grinds L6 and O1. Prefers an old appearance. **Prices:** $100 to $350; some to $700. **Remarks:** Full-time maker; first knife sold in 1975. Doing business as Trackers Forge. Knife-making school. Two-week course for beginners; covers forging, stock removal, hardening, tempering, case making. All materials supplied; $1250. **Mark:** Deer track.

ALDRETE, BOB,
PO Box 1471, Lomita, CA 90717, Phone: 310-326-3041

ALEXANDER, DARREL,
Box 381, Ten Sleep, WY 82442, Phone: 307-366-2699, dalexwyo@tctwest.net
Specialties: Traditional working straight knives. **Patterns:** Hunters, boots and fishing knives. **Technical:** Grinds D2, 440C, ATS-34 and 154CM. **Prices:** $75 to $120; some to $250. **Remarks:** Full-time maker; first knife sold in 1983. **Mark:** Name, city, state.

ALEXANDER, EUGENE,
Box 540, Ganado, TX 77962-0540, Phone: 512-771-3727

ALLEN, MIKE "WHISKERS",
12745 Fontenot Acres Rd, Malakoff, TX 75148, Phone: 903-489-1026, whiskersknives@aol.com; Web: www.whiskersknives.com
Specialties: Working and collector-quality lockbacks, liner locks and automatic folders to customer specs. **Patterns:** Folders, hunters, tantos, bowies, swords and miniatures. **Technical:** Grinds Damascus, 440C and ATS-34, engraves. **Prices:** $200 and up. **Remarks:** Full-time maker; first knife sold in 1984. **Mark:** Whiskers and date.

ALLRED, BRUCE F,
1764 N. Alder, Layton, UT 84041, Phone: 801-825-4612, allredbf@msn.com
Specialties: Custom hunting and utility knives. **Patterns:** Custom designs that include a unique grind line, thumb and mosaic pins. **Technical:** ATS-34, 154CM and 440C. **Remarks:** The handle material includes but not limited to Micarta (in various colors), natural woods and reconstituted stone.

ALVERSON, TIM (R.V.),
622 Homestead St., Moscow, ID 83843, Phone: 208-874-2277
Specialties: Fancy working knives to customer specs; other types on request. **Patterns:** Bowies, daggers, folders and miniatures. **Technical:** Grinds 440C, ATS-34; buys some Damascus. **Prices:** Start at $100. **Remarks:** Full-time maker; first knife sold in 1981. **Mark:** R.V.A. around rosebud.

AMERI, MAURO,
Via Riaello No. 20, Trensasco St Olcese, 16010 Genova, ITALY, Phone: 010-8357077
Specialties: Working and using knives of his design. **Patterns:** Hunters, Bowies and utility/camp knives. **Technical:** Grinds 440C, ATS-34 and 154CM. Handles in wood or Micarta; offers sheaths. **Prices:** $200 to $1200. **Remarks:** Spare-time maker; first knife sold in 1982. **Mark:** Last name, city.

AMMONS, DAVID C,
6225 N. Tucson Mtn. Dr, Tucson, AZ 85743, Phone: 520-307-3585
Specialties: Will build to suit. **Patterns:** Yours or his. **Prices:** $250 to $2000. **Mark:** AMMONS.

AMOUREUX, A W,
PO Box 776, Northport, WA 99157, Phone: 509-732-6292
Specialties: Heavy-duty working straight knives. **Patterns:** Bowies, fighters, camp knives and hunters for world-wide use. **Technical:** Grinds 440C, ATS-34 and 154CM. **Prices:** $80 to $2000. **Remarks:** Full-time maker; first knife sold in 1974. **Mark:** ALSTAR.

ANDERS, DAVID,
157 Barnes Dr, Center Ridge, AR 72027, Phone: 501-893-2294
Specialties: Working straight knives of his design. **Patterns:** Bowies, fighters and hunters. **Technical:** Forges 5160, 1080 and Damascus. **Prices:** $225 to $3200. **Remarks:** Part-time maker; first knife sold in 1988. Doing business as Anders Knives. **Mark:** Last name/MS.

ANDERS, JEROME,
14560 SW 37th St, Miramar, FL 33027, Phone: 305-613-2990, web:www.andersknives.com
Specialties: Case handles and pin work. **Patterns:** Layered and mosiac steel. **Prices:** $275 and up. **Remarks:** All his knives are truly one-of-a-kind. **Mark:** J. Anders in half moon.

ANDERSEN, HENRIK LEFOLII,
Jagtvej 8, Groenholt, 3480, Fredensborg, DENMARK, Phone: 0011-45-48483026
Specialties: Hunters and matched pairs for the serious hunter. **Technical:** Grinds A2; uses materials native to Scandinavia. **Prices:** Start at $250. **Remarks:** Part-time maker; first knife sold in 1985. **Mark:** Initials with arrow.

ANDERSON, GARY D,
2816 Reservoir Rd, Spring Grove, PA 17362-9802, Phone: 717-229-2665
Specialties: From working knives to collectors quality blades, some

folders. **Patterns:** Traditional and classic designs; customer patterns welcome. **Technical:** Forges Damascus carbon and stainless steels. Offers silver inlay, mokume, filework, checkering. **Prices:** $250 and up. **Remarks:** Part-time maker; first knife sold in 1985. Some engraving, scrimshaw and stone work. **Mark:** GAND, MS.

ANDERSON, MARK ALAN,
1176 Poplar St, Denver, CO 80220, mcantdrive95@comcast.net; Web: www.malancustomknives.com

Specialties: Stilettos. Automatics of several varieties and release mechanisms. **Patterns:** Drop point hunters, sub hilt fighters & drop point camp knives. **Technical:** Almost all my blades are hollow ground. **Prices:** $200 to $1800. **Remarks:** Focusing on fixed blade hunting, skinning & fighting knives now. **Mark:** Dragon head.

ANDERSON, MEL,
29505 P 50 Rd, Hotchkiss, CO 81419-8203, Phone: 970-872-4882, Fax: 970-872-4882, artnedge1@wmconnect.com

Specialties: Full-size, miniature and one-of-a-kind straight knives and folders of his design. **Patterns:** Tantos, Bowies, daggers, fighters, hunters and pressure folders. **Technical:** Grinds 440C, 5160, D2, 1095. **Prices:** Start at $145. **Remarks:** Knifemaker and sculptor, full-time maker; first knife sold in 1987. **Mark:** Scratchy Hand.

ANDERSON, TOM,
955 Canal Rd. Extd, Manchester, PA 17345, Phone: 717-266-6475, andersontech1@comcast.net; Web: www.andersoncustomknives.com

Specialties: High-tech one-hand folders. **Patterns:** Fighters, utility, and dress knives. **Technical:** Grinds BG-42, S30V and Damascus. Uses titanium, carbon fiber and select natural handle materials. **Prices:** Start at $400. **Remarks:** First knife sold in 1996. **Mark:** Stylized A over T logo with maker's name.

ANDRESS, RONNIE,
415 Audubon Dr N, Satsuma, AL 36572, Phone: 251-675-7604

Specialties: Working straight knives in standard patterns. **Patterns:** Boots, Bowies, hunters, friction folders and camp knives. **Technical:** Forges 1095, 5160, O1 and his own Damascus. Offers filework and inlays. **Prices:** $125 to $500. **Remarks:** Part-time maker; first knife sold in 1983. Doing business as Andress Knives. Jeweler, goldsmith, gold work, stone setter. Not currently making knives. **Mark:** Last name, J.S.

ANDREWS, ERIC,
132 Halbert Street, Grand Ledge, MI 48837, Phone: 517-627-7304

Specialties: Traditional working and using straight knives of his design. **Patterns:** Full-tang hunters, skinners and utility knives. **Technical:** Forges carbon steel; heat-treats. All knives come with sheath; most handles are of wood. **Prices:** $80 to $160. **Remarks:** Part-time maker; first knife sold in 1990. Doing business as The Tinkers Bench.

ANGELL, JON,
22516 East C R1474, Hawthorne, FL 32640, Phone: 352-475-5380, syrjon@aol.com

ANKROM, W.E.,
14 Marquette Dr, Cody, WY 82414, Phone: 307-587-3017, Fax: 307-587-3017

Specialties: Best quality folding knives of his design. Bowies, fighters, chute knives, boots and hunters. **Patterns:** Lock backs, liner locks, single high art. **Technical:** ATS-34 commercial Damascus. **Prices:** $500 and up. **Remarks:** Full-time maker; first knife sold in 1975. **Mark:** Name or name, city, state.

ANSO, JENS,
GL. Skanderborgvej, 116, 8472 Sporup, DENMARK, Phone: 45 86968826, info@ansoknives.com; Web: www.ansoknives.com

Specialties: Working knives of his own design. **Patterns:** Balisongs, swords, folders, drop-points, sheepsfoots, hawkbill, tanto, recurve. **Technical:** Grinds RWL-34 Damasteel S30V, CPM 154CM. Handrubbed or beadblasted finish. **Price:** $400 to $1200, some up to $3500. **Remarks:** Full-time maker since January 2002. First knife sold 1997. Doing business as ANSOKNIVES. **Mark:** ANSO and/or ANSO with logo.

ANTONIO JR., WILLIAM J,
6 Michigan State Dr, Newark, DE 19713-1161, Phone: 302-368-8211, antonioknives@aol.com

Specialties: Fancy working straight knives of his design. **Patterns:** Hunting, survival and fishing knives. **Technical:** Grinds D2, 440C and 154CM; offers stainless Damascus. **Prices:** $125 to $395; some to $900. **Remarks:** Part-time maker; first knife sold in 1978. **Mark:** Last name.

APELT, STACY E,
8076 Moose Ave, Norfolk, VA 23518, Phone: 757-583-5872, sapelt@cox.net

Specialties: Exotic wood and burls, ivories, Bowies, custom made knives to order. **Patterns:** Bowies, hunters, fillet, professional cutlery and Japanese style blades and swords. **Technical:** Hand forging, stock removal, scrimshaw, carbon, stainless and Damascus steels. **Prices:** $65 to $5000. **Remarks:** Professional Goldsmith. **Mark:** Stacy E. Apelt -Norfolk VA.

APPLEBY, ROBERT,
746 Municipal Rd, Shickshinny, PA 18655, Phone: 570-864-0879, r.appleby@juno.com; Web: www.applebyknives.com

Specialties: Working using straight knives and folders of his own and popular and historical designs. **Patterns:** Variety of straight knives and folders. **Technical:** Hand forged or grinds O1, 1084, 5160, 440C, ATS-34, commercial Damascus, makes own sheaths. **Prices:** Starting at $75. **Remarks:** Part-time maker, first knife sold in 1995. **Mark:** APPLEBY over SHICKSHINNY, PA.

APPLETON, RON,
315 Glenn St, Bluff Dale, TX 76433, Phone: 254-728-3039, ron@helovesher.com; Web: http://community.webshots.com/user/ angelic574

Specialties: One-of-a-kind folding knives. **Patterns:** Unique folding multi-locks and high-tech patterns. **Technical:** All parts machined, D2, S7, 416, 440C, 6A14V et.al. **Prices:** Start at $9500. **Remarks:** Spare-time maker; first knife sold in 1996. **Mark:** Initials with anvil or initials within arrowhead, signed and dated.

ARBUCKLE, JAMES M,
114 Jonathan Jct, Yorktown, VA 23693, Phone: 757-867-9578, a_r_bukckle@hotmail.com

Specialties: One-of-a-kind of his design; working knives. **Patterns:** Mostly chef's knives and hunters. **Technical:** Forged and stock removal blades using exotic hardwoods, natural materials, Micarta and stabilized woods. Forge 5160, 1084 and O1; stock remove D2, ATS-34, 440C. Makes own pattern welded steel. **Prices:** $175 to $900. **Remarks:** Forge, grind, heat-treat, finish and embellish all knives himself. Does own leatherwork. Part-time maker. ABS member; ASM member. **Mark:** J. Arbuckle or Arbuckle with maker below it.

ARCHER, RAY AND TERRI,
PO Box 129, Medicine Bow, WY 82329, Phone: 307-379-2567, archert@tribcsp.com; Web: http://www.archersknives.com

Specialties: High finish working straight knives and small one-of-a-kind. **Patterns:** Hunters/skinners, camping. **Technical:** Flat grinds ATS-34, 440C, S30V. Buys Damascus. **Price:** $100 to $1,000. Some to $2,000 **Remarks:** Full time makers. Make own sheaths; first knife sold 1994. Member of PKA & OK CA (Oregon Knife Collector Assoc.). **Mark:** Last name over city and state.

ARDWIN, COREY,
4700 North Cedar, North Little Rock, AR 72116, Phone: 501-791-0301, Fax: 501-791-2974, Boog@hotmail.com

ARM-KO KNIVES,
PO Box 76280, Marble Ray 4035 KZN, SOUTH AFRICA, Phone: 27 31 5771451, arm-koknives.co.za; Web: www.arm-koknives.co.za

Specialties: They will make what your fastidious taste desires. Be it cool collector or tenacious tactical with handles of mother-of-pearl, fossil & local ivories. Exotic dye/stabilized burls, giraffe bone, horns, carbon fiber, g10, and titanium etc. **Technical:** Via stock removal, grinding Damasteel, carbon & mosaic. Damascus, ATS-34, N690, 440A, 440B, 12C27, RWL34 and high carbon EN 8, 5160 all heat treated in house. **Prices:** From $200 and up. **Remarks:** Father a part-time maker for well over 10 years and member of Knifemakers Guild in SA. Son full-time maker over 3 years. **Mark:** Logo of initials A R M and H A R M "Edged Tools."

ARMS, ERIC,
11153 7 Mile Road, Tustin, MI 49688, Phone: 231-829-3726, ericarms@netonecom.net

Specialties: Working hunters, high performance straight knives. **Patterns:** Variety of hunters, scagel style, Ed Fowler design and drop point. **Technical:** Forge 52100, 5160, 1084 hand grind, heat treat, natural handle, stag horn, elk, big horn, flat grind, convex, all leather sheath work. **Prices:** Starting at $150 **Remarks:** Part-time maker **Mark:** Eric Arms

ARNOLD, JOE,
47 Patience Cres, London, Ont., CANADA N6E 2K7, Phone: 519-686-2623

Specialties: Traditional working and using straight knives of his design and to customer specs. **Patterns:** Fighters, hunters and Bowies. **Technical:** Grinds 440C, ATS-34 and 5160. **Prices:** $75 to $500; some to $2500. **Remarks:** Part-time maker; first knife sold in 1988. **Mark:** Last name, country.

ARROWOOD, DALE,
556 Lassetter Rd, Sharpsburg, GA 30277, Phone: 404-253-9672

Specialties: Fancy and traditional straight knives of his design and to customer specs. **Patterns:** Bowies, fighters and hunters. **Technical:** Grinds ATS-34 and 440C; forges high-carbon steel. Engraves and scrimshaws. **Prices:** $125 to $200; some to $245. **Remarks:** Part-time maker; first knife sold in 1989. **Mark:** Anvil with an arrow through it; Old English "Arrowood Knives."

ASHBY, DOUGLAS,
10123 Deermont, Dallas, TX 75243, Phone: 972-238-7531

Specialties: Traditional and fancy straight knives of his design or to customer specs. **Patterns:** Hunters, fighters and utility/camp knives. **Technical:** Grinds ATS-34 and commercial Damascus. **Prices:** $75 to $200; some to $500. **Remarks:** Part-time maker; first knife sold in 1990. **Mark:** Name, city.

ASHWORTH, BOYD,
1510 Bullard Place, Powder Springs, GA 30127, Phone: 770-422-9826, boydashworth@comcast.net; Web: www.boydashworthknives.com
Specialties: Turtle folders. Fancy Damascus locking folders. **Patterns:** Fighters, hunters and gents. **Technical:** Forges own Damascus; offers filework; uses exotic handle materials. **Prices:** $500 to $2500. **Remarks:** Part-time maker; first knife sold in 1993. **Mark:** Last name.

ATHEY, STEVE,
3153 Danube Way, Riverside, CA 92503, Phone: 951-850-8612, stevelonnie@yahoo.com
Specialties: Stock removal. **Patterns:** Hunters & Bowies. **Prices:** $100 to $500. **Remarks:** Part-time maker. **Mark:** Last name with number on blade.

ATKINSON, DICK,
General Delivery, Wausau, FL 32463, Phone: 850-638-8524
Specialties: Working straight knives and folders of his design; some fancy. **Patterns:** Hunters, fighters, boots; locking folders in interframes. **Technical:** Grinds A2, 440C and 154CM. Likes filework. **Prices:** $85 to $300; some exceptional knives. **Remarks:** Full-time maker; first knife sold in 1977. **Mark:** Name, city, state.

AYARRAGARAY, CRISTIAN L.,
Buenos Aires 250, (3100) Parana-Entre Rios, ARGENTINA, Phone: 043-231753
Specialties: Traditional working straight knives of his design. **Patterns:** Fishing and hunting knives. **Technical:** Grinds and forges carbon steel. Uses native Argentine woods and deer antler. **Prices:** $150 to $250; some to $400. **Remarks:** Full-time maker; first knife sold in 1980. **Mark:** Last name, signature.

B

BAARTMAN, GEORGE,
PO Box 1116, Bela-Bela 0480, Limpopo, SOUTH AFRICA, Phone: 27 14 736 4036, Fax: 086 636 3408, thabathipa@gmail.com
Specialties: Fancy and working LinerLock® folders of own design and to customers specs. Specialize in pattern filework on liners. **Patterns:** LinerLock® folders. **Technical:** Grinds 12C27, ATS-34, and Damascus, prefer working with stainless damasteel. Hollow grinds to hand-rubbed and polished satin finish. Enjoys working with mammoth, warthog tusk and pearls. **Prices:** Folders from $380 to $1000. **Remarks:** Part-time maker. Member of the Knifemakers Guild of South Africa since 1993. **Mark:** BAARTMAN.

BABCOCK, RAYMOND G.,
179 Lane Rd, Vincent, OH 45784, Phone: 614-678-2688
Specialties: Plain and fancy working straight knives. Will make knives to his design and to custom specifications. **Patterns:** Hunting knives and Bowies. **Technical:** Hollow grinds L6. **Prices:** $100 to $500. **Remarks:** Part-time maker; first knife sold in 1973. **Mark:** First initial and last name; R. Babcock.

BACHE-WIIG, TOM,
N-5966, Eivindvik, NORWAY, Phone: 475-778-4290, Fax: 475-778-1099, tom.bache-wiig@enivest.net; Web: tombaschewiig.com
Specialties: High-art and working knives of his design. **Patterns:** Hunters, utility knives, hatchets, axes and art knives. **Technical:** Grinds Uddeholm Elmax, powder metallurgy tool stainless steel. Handles made of rear burls of Nordic woods stabilized with vacuum/high-pressure technique. **Prices:** $430 to $900; some to $2300. **Remarks:** Part-time maker; first knife sold 1988. **Mark:** Etched name and eagle head.

BACON, DAVID R.,
906 136th St E, Bradenton, FL 34202-9694, Phone: 813-996-4289

BAGLEY, R. KEITH,
OLD PINE FORGE, 4415 Hope Acres Dr, White Plains, MD 20695, Phone: 301-932-0990, oldpineforge@hotmail.com
Specialties: High-carbon Damascus with semi-precious stones set in exotic wood handle; tactical and skinner knives. **Technical:** Use ATS-34, 5160, O1, 1085, 1095. **Patterns:** Various patterns; prefer all Tool-Steel and Nickel Damascus. **Price:** Damascus from $250 to $500; stainless from $100 to $225. **Remarks:** Farrier for 25 years, blacksmith for 25 years, knifemaker for 10 years.

BAILEY, JOSEPH D.,
3213 Jonesboro Dr, Nashville, TN 37214, Phone: 615-889-3172, jbknfemkr@aol.com
Specialties: Working and using straight knives; collector pieces. **Patterns:** Bowies, hunters, tactical, folders. **Technical:** 440C, ATS-34, Damascus and wire Damascus. Offers scrimshaw. **Prices:** $85 to $1200. **Remarks:** Part-time maker; first knife sold in 1988. **Mark:** Joseph D Bailey Nashville Tennessee.

BAILEY, KIRBY C.,
2055 F.M. 2790 W, Lytle, TX 78052, Phone: 830-709-9929
Specialties: All kinds of knives folders, fixed blade, fighters. **Patterns:** Hunters, folders, fighters, Bowies, miniatures. **Technical:** Does all his own work; heat treating, file work etc. **Prices:** $200 to $1000. Some increase in prices. **Remarks:** Has made knives for about 50 years, sold knives for 32 years. Has sold knives in Asia and all states in U.S. **Mark:** KCB and serial #.

BAILEY, RYAN,
4185 S. St. Rt. 605, Galena, OH 43021, Phone: 740-965-9970, dr@darrelralph.com; Web: www.darrelralph.com
Specialties: Fancy, high-art, high-tech, collectible straight knives and folders of his design and to customer specs; unique mechanisms, some disassemble. **Patterns:** Daggers, fighters and swords. **Technical:** Does own Damascus and forging from high-carbon. Embellishes with file work and gold work. **Prices:** $200 to $2500. **Remarks:** Full-time maker; first knife sold in 1999. Doing business as Briar Knives. **Mark:** RLB.

BAKER, HERB,
14104 NC 87 N, Eden, NC 27288, Phone: 336-627-0338

BAKER, RAY,
PO Box 303, Sapulpa, OK 74067, Phone: 918-224-8013
Specialties: High-tech working straight knives. **Patterns:** Hunters, fighters, Bowies, skinners and boots of his design and to customer specs. **Technical:** Grinds 440C, 1095 spring steel or customer request; heat-treats. Custom-made scabbards for any knife. **Prices:** $125 to $500; some to $1000. **Remarks:** Full-time maker; first knife sold in 1981. **Mark:** First initial, last name.

BAKER, VANCE,
574 Co. Rd 675, Riceville, TN 37370, Phone: 423-745-9157
Specialties: Traditional working straight knives of his design and to customer specs. Prefers drop-point hunters and small Bowies. **Patterns:** Hunters, utility and kitchen knives. **Technical:** Forges Damascus, cable, L6 and 5160. **Prices:** $100 to $250; some to $500. **Remarks:** Part-time maker; first knife sold in 1985. **Mark:** Initials connected.

BAKER, WILD BILL,
Box 361, Boiceville, NY 12412, Phone: 914-657-8646
Specialties: Primitive knives, buckskinners. **Patterns:** Skinners, camp knives and Bowies. **Technical:** Works with L6, files and rasps. **Prices:** $100 to $350. **Remarks:** Part-time maker; first knife sold in 1989. **Mark:** Wild Bill Baker, Oak Leaf Forge, or both.

BALBACH, MARKUS,
Heinrich -Worner -Str 3, 35789 Weilmunster-Laubuseschbach/Ts., GERMANY 06475-8911, Fax: 912986, Web: www.schmiede-balbach.de
Specialties: High-art knives and working/using straight knives and folders of his design and to customer specs. **Patterns:** Hunters and daggers. **Technical:** Stainless steel, one of Germany's greatest Smithies. Supplier for the forges of Solingen. **Remarks:** Full-time maker; first knife sold in 1984. Doing business as Schmiedewerkstatte M. Balbach. **Mark:** Initials stamped inside the handle.

BALL, KEN,
127 Sundown Manor, Mooresville, IN 46158, Phone: 317-834-4803
Specialties: Classic working/using straight knives of his design and to customer specs. **Patterns:** Hunters and utility/camp knives. **Technical:** Flat-grinds ATS-34. Offers filework. **Prices:** $150 to $400. **Remarks:** Part-time maker; first knife sold in 1994. Doing business as Ball Custom Knives. **Mark:** Last name.

BALLESTRA, SANTINO,
via D. Tempesta 11/17, 18039 Ventimiglia (IM), ITALY 0184-215228, ladasin@libero.it
Specialties: Using and collecting straight knives. **Patterns:** Hunting, fighting, skinners, Bowies, medieval daggers and knives. **Technical:** Forges ATS-34, D2, O2, 1060 and his own Damascus. Uses ivory and silver. **Prices:** $500 to $2000; some higher. **Remarks:** Full-time maker; first knife sold in 1979. **Mark:** First initial, last name.

BALLEW, DALE,
PO Box 1277, Bowling Green, VA 22427, Phone: 804-633-5701
Specialties: Miniatures only to customer specs. **Patterns:** Bowies, daggers and fighters. **Technical:** Files 440C stainless; uses ivory, abalone, exotic woods and some precious stones. **Prices:** $100 to $800. **Remarks:** Part-time maker; first knife sold in 1988. **Mark:** Initials and last name.

BANKS, DAVID L.,
99 Blackfoot Ave, Riverton, WY 82501, Phone: 307-856-3154/Cell: 307-851-5599
Specialties: Heavy-duty working straight knives. **Patterns:** Hunters, Bowies and camp knives. **Technical:** Forges Damascus 1084-15N20, L6-W1 pure nickel, 5160, 52100 and his own Damascus; differential heat treat and tempers. Handles made of horn, antlers and exotic wood. Hand-stitched harness leather sheaths. **Prices:** $300 to $2000. **Remarks:** Part-time maker. **Mark:** Banks Blackfoot forged Dave Banks and initials connected.

BARBARA BASKETT CUSTOM KNIVES,
427 Sutzer Ck Rd, Eastview, KY 42732, Phone: 270-862-5019, baskettknives@windstream; Web: www.geocities.com/baskettknives
Specialties: Fancy working knives and fantasy pieces, often set up in desk stands. **Patterns:** Fighters, Bowies and survival knives; locking folders and traditional styles. Cutting competition knives. **Technical:** Liner locks. Grinds O1, 440C, S30V, power CPM 154, CPM 4 buys

Damascus. Filework provided on most knives. **Prices:** Start at $250 and up. **Remarks:** Part-time maker; first knife sold in 1980. **Mark:** B. Baskett.

BARDSLEY, NORMAN P.,
197 Cottage St, Pawtucket, RI 02860, Phone: 401-725-9132, www.bardsleydistinctiveweaponry.com or www.bardsleycustomknives.com
Specialties: Working and fantasy knives. **Patterns:** Fighters, boots, fantasy, renaissance and native American in upscale and presentation fashion. **Technical:** Grinds all steels and Damascus. Uses exotic hides for sheaths. **Prices:** $100 to $15,000. **Remarks:** Full-time maker. **Mark:** Last name in script with logo.

BAREFOOT, JOE W.,
117 Oakbrook Dr, Liberty, SC 29657
Specialties: Working straight knives of his design. **Patterns:** Hunters, fighters and boots; tantos and survival knives. **Technical:** Grinds D2, 440C and ATS-34. Mirror finishes. Uses ivory and stag on customer request only. **Prices:** $50 to $160; some to $500. **Remarks:** Part-time maker; first knife sold in 1980. **Mark:** Bare footprint.

BARKER, REGGIE,
603 S Park Dr, Springhill, LA 71075, Phone: 318-539-2958, wrbarker@cmaaccess.com; Web: www.reggiebarkerknives.com
Specialties: Camp knives and hatchets. **Patterns:** Bowie, skinning, hunting, camping, fighters, kitchen or customer design. **Technical:** Forges carbon steel and own pattern welded steels. **Prices:** $225 to $2000. **Remarks:** Full-time maker. Winner of 1999 and 2000 Spring Hammering Cutting contest. Winner of Best Value of Show 2001; Arkansas Knife Show and Journeyman Smith. Border Guard Forge. **Mark:** Barker JS.

BARKER, ROBERT G.,
2311 Branch Rd, Bishop, GA 30621, Phone: 706-769-7827
Specialties: Traditional working/using straight knives of his design. **Patterns:** Bowies, hunters and utility knives, ABS Journeyman Smith. **Technical:** Hand forged carbon and Damascus. Forges to shape high-carbon 5160, cable and chain. Differentially heat-treats. **Prices:** $200 to $500; some to $1000. **Remarks:** Spare-time maker; first knife sold in 1987. **Mark:** BARKER/J.S.

BARKES, TERRY,
14844N.BluffRd.,Edinburgh,IN46124,Phone:812-526-6390,knifenpocket@sbcglobal.net; Web:http:// my.hsonline.net/ wizard/TerryBarkesKnives.htm
Specialties: Traditional working straight knives of his designs. **Patterns:** Drop point hunters, boot knives, skinning, fighter, utility, all purpose, camp, and grill knives. **Technical:** Grinds 1095 -1084 -52100 -01, Hollow grinds and flat grinds. Hand rubbed finish from 400 to 2000 grit or High polish buff. Hard edge and soft back, heat treat by maker. Likes File work, natural handle material, bone, stag, water buffalo horn, wildbeast bone, ironwood. **Prices:** $200 and up **Remarks:** Full-time maker, first knifge sold in 2005. Doing business as Barkes Knife Shop. **Marks:** Barkes -USA, Barkes Double Arrow -USA

BARLOW, JANA POIRIER,
3820 Borland Cir, Anchorage, AK 99517, Phone: 907-243-4581

BARNES, AUBREY G.,
11341 Rock Hill Rd, Hagerstown, MD 21740, Phone: 301-223-4587, a.barnes@myactv.net
Specialties: Classic Moran style reproductions and using knives of his own design. **Patterns:** Bowies, hunters, fighters, daggers and utility/camping knives. **Technical:** Forges 5160, 1085, L6 and Damascus, Silver wire inlays. **Prices:** $500 to $5000. **Remarks:** Full-time maker; first knife sold in 1992. Doing business as Falling Waters Forge. **Mark:** First and middle initials, last name, M.S.

BARNES, GARY L.,
Box 138, New Windsor, MD 21776-0138, Phone: 410-635-6243, Fax: 410-635-6243
Specialties: Ornate button lock Damascus folders. **Patterns:** Barnes original. **Technical:** Forges own Damascus. **Prices:** Average $2500. **Remarks:** ABS Master Smith since 1983. **Mark:** Hand engraved logo of letter B pierced by dagger.

BARNES, GREGORY,
266 W Calaveras St, Altadena, CA 91001, Phone: 626-398-0053, snake@annex.com

BARNES, JACK,
PO Box 1315, Whitefish, MT 59937-1315, Phone: 406-862-6078

BARNES, MARLEN R.,
904 Crestview Dr S, Atlanta, TX 75551-1854, Phone: 903-796-3668, MRBlives@worldnet.att.net
Specialties: Hammer forges random and mosaic Damascus. **Patterns:** Hatchets, straight and folding knives. **Technical:** Hammer forges carbon steel using 5160, 1084 and 52100 with 15N20 and 203E nickel. **Prices:** $150 and up. **Remarks:** Part-time maker; first knife sold 1999. **Mark:** Script M.R.B., other side J.S.

BARNES, WENDELL,
PO Box 272, Clinton, MT 59825, Phone: 406-825-0908
Specialties: Working straight knives. **Patterns:** Hunters, folders, neck knives. **Technical:** Grinds 440C, ATS-34, D2 and Damascus. **Prices:** Start at $75. **Remarks:** Spare-time maker; first knife sold in 1996. **Mark:** First initial and last name around broken heart.

BARNES, WILLIAM,
591 Barnes Rd, Wallingford, CT 06492-1805, Phone: 860-349-0443

BARNES JR., CECIL C.,
141 Barnes Dr, Center Ridge, AR 72027, Phone: 501-893-2267

BARNETT, VAN,
BARNETT INT'L INC, 1135 Terminal Way Ste #209, Reno, NV 89502, Phone: 866 ARTKNIFE or 304-727-5512, artknife@suddenlink.net; Web: www.VanBarnett.com
Specialties: Collector grade one-of-a-kind / embellished high art daggers and art folders. **Patterns:** Art daggers and folders. **Technical:** Forges and grinds own Damascus. **Prices:** Upscale. **Remarks:** Designs and makes one-of-a-kind highly embellished art knives using high karat gold, diamonds and other gemstones, pearls, stone and fossil ivories, carved steel guards and blades, all knives are carved and or engraved, does own engraving, carving and other embellishments, sole authorship; full-time maker since 1981. Does one high art collaboration a year with Dellana. Voting member of Knifemakers Guild. Member of ABS. Member Art Knife Invitational Group (AKI) **Mark:** V. H. Barnett or Van Barnett in script.

BARR, A.T.,
153 Madonna Dr, Nicholasville, KY 40356, Phone: 859-887-5400, Web: www.customknives.com
Specialties: Fine gent's user and collector grade LinerLock® folders and sheath knives. **Patterns:** LinerLock® folders and sheath knives. **Technical:** Flat grinds S30V, ATS-34, D2 commercial Damascus; all knives have a hand rubbed satin finish. Does all leather work. **Prices:** Start at $250 for folders and $200 for sheath knives. **Remarks:** Full-time maker, first knife sold in 1979. Knifemakers' Guild voting member. "Don't you buy no ugly knife." **Mark:** Full name.

BARR, JUDSON C.,
1905 Pickwick Circle, Irving, TX 75060, Phone: 972-790-7195, judsonbarrknives@yahoo.com
Specialties: Bowies. **Patterns:** Sheffield and Early American. **Technical:** Forged carbon steel and Damascus. Also stock removal. **Remarks:** Journeyman member of ABS. **Mark:** Barr.

BARRETT, CECIL TERRY,
2514 Linda Lane, Colorado Springs, CO 80909, Phone: 719-473-8325
Specialties: Working and using straight knives and folders of his design, to customer specs and in standard patterns. **Patterns:** Bowies, hunters, kitchen knives, locking folders and slip-joint folders. **Technical:** Grinds 440C, D2 and ATS-34. Wood and leather sheaths. **Prices:** $65 to $500; some to $750. **Remarks:** Full-time maker. **Mark:** Stamped middle name.

BARRETT, RICK L. (TOSHI HISA),
18943 CR 18, Goshen, IN 46528, Phone: 574-533-4297, barrettrick@hotmail.com
Specialties: Japanese-style blades from sushi knives to katana and fantasy pieces. **Patterns:** Swords, axes, spears/lances, hunter and utility knives. **Technical:** Forges and grinds Damascus and carbon steels, occasionally uses stainless. **Prices:** $250 to $4000+. **Remarks:** Full-time bladesmith, jeweler. **Mark:** Japanese mei on Japanese pieces and stylized initials.

BARRON, BRIAN,
123 12th Ave, San Mateo, CA 94402, Phone: 650-341-2683
Specialties: Traditional straight knives. **Patterns:** Daggers, hunters and swords. **Technical:** Grinds 440C, ATS-34 and 1095. Sculpts bolsters using an S-curve. **Prices:** $130 to $270; some to $1500. **Remarks:** Part-time maker; first knife sold in 1993. **Mark:** Diamond Drag "Barron."

BARRY, SCOTT,
Box 354, Laramie, WY 82073, Phone: 307-721-8038, scottyb@uwyo.edu
Specialties: Currently producing mostly folders, also make fixed blade hunters & fillet knives. **Technical:** Steels used are 440/C, ATS/34, 154/CM, S30V, Damasteel & Mike Norris stainless Damascus. **Prices:** Range from $300 $1000. **Remarks:** Part-time maker. First knife sold in 1972. **Mark:** DSBarry, etched on blade.

BARRY III, JAMES J.,
115 Flagler Promenade No., West Palm Beach, FL 33405, Phone: 561-832-4197
Specialties: High-art working straight knives of his design also high art tomahawks. **Patterns:** Hunters, daggers and fishing knives. **Technical:** Grinds 440C only. Prefers exotic materials for handles. Most knives embellished with filework, carving and scrimshaw. Many pieces designed to stand unassisted. **Prices:** $500 to $10,000. **Remarks:** Part-time maker; first knife sold in 1975. Guild member (Knifemakers) since 1991. **Mark:** Branded initials as a J and B together.

BARTH, J.D.,
101 4th St, PO Box 186, Alberton, MT 59820, Phone: 406-722-4557, mtdeerhunter@blackfoot.net; Web: www.jdbarthcustomknives.com
Specialties: Working and fancy straight knives of his design. LinerLock®

BELL, DON,
Box98,Lincoln,MT59639,Phone:406-362-3208,donbellcustomknivesmt@yahoo.com
Patterns: Folders, hunters and custom orders. **Technical:** Carbon steel 53100, 5160, 1095, 1084. Making own Damascus. Flat grinds. Natural handle material including fossil. ivory, pearl, & ironwork. **Remarks:** Full-time maker. First knife sold in 1999. **Mark:** Last name.

BELL, DONALD,
2 Division St, Bedford, Nova Scotia, CANADA B4A 1Y8, Phone: 902-835-2623, donbell@accesswave.ca; Web: www.bellknives.com
Specialties: Fancy knives: carved and pierced folders of his own design. **Patterns:** Locking folders, pendant knives, jewelry knives. **Technical:** Grinds Damascus, pierces and carves blades. **Prices:** $500 to $2000, some to $3000. **Remarks:** Spare-time maker; first knife sold in 1993. **Mark:** Bell symbol with first initial inside.

BELL, MICHAEL,
88321 N Bank Lane, Coquille, OR 97423, Phone: 541-396-3605, michael@dragonflyforge.com; Web: www. Dragonflyforge.com
Specialties: Full line of combat quality Japanese swords. **Patterns:** Traditional tanto to katana. **Technical:** Handmade steel and welded cable. **Prices:** Swords from bare blades to complete high art $4500 to $28,000. **Remarks:** Studied with Japanese master Nakajima Muneyoshi. Instruction in sword crafts. **Mark:** Dragonfly in shield or tombo kunimitsu.

BELL, TONY,
PO Box 24, Woodland, AL 36280, Phone: 256-449-2655, tbell905@aol.com
Specialties: Hand forged period knives and tomahawks. Art knives and knives made for everyday use.**Technical:**Makes own Damascus. Forges 1095, 5160,1080,L6 steels. Does own heat treating. **Prices:**$75-$1200. **Remarks:**Full time maker. **Mark:**Bell symbol with initial T in the middle.

BENDIK, JOHN,
7076 Fitch Rd, Olmsted Falls, OH 44138

BENJAMIN JR., GEORGE,
3001 Foxy Ln, Kissimmee, FL 34746, Phone: 407-846-7259
Specialties: Fighters in various styles to include Persian, Moro and military. **Patterns:** Daggers, skinners and one-of-a-kind grinds. **Technical:** Forges O1, D2, A2, 5160 and Damascus. Favors Pakkawood, Micarta, and mirror or Parkerized finishes. Makes unique para-military leather sheaths. **Prices:** $150 to $600; some to $1200. **Remarks:** Doing business as The Leather Box. **Mark:** Southern Pride Knives.

BENNETT, BRETT C,
4717 Sullivan St, Cheyenne, WY 82009, Phone: 307-220-3919, brett@bennettknives.com; Web: www.bennettknives.com
Specialties: Hand-rubbed finish on all blades. **Patterns:** Most fixed blade patterns. **Technical:** ATS-34, D-2, 1084/15N20 Damascus, 1084 forged. **Prices:** $100 and up. **Mark:** "B.C. Bennett" in script or "Bennett" stamped in script.

BENNETT, GLEN C,
5821 S Stewart Blvd, Tucson, AZ 85706

BENNETT, PETER,
PO Box 143, Engadine N.S.W. 2233, AUSTRALIA, Phone: 02-520-4975 (home), Fax: 02-528-8219 (work)
Specialties: Fancy and embellished working and using straight knives to customer specs and in standard patterns. **Patterns:** Fighters, hunters, bird/trout and fillet knives. **Technical:** Grinds 440C, ATS-34 and Damascus. Uses rare Australian desert timbers for handles. **Prices:** $90 to $500; some to $1500. **Remarks:** Full-time maker; first knife sold in 1985. **Mark:** First and middle initials, last name; country.

BENNICA, CHARLES,
11 Chemin du Salet, 34190 Moules et Baucels, FRANCE, Phone: +33 4 67 73 42 40, cbennica@bennica-knives.com; Web: www.bennica-knives.com
Specialties: Fixed blades and folding knives; the latter with slick closing mechanisms with push buttons to unlock blades. Unique handle shapes, signature to the maker. **Technical:** 416 stainless steel frames for folders and ATS-34 blades. Also specializes in Damascus.

BENSON, DON,
2505 Jackson St #112, Escalon, CA 95320, Phone: 209-838-7921
Specialties: Working straight knives of his design. **Patterns:** Axes, Bowies, tantos and hunters. **Technical:** Grinds 440C. **Prices:** $100 to $150; some to $400. **Remarks:** Spare-time maker; first knife sold in 1980. **Mark:** Name.

BENTLEY, C L,
2405 Hilltop Dr, Albany, GA 31707, Phone: 912-432-6656

BENTZEN, LEIF,
15 Apdalsvej, Aarhus N, DENMARK 8200
Technical: Blades are ground from Thyradur 2842 steel. **Remarks:** Part-time knifemaker and mostly makes hunter or collectors knives. **Prices:** $250 to $1600.

BER, DAVE,
656 Miller Rd, San Juan Island, WA 98250, Phone: 206-378-7230
Specialties: Working straight and folding knives for the sportsman; welcomes customer designs. **Patterns:** Hunters, skinners, Bowies, kitchen and fishing knives. **Technical:** Forges and grinds saw blade steel, wire Damascus, O1, L6, 5160 and 440C. **Prices:** $100 to $300; some to $500. **Remarks:** Full-time maker; first knife sold in 1985. **Mark:** Last name.

BERG, LOTHAR,
37 Hillcrest Ln, Kitchener ON, CANADA NZK 1S9, Phone: 519-745-3260; 519-745-3260

BERGER, MAX A.,
5716 John Richard Ct, Carmichael, CA 95608, Phone: 916-972-9229, bergerknives@aol.com
Specialties: Fantasy and working/using straight knives of his design. **Patterns:** Fighters, hunters and utility/camp knives. **Technical:** Grinds ATS-34 and 440C. Offers fileworks and combinations of mirror polish and satin finish blades. **Prices:** $200 to $600; some to $2500. **Remarks:** Part-time maker; first knife sold in 1992. **Mark:** Last name.

BERGH, ROGER,
Dalkarlsa 291, 91598 Bygdea, SWEDEN, Phone: 469-343-0061, knivroger@hotmail.com; Web: www.rogerbergh.com
Specialties: Collectible all-purpose straight-blade knives. Damascus steel blades, carving and artistic design knives are heavily influenced by nature and have an organic hand crafted feel.

BERGLIN, BRUCE D,
17441 Lake Terrace Place, Mount Vernon, WA 98274, Phone: 360-422-8603, bruce@berglins.com
Specialties: Working and using fixed blades and folders of his own design. **Patterns:** Hunters, boots, bowies, utility, liner locks and slip joints some with vintage finish. **Technical:** Forges carbon steel, grinds carbon steel. Prefers natural handle material and Micarta. **Prices:** Start at $300. **Remarks:** Part-time maker since 1998. **Mark:** First initial, middle initial and last name, sometimes surrounded with an oval.

BERTOLAMI, JUAN CARLOS,
Av San Juan 575, Neuquen, ARGENTINA 8300, fliabertolami@infovia.com.ar
Specialties: Hunting and country labor knives. All of them unique high quality pieces and supplies collectors too. **Technical:** Austrian stainless steel and elephant, hippopotamus and orca ivory, as well as ebony and other fine woods for the handles.

BERTUZZI, ETTORE,
Via Partigiani 3, 24068 Seriate (Bergamo), ITALY, Phone: 035-294262, Fax: 035-294262
Specialties: Classic straight knives and folders of his design, to customer specs and in standard patterns. **Patterns:** Bowies, hunters and locking folders. **Technical:** Grinds ATS-34, D3, D2 and various Damascus. **Prices:** $300 to $500. **Remarks:** Part-time maker; first knife sold in 1993. **Mark:** Name etched on ricasso.

BESEDICK, FRANK E,
195 Stillwagon Rd, Ruffsdale, PA 15679, Phone: 724-696-3312, bxtr.bez3@verizon.net
Specialties: Traditional working and using straight knives of his design. **Patterns:** Hunters, utility/camp knives and miniatures; buckskinner blades and tomahawks. **Technical:** Forges and grinds 5160, O1 and Damascus. Offers filework and scrimshaw. **Prices:** $75 to $300; some to $750. **Remarks:** Part-time maker; first knife sold in 1990. **Mark:** Name or initials.

BESHARA, BRENT (BESH),
207 Cedar St, PO Box 1046, Stayner, Ont., CANADA L0M 1S0, Phone: 705-428-3152, beshknives@sympatico.ca; Web: www.beshknives.com
Specialties: Tactical fighting fixed knives. **Patterns:** Tantos, fighters, neck and custom designs. **Technical:** Grinds 0-1, L6 and stainless upon request. Offers Kydex sheaths, does own Paragon heat treating. **Prices:** Start at $150. **Remarks:** Inventor of Besh wedge™. Part-time maker. Active serving military bomb disposal driver. **Mark:** "BESH" stamped.

BEST, RON,
1489 Adams Lane, Stokes, NC 27884, Phone: 252-714-1264, rebknives@webtv.net
Specialties: All integral fixed blades, interframe.**Patterns:** Bowies, hunters, fighters, fantasy, daggers & swords. **Technical:** Grinds 440C, D-2 and ATS-34. **Prices:** $600 to $8000.

BETHKE, LORA SUE,
13420 Lincoln St, Grand Haven, MI 49417, Phone: 616-842-8268, Fax: 616-844-2696, ibethke@sbcglobal.net
Specialties: Scagel style and straight knives of her design. **Patterns:** Hunters and miniatures **Technical:** Forges 1084 and Damascus. **Prices:** Start at $400. **Remarks:** Part-time maker; first knife sold in 1997. Journeyman Bladesmith, American Bladesmith Society. **Mark:** Full name -JS on reverse side.

BEUKES, TINUS,
83 Henry St, Risiville, Vereeniging 1939, SOUTH AFRICA, Phone: 27 16 423 2053
Specialties: Working straight knives. **Patterns:** Hunters, skinners and kitchen knives. **Technical:** Grinds D2, 440C and chain, cable and stainless Damascus. **Prices:** $80 to $180. **Remarks:** Part-time maker;

folders, stainless and Damascus, fully file worked, nitre bluing. **Technical:** Grinds ATS-34, 440-C, stainless and carbon Damascus. Uses variety of natural handle materials and Micarta. Likes dovetailed bolsters. Filework on most knives, full and tapered tangs. Makes custom fit sheaths for each knife. **Mark:** Name over maker, city and state.

BARTLOW, JOHN,
5078 Coffeen Ave, Sheridan, WY 82801, Phone: 307 673-4941, bartlow@bresnan.net
Specialties: Working hunters, greenriver skinners, classic capers and bird & trouts. **Technical:** ATS-34, CPM154, Damascus available on all linerlocks. **Prices:** Full-time maker, guild member from 1988. **Mark:** Bartlow, Sheridan WYO.

BARTRUG, HUGH E.,
2701 34th St N #142, St. Petersburg, FL 33713, Phone: 813-323-1136
Specialties: Inlaid straight knives and exotic folders; high-art knives and period pieces. **Patterns:** Hunters, Bowies and daggers; traditional patterns. **Technical:** Diffuses mokume. Forges 100 percent nickel, wrought iron, mosaic Damascus, shokeedo and O1 tool steel; grinds. **Prices:** $210 to $2500; some to $5000. **Remarks:** Retired maker; first knife sold in 1980. **Mark:** Ashley Forge or name.

BASKETT, BARBARA,
Custom Knives, 427 Sutzer Ck Rd, Eastview, KY 42732, Phone: 270-862-5019, baskettknives@windstream.net
Specialities: Hunters and LinerLocks. **Technical:** 440-C, CPM 154, S30V. **Prices:** $250 and up. **Mark:** B. Baskett.

BATLEY, MARK S.,
PO Box 217, Wake, VA 23176, Phone: 804 776-7794

BATSON, JAMES,
176 Brentwood Lane, Madison, AL 35758
Specialties: Forged Damascus blades and fittings in collectible period pieces. **Patterns:** Integral art knives, Bowies, folders, American-styled blades and miniatures. **Technical:** Forges carbon steel and his Damascus. **Prices:** $150 to $1800; some to $4500. **Remarks:** Semi retired full-time maker; first knife sold in 1978. **Mark:** Name, bladesmith with horse's head.

BATSON, RICHARD G.,
6591 Waterford Rd, Rixeyville, VA 22737, Phone: 540-937-2318
Specialties: Military, utility and fighting knives in working and presentation grade. **Patterns:** Daggers, combat and utility knives. **Technical:** Grinds O1, 1095 and 440C. Etches and scrimshaws; offers polished, Parkerized finishes. **Prices:** Active military, please inquire. **Remarks:** Semi-retired, limit production. First knife sold in 1958. **Mark:** Bat in circle, hand-signed and serial numbered.

BATTS, KEITH,
450 Manning Rd, Hooks, TX 75561, Phone: 903-832-1140, kbatts@quixnet.net
Specialties: Working straight knives of his design or to customer specs. **Patterns:** Bowies, hunters, skinners, camp knives and others. **Technical:** Forges 5160 and his Damascus; offers filework. **Prices:** $245 to $895. **Remarks:** Part-time maker; first knife sold in 1988. **Mark:** Last name.

BAUCHOP, PETER,
c/o BECK'S CUTLERY SPECIALTIES, 107 Edinburgh S #109, Cary, NC 27511, Phone: 919-460-0203, Fax: 919-460-7772, beckscutlery@mindspring.com
Specialties: Working straight knives and period pieces. **Patterns:** Fighters, swords and survival knives. **Technical:** Grinds O1, D2, G3, 440C and AST-34. Scrimshaws. **Prices:** $100 to $350; some to $1500. **Remarks:** Full-time maker; first knife sold in 1980. **Mark:** Bow and axe (BOW-CHOP).

BAUCHOP, ROBERT,
PO Box 330, Munster, Kwazulu-Natal 4278, SOUTH AFRICA, Phone: +27 39 3192449
Specialties: Fantasy knives; working and using knives of his design and to customer specs. **Patterns:** Hunters, swords, utility/camp knives, diver's knives and large swords. **Technical:** Grinds Sandvick 12C27, D2, 440C. Uses South African hardwoods red ivory, wild olive, African blackwood, etc. on handles. **Prices:** $200 to $800; some to $2000. **Remarks:** Full-time maker; first knife sold in 1986. Doing business as Bauchop Custom Knives and Swords. **Mark:** Viking helmet with Bauchop (bow and chopper) crest.

BAUMGARDNER, ED,
PO Box 81, Glendale, KY 42740, Phone: 502-435-2675
Specialties: Working fixed blades, some folders. **Patterns:** Drop point and clip point hunters, fighters, small Bowies, traditional slip joint folders, lockbacks, Liner locks and art folders with gold & gemstone inlays. **Technical:** Grinds O1, 154CM, ATS-34, and Damascus likes using natural handle materials. **Prices:** $100 to $2000. **Remarks:** Part-time maker, first knife sold in 2001. **Mark:** Last name.

BAXTER, DALE,
291 County Rd 547, Trinity, AL 35673, Phone: 256-355-3626, dale@baxterknives.com
Specialties: Bowies, fighters, and hunters. **Patterns:** No patterns: all unique true customs. **Technical:** Hand forge and hand finish. Steels: 1095 and L6 for carbon blades, 1095/L6 for Damascus. **Remarks:** Full-time bladesmith and sold first knife in 1998. **Mark:** Dale Baxter (script) and J.S. on reverse.

BEAM, JOHN R.,
1310 Foothills Rd, Kalispell, MT 59901, Phone: 406-755-2593
Specialties: Classic, high-art and working straight knives of his design. **Patterns:** Bowies and hunters. **Technical:** Grinds 440C, Damascus and scrap. **Prices:** $175 to $600; some to $3000. **Remarks:** Part-time maker; first knife sold in 1950. Doing business as Beam's Knives. **Mark:** Beam's Knives.

BEASLEY, GENEO,
PO Box 339, Wadsworth, NV 89442, Phone: 775-575-2584

BEATTY, GORDON H.,
121 Petty Rd, Seneca, SC 29672, Phone: 864-882-6278
Specialties: Working straight knives, some fancy. **Patterns:** Traditional patterns, mini-skinners and letter openers. **Technical:** Grinds 440C, D2 and ATS-34; makes knives one-at-a-time. **Prices:** $75 to $450. **Remarks:** Part-time maker; first knife sold in 1982. **Mark:** Name.

BEATY, ROBERT B.,
CUTLER, 1995 Big Flat Rd, Missoula, MT 59804, Phone: 406-549-1818
Specialties: Plain and fancy working knives and collector pieces; will accept custom orders. **Patterns:** Hunters, Bowies, utility, kitchen and camp knives; locking folders. **Technical:** Grinds D-2, ATS-34, Dendritie D-2, makes all tool steel Damascus, forges 1095, 5160, 52100. **Prices:** $100 to $450; some to $1100. **Remarks:** Full-time maker; first knife sold 1995. **Mark:** Stainless: First name, middle initial, last name, city and state. Carbon: Last name stamped on Ricasso.

BEAUCHAMP, GAETAN,
125 de la Rivire, Stoneham, PQ, CANADA G0A 4P0, Phone: 418-848-1914, Fax: 418-848-6859, knives@gbeauchamp.ca; Web: www.gbeauchamp.ca
Specialties: Working knives and folders of his design and to customer specs. **Patterns:** Hunters, fighters, fantasy knives. **Technical:** Grinds ATS-34, 440C, Damascus. Scrimshaws on ivory; specializes in buffalo horn and black backgrounds. Offers a variety of handle materials. **Prices:** Start at $250. **Remarks:** Full-time maker; first knife sold in 1992. **Mark:** Signature etched on blade.

BECKER, FRANZ,
AM Kreuzberg 2, 84533, Marktl/Inn, GERMANY 08678-8020
Specialties: Stainless steel knives in working sizes. **Patterns:** Semi- and full-integral knives; interframe folders. **Technical:** Grinds stainless steels; likes natural handle materials. **Prices:** $200 to $2000. **Mark:** Name, country.

BECKETT, NORMAN L.,
102 Tobago Ave, Satsuma, FL 32189, Phone: 386-325-3539, nbknives@yahoo.com
Specialties: Fancy, traditional and working folders and straight knives of his design. **Patterns:** Bowies, fighters, folders and hunters. **Technical:** Grinds CPM-S30V and Damascus. Fileworks blades; hollow and flat grinds. Prefers mirror finish; satin finish on working knives. Uses exotic handle material, stabilized woods and Micarta. Hand-tooled or inlaid sheaths. **Prices:** $125 to $900; some to $2500 and up. **Remarks:** Full-time maker; first knife sold in 1993. Doing business as Norm Beckett Knives. **Mark:** First and last name, maker, city and state.

BEERS, RAY,
2501 Lakefront Dr, Lake Wales, FL 33898, Phone: Winter 863-696-3036, rbknives@copper.net

BEERS, RAY,
8 Manorbrook Rd, Monkton, MD 21111, Phone: Summer 410-472-2229

BEETS, MARTY,
390 N 5th Ave, Williams Lake, BC, CANADA V2G 2G4, Phone: 250-392-7199
Specialties: Working and collectable straight knives of his own design. **Patterns:** Hunter, skinners, Bowies and utility knives. **Technical:** Grinds 440C-does all his own work including heat treating. Uses a variety of handle material specializing in exotic hardwoods, antler and horn. **Price:** $125 to $400. **Remarks:** Wife, Sandy does handmade/hand stitched sheaths. First knife sold in 1988. Business name Beets Handmade Knives.

BEGG, TODD M.,
420 169 St S, Spanaway, WA 98387, Phone: 253-531-2113, web:www.beggknives.com
Specialties: Hand rubbed satin finished 440c stainless steel. Mirror polished 426 stainless steel. Stabilized mardrone wood.

BEHNKE, WILLIAM,
8478 Dell Rd, Kingsley, MI 49649, Phone: 231-263-7447, wbehnke@michweb.net
Specialties: Hunters, belt knives, folders, hatchets and tomahawks. **Patterns:** Traditional styling in moderate-sized straight and folding knives. **Technical:** Forges his own Damascus, W-2 and 1095; likes natural material. **Prices:** $150 to $2000. **Remarks:** Part-time maker. **Mark:** Bill Behnke Knives.

first knife sold in 1993. **Mark:** Full name, city, logo.

BEVERLY II, LARRY H,
PO Box 741, Spotsylvania, VA 22553, Phone: 540-898-3951
Specialties: Working straight knives, slip-joints and liner locks. Welcomes customer designs. **Patterns:** Bowies, hunters, guard less fighters and miniatures. **Technical:** Grinds 440C, A2 and O1. **Prices:** $125 to $1000. **Remarks:** Part-time maker; first knife sold in 1986. **Mark:** Initials or last name in script.

BEZUIDENHOUT, BUZZ,
30 Surlingham Ave, Malvern, Queensburgh, Natal 4093, SOUTH AFRICA, Phone: 031-4632827, Fax: 031-3631259
Specialties: Traditional working and using straight knives of his design and to customer specs. **Patterns:** Boots, hunters, kitchen knives and utility/camp knives. **Technical:** Grinds 12C27, 440C and ATS-34. Uses local hardwoods, horn: kudu, impala, buffalo, giraffe bone and ivory for handles. **Prices:** $150 to $200; some to $1500. **Remarks:** Spare-time maker; first knife sold in 1988. **Mark:** First name with a bee emblem.

BIGGERS, GARY,
VENTURA KNIVES, 1278 Colina Vista, Ventura, CA 93003, Phone: 805-658-6610, Fax: 805-658-6610
Specialties: Fixed blade knives of his design. **Patterns:** Hunters, boots/fighters, Bowies and utility knives. **Technical:** Grinds ATS-34, O1 and commercial Damascus. **Prices:** $150 to $550. **Remarks:** Part-time maker: first knife sold in 1996. Doing business as Ventura Knives. **Mark:** First and last name, city and state.

BILLGREN, PER,
Stallgatan 9, S815 76 Soderfors, SWEDEN, Phone: +46 293 30600, Fax: +46 293 30124, mail@damasteel.se Web:www.damasteel.se
Specialties: Damasteel, stainless Damascus steels. **Patterns:** Bluetongue, Heimskringla, Muhammad's ladder, Rose, Twist, Odin's eye, Vinland, Hakkapelliitta. **Technical:** Modern Damascus steel made by patented powder metallurgy method. **Prices:** $80 to $180. **Remarks:** Damasteel is available through distributors around the globe.

BIRDWELL, IRA LEE,
PO Box 1135, Bagdad, AZ 86321, Phone: 928-633-2516
Specialties: Special orders. **Mark:** Engraved signature.

BIRNBAUM, EDWIN,
9715 Hamocks Blvd I 206, Miami, FL 33196

BISH, HAL,
9347 Sweetbriar Trace, Jonesboro, GA 30236, Phone: 770-477-2422, hal-bish@hp.com

BIZZELL, ROBERT,
145 Missoula Ave, Butte, MT 59701, Phone: 406-782-4403, patternweld2@cs.com
Specialties: Damascus Bowies. **Patterns:** Composite, mosaic and traditional. **Technical:** Fixed blades & LinerLock® folders. **Prices:** Fixed blades start at $275. Folders start at $500. **Remarks:** Currently not taking orders. **Mark:** Hand signed.

BLACK, EARL,
3466 South, 700 East, Salt Lake City, UT 84106, Phone: 801-466-8395
Specialties: High-art straight knives and folders; period pieces. **Patterns:** Boots, Bowies and daggers; lockers and gents. **Technical:** Grinds 440C and 154CM. Buys some Damascus. Scrimshaws and engraves. **Prices:** $200 to $1800; some to $2500 and higher. **Remarks:** Full-time maker; first knife sold in 1980. **Mark:** Name, city, state.

BLACK, SCOTT,
27100 Leetown Rd, Picayune, MS 39466, Phone: 601-799-5939, copperheadforge@telepak.net
Specialties: Friction folders; fighters. **Patterns:** Bowies, fighters, hunters, smoke hawks, friction folders, daggers. **Technical:** All forged, all work done by him, own hand-stitched leather work; own heat-treating. **Prices:** $100 to $2200. **Remarks:** ABS Journeyman Smith. Cabel / Damascus/ High Carbone. **Mark:** Hot Mark -Copperhead Snake.

BLACK, SCOTT,
570 Malcom Rd, Covington, GA 30209
Specialties: Working/using folders of his design. **Patterns:** Daggers, hunters, utility/camp knives and friction folders. **Technical:** Forges pattern welded, cable, 1095, O1 and 5160. **Prices:** $100 to $500. **Remarks:** Part-time maker; first knife sold in 1992. Doing business as Copperhead Forge. **Mark:** Hot mark on blade, copperhead snake.

BLACK, TOM,
921 Grecian NW, Albuquerque, NM 87107, Phone: 505-344-2549, tblackknives@aol.com
Specialties: Working knives to fancy straight knives of his design. **Patterns:** Drop-point skinners, folders, using knives, Bowies and daggers. **Technical:** Grinds 440C, 154CM, ATS-34, A2, D2 and Damascus. Offers engraving and scrimshaw. **Prices:** $250 and up; some over $8500. **Remarks:** Full-time maker; first knife sold in 1970. **Mark:** Name, city.

BLACKWOOD, NEIL,
7032 Willow Run, Lakeland, FL 33813, Phone: 863-701-0126, neil@blackwoodknives.com; Web: www.blackwoodknives.com
Specialties: Fixed blades and folders. **Technical:** Blade steels D2 Talonite, Stellite, CPM S30V and RWL 34. Handle materials: G-10 carbon fiber and Micarta in the synthetics: giraffe bone and exotic woods on the natural side. **Remarks:** Makes everything from the frames to the stop pins, pivot pins: everything but the stainless screws; one factory/custom collaboration (the Hybrid Hunter) with Outdoor Edge is in place and negotiations are under way for one with Benchmade.

BLANCHARD, G R (GARY),
PO Box 709, Pigeon Forge, TN 37868, Phone: 865-908-7466, Fax: 865-908-7466, blanchardscutlery@yahoo.com; Web: www.blanchardscutlery.com
Specialties: Fancy folders with patented button blade release and high-art straight knives of his design. **Patterns:** Boots, daggers and locking folders. **Technical:** Grinds 440C and ATS-34 and Damascus. Engraves his knives. **Prices:** $1500 to $18,000 or more. **Remarks:** Full-time maker; first knife sold in 1989. **Mark:** First and middle initials, last name or last name only.

BLASINGAME, ROBERT,
281 Swanson, Kilgore, TX 75662, Phone: 903-984-8144, rbblademastger@cablelynx.com Web:www.blasingameknives.com
Specialties: Classic working and using straight knives and folders of his design and to customer specs. **Patterns:** Bowies, daggers, fighters and hunters; one-of-a-kind historic reproductions. **Technical:** Hand-forges P.W. Damascus, cable Damascus and chain Damascus. **Prices:** $150 to $1000; some to $2000. **Remarks:** Full-time maker; first knife sold in 1968. **Mark:** 'B' inside anvil.

BLAUM, ROY,
319 N Columbia St, Covington, LA 70433, Phone: 985-893-1060
Specialties: Working straight knives and folders of his design; lightweight easy-open folders. **Patterns:** Hunters, boots, fishing and woodcarving/whittling knives. **Technical:** Grinds A2, D2, O1, 154CM and ATS-34. Offers leatherwork. **Prices:** $40 to $800; some higher. **Remarks:** Full-time maker; first knife sold in 1976. **Mark:** Engraved signature or etched logo.

BLOOMER, ALAN T,
PO Box 154, 116 E 6th St, Maquon, IL 61458, Phone: 309-875-3583, alant.bloomer@winco.net
Specialties: Folders & straight knives & custom pen maker. **Patterns:** All kinds. **Technical:** Does own heat treating. **Prices:** $400 to $1000. **Remarks:** Part-time maker. No orders. **Mark:** Stamp Bloomer.

BLOOMQUIST, R GORDON,
6206 Tiger Trail Dr, Olympia, WA 98512, Phone: 360-352-7162, bloomquistr@energy.wsu.edu

BLUM, CHUCK,
743 S Brea Blvd #10, Brea, CA 92621, Phone: 714-529-0484
Specialties: Art and investment daggers and Bowies. **Technical:** Flat-grinds; hollow-grinds 440C, ATS-34 on working knives. **Prices:** $125 to $8500. **Remarks:** Part-time maker; first knife sold in 1985. **Mark:** First and middle initials and last name with sailboat logo.

BLUM, KENNETH,
1729 Burleson, Brenham, TX 77833, Phone: 979-836-9577
Specialties: Traditional working straight knives of his design. **Patterns:** Camp knives, hunters and Bowies. **Technical:** Forges 5160; grinds 440C and D2. Uses exotic woods and Micarta for handles. **Prices:** $150 to $300. **Remarks:** Part-time maker; first knife sold in 1978. **Mark:** Last name on ricasso.

BOARDMAN, GUY,
39 Mountain Ridge R, New Germany 3619, SOUTH AFRICA, Phone: 031-726-921
Specialties: American and South African-styles. **Patterns:** Bowies, American and South African hunters, plus more. **Technical:** Grinds Bohler steels, some ATS-34. **Prices:** $100 to $600. **Remarks:** Part-time maker; first knife sold in 1986. **Mark:** Name, city, country.

BOCHMAN, BRUCE,
183 Howard Place, Grants Pass, OR 97526, Phone: 503-471-1985
Specialties: Working straight knives in standard patterns. **Patterns:** Bowies, hunters, fishing and bird knives. **Technical:** 440C; mirror or satin finish. **Prices:** $140 to $250; some to $750. **Remarks:** Part-time maker; first knife sold in 1977. **Mark:** Custom blades by B. Bochman.

BODEN, HARRY,
Via Gellia Mill, Bonsall Matlock, Derbyshire DE4 2AJ, ENGLAND, Phone: 0629-825176
Specialties: Traditional working straight knives and folders of his design. **Patterns:** Hunters, locking folders and utility/camp knives. **Technical:** Grinds Sandvik 12C27, D2 and O1. **Prices:** £70 to £150; some to £300. **Remarks:** Full-time maker; first knife sold in 1986. **Mark:** Full name.

BODNER, GERALD "JERRY",
4102 Spyglass Ct, Louisville, KY 40229, Phone: 502-968-5946
Specialties: Fantasy straight knives in standard patterns. **Patterns:** Bowies, fighters, hunters and micro-miniature knives. **Technical:** Grinds Damascus, 440C and D2. Offers filework. **Prices:** $35 to $180. **Remarks:** Part-time maker; first knife sold in 1993. **Mark:** Last name in script and JAB in oval above knives.

BODOLAY, ANTAL,
Rua Wilson Soares Fernandes #31, Planalto, Belo Horizonte MG-31730-700, BRAZIL, Phone: 031-494-1885
Specialties: Working folders and fixed blades of his design or to customer specs; some art daggers and period pieces. **Patterns:** Daggers, hunters, locking folders, utility knives and Khukris. **Technical:** Grinds D6, high-carbon steels and 420 stainless. Forges files on request. **Prices:** $30 to $350. **Remarks:** Full-time maker; first knife sold in 1965. **Mark:** Last name in script.

BOEHLKE, GUENTER,
Parkstrasse 2, 56412 Grossholbach, GERMANY 2602-5440, Boehlke-Messer@t-online.de; Web: www.boehlke-messer.de
Specialties: Classic working/using straight knives of his design. **Patterns:** Hunters, utility/camp knives and ancient remakes. **Technical:** Grinds Damascus, CPM-T-440V and 440C. Inlays gemstones and ivory. **Prices:** $220 to $700; some to $2000. **Remarks:** Spare-time maker; first knife sold in 1985. **Mark:** Name, address and bow and arrow.

BOGUSZEWSKI, PHIL,
PO Box 99329, Lakewood, WA 98499, Phone: 253-581-7096, knives01@aol.com
Specialties: Working folders—some fancy—mostly of his design. **Patterns:** Folders, slip-joints and lockers; also makes anodized titanium frame folders. **Technical:** Grinds BG42 and Damascus; offers filework. **Prices:** $550 to $3000. **Remarks:** Full-time maker; first knife sold in 1979. **Mark:** Name, city and state.

BOJTOS, ARPA D,
Dobsinskeho 10, 98403 Lucenec, SLOVAKIA, Phone: 00421-47 4333512, botjos@stonline.sk; Web: www.arpadbojtos.sk
Specialties: Art knives. **Patterns:** Daggers, fighters and hunters. **Technical:** Grinds ATS-34. Carves on steel, handle materials and sheaths. **Prices:** $2000 to $5000; some to $8000. **Remarks:** Full-time maker; first knife sold in 1990. **Mark:** AB.

BOLEWARE, DAVID,
PO Box 96, Carson, MS 39427, Phone: 601-943-5372
Specialties: Traditional and working/using straight knives of his design, to customer specs and in standard patterns. **Patterns:** Bowies, hunters and utility/camp knives. **Technical:** Grinds ATS-34, 440C and Damascus. **Prices:** $85 to $350; some to $600. **Remarks:** Part-time maker; first knife sold in 1989. **Mark:** First and last name, city, state.

BOLEY, JAMIE,
PO Box 477, Parker, SD 57053, Phone: 605-297-0014, jamie@polarbearforge.com
Specialties: Working knives and historical influenced reproductions. **Patterns:** Hunters, skinners, scramasaxes, and others.**Technical:** Forges 5160, O1, L6, 52100, W1, W2 makes own Damascus. **Prices:** Starts at $125. **Remarks:** Part-time maker. **Mark:** Polar bear paw print with name on the left side and Polar Bear Forge on the right.

BONASSI, FRANCO,
Via Nicoletta 4, Pordenone 33170, ITALY, Phone: 0434-550821, f.bonassi@faridindustrie.it
Specialties: Fancy and working one-of-a-kind folder knives of his design. **Patterns:** Folders, linerlocks and back locks. **Technical:** Grinds CPM, ATS-34, 154CM and commercial Damascus. Uses only titanium foreguards and pommels. **Prices:** Start at $350. **Remarks:** Spare-time maker; first knife sold in 1988. Has made cutlery for several celebrities; Gen. Schwarzkopf, Fuzzy Zoeller, etc. **Mark:** FRANK.

BOOCO, GORDON,
175 Ash St, PO Box 174, Hayden, CO 81639, Phone: 970-276-3195
Specialties: Fancy working straight knives of his design and to customer specs. **Patterns:** Hunters and Bowies. **Technical:** Grinds 440C, D2 and A2. Heat-treats. **Prices:** $150 to $350; some $600 and higher. **Remarks:** Part-time maker; first knife sold in 1984. **Mark:** Last name with push dagger artwork.

BOOS, RALPH,
6018-37A Avenue NW, Edmonton, Alberta, CANADA T6L 1H4, Phone: 780-463-7094
Specialties: Classic, fancy and fantasy miniature knives and swords of his design or to customer specs. **Patterns:** Bowies, daggers and swords. **Technical:** Hand files O1, stainless and Damascus. Engraves and carves. Does heat bluing and acid etching. **Prices:** $125 to $350; some to $1000. **Remarks:** Part-time maker; first knife sold in 1982. **Mark:** First initials back to back.

BOOTH, PHILIP W,
301 S Jeffery Ave, Ithaca, MI 48847, Phone: 989-875-2844, Web: wwwphilipbooth.com
Specialties: Automatics and lock back. Folding knives of his design, some liner locks. **Patterns:** Auto lock backs, liner locks, classic pattern multi-blades. **Technical:** Grinds ATS-34, 440C, 1095 and commercial Damascus. Prefers natural materials, offers file work and scrimshaw. **Prices:** $200 and up. **Remarks:** Part-time maker, first knife sold in 1991. **Mark:** Last name or name with city and map logo.

BORGER, WOLF,
Benzstrasse 8, 76676 Graben-Neudorf, GERMANY, Phone: 07255-72303, Fax: 07255-72304, wolf@messerschmied.de; Web: www.messerschmied.de
Specialties: High-tech working and using straight knives and folders, many with corkscrews or other tools, of his design. **Patterns:** Hunters, Bowies and folders with various locking systems. **Technical:** Grinds 440C, ATS-34 and CPM. Uses stainless Damascus. **Prices:** $250 to $900; some to $1500. **Remarks:** Full-time maker; first knife sold in 1975. **Mark:** Howling wolf and name; first name on Damascus blades.

BOSE, REESE,
PO Box 61, Shelburn, IN 47879, Phone: 812-397-5114
Specialties: Traditional working and using knives in standard patterns and multi-blade folders. **Patterns:** Multi-blade slip-joints. **Technical:** ATS-34, D2 and CPM 440V. **Prices:** $275 to $1500. **Remarks:** Full-time maker; first knife sold in 1992. Photos by Jack Busfield. **Mark:** R. Bose.

BOSE, TONY,
7252 N. County Rd, 300 E., Shelburn, IN 47879-9778, Phone: 812-397-5114
Specialties: Traditional working and using knives in standard patterns; multi-blade folders. **Patterns:** Multi-blade slip-joints. **Technical:** Grinds commercial Damascus, ATS-34 and D2. **Prices:** $400 to $1200. **Remarks:** Full-time maker; first knife sold in 1972. **Mark:** First initial, last name, city, state.

BOSSAERTS, CARL,
Rua Albert Einstein 906, 14051-110, Ribeirao Preto, S.P., BRAZIL, Phone: 016 633 7063
Specialties: Working and using straight knives of his design, to customer specs and in standard patterns. **Patterns:** Hunters, fighters and utility/camp knives. **Technical:** Grinds ATS-34, 440V and 440C; does filework. **Prices:** 60 to $400. **Remarks:** Part-time maker; first knife sold in 1992. **Mark:** Initials joined together.

BOST, ROGER E,
30511 Cartier Dr, Palos Verdes, CA 90275-5629, Phone: 310-541-6833, rogerbost@cox.net
Specialties: Hunters, fighters, boot, utility. **Patterns:** Loveless-style. **Technical:** ATS-34, 60-61RC, stock removal and forge. **Prices:** $300 and up. **Remarks:** First knife sold in 1990. Cal. Knifemakers Assn., ABS. **Mark:** Diamond with initials inside and Palos Verdes California around outside.

BOSTWICK, CHRIS T,
PO Box 491, Burlington, WI 53105
Specialties: Slip joints ATS-34. **Patterns:** English jack, gunstock jack, doctors, stockman. **Prices:** $300 and up. **Remarks:** Enjoy traditional patterns/history multiblade slipjoints. **Mark:** CTB.

BOSWORTH, DEAN,
329 Mahogany Dr, Key Largo, FL 33037, Phone: 305-451-1564
Specialties: Free hand hollow ground working knives with hand rubbed satin finish, filework and inlays. **Patterns:** Bird and Trout, hunters, skinners, fillet, Bowies, miniatures. **Technical:** Using 440C, ATS-34, D2, Meier Damascus, custom wet formed sheaths. **Prices:** $250 and up. **Remarks:** Part-time maker; first knife made in 1985. Member Florida Knifemakers Assoc. **Mark:** BOZ stamped in block letters.

BOURBEAU, JEAN YVES,
15 Rue Remillard, Notre Dame, Ile Perrot, Quebec, CANADA J7V 8M9, Phone: 514-453-1069
Specialties: Fancy/embellished and fantasy folders of his design. **Patterns:** Bowies, fighters and locking folders. **Technical:** Grinds 440C, ATS-34 and Damascus. Carves precious wood for handles. **Prices:** $150 to $1000. **Remarks:** Part-time maker; first knife sold in 1994. **Mark:** Interlaced initials.

BOUSE, D. MICHAEL,
1010 Victoria Pl, Waldorf, MD 20602, Phone: 301-843-0449
Specialties: Traditional and working/using straight knives of his design. **Patterns:** Daggers, fighters and hunters. **Technical:** Forges 5160 and Damascus; grinds D2; differential hardened blades; decorative handle pins. **Prices:** $125 to $350. **Remarks:** Spare-time maker; first knife sold in 1992. Doing business as Michael's Handmade Knives. **Mark:** Etched last name.

BOWEN, TILTON,
189 Mt Olive Rd, Baker, WV 26801, Phone: 304-897-6159
Specialties: Straight, stout working knives. **Patterns:** Hunters, fighters and boots; also offers buckskinner and throwing knives. All his D2-blades since 1st of year, 1997 are Deep Cryogenic processed. **Technical:** Grinds D2 and 4140. **Prices:** $70 to $295. **Remarks:** Full-time maker; first knife sold in 1982-1983. Sells wholesale to dealers. **Mark:** Initials and BOWEN BLADES, WV.

BOWLES, CHRIS,
PO Box 985, Reform, AL 35481, Phone: 205-375-6162
Specialties: Working/using straight knives, and period pieces. **Patterns:** Utility, tactical, hunting, neck knives, machetes, and swords. **Grinds:** 0-1, 154 cm, BG-42, 440V. **Prices:** $50 to $400 some higher. **Remarks:** Full-time maker. **Mark:** Bowles stamped or Bowles etched in script.

BOXER, BO,
LEGEND FORGE, 6477 Hwy 93 S #134, Whitefish, MT 59937, Phone: 505-799-0173, legendforge@aol.com; Web: www.legendforgesknives.com
Specialties: Handmade hunting knives, Damascus hunters. Most are antler handled. Also, hand forged Damascus steel. **Patterns:** Hunters and Bowies. **Prices:** $125 to $2500 on some very exceptional Damascus knives. **Remarks:** Makes his own custom leather sheath stamped with maker stamp. His knives are used by the outdoorsman of the Smoky Mountains, North Carolina, and the Rockies of Montana and New Mexico. Spends one-half of the year in Montana and the other part of the year in Taos, New Mexico. **Mark:** The name "Legend Forge" hand engraved on every blade.

BOYD, FRANCIS,
1811 Prince St, Berkeley, CA 94703, Phone: 510-841-7210
Specialties: Folders and kitchen knives, Japanese swords. **Patterns:** Push-button sturdy locking folders; San Francisco-style chef's knives. **Technical:** Forges and grinds; mostly uses high-carbon steels. **Prices:** Moderate to heavy. **Remarks:** Designer. **Mark:** Name.

BOYE, DAVID,
PO Box 1238, Dolan Springs, AZ 86441, Phone: 800-853-1617, Fax: 928-767-4273, boye@cltlink.net; Web: www.boyeknives.com
Specialties: Folders and Boye Basics. Forerunner in the use of dendritic steel and dendritic cobalt for blades. **Patterns:** Lockback folders and fixed blade sheath knives in cobalt. **Technical:** Casts blades in cobalt. **Prices:** From $129 to $360. **Remarks:** Part-time maker; author of *Step-by-Step Knifemaking*. **Mark:** Name.

BOYER, MARK,
10515 Woodinville Dr #17, Bothell, WA 98011, Phone: 206-487-9370, boyerbl@mail.eskimo.com
Specialties: High-tech and working/using straight knives of his design. **Patterns:** Fighters and utility/camp knives. **Technical:** Grinds 1095 and D2. Offers Kydex sheaths; heat-treats. **Prices:** $45 to $120. **Remarks:** Part-time maker; first knife sold in 1994. Doing business as Boyer Blades. **Mark:** Eagle holding two swords with name.

BOYSEN, RAYMOND A,
125 E St Patrick, Rapid Ciy, SD 57701, Phone: 605-341-7752
Specialties: Hunters and Bowies. **Technical:** High performance blades forged from 52100 and 5160. **Prices:** $200 and up. **Remarks:** American Bladesmith Society Journeyman Smith. Part-time bladesmith. **Mark:** BOYSEN.

BRACK, DOUGLAS D,
1591 Los Angeles Ave #8, Ventura, CA 93004, Phone: 805-659-1505
Specialties: Fighters, daggers, boots, Bowies. **Patterns:** One of a kind. **Technical:** Grinds 440-ATS, own Damascus. **Prices:** $300 to $3000. **Remarks:** Full-time maker; first knife sold in 1984. **Mark:** tat.

BRADBURN, GARY,
BRADBURNCUSTOMCUTLERY,1714ParkPlace,Wichita,KS67203,Phone: 316-640-5684, gary@bradburnknives.com; Web:www.bradburnknives.com
Specialties: Specialize in clay-tempered Japanese-style knives and swords. **Patterns:** Also Bowies and fighters. **Technical:** Forge and/or grind carbon steel only. **Prices:** $150 to $1200. **Mark:** Initials GB stylized to look like Japanese character.

BRADFORD, GARRICK,
582 Guelph St, Kitchener ON, CANADA N2H-5Y4, Phone: 519-576-9863

BRADLEY, DENNIS,
2410 Bradley Acres Rd, Blairsville, GA 30512, Phone: 706-745-4364
Specialties: Working straight knives and folders, some high-art. **Patterns:** Hunters, boots and daggers; slip-joints and two-blades. **Technical:** Grinds ATS-34, D2, 440C and commercial Damascus. **Prices:** $100 to $500; some to $2000. **Remarks:** Part-time maker; first knife sold in 1973. **Mark:** BRADLEY KNIVES in double heart logo.

BRADLEY, JOHN,
PO Box 33, Pomona Park, FL 32181, Phone: 904-649-4739, yeldarbj@bellsouth.net
Specialties: Fixed-blade using knives. **Patterns:** Skinners, Bowies, camp knives and primitive knives. **Technical:** Hand forged from 52100, 1095 and own Damascus. **Prices:** $150 to $1000; some higher. **Remarks:** Part-time maker; first knife sold in 1988. **Mark:** Last name.

BRADSHAW, BAILEY,
PO Box 564, Diana, TX 75640, Phone: 903-968-2029, bailey@bradshawcutlery.com
Specialties: Traditional folders and contemporary front lock folders. **Patterns:** Single or multi-blade folders, Bowies. **Technical:** Grind CPM 3V, CPM 440V, CPM 420V, Forge Damascus, 52100. **Prices:** $250 to $3000. **Remarks:** Engraves, carves and does sterling silver sheaths. **Mark:** Tori arch over initials back to back.

BRANDON, MATTHEW,
4435 Meade St, Denver, CO 80211, Phone: 303-458-0786, mtbrandon@hotmail.com
Specialties: Hunters, skinners, full-tang Bowies. **Prices:** $150 to $1000. **Remarks:** Satisfaction or full refund. **Mark:** MTB.

BRANDSEY, EDWARD P,
4441 Hawkridge Ct, Janesville, WI 53546, Phone: 608-868-9010, ebrandsey@centurytel.com
Patterns: Large bowies, hunters, neck knives and buckskinner-styles. Native American influence on some. An occasional tanto, art piece. Does own scrimshaw. See Egnath's second book. Now making locking liner folders. **Technical:** ATS-34, S530V, 440-C, 0-1, and some Damascus. Paul Bos treating past 20 years. **Prices:** $250 to $600; some to $3000. **Remarks:** Full-time maker. First knife sold in 1973. **Mark:** Initials connected -registered Wisc. Trademark since March 1983.

BRANDT, MARTIN W,
833 Kelly Blvd, Springfield, OR 97477, Phone: 541-747-5422, oubob747@aol.com

BRANTON, ROBERT,
4976 Seewee Rd, Awendaw, SC 29429, Phone: 843-928-3624
Specialties: Working straight knives of his design or to customer specs; throwing knives. **Patterns:** Hunters, fighters and some miniatures. **Technical:** Grinds ATS-34, A2 and 1050; forges 5160, O1. Offers hollow- or convex-grinds. **Prices:** $25 to $400. **Remarks:** Part-time maker; first knife sold in 1985. Doing business as Pro-Flyte, Inc. **Mark:** Last name; or first and last name, city, state.

BRATCHER, BRETT,
11816 County Rd 302, Plantersville, TX 77363, Phone: 936-894-3788, Fax: (936) 894-3790, brett_bratcher@msn.com
Specialties: Hunting and skinning knives. **Patterns:** Clip and drop point. Hand forged. **Technical:** Material 5160, D2, 1095 and Damascus. **Price:** $200 to $500. **Mark:** Bratcher.

BRAY JR., W LOWELL,
6931 Manor Beach Rd, New Port Richey, FL 34652, Phone: 727-846-0830, brayknives@aol.com
Specialties: Traditional working and using straight knives and folders of his design. **Patterns:** Hunters, fighters and utility knives. **Technical:** Grinds 440C and ATS-34; forges 52100 and Damascus. **Prices:** $125 to $800. **Remarks:** Spare-time maker; first knife sold in 1992. **Mark:** Lowell Bray Knives in shield or Bray Primative in shield.

BREED, KIM,
733 Jace Dr, Clarksville, TN 37040, Phone: 931-645-9171, sfbreed@yahoo.com
Specialties: High end through working folders and straight knives. **Patterns:** Hunters, fighters, daggers, Bowies. His design or customers. Likes one-of-a-kind designs. **Technical:** Makes own Mosiac and regular Damascus, but will use stainless steels. Offers filework and sculpted material. **Prices:** $150 to $2000. **Remarks:** Full-time maker. First knife sold in 1990. **Mark:** Last name.

BREND, WALTER,
353 Co Rd 1373, Vinemont, AL 35179, Phone: 256-739-1987, walterbrend@hotmail.com
Specialties: Tactical-style knives, fighters, automatics. **Technical:** Grinds D-Z and 440C blade steels, 154CM steel. **Prices:** Micarta handles, titanium handles.

BRENNAN, JUDSON,
PO Box 1165, Delta Junction, AK 99737, Phone: 907-895-5153, Fax: 907-895-5404
Specialties: Period pieces. **Patterns:** All kinds of Bowies, rifle knives, daggers. **Technical:** Forges miscellaneous steels. **Prices:** Upscale, good value. **Remarks:** Muzzle-loading gunsmith; first knife sold in 1978. **Mark:** Name.

BRESHEARS, CLINT,
1261 Keats, Manhattan Beach, CA 90266, Phone: 310-372-0739, Fax: 310-372-0739, breshears@mindspring.com; Web: www.clintknives.com
Specialties: Working straight knives and folders. **Patterns:** Hunters, Bowies and survival knives. Folders are mostly hunters. **Technical:** Grinds 440C, 154CM and ATS-34; prefers mirror finishes. **Prices:** $125 to $750; some to $1800. **Remarks:** Part-time maker; first knife sold in 1978. **Mark:** First name.

BREUER, LONNIE,
PO Box 877384, Wasilla, AK 99687-7384
Specialties: Fancy working straight knives. **Patterns:** Hunters, camp knives and axes, folders and Bowies. **Technical:** Grinds 440C, AEB-L and D2; likes wire inlay, scrimshaw, decorative filing. **Prices:** $60 to $150; some to $300. **Remarks:** Part-time maker; first knife sold in 1977. **Mark:** Signature.

BRITTON, TIM,
PO Box 71, Bethania, NC 27010, Phone: 366-923-2062; 336-922-9582, timbritton@yahoo.com; Web: www.timbritton.com
Specialties: Small and simple working knives, sgian dubhs, slip joint folders and special tactical designs. **Technical:** Forges and grinds stainless steel. **Prices:** $165 to ???. **Remarks:** Veteran knifemaker. **Mark:** Etched signature.

BROADWELL, DAVID,
PO Box 4314, Wichita Falls, TX 76308, Phone: 940-692-1727, Fax: 940-692-4003, david@broadwell.com; Web: www.david.broadwell.com
Specialties: Sculpted high-art straight and folding knives. **Patterns:** Daggers, sub-hilted fighters, folders, sculpted art knives and some Bowies. **Technical:** Grinds mostly Damascus; carves; prefers natural handle materials, including stone. Some embellishment. **Prices:** $350 to $3000; some higher. **Remarks:** Full-time maker; first knife sold in 1982. **Mark:** Stylized emblem bisecting "B"/with last name below.

BROCK, KENNETH L,
PO Box 375, 207 N Skinner Rd, Allenspark, CO 80510, Phone: 303-747-2547, brockknives@nedernet.net
Specialties: Custom designs, full-tang working knives and button lock folders of his design. **Patterns:** Hunters, miniatures and minis. **Technical:** Flat-grinds D2 and 440C; makes own sheaths; heat-treats. **Prices:** $75 to $800. **Remarks:** Full-time maker; first knife sold in 1978. **Mark:** Last name, city, state and serial number.

BRODZIAK, DAVID,
27 Stewart St, Albany, Western Australia, AUSTRALIA 6330, Phone: 61 8 9841 3314, Fax: 61898115065, brodziakomninet.net.au; Web: www.brodziakcustomknives.com

BROMLEY, PETER,
BROMLEY KNIVES, 1408 S Bettman, Spokane, WA 99212, Phone: 509-534-4235, Fax: 509-536-2666
Specialties: Period Bowies, folder, hunting knives; all sizes and shapes. **Patterns:** Bowies, boot knives, hunters, utility, folder, working knives. **Technical:** High-carbon steel (1084, 1095 and 5160). Stock removal and forge. **Prices:** $85 to $750. **Remarks:** Almost full-time, first knife sold in 1987. A.B.S. Journeyman Smith. **Mark:** Bromley, Spokane, WA.

BROOKER, DENNIS,
Rt 1, Box 12A, Derby, IA 50068, Phone: 515-533-2103
Specialties: Fancy straight knives and folders of his design. **Patterns:** Hunters, folders and boots. **Technical:** Forges and grinds. Full-time engraver and designer; instruction available. **Prices:** Moderate to upscale. **Remarks:** Part-time maker. Takes no orders; sells only completed work. **Mark:** Name.

BROOKS, BUZZ,
2345 Yosemite Dr, Los Angles, CA 90041, Phone: 323-256-2892

BROOKS, MICHAEL,
2811 64th St, Lubbock, TX 79413, Phone: 806-799-3088, chiang@nts-online.net
Specialties: Working straight knives of his design or to customer specs. **Patterns:** Martial art, Bowies, hunters, and fighters. **Technical:** Grinds 440C, D2 and ATS-34; offers wide variety of handle materials. **Prices:** $75 & up. **Remarks:** Part-time maker; first knife sold in 1985. **Mark:** Initials.

BROOKS, STEVE R,
1610 Dunn Ave, Walkerville, MT 59701, Phone: 406-782-5114, Fax: 406-782-5114, steve@brooksmoulds.com; Web: brooksmoulds.com
Specialties: Working straight knives and folders; period pieces. **Patterns:** Hunters, Bowies and camp knives; folding lockers; axes, tomahawks and buckskinner knives; swords and stilettos. **Technical:** Damascus and mosaic Damascus. Some knives come embellished. **Prices:** $400 to $2000. **Remarks:** Full-time maker; first knife sold in 1982. **Mark:** Lazy initials.

BROOME, THOMAS A,
1212 E. Aliak Ave, Kenai, AK 99611-8205, Phone: 907-283-9128, tomlei@ptialaska.ent; Web: www.alaskanknives.com
Specialties: Working hunters and folders **Patterns:** Traditional and custom orders. **Technical:** Grinds ATS-34, BG-42, CPM-S30V. **Prices:** $175 to $350. **Remarks:** Full-time maker; first knife sold in 1979. Doing business as Thom's Custom Knives, Alaskan Man O; Steel Knives. **Mark:** Full name, city, state.

BROTHERS, ROBERT L,
989 Philpott Rd, Colville, WA 99114, Phone: 509-684-8922
Specialties: Traditional working and using straight knives and folders of his design and to customer specs. **Patterns:** Bowies, fighters and hunters. **Technical:** Grinds D2; forges Damascus. Makes own Damascus from saw steel wire rope and chain; part-time goldsmith and stone-setter. **Prices:** $100 to $400; some higher. **Remarks:** Part-time maker; first knife sold in 1986. **Mark:** Initials and year made.

BROWER, MAX,
2016 Story St, Boone, IA 50036, Phone: 515-432-2938, mbrower@mchsi.com
Specialties: Working/using straight knives. **Patterns:** Bowies, hunters and boots. **Technical:** Grinds 440C and ATS-34. **Prices:** Start at $150. **Remarks:** Spare-time maker; first knife sold in 1981. **Mark:** Last name.

BROWN, DENNIS G,
1633 N 197th Pl, Shoreline, WA 98133, Phone: 206-542-3997, denjilbro@msn.com

BROWN, HAROLD E,
3654 NW Hwy 72, Arcadia, FL 34266, Phone: 863-494-7514, brknives@strato.net
Specialties: Fancy and exotic working knives. **Patterns:** Folders, slip-lock, locking several kinds. **Technical:** Grinds D2 and ATS-34. Embellishment available. **Prices:** $175 to $1000. **Remarks:** Part-time maker; first knife sold in 1976. **Mark:** Name and city with logo.

BROWN, JIM,
1097 Fernleigh Cove, Little Rock, AR 72210

BROWN, ROB E,
PO Box 15107, Emerald Hill 6011, Port Elizabeth, SOUTH AFRICA, Phone: 27-41-3661086, Fax: 27-41-4511731, rbknives@global.co.za
Specialties: Contemporary-designed straight knives and period pieces. **Patterns:** Utility knives, hunters, boots, fighters and daggers. **Technical:** Grinds 440C, D2, ATS-34 and commercial Damascus. Knives mostly mirror finished; African handle materials. **Prices:** $100 to $1500. **Remarks:** Full-time maker; first knife sold in 1985. **Mark:** Name and country.

BROWNE, RICK,
980 West 13th St, Upland, CA 91786, Phone: 909-985-1728
Specialties: Sheffield pattern pocket knives. **Patterns:** Hunters, fighters and daggers. No heavy-duty knives. **Technical:** Grinds ATS-34. **Prices:** Start at $450. **Remarks:** Part-time maker; first knife sold in 1975. **Mark:** R.E. Browne, Upland, CA.

BROWNING, STEVEN W,
3400 Harrison Rd, Benton, AR 72015, Phone: 501-316-2450

BRUNCKHORST, LYLE,
COUNTRY VILLAGE, 23706 7th Ave SE Ste B, Bothell, WA 98021, Phone: 425-402-3484, bronks@bronksknifeworks.com; Web: www.bronksknifeworks.com
Specialties: Forges own Damascus with 1084 and 15N20, forges 5160, 52100. Grinds CPM 154 CM, ATS-34, S30V. Hosts Biannual Northwest School of Knifemaking and Northwest Hammer In. Offers online and in-house sharpening services and knife sharpeners. Maker of the Double L Hoofknife. Traditional working and using knives, the new patent pending Xross-Bar Lock folders, tomahawks and irridescent RR spike knives. **Patterns:** Damascus Bowies, hunters, locking folders and featuring the ultra strong locking tactical folding knnives. **Technical:** Offers scrimshaw, inlays and animal carvings in horn handles. **Prices:** $185 to $1500; some to $3750. **Remarks:** Full-time maker; first knife made in 1976. **Mark:** Bucking horse or bronk.

BRUNER JR., FRED BRUNER BLADES,
E10910W Hilldale Dr, Fall Creek, WI 54742, Phone: 715-877-2496, brunerblades@msn.com
Specialties: Pipe tomahawks, swords, makes his own. **Patterns:** Drop point hunters. **Prices:** $65 to $1500. **Remarks:** Voting member of the Knifemakers Guild. **Mark:** Fred Bruner.

BRUNETTA, DAVID,
PO Box 4972, Laguna Beach, CA 92652, Phone: 714-497-9611
Specialties: Straights, folders and art knives. **Patterns:** Bowies, camp/hunting, folders, fighters. **Technical:** Grinds ATS-34, D2, BG42. forges O1, 52100, 5160, 1095, makes own Damascus. **Prices:** $300 to $9000. **Mark:** Circle DB logo with last name straight or curved.

BRYAN, TOM,
14822 S Gilbert Rd, Gilbert, AZ 85296, Phone: 480-812-8529
Specialties: Straight and folding knives. **Patterns:** Drop-point hunter fighters. **Technical:** ATS-34, 154CM, 440C and A2. **Prices:** $150 to $800. **Remarks:** Part-time maker; sold first knife in 1994. DBA as T. Bryan Knives. **Mark:** T. Bryan.

BUCHANAN, THAD,
THAD BUCHANAN CUSTOM KNIVES, 915 NW Perennial Way, Prineville, OR 97754, Phone: 541-416-2556, knives@crestviewcable.com; Web: www.buchananblades.com
Specialties: Fixed blades & slip joints. **Patterns:** Various hunters, trout, bird, utility, boots & fighters. **Technical:** Stock removal, high polish, variety handle materials. **Prices:** $450 to $1100. **Remarks:** 2005 Blade in magazine handmade award for hunter/utility. 2006 Blade West best fixed blade award. **Mark:** Thad Buchanan Oregon USA.

BUCHMAN, BILL,
63312 South Rd, Bend, OR 97701-9027, Phone: 541-382-8851
Specialties: Leather cutting knives for saddle makers and leather crafters. **Patterns:** Many. **Technical:** Sandkik-Swedish carbon steel. **Prices:** Varies: $35 to $130. **Remarks:** Full-time maker; first knife sold in 1982. **Mark:** BB & # of knife on large knives -no mark on small knives.

BUCHNER, BILL,
PO Box 73, Idleyld Park, OR 97447, Phone: 541-498-2247, blazinhammer@earthlink.net; Web: www.home.earthlin.net/~blazinghammer
Specialties: Working straight knives, kitchen knives and high-art knives of his design. **Technical:** Uses W1, L6 and his own Damascus. Invented "spectrum metal" for letter openers, folder handles and jewelry. Likes sculpturing and carving in Damascus. **Prices:** $40 to $3000; some higher. **Remarks:** Full-time maker; first knife sold in 1978. **Mark:** Signature.

BUCHOLZ, MARK A,
PO Box 82, Holualoa, HI 96725, Phone: 808-322-4045
Specialties: LinerLock® folders. Patterns: Hunters and fighters. **Technical:** Grinds ATS-34. **Prices:** Upscale. **Remarks:** Full-time maker; first knife sold in 1976. **Mark:** Name, city and state in buffalo skull logo

or signature.

BUCKBEE, DONALD M,
243 South Jackson Trail, Grayling, MI 49738, Phone: 517-348-1386
Specialties: Working straight knives, some fancy, in standard patterns; concentrating on kitchen knives. **Patterns:** Kitchen knives, hunters, Bowies. **Technical:** Grinds D2, 440C, ATS-34. Makes ultra-lights in hunter patterns. **Prices:** $100 to $250; some to $350. **Remarks:** Part-time maker; first knife sold in 1984. **Mark:** Antlered bee—a buck bee.

BUCKNER, JIMMIE H,
PO Box 162, Putney, GA 31782, Phone: 229-436-4182
Specialties: Camp knives, Bowies (one-of-a-kind), liner-lock folders, tomahawks, camp axes, neck knives for law enforcement and hide-out knives for body guards and professional people. **Patterns:** Hunters, camp knives, Bowies. **Technical:** Forges 1084, 5160 and Damascus (own), own heat treats. **Prices:** $195 to $795 and up. **Remarks:** Full-time maker; first knife sold in 1980, ABS Master Smith. **Mark:** Name over spade.

BUEBENDORF, ROBERT E,
108 Lazybrooke Rd, Monroe, CT 06468, Phone: 203-452-1769
Specialties: Traditional and fancy straight knives of his design. **Patterns:** Hand-makes and embellishes belt buckle knives. **Technical:** Forges and grinds 440C, O1, W2, 1095, his own Damascus and 154CM. **Prices:** $200 to $500. **Remarks:** Full-time maker; first knife sold in 1978. **Mark:** First and middle initials, last name and MAKER.

BULLARD, BILL,
Rt 5, Box 35, Andalusia, AL 36420, Phone: 334-222-9003
Specialties: Traditional working and using straight knives and folders of his design. **Patterns:** Hunters, slip-joint folders and utility/camp knives and folders to customer specs. **Technical:** Forges Damascus, cable. Offers filework. **Prices:** $100 to $500; some to $1500. **Remarks:** Part-time maker; first knife sold in 1974. Doing business as Five Runs Forge. **Mark:** Last name stamped on ricasso.

BULLARD, RANDALL,
7 Mesa Dr., Canyon, TX 79015, Phone: 806-655-0590
Specialties: Working/using straight knives and folders of his design or to customer specs. **Patterns:** Hunters, locking folders and slip-joint folders. **Technical:** Grinds O1, ATS-34 and 440C. Does file work. **Prices:** $125 to $300; some to $500. **Remarks:** Part-time maker; first knife sold in 1993. Doing business as Bullard Custom Knives. **Mark:** First and middle initials, last name, maker, city and state.

BULLARD, TOM,
117 MC 8068, Flippin, AR 72634, Phone: 870-453-3421, tbullard@southshore.com; Web: www.southshore.com/~tombullard
Specialties: Traditional folders and hunters. **Patterns:** Bowies, hunters, single and 2-blade trappers, lockback folders. **Technical:** Grinds 440-C, ATS-34, 0-1, commercial Damascus. **Prices:** $150 and up. **Remarks:** Offers filework and engraving by Norvell Foster and Terry Thies. Does not make screw-together knives. **Mark:** T Bullard.

BUMP, BRUCE D.,
1103 Rex Ln, Walla Walla, WA 99362, Phone: 509 522-2219, bruceandkaye@charter.net; Web: www.brucebumpknives.com
Specialties: Complete range of knives from field grade to "one-of-a-kind" cut and shoots. **Patterns:** Black Powder pistol/folders, "Brutus" axe/gun, shooting swords. **Technical:** Dual threat weapons of his own design inspired from early centuries. **Prices:** $250 to $20,000. **Remarks:** Full-time maker ABS mastersmith 2003. **Mark:** Bruce D. Bump, Bruce D Bump Custom Walla Walla WA.

BURDEN, JAMES,
405 Kelly St, Burkburnett, TX 76354

BURGER, FRED,
Box 436, Munster 4278, Kwa-Zulu Natal, SOUTH AFRICA, Phone: 27 39 3192316, info@swordcane.com; Web: www.swordcane.com
Specialties: Sword canes, folders, and fixed blades. **Patterns:** 440C and carbon steel blades. **Technical:** Double hollow ground and Poniard-style blades. **Prices:** $300 to $3000. **Remarks:** Full-time maker with son, Barry, since 1987. Member South African Guild. **Mark:** Last name in oval pierced by a dagger.

BURGER, PON,
12 Glenwood Ave, Woodlands, Bulawayo, ZIMBABWE 75514
Specialties: Collector's items. **Patterns:** Fighters, locking folders of traditional styles, buckles. **Technical:** Scrimshaws 440C blade. Uses polished buffalo horn with brass fittings. Cased in buffalo hide book. **Prices:** $450 to $1100. **Remarks:** Full-time maker; first knife sold in 1973. Doing business as Burger Products. **Mark:** Spirit of Africa.

BURKE, BILL,
12 Chapman ln, Boise, ID 83716, Phone: 208-756-3797, burke531@salmoninternet.com
Specialties: Hand-forged working knives. Patterns: Fowler pronghorn, clip point and drop point hunters. **Technical:** Forges 52100 and 5160. Makes own Damascus from 15N20 and 1084. **Prices:** $450 and up. **Remarks:** Dedicated to fixed-blade high-performance knives. ABS Journeyman. Also makes "Ed Fowler" miniatures. **Mark:** Initials connected.

BURKE, DAN,
22001 Ole Barn Rd, Edmond, OK 73003, Phone: 405-341-3406, Fax: 405-340-3333, burkeknives@aol.com
Specialties: Slip joint folders. **Patterns:** Traditional folders. **Technical:** Grinds D2 and BG-42. Prefers natural handle materials; heat-treats. **Prices:** $440 to $1900. **Remarks:** Full-time maker; first knife sold in 1976. **Mark:** First initial and last name.

BURRIS, PATRICK R,
11078 Crystal Lynn Ct, Jacksonville, FL 32226, Phone: 904-757-3938, keenedge@comcast.net
Specialties: Traditional straight knives. **Patterns:** Hunters, Bowies, locking liner folders. **Technical:** Flat grinds CPM stainless and Damascus. **Remarks:** Offers filework, embellishment, exotic materials and Damascus **Mark:** Last name in script.

BURROWS, CHUCK,
WILD ROSE TRADING CO, 289 La Posta Canyon Rd, Durango, CO 81303, Phone: 970-259-8396, chuck@wrtcleather.com; Web: www.wrtcleather.com
Specialties: Presentation knives, hawks, and sheaths based on the styles of the American frontier incorporating carving, beadwork, rawhide, braintan, and other period correct materials. Also makes other period style knives such as Scottish Dirks and Moorish jambiyahs. **Patterns:** Bowies, Dags, tomahawks, war clubs, and all other 18th and 19th century frontier style edged weapons and tools. **Technical:** Carbon steel only: 5160, 1080/1084, 1095, O1, Damascus-Our Frontier Shear Steel, plus other styles available on request. Forged knives, hawks, etc. are made in collaborations with bladesmiths. Gib Guignard (under the name of Cactus Rose) and Mark Williams (under the name UB Forged). Blades are usually forge finished and all items are given an aged period look. **Prices:** $500 plus. **Remarks:** Full-time maker, first knife sold in 1973. 40+ years experience working leather. **Mark:** A lazy eight or lazy eight with a capital T at the center. On leather either the lazy eight with T or a WRTC makers stamp.

BURROWS, STEPHEN R,
1020 Osage St, Humboldt, KS 66748, Phone: 816-921-1573
Specialties: Fantasy straight knives of his design, to customer specs and in standard patterns; period pieces. **Patterns:** Fantasy, bird and trout knives, daggers, fighters and hunters. **Technical:** Forges 5160 and 1095 high-carbon steel, O1 and his Damascus. Offers lost wax casting in bronze or silver of cross guards and pommels. **Prices:** $65 to $600; some to $2000. **Remarks:** Full-time maker; first knife sold in 1983. Doing business as Gypsy Silk. **Mark:** Etched name.

BUSCH, STEVE,
1989 Old Town Loop, Oakland, OR 97462, Phone: 541-459-2833, steve@buschcustomknives.com; Web: wwwbuschcustomknives.blademakers.com
Specialties: D/A automatic right and left handed, folders, fixed blade working mainly in Damascus file work, functional art knives, nitrate bluing, heat bluing most all scale materials. **Prices:** $150 to $2000. **Remarks:** Trained under Vallotton family 3 1/2 years on own since 2002. **Mark:** Signature and date of completion on all knives.

BUSFIELD, JOHN,
153 Devonshire Circle, Roanoke Rapids, NC 27870, Phone: 252-537-3949, Fax: 252-537-8704, busfield@charter.net; Web: www.busfieldknives.com
Specialties: Investor-grade folders; high-grade working straight knives. **Patterns:** Original price-style and trailing-point interframe and sculpted-frame folders, drop-point hunters and semi-skinners. **Technical:** Grinds 154CM and ATS-34. Offers interframes, gold frames and inlays; uses jade, agate and lapis. **Prices:** $275 to $2000. **Remarks:** Full-time maker; first knife sold in 1979. **Mark:** Last name and address.

BUSSE, JERRY,
11651 Co Rd 12, Wauseon, OH 43567, Phone: 419-923-6471
Specialties: Working straight knives. **Patterns:** Heavy combat knives and camp knives. **Technical:** Grinds D2, A2, INFI. **Prices:** $1100 to $3500. **Remarks:** Full-time maker; first knife sold in 1983. **Mark:** Last name in logo.

BUTLER, BART,
822 Seventh St, Ramona, CA 92065, Phone: 760-789-6431

BUTLER, JOHN,
777 Tyre Rd, Havana, FL 32333, Phone: 850-539-5742
Specialties: Hunters, Bowies, period. **Technical:** Damascus, 52100, 5160, L6 steels. **Prices:** $80 and up. **Remarks:** Making knives since 1986. Journeyman (ABS). **Mark:** JB.

BUTLER, JOHN R,
20162 6th Ave N E, Shoreline, WA 98155, Phone: 206-362-3847, rjjjrb@sprynet.com

BUXTON, BILL,
155 Oak Bend Rd, Kaiser, MO 65047, Phone: 573-348-3577, camper@yhti.net; Web: www.geocities.com/buxtonknives
Specialties: Forged fancy and working straight knives and folders. Mostly one-of-a-kind pieces. **Patterns:** Fighters, daggers, Bowies, hunters, linerlock folders, axes and tomahawks. **Technical:** Forges 52100, 0-1,

1080. Makes own Damascus (mosaic and random patterns) from 1080, 1095, 15n20, and powdered metals 1084 and 4800a. Offers sterling silver inlay, n/s pin patterning and pewter pouring on axe and hawk handles. **Prices:** $300 to $1500. **Remarks:** Full-time maker, sold first knife in 1998. **Mark:** First and last name.

BYBEE, BARRY J,
795 Lock Rd. E, Cadiz, KY 42211-8615
Specialties: Working straight knives of his design. **Patterns:** Hunters, fighters, boot knives, tantos and Bowies. **Technical:** Grinds ATS-34, 440C. Likes stag and Micarta for handle materials. **Prices:** $125 to $200; some to $1000. **Remarks:** Part-time maker; first knife sold in 1968. **Mark:** Arrowhead logo with name, city and state.

BYRD, WESLEY L,
189 Countryside Dr, Evensville, TN 37332, Phone: 423-775-3826, w.l.byrd@worldnet.att.net
Specialties: Hunters, fighters, Bowies, dirks, sgian dubh, utility, and camp knives. **Patterns:** Wire rope, random patterns. Twists, W's, Ladder, Kite Tail. **Technical:** Uses 52100, 1084, 5160, L6, and 15n20. **Prices:** Starting at $180. **Remarks:** Prefer to work with customer for their design preferences. ABS Journeyman Smith. **Mark:** BYRD, WB <X.

C

CABE, JERRY (BUDDY),
62 McClaren Ln, Hattieville, AR 72063, Phone: 501-354-3581

CABRERA, SERGIO B,
24500 Broad Ave, Wilmington, CA 90744

CAFFREY, EDWARD J,
2608 Central Ave West, Great Falls, MT 59404, Phone: 406-727-9102, ed@caffreyknives.net; Web: www.caffreyknives.net
Specialties: One-of-a-kind using and collector quality pieces. Will accept some customer designs. **Patterns:** Bowies, folders, hunters, fighters, camp/utility, tomahawks and hatchets. **Technical:** Forges all types of Damascus, specializing in Mosaic Damascus, 52100, 5160, 1080/1084 and most other commonly forged steels. Offers S30V for those who demand stainless. **Prices:** Starting at $165; typical hunters start at $375; Collector pieces can range into the thousands. **Remarks:** Offers one-on-one basic and advanced bladesmithing classes. ABS Mastersmith. Full-time maker. **Mark:** Stamped last name and MS on straight knives. Etched last name with MS on folders.

CAIRNES JR., CARROLL B,
Rt. 1 Box 324, Palacios, TX 77465, Phone: 369-588-6815

CALDWELL, BILL,
255 Rebecca, West Monroe, LA 71292, Phone: 318-323-3025
Specialties: Straight knives and folders with machined bolsters and liners. **Patterns:** Fighters, Bowies, survival knives, tomahawks, razors and push knives. **Technical:** Owns and operates a very large, well-equipped blacksmith and bladesmith shop with six large forges and eight power hammers. **Prices:** $400 to $3500; some to $10,000. **Remarks:** Full-time maker and self-styled blacksmith; first knife sold in 1962. **Mark:** Wild Bill and Sons.

CALLAHAN, ERRETT,
2 Fredonia, Lynchburg, VA 24503, Phone: 434-528-3444
Specialties: Obsidian knives. **Patterns:** Modern-styles and Stone Age replicas. **Technical:** Flakes and knaps to order. **Prices:** $100 to $3400. **Remarks:** Part-time maker; first flint blades sold in 1974. **Mark:** Blade— engraved name, year and arrow; handle—signed edition, year and unit number.

CALLAHAN, F TERRY,
PO Box 880, Boerne, TX 78006, Phone: 830-981-8274, Fax: 830-981-8279, ftclaw@gvtc.com
Specialties: Custom hand-forged edged knives, collectible and functional. **Patterns:** Bowies, folders, daggers, hunters & camp knives . **Technical:** Forges 5160, 1095 and his own Damascus. Offers filework and handmade sheaths. **Prices:** $125 to $2000. **Remarks:** First knife sold in 1990. ABS/Journeyman Bladesmith. **Mark:** Initials inside a keystone symbol.

CALVERT JR., ROBERT W (BOB),
911 Julia, PO Box 858, Rayville, LA 71269, Phone: 318-728-4113, Fax: (318) 728-0000, rcalvert@fredmorganins.com
Specialties: Using and hunting knives; your design or his. Since 1990. **Patterns:** Forges own Damascus; all patterns. **Technical:** 5160, D2, 52100, 1084. Prefers natural handle material. **Prices:** $250 and up. **Remarks:** TOMB Member ABS, Journeyman Smith. Board of directors-ABS.**Mark:** Calvert (Block) J S.

CAMERER, CRAIG,
3766 Rockbridge Rd, Chesterfield, IL 62630, Phone: 618-753-2147, craig@camererknives.com; Web: www.camererknives.com
Specialties: Everyday carry knives, hunters and Bowies. Patterns: D-guard, historical recreations and fighters. **Technical:** Most of his knives are forged to shape. **Prices:** $100 and up. **Remarks:** Member of the ABS and PKA. Journeymen Smith ABS.

CAMERON, RON G,
PO Box 183, Logandale, NV 89021, Phone: 702-398-3356, rntcameron@mvdsl.com
Specialties: Fancy and embellished working/using straight knives and folders of his design. **Patterns:** Bowies, hunters and utility/camp knives. **Technical:** Grinds ATS-34, AEB-L and Devin Thomas Damascus or own Damascus from 1084 and 15N20. Does filework, fancy pins, mokume fittings. Uses exotic hardwoods, stag and Micarta for handles. Pearl & mammoth ivory. **Prices:** $175 to $850 some to $1000. **Remarks:** Part-time maker; first knife sold in 1994. Doing business as Cameron Handmade Knives. **Mark:** Last name, town, state or last name.

CAMERON HOUSE,
2001 Delaney Rd Se, Salem, OR 97306, Phone: 503-585-3286
Specialties: Working straight knives. **Patterns:** Hunters, Bowies, fighters. **Technical:** Grinds ATS-34, 530V, 154CM. **Remarks:** Part-time maker, first knife sold in 1993. **Prices:** $150 and up. **Mark:** HOUSE.

CAMPBELL, COURTNAY M,
PO Box 23009, Columbia, SC 29224, Phone: 803-787-0151

CAMPBELL, DICK,
196 Graham Rd, Colville, WA 99114, Phone: 509-684-6080, dicksknives@aol.com
Specialties: Working straight knives, folders & period pieces. **Patterns:** Hunters, fighters, boots: 19th century Bowies, Japanese swords and daggers. **Technical:** Grinds 440C, 154CM. **Prices:** $200 to $2500. **Remarks:** Full-time maker. First knife sold in 1975. **Mark:** Name.

CAMPOS, IVAN,
R.XI de Agosto 107, Tatui, SP, BRAZIL 18270-000, Phone: 00-55-15-2518092, Fax: 00-55-15-2594368, ivan@ivancampos.com; Web: www.ivancampos.com
Specialties: Brazilian handmade and antique knives.

CANDRELLA, JOE,
1219 Barness Dr, Warminster, PA 18974, Phone: 215-675-0143
Specialties: Working straight knives, some fancy. **Patterns:** Daggers, boots, Bowies. **Technical:** Grinds 440C and 154CM. **Prices:** $100 to $200; some to $1000. **Remarks:** Part-time maker; first knife sold in 1985. Does business as Franjo. **Mark:** FRANJO with knife as J.

CANNADY, DANIEL L,
Box 301, 358 Parkwood Terrace, Allendale, SC 29810, Phone: 803-584-2813, Fax: 803-584-2813
Specialties: Working straight knives and folders in standard patterns. **Patterns:** Drop-point hunters, Bowies, skinners, fishing knives with concave grind, steak knives and kitchen cutlery. **Technical:** Grinds D2, 440C and ATS-34. **Prices:** $65 to $325; some to $1000. **Remarks:** Full-time maker; first knife sold in 1980. **Mark:** Last name above Allendale, S.C.

CANNON, RAYMOND W,
PO Box 1412, Homer, AK 99603, Phone: 907-235-7779, Web: www.cannon@xyz.net
Specialties: Fancy working knives, folders and swords of his design or to customer specs; many one-of-a-kind pieces. **Patterns:** Bowies, daggers and skinners. **Technical:** Forges & grinds O1, A6, 52100, 5160, 1050, 1084 and his own combinations for Damascus. **Remarks:** First knife sold in 1984. **Mark:** Cannon Alaska or "Hand forged by Wes Cannon."

CANOY, ANDREW B,
3420 Fruchey Ranch Rd, Hubbard Lake, MI 49747, Phone: 810-266-6039, canoy1@shianet.org

CANTER, RONALD E,
96 Bon Air Circle, Jackson, TN 38305, Phone: 731-668-1780, canterr@charter.net
Specialties: Traditional working knives to customer specs. **Patterns:** Beavertail skinners, Bowies, hand axes and folding lockers. **Technical:** Grinds 440C, Micarta & deer antler. **Prices:** $75 and up. **Remarks:** Spare-time maker; first knife sold in 1973. **Mark:** Three last initials intertwined.

CANTRELL, KITTY D,
19720 Hwy 78, Ramona, CA 92076, Phone: 760-788-8304

CAPDEPON, RANDY,
553 Joli Rd, Carencro, LA 70520, Phone: 318-896-4113, Fax: 318-896-8753
Specialties: Straight knives and folders of his design. **Patterns:** Hunters and locking folders. **Technical:** Grinds ATS-34, 440C and D2. **Prices:** $200 to $600. **Remarks:** Part-time maker; first knife made in 1992. Doing business as Capdepon Knives. **Mark:** Last name.

CAPDEPON, ROBERT,
829 Vatican Rd, Carencro, LA 70520, Phone: 337-896-8753, Fax: 318-896-8753
Specialties: Traditional straight knives and folders of his design. **Patterns:** Boots, hunters and locking folders. **Technical:** Grinds ATS-34, 440C and D2. Hand-rubbed finish on blades. Likes natural horn materials for handles, including ivory. Offers engraving. **Prices:** $250 to $750. **Remarks:** Full-time maker; first knife made in 1992. **Mark:** Last name.

CARLISLE, JEFF,
PO Box 282 12753 Hwy 200, Simms, MT 59477, Phone: 406-264-5693

CARLSON, KELLY,
54 S Holt Hill, Antrim, NH 03440, Phone: 603-588-2765, kellycarlson@tds.net; Web: www.carlsonknives.com
Specialties: Unique folders of maker's own design. **Patterns:** One-of-a-kind, artistic folders, mostly of liner-lock design, along with interpretations of traditional designs. **Technical:** Grinds and heat treats S30V, D2, ATS-34, stainless and carbon Damascus steels. Prefers hand sanded finishes and natural ivories and pearls, in conjunction with decorative accents obtained from mosaic Damascus, Damascus and various exotic materials. **Prices:** $600 to $3500. **Remarks:** Full-time maker as of 2002, first knife sold in 1975. New mechanism designs include assisted openers, top locks, and galvanic slipjoints powered by neodymium magnets, patent pending.

CAROLINA CUSTOM KNIVES, SEE TOMMY MCNABB,

CARPENTER, RONALD W,
Rt. 4 Box 323, Jasper, TX 75951, Phone: 409-384-4087

CARR, TIM,
3660 Pillon Rd, Muskegon, MI 49445, Phone: 231-766-3582
Specialties: Hunters, camp knives. **Patterns:** His or yours. **Technical:** Hand forges 5160, 52100 and Damascus. **Prices:** $125 to $700. **Remarks:** Part-time maker. **Mark:** The letter combined from maker's initials TRC.

CARRILLO, DWAINE,
C/O AIRKAT KNIVES, 1021 SW 15th St, Moore, OK 73160, Phone: 405-503-5879, Web: www.airkatknives.com

CARROLL, CHAD,
12182 McClelland, Grant, MI 49327, Phone: 231-834-9183, CHAD724@msn.com
Specialties: Hunters, Bowies, folders, swords, tomahawks. **Patterns:** Fixed blades, folders. **Prices:** $100 to $2000. **Remarks:** ABS Journeyman May 2002. **Mark:** A backwards C next to a forward C, maker's initials.

CARSON, HAROLD J "KIT",
1076 Brizendine Lane, Vine Grove, KY 40175, Phone: 270 877-6300, Fax: 270 877 6338, KCKnives@bbtel.com; Web: http://ww.kvnet.org/knives; album-www.kitcarsonknives.com/album
Specialties: Military fixed blades and folders; art pieces. **Patterns:** Fighters, D handles, daggers, combat folders and Crosslock-styles, tactical folders, tactical fixed blades. **Technical:** Grinds Stellite 6K, Talonite, CPM steels, Damascus. **Prices:** $400 to $750; some to $5000. **Remarks:** Full-time maker; first knife sold in 1973. **Mark:** Name stamped or engraved.

CARTER, FRED,
5219 Deer Creek Rd, Wichita Falls, TX 76302, Phone: 904-723-4020
Specialties: High-art investor-class straight knives; some working hunters and fighters. **Patterns:** Classic daggers, Bowies; interframe, stainless and blued steel folders with gold inlay. **Technical:** Grinds a variety of steels. Uses no glue or solder. Engraves and inlays. **Prices:** Generally upscale. **Remarks:** Full-time maker. **Mark:** Signature in oval logo.

CARTER, MURRAY M,
PO Box 307, Vernonia, OR 97064, Phone: 503-429-0447, murray@cartercutlery.com; Web:www.cartercutlery.com
Specialties: Traditional Japanese cutlery, utilizing San soh ko (three layer) or Kata-ha (two layer) blade construction. Laminated neck knives, traditional Japanese etc. **Patterns:** Works from over 200 standard Japanese and North American designs. **Technical:** Hot forges and cold forges Hitachi white steel #1, Hitachi blue super steel exclusively. **Prices:** $100 to $3000. **Remarks:** Full-time Bladesmith. First knife sold in 1989. **Mark:** Name in cursive, often appearing with Japanese characters. **Other:** Very interestng and informative monthly newsletter.

CASHEN, KEVIN R,
5615 Tyler St, Hubbardston, MI 48845, Phone: 989-981-6780, kevin@cashenblades.com; Web: www.cashenblades.com
Specialties: Working straight knives, high art pattern welded swords, traditional renaissance and ethnic pieces. **Patterns:** Hunters, Bowies, utility knives, swords, daggers. **Technical:** Forges 1095, 1084 and his own O1/ L6 Damascus. **Prices:** $100 to $4000+. **Remarks:** Full-time maker; first knife sold in 1985. Doing business as Matherton Forge. **Mark:** Black letter Old English initials and Master Smith stamp.

CASTEEL, DIANNA,
PO Box 63, Monteagle, TN 37356, Phone: 931-212-4341, ddcasteel@charter.net; Web: www.casteelcustomknives.com
Specialties: Small, delicate daggers and miniatures; most knives one-of-a-kind. **Patterns:** Daggers, boot knives, fighters and miniatures. **Technical:** Grinds 440C. Offers stainless Damascus. **Prices:** Start at $350; miniatures start at $250. **Remarks:** Full-time maker. **Mark:** Di in script.

CASTEEL, DOUGLAS,
PO Box 63, Monteagle, TN 37356, Phone: 931-212-4341, Fax: 931-723-1856, ddcasteel@charter.net; Web: www.casteelcustomknives.com
Specialties: One-of-a-kind collector-class period pieces. **Patterns:** Daggers, Bowies, swords and folders. **Technical:** Grinds 440C. Offers gold and silver castings.Offers stainless Damascus **Prices:** Upscale. **Remarks:** Full-time maker; first knife sold in 1982. **Mark:** Last name.

CASTELLUCIO, RICH,
220 Stairs Rd, Amsterdam, NY 12010, Phone: 518-843-5540, rcastellucio@nycap.rr.com
Patterns: Bowies, push daggers, and fantasy knives. **Technical:** Uses ATS-34, 440C, 154CM. I use stabilized wood, bone for the handles. Guards are made of copper, brass, stainless, nickle, and mokume.

CASTON, DARRIEL,
3725 Duran Circle, Sacramento, CA 95821, Phone: 916-359-0613, dcaston@surewest.net
Specialties: Investment grade jade handle folders of his design and gentleman folders. **Patterns:** Folders: slipjoints and lockback. Will be making linerlocks in the near future. **Technical:** Small gentleman folders for office and desk warriors. Grinds ATS-34, 154CM, S30V and Damascus. **Prices:** $250 to $900. **Remarks:** Part-time maker; won best new maker at first show in Sept 2004. **Mark:** Etched rocket ship with "Darriel Caston" or just "Caston" on inside spring on Damascus and engraved knives.

CASWELL, JOE,
173 S Ventu Park Rd, Newbury, CA 91320, Phone: 805-499-0707, Web:www.caswellknives.com
Specialties: Historic pattern welded knives and swords, hand forged. Also high precision folding and fixed blade "gentleman" and "tactical" knives of his design, period firearms. Inventor of the "In-Line" retractable pocket clip for folding knives. **Patterns:**Hunters, tactical/utility, fighters, bowies, daggers, pattern welded medieval swords, precision folders. **Technical:**Forges own Damascus especially historic forms. Sometimes uses modern stainless steels and Damascus of other makers. Makes some pieces entirely by hand, others using the latest CNC techniques and by hand. Makes sheaths too.**Prices:**$100-$5,500. **Remarks:**Full time makers since 1995. Making mostly historic recreations for exclusive clientele. Recently moving into folding knives and 'modern' designs. **Mark:**CASWELL or CASWELL USA Accompanied by a mounted knight logo.

CATOE, DAVID R,
4024 Heutte Dr, Norfolk, VA 23518, Phone: 757-480-3191
Technical: Does own forging, Damascus and heat treatments. **Price:** $200 to $500; some higher. **Remarks:** Part-time maker; trained by Dan Maragni 1985-1988; first knife sold 1989. **Mark:** Leaf of a camellia.

CAWTHORNE, CHRISTOPHER A,
PO Box 604, Wrangell, AK 99929
Specialties: High-carbon steel, cable wire rope, silver wire inlay. **Patterns:** Forge welded Damascus and wire rope, random pattern. **Technical:** Hand forged, 50 lb. little giant power hammer, W-2, 0-1, L6, 1095. **Prices:** $650 to $2500. **Remarks:** School ABS 1985 w/Bill Moran, hand forged, heat treat. **Mark:** Cawthorne, forged in stamp.

CENTOFANTE, FRANK,
PO Box 928, Madisonville, TN 37354-0928, Phone: 423-442-5767, Fax: 423-420-0871, frankcentofante@bellsouth.net
Specialties: Fancy working folders. **Patterns:** Lockers and liner locks. **Technical:** Grinds ATS-34 and CPM154; hand-rubbed satin finish on blades. **Prices:** $600 to $1200. **Remarks:** Full-time maker; first knife sold in 1968. **Mark:** Name, city, state.

CHAFFEE, JEFF L,
14314 N. Washington St, PO Box 1, Morris, IN 47033, Phone: 812-934-6350
Specialties: Fancy working and utility folders and straight knives. **Patterns:** Fighters, dagger, hunter and locking folders. **Technical:** Grinds commercial Damascus, 440C, ATS-34, D2 and O1. Prefers natural handle materials. **Prices:** $350 to $2000. **Remarks:** Part-time maker; first knife sold in 1988. **Mark:** Last name.

CHAMBERLAIN, CHARLES R,
PO Box 156, Barren Springs, VA 24313-0156, Phone: 703-381-5137

CHAMBERLAIN, JON A,
15 S. Lombard, E. Wenatchee, WA 98802, Phone: 509-884-6591
Specialties: Working and kitchen knives to customer specs; exotics on special order. **Patterns:** Over 100 patterns in stock. **Technical:** Prefers ATS-34, D2, L6 and Damascus. **Prices:** Start at $50. **Remarks:** First knife sold in 1986. Doing business as Johnny Custom Knifemakers. **Mark:** Name in oval with city and state enclosing.

CHAMBERLIN, JOHN A,
11535 Our Rd., Anchorage, AK 99516, Phone: 907-346-1524, Fax: 907-562-4583
Specialties: Art and working knives. Patterns: Daggers and hunters; some folders. **Technical:** Grinds ATS-34, 440C, A2, D2 and Damascus. Uses Alaskan handle materials such as oosic, jade, whale jawbone,

fossil ivory. **Prices:** Start at $150. **Remarks:** Does own heat treating and cryogenic deep freeze. Full-time maker; first knife sold in 1984. **Mark:** Name over English shield and dagger.

CHAMBLIN, JOEL,
960 New Hebron Church Rd, Concord, GA 30206, Phone: 770-884-9055, Web: chamblinknives.com
Specialties: Fancy and working folders. **Patterns:** Fancy locking folders, traditional, multi-blades and utility. **Technical:** Grinds ATS-34, 440V, BG-42 and commercial Damascus. Offers filework. **Prices:** Start at $300. **Remarks:** Full-time maker; first knife sold in 1989. **Mark:** Last name.

CHAMPION, ROBERT,
1806 Plateau Ln, Amarillo, TX 79106, Phone: 806-359-0446, championknives@arn.net
Specialties: Traditional working straight knives. **Patterns:** Hunters, skinners, camp knives, Bowies, daggers. **Technical:** Grinds 440C and D2. **Prices:** $100 to $600. **Remarks:** Part-time maker; first knife sold in 1979. Stream-line hunters. **Mark:** Last name with dagger logo, city and state.

CHAPO, WILLIAM G,
45 Wildridge Rd, Wilton, CT 06897, Phone: 203-544-9424
Specialties: Classic straight knives and folders of his design and to customer specs; period pieces. **Patterns:** Boots, Bowies and locking folders. **Technical:** Forges stainless Damascus. Offers filework. **Prices:** $750 and up. **Remarks:** Full-time maker; first knife sold in 1989. **Mark:** First and middle initials, last name, city, state.

CHARD, GORDON R,
104 S. Holiday Lane, Iola, KS 66749, Phone: 620-365-2311, Fax: 620-365-2311, gchard@cox.net
Specialties: High tech folding knives in one-of-a-kind styles. **Patterns:** Liner locking folders of own design. Also fixed blade Art Knives. **Technical:** Clean work with attention to fit and finish. Blade steel mostly ATS-34 and 154CM, some CPM440V Vaso Wear and Damascus. **Prices:** $150 to $2500. **Remarks:** First knife sold in 1983. **Mark:** Name, city and state surrounded by wheat on each side.

CHASE, ALEX,
208 E. Pennsylvania Ave., DeLand, FL 32724, Phone: 386-734-9918, chase8578@bellsouth.net
Specialties: Historical steels, classic and traditional straight knives of his design and to customer specs. **Patterns:** Art, fighters, hunters and Japanese style. **Technical:** Forges O1-L6 Damascus, meteoric Damascus, 52100, 5160; uses fossil walrus and mastodon ivory etc. **Prices:** $150 to $1000; some to $3500. **Remarks:** Full-time maker; Guild member since 1996. Doing business as Confederate Forge. **Mark:** Stylized initials-A.C.

CHASE, JOHN E,
217 Walnut, Aledo, TX 76008, Phone: 817-441-8331, jchaseknives@sbcglobal.net
Specialties: Straight high-tech working knives in standard patterns or to customer specs. **Patterns:** Hunters, fighters, daggers and Bowies. **Technical:** Grinds D2, O1, 440C; offers mostly satin finishes. **Prices:** Start at $265. **Remarks:** Part-time maker; first knife sold in 1974. **Mark:** Last name in logo.

CHAUVIN, JOHN,
200 Anna St, Scott, LA 70583, Phone: 337-237-6138, Fax: 337-230-7980
Specialties: Traditional working and using straight knives of his design, to customer specs and in standard patterns. **Patterns:** Bowies, fighters, and hunters. **Technical:** Grinds ATS-34, 440C and O1 high-carbon. Paul Bos heat treating. Uses ivory, stag, oosic and stabilized Louisiana swamp maple for handle materials. Makes sheaths using alligator and ostrich. **Prices:** $200 and up. Bowies start at $500. **Remarks:** Part-time maker; first knife sold in 1995. **Mark:** Full name, city, state.

CHAUZY, ALAIN,
1 Rue de Paris, 21140 Seur-en-Auxios, FRANCE, Phone: 03-80-97-03-30, Fax: 03-80-97-34-14
Specialties: Fixed blades, folders, hunters, Bowies-scagel-style. **Technical:** Forged blades only. Steels used XC65, 07C, and own Damascus. **Prices:** Contact maker for quote. **Remarks:** Part-time maker. **Mark:** Number 2 crossed by an arrow and name.

CHAVAR, EDWARD V,
1830 Richmond Ave, Bethlehem, PA 18018, Phone: 610-865-1806
Specialties: Working straight knives to his or customer design specifications, folders, high art pieces and some forged pieces. **Patterns:** Fighters, hunters, tactical, straight and folding knives and high art straight and folding knives for collectors. **Technical:** Grinds ATS-34, 440C, L6, Damascus from various makers and uses Damascus steel and mokume of his own creation. **Prices:** Standard models range from $95 to $1500, custom and specialty up to $3000. **Remarks:** Full-time maker; first knife sold in 1990. **Mark:** Name, city, state or signature.

CHEATHAM, BILL,
PO Box 636, Laveen, AZ 85339, Phone: 602-237-2786, blademan76@aol.com
Specialties: Working straight knives and folders. Patterns: Hunters, fighters, boots and axes; locking folders. **Technical:** Grinds 440C. **Prices:** $150 to $350; exceptional knives to $600. **Remarks:** Full-time maker; first knife sold in 1976. **Mark:** Name, city, state.

CHERRY, FRANK J,
3412 Tiley N.E., Albuquerque, NM 87110, Phone: 505-883-8643

CHEW, LARRY,
515 Cleveland Rd Unit A-9, Granbury, TX 76049, Phone: 817-573-8035, chewman@swbell.net; Web: www.voodooinside.com
Specialties: High-tech folding knives. **Patterns:** Double action automatic and manual folding patterns of his design. **Technical:** CAD designed folders utilizing roller bearing pivot design known as "VooDoo." Double action automatic folders with a variety of obvious and disguised release mechanisms, some with lock-outs. **Prices:** Manual folders start at $475, double action autos start at $750. **Remarks:** Made and sold first knife in 1988, first folder in 1989. Full-time maker since 1997. **Mark:** Name and location etched in blade, Damascus autos marked on spring inside frame. Earliest knives stamped LC.

CHOATE, MILTON,
1665 W. County 17-1/2, Somerton, AZ 85350, Phone: 928-627-7251, mccustom@juno.com
Specialties: Classic working and using straight knives of his design, to customer specs and in standard patterns. **Patterns:** Bowies, hunters and utility/camp knives. **Technical:** Grinds 440C; grinds and forges 1095 and 5160. Does filework on top and guards on request. **Prices:** $200 to $800. **Remarks:** Full-time maker, first knife made in 1990. All knives come with handmade sheaths by Judy Choate. **Mark:** Knives marked "Choate."

CHRISTENSEN, JON P,
7814 Spear Dr, Shepherd, MT 59079, Phone: 406-373-0253, jbchris@aol.com; Web: www.jonchristensenknives.com
Specialties: Patch knives, hunter/utility knives, Bowies, tomahawks. **Technical:** All blades forged, does all own work including sheaths. Forges O1, 1084, 52100, 5160. Damascus from 1084/15N20. **Prices:** $220 and up. **Remarks:** ABS Mastersmith, first knife sold in 1999. **Mark:** First and middle initial surrounded by last initial.

CHURCHMAN, T W (TIM),
475 Saddle Horn Drive, Bandera, TX 78003, Phone: 830-796-8350
Specialties: Fancy and traditional straight knives and single blade liner locking folders. Bird/trout knives of his design and to customer specs. **Patterns:** Bird/trout knives, fillet, Bowies, daggers, fighters, boot knives, some miniatures. **Technical:** Grinds 440C, D2 and 154CM. Offers stainless fittings, fancy filework, exotic and stabilized woods and hand sewed lined sheaths. Also flower pins as a style. **Prices:** $80 to $650; some to $1500. **Remarks:** Part-time maker; first knife made in 1981 after reading *"KNIVES '81."* Doing business as "Custom Knives Churchman Made." **Mark:** Last name, dagger.

CLAIBORNE, JEFF,
1470 Roberts Rd, Franklin, IN 46131, Phone: 317-736-7443, jeff@claiborneknives.com; Web: www.claiborneknives.com
Specialties: Multi blade slip joint folders. All one-of-a-kind by hand, no jigs or fixtures, swords, straight knives, period pieces, camp knives, hunters, fighters, ethnic swords all periods. Handle: uses stag, pearl, oosic, bone ivory, mastadon-mammoth, elephant or exotic woods. **Technical:** Forges high-carbon steel, makes Damascus, forges cable grinds, O1, 1095, 5160, 52100, L6. **Prices:** $250 and up. **Remarks:** Part-time maker; first knife sold in 1989. **Mark:** Stylized initials in an oval.

CLAIBORNE, RON,
2918 Ellistown Rd, Knox, TN 37924, Phone: 615-524-2054, Bowie@icy.net
Specialties: Multi-blade slip joints, swords, straight knives. **Patterns:** Hunters, daggers, folders. **Technical:** Forges Damascus: mosaic, powder mosaic. Prefers bone and natural handle materials; some exotic woods. **Prices:** $125 to $2500. **Remarks:** Part-time maker; first knife sold in 1979. Doing business as Thunder Mountain Forge Claiborne Knives. **Mark:** Claiborne.

CLARK, D E (LUCKY),
413 Lyman Lane, Johnstown, PA 15909-1409
Specialties: Working straight knives and folders to customer specs. **Patterns:** Customer designs. **Technical:** Grinds D2, 440C, 154CM. **Prices:** $100 to $200; some higher. **Remarks:** Part-time maker; first knife sold in 1975. **Mark:** Name on one side; "Lucky" on other.

CLARK, HOWARD F,
115 35th Pl, Runnells, IA 50237, Phone: 515-966-2126, howard@mvforge.com; Web: mvforge.com
Specialties: Currently Japanese-style swords. **Patterns:** Katana. **Technical:** Forges L6 and 1086. **Prices:** $1200 to 5000. **Remarks:** Full-time maker; first knife sold in 1979. Doing business as Morgan Valley Forge. **Prior Mark:** Block letters and serial number on folders; anvil/initials logo on straight knives. **Current Mark:** Two character kanji "Big Ear."

CLARK, NATE,
604 Baird Dr, Yoncalla, OR 97499, nateclarkknives@hotmail.com; Web: www.nateclarkknives.com
Specialties: Automatics (push button and hidden release) ATS-34 mirror polish or satin finish, Damascus, pearl, ivory, abalone, woods, bone,

Micarta, G-10, filework and carving and sheath knives. **Prices:** $100 to $2500. **Remarks:** Full-time knifemaker since 1996. **Mark:** Nate Clark on spring, spacer or blade.

CLARK, R W,
R.W. CLARK CUSTOM KNIVES, 1069 Golden Meadow, Corona, CA 92882, Phone: 909-279-3494, Fax: 909-279-4394, info@rwclarkknives.com; Web: www.rwclarkknives.com
Specialties: Military field knives and Asian hybrids. Hand carved leather sheaths. **Patterns:** Fixed blade hunters, field utility and military. Also presentation and collector grade knives. **Technical:** First maker to use liquid metals LM1 material in knives. Other materials include S30V, O1, stainless and carbon Damascus. **Prices:** $75 to $2000. Average price $300. **Remarks:** Started knifemaking in 1990, full-time in 2000. **Mark:** R.W. Clark, Custom, Corona, CA in standard football shape. Also uses three Japanese characters, spelling Clark, on Asian Hybrids.

CLAY, J D,
65 Ellijay Rd, Greenup, KY 41144, Phone: 606-473-6769, Web: wwwaawc.net-photogallery
Specialties: Long known for cleanly finished, collector quality knives of functional design. **Patterns:** Practical hunters in field and collector grade. **Technical:** Grinds 440C, high mirror finishes. **Prices:** Start at $145. **Remarks:** Full-time maker; first knife sold in 1972. **Mark:** Name stamp in script on blade.

CLAY, WAYNE,
Box 125B, Pelham, TN 37366, Phone: 931-467-3472, Fax: 931-467-3076
Specialties: Working straight knives and folders in standard patterns. **Patterns:** Hunters and kitchen knives; gents and hunter patterns. **Technical:** Grinds ATS-34. **Prices:** $125 to $500; some to $1000. **Remarks:** Full-time maker; first knife sold in 1978. **Mark:** Name.

COATS, KEN,
317 5th Ave, Stevens Point, WI 54481, Phone: 715-544-0115, kandk_c@charter.net
Technical: Grinds ATS-34, 440C. Stainless blades and backsprings. Does all own heat treating and freeze cycle. Blades are drawn to 60RC. Nickel silver or brass bolsters on folders are soldered, neutralized and pinned. Handles are jigged bone, hardwoods antler, and Micarta. Cuts and jigs own bone, usually shades of brown or green.

COCKERHAM, LLOYD,
1717 Carolyn Ave, Denham Springs, IA 70726, Phone: 225-665-1565

COFFEY, BILL,
68 Joshua Ave, Clovis, CA 93611, Phone: 559-299-4259
Specialties: Working and fancy straight knives and folders of his design. **Patterns:** Hunters, fighters, utility, LinerLock® folders and fantasy knives. **Technical:** Grinds 440C, ATS-34, A-Z and commercial Damascus. **Prices:** $250 to $1000; some to $2500. **Remarks:** Full-time maker. First knife sold in 1993. **Mark:** First and last name, city, state.

COFFMAN, DANNY,
541 Angel Dr S, Jacksonville, AL 36265-5787, Phone: 256-435-1619
Specialties: Straight knives and folders of his design. Now making liner locks for $650 to $1200 with natural handles and contrasting Damascus blades and bolsters. **Patterns:** Hunters, locking and slip-joint folders. **Technical:** Grinds Damascus, 440C and D2. Offers filework and engraving. **Prices:** $100 to $400; some to $800. **Remarks:** Spare-time maker; first knife sold in 1992. Doing business as Customs by Coffman. **Mark:** Last name stamped or engraved.

COHEN, N J (NORM),
2408 Sugarcone Rd, Baltimore, MD 21209, Phone: 410-998-2768, njcohen@verizon.net; Web:www.njcknives.com
Specialties: Working class knives. **Patterns:** Hunters, skinners, bird knives, push daggers, boots, kitchen and practical customer designs. **Technical:** Stock removal 440C, ATS-34. Uses Micarta, Corian. Some woods in handles. **Prices:** $50 to $250. **Remarks:** Part-time maker; first knife sold in 1982. **Mark:** Etched initials or NJC MAKER.

COHEN, TERRY A,
PO Box 406, Laytonville, CA 95454
Specialties: Working straight knives and folders. **Patterns:** Bowies to boot knives and locking folders; mini-boot knives. **Technical:** Grinds stainless; hand rubs; tries for good balance. **Prices:** $85 to $150; some to $325. **Remarks:** Part-time maker; first knife sold in 1983. **Mark:** TERRY KNIVES, city and state.

COIL, JIMMIE J,
2936 Asbury Pl, Owensboro, KY 42303, Phone: 270-684-7827
Specialties: Traditional working and straight knives of his design. **Patterns:** Hunters, Bowies and fighters. **Technical:** Grinds 440C, ATS-34 and D2. Blades are flat-ground with brush finish; most have tapered tang. Offers filework. **Prices:** $65 to $250; some to $750. **Remarks:** Spare-time maker; first knife sold in 1974. **Mark:** Name.

COLE, DAVE,
620 Poinsetta Dr, Satellite Beach, FL 32937, Phone: 321-773-1687
Specialties: Fixed blades and friction folders of his design or customers. Patterns: Utility, hunters, and Bowies. **Technical:** Grinds O1, 1095. 440C stainless Damascus; prefers natural handle materials, handmade sheaths. **Prices:** $100 and up. **Remarks:** Part-time maker, member of FKA; first knife sold in 1991. **Mark:** D Cole.

COLE, JAMES M,
505 Stonewood Blvd, Bartonville, TX 76226, Phone: 817-430-0302, dogcole@swbell.net

COLE, WELBORN I,
365 Crystal Ct, Athens, GA 30606, Phone: 404-261-3977
Specialties: Traditional straight knives of his design. **Patterns:** Hunters. **Technical:** Grinds 440C, ATS-34 and D2. Good wood scales. **Prices:** NA. **Remarks:** Full-time maker; first knife sold in 1983. **Mark:** Script initials.

COLEMAN, JOHN A,
7233 Camel Rock Way, Citrus Heightss, CA 95610, Phone: 916-335-1568
Specialties: Traditional working straight knives of his design or yours. **Patterns:** Plain to fancy file back working knives hunters, bird, trout, camp knives, skinners. Trout knives miniatures of Bowies and cappers. **Technical:** Grinds 440C, ATS-34, 145CM and D2. Exotic woods bone, antler and some ivory. **Prices:** $80 to $200, some to $450. **Remarks:** Part-time maker. First knife sold in 1989. Doing business as Slim's Custom Knives. Enjoys making knives to your specs; all knives come with handmade sheath by Slim's Leather. **Mark:** Cowboy setting on log whittling Slim's Custom Knives above cowboy and name and state under cowboy.

COLEMAN, KEITH E,
5001 Starfire Pl NW, Albuquerque, NM 87120-2010, Phone: 505-899-3783, keith@kecenterprises.com; Web: kecenterprises.com
Specialties: Affordable collector-grade straight knives and folders; some fancy. **Patterns:** Fighters, tantos, combat folders, gents folders and boots. **Technical:** Grinds ATS-34 and Damascus. Prefers specialty woods; offers filework. **Prices:** $150 to $700; some to $1500. **Remarks:** Full-time maker; first knife sold in 1980. **Mark:** Name, city and state.

COLLINS, LYNN M,
138 Berkley Dr, Elyria, OH 44035, Phone: 440-366-7101
Specialties: Working straight knives. **Patterns:** Field knives, boots and fighters. **Technical:** Grinds D2, 154CM and 440C. **Prices:** Start at $150. **Remarks:** Spare-time maker; first knife sold in 1980. **Mark:** Initials, asterisks.

COLTER, WADE,
PO Box 2340, Colstrip, MT 59323, Phone: 406-748-4573
Specialties: Fancy and embellished straight knives, folders and swords of his design; historical and period pieces. **Patterns:** Bowies, swords and folders. **Technical:** Hand forges 52100 ball bearing steel and L6, 1090, cable and chain Damascus from 5N20 and 1084. Carves and makes sheaths. **Prices:** $250 to $3500. **Remarks:** Part-time maker; first knife sold in 1990. Doing business as "Colter's Hell" Forge. **Mark:** Initials on left side ricasso.

COLTRAIN, LARRY D,
PO Box 1331, Buxton, NC 27920

CONKLIN, GEORGE L,
Box 902, Ft. Benton, MT 59442, Phone: 406-622-3268, Fax: 406-622-3410, 7bbgrus@3rivers.net
Specialties: Designer and manufacturer of the "Brisket Breaker." **Patterns:** Hunters, utility/camp knives and hatchets. **Technical:** Grinds 440C, ATS-34, D2, 1095, 154CM and 5160. Offers some forging and heat-treats for others. Offers some jewelling. **Prices:** $65 to $200; some to $1000. **Remarks:** Full-time maker. Doing business as Rocky Mountain Knives. **Mark:** Last name in script.

CONLEY, BOB,
1013 Creasy Rd, Jonesboro, TN 37659, Phone: 423-753-3302
Specialties: Working straight knives and folders. **Patterns:** Lockers, two-blades, gents, hunters, traditional-styles, straight hunters. **Technical:** Grinds 440C, 154CM and ATS-34. Engraves. **Prices:** $250 to $450; some to $600. **Remarks:** Full-time maker; first knife sold in 1979. **Mark:** Full name, city, state.

CONN JR., C T,
206 Highland Ave, Attalla, AL 35954, Phone: 205-538-7688
Specialties: Working folders, some fancy. **Patterns:** Full range of folding knives. **Technical:** Grinds O2, 440C and 154CM. **Prices:** $125 to $300; some to $600. **Remarks:** Part-time maker; first knife sold in 1982. **Mark:** Name.

CONNOLLY, JAMES,
2486 Oro-Quincy Hwy, Oroville, CA 95966, Phone: 530-534-5363, rjconnolly@sbcglobal.net
Specialties: Classic working and using knives of his design. **Patterns:** Boots, Bowies, daggers and swords. **Technical:** Grinds ATS-34, BG42, A2, O1. **Prices:** $100 to $500; some to $1500. **Remarks:** Part-time maker; first knife sold in 1980. Doing business as Gold Rush Designs. **Mark:** First initial, last name, Handmade.

CONNOR, JOHN W,
PO Box 12981, Odessa, TX 79768-2981, Phone: 915-362-6901

CONNOR, MICHAEL,
Box 502, Winters, TX 79567, Phone: 915-754-5602
Specialties: Straight knives, period pieces, some folders. Patterns: Hunters to camp knives to traditional locking folders to Bowies. **Technical:** Forges 5160, O1, 1084 steels and his own Damascus. **Prices:**

Moderate to upscale. **Remarks:** Spare-time maker; first knife sold in 1974. ABS Master Smith 1983. **Mark:** Last name, M.S.

CONTI, JEFFREY D,
21104 75th St E, Bonney Lake, WA 98390, Phone: 253-447-4660, Fax: 253-512-8629
Specialties: Working straight knives. **Patterns:** Fighters and survival knives; hunters, camp knives and fishing knives. **Technical:** Grinds D2, 154CM and O1. Engraves. **Prices:** Start at $80. **Remarks:** Part-time maker; first knife sold in 1980. Does own heat treating. **Mark:** Initials, year, steel type, name and number of knife.

CONWAY, JOHN,
13301 100th Place NE, Kirkland, WA 98034, Phone: 425-823-2821, jcknives@verizon.net
Specialities: Folders; working and Damascus. Straight knives, camp, utility and fighting knives. **Patterns:** LinerLock® folders of own design. Hidden tang straight knives of own design. **Technical:** Flat grinds forged carbon steels and own Damascus steel, including mosaic. **Prices:** $300 to $850. **Remarks:** Part-time maker since 1999. **Mark:** Oval with stylized initials J C inset.

COOGAN, ROBERT,
1560 Craft Center Dr, Smithville, TN 37166, Phone: 615-597-6801, http://iweb.tntech.edu/rcoogan/
Specialties: One-of-a-kind knives. **Patterns:** Unique items like ulu-style Appalachian herb knives. **Technical:** Forges; his Damascus is made from nickel steel and W1. **Prices:** Start at $100. **Remarks:** Part-time maker; first knife sold in 1979. **Mark:** Initials or last name in script.

COOK, JAMES R,
455 Anderson Rd, Nashville, AR 71852, Phone: 870 845 5173, jr@jrcookknives.com; Web: www.jrcrookknives.com
Specialties: Working straight knives and folders of his design or to customer specs. **Patterns:** Bowies, hunters and camp knives. **Technical:** Forges 1084 and high-carbon Damascus. **Prices:** $195 to $5500. **Remarks:** Full-time maker; first knife sold in 1986. **Mark:** First and middle initials, last name.

COOK, LOUISE,
475 Robinson Ln, Ozark, IL 62972, Phone: 618-777-2932
Specialties: Working and using straight knives of her design and to customer specs; period pieces. **Patterns:** Bowies, hunters and utility/camp knives. **Technical:** Forges 5160. Filework; pin work; silver wire inlay. **Prices:** Start at $50/inch. **Remarks:** Part-time maker; first knife sold in 1990. Doing business as Panther Creek Forge. **Mark:** First name and Journeyman stamp on one side; panther head on the other.

COOK, MIKE,
475 Robinson Ln, Ozark, IL 62972, Phone: 618-777-2932
Specialties: Traditional working and using straight knives of his design and to customer specs. **Patterns:** Bowies, hunters and utility/camp knives. **Technical:** Forges 5160. Filework; pin work. **Prices:** Start at $50/ inch. **Remarks:** Spare-time maker; first knife sold in 1991. **Mark:** First initial, last name and Journeyman stamp on one side; panther head on the other.

COOK, MIKE A,
10927 Shilton Rd, Portland, MI 48875, Phone: 517-647-2518
Specialties: Fancy/embellished and period pieces of his design. **Patterns:** Daggers, fighters and hunters. **Technical:** Stone bladed knives in agate, obsidian and jasper. Scrimshaws; opal inlays. **Prices:** $60 to $300; some to $800. **Remarks:** Part-time maker; first knife sold in 1988. Doing business as Art of Ishi. **Mark:** Initials and year.

COOMBS JR., LAMONT,
546 State Rt 46, Bucksport, ME 04416, Phone: 207-469-3057, Fax: 207-469-3057, theknifemaker@hotmail.com; Web: www.knivesby.com/coomb-knives.html
Specialties: Classic fancy and embellished straight knives; traditional working and using straight knives. Knives of his design and to customer specs. **Patterns:** Hunters, folders and utility/camp knives. **Technical:** Hollow-and flat-grinds ATS-34, 440C, A2, D2 and O1; grinds Damascus from other makers. **Prices:** $100 to $500; some to $3500. **Remarks:** Full-time maker; first knife sold in 1988. **Mark:** Last name on banner, handmade underneath.

COON, RAYMOND C,
21135 S.E. Tillstrom Rd, Gresham, OR 97080, Phone: 503-658-2252, Raymond@damascusknife.com; Web: Damascusknife.com
Specialties: Working straight knives in standard patterns. **Patterns:** Hunters, Bowies, daggers, boots and axes. **Technical:** Forges high-carbon steel and Damascus or 97089. **Prices:** Start at $235. **Remarks:** Full-time maker; does own leatherwork, makes own Damascus, daggers; first knife sold in 1995. **Mark:** First initial, last name.

COPELAND, GEORGE STEVE,
220 Pat Carr Lane, Alpine, TN 38543, Phone: 931-823-5214, nifmakr@twlakes.net
Specialties: Traditional and fancy working straight knives and folders. **Patterns:** Friction folders, Congress two-and four-blade folders, button locks and one-and two-blade automatics. **Technical:** Stock removal of 440C, S300, ATS-34 and A2; heat-treats. **Prices:** $180 to $950; some higher. **Remarks:** Full-time maker; first knife sold in 1979. Doing business as Alpine Mountain Knives. **Mark:** G.S. Copeland (HANDMADE); some with four-leaf clover stamp.

COPELAND, THOM,
171 Country Line Rd S, Nashville, AR 71852, tcope@cswnet.com
Specialties: Hand forged fixed blades; hunters, Bowies and camp knives. **Remarks:** Member of ABS and AKA (Arkansas Knifemakers Association). **Mark:** Copeland.

COPPINS, DANIEL,
7303 Sherrard Rd, Cambridge, OH 43725, Phone: 740-439-4199
Specialties: Grinds 440 C, D-2. Antler handles. **Patterns:** Drop point hunters, fighters, Bowies, bird and trout daggers. **Prices:** $40 to $800. **Remarks:** Sold first knife in 2002. **Mark:** DC.

CORBY, HAROLD,
218 Brandonwood Dr, Johnson City, TN 37604, Phone: 615-926-9781
Specialties: Large fighters and Bowies; self-protection knives; art knives. Along with art knives and combat knives, Corby now has a all new automatic MO.PB1, also side lock MO LL-1 with titanium liners G-10 handles. **Patterns:** Sub-hilt fighters and hunters. **Technical:** Grinds 154CM, ATS-34 and 440C. **Prices:** $200 to $6000. **Remarks:** Full-time maker; first knife sold in 1969. Doing business as Knives by Corby. **Mark:** Last name.

CORDOVA, JOSEPH G,
PO Box 977, Peralta, NM 87042, Phone: 505-869-3912, kcordova@rt66.com
Specialties: One-of-a-kind designs, some to customer specs. **Patterns:** Fighter called the 'Gladiator', hunters, boots and cutlery. **Technical:** Forges 1095, 5160; grinds ATS-34, 440C and 154CM. **Prices:** Moderate to upscale. **Remarks:** Full-time maker; first knife sold in 1953. Past chairman of American Bladesmith Society. **Mark:** Cordova made.

CORKUM, STEVE,
34 Basehoar School Rd, Littlestown, PA 17340, Phone: 717-359-9563, sco7129849@aol.com; Web: www.hawknives.com

COSGROVE, CHARLES G,
7606 Willow Oak Ln, Arlington, TX 76001, Phone: 817-472-6505, charles.barchar@gmail.com
Specialties: Traditional fixed or locking blade working knives. **Patterns:** Hunters, Bowies and locking folders. **Technical:** Stock removal using 440C, ATS-34 and D2. Makes heavy, hand-stitched sheaths. **Prices:** $250 to $2500. **Remarks:** Full-time maker; first knife sold in 1968. No longer accepting customer designs. **Mark:** C. Cosgrove.

COSTA, SCOTT,
409 Coventry Rd, Spicewood, TX 78669, Phone: 830-693-3431
Specialties: Working straight knives. **Patterns:** Hunters, skinners, axes, trophy sets, custom boxed steak sets, carving sets and bar sets. **Technical:** Grinds D2, ATS-34, 440 and Damascus. Heat-treats. **Prices:** $225 to $2000. **Remarks:** Full-time maker; first knife sold in 1985. **Mark:** Initials connected.

COTTRILL, JAMES I,
1776 Ransburg Ave, Columbus, OH 43223, Phone: 614-274-0020
Specialties: Working straight knives of his design. **Patterns:** Caters to the boating and hunting crowd; cutlery. **Technical:** Grinds O1, D2 and 440C. Likes filework. **Prices:** $95 to $250; some to $500. **Remarks:** Full-time maker; first knife sold in 1977. **Mark:** Name, city, state, in oval logo.

COURTNEY, ELDON,
2718 Bullinger, Wichita, KS 67204, Phone: 316-838-4053
Specialties: Working straight knives of his design. **Patterns:** Hunters, fighters and one-of-a-kinds. **Technical:** Grinds and tempers L6, 440C and spring steel. **Prices:** $100 to $500; some to $1500. **Remarks:** Full-time maker; first knife sold in 1977. **Mark:** Full name, city and state.

COURTOIS, BRYAN,
3 Lawn Ave, Saco, ME 04072, Phone: 207-282-3977, bryancourtois@verizon.net; Web: http://mysite.verizon.net/ vzeui2z01
Specialties: Working straight knives; prefers customer designs, no standard patterns. **Patterns:** Functional hunters; everyday knives. **Technical:** Grinds 440C or customer request. Hollow-grinds with a variety of finishes. Specializes in granite handles and custom skeleton knives. **Prices:** Start at $75. **Remarks:** Part-time maker; first knife sold in 1988. Doing business as Castle Knives. **Mark:** A rook chess piece machined into blade using electrical discharge process.

COUSINO, GEORGE,
7818 Norfolk, Onsted, MI 49265, Phone: 517-467-4911, gcousino@frontiernet.net; Web: www.cousinoknives.com
Specialties: Hunters, Bowies using knives. **Patterns:** Hunters, Bowies, buckskinners, folders and daggers. **Technical:** Grinds 440C. **Prices:** $95 to $300. **Remarks:** Part-time maker; first knife sold in 1981. **Mark:** Last name.

COVER, RAYMOND A,
1206 N Third St, Festus, MO 63028-1628, Phone: 636-937-5955
Specialties: High-tech working straight knives and folders in standard patterns. Patterns: Slip joint folders, two-bladed folders. **Technical:** Grinds D2, and ATS-34. **Prices:** $165 to $250; some to $400. **Remarks:** Part-time maker; first knife sold in 1974. **Mark:** Name.

COWLES, DON,
1026 Lawndale Dr, Royal Oak, MI 48067, Phone: 248-541-4619, don@cowlesknives.com; Web: www.cowlesknives.com
Specialties: Straight, non-folding pocket knives of his design. **Patterns:** Gentlemen's pocket knives. **Technical:** Grinds CPM154, S30V, Damascus, Talonite. Engraves; pearl inlays in some handles. **Prices:** Start at $300. **Remarks:** Full-time maker; first knife sold in 1994. **Mark:** Full name with oak leaf.

COX, COLIN J,
107 N. Oxford Dr, Raymore, MO 64083, Phone: 816-322-1977, colin4knives@aol.com; Web: www.colincoxknives.com
Specialties: Working straight knives and folders of his design; period pieces. **Patterns:** Hunters, fighters and survival knives. Folders, two-blades, gents and hunters. **Technical:** Grinds D2, 440C, 154CM and ATS-34. **Prices:** $125 to $750; some to $4000. **Remarks:** Full-time maker; first knife sold in 1981. **Mark:** Full name, city and state.

COX, SAM,
1756 Love Springs Rd, Gaffney, SC 29341, Phone: 864-489-1892, Fax: 864-489-0403, artcutlery@yahoo.com; Web: www.samcox.us
Specialties: Classic high-art working straight knives of his design. Duck knives copyrighted. **Patterns:** Diverse. **Technical:** Grinds 154CM and S30V. **Prices:** $300 to $1400. **Remarks:** Full-time maker; first knife sold in 1983. **Mark:** Cox Call, Sam, Sam Cox, unique 2000 logo, artistic cutlery logo (beginning 2007).

CRAIG, ROGER L,
2617 SW Seabrook Ave, Topeka, KS 66614, Phone: 785-249-4109
Specialties: Working and camp knives, some fantasy; all his design. **Patterns:** Fighters, hunter. **Technical:** Grinds 1095 and 5160. Most knives have file work. **Prices:** $50 to $250. **Remarks:** Part-time maker; first knife sold in 1991. Doing business as Craig Knives. **Mark:** Last name-Craig.

CRAIN, FRANK,
1127 W Dalke, Spokane, WA 99205, Phone: 509-325-1596

CRAIN, JACK W,
PO Box 212, Granbury, TX 76048, Phone: 817-599-6414, Web: www.crainknives.com -Site 9291 jackwcrain@crainkinves.com
Specialties: Fantasy and period knives; combat and survival knives. **Patterns:** One-of-a-kind art or fantasy daggers, swords and Bowies; survival knives. **Technical:** Forges Damascus; grinds stainless steel. Carves. **Prices:** $350 to $2500; some to $20,000. **Remarks:** Full-time maker; first knife sold in 1969. Designer and maker of the knives seen in the films *Dracula 2000*, *Executive Decision*, *Demolition Man*, *Predator I* and *II*, *Commando*, *Die Hard I* and *II*, *Road House*, *Ford Fairlane* and *Action Jackson*, and television shows *War of the Worlds*, *Air Wolf*, *Kung Fu: The Legend Cont.* and *Tales of the Crypt*. **Mark:** Stylized crane.

CRAWFORD, PAT AND WES,
205 N. Center, West Memphis, AR 72301, Phone: 870-732-2452, patcrawford1@earthlink.com
Specialties: Stainless steel Damascus. High-tech working self-defense and combat types and folders. **Patterns:** Tactical-more fancy knives now. **Technical:** Grinds S30V. **Prices:** $400 to $2000. **Remarks:** Full-time maker; first knife sold in 1973. **Mark:** Last name.

CRAWLEY, BRUCE R,
16 Binbrook Dr, Croydon 3136 Victoria, AUSTRALIA
Specialties: Folders. **Patterns:** Hunters, lockback folders and Bowies. **Technical:** Grinds 440C, ATS-34 and commercial Damascus. Offers filework and mirror polish. **Prices:** $160 to $3500. **Remarks:** Part-time maker; first knife sold in 1990. **Mark:** Initials.

CRENSHAW, AL,
Rt 1 Box 717, Eufaula, OK 74432, Phone: 918-452-2128
Specialties: Folders of his design and in standard patterns. **Patterns:** Hunters, locking folders, slip-joint folders, multi blade folders. **Technical:** Grinds 440C, D2 and ATS-34. Does filework on back springs and blades; offers scrimshaw on some handles. **Prices:** $150 to $300; some higher. **Remarks:** Full-time maker; first knife sold in 1981. Doing business as A. Crenshaw Knives. **Mark:** First initial, last name, Lake Eufaula, state stamped; first initial last name in rainbow; Lake Eufaula across bottom with Okla. in middle.

CROCKFORD, JACK,
1859 Harts Mill Rd, Chamblee, GA 30341, Phone: 770-457-4680
Specialties: Lockback folders. **Patterns:** Hunters, fishing and camp knives, traditional folders. **Technical:** Grinds A2, D2, ATS-34 and 440C. Engraves and scrimshaws. **Prices:** Start at $175. **Remarks:** Part-time maker; first knife sold in 1975. **Mark:** Name.

CROSS, ROBERT,
RMB 200B, Manilla Rd, Tamworth 2340, NSW, AUSTRALIA, Phone: 067-618385

CROWDER, ROBERT,
Box 1374, Thompson Falls, MT 59873, Phone: 406-827-4754
Specialties: Traditional working knives to customer specs. **Patterns:** Hunters, Bowies, fighters and fillets. **Technical:** Grinds ATS-34, 154CM, 440C, Vascowear and commercial Damascus. **Prices:** $225 to $500; some to $2500. **Remarks:** Full-time maker; first knife sold in 1985. **Mark:** R Crowder signature & Montana.

CROWELL, JAMES L,
PO Box 822, Mtn. View, AR 72560, Phone: 870-746-4215, crowellknives@yahoo.com
Specialties: Bowie knives; fighters and working knives. **Patterns:** Hunters, fighters, Bowies, daggers and folders. Period pieces: War hammers, Japanese and European. **Technical:** Forges 10 series carbon steels as well as O1, L6 and his own Damascus. **Prices:** $425 to $4500; some to $7500. **Remarks:** Full-time maker; first knife sold in 1980. Earned ABS Master Bladesmith in 1986. **Mark:** A shooting star.

CROWTHERS, MARK F,
PO Box 4641, Rolling Bay, WA 98061-0641, Phone: 206-842-7501

CULPEPPER, JOHN,
2102 Spencer Ave, Monroe, LA 71201, Phone: 318-323-3636
Specialties: Working straight knives. **Patterns:** Hunters, Bowies and camp knives in heavy-duty patterns. **Technical:** Grinds O1, D2 and 440C; hollow-grinds. **Prices:** $75 to $200; some to $300. **Remarks:** Part-time maker; first knife sold in 1970. Doing business as Pepper Knives. **Mark:** Pepper.

CULVER, STEVE,
5682 94th St, Meriden, KS 66512, Phone: 866-505-0146, Web: www.culverart.com
Specialties: Edged tools and weapons, collectible and functional. **Patterns:** Bowies, daggers, swords, hunters, folders and edged tools. **Technical:** Forges carbon steels and his own pattern welded steels. **Prices:** $200 to $1500; some to $4000. **Remarks:** Full-time maker; first knife sold in 1989. **Mark:** Last name, M. S.

CUMMING, BOB,
CUMMING KNIVES, 35 Manana Dr, Cedar Crest, NM 87008, Phone: 505-286-0509, cumming@comcast.net; Web: www.cummingknives.com
Specialties: One-of-a-kind exhibition grade custom Bowie knives, exhibition grade and working hunters, bird & trout knives, salt and fresh water fillet knives. Low country oyster knives, custom tanto's plains Indian style sheaths & custom leather, all types of exotic handle materials, scrimshaw and engraving. Added folders in 2006. **Prices:** $90 to $2500 and up. **Remarks:** Mentored by the late Jim Nolen, sold first knife in 1978 in Denmark. Retired U.S. Foreign Service Officer. Member NCCKG. **Mark:** Stylized CUMMING.

CURTISS, STEVE L,
PO Box 448, Eureka, MT 59914, Phone: 406-889-5510, Fax: 406-889-5510, slc@bladerigger.com; Web: http://www.bladerigger.com
Specialties: True custom and semi-custom production (SCP), specialized concealment blades; advanced sheaths and tailored body harnessing systems. **Patterns:** Tactical/personal defense fighters, swords, utility and custom patterns. **Technical:** Grinds A2 and Talonite®; heat-treats. Sheaths: Kydex or Kydex-lined leather laminated or Kydex-lined with Rigger Coat™. Exotic materials available. **Prices:** $50 to $10,000. **Remarks:** Full-time maker. Doing business as Blade Rigger L.L.C. Martial artist and unique defense industry tools and equipment. **Mark:** For true custom: Initials and for SCP: Blade Rigger.

CUTE, THOMAS,
State Rt 90-7071, Cortland, NY 13045, Phone: 607-749-4055
Specialties: Working straight knives. **Patterns:** Hunters, Bowies and fighters. **Technical:** Grinds O1, 440C and ATS-34. **Prices:** $100 to $1000. **Remarks:** Full-time maker; first knife sold in 1974. **Mark:** Full name.

CUTTING EDGE, THE, Mark,
1971 Fox Ave, Fairbanks, AK 99701, Phone: 907-452-7477, cuttingedge@gcil.net www.markknappcustomeknives.com
Specialties: Mosaic handles of exotic natural materials from Alaska and around the world. Folders, fixed blades, full and hidden tangs. **Patterns:** Folders, hunters, skinners and camp knives. **Technical:** Forges own Damascus, uses both forging and stock removal with ATS-34, 154CM, stainless Damascus, carbon steel and carbon Damascus. **Prices:** $800-$2000. **Remarks:** Full time maker, sold first knife in 2000. **Mark:** Mark Knapp Custom Knives Fairbanks AK.

D

DAILEY, G E,
577 Lincoln St, Seekonk, MA 02771, Phone: 508-336-5088, gedailey@msn.com; Web: www.gedailey.com
Specialties: One-of-a-kind exotic designed edged weapons. **Patterns:** Folders, daggers and swords. **Technical:** Reforges and grinds Damascus; prefers hollow-grinding. Engraves, carves, offers filework and sets stones and uses exotic gems and gold. **Prices:** Start at $1100. **Remarks:** Full-time maker. First knife sold in 1982. **Mark:** Last name or stylized initialed logo.

DAKE, C M,
19759 Chef Menteur Hwy, New Orleans, LA 70129-9602, Phone: 504-254-0357, Fax: 504-254-9501
Specialties: Fancy working folders. Patterns: Front-lock lockbacks, button-lock folders. **Technical:** Grinds ATS-34 and Damascus. **Prices:**

$500 to $2500; some higher. **Remarks:** Full-time maker; first knife sold in 1988. Doing business as Bayou Custom Cutlery. **Mark:** Last name.

DAKE, MARY H,
Rt 5 Box 287A, New Orleans, LA 70129, Phone: 504-254-0357

DALLYN, KELLY,
14695 Deerridge Dr SE, Calgary, AB, CANADA T2J 6A8, Phone: 403-278-3056

DAMASTEEL STAINLESS DAMASCUS,
3052 Isim Rd., Norman, OK 73026, Phone: 888-804-0683; 405-321-3614, damascus@newmex.com; Web: www.ssdamacus.com
Patterns: Rose, Odin's eye, 5, 20, 30 twists Hakkapelitta, TNT, and infinity

DAMLOVAC, SAVA,
10292 Bradbury Dr, Indianapolis, IN 46231, Phone: 317-839-4952
Specialties: Period pieces, fantasy, Viking, Moran type all Damascus daggers. **Patterns:** Bowies, fighters, daggers, Persian-style knives. **Technical:** Uses own Damascus, some stainless, mostly hand forges. **Prices:** $150 to $2500; some higher. **Remarks:** Full-time maker; first knife sold in 1993. Specialty, Bill Moran all Damascus dagger sets, in Moran-style wood case. **Mark:** "Sava" stamped in Damascus or etched in stainless.

D'ANDREA, JOHN,
8517 N Linwood Loop, Citrus Springs, FL 34433-5045, Phone: 352-489-2803, jpda@optonline.net
Specialties: Fancy working straight knives and folders with filework and distinctive leatherwork. **Patterns:** Hunters, fighters, daggers, folders and an occasional sword. **Technical:** Grinds ATS-34, 154CM, 440C and D2. **Prices:** $180 to $600; some to $1000. **Remarks:** Part-time maker; first knife sold in 1986. **Mark:** First name, last initial imposed on samurai sword.

D'ANGELO, LAURENCE,
14703 NE 17th Ave, Vancouver, WA 98686, Phone: 360-573-0546
Specialties: Straight knives of his design. **Patterns:** Bowies, hunters and locking folders. **Technical:** Grinds D2, ATS-34 and 440C. Hand makes all sheaths. **Prices:** $100 to $200. **Remarks:** Full-time maker; first knife sold in 1987. **Mark:** Football logo—first and middle initials, last name, city, state, Maker.

DANIEL, TRAVIS E,
1655 Carrow Rd, Chocowinity, NC 27817, Phone: 252-940-0807, tedsknives@mail.com
Specialties: Traditional working straight knives of his design or to customer specs. **Patterns:** Hunters, fighters and utility/camp knives. **Technical:** Grinds ATS-34, 440-C, 154CM, forges his own Damascus. Stock removal. **Prices:** $90 to $1200. **Remarks:** Full-time maker; first knife sold in 1976. **Mark:** TED.

DANIELS, ALEX,
1416 County Rd 415, Town Creek, AL 35672, Phone: 256-685-0943, akdknives@aol.com
Specialties: Working and using straight knives and folders; period pieces, reproduction Bowies. **Patterns:** Mostly reproduction Bowies but offers full line of knives. **Technical:** Now also using BG-42 along with 440C and ATS-34. **Prices:** $200 to $2500. **Remarks:** Full-time maker; first knife sold in 1963. **Mark:** First and middle initials, last name, city and state.

DANNEMANN, RANDY,
RIM RANCH, 27752 P25 Rd, Hotchkiss, CO 81419, danneman@sopris.net
Specialties: Classic pattern working hunters, skinners, bird, trout, kitchen & utility knives. **Technical:** Grinds 440C, 154CM, & D2 steel, in house heat treating and cryogenic enhancement. Most are full tapered tang with finger guard and working satin finish. Custom fitted leather sheath for every hunting style knife, both serialized. Uses imported hardwoods, stag, or Micarta for handles. **Price:** $140 to $240 some higher. **Remarks:** First knife sold 1974. Catalog $2.00 email dannknife@tds.net. **Mark:** R. Dannemann Colorado or stamped Dannemann.

DARBY, DAVID T,
30652 S 533 Rd, Cookson, OK 74427, Phone: 918-457-4868, knfmkr@fullnet.net
Specialties: Forged blades only, all styles. **Prices:** $350 and up. **Remarks:** ABS Journeyman Smith. **Mark:** Stylized quillion dagger incorporates last name (Darby).

DARBY, JED,
7878 E Co Rd 50 N, Greensburg, IN 47240, Phone: 812-663-2696
Specialties: Traditional working/using straight knives of his design and to customer specs. **Patterns:** Bowies, hunters and utility/camp knives. **Technical:** Grinds 440C, ATS-34 and Damascus. **Prices:** $70 to $550; some to $1000. **Remarks:** Full-time maker; first knife sold in 1992. Doing business as Darby Knives. **Mark:** Last name and year.

DARBY, RICK,
71 Nestingrock Ln, Levittown, PA 19054
Specialties: Working straight knives. Patterns: Boots, fighters and hunters with mirror finish. **Technical:** Grinds 440C and CPM440V. **Prices:** $125 to $300. **Remarks:** Part-time maker; first knife sold in 1974. **Mark:** First and middle initials, last name.

DARCEY, CHESTER L,
1608 Dominik Dr, College Station, TX 77840, Phone: 979-696-1656, DarceyKnives@yahoo.com
Specialties: Lockback, LinerLock® and scale release folders. **Patterns:** Bowies, hunters and utilities. **Technical:** Stock removal on carbon and stainless steels, forge own Damascus. **Prices:** $200 to $1000. **Remarks:** Part-time maker, first knife sold in 1999. **Mark:** Last name in script.

DARK, ROBERT,
2218 Huntington Court, Oxford, AL 36203, Phone: 256-831-4645, dark@darkknives.com; Web: www.darknives.com
Specialties: Fixed blade working knives of maker's designs. Works with customer designed specifications. **Patterns:** Hunters, Bowies, camp knives, kitchen/utility, bird and trout. Standard patterns and customer designed. **Technical:** Forged and stock removal. Works with high carbon, stainless and Damascus steels. Hollow and flat grinds. **Prices:** $175 to $750. **Remarks:** Sole authorship knives and custom leather sheaths. Full-time maker. **Mark:** "R Dark" on left side of blade.

DARPINIAN, DAVE,
12484 S Greenwood St, Olathe, KS 66062, Phone: 913-244-7114, darpo1956@yahoo.com; Web: www.darpinianknives.com
Specialties: Working knives and fancy pieces to customer specs. **Patterns:** Full range of straight knives including art daggers and short swords. **Technical:** Art grinds ATS-34, 440C, 154CM, 5160, 1095. **Prices:** $300 to $1000. **Remarks:** First knife sold in 1986, part-time maker. **Mark:** Last name.

DAVEY, KEVIN,
105 Joey Dr, Boerne, TX 78006, kevin_n_davey@yahoo.com; Web: www.coutelforge.com
Specialties: Bowies, camp, drop point hunters, forged integrals, daggers, mostly one-of-a-kind designs by maker, sole authorship. **Technical:** Bladesmith, forges mostly 52100 with flat or convex grinds but can also grind hollow, makes own pattern welded steel and own heat treatment. **Prices:** Between $200 to $800. **Remarks:** Part-time maker, current American Bladesmith Society Apprentice working towards journeyman status. See samples of work at www.coutelcutlery.com. **Mark:** Kevin Davey stamped in circle with 5 point star in center.

DAVIDSON, EDMUND,
3345 Virginia Ave, Goshen, VA 24439, Phone: 540-997-5651, Web: www.edmunddavidson.com
Specialties: Working straight knives; many integral patterns and upgraded models. **Patterns:** Heavy-duty skinners and camp knives. **Technical:** Grinds A2, ATS-34, BG-42, S7, 440C. **Prices:** $100 to infinity. **Remarks:** Full-time maker; first knife sold in 1986. **Mark:** Name in deer head or custom logos.

DAVIDSON, JEFF,
PO Box 14708, Haltom City, TX 76117, Phone: 8175282416, davidsonknives@sbcglobal.net; Web: davidsoncustomknives.net
Specialties: High-performance working fixed blades. **Patterns:** Hunters, camp knives and Bowies. **Technical:** Low temperature forged 5160 and 52100 blades. Multiple quench heat treating, handle materials hardwoods, deer, elk and other types of horn. Makes heavy duty hand stitched waxed harness leather pouch type sheaths. **Prices:** Start at $300. **Remarks:** Full-time maker dedicated to the high performance using knife. **Mark:** First and last name.

DAVIDSON, LARRY,
921 Bennett St, Cedar Hill, TX 75104, Phone: 972-291-3904, dson@swbell.net; Web: www.davidsonknives.com

DAVIS, BARRY L,
4262 US 20, Castleton, NY 12033, Phone: 518-477-5036, daviscustomknives@yahoo.com
Specialties: Collector grade Damascus folders. Traditional designs with focus on turn-of-the-century techniques employed. Sole authorship. Forges own Damascus, does all carving, filework, gold work and piquet. Uses only natural handle material. Enjoys doing multi-blade as well as single blade folders and daggers. **Prices:** Prices range from $2000 to $7000. **Remarks:** First knife sold in 1980.

DAVIS, CHARLIE,
ANZA KNIVES, PO Box 710806, Santee, CA 92072, Phone: 619-561-9445, Fax: 619-390-6283, sales@anzaknives.com; Web: www.anzaknives.com
Specialties: Fancy and embellished working straight knives of his design. **Patterns:** Hunters, camp and utility knives. **Technical:** Grinds high-carbon files. **Prices:** $20 to $185, custom depends. **Remarks:** Full-time maker; first knife sold in 1980. Now offers custom. **Mark:** ANZA U.S.A.

DAVIS, DON,
8415 Coyote Run, Loveland, CO 80537-9665, Phone: 970-669-9016, Fax: 970-669-8072
Specialties: Working straight knives in standard patterns or to customer specs. Patterns: Hunters, utility knives, skinners and survival knives. **Technical:** Grinds 440C, ATS-34. **Prices:** $75 to $250. **Remarks:** Full-time maker; first knife sold in 1985. **Mark:** Signature, city and state.

DAVIS, JESSE W,
7398A Hwy 3, Sarah, MS 38665, Phone: 662-382-7332, jandddvais1@earthlink.net
Specialties: Working straight knives and boots in standard patterns and to customer specs. **Patterns:** Boot knives, daggers, fighters, subhilts & Bowies. **Technical:** Grinds A2, D2, 440C and commercial Damascus. **Prices:** $125 to $1000. **Remarks:** Full-time maker; first knife sold in 1977. Former member Knifemakers Guild (in good standing). **Mark:** Name or initials.

DAVIS, JOEL,
74538 165th, Albert Lea, MN 56007, Phone: 507-377-0808, joelknives@yahoo.com
Specialties: Completesoleauthorshippresentationgradehighlycomplex pattern-welded mosaic Damascus blade and bolster stock. **Patterns:** To date Joel has executed over 900 different mosaic Damascus patterns in the past four years. Anything conceived by maker's imagination. **Technical:** Uses various heat colorable "high vibrancy" steels, nickel 200 and some powdered metal for bolster stock only. Uses 1095, 1075 and 15N20. High carbon steels for cutting edge blade stock only. **Prices:** 15 to $50 per square inch and up depending on complexity of pattern. **Remarks:** Full-time mosaic Damascus metal smith focusing strictly on never-before-seen mosaic patterns. Most of maker's work is used for art knives ranging between $1500 to $4500.

DAVIS, JOHN,
235 Lampe Rd, Selah, WA 98942, Phone: 509-697-3845, Fax: 509-697-8087
Specialties: Working and using straight knives of his own design, to customer specs and in standard patterns. **Patterns:** Boots, hunters, kitchen and utility/camp knives. **Technical:** Grinds ATS-34, 440C and commercial Damascus; makes own Damascus and mosaic Damascus. Embellishes with stabilized wood, mokume and nickel-silver. **Prices:** Start at $150. **Remarks:** Part-time maker; first knife sold in 1996. **Mark:** Name city and state on Damascus stamp initials.

DAVIS, STEVE,
3370 Chatsworth Way, Powder Springs, GA 30127, Phone: 770-427-5740
Specialties: Traditional gents and ladies folders of his design and to customer specs. **Patterns:** Slip-joint folders, locking-liner folders, lock back folders. **Technical:** Grinds ATS-34, 440C and Damascus. Offers filework; prefers hand-rubbed finishes and natural handle materials. Uses pearl, ivory, stag and exotic woods. **Prices:** $250 to $600; some to $1500. **Remarks:** Part-time maker; first knife sold in 1988. Doing business as Custom Knives by Steve Davis. **Mark:** Name engraved on blade.

DAVIS, TERRY,
Box 111, Sumpter, OR 97877, Phone: 541-894-2307
Specialties: Traditional and contemporary folders. **Patterns:** Multi-blade folders, whittlers and interframe multiblades; sunfish patterns. **Technical:** Flat-grinds ATS-34. **Prices:** $400 to $1000; some higher. **Remarks:** Full-time maker; first knife sold in 1985. **Mark:** Name in logo.

DAVIS, VERNON M,
2020 Behrens Circle, Waco, TX 76705, Phone: 254-799-7671
Specialties: Presentation-grade straight knives. **Patterns:** Bowies, daggers, boots, fighters, hunters and utility knives. **Technical:** Hollow-grinds 440C, ATS-34 and D2. Grinds an aesthetic grind line near choil. **Prices:** $125 to $550; some to $5000. **Remarks:** Part-time maker; first knife sold in 1980. **Mark:** Last name and city inside outline of state.

DAVIS, W C,
1955 S 1251 Rd, El Dorado Springs, MO 64744, Phone: 417-876-1259
Specialties: Fancy working straight knives and folders. **Patterns:** Folding lockers and slip-joints; straight hunters, fighters and Bowies. **Technical:** Grinds A2, ATS-34, 154, CPM T490V and CPM 530V. **Prices:** $100 to $300; some to $1000. **Remarks:** Full-time maker; first knife sold in 1972. **Mark:** Name.

DAVIS JR., JIM,
5129 Ridge St, Zephyrhills, FL 33541, Phone: 813-779-9213 813-469-4241 Cell, jimdavisknives@aol.com
Specialties: Presentation-grade fixed blade knives w/composite hidden tang handles. Employs a variety of ancient and contemporary ivories. **Patterns:** One-of-a-kind gents, personal, and executive knives and hunters w/unique cam-lock pouch sheaths and display stands. **Technical:** Flat grinds ATS-34 and stainless Damascus w/most work by hand w/ assorted files. **Prices:** $300 and up. **Remarks:** Full-time maker, first knives sold in 2000. **Mark:** Signature w/printed name over "HANDCRAFTED."

DAWKINS, DUDLEY L,
221 NW Broadmoor Ave., Topeka, KS 66606-1254, Phone: 785-235-0468, Fax: 785-235-3871, dawkind@sbcglobal.net
Specialties: Stylized old or "Dawkins Forged" with anvil in center. New tang stamps. Patterns: Straight knives. **Technical:** Mostly carbon steel; some Damascus-all knives forged. **Prices:** $175 and up. **Remarks:** All knives supplied with wood-lined sheaths. Also make custom wood-lined sheaths $55 and up. ABS Member, sole authorship. **Mark:** Stylized "DLD or Dawkins Forged with anvil in center.

DAWSON, BARRY,
10A Town Plaza Suite 303, Durango, CO 81301, lindad@northlink.com; Web: www.knives.com
Specialties: Samurai swords, combat knives, collector daggers, tactical, folding and hunting knives. **Patterns:** Offers over 60 different models. **Technical:** Grinds 440C, ATS-34, own heat-treatment. **Prices:** $75 to $1500; some to $5000. **Remarks:** Full-time maker; first knife sold in 1975. **Mark:** Last name, USA in print or last name in script.

DAWSON, LYNN,
7760 E Hwy 69 #C-5 157, Prescott Valley, AZ 86314, Phone: 928-713-7548/928/713/8493, Fax: 928-772-1729, lynnknives@commspeed.net; Web: www.lynnknives.com
Specialties: Swords, hunters, utility, and art pieces. **Patterns:** Over 25 patterns to choose from. **Technical:** Grinds 440C, ATS-34, own heat treating. **Prices:** $80 to $1000. **Remarks:** Custom work and her own designs. **Mark:** The name "Lynn" in print or script.

DE MARIA JR., ANGELO,
12 Boronda Rd, Carmel Valley, CA 93924, Phone: 831-659-3381, Fax: 831-659-1315, angelodemaria1@mac.com
Specialties: Damascus, fixed and folders, sheaths. **Patterns:** Mosiac and random. **Technical:** Forging 5160, 1084 and 15N20. **Prices:** $200+. **Remarks:** Part-time maker. **Mark:** Angelo de Maria Carmel Valley, CA etch or AdM stamp.

DEAN, HARVEY J,
3266 CR 232, Rockdale, TX 76567, Phone: 512-446-3111, Fax: 512-446-5060, dean@tex1.net; Web: www.harveydean.com
Specialties: Collectible, functional knives. **Patterns:** Bowies, hunters, folders, daggers, swords, battle axes, camp and combat knives. **Technical:** Forges 1095, O1 and his Damascus. **Prices:** $350 to $10,000. **Remarks:** Full-time maker; first knife sold in 1981. **Mark:** Last name and MS.

DEBRAGA, JOSE C,
76 Rue de La Pointe, Aux Lievres, Quebec, CANADA G1K 5Y3, Phone: 418-948-0105, Fax: 418-948-0105, josecdebragaglovetrotter.net; Web: www.gcaq.ga
Specialties: Art knives, fantasy pieces and working knives of his design or to customer specs. **Patterns:** Knives with sculptured or carved handles, from miniatures to full-size working knives. **Technical:** Grinds and hand-files 440C and ATS-34. A variety of steels and handle materials available. Offers lost wax casting. **Prices:** Start at $300. **Remarks:** Full-time maker; wax modeler, sculptor and knifemaker; first knife sold in 1984. **Mark:** Initials in stylized script and serial number.

DEBRAGA, JOVAN,
141 Notre Dame des Victoir, Quebec, CANADA G2G 1J3, Phone: 418-997-0819/418-877-1915, jovancdebraga@msn.com
Specialties: Art knives, fantasy pieces and working knives of his design or to customer specs. **Patterns:** Knives with sculptured or carved handles, from miniatures to full-sized working knives. **Technical:** Grinds and hand-files 440C, and ATS-34. A variety of steels and handle materials available. **Prices:** Start at $300. **Remarks:** Full time maker. Sculptor and knifemaker. First knife sold in 2003. **Mark:** Initials in stylized script and serial number.

DEL RASO, PETER,
28 Mayfield Dr, Mt. Waverly, Victoria, 3149, AUSTRALIA, Phone: 613 98060644, delrasofamily@optusnet.com.au
Specialties: Fixed blades, some folders, art knives. **Patterns:** Daggers, Bowies, tactical, boot, personal and working knives. **Technical:** Grinds ATS-34, commercial Damascus and any other type of steel on request. **Prices:** $100 to $1500. **Remarks:** Part-time maker, first show in 1993. **Mark:** Maker's surname stamped.

DELAROSA, JIM,
2116 N Pontiac Dr, Janesville, WI 53545, Phone: 608-314-0311
Specialties: Working straight knives and folders of his design or customer specs. **Patterns:** Hunters, skinners, fillets, utility and locking folders. **Technical:** Grinds ATS-34, 440-C, D2, O1 and commercial Damascus. **Prices:** $75 to $450; some higher. **Remarks:** Part-time maker. **Mark:** First and last name.

DELL, WOLFGANG,
Am Alten Berg 9, D-73277 Owen-Teck, GERMANY, Phone: 49-7021-81802, dellknives@compuserve.de; Web: www.dell-knives.de
Specialties: Fancy high-art straight of his design and to customer specs. **Patterns:** Fighters, hunters, Bowies and utility/camp knives. **Technical:** Grinds ATS-34, RWL-34, Elmax, Damascus (Fritz Schneider). Offers high gloss finish and engraving. **Prices:** $500 to $1000; some to $1600. **Remarks:** Full-time maker; first knife sold in 1992. Member of German Knifemaker Guild since 1993. Member of the Italian Knifemaker Guild since 2000. **Mark:** Hopi hand of peace.

DELLANA,
STARLANI INT'L INC, 1135 Terminal Way Ste #209, Reno, NV 89502, Phone: 877-88dellana or 304-727-5512, dellana@suddenlink.net; Web: www.knivesbydellana.com
Specialties: Collector grade fancy/embellished high art folders and art

daggers. **Patterns:** Locking folders and art daggers. **Technical:** Forges her own Damascus and W-2. Engraves, does stone setting, filework, carving and gold/platinum fabrication. Prefers exotic, high karat gold, platinum, silver, gemstone and mother-of-pearl handle materials. **Price:** Upscale. **Remarks:** Sole authorship, full-time maker, first knife sold in 1994. Also does one high art collaboration a year with Van Barnett. Member: Art Knife Invitational and ABS. **Mark:** First name.

DELONG, DICK,
17561 E. Ohio Circle, Aurora, CO 80017, Phone: 303-745-2652
Specialties: Fancy working knives and fantasy pieces. **Patterns:** Hunters and small skinners. **Technical:** Grinds and files O1, D2, 440C and Damascus. Offers cocobolo and Osage orange for handles. **Prices:** Start at $50. **Remarks:** Part-time maker. Member of Art Knife Invitational. Voting member of Knifemakers Guild. Member of ABS. **Mark:** Last name; some unmarked.

DEMENT, LARRY,
PO Box 1807, Prince Fredrick, MD 20678, Phone: 410-586-9011
Specialties: Fixed blades. **Technical:** Forged and stock removal. **Prices:** $75 to $200. **Remarks:** Affordable, good feelin', quality knives. Part-time maker.

DEMPSEY, DAVID,
1644 Bass Rd, Apt 2202, Macon, GA 31210, Phone: 229-244-9101, dempsey@dempseyknives.com; Web: www.dempseyknives.com
Specialties: Tactical, utility, working, classic straight knives. **Patterns:** Fighters, tantos, hunters, neck, utility or customer design. **Technical:** Grinds carbon steel and stainless including S30V (differential heat treatment), stainless steel. **Prices:** Start at $150 for neck knives. **Remarks:** Full-time maker. First knife sold 1998. **Mark:** First and last name over knives.

DEMPSEY, GORDON S,
PO Box 7497, N. Kenai, AK 99635, Phone: 907-776-8425
Specialties: Working straight knives. **Patterns:** Pattern welded Damascus and carbon steel blades. **Technical:** Pattern welded Damascus and carbon steel. **Prices:** $80 to $250. **Remarks:** Part-time maker; first knife sold in 1974. **Mark:** Name.

DENNEHY, DAN,
PO Box 470, Del Norte, CO 81132, Phone: 719-657-2545
Specialties: Working knives, fighting and military knives, throwing knives. **Patterns:** Full range of straight knives, tomahawks, buckle knives. **Technical:** Forges and grinds A2, O1 and D2. **Prices:** $200 to $500. **Remarks:** Full-time maker; first knife sold in 1942. Latest inductee into cutlery hall of fame, #44 **Mark:** First name and last initial, city, state and shamrock.

DENNEHY, JOHN D,
8463 Woodlands Way, Wellington, CO 80549, Phone: 970-568-3697, jd@thewildirishrose.com
Specialties: Working straight knives, throwers, and leatherworker's knives. **Technical:** 440C, & O1, heat treats own blades, part-time maker, first knife sold in 1989. **Patterns:** Small hunting to presentation Bowies, leatherworks round and head knives. **Prices:** $200 and up. **Remarks:** Custom sheath maker, sheath making seminars at the Blade Show.

DENNING, GENO,
CAVEMAN ENGINEERING, 135 Allenvalley Rd, Gaston, SC 29053, Phone: 803-794-6067, cden101656@aol.com; Web: www.cavemanengineering.com
Specialties: Mirror finish. **Patterns:** Hunters, fighters, folders. **Technical:** ATS-34, 440V, S-30-V D2. **Prices:** $100 and up. **Remarks:** Full-time maker since 1996. Sole income since 1999. Instructor at Montgomery Community College (Grinding Blades). A director of SCAK: South Carolina Association of Knifemakers. **Mark:** Troy NC.

DERINGER, CHRISTOPH,
625 Chemin Lower, Cookshire, Quebec, CANADA J0B 1M0, Phone: 819-345-4260, cdsab@sympatico.ca
Specialties: Traditional working/using straight knives and folders of his design and to customer specs. **Patterns:** Boots, hunters, folders, art knives, kitchen knives and utility/camp knives. **Technical:** Forges 5160, O1 and Damascus. Offers a variety of filework. **Prices:** Start at $250. **Remarks:** Full-time maker; first knife sold in 1989. **Mark:** Last name stamped/engraved.

DERR, HERBERT,
413 Woodland Dr, St. Albans, WV 25177, Phone: 304-727-3866
Specialties: Damascus one-of-a-kind knives, carbon steels also. **Patterns:** Birdseye, ladder back, mosaics. **Technical:** All styles functional as well as artistically pleasing. **Prices:** $90 to $175 carbon, Damascus $250 to $800. **Remarks:** All Damascus made by maker. **Mark:** H.K. Derr.

DETMER, PHILLIP,
14140 Bluff Rd, Breese, IL 62230, Phone: 618-526-4834
Specialties: Working knives. Patterns: Bowies, daggers and hunters. **Technical:** Grinds ATS-34 and D2. **Prices:** $60 to $400. **Remarks:** Part-time maker; first knife sold in 1977. **Mark:** Last name with dagger.

DI MARZO, RICHARD,
1417 10th St S, Birmingham, AL 35205, Phone: 205-252-3331
Specialties: Handle artist. Scrimshaw carvings.

DICK, DAN,
P.O. Box 2303, Hutchinson, KS 67504-2303, Phone: 620-669-6805, Dan@DanDickKnives.com; Web: www.dandickknives.com
Specialties: Traditional working/using fixed bladed knives of maker's design. **Patterns:**Hunters, Skinners, Utility, Kitchen, Tactical, Bowies. **Technical:**Stock removal maker using D2, forges his own Damascus and is dabbling in forging knives. Prefers natural handle materials such as: exotic and fancy burl woods and some horn. Makes his own leather sheaths, many with tooling, also makes sheaths from Kydex for his tacticals. **Prices:**$80 and up. **Remarks:**Part-time maker since 2006. **Marks:** Dan Dick using one D with first name over last.

DICKERSON, GAVIN,
PO Box 7672, Petit 1512, SOUTH AFRICA, Phone: +27 011-965-0988, Fax: +27 011-965-0988
Specialties: Straight knives of his design or to customer specs. **Patterns:** Hunters, skinners, fighters and Bowies. **Technical:** Hollow-grinds D2, 440C, ATS-34, 12C27 and Damascus upon request. Prefers natural handle materials; offers synthetic handle materials. **Prices:** $190 to $2500. **Remarks:** Part-time maker; first knife sold in 1982. **Mark:** Name in full.

DICKERSON, GORDON S,
47 S Maple St, New Augusta, MS 38462, Phone: 931-796-1187
Specialties: Traditional working straight knives; Civil War era period pieces. **Patterns:** Bowies, hunters, tactical, camp/utility knives; some folders. **Technical:** Forges carbon steel; pattern welded and cable Damascus. **Prices:** $150 to $500; some to $3000. ABS member. **Mark:** Last name.

DICKISON, SCOTT S,
179 Taylor Rd, Fisher Circle, Portsmouth, RI 02871, Phone: 401-847-7398, squared22@cox .net; Web: http://members.cox.net/squared22
Specialties: Working and using straight knives and locking folders of his design and automatics. **Patterns:** Trout knives, fishing and hunting knives. **Technical:** Forges and grinds commercial Damascus and D2, O1. Uses natural handle materials. **Prices:** $400 to $750; some higher. **Remarks:** Part-time maker; first knife sold in 1989. **Mark:** Stylized initials.

DICRISTOFANO, ANTHONY P,
PO Box 2369, Northlake, IL 60164, Phone: 847-845-9598, sukemitsu@sbcglobal.net Web: www.namahagesword.com
Specialties: Japanese-style swords. **Patterns:** Katana, Wakizashi, Otanto, Kozuka. **Technical:** Tradition and some modern steels. All clay tempered and traditionally hand polished using Japanese wet stones. **Remarks:** Part-time maker. **Prices:** Varied, available on request. **Mark:** Blade tang signed in "SUKEMITSU."

DIEBEL, CHUCK,
PO Box 13, Broussard, LA 70516-0013

DIETZ, HOWARD,
421 Range Rd, New Braunfels, TX 78132, Phone: 830-885-4662
Specialties: Lock-back folders, working straight knives. **Patterns:** Folding hunters, high-grade pocket knives. ATS-34, 440C, CPM 440V, D2 and stainless Damascus. **Prices:** $300 to $1000. **Remarks:** Full-time gun and knifemaker; first knife sold in 1995. **Mark:** Name, city, and state.

DIETZEL, BILL,
PO Box 1613, Middleburg, FL 32068, Phone: 904-282-1091
Specialties: Forged straight knives and folders. **Patterns:** His interpretations. **Technical:** Forges his Damascus and other steels. **Prices:** Middle ranges. **Remarks:** Likes natural materials; uses titanium in folder liners. Master Smith (1997). **Mark:** Name.

DIGANGI, JOSEPH M,
Box 950, Santa Cruz, NM 87567, Phone: 505-753-6414, Fax: 505-753-8144, Web: www.digangidesigns.com
Specialties: Kitchen and table cutlery. **Patterns:** French chef's knives, carving sets, steak knife sets, some camp knives and hunters. Holds patents and trademarks for "System II" kitchen cutlery set. **Technical:** Grinds ATS-34. **Prices:** $150 to $595; some to $1200. **Remarks:** Full-time maker; first knife sold in 1983. **Mark:** DiGangi Designs.

DILL, DAVE,
7404 NW 30th St, Bethany, OK 73008, Phone: 405-789-0750
Specialties: Folders of his design. **Patterns:** Various patterns. **Technical:** Hand-grinds 440C, ATS-34. Offers engraving and filework on all folders. **Prices:** Starting at $450. **Remarks:** Full-time maker; first knife sold in 1987. **Mark:** First initial, last name.

DILL, ROBERT,
1812 Van Buren, Loveland, CO 80538, Phone: 970-667-5144, Fax: 970-667-5144, dillcustomknives@msn.com
Specialties: Fancy and working knives of his design. **Patterns:** Hunters, Bowies and fighters. **Technical:** Grinds 440C and D2. **Prices:** $100 to $800. **Remarks:** Full-time maker; first knife sold in 1984. **Mark:** Logo stamped into blade.

DILLUVIO, FRANK J,
13611 Murthum, Warren, MI 48088, Phone: 586-294-5280, frankscustomknives@hotmail.com; Web: www.fdilluviocustomknives.com
Specialties: Traditional working straight knives, some high-tech. **Patterns:** Hunters, Bowies, fishing knives, sub-hilts, LinerLock® folders and miniatures. **Technical:** Grinds D2, 440C, CPM; works for precision fits— no solder. **Prices:** $95 to $450; some to $800. **Remarks:** Full-time maker; first knife sold in 1984. **Mark:** Name and state.

DION, GREG,
3032 S Jackson St, Oxnard, CA 93033, Phone: 805-483-1781
Specialties: Working straight knives, some fancy. Welcomes special orders. **Patterns:** Hunters, fighters, camp knives, Bowies and tantos. **Technical:** Grinds ATS-34, 154CM and 440C. **Prices:** $85 to $300; some to $600. **Remarks:** Part-time maker; first knife sold in 1985. **Mark:** Name.

DIOTTE, JEFF,
DIOTTE KNIVES, 159 Laurier Dr, LaSalle Ontario, CANADA N9J 1L4, Phone: 519-978-2764

DIPPOLD, AL,
90 Damascus Ln, Perryville, MO 63775, Phone: 573-547-1119, adippold@midwest.net
Specialties: Fancy one-of-a-kind locking folders. **Patterns:** Locking folders. **Technical:** Forges and grinds mosaic and pattern welded Damascus. Offers filework on all folders. **Prices:** $500 to $3500; some higher. **Remarks:** Full-time maker; first knife sold in 1980. **Mark:** Last name in logo inside of liner.

DISKIN, MATT,
PO Box 653, Freeland, WA 98249, Phone: 360-730-0451
Specialties: Damascus autos. **Patterns:** Dirks and daggers. **Technical:** Forges mosaic Damascus using 15N20, 1084, 02, 06, L6; pure nickel. **Prices:** Start at $500. Remarks; Full-time maker. **Mark:** Last name.

DIXON JR., IRA E,
PO Box 2581, Ventura, CA 93002-2581, irasknives@yahoo.com
Specialties: Utilitarian straight knives of his design. **Patterns:** Camp, hunters, fighters, utility knives and art knives. **Technical:** Grinds CPM, S30V, 1095, Damascus and D2. **Prices:** $200 to $1500. **Remarks:** Part-time maker; first knife sold in 1993. **Mark:** First name, Handmade.

DODD, ROBERT F,
4340 E Canyon Dr, Camp Verde, AZ 86322, Phone: 928-567-3333, rfdknives@commspeed.net; Web: www.rfdoddknives.com
Specialties: Folders, fixed blade hunter/skinners, Bowies, daggers. **Patterns:** Drop point. **Technical:** ATS-34 and Damascus. **Prices:** $250 and up. **Remarks:** Hand tooled leather sheaths. **Mark:** R. F. Dodd, Camp Verde AZ.

DOGGETT, BOB,
1310 Vinetree Rd, Brandon, FL 33510, Phone: 813-786-9057, dogman@tampabay.rr.com; Web: www.doggettcustomknives.com
Specialties: Clean, functional working knives. **Patterns:** Classic-styled hunter, fighter and utility fixed blades; liner locking folders. **Technical:** Uses stainless steel and commercial Damascus, 416 stainless for bolsters and hardware, hand-rubbed satin finish, top quality handle materials and titanium liners on folders. **Prices:** Start at $175. **Remarks:** Part-time maker. **Mark:** Last name.

DOIRON, DONALD,
6 Chemin Petit Lac des Ced, Messines, PQ, CANADA JOX-2JO, Phone: 819-465-2489

DOLAN, ROBERT L.,
220—B Naalae Rd, Kula, HI 96790, Phone: 808-878-6406
Specialties: Working straight knives in standard patterns, his designs or to customer specs. **Patterns:** Fixed blades and potter's tools, ceramic saws. **Technical:** Grinds O1, D2, 440C and ATS-34. Heat-treats and engraves. **Prices:** Start at $75. **Remarks:** Full-time tool and knifemaker; first knife sold in 1985. **Mark:** Last name, USA.

DOLE, ROGER,
DOLE CUSTOM KNIFE WORKS, PO Box 323, Buckley, WA 98321, Phone: 253-862-6770
Specialties: Folding knives. They include slip joint, lock back and locking liner type knives. Most have integral bolster and liners. The locking liner knives have a removable titanium side lock that is machined into the integral liner, they are also available with a split liner lock. **Technical:** Makes ATS-34, 440-C and BG-42 stainless steel. Has in stock or available all types of natural and synthetic handle materials. Uses 416, 303, and 304 stainless steel, 7075-T6 aluminum and titanium for the guards on the fixed blade knives and integral liners on the folding knives. The locking LinerLock® mechanisms are made from 6AL4V titanium. Uses the stock removal method to fabricate all of the blades produced. The blades are ground on a 2 X 72 inch belt grinder. Not a bladesmith. **Patterns:** 51 working designs for fixed blade knives. They include small bird and trout knives to skinning axes. Most are working designs. All come with hand crafted leather sheath Kydex sheaths; can be special ordered. **Remarks:** First knife sold in 1975.

DOMINY, CHUCK,
PO Box 593, Colleyville, TX 76034, Phone: 817-498-4527
Specialties: Titanium LinerLock® folders. **Patterns:** Hunters, utility/camp knives and LinerLock® folders. **Technical:** Grinds 440C and ATS-34. **Prices:** $250 to $3000. **Remarks:** Full-time maker; first knife sold in 1976. **Mark:** Last name.

DOOLITTLE, MIKE,
13 Denise Ct, Novato, CA 94947, Phone: 415-897-3246
Specialties: Working straight knives in standard patterns. **Patterns:** Hunters and fishing knives. **Technical:** Grinds 440C, 154CM and ATS-34. **Prices:** $125 to $200; some to $750. **Remarks:** Part-time maker; first knife sold in 1981. **Mark:** Name, city and state.

DORNELES, LUCIANO OLIVERIRA,
Rua 15 De Novembro 2222, Nova Petropolis, RS, BRAZIL 95150-000, Phone: 011-55-54-303-303-90, tchebufalo@hotmail.com
Specialties: Traditional "true" Brazilian-style working knives and to customer specs. **Patterns:** Brazilian hunters, utility and camp knives, Bowies, Dirk. A master at the making of the true "Faca Campeira Gaucha," the true camp knife of the famous Brazilian Gauchos. A Dorneles knife is 100 percent hand-forged with sledge hammers only. Can make spectacular Damascus hunters/daggers. **Technical:** Forges only 52100 and his own Damascus, can put silver wire inlay on customer design handles on special orders; uses only natural handle materials. **Prices:** $250 to $1000. **Mark:** Symbol with L. Dorneles.

DOTSON, TRACY,
1280 Hwy C-4A, Baker, FL 32531, Phone: 850-537-2407
Specialties: Folding fighters and small folders. **Patterns:** LinerLock® and lockback folders. **Technical:** Hollow-grinds ATS-34 and commercial Damascus. **Prices:** Start at $250. **Remarks:** Part-time maker; first knife sold in 1995. **Mark:** Last name.

DOUCETTE, R,
CUSTOM KNIVES, 112 Memorial Dr, Brantford, Ont., CANADA N3R 5S3, Phone: 519-756-9040, randy@randydoucetteknives.com; Web: www.randydoucetteknives.com
Specialties: Filework, tactical designs, multiple grinds. **Patterns:** Tactical folders, Bowies, daggers, tantos, karambits, balisongs. **Technical:** All knives are handmade. The only outsourcing is heat treatment. **Prices:** $200 to $2,500. **Remarks:** Custom orders welcome. **Mark:** R. Doucette

DOUGLAS, JOHN J,
506 Powell Rd, Lynch Station, VA 24571, Phone: 804-369-7196
Specialties: Fancy and traditional straight knives and folders of his design and to customer specs. **Patterns:** Locking folders, swords and sgian dubhs. **Technical:** Grinds 440C stainless, ATS-34 stainless and customer's choice. Offers newly designed non-pivot uni-lock folders. Prefers highly polished finish. **Prices:** $160 to $1400. **Remarks:** Full-time maker; first knife sold in 1975. Doing business as Douglas Keltic. **Mark:** Stylized initial. Folders are numbered; customs are dated.

DOURSIN, GERARD,
Chemin des Croutoules, F 84210, Pernes les Fontaines, FRANCE
Specialties: Period pieces. **Patterns:** Liner locks and daggers. **Technical:** Forges mosaic Damascus. **Prices:** $600 to $4000. **Remarks:** First knife sold in 1983. **Mark:** First initial, last name and I stop the lion.

DOUSSOT, LAURENT,
6262 De La Roche, Montreal, Quebec, CANADA H2H 1W9, Phone: 516-270-6992, Fax: 516-722-1641
Specialties: Fancy and embellished folders and fantasy knives. **Patterns:** Fighters and locking folders. **Technical:** Grinds ATS-34 and commercial Damascus. Scale carvings on all knives; most bolsters are carved titanium. **Prices:** $350 to $3000. **Remarks:** Part-time maker; first knife was sold in 1992. **Mark:** Stylized initials inside circle.

DOWELL, T M,
139 NW St Helen's Pl, Bend, OR 97701, Phone: 541-382-8924, Fax: 541-382-8924, tmdknives@webtv.net
Specialties: Integral construction in hunting knives. **Patterns:** Limited to featherweights, lightweights, integral hilt and caps. **Technical:** Grinds D-2, BG-42 and Vasco wear. **Prices:** $275 and up. **Remarks:** Full-time maker; first knife sold in 1967. **Mark:** Initials logo.

DOWNIE, JAMES T,
10076 Estate Dr, Port Franks, Ont., CANADA NOM 2LO, Phone: 519-243-1488, Web: www.ckg.org (click on members page)
Specialties: Serviceable straight knives and folders; period pieces. **Patterns:** Hunters, Bowies, camp knives, fillet and miniatures. **Technical:** Grinds D2, 440C and ATS-34, Damasteel, stainless steel Damascus. **Prices:** $100 to $500; some higher. **Remarks:** Full-time maker, first knife sold in 1978. **Mark:** Signature of first and middle initials, last name.

DOWNING, LARRY,
12268 Hwy 181N, Bremen, KY 42325, Phone: 270-525-3523, larrydowning@bellsouth.net; Web: www.downingcustomknives.com
Specialties: Working straight knives and folders. Patterns: From mini-knives to daggers, folding lockers to interframes. **Technical:** Forges and grinds 154CM, ATS-34 and his own Damascus. **Prices:** $195 to $950; some higher. **Remarks:** Part-time maker; first knife sold in 1979. **Mark:** Name in arrowhead.

DOWNING, TOM,
2675 12th St, Cuyahoga Falls, OH 44223, Phone: 330-923-7464
Specialties: Working straight knives; period pieces. **Patterns:** Hunters, fighters and tantos. **Technical:** Grinds 440C, ATs-34 and CPM-T-440V. Prefers natural handle materials. **Prices:** $150 to $900, some to $1500. **Remarks:** Part-time maker; first knife sold in 1979. **Mark:** First and middle initials, last name.

DOWNS, JAMES F,
2247 Summit View Rd, Powell, OH 43065, Phone: 614-766-5350, jfdowns1@yahoo.com
Specialties: Working straight knives of his design or to customer specs. **Patterns:** Folders, Bowies, boot, hunters, utility. **Technical:** Grinds 440C and other steels. Prefers mastodon ivory, all pearls, stabilized wood and elephant ivory. **Prices:** $75 to $1200. **Remarks:** Full-time maker; first knife sold in 1980. **Mark:** Last name.

DOX, JAN,
Zwanebloemlaan 27, B 2900 Schoten, BELGIUM, Phone: 32 3 658 77 43, jan.dox@pi.be
Specialties: Working/using knives, from kitchen to battlefield. **Patterns:** Own designs, some based on traditional ethnic patterns (Scots, Celtic, Scandinavian and Japanese) or to customer specs. **Technical:** Grinds D2/A2 and stainless, forges carbon steels, convex edges. Handles: Wrapped in modern or traditional patterns, resin impregnated if desired. Natural or synthetic materials, some carved. **Prices:** Start at 25 to 50 Euro (USD) and up. **Remarks:** Spare-time maker, first knife sold 2001. **Mark:** Name or stylized initials.

DOZIER, BOB,
PO Box 1941, Springdale, AR 72765, Phone: 888-823-0023/479-756-0023, Fax: 479-756-9139, info@dozierknives.com; Web www.dozierknives.com
Specialties: Using knives (fixed blades and folders). **Patterns:** Some fine collector-grade knives. **Technical:** Uses D2. Prefers Micarta handle material. **Prices:** Using knives: $145 to $595. **Remarks:** Full-time maker; first knife sold in 1965. Also sells a semi-handmade line of fixed blade with mark; state, knives, last name in circle. **Mark:** State, made, last name in a circle (for fixed blades); Last name with arrow through 'D' and year over name (for folders).

DRAPER, AUDRA,
#10 Creek Dr, Riverton, WY 82501, Phone: 307-856-6807 or 307-851-0426 cell, adraper@wyoming.com; Web: www.draperknives.com
Specialties: One-of-a-kind straight and folding knives. Also pendants, earring and bracelets of Damascus. **Patterns:** Design custom knives, using, Bowies, and minis. **Technical:** Forge Damascus; heat-treats all knives. **Prices:** Vary depending on item. **Remarks:** Full-time maker; master bladesmith in the ABS. Member of the PKA; first knife sold in 1995. **Mark:** Audra.

DRAPER, MIKE,
#10 Creek Dr, Riverton, WY 82501, Phone: 307-856-6807, adraper@wyoming.com
Specialties: Mainly folding knives in tactical fashion, occasonal fixed blade. **Patterns:** Hunters, Bowies and camp knives, tactical survival. **Technical:** Grinds S30V stainless steel. **Prices:** Starting at $250+. **Remarks:** Full-time maker; first knife sold in 1996. **Mark:** Initials M.J.D. or name, city and state.

DREW, GERALD,
213 Hawk Ridge Dr, Mill Spring, NC 28756, Phone: 828-713-4762
Specialties: Blade ATS-34 blades. Straight knives. **Patterns:** Hunters, camp knives, some Bowies and tactical. **Technical:** ATS-34 preferred. **Price:** $65 to $400. **Mark:** GL DREW.

DRISCOLL, MARK,
4115 Avoyer Pl, La Mesa, CA 91941, Phone: 619-670-0695
Specialties: High-art, period pieces and working/using knives of his design or to customer specs; some fancy. **Patterns:** Swords, Bowies, fighters, daggers, hunters and primitive (mountain man-styles). **Technical:** Forges 52100, 5160, O1, L6, 1095, and maker his own Damascus and mokume; also does multiple quench heat treating. Uses exotic hardwoods, ivory and horn, offers fancy file work, carving, scrimshaws. **Prices:** $150 to $550; some to $1500. **Remarks:** Part-time maker; first knife sold in 1986. Doing business as Mountain Man Knives. **Mark:** Double "M."

DROST, JASON D,
Rt 2 Box 49, French Creek, WV 26218, Phone: 304-472-7901
Specialties: Working/using straight knives of his design. **Patterns:** Hunters and utility/camp knives. **Technical:** Grinds 154CM and D2. **Prices:** $125 to $5000. **Remarks:** Spare-time maker; first knife sold in 1995. **Mark:** First and middle initials, last name, maker, city and state.

DROST, MICHAEL B,
Rt 2 Box 49, French Creek, WV 26218, Phone: 304-472-7901
Specialties: Working/using straight knives and folders of all designs. Patterns: Hunters, locking folders and utility/camp knives. **Technical:** Grinds ATS-34, D2 and CPM-T-440V. Offers dove-tailed bolsters and spacers, filework and scrimshaw. **Prices:** $125 to $400; some to $740. **Remarks:** Full-time maker; first knife sold in 1990. Doing business as Drost Custom Knives. **Mark:** Name, city and state.

DUBLIN, DENNIS,
728 Stanley St, Box 986, Enderby, B.C., CANADA V0E 1V0, Phone: 604-838-6753
Specialties: Working straight knives and folders, plain or fancy. **Patterns:** Hunters and Bowies, locking hunters, combination knives/axes. **Technical:** Forges and grinds high-carbon steels. **Prices:** $100 to $400; some higher. **Remarks:** Full-time maker; first knife sold in 1970. **Mark:** Name.

DUFF, BILL,
2801 Ash St, Poteau, OK 74953, Phone: 918-647-4458
Specialties: Straight knives and folders, some fancy. **Patterns:** Hunters, folders and miniatures. **Technical:** Grinds 440-C and commercial Damascus. **Prices:** $200 to $1000 some higher. **Remarks:** First knife some in 1976. **Mark:** Bill Duff.

DUFOUR, ARTHUR J,
8120 De Armoun Rd, Anchorage, AK 99516, Phone: 907-345-1701
Specialties: Working straight knives from standard patterns. **Patterns:** Hunters, Bowies, camp and fishing knives—grinded thin and pointed. **Technical:** Grinds 440C, ATS-34, AEB-L. Tempers 57-58R; hollow-grinds. **Prices:** $135; some to $250. **Remarks:** Part-time maker; first knife sold in 1970. **Mark:** Prospector logo.

DUGGER, DAVE,
2504 West 51, Westwood, KS 66205, Phone: 913-831-2382
Specialties: Working straight knives; fantasy pieces. **Patterns:** Hunters, boots and daggers in one-of-a-kind styles. **Technical:** Grinds D2, 440C and 154CM. **Prices:** $75 to $350; some to $1200. **Remarks:** Part-time maker; first knife sold in 1979. Not currently accepting orders. Doing business as Dog Knives. **Mark:** DOG.

DUNKERLEY, RICK,
PO Box 582, Seeley Lake, MT 59868, Phone: 406-677-5496, rick@dunkerleyhandmadeknives.com
Specialties: Mosaic Damascus folders and carbon steel utility knives. **Patterns:** One-of-a-kind folders, standard hunters and utility designs. **Technical:** Forges 52100, Damascus and mosaic Damascus. Prefers natural handle materials. **Prices:** $200 and up. **Remarks:** Full-time maker; first knife sold in 1984, ABS Master Smith. Doing business as Dunkerley Custom Knives. Dunkerley handmade knives, sole authorship. **Mark:** Dunkerley, MS.

DUNN, CHARLES K,
17740 GA Hwy 116, Shiloh, GA 31826, Phone: 706-846-2666
Specialties: Fancy and working straight knives and folders of his design and to customer specs. **Patterns:** Bowies, hunters and locking folders. **Technical:** Grinds 440C and ATS-34. Engraves; filework offered. **Prices:** $75 to $300. **Remarks:** Part-time maker; first knife sold in 1988. **Mark:** First initial, last name, city, state.

DUNN, STEVE,
376 Biggerstaff Rd, Smiths Grove, KY 42171, Phone: 270-563-9830, dunndeal@verizon.net; Web: www.stevedunnknives.com
Specialties: Working and using straight knives of his design; period pieces. Also offer engraving & gold inlays. **Patterns:** Hunters, skinners, Bowies, fighters, camp knives, folders, swords and battle axes. **Technical:** Forges own Damascus, 1075, 15N20, 52100, 1084, L6. **Prices:** Moderate to upscale. **Remarks:** Full-time maker; first knife sold in 1990. **Mark:** Last name and MS.

DURAN, JERRY T,
PO Box 80692, Albuquerque, NM 87198-0692, Phone: 505-873-4676, jtdknives@hotmail.com; Web: www.kmg.org/jtdknives
Specialties: Tactical folders, Bowies, fighters, liner locks, autopsy and hunters. **Patterns:** Folders, Bowies, hunters and tactical knives. **Technical:** Forges own Damascus and forges carbon steel. **Prices:** Moderate to upscale. **Remarks:** Full-time maker; first knife sold in 1978. **Mark:** Initials in elk rack logo.

DURHAM, KENNETH,
BUZZARD ROOST FORGE, 10495 White Pike, Cherokee, AL 35616, Phone: 256-359-4287, www.home.hiwaay.net/~jamesd/
Specialties: Bowies, dirks, hunters. **Patterns:** Traditional patterns. **Technical:** Forges 1095, 5160, 52100 and makes own Damascus. **Prices:** $85 to $1600. **Remarks:** Began making knives about 1995. Received Journeyman stamp 1999. Got Master Smith stamp in 2004. **Mark:** Bull's head with Ken Durham above and Cherokee AL below.

DURIO, FRED,
144 Gulino St, Opelousas, LA 70570, Phone: 337-948-4831/cell 337-351-2652, fdurio@yahoo.com
Specialties: Folders. **Patterns:** Liner locks; plain and fancy. **Technical:** Makes own Damascus. **Prices:** Moderate to upscale. **Remarks:** Full-time maker. **Mark:** Last name-Durio.

DUVALL, FRED,
10715 Hwy 190, Benton, AR 72015, Phone: 501-778-9360
Specialties: Working straight knives and folders. **Patterns:** Locking folders, slip joints, hunters, fighters and Bowies. **Technical:** Grinds D2 and CPM440V; forges 5160. **Prices:** $100 to $400; some to $800. **Remarks:** Part-time maker; first knife sold in 1973. **Mark:** Last name.

DYER, DAVID,
4531 Hunters Glen, Granbury, TX 76048, Phone: 817-573-1198
Specialties: Working skinners and early period knives. **Patterns:** Customer designs, his own patterns. **Technical:** Coal forged blades; 5160 and 52100 steels. Grinds D2, 1095, L6. **Prices:** $150 for neck knives and small (3" to 3-1/2"). To $600 for large blades and specialty blades. **Mark:** Last name DYER electro etched.

DYESS, EDDIE,
1005 Hamilton, Roswell, NM 88201, Phone: 505-623-5599, eddyess@msn.com
Specialties: Working and using straight knives in standard patterns. **Patterns:** Hunters and fighters. **Technical:** Grinds 440C, 154CM and D2 on request. **Prices:** $150 to $300, some higher. **Remarks:** Spare-time maker; first knife sold in 1980. **Mark:** Last name.

DYRNOE, PER,
Sydskraenten 10, Tulstrup, DK 3400 Hilleroed, DENMARK, Phone: +45 42287041
Specialties: Hand-crafted knives with zirconia ceramic blades. **Patterns:** Hunters, skinners, Norwegian-style tolle knives, most in animal-like ergonomic shapes. **Technical:** Handles of exotic hardwood, horn, fossil ivory, etc. Norwegian-style sheaths. **Prices:** Start at $500. **Remarks:** Part-time maker in cooperation with Hans J. Henriksen; first knife sold in 1993. **Mark:** Initial logo.

E

EAKER, ALLEN L,
416 Clinton Ave Dept KI, Paris, IL 61944, Phone: 217-466-5160
Specialties: Traditional straight knives and folders of his design. **Patterns:** Hunters, locking folders and slip-joint folders. **Technical:** Grinds 440C; inlays. **Prices:** $125 to $325; some to $500. **Remarks:** Spare-time maker; first knife sold in 1994. **Mark:** Initials in tankard logo stamped on tang, serial number on back side.

EALY, DELBERT,
PO Box 121, Indian River, MI 49749, Phone: 231-238-4705

EASLER JR., RUSSELL O,
PO Box 301, Woodruff, SC 29388, Phone: 864-476-7830
Specialties: Working straight knives and folders. **Patterns:** Hunters, tantos and boots; locking folders and interframes. **Technical:** Grinds 440C, 154CM and ATS-34. **Prices:** $100 to $350; some to $800. **Remarks:** Part-time maker; first knife sold in 1973. **Mark:** Name or name with bear logo.

EATON, FRANK L JR,
41 Vista Woods Rd, Stafford, VA 22556, Phone: 540-657-6160, FEton2@aol.com
Specialties: Full tang/hidden tang fixed working and art knives of his own design. **Patterns:** Hunters, skinners, fighters, Bowies, tacticals and daggers. **Technical:** Stock removal maker, prefer using natural materials. **Prices:** $175 to $400. **Remarks:** Part-time maker -Active Duty Airborn Ranger-Making 4 years. **Mark:** Name over 75th Ranger Regimental Crest.

EATON, RICK,
313 Dailey Rd, Broadview, MT 59015, Phone: 406-667-2405, rick@eatonknives.com; Web: www.eatonknives.com
Specialties: Interframe folders and one-hand-opening side locks. **Patterns:** Bowies, daggers, fighters and folders. **Technical:** Grinds 154CM, ATS-34, 440C and other maker's Damascus. Offers high-quality hand engraving, Bulino and gold inlay. **Prices:** Upscale. **Remarks:** Full-time maker; first knife sold in 1982. **Mark:** Full name or full name and address.

EBISU, HIDESAKU,
3-39-7 Koi Osako Nishi Ku, Hiroshima City, JAPAN 733 0816

ECHOLS, ROGER,
46 Channing Rd, Nashville, AR 71852-8588, Phone: 870-451-9089, blademanechols@aol.com
Specialties: Liner locks, auto-scale release, lock backs. **Patterns:** His or yours. **Technical:** Autos. **Prices:** $500 to $1700. **Remarks:** Likes to use pearl, ivory and Damascus the most. Made first knife in 1984. Part-time maker; tool and die maker by trade. **Mark:** Name.

EDDY, HUGH E,
211 E Oak St, Caldwell, ID 83605, Phone: 208-459-0536

EDEN, THOMAS,
PO Box 57, Cranbury, NJ 08512, Phone: 609-371-0774, njirrigation@msn.com
Specialties: Chef's knives. **Patterns:** Fixed blade, working patterns, hand forged. **Technical:** Damascus. **Remarks:** ABS Smith. **Mark:** Eden (script).

EDGE, TOMMY,
1244 County Road 157, Cash, AR 72421, Phone: 501-477-5210, tedge@tex.net
Specialties: Fancy/embellished working knives of his design. **Patterns:** Bowies, hunters and utility/camping knives. **Technical:** Grinds 440C, ATS-34 and D2. Makes own cable Damascus; offers filework. **Prices:** $70 to $250; some to $1500. **Remarks:** Part-time maker; first knife sold in 1973. **Mark:** Stamped first initial, last name and stenciled name, city and state in oval shape.

EDWARDS, FAIN E,
PO Box 280, Topton, NC 28781, Phone: 828-321-3127

EDWARDS, MITCH,
303 New Salem Rd, Glasgow, KY 42141, Phone: 270-404-0758 / 270-404-0758, medwards@glasgow-ky.com; Web: www.traditionalknives.com
Specialties: Period pieces. **Patterns:** Neck knives, camp, rifleman and Bowie knives. **Technical:** All hand forged, forges own Damascus O1, 1084, 1095, L6, 15N20. **Prices:** $200 to $1000. **Remarks:** Journeyman Smith. **Mark:** Broken heart.

EHRENBERGER, DANIEL ROBERT,
1213 S Washington St, Mexico, MO 65265, Phone: 573-633-2010
Specialties: Affordable working/using straight knives of his design and to custom specs. Patterns: 10" western Bowie, fighters, hunting and skinning knives. **Technical:** Forges 1085, 1095, his own Damascus and cable Damascus. **Prices:** $80 to $500. **Remarks:** Full-time maker, first knife sold 1994. **Mark:** Ehrenberger JS.

EKLUND, MAIHKEL,
Fone Stam V9, S-820 41 Farila, SWEDEN, info@art-knives.com; Web: www.art-knives.com
Specialties: Collector-grade working straight knives. **Patterns:** Hunters, Bowies and fighters. **Technical:** Grinds ATS-34, Uddeholm and Dama steel. Engraves and scrimshaws. **Prices:** $200 to $2000. **Remarks:** Full-time maker; first knife sold in 1983. **Mark:** Initials or name.

ELDER JR., PERRY B,
1321 Garrettsburg Rd, Clarksville, TN 37042-2516, Phone: 931-647-9416, pbebje@bellsouth.net
Specialties: Hunters, combat Bowies bird and trout. **Technical:** High-carbon steel and Damascus blades. **Prices:** $350 and up depending on blade desired. **Mark:** ELDER.

ELDRIDGE, ALLAN,
7731 Four Winds Dr, Ft. Worth, TX 76133, Phone: 817-370-7778
Specialties: Fancy classic straight knives in standard patterns. **Patterns:** Hunters, Bowies, fighters, folders and miniatures. **Technical:** Grinds O1 and Damascus. Engraves silver-wire inlays, pearl inlays, scrimshaws and offers filework. **Prices:** $50 to $500; some to $1200. **Remarks:** Spare-time maker; first knife sold in 1965. **Mark:** Initials.

ELISHEWITZ, ALLEN,
PO Box 3059, Canyon Lake, TX 78133, Phone: 830-899-5356, allen@elishewitzknives.com; Web: elishewitzknives.com
Specialties: Collectible high-tech working straight knives and folders of his design. **Patterns:** Working, utility and tactical knives. **Technical:** Designs and uses innovative locking mechanisms. All designs drafted and field-tested. **Prices:** $600 to $1000. **Remarks:** Full-time maker; first knife sold in 1989. **Mark:** Gold medallion inlaid in blade.

ELKINS, VAN,
3596 New Monroe Rd., Bastrop, LA 71220, Phone: 318-614-0543/318-283-2374
Specialties: Folders, from liner-locks to one-of-a-kind damascus button-locks. **Patterns:** Bowies and folders. **Technical:** Forges own damascus in several patterns. Uses high-tech stainless in tactical designs. **Prices:** $595 to $5800. **Remarks:** Believes in sole authorship. First knife sold in 1984. **Mark:** Elkins.

ELLEFSON, JOEL,
PO Box 1016, 310 S 1st St, Manhattan, MT 59741, Phone: 406-284-3111
Specialties: Working straight knives, fancy daggers and one-of-a-kinds. **Patterns:** Hunters, daggers and some folders. **Technical:** Grinds A2, 440C and ATS-34. Makes own mokume in bronze, brass, silver and shibuishi; makes brass/steel blades. **Prices:** $100 to $500; some to $2000. **Remarks:** Part-time maker; first knife sold in 1978. **Mark:** Stylized last initial.

ELLERBE, W B,
3871 Osceola Rd, Geneva, FL 32732, Phone: 407-349-5818
Specialties: Period and primitive knives and sheaths. **Patterns:** Bowies to patch knives, some tomahawks. **Technical:** Grinds Sheffield O1 and files. **Prices:** Start at $35. **Remarks:** Full-time maker; first knife sold in 1971. Doing business as Cypress Bend Custom Knives. **Mark:** Last name or initials.

ELLIOTT, JERRY,
4507 Kanawha Ave, Charleston, WV 25304, Phone: 304-925-5045, elliottknives@verizon.net
Specialties: Classic and traditional straight knives and folders of his design and to customer specs. **Patterns:** Hunters, locking folders and Bowies. **Technical:** Grinds ATS-34, 154CM, O1, D2 and T-440-V. All guards silver-soldered; bolsters are pinned on straight knives, spot-welded on folders. **Prices:** $80 to $265; some to $1000. **Remarks:** Full-time maker; first knife sold in 1972. **Mark:** First and middle initials, last name, knife maker, city, state.

ELLIS, DAVE/ABS MASTERSMITH,
380 South Melrose Dr #407, Vista, CA 92083, Phone: 760-643-4032 Eves: 760-945-7177, www.exquisiteknives.com
Specialties: Bowies, utility and combat knives. **Patterns:** Using knives to art quality pieces. **Technical:** Forges 5160, L6, 52100, cable and his own Damascus steels. **Prices:** $300 to $4000. **Remarks:** Part-time maker. California's first ABS Master Smith. **Mark:** Dagger-Rose with name and M.S. mark.

ELLIS, WILLIAM DEAN,
2767 Edgar Ave, Sanger, CA 93657, Phone: 559-314-4459, urleebird@comcast.net; Web: www.billysblades.com
Specialties: Classic and fancy knives of his design. **Patterns:** Boots, fighters and utility knives. **Technical:** Grinds ATS-34, D2 and Damascus. Offers tapered tangs and six patterns of filework; tooled multi-colored sheaths. **Prices:** $250 to $500; some to $1500. **Remarks:** Part-time maker; first knife sold in 1991. Doing business as Billy's Blades. **Mark:** "B" in a five-point star next to "Billy," city and state within a rounded-corner rectangle.

ELLIS, WILLY B,
4941 Cardinal Trail, Palm Harbor, FL 34683, Phone: 727-942-6420, Web: www.willyb.com
Specialties: One-of-a-kind high art and fantasy knives of his design. Occasional customs full size and miniatures. **Patterns:** Bowies, fighters, hunters and others. **Technical:** Grinds 440C, ATS-34, 1095, carbon Damascus, ivory bone, stone and metal carving. **Prices:** $175 to $15,000. **Remarks:** Full-time maker, first knife made in 1973. Member Knifemakers Guild. Jewel setting inlays. **Mark:** Willy B. or WB'S C etched or carved.

ELROD, ROGER R,
58 Dale Ave, Enterprise, AL 36330, Phone: 334-347-1863

EMBRETSEN, KAJ,
FALUVAGEN 67, S-82821 Edsbyn, SWEDEN, Phone: 46-271-21057, Fax: 46-271-22961, kay.embretsen@telia.com Web:www.embretsenknives.com
Specialties: Large bowies, hunting, fishing, fancy collector knives. **Patterns:**Using exotic handle materials of hard to find natural materials. **Technical:** Uses D2, 6K stellite, 440C, 52160, Damascus, cable. Forges & stock removal. **Remarks:**First knife sold in 1978. **Prices:**$150-$750 some to $5000. **Mark:**Ross Custom Knives. Tang Stamp.

EMERSON, ERNEST R,
PO Box 4180, Torrance, CA 90510-4180, Phone: 310-212-7455, info@emersonknives.com; Web: www.emersonknives.com
Specialties: High-tech folders and combat fighters. **Patterns:** Fighters, LinerLock® combat folders and SPECWAR combat knives. **Technical:** Grinds 154CM and Damascus. Makes folders with titanium fittings, liners and locks. Chisel grind specialist. **Prices:** $550 to $850; some to $10,000. **Remarks:** Full-time maker; first knife sold in 1983. **Mark:** Last name and Specwar knives.

ENCE, JIM,
145 S 200 East, Richfield, UT 84701, Phone: 435-896-6206
Specialties: High-art period pieces (spec in California knives) art knives. **Patterns:** Art, boot knives, fighters, Bowies and occasional folders. **Technical:** Grinds 440C for polish and beauty boys; makes own Damascus. **Prices:** Upscale. **Remarks:** Full-time maker; first knife sold in 1977. Does own engraving, gold work and stone work. Guild member since 1977. Founding member of the AKI. **Mark:** Ence, usually engraved.

ENGLAND, VIRGIL,
1340 Birchwood St, Anchorage, AK 99508, Phone: 907-274-9494, WEB: www.virgilengland.com
Specialties: Edged weapons and equipage, one-of-a-kind only. **Patterns:** Axes, swords, lances and body armor. **Technical:** Forges and grinds as pieces dictate. Offers stainless and Damascus. **Prices:** Upscale. **Remarks:** A veteran knifemaker. No commissions. **Mark:** Stylized initials.

ENGLE, WILLIAM,
16608 Oak Ridge Rd, Boonville, MO 65233, Phone: 816-882-6277
Specialties: Traditional working and using straight knives of his design. **Patterns:** Hunters, Bowies and fighters. **Technical:** Grinds 440C, ATS-34 and 154 CM. **Prices:** $250 to $500; some higher. **Remarks:** Part-time maker; first knife sold in 1982. All knives come with certificate of authenticity. **Mark:** Last name in block lettering.

ENGLEBRETSON, GEORGE,
1209 NW 49th St, Oklahoma City, OK 73118, Phone: 405-840-4784
Specialties: Working straight knives. **Patterns:** Hunters and Bowies. **Technical:** Grinds A2, D2, 440C and ATS-34. **Prices:** Start at $150. **Remarks:** Full-time maker; first knife sold in 1967. **Mark:** "By George," name and city.

ENGLISH, JIM,
14586 Olive Vista Dr, Jamul, CA 91935, Phone: 619-669-0833
Specialties: Traditional working straight knives to customer specs. Patterns: Hunters, Bowies, fighters, tantos, daggers, boot and utility/camp knives. **Technical:** Grinds 440C, ATS-34, commercial Damascus and customer choice. **Prices:** $130 to $350. **Remarks:** Part-time maker; first knife sold in 1985. In addition to custom line, also does business as Mountain Home Knives. **Mark:** Double "A," Double "J" logo.

ENNIS, RAY,
1220S 775E, Ogden, UT 84404, Phone: 800-410-7603, Fax: 501-621-2683, nifmakr@hotmail.com; Web:www.ennis-entrekusa.com

ENOS III, THOMAS M,
12302 State Rd 535, Orlando, FL 32836, Phone: 407-239-6205, tmenos3@att.net
Specialties: Heavy-duty working straight knives; unusual designs. **Patterns:** Swords, machetes, daggers, skinners, filleting, period pieces. **Technical:** Grinds 440C, D2, 154CM. **Prices:** $75 to $1500. **Remarks:** Full-time maker; first knife sold in 1972. No longer accepting custom requests. Will be making his own designs. Send SASE for listing of items for sale. **Mark:** Name in knife logo and year, type of steel and serial number.

ENTIN, ROBERT,
127 Pembroke St 1, Boston, MA 02118

EPTING, RICHARD,
4021 Cody Dr, College Station, TX 77845, Phone: 979-690-6496, rgeknives@hotmail.com; Web: www.eptingknives.com
Specialties: Folders and working straight knives. **Patterns:** Hunters, Bowies, and locking folders. **Technical:** Forges high-carbon steel and his own Damascus. **Prices:** $200 to $800; some to $1800. **Remarks:** Part-time maker, first knife sold 1996. **Mark:** Name in arch logo.

ERICKSON, L.M.,
1379 Black Mountain Cir, Ogden, UT 84404, Phone: 801-737-1930
Specialties: Straight knives; period pieces. **Patterns:** Bowies, fighters, boots and hunters. **Technical:** Grinds 440C, 154CM and commercial Damascus. **Prices:** $200 to $900; some to $5000. **Remarks:** Part-time maker; first knife sold in 1981. **Mark:** Name, city, state.

ERICKSON, WALTER E.,
22280 Shelton Tr, Atlanta, MI 49709, Phone: 989-785-5262, wberic@racc2000.com
Specialties: Unusual survival knives and high-tech working knives. **Patterns:** Butterflies, hunters, tantos. **Technical:** Grinds ATS-34 or customer choice. **Prices:** $150 to $500; some to $1500. **Remarks:** Full-time maker; first knife sold in 1981. **Mark:** Using pantograph with assorted fonts (no longer stamping).

ERIKSEN, JAMES THORLIEF,
dba VIKING KNIVES, 3830 Dividend Dr, Garland, TX 75042, Phone: 972-494-3667, Fax: 972-235-4932, VikingKnives@aol.com
Specialties: Heavy-duty working and using straight knives and folders utilizing traditional, Viking original and customer specification patterns. Some high-tech and fancy/embellished knives available. **Patterns:** Bowies, hunters, skinners, boot and belt knives, utility/camp knives, fighters, daggers, locking folders, slip-joint folders and kitchen knives. **Technical:** Hollow-grinds 440C, D2, ASP-23, ATS-34, 154CM, Vascowear. **Prices:** $150 to $300; some to $600. **Remarks:** Full-time maker; first knife sold in 1985. Doing business as Viking Knives. For a color catalog showing 50 different models, mail $5 to above address. **Mark:** VIKING or VIKING USA for export.

ERNEST, PHIL,
PO 5240, Wittier, CA 90607-5240, Phone: 562-556-2324, hugger883562@yahoo.com Web:http://ernestcustomknives.com
Specialties: Fixed Blades. **Patterns:** Wide range. Many original as well as hunters, camp, fighters, daggers, bowies and tactical. Specializing in Wharncliff's of all sizes. **Technical:** Grinds commercial Damascus, mosaic Damascus, ATS-34 and 440C. Full tangs with bolsters. Handle material includes all types of exotic hardwood, abalone, pearl, mammoth tooth, mammoth ivory, Damascus steel and mosaic Damascus. **Remarks:** Full time maker. First knife sold in 1999. **Prices:**$200 to $1800. Some to $2500. **Mark:** Owl logo with PJ Ernest Whittier CA or PJ Ernest.

ERNEST, PHIL (PJ),
PO Box 5240, Whittier, CA 90607-5240, Phone: 562-556-2324, hugger883562@yahoo.com; Web:www.ernestcustomknives.com
Specialties: Fixed blades. **Patterns:** Wide range. Many original as well as hunters, camp, fighters, daggers, bowies and tactical. Specialzin in Wharncliff's of all sizes. **Technical:** Grinds commercial Damascus, Mosaid Damascus. ATS-34, and 440C. Full Tangs with bolsters. Handle material includes all types of exotic hardwood, abalone, peal mammoth tooth, mammoth ivory, Damascus steel and Mosaic Damascus. **Remarks:** Full time maker. First knife sold in 1999. **Prices:** $200 to $1800. Some to $2500. **Mark:** Owl logo with PJ Ernest Whittier CA or PJ Ernest.

ESSEGIAN, RICHARD,
7387 E Tulare St, Fresno, CA 93727, Phone: 309-255-5950
Specialties: Fancy working knives of his design; art knives. **Patterns:** Bowies and some small hunters. **Technical:** Grinds A2, D2, 440C and 154CM. Engraves and inlays. **Prices:** Start at $600. **Remarks:** Part-time maker; first knife sold in 1986. **Mark:** Last name, city and state.

ETZLER, JOHN,
11200 N Island, Grafton, OH 44044, Phone: 440-748-2460, jetzler@bright.net; Web: members.tripod.com/~etzlerknives/
Specialties: High-art and fantasy straight knives and folders of his design and to customer specs. **Patterns:** Folders, daggers, fighters, utility knives. **Technical:** Forges and grinds nickel Damascus and tool

steel; grinds stainless steels. Prefers exotic, natural materials. **Prices:** $250 to $1200; some to $6500. **Remarks:** Full-time maker; first knife sold in 1992. **Mark:** Name or initials.

EVANS, BRUCE A,
409 CR 1371, Booneville, MS 38829, Phone: 662-720-0193, beknives@avsia.com; Web: www.bruceevans.homestead.com/open.html
Specialties: Forges blades. **Patterns:** Hunters, Bowies, or will work with customer. **Technical:** 5160, cable Damascus, pattern welded Damascus. **Prices:** $200 and up. **Mark:** Bruce A. Evans Same with JS on reverse of blade.

EVANS, CARLTON,
PO Box 72, Fort Davis, TX 79734, Phone: 817-886-9231, carlton@carltonevans.com; Web: www.evanshandmakeknives.com
Specialties: High end folders and fixed blades. **Technical:** Uses the stock removal methods. The materials used are of the highest quality. **Remarks:** Full-time knifemaker, voting member of Knifemakers Guild, member of the Texas Knifemakers and Collectors Association.

EVANS, RONALD B,
209 Hoffer St, Middleton, PA 17057-2723, Phone: 717-944-5464

EVANS, VINCENT K AND GRACE,
35 Beaver Creek Rd, Cathlamet, WA 98612, Phone: 360-795-0096, evansvk@gmail.com
Specialties: Period pieces; swords. **Patterns:** Scottish, Viking, central Asian. **Technical:** Forges 5160 and his own Damascus. **Prices:** $700 to $4000; some to $8000. **Remarks:** Full-time maker; first knife sold in 1983. **Mark:** Last initial with fish logo.

EWING, JOHN H,
3276 Dutch Valley Rd, Clinton, TN 37716, Phone: 865-457-5757, johnja@comcast.net
Specialties: Working straight knives, hunters, camp knives. **Patterns:** Hunters. **Technical:** Grinds 440-D2. Forges 5160, 1095 prefers forging. **Prices:** $150 to $2000. **Remarks:** Part-time maker; first knife sold in 1985. **Mark:** First initial, last name, some embellishing done on knives.

F

FAGAN, JAMES A,
109 S 17 Ave, Lake Worth, FL 33460, Phone: 561-585-9349

FANT JR., GEORGE,
1983 CR 3214, Atlanta, TX 75551-6515, Phone: (903) 846-2938

FARID R, MEHR,
8 Sidney Close, Tunbridge Wells, Kent, ENGLAND TN2 5QQ, Phone: 011-44-1892 520345, farid@faridknives.com; Web: www.faridknives.com
Specialties: Hollow handle survival knives. High tech folders. **Patterns:** Flat grind blades & chisel ground LinerLock® folders. **Technical:** Grinds 440C, CPMT-440V, CPM-420V, CPM-15V, CPM5125V, and T-1 high speed steel. **Prices:** $550 to $5000. **Remarks:** Full-time maker; first knife sold in 1991. **Mark:** First name stamped.

FARR, DAN,
285 Glen Ellyn Way, Rochester, NY 14618, Phone: 585-721-1388
Specialties: Hunting, camping, fighting and utility. **Patterns:** Fixed blades. **Technical:** Forged or stock removal. **Prices:** $150 to $750.

FASSIO, MELVIN G,
420 Tyler Way, Lolo, MT 59847, Phone: 406-273-9143
Specialties: Working folders to customer specs. **Patterns:** Locking folders, hunters and traditional-style knives. **Technical:** Grinds 440C. **Prices:** $125 to $350. **Remarks:** Part-time maker; first knife sold in 1975. **Mark:** Name and city, dove logo.

FAUCHEAUX, HOWARD J,
PO Box 206, Loreauville, LA 70552, Phone: 318-229-6467
Specialties: Working straight knives and folders; period pieces. Also a hatchet with capping knife in the handle. **Patterns:** Traditional locking folders, hunters, fighters and Bowies. **Technical:** Forges W2, 1095 and his own Damascus; stock removal D2. **Prices:** Start at $200. **Remarks:** Full-time maker; first knife sold in 1969. **Mark:** Last name.

FAUST, DICK,
624 Kings Hwy N, Rochester, NY 14617, Phone: 585-544-1948, dickfaustknives@mac.com
Specialties: High-performance working straight knives. **Patterns:** Hunters and utility/camp knives. **Technical:** Hollow grinds 154CM full tang. Exotic woods, stag and Micarta handles. Provides a custom leather sheath with each knife. **Prices:** From $200 to $600, some higher. **Remarks:** Full-time maker. **Mark:** Signature.

FAUST, JOACHIM,
Kirchgasse 10, 95497 Goldkronach, GERMANY

FECAS, STEPHEN J,
1312 Shadow Lane, Anderson, SC 29625, Phone: 864-287-4834, Fax: 864-287-4834
Specialties: Front release lock backs, liner locks. Folders only. **Patterns:** Gents folders. **Technical:** Grinds ATS-34, Damascus-Ivories and pearl handles. **Prices:** $650 to $1200. **Remarks:** Full-time maker since 1980. First knife sold in 1977. All knives hand finished to 1500 grit. **Mark:** Last name signature.

FELIX, ALEXANDER,
PO Box 4036, Torrance, CA 90510, Phone: 310-320-1836, sgiandubh@dslextreme.com
Specialties: Straight working knives, fancy ethnic designs. **Patterns:** Hunters, Bowies, daggers, period pieces. **Technical:** Forges carbon steel and Damascus; forged stainless and titanium jewelry, gold and silver casting. **Prices:** $110 and up. **Remarks:** Jeweler, ABS Journeyman Smith. **Mark:** Last name.

FELLOWS, MIKE,
PO Box 162, Mosselbay 6500, SOUTH AFRICA, Phone: 27 82 960 3868, karatshin@gmail.com
Specialties: Miniatures, art knives and folders with occasionally hunters and skinners. **Patterns:** Own designs. **Technical:** Uses own Damascus. **Prices:** R2,000 and up. **Remarks:** Use only indigenous materials. Exotic hard woods, horn & ivory. Does all own embellishments. **Mark:** "SHIN" letter from Hebrew alphabet over Hebrew work "Karat." **Other:** Member of knifemakers guild of Southern Africa.

FERGUSON, JIM,
PO Box 301, San Angelo, TX 76902, Phone: 915-651-6656
Specialties: Straight working knives and folders. **Patterns:** Working belt knives, hunters, Bowies and some folders. **Technical:** Grinds ATS-34, D2 and Vascowear. Flat-grinds hunting knives. **Prices:** $200 to $600; some to $1000. **Remarks:** Full-time maker; first knife sold in 1987. **Mark:** First and middle initials, last name.

FERGUSON, JIM,
32131 Via Bande, Temecula, CA 92592, Phone: 951-302-0267, jim@twistednickel.com; Web: www.twistednickel.com
Specialties: Nickel Damascus, Bowies, daggers, push blades. **Patterns:** All styles. **Technical:** Forges Damascus and sells in U.S. and Canada. **Prices:** $120 to $5000. **Remarks:** 1200 sq. ft. commercial shop, 75 ton press. Has made over 11,000 lbs of Damascus. **Mark:** Jim Ferguson over push blade. Also make swords, battle axes and utilities.

FERGUSON, LEE,
1993 Madison 7580, Hindsville, AR 72738, Phone: 479-443-0084, info@fergusonknives.com; Web: www.fergusonknives.com
Specialties: Straight working knives and folders, some fancy. **Patterns:** Hunters, daggers, swords, locking folders and slip-joints. **Technical:** Grinds D2, 440C and ATS-34; heat-treats. **Prices:** $50 to $600; some to $4000. **Remarks:** Full-time maker; first knife sold in 1977. **Mark:** Full name.

FERGUSON, LINDA,
1993 Madison 7580, Hindsville, AR 72738, Phone: 479-443-0084, info@fergusonknives.com: Web: www.fergusonknives.com
Specialties: Mini knives. **Patterns:** Daggers & hunters. **Technical:** Hollow ground, stainless steel or Damascus. **Prices:** $65 to $250. **Remarks:** 2004 member Knifemakers Guild, Miniature Knifemakers Society. **Mark:** LF inside a Roman numeral 2.

FERRARA, THOMAS,
122 Madison Dr, Naples, FL 33942, Phone: 813-597-3363, Fax: 813-597-3363
Specialties: High-art, traditional and working straight knives and folders of all designs. **Patterns:** Boots, Bowies, daggers, fighters and hunters. **Technical:** Grinds 440C, D2 and ATS-34; heat-treats. **Prices:** $100 to $700; some to $1300. **Remarks:** Part-time maker; first knife sold in 1983. **Mark:** Last name.

FERRIER, GREGORY K,
3119 Simpson Dr, Rapid City, SD 57702, Phone: 605-342-9280

FERRIS, BILL,
186 Thornton Dr, Palm Beach Garden, FL 33418

FERRY, TOM,
16005 SE 322nd St, Auburn, WA 98092, Phone: 255-217-2569, knfesmth71@aol.com; Web: www.tferryknives.com
Specialties: Presentation grade knives. **Patterns:** Folders and fixed blades. **Technical:** Specialize in Damascus and Timascus™ (Titanium Damascus). **Prices:** $250 and up **Remarks:** Name Tom Ferry DBA: Soos Creek Ironworks. ABS Master Smith co-developer of Timascus™. **Mark:** Combined T and F in a circle and/or last name.

FIKES, JIMMY L,
PO Box 3457, Jasper, AL 35502, Phone: 205-387-9302, Fax: 205-221-1980, oleyfermo@aol.com
Specialties: High-art working knives; artifact knives; using knives with cord-wrapped handles; swords and combat weapons. **Patterns:** Axes to buckskinners, camp knives to miniatures, tantos to tomahawks; springless folders. **Technical:** Forges W2, O1 and his own Damascus. **Prices:** $135 to $3000; exceptional knives to $7000. **Remarks:** Full-time maker. **Mark:** Stylized initials.

FILIPPOU, IOANNIS-MINAS,
7 Krinis Str Nea Smyrni, Athens 17122, GREECE, Phone: (1) 935-2093

FINCH, RICKY D,
2446 Hwy. 191, West Liberty, KY 41472, Phone: 606-743-7151, finchknives@mrtc.com; Web: www.finchknives.com
Specialties: Traditional working/using straight knives of his design or

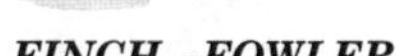

to customer spec. **Patterns:** Hunters, skinners and utility/camp knives. LinerLock® of his design. **Technical:** Grinds 44C, ATS-34 and CPM154, hand rubbed stain finish, use Micarta, stabilized wood, natural and exotic. **Prices:** $85 to $225. **Remarks:** Part-time maker, first knife made 1994. Doing business as Finch Knives. **Mark:** Last name inside outline of state of Kentucky.

FIORINI, BILL,
E2173 Axlen Rd., DeSoto, WI 54624, Phone: 608-780-5898, fiorini.will@uwlax.edu; Web: www.billfiorini.com
Specialties: Fancy working knives. **Patterns:** Hunters, boots, Japanese-style knives and kitchen/utility knives and folders. **Technical:** Forges own Damascus, mosaic and mokune-gane. **Prices:** Full range. **Remarks:** Full-time metal smith researching pattern materials. **Mark:** Orchid crest with name KOKA in Japanese.

FISHER, JAY,
1405 Edwards, Clovis, NM 88101, Phone: 575-763-2268, jayfisher@jayfisher.com Web: www.JayFisher.com
Specialties: High-art, working and collector's knives of his design and client's designs. Military working and commemoratives. **Patterns:** Hunters, daggers, folding knives, museum pieces and high-art sculptures. **Technical:** Grinds 440C, ATS-34, O1and D2. Prolific maker of stone-handled knives and swords. **Prices:** $400 to $50,000; some higher. **Remarks:** Full-time maker; first knife sold in 1980. High resolution etching, computer and manual engraving. **Mark:** Signature JaFisher"

FISHER, THEO (TED),
8115 Modoc Lane, Montague, CA 96064, Phone: 916-459-3804
Specialties: Moderately priced working knives in carbon steel. **Patterns:** Hunters, fighters, kitchen and buckskinner knives, Damascus miniatures. **Technical:** Grinds ATS-34, L6 and 440C. **Prices:** $65 to $165; exceptional knives to $300. **Remarks:** First knife sold in 1981. **Mark:** Name in banner logo.

FISK, JERRY,
10095 Hwy 278 W, Nashville, AR 71852, Phone: 870-845-4456, jerry@fisk-knives.com; Web: wwwfisk-knives.com
Specialties: Edged weapons, collectible and functional. **Patterns:** Bowies, daggers, swords, hunters, camp knives and others. **Technical:** Forges carbon steels and his own pattern welded steels. **Prices:** $250 to $15,000. **Remarks:** National living treasure. **Mark:** Name, MS.

FISTER, JIM,
PO Box 307, Simpsonville, KY 40067
Specialties: One-of-a-kind collectibles and period pieces. **Patterns:** Bowies, camp knives, hunters, buckskinners, and daggers. **Technical:** Forges, 1085, 5160, 52100, his own Damascus, pattern and turkish. **Prices:** $150 to $2500. **Remarks:** Part-time maker; first knife sold in 1982. **Mark:** Name and MS.

FITCH, JOHN S,
45 Halbrook Rd, Clinton, AR 72031-8910, Phone: 501-893-2020

FITZGERALD, DENNIS M,
4219 Alverado Dr, Fort Wayne, IN 46816-2847, Phone: 219-447-1081
Specialties: One-of-a-kind collectibles and period pieces. **Patterns:** Skinners, fighters, camp and utility knives; period pieces. **Technical:** Forges 1085, 1095, L6, 5160, 52100, his own pattern and Turkish Damascus. **Prices:** $100 to $500. **Remarks:** Part-time maker; first knife sold in 1985. Doing business as The Ringing Circle. **Mark:** Name and circle logo.

FLINT, ROBERT,
2902 Aspen, Anchorage, AK 99517, Phone: 907-243-6706
Specialties: Working straight knives and folders. **Patterns:** Utility, hunters, fighters and gents. **Technical:** Grinds ATS-34, BG-42, D2 and Damascus. **Prices:** $150 and up. **Remarks:** Part-time maker, first knife sold in 1998. **Mark:** Last name; stylized initials.

FLOURNOY, JOE,
5750 Lisbon Rd, El Dorado, AR 71730, Phone: 870-863-7208, flournoy@ipa.net
Specialties: Working straight knives and folders. **Patterns:** Hunters, Bowies, camp knives, folders and daggers. **Technical:** Forges only high-carbon steel, steel cable and his own Damascus. **Prices:** $350 Plus. **Remarks:** First knife sold in 1977. **Mark:** Last name and MS in script.

FOGARIZZU, BOITEDDU,
via Crispi 6, 07016 Pattada, ITALY
Specialties: Traditional Italian straight knives and folders. **Patterns:** Collectible folders. **Technical:** forges and grinds 12C27, ATS-34 and his Damascus. **Prices:** $200 to $3000. **Remarks:** Full-time maker; first knife sold in 1958. **Mark:** Full name and registered logo.

FOGG, DON,
40 Alma Rd, Jasper, AL 35501-8813, Phone: 205-483-0822, dfogg@dfoggknives.com; Web: www.dfoggknives.com
Specialties: Swords, daggers, Bowies and hunting knives. Patterns: Collectible folders. **Technical:** Hand-forged high-carbon and Damascus steel. **Prices:** $200 to $5000. **Remarks:** Full-time maker; first knife sold in 1976. **Mark:** 24K gold cherry blossom.

FONTENOT, GERALD J,
901 Maple Ave, Mamou, LA 70554, Phone: 318-468-3180

FORREST, BRIAN,
FORREST KNIVES, PO Box 203, Descanso, CA 91916, Phone: 619-445-6343, forrestknives@hotmail.com; Web: www.forrestknives.com
Specialties: Forged tomahawks, working knives, big Bowies. **Patterns:** Traditional and extra large Bowies. **Technical:** Hollow grinds: 440C, 1095, S160 Damascus. **Prices"**$125 and up. **Remarks:** Member of California Knifemakers Association. Full-time maker. First knife sold in 1971. **Mark:** Forrest USA/Tomahawks marked FF (Forrest Forge).

FORTHOFER, PETE,
5535 Hwy 93S, Whitefish, MT 59937, Phone: 406-862-2674
Specialties: Interframes with checkered wood inlays; working straight knives. **Patterns:** Interframe folders and traditional-style knives; hunters, fighters and Bowies. **Technical:** Grinds D2, 440C, 154CM and ATS-34. **Prices:** $350 to $2500; some to $1500. **Remarks:** Part-time maker; full-time gunsmith. First knife sold in 1979. **Mark:** Name and logo.

FORTUNE PRODUCTS, INC.,
205 Hickory Creek Rd, Marble Falls, TX 78654, Phone: 830-693-6111, Fax: 830-693-6394, Web: www.accusharp.com
Specialties: Knife sharpeners.

FOSTER, AL,
118 Woodway Dr, Magnolia, TX 77355, Phone: 936-372-9297
Specialties: Straight knives and folders. **Patterns:** Hunting, fishing, folders and Bowies. **Technical:** Grinds 440-C, ATS-34 and D2. **Prices:** $100 to $1000. **Remarks:** Full-time maker; first knife sold in 1981. **Mark:** Scorpion logo and name.

FOSTER, BURT,
23697 Archery Range Rd, Bristol, VA 24202, Phone: 276-669-0121, burtfoster@bvunet.net; Web:www.burt@burtfoster.com
Specialties: Working straight knives, laminated blades, and some art knives of his design. **Patterns:** Bowies, hunters, daggers. **Technical:** Forges 52100, W-2 and makes own Damascus. Does own heat treating. **Remarks:** ABS MasterSmith. Full-time maker, believes in sole authorship. **Mark:** Signed "BF" initials.

FOSTER, NORVELL C,
7945 Youngsford Rd, Marion, TX 78124-1713, Phone: 830-914-2078
Specialties: Engraving; ivory handle carving. **Patterns:** American-large and small scroll-oak leaf and acorns. **Prices:** $25 to $400. **Remarks:** Have been engraving since 1957. **Mark:** N.C. Foster -Marion -Tex and current year.

FOSTER, R L (BOB),
745 Glendale Blvd, Mansfield, OH 44907, Phone: 419-756-6294

FOSTER, RONNIE E,
95 Riverview Rd., Morrilton, AR 72110, Phone: 501-354-5389
Specialties: Working, using knives, some period pieces, work with customer specs. **Patterns:** Hunters, fighters, Bowies, liner-lock folders, camp knives. **Technical:** Forge-5160, 1084, O1, 15N20-makes own Damascus. **Prices:** $200 (start). **Remarks:** Part-time maker. First knife sold 1994. **Mark:** Ronnie Foster MS.

FOSTER, TIMOTHY L,
723 Sweet Gum Acres Rd, El Dorado, AR 71730, Phone: 870-863-6188

FOWLER, CHARLES R,
226 National Forest Rd 48, Ft McCoy, FL 32134-9624, Phone: 904-467-3215

FOWLER, ED A.,
Willow Bow Ranch, PO Box 1519, Riverton, WY 82501, Phone: 307-856-9815
Specialties: High-performance working and using straight knives. **Patterns:** Hunter, camp, bird, and trout knives and Bowies. New model, the gentleman's Pronghorn. **Technical:** Low temperature forged 52100 from virgin 5-1/2 round bars, multiple quench heat treating, engraves all knives, all handles domestic sheep horn processed and aged at least 5 years. Makes heavy duty hand-stitched waxed harness leather pouch type sheathes. **Prices:** $800 to $7000. **Remarks:** Full-time maker. First knife sold in 1962. **Mark:** Initials connected.

FOWLER, JERRY,
610 FM 1660 N, Hutto, TX 78634, Phone: 512-846-2860, fowler@inetport.com
Specialties: Using straight knives of his design. **Patterns:** A variety of hunting and camp knives, combat knives. Custom designs considered. **Technical:** Forges 5160, his own Damascus and cable Damascus. Makes sheaths. Prefers natural handle materials. **Prices:** Start at $150. **Remarks:** Part-time maker; first knife sold in 1986. Doing business as Fowler Forge Knife Works. **Mark:** First initial, last name, date and J.S.

FOWLER, RICKY AND SUSAN,
FOWLER CUSTOM KNIVES, 18535-B Co. Rd. 48, Robertsdale, AL 36567, Phone: 251-947-5648, theknifeshop@gulftel.com; Web: www.fowlerknives.net
Specialties: Traditional working/using straight knives of his design or to customer specifications. Patterns: Skinners, fighters, tantos, Bowies and utility/camp knives. **Technical:** Grinds O1, exclusively. **Prices:** Start at $150. **Remarks:** Full-time maker; first knife sold in 1994. Doing business as Fowler Custom Knives. **Mark:** Last name tang stamped.

FOX, PAUL,
4721 Rock Barn Rd, Claremont, NC 28610, Phone: 828-459-2000, pfox@charter.net
Specialties: Unique locking mechanisms. **Patterns:** Pen knives, one-of-a-kind tactical knives. **Technical:** All locking mechanisms are his. **Prices:** $350 and up. **Remarks:** First knife sold in 1976. Guild member since 1977. **Mark:** Fox, P Fox, Paul Fox. Cuts out all parts of knives in shop.

FRALEY, D B,
1355 Fairbanks Ct, Dixon, CA 95620, Phone: 707-678-0393, dbtfnives@sbcglobal.net; Web:www.dbfraleyknives.com
Specialties Usable gentleman's fixed blades and folders. **Patterns:** Foure folders in four different sizes in liner lock and frame lock. **Technical:** Grinds CPMS30V, 154, 6K stellite. **Prices:** $250 and up. **Remarks:** Part time maker. First knife sold in 1990. **Mark:** First and middle initials, last name over a buffalo.

FRALEY, D B,
1355 Fairbanks Ct, Dixon, CA 95620, Phone: 707-678-0393, dbfknives@aol
Specialties: Traditional working/using straight knives and folders of his design and in standard patterns. **Patterns:** Fighters, hunters, utility/camp knives. **Technical:** Grinds ATS-34. Offers hand-stitched sheaths. **Prices:** Start at $100. **Remarks:** Part-time maker; first knife sold in 1990. **Mark:** First and middle initials, last name over buffalo.

FRAMSKI, WALTER P,
24 Rek Ln, Prospect, CT 06712, Phone: 203-758-5634

FRANCE, DAN,
Box 218, Cawood, KY 40815, Phone: 606-573-6104
Specialties: Traditional working and using straight knives of his design. **Patterns:** Hunters, Bowies and utility/camp knives. **Technical:** Forges and grinds O1, 5160 and L6. **Prices:** $35 to $125; some to $350. **Remarks:** Spare-time maker; first knife sold in 1985. **Mark:** First name.

FRANCIS, JOHN D,
FRANCIS KNIVES, 18 Miami St., Ft. Loramie, OH 45845, Phone: 937-295-3941, jdfrancis@roadrunner.com
Specialties: Utility and hunting-style fixed bladed knives of 440 C and ATS-34 steel; Micarta, exotic woods, and other types of handle materials. **Prices:** $90 to $150 range. **Remarks:** Exceptional quality and value at factory prices. **Mark:** Francis-Ft. Loramie, OH stamped on tang.

FRANCIS, VANCE,
2612 Alpine Blvd, Alpine, CA 91901, Phone: 619-445-0979
Specialties: Working straight knives. **Patterns:** Bowies and utility knives. **Technical:** Uses ATS-34, A2, D2 and Damascus; differentially tempers large blades. **Prices:** $175 to $600. **Remarks:** Part-time maker. **Mark:** First name, last name, city and state under feather in oval.

FRANK, HEINRICH H,
1147 SW Bryson St, Dallas, OR 97338, Phone: 503-831-1489, Fax: 503-831-1489
Specialties: High-art investor-class folders, handmade and engraved. **Patterns:** Folding daggers, hunter-size folders and gents. **Technical:** Grinds 07 and O1. **Prices:** $4800 to $16,000. **Remarks:** Full-time maker; first knife sold in 1965. Doing business as H.H. Frank Knives. **Mark:** Name, address and date.

FRANKLIN, MIKE,
9878 Big Run Rd, Aberdeen, OH 45101, Phone: 937-549-2598
Specialties: High-tech tactical folders. **Patterns:** Tactical folders. **Technical:** Grinds CPM-T-440V, 440-C, ATS-34; titanium liners and bolsters; carbon fiber scales. Uses radical grinds and severe serrations. **Prices:** $275 to $600. **Remarks:** Full-time maker; first knife sold in 1969. **Mark:** Stylized boar with HAWG.

FRAPS, JOHN R,
3810 Wyandotte Tr, Indianpolis, IN 46240-3422, Phone: 317-849-9419, Fax: 317-842-2224, jfraps@att.net; Web: www.frapsknives.com
Specialties: Working and collector grade LinerLock® and slip joint folders. **Patterns:** One-of-a kind linerlocks and traditional slip joints. **Technical:** Flat and hollow grinds ATS-34, Damascus, Talonite, CPM S30V, 154Cm, Stellite 6K; hand rubbed or mirror finish. **Prices:** $200 to $1500, some higher. **Remarks:** Voting member of the Knifemaker's Guild; Full-time maker; first knife sold in 1997. **Mark:** Cougar Creek Knives and/or name.

FRAZIER, RON,
2107 Urbine Rd, Powhatan, VA 23139, Phone: 804-794-8561
Specialties: Classy working knives of his design; some high-art straight knives. **Patterns:** Wide assortment of straight knives, including miniatures and push knives. **Technical:** Grinds 440C; offers satin, mirror or sand finishes. **Prices:** $85 to $700; some to $3000. **Remarks:** Full-time maker; first knife sold in 1976. **Mark:** Name in arch logo.

FRED, REED WYLE,
3149 X S, Sacramento, CA 95817, Phone: 916-739-0237
Specialties: Working using straight knives of his design. **Patterns:** Hunting and camp knives. **Technical:** Forges any 10 series, old files and carbon steels. Offers initialing upon request; prefers natural handle materials. **Prices:** $30 to $300. **Remarks:** Part-time maker; first knife sold in 1994. Doing business as R.W. Fred Knifemaker. **Mark:** Engraved first and last initials.

FREDERICK, AARON,
459 Brooks Ln, West Liberty, KY 41472-8961, Phone: 606-7432015, aaronf@mrtc.com; Web: www.frederickknives.com
Specialties: Makes most types of knives, but as for now specializes in the Damascus folder. Does all own Damascus and forging of the steel. Also prefers natural handle material such as ivory and pearl. Prefers 14k gold screws in most of the knives he do. Also offer several types of file work on blades, spacers, and liners. Has just recently started doing carving and can do a limited amount of engraving.

FREEMAN, JOHN,
160 Concession St, Cambridge, Ont., CANADA N1R 2H7, Phone: 519-740-2767, Fax: 519-740-2785, freeman@golden.net; Web: www.freemanknives.com
Specialties: Kitchen knives, outdoor knives, sharpeners and folders. **Patterns:** Hunters, skinners, utilities, backpackers. **Technical:** Flat ground 440C. **Prices:** Start at $135 and up. **Remarks:** Full-time maker; first knife sold in 1985. **Mark:** Last name, country.

FREER, RALPH,
114 12th St, Seal Beach, CA 90740, Phone: 562-493-4925, Fax: same, ralphfreer@adelphia.net
Specialties: Exotic folders, liner locks, folding daggers, fixed blades. **Patters:** All original. **Technical:** Lots of Damascus, ivory, pearl, jeweled, thumb studs, carving ATS-34, 420V, 530V. **Prices:** $400 to $2500 and up. **Mark:** Freer in German-style text, also Freer shield.

FREILING, ALBERT J,
3700 Niner Rd, Finksburg, MD 21048, Phone: 301-795-2880
Specialties: Working straight knives and folders; some period pieces. **Patterns:** Boots, Bowies, survival knives and tomahawks in 4130 and 440C; some locking folders and interframes; ball-bearing folders. **Technical:** Grinds O1, 440C and 154CM. **Prices:** $100 to $300; some to $500. **Remarks:** Part-time maker; first knife sold in 1966. **Mark:** Initials connected.

FREY, STEVE,
19103 131st Drive SE, Snohomish, WA 98296, Phone: 360-668-7351, sfrey2@aol.com
Remarks: Custom crafted knives-all styles.

FREY JR., W FREDERICK,
305 Walnut St, Milton, PA 17847, Phone: 570-742-9576, wffrey@ptd.net
Specialties: Working straight knives and folders, some fancy. **Patterns:** Wide range miniatures, boot knives and lock back folders. **Technical:** Grinds A2, O1 and D2; vaseo wear, cru-wear and CPM 560V and CPM 590V. **Prices:** $100 to $250; some to $1200. **Remarks:** Spare-time maker; first knife sold in 1983. All knives include quality hand stitched sheaths. **Mark:** Last name in script.

FRIEDLY, DENNIS E,
12 Cottontail Ln E, Cody, WY 82414, Phone: 307-527-6811, friedly_knives@hotmail.com
Specialties: Fancy working straight knives and daggers, lock back folders and liner locks. Also embellished bowies. **Patterns:** Hunters, fighters, short swords, minis and miniatures; new line of full-tang hunters/boots. **Technical:** Grinds 440C, commercial Damascus, mosaic Damascus and ATS-34 blades; prefers hidden tangs and full tangs. Both flat and hollow grinds. **Prices:** $350 to $2500. Some to $10,000. **Remarks:** Full-time maker; first knife sold in 1972. **Mark:** D.E. Friedly-Cody, WY. Friedly Knives

FRIGAULT, RICK,
3584 Rapidsview Dr, Niagara Falls, Ont., CANADA L2G 6C4, Phone: 905-295-6695, rfrigualt@cogeco.ca; Web: www.rfrigaultknives.com
Specialties: Fixed blades. **Patterns:** Hunting, tactical and large Bowies. **Technical:** Grinds ATS-34, 440-C, D-2, CPMS30V, CPMS60V, CPMS90V, BG42 and Damascus. Use G-10, Micarta, ivory, antler, ironwood and other stabilized woods for carbon fiber handle material. Makes leather sheaths by hand. Tactical blades include a Concealex sheath made by "On Scene Tactical." **Remarks:** Sold first knife in 1997. Member of Canadian Knifemakers Guild. **Mark:** RFRIGAULT.

FRITZ, ERIK L,
837 River St Box 1203, Forsyth, MT 59327, Phone: 406-351-1101, tacmedic45@yahoo.com
Specialties: Forges carbon steel 1084, 5160, 52100 and Damascus. **Patterns:** Hunters, camp knives, bowies and folders as well as forged tactical. **Technical:** Forges own Mosaic and pattern welded Damascus as well as doing own heat treat. **Prices:** A$200 and up. **Remarks:** Sole authorship knives and sheaths. Part time maker first knife sold in 2004. ABS member. **Mark:** E. Fritz in arc on left side ricasso.

FRITZ, JESSE,
900 S. 13th St, Slaton, TX 79364, Phone: 806-828-5083
Specialties: Working and using straight knives in standard patterns. **Patterns:** Hunters, utility/camp knives and skinners with gut hook, Bowie knives, kitchen carving sets by request. **Technical:** Grinds 440C, O1 and 1095. Uses 1095 steel. Fline-napped steel design, blued blades, filework

and machine jewelling. Inlays handles with turquoise, coral and mother-of-pearl. Makes sheaths. **Prices:** $85 to $275; some to $500. **Mark:** Last name only (FRITZ).

FRIZZELL, TED,
14056 Low Gap Rd, West Fork, AR 72774, Phone: 501-839-2516
Specialties: Swords, axes and self-defense weapons. **Patterns:** Small skeleton knives to large swords. **Technical:** Grinds 5160 almost exclusively—1/4" to 1/2"— bars some O1 and A2 on request. All knives come with Kydex sheaths. **Prices:** $45 to $1200. **Remarks:** Full-time maker; first knife sold in 1984. Doing business as Mineral Mountain Hatchet Works. Wholesale orders welcome. **Mark:** A circle with line in the middle; MM and HW within the circle.

FRONEFIELD, DANIEL,
20270 Warriors Path, Peyton, CO 80831, Phone: 719-749-0226, dfronfld@hiwaay.com
Specialties: Fixed and folding knives featuring meteorites and other exotic materials. **Patterns:** San-mai Damascus, custom Damascus. **Prices:** $500 to $3000.

FROST, DEWAYNE,
1016 Van Buren Rd, Barnesville, GA 30204, Phone: 770-358-1426, lbrtyhill@aol.com
Specialties: Working straight knives and period knives. **Patterns:** Hunters, Bowies and utility knives. **Technical:** Forges own Damascus, cable, etc. as well as stock removal. **Prices:** $150 to $500. **Remarks:** Part-time maker ABS Journeyman Smith. **Mark:** Liberty Hill Forge Dewayne Frost w/liberty bell.

FRUHMANN, LUDWIG,
Stegerwaldstr 8, 84489 Burghausen, GERMANY
Specialties: High-tech and working straight knives of his design. **Patterns:** Hunters, fighters and boots. **Technical:** Grinds ATS-34, CPM-T-440V and Schneider Damascus. Prefers natural handle materials. **Prices:** $200 to $1500. **Remarks:** Spare-time maker; first knife sold in 1990. **Mark:** First initial and last name.

FUEGEN, LARRY,
617 N Coulter Circle, Prescott, AZ 86303, Phone: 928-776-8777, fuegen@cableone.net; Web: www.larryfuegen.com
Specialties: High-art folders and classic and working straight knives. **Patterns:** Forged scroll folders, lockback folders and classic straight knives. **Technical:** Forges 5160, 1095 and his own Damascus. Works in exotic leather; offers elaborate filework and carving; likes natural handle materials, now offers own engraving. **Prices:** $575 to $9000. **Remarks:** Full-time maker; first knife sold in 1975. Sole authorship on all knives. ABS Mastersmith. **Mark:** Initials connected.

FUJIKAWA, SHUN,
Sawa 1157 Kaizuka, Osaka 597 0062, JAPAN, Phone: 81-724-23-4032, Fax: 81-726-23-9229
Specialties: Folders of his design and to customer specs. **Patterns:** Locking folders. **Technical:** Grinds his own steel. **Prices:** $450 to $2500; some to $3000. **Remarks:** Part-time maker.

FUJISAKA, STANLEY,
45-004 Holowai St, Kaneohe, HI 96744, Phone: 808-247-0017
Specialties: Fancy working straight knives and folders. **Patterns:** Hunters, boots, personal knives, daggers, collectible art knives. **Technical:** Grinds 440C, 154CM and ATS-34; clean lines, inlays. **Prices:** $150 to $1200; some to $3000. **Remarks:** Full-time maker; first knife sold in 1984. **Mark:** Name, city, state.

FUKUTA, TAK,
38-Umeagae-cho, Seki-City, Gifu-Pref, JAPAN, Phone: 0575-22-0264
Specialties: Bench-made fancy straight knives and folders. **Patterns:** Sheffield-type folders, Bowies and fighters. **Technical:** Grinds commercial Damascus. **Prices:** Start at $300. **Remarks:** Full-time maker. **Mark:** Name in knife logo.

FULLER, BRUCE A,
1305 Airhart Dr, Baytown, TX 77520, Phone: 281-427-1848, fullcoforg@aol.com
Specialties: One-of-a-kind working/using straight knives and folders of his designs. **Patterns:** Bowies, hunters, folders, and utility/camp knives. **Technical:** Forges high-carbon steel and his own Damascus. Prefers El Solo Mesquite and natural materials. Offers filework. **Prices:** $200 to $500; some to $1800. **Remarks:** Spare-time maker; first knife sold in 1991. Doing business as Fullco Forge. **Mark:** Fullco, M.S.

FULLER, JACK A,
7103 Stretch Ct, New Market, MD 21774, Phone: 301-798-0119
Specialties: Straight working knives of his design and to customer specs. **Patterns:** Fighters, camp knives, hunters, tomahawks and art knives. **Technical:** Forges 5160, O1, W2 and his own Damascus. Does silver wire inlay and own leather work, wood lined sheaths for big camp knives. **Prices:** $300 to $850. **Remarks:** Part-time maker. Master Smith in ABS; first knife sold in 1979. **Mark:** Fuller's Forge, MS.

FULTON, MICKEY,
406 S Shasta St, Willows, CA 95988, Phone: 530-934-5780
Specialties: Working straight knives and folders of his design. **Patterns:** Hunters, Bowies, lockback folders and steak knife sets. **Technical:** Hand-filed, sanded, buffed ATS-34, 440C and A2. **Prices:** $65 to $600; some to $1200. **Remarks:** Full-time maker; first knife sold in 1979. **Mark:** Signature.

G

GADBERRY, EMMET,
82 Purple Plum Dr, Hattieville, AR 72063, Phone: 501-354-4842

GADDY, GARY LEE,
205 Ridgewood Lane, Washington, NC 27889, Phone: 252-946-4359
Specialties: Working/using straight knives of his design; period pieces. **Patterns:** Bowies, hunters, utility/camp knives. **Technical:** Grinds ATS-34, O1; forges 1095. **Prices:** $100 to $225; some to $400. **Remarks:** Spare-time maker; first knife sold in 1991. **Mark:** Quarter moon logo.

GAETA, ANGELO,
R. Saldanha Marinho, 1295 Centro Jau, SP-17201-310, BRAZIL, Phone: 0146-224543, Fax: 0146-224543
Specialties: Straight using knives to customer specs. **Patterns:** Hunters, fighting, daggers, belt push dagger. **Technical:** Grinds D6, ATS-34 and 440C stainless. Titanium nitride golden finish upon request. **Prices:** $60 to $300. **Remarks:** Full-time maker; first knife sold in 1992. **Mark:** First initial, last name.

GAETA, ROBERTO,
Rua Mandissununga 41, Sao Paulo, BRAZIL 05619-010, Phone: 11-37684626, karlaseno@uol.com.br
Specialties: Wide range of using knives. **Patterns:** Brazilian and North American hunting and fighting knives. **Technical:** Grinds stainless steel; likes natural handle materials. **Prices:** $100 to $250; some to $600. **Remarks:** Full-time maker; first knife sold in 1979. **Mark:** BOB'G.

GAINES, BUDDY,
GAINES KNIVES, 155 Red Hill Rd., Commerce, GA 30530, Web: www.gainesknives.com
Specialties: Collectible and working folders and straight knives. **Patterns:** Folders, hunters, Bowies, tactical knives. **Technical:** Forges own Damascus, grinds ATS-34, D2, commercial Damascus. Prefers mother-of-pearl and stag. **Prices:** Start at $200. **Remarks:** Part-time maker, sold first knife in 1985. **Mark:** Last name.

GAINEY, HAL,
904 Bucklevel Rd, Greenwood, SC 29649, Phone: 864-223-0225, Web: www.scak.org
Specialties: Traditional working and using straight knives and folders. **Patterns:** Hunters, slip-joint folders and utility/camp knives. **Technical:** Hollow-grinds ATS-34 and D2; makes sheaths. **Prices:** $95 to $145; some to $500. **Remarks:** Full-time maker; first knife sold in 1975. **Mark:** Eagle head and last name.

GALLAGHER, BARRY,
135 Park St, Lewistown, MT 59457, Phone: 406-538-7056, Web: www.gallagherknives.com
Specialties: One-of-a-kind Damascus folders. **Patterns:** Folders, utility to high art, some straight knives, hunter, Bowies, and art pieces. **Technical:** Forges own mosaic Damascus and carbon steel, some stainless. **Prices:** $400 to $5000+. **Remarks:** Full-time maker; first knife sold in 1993. Doing business as Gallagher Custom Knives. **Mark:** Last name.

GAMBLE, FRANK,
4676 Commercial St SE #26, Salem, OR 97302, Phone: 503-581-7993, gamble6831@comcast.net
Specialties: Fantasy and high-art straight knives and folders of his design. **Patterns:** Daggers, fighters, hunters and special locking folders. **Technical:** Grinds 440C and ATS-34; forges Damascus. Inlays; offers jewelling. Prices $150 to $10,000. **Remarks:** Full-time maker; first knife sold in 1976. **Mark:** First initial, last name.

GAMBLE, ROGER,
2801 65 Way N, St. Petersburg, FL 33710, Phone: 727-384-1470, rlgamble2@netzero.net
Specialties: Traditional working/using straight knives and folders of his design. **Patterns:** Liner locks and hunters. **Technical:** Grinds ATS-34 and Damascus. **Prices:** $150 to $2000. **Remarks:** Part-time maker; first knife sold in 1982. Doing business as Gamble Knives. **Mark:** First name in a fan of cards over last name.

GANSTER, JEAN-PIERRE,
18, Rue du Vieil Hopital, F-67000 Strasbourg, FRANCE, Phone: (0033) 388 32 65 61, Fax: (0033) 388 32 52 79
Specialties: Fancy and high-art miniatures of his design and to customer specs. **Patterns:** Bowies, daggers, fighters, hunters, locking folders and miniatures. **Technical:** Forges and grinds stainless Damascus, ATS-34, gold and silver. **Prices:** $100 to $380; some to $2500. **Remarks:** Part-time maker; first knife sold in 1972. **Mark:** Stylized first initials.

GARCIA, MARIO EIRAS,
R. Edmundo Scanapieco, 300 Caxingui, Sao Paulo SP-05516-070, BRAZIL, Fax: 011-37214528
Specialties: Fantasy knives of his design; one-of-a-kind only. Patterns: Fighters, daggers, boots and two-bladed knives. **Technical:** Forges car leaf springs. Uses only natural handle material. **Prices:** $100 to $200. **Remarks:** Part-time maker; first knife sold in 1976. **Mark:** Two "B"s, one opposite the other.

GARNER, LARRY W,
13069 FM 14, Tyler, TX 75706, Phone: 903-597-6045, lwgarner@classicnet.net

Specialties: Fixed blade hunters and Bowies. **Patterns:** His designs or yours. **Technical:** Hand forges 5160. **Prices:** $200 to $500. **Remarks:** Apprentice bladesmith. **Mark:** Last name.

GARNER JR., WILLIAM O,
2803 East DeSoto St, Pensacola, FL 32503, Phone: 850-438-2009

Specialties: Working straight and art knives. **Patterns:** Hunters and folders. **Technical:** Grinds 440C and ATS-34 steels. **Prices:** $235 to $600. **Remarks:** Full-time maker; first knife sold in 1985. **Mark:** First and last name in oval logo or last name.

GARVOCK, MARK W,
RR 1, Balderson, Ont., CANADA K1G 1A0, Phone: 613-833-2545, Fax: 613-833-2208, garvock@travel-net.com

Specialties: Hunters, Bowies, Japanese, daggers and swords. **Patterns:** Cable Damascus, random pattern welded or to suit. **Technical:** Forged blades; hi-carbon. **Prices:** $250 to $900. **Remarks:** CKG member and ABS member. Shipping and taxes extra. **Mark:** Big G with M in middle.

GAUDETTE, LINDEN L,
5 Hitchcock Rd, Wilbraham, MA 01095, Phone: 413-596-4896

Specialties: Traditional working knives in standard patterns. **Patterns:** Broad-bladed hunters, Bowies and camp knives; wood carver knives; locking folders. **Technical:** Grinds ATS-34, 440C and 154CM. **Prices:** $150 to $400; some higher. **Remarks:** Full-time maker; first knife sold in 1975. **Mark:** Last name in Gothic logo; used to be initials in circle.

GAULT, CLAY,
#1225 PR 7022, Lexington, TX 78947, Phone: 979-773-3305

Specialties: Classic straight and folding hunting knives and multi-blade folders of his design. **Patterns:** Folders and hunting knives. **Technical:** Grinds BX-NSM 174 steel, custom rolled from billets to his specifications. Uses exotic leathers for sheaths, and fine natural materials for all knives. **Prices:** $325 to $600; some higher. **Remarks:** Full-time maker; first knife sold in 1970. **Mark:** Name or name with cattle brand.

GEDRAITIS, CHARLES J,
GEDRAITIS HAND CRAFTED KNIVES, 444 Shrewsbury St, Holden, MA 01520, Phone: 508-963-1861, knifemaker_1999@yahoo.com; Web: http://cgknives.blademakers.com

Specialties: One-of-a-kind folders & automatics of his own design. **Patterns:** One-of-a-kind. **Technical:** Forges to shape mostly stock removal. **Prices:** $300 to $2500. **Remarks:** Full-time maker. **Mark:** 3 scallop shells with an initial inside each one: CJG.

GEISLER, GARY R,
PO Box 294, Clarksville, OH 45113, Phone: 937-383-4055, ggeisler@in-touch.net

Specialties: Period Bowies and such; flat ground. **Patterns:** Working knives usually modeled close after an existing antique. **Technical:** Flat grinds 440C, A2 and ATS-34. **Prices:** $300 and up. **Remarks:** Part-time maker; first knife sold in 1982. **Mark:** G.R. Geisler Maker; usually in script on reverse side because maker is left-handed.

GENSKE, JAY,
283 Doty St, Fond du Lac, WI 54935, Phone: 920-921-8019/Cell Phone 920-579-0144, jaygenske@hotmail.com

Specialties: Working/using knives and period pieces of his design and to customer specs. **Patterns:** Bowies, fighters, hunters. **Technical:** Grinds ATS-34 and 440C, O1 and 1095 forges and grinds Damascus and 1095. Offers custom-tooled sheaths, scabbards and hand carved handles. **Prices:** $95 to $500; some to $1000. **Remarks:** Full-time maker; first knife sold in 1985. Doing business as Genske Knives. **Mark:** Stamped or engraved last name.

GEORGE, HARRY,
3137 Old Camp Long Rd, Aiken, SC 29805, Phone: 803-649-1963, hdkk-george@scescape.net

Specialties: Working straight knives of his design or to customer specs. **Patterns:** Hunters, skinners and utility knives. **Technical:** Grinds ATS-34. Prefers natural handle materials, hollow-grinds and mirror finishes. **Prices:** Start at $70. **Remarks:** Part-time maker; first knife sold in 1985. Trained under George Herron. Member SCAK. Member Knifemakers Guild. **Mark:** Name, city, state.

GEORGE, LES,
46-445 Kahuhipa St A, Kaneohe, HI 96744, Phone: 808-234-1589, les@georgeknives.com; Web: www.georgeknives.com

Specialties: Balisongs, straight knives and folders. **Patterns:** Swords, miniatures, folders, hunters and fighters. **Technical:** Grinds D2, A2, CPM154, forges own Damascus and mokume-gane. **Prices:** $100 to $600. **Remarks:** Part-time maker, first knife sold in 1992. Doing business as www.georgeknives.com. **Mark:** Last name with logo.

GEORGE, TOM,
550 Aldbury Dr, Henderson, NV 89014, tagmaker@aol.com

Specialties: Working straight knives, display knives, custom meat cleavers, and folders of his design. **Patterns:** Hunters, Bowies, daggers, buckskinners, swords and folders. **Technical:** Uses D2, 440C, ATS-34 and 154CM. **Prices:** $500 to $13,500. **Remarks:** Custom orders not accepted "at this time". Full-time maker. First knife1982; first 350 knives were numbered; after that no numbers. Almost all his knives today are Bowies and swords. **Mark:** Tom George maker.

GEPNER, DON,
2615 E Tecumseh, Norman, OK 73071, Phone: 405-364-2750

Specialties: Traditional working and using straight knives of his design. **Patterns:** Bowies and daggers. **Technical:** Forges his Damascus, 1095 and 5160. **Prices:** $100 to $400; some to $1000. **Remarks:** Spare-time maker; first knife sold in 1991. Has been forging since 1954; first edged weapon made at 9 years old. **Mark:** Last initial.

GERNER, THOMAS,
PO Box 301 Walpole, Western Australia, AUSTRALIA 6398, gerner@bordernet.com.au; Web: www.deepriverforge.com

Specialties: Forged working knives; plain steel and pattern welded. **Patterns:** Tries most patterns heard or read about. **Technical:** 5160, L6, O1, 52100 steels; Australian hardwood handles. **Prices:** $220 and up. **Remarks:** Achieved ABS Master Smith rating in 2001. **Mark:** Like a standing arrow and a leaning cross, T.G. in the Runic (Viking) alphabet.

GEVEDON, HANNERS (HANK),
1410 John Cash Rd, Crab Orchard, KY 40419-9770

Specialties: Traditional working and using straight knives. **Patterns:** Hunters, swords, utility and camp knives. **Technical:** Forges and grinds his own Damascus, 5160 and L6. Cast aluminum handles. **Prices:** $50 to $250; some to $400. **Remarks:** Part-time maker; first knife sold in 1983. **Mark:** Initials and LBF tang stamp.

GIAGU, SALVATORE AND DEROMA MARIA ROSARIA,
Via V Emanuele 64, 07016 Pattada (SS), ITALY, Phone: 079-755918, Fax: 079-755918, coltelligiagu@jumpy.it

Specialties: Using and collecting traditional and new folders from Sardegna. **Patterns:** Folding, hunting, utility, skinners and kitchen knives. **Technical:** Forges ATS-34, 440, D2 and Damascus. **Prices:** $200 to $2000; some higher. **Mark:** First initial, last name and name of town and muflon's head.

GIBERT, PEDRO,
Gutierrez 5189, 5603 Rama Caida, San Rafael Mendoza, ARGENTINA, Phone: 054-2627-441138, rosademayo@infovia.com.ar

Specialties: Hand forges: Stock removal and integral. High quality artistic knives of his design and to customer specifications. **Patterns:** Country (Argentine gaucho-style), knives, folders, Bowies, daggers, hunters. Others upon request. **Technical:** Blade: Bohler k110 Austrian steel (high resistance to waste). Handles: (Natural materials) ivory elephant, killer whale, hippo, walrus tooth, deer antler, goat, ram, buffalo horn, bone, rhea, goat, sheep, cow, exotic woods (South America native woods) hand carved and engraved guards and blades. Stainless steel guards, finely polished: semi-matte or shiny finish. Sheaths: Raw or tanned leather, hand-stitched; rawhide or cotton yarn embroidered. Box: One wood piece, hand carved. Wooden hinges and locks. **Prices:** $400 and up. **Remarks:** Full-time maker. Supply contractors. **Mark:** Only a rose logo. Buyers initials upon request.

GIBO, GEORGE,
PO Box 4304, Hilo, HI 96720, Phone: 808-987-7002, geogibo@interpac.net

Specialties: Straight knives and folders. **Patterns:** Hunters, bird and trout, utility, gentlemen and tactical folders. **Technical:** Grinds ATS-34, BG-42, Talonite, Stainless Steel Damascus. **Prices:** $250 to $1000. **Remarks:** Spare-time maker; first knife sold in 1995. **Mark:** Name, city and state around Hawaiian "Shaka" sign.

GIBSON SR., JAMES HOOT,
90 Park Place Ave., Bunnell, FL 32110, Phone: 386-437-4383, hootsknives.aol.com

Specialties: Bowies, folders, daggers, and hunters. **Patterns:** Most all. **Technical:** ATS-440C hand cut and grind. Also traditional old fashioned folders. **Prices:** $250 to $3000. **Remarks:** 100 percent handmade. **Mark:** Hoot.

GILBERT, CHANTAL,
291 Rue Christophe-Colomb est #105, Quebec City Quebec, CANADA G1K 3T1, Phone: 418-525-6961, Fax: 418-525-4666, gilbertc@medion.qc.ca; Web:www.chantalgilbert.com

Specialties: Straight art knives that may resemble creatures, often with wings, shells and antennae, always with a beak of some sort, fixed blades in a feminine style. **Technical:** ATS-34 and Damascus. Handle materials usually silver that she forms to shape via special molds and a press; ebony and fossil ivory. **Prices:** Range from $500 to $4000. **Remarks:** Often embellishes her art knives with rubies, meteorite, 18k gold and similar elements.

GILBREATH, RANDALL,
55 Crauswell Rd, Dora, AL 35062, Phone: 205-648-3902

Specialties: Damascus folders and fighters. Patterns: Folders and fixed blades. **Technical:** Forges Damascus and high-carbon; stock removal stainless steel. **Prices:** $300 to $1500. **Remarks:** Full-time maker; first knife sold in 1979. **Mark:** Name in ribbon.

GILJEVIC, BRANKO,
35 Hayley Crescent, Queanbeyan 2620, N.S.W., AUSTRALIA 0262977613
Specialties: Classic working straight knives and folders of his design. **Patterns:** Hunters, Bowies, skinners and locking folders. **Technical:** Grinds 440C. Offers acid etching, scrimshaw and leather carving. **Prices:** $150 to $1500. **Remarks:** Part-time maker; first knife sold in 1987. Doing business as Sambar Custom Knives. **Mark:** Company name in logo.

GIRAFFEBONE INC.,
3052 Isim Road, Norman, OK 73026, Phone: 888-804-0683; 405-321-3614, sandy@giraffebone.com; Web: www.giraffebone.com
Specialties: Giraffebone, horns, African hardwoods, and mosaic Damascus

GIRTNER, JOE,
409 Catalpa Ave, Brea, CA 92821, Phone: 714-529-2388, conceptsinknives@aol.com
Specialties: Art knives and miniatures. **Patterns:** Mainly Damascus (some carved). **Technical:** Many techniques and materials combines. **Prices:** $55 to $3000. **Mark:** Name.

GITTINGER, RAYMOND,
6940 S Rt 100, Tiffin, OH 44883, Phone: 419-397-2517

GLOVER, RON,
7702 Misty Springs Ct, Mason, OH 45040, Phone: 513-398-7857
Specialties: High-tech working straight knives and folders. **Patterns:** Hunters to Bowies; some interchangeable blade models; unique locking mechanisms. **Technical:** Grinds 440C, 154CM; buys Damascus. **Prices:** $70 to $500; some to $800. **Remarks:** Part-time maker; first knife sold in 1981. **Mark:** Name in script.

GLOVER, WARREN D,
dba BUBBA KNIVES, PO Box 475, Cleveland, GA 30528, Phone: 706-865-3998, Fax: 706-348-7176, warren@bubbaknives.net; Web: www.bubbaknives.net
Specialties: Traditional and custom working and using straight knives of his design and to customer request. **Patterns:** Hunters, skinners, bird and fish, utility and kitchen knives. **Technical:** Grinds 440, ATS-34 and stainless steel Damascus. **Prices:** $75 to $400 and up. **Remarks:** Full-time maker; sold first knife in 1995. **Mark:** Bubba, year, name, state.

GODDARD, WAYNE,
473 Durham Ave, Eugene, OR 97404, Phone: 541-689-8098, wgoddard44@comcast.net
Specialties: Working/using straight knives and folders. **Patterns:** Hunters and folders. **Technical:** Works exclusively with wire Damascus and his own-pattern welded material. **Prices:** $250 to $4000. **Remarks:** Full-time maker; first knife sold in 1963. **Mark:** Blocked initials on forged blades; regular capital initials on stock removal.

GOERS, BRUCE,
3423 Royal Ct S, Lakeland, FL 33813, Phone: 941-646-0984
Specialties: Fancy working and using straight knives of his design and to customer specs. **Patterns:** Hunters, fighters, Bowies and fantasy knives. **Technical:** Grinds ATS-34, some Damascus. **Prices:** $195 to $600; some to $1300. **Remarks:** Part-time maker; first knife sold in 1990. Doing business as Vulture Cutlery. **Mark:** Buzzard with initials.

GOFOURTH, JIM,
3776 Aliso Cyn Rd, Santa Paula, CA 93060, Phone: 805-659-3814
Specialties: Period pieces and working knives. **Patterns:** Bowies, locking folders, patent lockers and others. **Technical:** Grinds A2 and 154CM. **Prices:** Moderate. **Remarks:** Spare-time maker. **Mark:** Initials interconnected.

GOGUEN, SCOTT,
166 Goguen Rd, Newport, NC 28570, Phone: 252-393-6013, goguenknives.com
Specialties: Classic and traditional working knives. **Patterns:** Kitchen, camp, hunters, Bowies. **Technical:** Forges high-carbon steel and own Damascus. Offers clay tempering and cord wrapped handles. **Prices:** $85 to $1500. **Remarks:** Spare-time maker; first knife sold in1988. **Mark:** Last name or name in Japanese characters.

GOLDBERG, DAVID,
321 Morris Rd, Ft Washington, PA 19034, Phone: 215-654-7117, david@goldmountainforge.com; Web: www.goldmountainforge.com
Specialties: Japanese-style designs, will work with special themes in Japanese genre. **Patterns:** Kozuka, Tanto, Wakazashi, Katana, Tachi, Sword canes, Yari and Naginata. **Technical:** Forges his own Damascus and makes his own handmade tamehagane steel from straw ash, iron, carbon and clay. Uses traditional materials, carves fittings handles and cases. Hardens all blades in traditional Japanese clay differential technique. **Remarks:** Full-time maker; first knife sold in 1987. Japanese swordsmanship teacher (jaido) and Japanese self-defense teach (aikido). **Mark:** Name (kinzan) in Japanese Kanji on Tang under handle.

GOLDEN, RANDY,
6492 Eastwood Glen Dr, Montgomery, AL 36117, Phone: 334-271-6429, rgolden1@mindspring.com
Specialties: Collectable quality hand rubbed finish, hunter, camp, Bowie straight knives, custom leather sheaths with exotic skin inlays and tooling. **Technical:** Stock removal ATS-34, CPM154, S30V and BG-42. Natural handle materials primarily stag and ivory. **Prices:** $250 to $1500. **Remarks:** Full-time maker, member Knifemakers Guild, first knife sold in 2000. **Mark:** R. R. Golden Montgomery, AL.

GOLTZ, WARREN L,
802 4th Ave E, Ada, MN 56510, Phone: 218-784-7721, sspexp@loretel.net
Specialties: Fancy working knives in standard patterns. **Patterns:** Hunters, Bowies and camp knives. **Technical:** Grinds 440C and ATS-34. **Prices:** $120 to $595; some to $950. **Remarks:** Part-time maker; first knife sold in 1984. **Mark:** Last name.

GONZALEZ, LEONARDO WILLIAMS,
Ituzaingo 473, Maldonado, CP 20000, URUGUAY, Phone: 598 4222 1617, Fax: 598 4222 1617, willyknives@hotmail.com
Specialties: Classic high-art and fantasy straight knives; traditional working and using knives of his design, in standard patterns or to customer specs. **Patterns:** Hunters, Bowies, daggers, fighters, boots, swords and utility/camp knives. **Technical:** Forges and grinds high-carbon and stainless Bohler steels. **Prices:** $100 to $2500. **Remarks:** Full-time maker; first knife sold in 1985. **Mark:** Willy, whale, R.O.U.

GOO, TAI,
5920 W Windy Lou Ln, Tucson, AZ 85742, Phone: 520-744-9777, taigoo@msn.com; Web: www.taigoo.com
Specialties: High art, neo-tribal, bush and fantasy. **Technical:** Hand forges, does own heat treating, makes own Damascus. **Prices:** $150 to $500 some to $10,000. **Remarks:** Full-time maker; first knife sold in 1978. **Mark:** Chiseled signature.

GOODE, BEAR,
PO Box 6474, Navajo Dam, NM 87419, Phone: 505-632-8184
Specialties: Working/using straight knives of his design and in standard patterns. **Patterns:** Bowies, hunters and utility/camp knives. **Technical:** Grinds 440C, ATS-34, 154-CM; forges and grinds 1095, 5160 and other steels on request; uses Damascus. **Prices:** $60 to $225; some to $500 and up. **Remarks:** Part-time maker; first knife sold in 1993. Doing business as Bear Knives. **Mark:** First and last name with a three-toed paw print.

GOODE, BRIAN,
203 Gordon Ave, Shelby, NC 28152, Phone: 704-434-6496, web:www.bgoodeknives.com
Specialties: Flat ground working knives with etched/antique or brushed finish. **Patterns:** Field, camp, hunters, skinners, survival, maker's design or yours. Currently full tang only with supplied leather sheath or kydex. **Technical:** 0-1, D2 and other ground flat stock. Stock removal and differential heat treat preferred. Etched antique/etched satin working finish preferred. Micarta and hardwoods for strength. **Prices:** $150 to $700. **Remarks:** Part-time maker and full-time knife lover. First knife sold in 2004. **Mark:** B. Goode with NC separated by a feather.

GOODLING, RODNEY W,
6640 Old Harrisburg Rd, York Springs, PA 17372

GORDON, LARRY B,
23555 Newell Cir W, Farmington Hills, MI 48336, Phone: 248-477-5483, lbgordon1@aol.com
Specialties: Folders, small fixed blades. New design rotating scale release automatic. **Patterns:** Rotating handle locker. Ambidextrous fire (R&L) **Prices:** $450 minimum. **Remarks:** High line materials preferred. **Mark:** Gordon.

GORENFLO, GABE,
9145 Sullivan Rd, Baton Rouge, LA 70818, Phone: 504-261-5868

GORENFLO, JAMES T (JT),
9145 Sullivan Rd, Baton Rouge, LA 70818, Phone: 225-261-5868
Specialties: Traditional working and using straight knives of his design. **Patterns:** Bowies, hunters and utility/camp knives. **Technical:** Forges 5160, 1095, 52100 and his own Damascus. **Prices:** Start at $200. **Remarks:** Part-time maker; first knife sold in 1992. **Mark:** Last name or initials, J.S. on reverse.

GOSSMAN, SCOTT,
, PO Box 815, Forest Hill, MD 21050, Phone: 410-452-8456, scott@gossmanknives.com Web:www.gossmanknives.com
Specialties: Heavy duty knives for big game hunting and survival. **Patterns:** Drop point spear point hunters. Large camp/survival knives. **Technical:** Grinds D-2, A2, O1 and 57 convex grinds and edges. **Price:** $100 to $350 some higher. **Remarks:** Full time maker does business as Gossman Knives. **Mark:** Gossman and steel type.

GOTTAGE, DANTE,
43227 Brooks Dr, Clinton Twp., MI 48038-5323, Phone: 810-286-7275
Specialties: Working knives of his design or to customer specs. Patterns: Large and small skinners, fighters, Bowies and fillet knives. **Technical:** Grinds O1, 440C and 154CM and ATS-34. **Prices:** $150 to $600. **Remarks:** Part-time maker; first knife sold in 1975. **Mark:** Full name in script letters.

GOTTAGE, JUDY,
43227 Brooks Dr, Clinton Twp., MI 48038-5323, Phone: 810-286-7275, jgottage@remaxmetropolitan.com
Specialties: Custom folders of her design or to customer specs.

Patterns: Interframes or integral. **Technical:** Stock removal. **Prices:** $300 to $3000. **Remarks:** Full-time maker; first knife sold in 1980. **Mark:** Full name, maker in script.

GOTTSCHALK, GREGORY J,
12 First St. (Ft. Pitt), Carnegie, PA 15106, Phone: 412-279-6692
Specialties: Fancy working straight knives and folders to customer specs. **Patterns:** Hunters to tantos, locking folders to minis. **Technical:** Grinds 440C, 154CM, ATS-34. Now making own Damascus. Most knives have mirror finishes. **Prices:** Start at $150. **Remarks:** Part-time maker; first knife sold in 1977. **Mark:** Full name in crescent.

GOUKER, GARY B,
PO Box 955, Sitka, AK 99835, Phone: 907-747-3476
Specialties: Hunting knives for hard use. **Patterns:** Skinners, semi-skinners, and such. **Technical:** Likes natural materials, inlays, stainless steel. **Prices:** Moderate. **Remarks:** New Alaskan maker. **Mark:** Name.

GOYTIA, ENRIQUE,
2120 E Paisano Ste 276, El Paso, TX 79905

GRAHAM, GORDON,
3145 CR 4008, New Boston, TX 75570, Phone: 903-293-2610, Web: www.grahamknives.com
Prices: $200 to $500. **Mark:** Graham.

GRANGER, PAUL J,
2820 St Charles Ln, Kennesaw, GA 30144, Phone: 770-426-6298, grangerknives@hotmail.com; Web: www.geocities.com/ grangerknives Web: www.grangerknives.com
Specialties: Working straight knives of his own design and a few folders. **Patterns:** 2.75" to 4" work knives, skinners, tactical knives and Bowies from 5"-9." **Technical:** Forges 52100 and 5160 and his own carbon steel Damascus. Offers filework. **Prices:** $95 to $400. **Remarks:** Part-time maker since 1997. Sold first knife in 1997. Doing business as Granger Knives and Pale Horse Fighters. Member of ABS and OBG. **Mark:** "Granger" or "Palehorse Fighters."

GRAVELINE, PASCAL AND ISABELLE,
38, Rue de Kerbrezillic, 29350 Moelan-sur-Mer, FRANCE, Phone: 33 2 98 39 73 33, Fax: 33 2 98 39 73 33, atelier.graveline@wanadso.fr; Web: www.graveline-couteliers.com
Specialties: French replicas from the 17th, 18th and 19th centuries. **Patterns:** Traditional folders and multi-blade pocket knives; traveling knives, fruit knives and fork sets; puzzle knives and friend's knives; rivet less knives. **Technical:** Grind 12C27, ATS-34, Damascus and carbon steel. **Prices:** $500 to $5000. **Remarks:** Full-time makers; first knife sold in 1992. **Mark:** Last name over head of ram.

GRAY, BOB,
8206 N Lucia Court, Spokane, WA 99208, Phone: 509-468-3924
Specialties: Straight working knives of his own design or to customer specs. **Patterns:** Hunter, fillet and carving knives. **Technical:** Forges 5160, L6 and some 52100; grinds 440C. **Prices:** $100 to $600. **Remarks:** Part-time knifemaker; first knife sold in 1991. Doing business as Hi-Land Knives. **Mark:** HI-L.

GRAY, DANIEL,
GRAY KNIVES, 686 Main Rd., Brownville, ME 04414, Phone: 207-965-2191, mail@grayknives.com; Web: www.grayknives.com
Specialties: Straight knives, fantasy, folders, automatics and traditional of his own design. **Patterns:** Automatics, fighters, hunters. **Technical:** Grinds O1, 154CM and D2. **Prices:** From $155 to $750. **Remarks:** Full-time maker; first knife sold in 1974. **Mark:** Gray Knives.

GREBE, GORDON S,
PO Box 296, Anchor Point, AK 99556-0296, Phone: 907-235-8242
Specialties: Working straight knives and folders, some fancy. **Patterns:** Tantos, Bowies, boot fighter sets, locking folders. **Technical:** Grinds stainless steels; likes 1/4" inch stock and glass-bead finishes. **Prices:** $75 to $250; some to $2000. **Remarks:** Full-time maker; first knife sold in 1968. **Mark:** Initials in lightning logo.

GRECO, JOHN,
100 Mattie Jones Rd, Greensburg, KY 42743, Phone: 270-932-3335, Fax: 270-932-2225, johngreco@grecoknives.com; Web: www.grecoknives.com
Specialties: Limited edition knives and swords. **Patterns:** Tactical, fighters, camp knives, short swords. **Technical:** Stock removal carbon steel. **Prices:** Affordable. **Remarks:** Full-time maker since 1986. First knife sold in 1979. **Mark:** Greco and steroc w/mo mark.

GREEN, BILL,
6621 Eastview Dr, Sachse, TX 75048, Phone: 972-463-3147
Specialties: High-art and working straight knives and folders of his design and to customer specs. **Patterns:** Bowies, hunters, kitchen knives and locking folders. **Technical:** Grinds ATS-34, D2 and 440V. Hand-tooled custom sheaths. **Prices:** $70 to $350; some to $750. **Remarks:** Part-time maker; first knife sold in 1990. **Mark:** Last name.

GREEN, WILLIAM (BILL),
46 Warren Rd, View Bank Vic., AUSTRALIA 3084, Fax: 03-9459-1529
Specialties: Traditional high-tech straight knives and folders. **Patterns:** Japanese-influenced designs, hunters, Bowies, folders and miniatures. **Technical:** Forges O1, D2 and his own Damascus. Offers lost wax castings for bolsters and pommels. Likes natural handle materials, gems, silver and gold. **Prices:** $400 to $750; some to $1200. **Remarks:** Full-time maker. **Mark:** Initials.

GREENAWAY, DON,
3325 Dinsmore Tr, Fayetteville, AR 72704, Phone: 501-521-0323

GREENE, CHRIS,
707 Cherry Lane, Shelby, NC 28150, Phone: 704-434-5620

GREENE, DAVID,
570 Malcom Rd, Covington, GA 30209, Phone: 770-784-0657
Specialties: Straight working using knives. **Patterns:** Hunters. **Technical:** Forges mosaic and twist Damascus. Prefers stag and desert ironwood for handle material.

GREENE, STEVE,
DUNN KNIVES INC, PO Box 204, Rossville, KS 66533, Phone: 785-584-6856, Fax: 785-584-6020, s.greene@earthlink.net; Web: www.dunnknives.com
Specialties: Skinning & fillet knives. **Patterns:** Skinners, drop points, clip points and fillets. **Technical:** S60V, S90V and 20 CV powdered metal steel. **Prices:** $90 to $250. **Mark:** Dunn by Greene and year. **Remarks:** Full-time knifemaker. First knife sold in 1972.

GREENFIELD, G O,
2605 15th St #113, Everett, WA 98201, garyg1946@yahoo.com
Specialties: High-tech and working straight knives and folders of his design. **Patterns:** Boots, daggers, hunters and one-of-a-kinds. **Technical:** Grinds ATS-34, D2, 440C and T-440V. Makes sheaths for each knife. **Prices:** $100 to $800; some to $10,000. **Remarks:** Part-time maker; first knife sold in 1978. **Mark:** Springfield®, serial number.

GREGORY, MICHAEL,
211 Calhoun Rd, Belton, SC 29627, Phone: 864-338-8898
Specialties: Working straight knives and folders. **Patterns:** Hunters, tantos, locking folders and slip-joints, boots and fighters. **Technical:** Grinds 440C, 154CM and ATS-34; mirror finishes. **Prices:** $95 to $200; some to $1000. **Remarks:** Part-time maker; first knife sold in 1980. **Mark:** Name, city in logo.

GREINER, RICHARD,
1073 E County Rd 32, Green Springs, OH 44836

GREISS, JOCKL,
Herrenwald 15, D 77773 Schenkenzell, GERMANY, Phone: +49 7836 95 71 69 or +49 7836 95 55 76, www.jocklgreiss@yahoo.com
Specialties: Classic and working using straight knives of his design. **Patterns:** Bowies, daggers and hunters. **Technical:** Uses only Jerry Rados Damascus. All knives are one-of-a-kind made by hand; no machines are used. **Prices:** $700 to $2000; some to $3000. **Remarks:** Full-time maker; first knife sold in 1984. **Mark:** An "X" with a long vertical line through it.

GREY, PIET,
PO Box 363, Naboomspruit 0560, SOUTH AFRICA, Phone: 014-743-3613
Specialties: Fancy working and using straight knives of his design. **Patterns:** Fighters, hunters and utility/camp knives. **Technical:** Grinds ATS-34 and AEB-L; forges and grinds Damascus. Solder less fitting of guards. Engraves and scrimshaws. **Prices:** $125 to $750; some to $1500. **Remarks:** Part-time maker; first knife sold in 1970. **Mark:** Last name.

GRIFFIN, RENDON AND MARK,
9706 Cedardale, Houston, TX 77055, Phone: 713-468-0436
Specialties: Working folders and automatics of their designs. **Patterns:** Standard lockers and slip-joints. **Technical:** Most blade steels; stock removal. **Prices:** Start at $350. **Remarks:** Rendon's first knife sold in 1966; Mark's in 1974. **Mark:** Last name logo.

GRIFFIN, THOMAS J,
591 Quevli Ave., Windom, MN 56101, Phone: 507-831-1089
Specialties: Period pieces and fantasy straight knives of his design. **Patterns:** Daggers and swords. **Technical:** Forges 1095, 52100 and L6. Most blades are his own Damascus; turned fittings and wire-wrapped grips. **Prices:** $250 to $800; some to $2000. **Remarks:** Full-time maker; first knife sold in 1991. Doing business as Griffin Knives. **Mark:** Last name etched.

GRIFFIN JR., HOWARD A,
14299 SW 31st Ct, Davie, FL 33330, Phone: 954-474-5406, mgriffin18@aol.com
Specialties: Working straight knives and folders. **Patterns:** Hunters, Bowies, locking folders with his own push-button lock design. **Technical:** Grinds 440C. **Prices:** $100 to $200; some to $500. **Remarks:** Part-time maker; first knife sold in 1983. **Mark:** Initials.

GROSPITCH, ERNIE,
18440 Amityville Dr, Orlando, FL 32820, Phone: 407-568-5438, shrpknife@aol.com; Web: www.erniesknives.com
Specialties: Bowies, hunting, fishing, kitchen, lockback folders, leather craft. Patterns: His design or customer. **Technical:** Stock removal using most available steels. **Prices:** $140 and up. **Remarks:** Full-time maker, sold first knife in 1990. **Mark:** Etched name/maker city and state.

GROSS, W W,
109 Dylan Scott Dr, Archdale, NC 27263-3858
Specialties: Working knives. **Patterns:** Hunters, boots, fighters. **Technical:** Grinds. **Prices:** Moderate. **Remarks:** Full-time maker. **Mark:** Name.

GROSSMAN, STEWART,
24 Water St #419, Clinton, MA 01510, Phone: 508-365-2291; 800-mysword
Specialties: Miniatures and full-size knives and swords. **Patterns:** One-of-a-kind miniatures—jewelry, replicas—and wire-wrapped figures. Full-size art, fantasy and combat knives, daggers and modular systems. **Technical:** Forges and grinds most metals and Damascus. Uses gems, crystals, electronics and motorized mechanisms. **Prices:** $20 to $300; some to $4500 and higher. **Remarks:** Full-time maker; first knife sold in 1985. **Mark:** G1.

GRUSSENMEYER, PAUL G,
310 Kresson Rd, Cherry Hill, NJ 08034, Phone: 856-428-1088, pgrussentne@comcast.net; Web: www.pgcarvings.com
Specialties: Assembling fancy and fantasy straight knives with his own carved handles. **Patterns:** Bowies, daggers, folders, swords, hunters and miniatures. **Technical:** Uses forged steel and Damascus, stock removal and knapped obsidian blades. **Prices:** $250 to $4000. **Remarks:** Spare-time maker; first knife sold in 1991. **Mark:** First and last initial hooked together on handle.

GUARNERA, ANTHONY R,
42034 Quail Creek Dr, Quartzhill, CA 93536, Phone: 661-722-4032
Patterns: Hunters, camp, Bowies, kitchen, fighter knives. **Technical:** Forged and stock removal. **Prices:** $100 and up.

GUESS, RAYMOND L,
7214 Salineville Rd NE, Mechanicstown, OH 44651, Phone: 330-738-2793
Specialties: Working straight knives and folders of his design or to customer specs. **Patterns:** Hunters, Bowies, fillet knives, steak and paring knife sets. **Technical:** Grinds 440C. Offers silver inlay work and mirror finishes. Custom-made leather sheath for each knife. **Prices:** $65 to $850; some to $700. **Remarks:** Spare-time maker; first knife sold in 1985. **Mark:** First initial, last name.

GUIDRY, BRUCE,
24550 Adams Ave, Murrieta, CA 92562, Phone: 909-677-2384

GUNTER, BRAD,
13 Imnaha Rd., Tijeras, NM 87059, Phone: 505-281-8080

GURGANUS, CAROL,
2553 NC 45 South, Colerain, NC 27924, Phone: 252-356-4831, Fax: 252-356-4650
Specialties: Working and using straight knives. **Patterns:** Fighters, hunters and kitchen knives. **Technical:** Grinds D2, ATS-34 and Damascus steel. Uses stag, and exotic wood handles. **Prices:** $100 to $300. **Remarks:** Part-time maker; first knife sold in 1992. **Mark:** Female symbol, last name, city, state.

GURGANUS, MELVIN H,
2553 NC 45 South, Colerain, NC 27924, Phone: 252-356-4831, Fax: 252-356-4650
Specialties: High-tech working folders. **Patterns:** Leaf-lock and back-lock designs, bolstered and interframe. **Technical:** D2 and 440C; Heat-treats, carves and offers lost wax casting. **Prices:** $300 to $3000. **Remarks:** Part-time maker; first knife sold in 1983. **Mark:** First initial, last name and maker.

GUTHRIE, GEORGE B,
1912 Puett Chapel Rd, Bassemer City, NC 28016, Phone: 704-629-3031
Specialties: Working knives of his design or to customer specs. **Patterns:** Hunters, boots, fighters, locking folders and slip-joints in traditional styles. **Technical:** Grinds D2, 440C and 154CM. **Prices:** $105 to $300; some to $450. **Remarks:** Part-time maker; first knife sold in 1978. **Mark:** Name in state.

H

HAGEN, DOC,
PO Box 58, 41780 Kansas Point Ln, Pelican Rapids, MN 56572, Phone: 218-863-8503, dhagen@prtel.com; Web: www.dochagencustomknives.com
Specialties: Folders. Autos:bolster release-dual action. Slipjoint folders**Patterns:** Defense-related straight knives; wide variety of folders. **Technical:** Dual action release, bolster release autos. **Prices:** $300 to $800; some to $3000. **Remarks:** Full-time maker; first knife sold in 1975. Makes his own Damascus. **Mark:** DOC HAGEN in shield, knife, banner logo; or DOC.

HAGGERTY, GEORGE S,
PO Box 88, Jacksonville, VT 05342, Phone: 802-368-7437, swewater@sover.net
Specialties: Working straight knives and folders. Patterns: Hunters, claws, camp and fishing knives, locking folders and backpackers. **Technical:** Forges and grinds W2, 440C and 154CM. **Prices:** $85 to $300. **Remarks:** Part-time maker; first knife sold in 1981. **Mark:** Initials or last name.

HAGUE, GEOFF,
Unit 5, Project Workshops, Laines Farm, Quarley, SP11 8PX, UK, Phone: (+44) 01672-870212, Fax: (+44) 01672 870212, geoff@hagueknives.com; Web: www.hagueknives.com
Specialties: Quality folding knives. **Patterns:** Back lock, locking liner, slip joint, and friction folders. **Technical:** RWL34, D2, titanium, and some gold decoraqtion. Mainly natural handle materials. **Prices:** $900 to $2,000. **Remarks:** Full-time maker. **Mark:** Last name.

HAINES, JEFF HAINES CUSTOM KNIVES,
302 N Mill St, Wauzeka, WI 53826, Phone: 608-875-5325, jeffhaines@centurytel.net
Patterns: Hunters, skinners, camp knives, customer designs welcome. **Technical:** Forges 1095, 5160, and Damascus, grinds A2. **Prices:** $50 and up. **Remarks:** Part-time maker since 1995. **Mark:** Last name.

HALFRICH, JERRY,
340 Briarwood, San Marcos, TX 78666, Phone: 512-353-2582, Fax: 512-392-3659, jerryhalfrich@earthlink.net; Web: www.halfrichknives.com
Specialties: Working knives and specialty utility knives for the professional and serious hunter. Uses proven designs in both straight and folding knives. Plays close attention to fit and finish. Art knives on special request. **Patterns:** Hunters, skinners, lock back liner lock. **Technical:** Grinds both flat and hollow D2, damasteel, BG42 makes high precision folders. **Prices:** $300 to $600, sometimes $1000. **Remarks:** Full-time maker since 2000. DBA Halfrich Custom Knives. **Mark:** Halfrich, San Marcos, TX in a football shape.

HALL, JEFF,
PO Box 435, Los Alamitos, CA 90720, Phone: 562-594-4740, jhall10176@aol.com
Specialties: Collectible and working folders of his design. **Technical:** Grinds S30V, ATS-34, and various makers' Damascus. **Patterns:** Fighters, gentleman's, hunters and utility knives. **Prices:** $300 to $500; some to $1000. **Remarks:** Full-time maker. First knife sold 1998. **Mark:** Last name.

HALLIGAN, ED,
14 Meadow Way, Sharpsburg, GA 30277, Phone: 770-251-7720, Fax: 770-251-7720
Specialties: Working straight knives and folders, some fancy. **Patterns:** Liner locks, hunters, skinners, boots, fighters and swords. **Technical:** Grinds ATS-34; forges 5160; makes cable and pattern Damascus. **Prices:** $160 to $2500. **Remarks:** Full-time maker; first knife sold in 1985. Doing business as Halligan Knives. **Mark:** Last name, city, state and USA.

HAMLET JR., JOHNNY,
300 Billington, Clute, TX 77531, Phone: 979-265-6929, nifeman@swbell.net; Web: www.hamlets-handmade-knives.com
Specialties: Working straight knives and folders. **Patterns:** Hunters, fighters, fillet and kitchen knives, locking folders. Likes upswept knives and trailing-points. **Technical:** Grinds 440C, D2, ATS-34. Makes sheaths. **Prices:** $125 and up. **Remarks:** Full-time maker; sold first knife in 1988. **Mark:** Hamlet's Handmade in script.

HAMMOND, HANK,
189 Springlake Dr, Leesburg, GA 31763, Phone: 229-434-1295, godogs57@bellsouth.net
Specialties: Traditional hunting and utility knives of his design. Will also design and produce knives to customer's specifications. **Patterns:** Straight or sheath knives, hunters skinners as well as Bowies and fighters. **Technical:** Grinds (hollow and flat grinds) CPM 154CM, ATS-34. Also uses Damascus and forges 52100. Offers filework on blades. Handle materials include all exotic woods, red stag, sambar stag, deer, elk, oosic, bone, fossil ivory, Micarta, etc. All knives come with sheath handmade for that individual knife. **Prices:** $100 up to $500. **Remarks:** Part-time maker. Sold first knife in 1981. Doing business as Double H Knives. **Mark:** "HH" inside 8 point deer rack.

HAMMOND, JIM,
PO Box 486, Arab, AL 35016, Phone: 256-586-4151, Fax: 256-586-0170, jim@jimhammondknives.com; Web: www.jimhammondkinves.com
Specialties: High-tech fighters and folders. **Patterns:** Proven-design fighters. **Technical:** Grinds 440C, 440V, ATS-34 and other specialty steels. **Prices:** $385 to $1200; some to $9200. **Remarks:** Full-time maker; first knife sold in 1977. Designer for Columbia River Knife and Tool. **Mark:** Full name, city, state in shield logo.

HANCOCK, TIM,
10805 N. 83rd St, Scottsdale, AZ 85260, Phone: 480-998-8849
Specialties: High-art and working straight knives and folders of his design and to customer preferences. **Patterns:** Bowies, fighters, daggers, tantos, swords, folders. **Technical:** Forges Damascus and 52100; grinds ATS-34. Makes Damascus. Silver-wire inlays; offers carved fittings and file work. **Prices:** $500 to $10,000. **Remarks:** Full-time maker; first knife sold in 1988. Master Smith ABS. **Mark:** Last name or heart.

HAND, BILL,
PO Box 717, 1103 W. 7th St., Spearman, TX 79081, Phone: 806-659-2967, Fax: 806-659-5139, klinker@arn.net
Specialties: Traditional working and using straight knives and folders of

his design or to customer specs. **Patterns:** Hunters, Bowies, folders and fighters. **Technical:** Forges 5160, 52100 and Damascus. **Prices:** Start at $150. **Remarks:** Part-time maker; Journeyman Smith. Current delivery time 12 to 16 months. **Mark:** Stylized initials.

HANKINS, R,
9920 S Rural Rd #10859, Tempe, AZ 85284, Phone: 480-940-0559, pamhankins@uswest.net; Web: http://albums.photopoint.com/ j/
Specialties: Completely handmade tactical, practical and custom Bowie knives. **Technical:** Use Damascus, ATS-34 and 440C stainless steel for blades. Stock removal method of grinding. Handle material varies from ivory, stag to Micarta, depending on application and appearance. **Remarks:** Part-time maker.

HANSEN, LONNIE,
PO Box 4956, Spanaway, WA 98387, Phone: 253-847-4632, lonniehansen@msn.com; Web: lchansen.com
Specialties: Working straight knives of his design. **Patterns:** Tomahawks, tantos, hunters, fillet. **Technical:** Forges 1086, 52100, grinds 440V, BG-42. **Prices:** Starting at $300. **Remarks:** Part-time maker since 1989. **Mark:** First initial and last name. Also first and last initial.

HANSEN, ROBERT W,
35701 University Ave NE, Cambridge, MN 55008, Phone: 612-689-3242
Specialties: Working straight knives, folders and integrals. **Patterns:** From hunters to minis, camp knives to miniatures; folding lockers and slip-joints in original styles. **Technical:** Grinds O1, 440C and 154CM; likes filework. **Prices:** $75 to $175; some to $550. **Remarks:** Part-time maker; first knife sold in 1983. **Mark:** Fish with last initial inside.

HANSON III, DON L.,
PO Box 13, Success, MO 65570-0013, Phone: 573-674-3045, Web: www.sunfishforge.com; Web: www.donhansonknives.com
Specialties: One-of-a-kind Damascus folders and forged fixed blades. **Patterns:** Small, fancy pocket knives, large folding fighters and Bowies. **Technical:** Forges own pattern welded Damascus, file work and carving also carbon steel blades with hamons. **Prices:** $800 and up. **Remarks:** Full-time maker, first knife sold in 1984. ABS mastersmith. **Mark:** Sunfish.

HARA, KOUJI,
292-2 Osugi, Seki-City, Gifu-Pref. 501-3922, JAPAN, Phone: 0575-24-7569, Fax: 0575-24-7569, info@knifehousehara.com; Web: www.knifehousehara.com
Specialties: High-tech and working straight knives of his design; some folders. **Patterns:** Hunters, locking folders and utility/camp knives. **Technical:** Grinds Cowry X, Cowry Y and ATS-34. Prefers high mirror polish; pearl handle inlay. **Prices:** $400 to $2500. **Remarks:** Full-time maker; first knife sold in 1980. Doing business as Knife House "Hara." **Mark:** First initial, last name in fish.

HARDY, DOUGLAS E,
114 Cypress Rd, Franklin, GA 30217, Phone: 706-675-6305

HARDY, SCOTT,
639 Myrtle Ave, Placerville, CA 95667, Phone: 530-622-5780, Web: www.innercite.com/~shardy
Specialties: Traditional working and using straight knives of his design. **Patterns:** Most anything with an edge. **Technical:** Forges carbon steels. Japanese stone polish. Offers mirror finish; differentially tempers. **Prices:** $100 to $1000. **Remarks:** Part-time maker; first knife sold in 1982. **Mark:** First initial, last name and Handmade with bird logo.

HARKINS, J A,
PO Box 218, Conner, MT 59827, Phone: 406-821-1060, kutter@customknives.net; Web: customknives.net
Specialties: Investment grade folders. **Patterns:** Flush buttons, lockers. **Technical:** Grinds ATS-34. Engraves; offers gem work. **Prices:** Start at $550. **Remarks:** Full-time maker and engraver; first knife sold in 1988. **Mark:** First and middle initials, last name.

HARLEY, LARRY W,
348 Deerfield Dr, Bristol, TN 37620, Phone: 423-878-5368 (shop)/Cell 423-571-0638, Fax: 276-466-6771, Web: www.lonesomepineknives.com
Specialties: One-of-a-kind Persian in one-of-a-kind Damascus. Working knives, period pieces. **Technical:** Forges and grinds ATS-34, 440c, L6, 15, 20, 1084, and 52100. **Patterns:** Full range of straight knives, tomahawks, razors, buck skinners and hog spears. **Prices:** $200 and up. **Mark:** Pine tree.

HARLEY, RICHARD,
348 Deerfield Dr, Bristol, TN 37620, Phone: 423-878-5368/423-571-0638
Specialties: Hunting knives, Bowies, friction folders, one-of-a-kind. **Technical:** Forges 1084, S160, 52100, Lg. **Prices:** $150 to $1000. **Mark:** Pine tree with name.

HARM, PAUL W,
818 Young Rd, Attica, MI 48412, Phone: 810-724-5582, harm@blclinks.net
Specialties: Early American working knives. Patterns: Hunters, skinners, patch knives, fighters, folders. **Technical:** Forges and grinds 1084, O1, 52100 and own Damascus. **Prices:** $75 to $1000. **Remarks:** First knife sold in 1990. **Mark:** Connected initials.

HARRINGTON, ROGER,
3 Beech Farm Cottages, Bugsell Ln., East Sussex, ENGLAND TN 32 5 EN, Phone: 44 0 1580 882194, info@bisonbushcraft.co.uk; Web: www.bisonbushcraft.co.uk
Specialties: Working straight knives to his or customer's designs, flat saber Scandinavia-style grinds on full tang knives, also hollow and convex grinds. **Technical:** Grinds O1, D2, Damascus. **Prices:** $200 to $800. **Remarks:** First knife made by hand in 1997 whilst traveling around the world. **Mark:** Bison with bison written under.

HARRIS, CASS,
19855 Fraiser Hill Ln, Bluemont, VA 20135, Phone: 540-554-8774, Web: www.tdogforge.com
Prices: $160 to $500.

HARRIS, JAY,
991 Johnson St, Redwood City, CA 94061, Phone: 415-366-6077
Specialties: Traditional high-tech straight knives and folders of his design. **Patterns:** Daggers, fighters and locking folders. **Technical:** Uses 440C, ATS-34 and CPM. **Prices:** $250 to $850. **Remarks:** Spare-time maker; first knife sold in 1980.

HARRIS, JEFFERY A,
214 Glen Cove Dr, Chesterfield, MO 63017, Phone: 314-469-6317, Fax: 314-469-6374, jeffro135@aol.com
Remarks: Purveyor and collector of handmade knives.

HARRIS, JOHN,
14131 Calle Vista, Riverside, CA 92508, Phone: 951-653-2755, johnharrisknives@yahoo.com
Specialties: Hunters, daggers, Bowies, bird and trout, period pieces, Damascus and carbon steel knives, forged and stock removal. **Prices:** $200 to $1000.

HARRIS, RALPH DEWEY,
2607 Bell Shoals Rd, Brandon, FL 33511, Phone: 813-681-5293, Fax: 813-654-8175
Specialties: Collector quality interframe folders. **Patterns:** High tech locking folders of his own design with various mechanisms. **Technical:** Grinds 440C, ATS-34 and commercial Damascus. Offers various frame materials including 416ss, and titanium; file worked frames and his own engraving. **Prices:** $400 to $3000. **Remarks:** Full-time maker; first knife sold in 1978. **Mark:** Last name, or name and city.

HARRISON, BRIAN,
BFH KNIVES, 2359 E Swede Rd, Cedarville, MI 49719, Phone: 906-484-2011, bfhknives@easternup.net; Web: www.bfhknives.com
Specialties: High grade fixed blade knives. **Patterns:** Many sizes & variety of patterns from small pocket carries to large combat and camp knives. Mirror and bead blast finishes. All handles of high grade materials from ivory to highly figured stabilized woods to stag, deer & moose horn and Micarta. Hand sewn fancy sheaths for pocket or belt. **Technical:** Flat & hollow grinds usually ATS-34 but some O1, L6 and stellite 6K. **Prices:** $150 to $1200. **Remarks:** Full-time maker, sole authorship. Made first knife in 1980, sold first knife in 1999. Received much knowledge from the following makers: George Young, Eric Erickson, Webster Wood, Ed Kalfayan who are all generous men.**Mark:** Engraved blade outline w/BFH Knives over the top edge, signature across middle & Cedarville, MI underneath.

HARRISON, JIM (SEAMUS),
721 Fairington View Dr, St. Louis, MO 63129, Phone: 314-894-2525; Cell: 314-791-6350, jrh@seamusknives.com; Web: www.seamusknives.com
Specialties: Gents and fancy tactical locking-liner folders. Compact straight blades for hunting, backpacking and canoeing. **Patterns:** LinerLock® folders. Compact 3 fingered fixed blades often with modified wharncliffes. Survival knife with mortised handles. **Technical:** Grinds talonite, S30V, Mike Norris and Devin Thomas S.S. Damascus, 440-C. Heat treats. **Prices:** Folders $400 to $1,200. Fixed blades $400 to $600. **Remarks:** Full-time maker. **Mark:** Seamus

HARSEY, WILLIAM H,
82710 N. Howe Ln, Creswell, OR 97426, Phone: 519-895-4941, harseyjr@cs.com
Specialties: High-tech kitchen and outdoor knives. **Patterns:** Folding hunters, trout and bird folders; straight hunters, camp knives and axes. **Technical:** Grinds; etches. **Prices:** $125 to $300; some to $1500. Folders start at $350. **Remarks:** Full-time maker; first knife sold in 1979. **Mark:** Full name, state, U.S.A.

HART, BILL,
647 Cedar Dr, Pasadena, MD 21122, Phone: 410-255-4981
Specialties: Fur-trade era working straight knives and folders. **Patterns:** Springback folders, skinners, Bowies and patch knives. **Technical:** Forges and stock removes 1095 and 5160 wire Damascus. **Prices:** $100 to $600. **Remarks:** Part-time maker; first knife sold in 1986. **Mark:** Name.

HARTMAN, ARLAN (LANNY),
6102 S Hamlin Cir, Baldwin, MI 49304, Phone: 231-745-4029
Specialties: Working straight knives and folders. Patterns: Drop-point hunters, coil spring lockers, slip-joints. **Technical:** Flat-grinds D2, 440C and ATS-34. **Prices:** $300 to $2000. **Remarks:** Part-time maker; first knife sold in 1982. **Mark:** Last name.

HARTMAN, TIM,
3812 Pedroncelli Rd NW, Albuquerque, NM 87107, Phone: 505-385-6924, tbonz1@comcast.net
Specialties: Exotic wood scales, sambar stag, filework, hunters. **Patterns:**Fixed blade hunters, skinners, utility and hiking. **Technical:** 154CM, Ats-34 and D2. Mirror finish and contoured scales. **Prices:** Start at $200-$450. **Remarks:** Started making knives in 2004. **Mark:** 3 lines Ti Hartman, Maker, Albuquerque NM

HARTSFIELD, PHILL,
PO Box 1637, Newport Beach, CA 92659-0637, Phone: 949-722-9792 and 714-636-7633, phartsfield@att.net; Web: www.phillhartsfield.com
Specialties: Heavy-duty working and using straight knives. **Patterns:** Fighters, swords and survival knives, most in Japanese profile. **Technical:** Grinds A2. **Prices:** $450 to $20,000. **Remarks:** Full-time maker; first knife sold about 1976. Doing business as A Cut Above. The Hartsfield folder is now available. Color catalog. **Mark:** Initials, chiseled character plus register mark.

HARVEY, HEATHER,
HEAVIN FORGE, PO Box 768, Belfast 1100, SOUTH AFRICA, Phone: 27-13-253-0914, heavin.knives@mweb.co.za; Web: www.africut.co.za
Specialties: Integral hand forged knives, traditional African weapons, primitive folders and by-gone forged-styles. **Patterns:** All forged knives, war axes, spears, arrows, forks, spoons, and swords. **Technical:** Own carbon Damascus and mokume. Also forges stainless, brass, copper and titanium. Traditional forging and heat-treatment methods used. **Prices:** $300 to $5000, average $1000. **Remarks:** Full-time maker and knifemaking instructor. Master bladesmith with ABS. First Damascus sold in 1995, first knife sold in 1998. Often collaborate with husband, Kevin (ABS MS) using the logo "Heavin." **Mark:** First name and sur name, oval shape with "M S" in middle.

HARVEY, KEVIN,
HEAVIN FORGE, PO Box 768, Belfast 1100, SOUTH AFRICA, Phone: 27-13-253-0914, info@heavinforge.co.za Web: www.heavinforge.co.za
Specialties: Large knives of presentation quality and creative art knives. **Patterns:** Fixed blades of Bowie, dagger and fighter-styles, occasionally folders and swords. **Technical:** Stock removal of stainless and forging of carbon steel and own Damascus. Indigenous African handle materials preferred. Own engraving Often collaborate with wife, Heather (ABS MS) under the logo "Heavin." **Prices:** $500 to $5000 average $1500. **Remarks:** Full-time maker and knifemaking instructor. Master bladesmith with ABS. First knife sold in 1984. **Mark:** First name and surname, oval with "M S" in the middle.

HARVEY, MAX,
14 Bass Rd, Bull Creek, Perth 6155, Western Australia, AUSTRALIA, Phone: 09-332-7585
Specialties: Daggers, Bowies, fighters and fantasy knives. **Patterns:** Hunters, Bowies, tantos and skinners. **Technical:** Hollow-and flat-grinds 440C, ATS-34, 154CM and Damascus. Offers gem work. **Prices:** $250 to $4000. **Remarks:** Part-time maker; first knife sold in 1981. **Mark:** First and middle initials, last name.

HARVEY, MEL,
Chrome Fang Custom Cutlery

HASLINGER, THOMAS,
164 Fairview Dr SE, Calgary, AB, CANADA T2H 1B3, Phone: 403-253-9628, Web: www.haslinger-knives.com
Specialties: One-of-a-kind using, working and art knives HCK signature sweeping grind lines. Maker of New Generation Chef series. Differential heat treated stainless steel. **Patterns:** No fixed patterns, likes to work with customers on design. **Technical:** Grinds various specialty alloys, including Damascus, High end satin finish. Prefers natural handle materials e.g. ancient ivory stag, pearl, abalone, stone and exotic woods. Does inlay work with stone, some sterling silver, niobium and gold wire work. Custom sheaths using matching woods or hand stitched with unique leather like sturgeon, Nile perch or carp. Offers engraving. **Prices:** Starting at $150. **Remarks:** Full-time maker; first knife sold in 1994. Doing business as Haslinger Custom Knives. **Mark:** Two marks used, high end work uses stylized initials, other uses elk antler with Thomas Haslinger, Canada, handcrafted above.

HAWES, CHUCK,
HAWES FORGE, PO Box 176, Weldon, IL 61882, Phone: 217-736-2479
Specialties: 95 percent of all work in own Damascus. **Patterns:** Slip-joints liner locks, hunters, Bowie's, swords, anything in between. **Technical:** Forges everything, uses all high-carbon steels, no stainless. **Prices:** $150 to $4000. **Remarks:** Like to do custom orders, his style or yours. Sells Damascus. Full-time maker since 1995. **Mark:** Small football shape. Chuck Hawes maker Weldon, IL.

HAWK, GRANT AND GAVIN,
Box 401, Idaho City, ID 83631, Phone: 208-392-4911, Web: www.9-hawkknives.com
Specialties: Large folders with unique locking systems D.O.G. lock, toad lock. **Technical:** Grinds ATS-34, titanium folder parts. **Prices:** $450 and up. **Remarks:** Full-time maker. **Mark:** First initials and last names.

HAWKINS, BUDDY,
PO Box 5969, Texarkana, TX 75505-5969, Phone: 903-838-7917, buddyhawkins@cableone.net

HAWKINS, RADE,
110 Buckeye Rd, Fayetteville, GA 30214, Phone: 770-964-1177, Fax: 770-306-2877, radeh@bellsouth.net; Web: wwwhawkinscustomknives.com
Specialties: All styles. **Patterns:** All styles. **Technical:** Grinds and forges. Makes own Damascus **Prices:** Start at $190. **Remarks:** Full-time maker; first knife sold in 1972. Member knifemakers guild, ABS Journeyman Smith. **Mark:** Rade Hawkins Custom Knives.

HAYES, DOLORES,
PO Box 41405, Los Angeles, CA 90041, Phone: 213-258-9923
Specialties: High-art working and using straight knives of her design. **Patterns:** Art knives and miniatures. **Technical:** Grinds 440C, stainless AEB, commercial Damascus and ATS-34. **Prices:** $50 to $500; some to $2000. **Remarks:** Spare-time maker; first knife sold in 1978. **Mark:** Last name.

HAYES, SCOTTY,
Texarkana College, 2500 N Robinson Rd., Tesarkana, TX 75501, Phone: 903-838-4541, ext. 3236, Fax: 903-832-5030, shayes@texakanacollege.edu; Web: www.americanbladesmith.com/ 2005ABSo/o20schedule.htm
Specialties: ABS School of Bladesmithing.

HAYES, WALLY,
1026 Old Montreal Rd, Orleans, Ont., CANADA K4A-3N2, Phone: 613-824-9520, Web: www.hayesknives.com
Specialties: Classic and fancy straight knives and folders. **Patterns:** Daggers, Bowies, fighters, tantos. **Technical:** Forges own Damascus and O1; engraves. **Prices:** $150 to $14,000. **Mark:** Last name, M.S. and serial number.

HAYNES, JERRY,
260 Forest Meadow Dr, Gunter, TX 75058, Phone: 210-599-2928, jhaynes@arrow-head.com; Web: http://www.arrow-head.com
Specialties: Working straight knives and folders of his design, also historical blades. **Patterns:** Hunters, skinners, carving knives, fighters, renaissance daggers, locking folders and kitchen knives. **Technical:** Grinds ATS-34, CPM, Stellite 6K, D2 and acquired Damascus. Prefers exotic handle materials. Has B.A. in design. Studied with R. Buckminster Fuller. **Prices:** $200 to $1200. **Remarks:** Part-time maker, will go full-time after retirement in 2007. First knife sold in 1953. **Mark:** Arrowhead and last name.

HAYS, MARK,
HAYS HANDMADE KNIVES, 1008 Kavanagh Dr., Austin, TX 78748, Phone: 512-292-4410, markhays@austin.rr.com
Specialties: Working straight knives and folders. Patterns inspired by Randall and Stone. **Patterns:** Bowies, hunters and slip-joint folders. **Technical:** 440C stock removal. Repairs and restores Stone knives. **Prices:** Start at $200. **Remarks:** Part-time maker, brochure available, with Stone knives 1974-1983, 1990-1991. **Mark:** First initial, last name, state and serial number.

HAZEN, MARK,
9600 Surrey Rd, Charlotte, NC 28227, Phone: 704-573-0052, Fax: 704-573-0052, mhazen@carolina.rr.com
Specialties: Working/using straight knives of his design. **Patterns:** Hunters/skinners, fillet, utility/camp, fighters, short swords. **Technical:** Grinds 154 CM, ATS-34, 440C. **Prices:** $75 to $450; some to $1500. **Remarks:** Part-time maker. First knife sold 1982. **Mark:** Name with cross in it, etched in blade.

HEADRICK, GARY,
122 Wilson Blvd, Juane Les Pins, FRANCE 06160, Phone: 033 0610282885, headrick-gary@wanadoo.fr
Specialties: Hi-tech folders with natural furnishings. Back lock & back spring. **Patterns:** Damascus and mokumes. **Technical:** Self made Damascus all steel (no nickel). **Prices:** $500 to $2000. **Remarks:** Full-time maker for last 7 years. German Guild-French Federation. 10 years active. **Mark:** G/P in a circle.

HEANEY, JOHN D,
9 Lefe Court, Haines City, FL 33844, Phone: 863-422-5823, jdh199@msn.com; Web: www.heaneyknives.com
Specialties: Forged 5160, O1 and Damascus. Prefers using natural handle material such as bone, stag and oosic. Plans on using some of the various ivories on future knives. **Prices:** $250 and up. **Remarks:** ABS member. Received journeyman smith stamp in June. **Mark:** Heaney JS.

HEASMAN, H G,
28 St Mary's Rd, Llandudno, N. Wales, UNITED KINGDOM LL302UB, Phone: (UK)0492-876351
Specialties: Miniatures only. **Patterns:** Bowies, daggers and swords. **Technical:** Files from stock high-carbon and stainless steel. **Prices:** $400 to $600. **Remarks:** Part-time maker; first knife sold in 1975. Doing business as Reduced Reality. **Mark:** NA.

HEATH, WILLIAM,
PO Box 131, Bondville, IL 61815, Phone: 217-863-2576
Specialties: Classic and working straight knives, folders. **Patterns:**

Hunters and Bowies LinerLock® folders. **Technical:** Grinds ATS-34, 440C, 154CM, Damascus, handle materials Micarta, woods to exotic materials snake skins cobra, rattle snake, African flower snake. Does own heat treating. **Prices:** $75 to $300 some $1000. **Remarks:** Full-time maker. First knife sold in 1979. **Mark:** W. D. HEATH.

HEDRICK, DON,
131 Beechwood Hills, Newport News, VA 23608, Phone: 757-877-8100, donaldhedrick@cox.net
Specialties: Working straight knives; period pieces and fantasy knives. **Patterns:** Hunters, boots, Bowies and miniatures. **Technical:** Grinds 440C and commercial Damascus. Also makes micro-mini Randall replicas. **Prices:** $150 to $550; some to $1200. **Remarks:** Part-time maker; first knife sold in 1982. **Mark:** First initial, last name in oval logo.

HEFLIN, CHRISTOPHER M,
6013 Jocely Hollow Rd, Nashville, TN 37205, Phone: 615-352-3909, blix@bellsouth.net

HEGWALD, J L,
1106 Charles, Humboldt, KS 66748, Phone: 316-473-3523
Specialties: Working straight knives, some fancy. **Patterns:** Makes Bowies, miniatures. **Technical:** Forges or grinds O1, L6, 440C; mixes materials in handles. **Prices:** $35 to $200; some higher. **Remarks:** Part-time maker; first knife sold in 1983. **Mark:** First and middle initials.

HEHN, RICHARD KARL,
Lehnmuehler Str 1, 55444 Dorrebach, GERMANY, Phone: 06724 3152
Specialties: High-tech, full integral working knives. **Patterns:** Hunters, fighters and daggers. **Technical:** Grinds CPM T-440V, CPM T-420V, forges his own stainless Damascus. **Prices:** $1000 to $10,000. **Remarks:** Full-time maker; first knife sold in 1963. **Mark:** Runic last initial in logo.

HEIMDALE, J E,
7749 E 28 CT, Tulsa, OK 74129, Phone: 918-640-0784, heimdale@sbcglobal.net
Specialties: Art knives **Patterns:** Bowies, daggers **Technical:** Makes allcomponents and handles -exotic woods and sheaths. Uses Damascus blades by other Blademakers, notably R.W. Wilson. **Prices:** $300 and up. **Remarks:** Part-time maker. First knife sold in 1999. **Marks:** JEHCO

HEINZ, JOHN,
611 Cafferty Rd, Upper Black Eddy, PA 18972, Phone: 610-847-8535, Web: www.herugrim.com
Specialties: Historical pieces / copies. **Technical:** Makes his own steel. **Prices:** $150 to $800. **Mark:** "H."

HEITLER, HENRY,
8106 N Albany, Tampa, FL 33604, Phone: 813-933-1645
Specialties: Traditional working and using straight knives of his design and to customer specs. **Patterns:** Fighters, hunters, utility/camp knives and fillet knives. **Technical:** Flat-grinds ATS-34; offers tapered tangs. **Prices:** $135 to $450; some to $600. **Remarks:** Part-time maker; first knife sold in 1990. **Mark:** First initial, last name, city, state circling double H's.

HELSCHER, JOHN W,
2645 Highway 1, Washington, IA 52353, Phone: 319-653-7310

HELTON, ROY,
HELTON KNIVES, 2941 Comstock St., San Diego, CA 92111, Phone: 858-277-5024

HEMBROOK, RON,
HEMBROOK KNIVES, PO Box 201, Neosho, WI 53059, Phone: 920-625-3607, rhembrook3607@charter.net; Web: www.hembrookcustomknives.com
Specialties: Hunters, working knives. **Technical:** Grinds ATS-34, 440C, O1 and Damascus. **Prices:** $125 to $750, some to $1000. **Remarks:** First knife sold in 1980. **Mark:** Hembrook plus a serial number. Part-time maker, makes hunters, daggers, Bowies, folders and miniatures.

HEMPERLEY, GLEN,
13322 Country Run Rd, Willis, TX 77318, Phone: 936-228-5048, hemperley.com
Specialties: Specializes in hunting knives, does fixed and folding knives.

HENDRICKS, SAMUEL J,
2162 Van Buren Rd, Maurertown, VA 22644, Phone: 703-436-3305
Specialties: Integral hunters and skinners of thin design. **Patterns:** Boots, hunters and locking folders. **Technical:** Grinds ATS-34, 440C and D2. Integral liners and bolsters of N-S and 7075 T6 aircraft aluminum. Does leatherwork. **Prices:** $50 to $250; some to $500. **Remarks:** Full-time maker; first knife sold in 1992. **Mark:** First and middle initials, last name, city and state in football-style logo.

HENDRICKSON, E JAY,
4204 Ballenger Creek Pike, Frederick, MD 21703, Phone: 301-663-6923, Fax: 301-663-6923, ejayhendrickson@comcast.net
Specialties: Specializes in silver wire inlay. Patterns: Bowies, Kukri's, camp, hunters, and fighters. **Technical:** Forges 06, 1084, 5160, 52100, D2, L6 and W2; makes Damascus. Moran-styles on order. **Prices:** $400 to $5000. **Remarks:** Full-time maker; first knife sold in 1975. **Mark:** Last name, M.S.

HENDRICKSON, SHAWN,
2327 Kaetzel Rd, Knoxville, MD 21758, Phone: 301-432-4306
Specialties: Hunting knives. **Patterns:** Clip points, drop points and trailing point hunters. **Technical:** Forges 5160, 1084 and L6. **Prices:** $175 to $400.

HENDRIX, JERRY,
HENDRIX CUSTOM KNIVES, 175 Skyland Dr. Ext., Clinton, SC 29325, Phone: 864-833-2659, jhendrix@backroads.net
Specialties: Traditional working straight knives of all designs. **Patterns:** Hunters, utility, boot, bird and fishing. **Technical:** Grinds ATS-34 and 440C. **Prices:** $85 to $275. **Remarks:** Full-time maker. Hand stitched, waxed leather sheaths. **Mark:** Full name in shape of knife.

HENDRIX, WAYNE,
9636 Burton's Ferry Hwy, Allendale, SC 29810, Phone: 803-584-3825, Fax: 803-584-3825, knives@barnwellsc.com; Web: www.hendrixknives.com
Specialties: Working/using knives of his design. **Patterns:** Hunters and fillet knives. **Technical:** Grinds ATS-34, D2 and 440C. **Prices:** $100 and up. **Remarks:** Full-time maker; first knife sold in 1985. **Mark:** Last name.

HENRIKSEN, HANS J,
Birkegaardsvej 24, DK 3200 Helsinge, DENMARK, Fax: 45 4879 4899
Specialties: Zirconia ceramic blades. **Patterns:** Customer designs. **Technical:** Slip-cast zirconia-water mix in plaster mould; offers hidden or full tang. **Prices:** White blades start at $10cm; colored +50 percent. **Remarks:** Part-time maker; first ceramic blade sold in 1989. **Mark:** Initial logo.

HENSLEY, WAYNE,
PO Box 904, Conyers, GA 30012, Phone: 770-483-8938
Specialties: Period pieces and fancy working knives. **Patterns:** Boots to Bowies, locking folders to miniatures. Large variety of straight knives. **Technical:** Grinds ATS-34, 440C, D2 and commercial Damascus. **Prices:** $85 and up. **Remarks:** Full-time maker; first knife sold in 1974. **Mark:** Last name.

HERB, MARTIN,
2500 Starwood Dr, Richmond, VA 23229

HERBST, PETER,
Komotauer Strasse 26, 91207 Lauf a.d. Pegn., GERMANY, Phone: 09123-13315, Fax: 09123-13379
Specialties: Working/using knives and folders of his design. **Patterns:** Hunters, fighters and daggers; interframe and integral. **Technical:** Grinds CPM-T-440V, UHB-Elmax, ATS-34 and stainless Damascus. **Prices:** $300 to $3000; some to $8000. **Remarks:** Full-time maker; first knife sold in 1981. **Mark:** First initial, last name.

HERBST, THINUS,
PO Box 59158, Karenpark 0118, Akasia, South Africa, Phone: +27 82 254 8016, thinus@herbst.co.za; Web: www.herbst.co.za
Specialties: Plain and fancy working straight knives of own design and liner lock folders. **Patterns:** Hunters, utility knives, art knives, and liner lock folders. **Technical:** Prefer exotic materials for handles. Most knives embellished with file work, carving and scrimshaw. **Prices:** $200 to $2000. **Remarks:** Full-time maker, member of the Knifemakers Guild of South Africa.

HERMAN, TIM,
7721 Foster, Overland Park, KS 66204, Phone: 913-649-3860, Fax: 913-649-0603
Specialties: Investment-grade folders of his design; interframes and bolster frames. **Patterns:** Interframes and new designs in carved stainless. **Technical:** Grinds ATS-34 and damasteel Damascus. Engraves and gold inlays with pearl, jade, lapis and Australian opal. **Prices:** $1000 to $15,000. **Remarks:** Full-time maker; first knife sold in 1978. **Mark:** Etched signature.

HERNDON, WM R "BILL",
32520 Michigan St, Acton, CA 93510, Phone: 661-269-5860, bherndons1@earthlink.net
Specialties: Straight knives, plain and fancy. **Technical:** Carbon steel (white and blued), Damascus, stainless steels. **Prices:** Start at $175. **Remarks:** Full-time maker; first knife sold in 1976. American Bladesmith Society journeyman smith. **Mark:** Signature and/or helm logo.

HERRING, MORRIS,
Box 85 721 W Line St, Dyer, AR 72935, Phone: 501-997-8861, morrish@ipa.com

HETHCOAT, DON,
Box 1764, Clovis, NM 88101, Phone: 575-762-5721, dhethcoat@plateautel.net
Specialties: Liner lock-locking and multi-blade folders **Patterns:** Hunters, Bowies. **Technical:** Grinds stainless; forges Damascus. **Prices:** Moderate to upscale. **Remarks:** Full-time maker; first knife sold in 1969. **Mark:** Last name on all.

HIBBEN, DARYL,
PO Box 172, LaGrange, KY 40031-0172, Phone: 502-222-0983, dhibben1@bellsouth.net
Specialties: Working straight knives, some fancy to customer specs. **Patterns:** Hunters, fighters, Bowies, short sword, art and fantasy.

Technical: Grinds 440C, ATS-34, 154CM, Damascus; prefers hollow-grinds. **Prices:** $175 to $3000. **Remarks:** Full-time maker; first knife sold in 1979. Teaches 3-or 5-day knife making classes for beginners or advanced students. **Mark:** Etched full name in script.

HIBBEN, GIL,
PO Box 13, LaGrange, KY 40031, Phone: 502-222-1397, Fax: 502-222-2676, hibbenknives.com; Web: www.gil_hibben@bellsouth.net
Specialties: Working knives and fantasy pieces to customer specs. **Patterns:** Full range of straight knives, including swords, axes and miniatures; some locking folders. **Technical:** Grinds ATS-34, 440C and D2. **Prices:** $300 to $2000; some to $10,000. **Remarks:** Full-time maker; first knife sold in 1957. Maker and designer of *Rambo III* knife; made swords for movie *Marked for Death* and throwing knife for movie *Under Seige*; made belt buckle knife and knives for movie *Perfect Weapon*; made knives featured in movie *Star Trek the Next Generation* , *Star Trek Nemesis*. 1990 inductee Cutlery Hall of Fame; designer for United Cutlery. Official klingon armourer for Star Trek, over 37 movies and TV productions. Celebrating 50 years since first knife sold. **Mark:** Hibben Knives. City and state, or signature.

HIBBEN, JOLEEN,
PO Box 172, LaGrange, KY 40031, Phone: 502-222-0983, dhibben1@bellsouth.net
Specialties: Miniature straight knives of her design; period pieces. **Patterns:** Hunters, axes and fantasy knives. **Technical:** Grinds Damascus, 1095 tool steel and stainless 440C or ATS-34. Uses wood, ivory, bone, feathers and claws on/for handles. **Prices:** $60 to $600. **Remarks:** Spare-time maker; first knife sold in 1991. Design knives, make & tool leather sheathes. Produced first inlaid handle in 2005, used by Daryl on a dagger. **Mark:** Initials or first name.

HIBBEN, WESTLEY G,
14101 Sunview Dr, Anchorage, AK 99515
Specialties: Working straight knives of his design or to customer specs. **Patterns:** Hunters, fighters, daggers, combat knives and some fantasy pieces. **Technical:** Grinds 440C mostly. Filework available. **Prices:** $200 to $400; some to $3000. **Remarks:** Part-time maker; first knife sold in 1988. **Mark:** Signature.

HICKS, GARY,
341 CR 275, Tuscola, TX 79562, Phone: 325-554-9762

HIGH, TOM,
5474 S 1128 Rd, Alamosa, CO 81101, Phone: 719-589-2108, www.rockymountainscrimshaw.com
Specialties: Hunters, some fancy. **Patterns:** Drop-points in several shapes; some semi-skinners. Knives designed by and for top outfitters and guides. **Technical:** Grinds ATS-34; likes hollow-grinds, mirror finishes; prefers scrimable handles. **Prices:** $175 to $8000. **Remarks:** Full-time maker; first knife sold in 1965. Limited edition wildlife series knives. **Mark:** Initials connected; arrow through last name.

HILKER, THOMAS N,
PO Box 409, Williams, OR 97544, Phone: 541-846-6461
Specialties: Traditional working straight knives and folders. **Patterns:** Folding skinner in two sizes, Bowies, fork and knife sets, camp knives and interchangeable. **Technical:** Grinds D2, 440C and ATS-34. Heat-treats. **Prices:** $50 to $350; some to $400. Doing business as Thunderbolt Artisans. Only limited production models available; not currently taking orders. **Remarks:** Full-time maker; first knife sold in 1983. **Mark:** Last name.

HILL, HOWARD E,
111 Mission Lane, Polson, MT 59860, Phone: 406-883-3405, Fax: 406-883-3486, knifeman@bigsky.net
Specialties: Autos, complete new design, legal in Montana (with permit). **Patterns:** Bowies, daggers, skinners and lockback folders. **Technical:** Grinds 440C; uses micro and satin finish. **Prices:** $150 to $1000. **Remarks:** Full-time maker; first knife sold in 1981. **Mark:** Persuader.

HILL, RICK,
20 Nassau, Maryville, IL 62062-5618, Phone: 618-288-4370
Specialties: Working knives and period pieces to customer specs. **Patterns:** Hunters, locking folders, fighters and daggers. **Technical:** Grinds D2, 440C and 154CM; forges his own Damascus. **Prices:** $75 to $500; some to $3000. **Remarks:** Part-time maker; first knife sold in 1983. **Mark:** Full name in hill shape logo.

HILL, STEVE E,
40 Rand Pond Rd, Goshen, NH 03752, Phone: 603-863-4762, Fax: 603-863-4762, kingpirateboy2@juno.com; Web: google or yahoo search: stevehillknives
Specialties: Fancy manual and automatic LinerLock® folders, small fixed blades and classic Bowie knives. Patterns: Classic to cool folding and fixed blade designs. **Technical:** Grinds Damascus and occasional 440C, D2. Prefers natural handle materials; offers elaborate filework, carving, and inlays. **Prices:** $200 to $5000, some higher. **Remarks:** Full-time maker; first knife sold in 1978. Google search: Steve Hill custom knives. **Mark:** First initial, last name and handmade. (4400, D2). Damascus folders: mark inside handle.

HILLMAN, CHARLES,
225 Waldoboro Rd, Friendship, ME 04547, Phone: 207-832-4634
Specialties: Working knives of his own or custom design. Heavy Scagel influence. **Patterns:** Hunters, fishing, camp and general utility. Occasional folders. **Technical:** Grinds D2 and 440C. File work, blade and handle carving, engraving. Natural handle materials-antler, bone, leather, wood, horn. Sheaths made to order. **Prices:** $60 to $500. **Remarks:** Part-time maker; first knife sold 1986. **Mark:** Last name in oak leaf.

HINDERER, RICK,
5423 Kister Rd, Wooster, OH 44691, Phone: 330-263-0962, Fax: 330-263-0962, rhind64@earthlink.net; Web: www.rhknives.com
Specialties: Working tactical knives, and some one-of-a kind. **Patterns:** Makes his own. **Technical:** Grinds CPM S30V. **Prices:** $150 to $4000. **Remarks:** Full-time maker doing business as Rick Hinderer Knives, first knife sold in 1988. **Mark:** R. Hinderer.

HINDMARCH, G,
PO Box 135, Carlyle SK S0C 0R0, CANADA, Phone: 306-453-2568
Specialties: Working and fancy straight knives, Bowies. **Patterns:** Hunters, fillet, skinners, Bowies. **Technical:** Grind 440C, ATS-34, some Damascus. **Prices:** $175 -$700. **Remarks:** Part-time maker; first knife sold 1994. All knives satin finish. Does file work, offers engraving, stabilized wood, Giraffe bone, some Micarta. **Mark:** First initial last name, city, province.

HINK III, LES,
1599 Aptos Lane, Stockton, CA 95206, Phone: 209-547-1292
Specialties: Working straight knives and traditional folders in standard patterns or to customer specs. **Patterns:** Hunting and utility/camp knives; others on request. **Technical:** Grinds carbon and stainless steels. **Prices:** $80 to $200; some higher. **Remarks:** Part-time maker; first knife sold in 1980. **Mark:** Last name, or last name 3.

HINMAN, TED,
183 Highland Ave, Watertown, MA 02472

HINSON AND SON, R,
2419 Edgewood Rd, Columbus, GA 31906, Phone: 706-327-6801
Specialties: Working straight knives and folders. **Patterns:** Locking folders, liner locks, combat knives and swords. **Technical:** Grinds 440C and commercial Damascus. **Prices:** $200 to $450; some to $1500. **Remarks:** Part-time maker; first knife sold in 1983. Son Bob is co-worker. **Mark:** HINSON, city and state.

HINTZ, GERALD M,
5402 Sahara Ct, Helena, MT 59602, Phone: 406-458-5412
Specialties: Fancy, high-art, working/using knives of his design. **Patterns:** Bowies, hunters, daggers, fish fillet and utility/camp knives. **Technical:** Forges ATS-34, 440C and D2. Animal art in horn handles or in the blade. **Prices:** $75 to $400; some to $1000. **Remarks:** Part-time maker; first knife sold in 1980. Doing business as Big Joe's Custom Knives. Will take custom orders. **Mark:** F.S. or W.S. with first and middle initials and last name.

HIRAYAMA, HARUMI,
4-5-13 Kitamachi, Warabi City, Saitama Pref. 335-0001, JAPAN, Phone: 048-443-2248, Fax: 048-443-2248, Web: www.ne.jp/asahi/harumi/knives
Specialties: High-tech working knives of her design. **Patterns:** Locking folders, interframes, straight gents and slip-joints. **Technical:** Grinds 440C or equivalent; uses natural handle materials and gold. **Prices:** Start at $1500. **Remarks:** Part-time maker; first knife sold in 1985. **Mark:** First initial, last name.

HIROTO, FUJIHARA,
, 2-34-7 Koioosako Nishi-ku Hiroshima-city, Hiroshima, JAPAN, Phone: 082-271-8389, fjhr8363@crest.ocn.ne.jp

HITCHMOUGH, HOWARD,
95 Old Street Rd, Peterborough, NH 03458-1637, Phone: 603-924-9646, Fax: 603-924-9595, howard@hitchmoughknives.com; Web: www.hitchmoughknives.com
Specialties: High class folding knives. **Patterns:** Lockback folders, liner locks, pocket knives. **Technical:** Uses ATS-34, stainless Damascus, titanium, gold and gemstones. Prefers hand-rubbed finishes and natural handle materials. **Prices:** $1850 -$5000. **Remarks:** Full-time maker; first knife sold in 1967. **Mark:** Last name.

HOBART, GENE,
100 Shedd Rd, Windsor, NY 13865, Phone: 607-655-1345

HOCKENSMITH, DAN,
390 SB Road, Morrill, NE 69358, Phone: 308-247-2719, Web: hockensmithknives.com
Specialties: Traditional working and using straight knives of his design. **Patterns:** Hunters, Bowies, folders and utility/camp knives. **Technical:** Uses his Damascus, 5160, carbon steel, 52100 steel and 1084 steel. Hand forged. **Prices:** $250 to $1500. **Remarks:** Part-time maker; first knife sold in 1987. **Mark:** Last name or stylized "D" with H inside.

HODGE III, JOHN,
422 S 15th St, Palatka, FL 32177, Phone: 904-328-3897
Specialties: Fancy straight knives and folders. Patterns: Various. **Technical:** Pattern-welded Damascus—"Southern-style." **Prices:** To $1000. **Remarks:** Part-time maker; first knife sold in 1981. **Mark:** JH3 logo.

HOEL, STEVE,
PO Box 283, Pine, AZ 85544, Phone: 602-476-4278
Specialties: Investor-class folders, straight knives and period pieces of his design. **Patterns:** Folding interframes lockers and slip-joints; straight Bowies, boots and daggers. **Technical:** Grinds 154CM, ATS-34 and commercial Damascus. **Prices:** $600 to $1200; some to $7500. **Remarks:** Full-time maker. **Mark:** Initial logo with name and address.

HOFER, LOUIS,
Gen Del, Rose Prairie, B.C., CANADA V0C 2H0, Phone: 250-630-2513

HOFFMAN, KEVIN L,
28 Hopeland Dr, Savannah, GA 31419, Phone: 912-920-3579, Fax: 912-920-3579, kevh052475@aol.com; Web: www.KLHoffman.com
Specialties: Distinctive folders and fixed blades. **Patterns:** Titanium frame lock folders. **Technical:** Sculpted guards and fittings cast in sterling silver and 14k gold. Grinds ATS-34, CPM S30V Damascus. Makes kydex sheaths for his fixed blade working knives. **Prices:** $400 and up. **Remarks:** Full-time maker since 1981. **Mark:** KLH.

HOGAN, THOMAS R,
2802 S. Heritage Ave, Boise, ID 83709, Phone: 208-362-7848

HOGSTROM, ANDERS T,
Granvagen 2, 135 52 Tyreso, SWEDEN, Phone: 46 8 798 5802, andershogstrom@hotmail.com or andershogstrom@rixmail.se; Web: www.andershogstrom.com
Specialties: Short and long daggers, fighters and swords For select pieces makes wooden display boxes. **Patterns:** Daggers, fighters, short knives and swords and an occasional sword. **Technical:** Grinds 1050 High Carbon, Damascus and stainless, forges own Damasus on occasion. Does clay tempering and uses exotic hardwoods. **Prices:** Start at $500. **Marks:** Last name in various typefaces.

HOKE, THOMAS M,
3103 Smith Ln, LaGrange, KY 40031, Phone: 502-222-0350
Specialties: Working/using knives, straight knives. Own designs and customer specs. **Patterns:** Daggers, Bowies, hunters, fighters, short swords. **Technical:** Grind 440C, Damascus and ATS-34. Filework on all knives. Tooling on sheaths (custom fit on all knives). Any handle material, mostly exotic. **Prices:** $100 to $700; some to $1500. **Remarks:** Full-time maker, first knife sold in 1986. **Mark:** Dragon on banner which says T.M. Hoke.

HOLBROOK, H L,
PO Box 483, Sandy Hook, KY 41171, Phone: 606-738-9922 home/606-738-6842 Shop, hhknives@mrtc.com
Specialties: Traditional working using straight knives and folders of his design, to customer specs and in standard patterns. Stablized wood. **Patterns:** Hunters, folders. **Technical:** Grinds 440C, ATS-34 and D2. Blades have hand-rubbed satin finish. Uses exotic woods, stag and Micarta. Hand-sewn sheath with each straight knife. **Prices:** $90 to $270; some to $400. **Remarks:** Part-time maker; first knife sold in 1983. Doing business as Holbrook Knives. **Mark:** Name, city, state.

HOLDER, D'ALTON,
7148 W Country Gables Dr, Peoria, AZ 85381, Phone: 623-878-3064, Fax: 623-878-3964, dholderknives@cox.net; Web: d'holder.com
Specialties: Deluxe working knives and high-art hunters. **Patterns:** Drop-point hunters, fighters, Bowies. **Technical:** Grinds ATS-34; uses amber and other materials in combination on stick tangs. **Prices:** $400 to $1000; some to $2000. **Remarks:** Full-time maker; first knife sold in 1966. **Mark:** D'HOLDER, city and state.

HOLLAND, JOHN H,
1580 Nassau St, Titusville, FL 32780, Phone: 321-267-4378
Specialties: Traditional and fancy working/using straight knives and folders of his design, to customer specs and in standard patterns. **Patterns:** Hunters, and slip-joint folders. **Technical:** Grinds 440V and 440C. Offers engraving. **Prices:** $200 to $500; some to $1000. **Remarks:** Part-time maker; first knife sold in 1988. Doing business as Holland Knives. **Mark:** First and last name, city, state.

HOLLOWAY, PAUL,
714 Burksdale Rd, Norfolk, VA 23518, Phone: 804-588-7071
Specialties: Working straight knives and folders to customer specs. **Patterns:** Lockers and slip-joints; fighters and boots; fishing and push knives, from swords to miniatures. **Technical:** Grinds A2, D2, 154CM, 440C and ATS-34. **Prices:** $125 to $400; some to $1200. **Remarks:** Part-time maker; first knife sold in 1981. **Mark:** Last name, or last name and city in logo.

HOOK, BOB,
3247 Wyatt Rd, North Pole, AK 99705, Phone: 907-488-8886, grayling@alaska.net
Specialties: Forged carbon steel. Damascus blades. Patterns: Pronghorns, bowies, drop point hunters and knives for the kitchen. **Technical:** 5160, 52100, carbon steel and 1084 and 15N20 pattern welded steel blades are hand forged. Heat treated and ground by maker. Handles are natural materials from Alaska. I favor sole authorship of each piece. **Prices:** $300-$1000. **Remarks:** Apprentice with ABS. I have attended the Bill Moran School of Bladesmithing. Knife maker since 2000. **Mark:** Hook.

HOOK, BOB,
3247 Wyatt Rd, North Pole, AK 99705, Phone: 907-488-8886

HORN, DES,
PO Box 322, Onrusrivier 7201, SOUTH AFRICA, Phone: 27283161795, Fax: 27283161795, deshorn@usa.net
Specialties: Folding knives. **Patterns:** Ball release side lock mechanism and interframe automatics. **Technical:** Prefers working in totally stainless materials. **Prices:** $800 to $4000. **Remarks:** Full-time maker. Enjoys working in gold, titanium, meteorite, pearl and mammoth. **Mark:** Des Horn.

HORN, JESS,
2526 Lansdown Rd, Eugene, OR 97404, Phone: 541-463-1510, jandahorn@earthlink.net
Specialties: Investor-class working folders; period pieces; collectibles. **Patterns:** High-tech design and finish in folders; liner locks, traditional slip-joints and featherweight models. **Technical:** Grinds ATS-34, 154CM. **Prices:** Start at $1000. **Remarks:** Full-time maker; first knife sold in 1968. **Mark:** Full name or last name.

HORNE, GRACE,
182 Crimicar Ln, Sheffield Britain, UNITED KINGDOM S10 4EJ, gracehorne@hotmail.co.uk
Specialties: Knives of own design including kitchen and utility knives for people with reduced hand use. **Technical:** Working at Sheffield Hallam University researching innovative, contemporary Damascus steels using non-traditional methods of manufacture. **Remarks:** Spare-time maker/full-time researcher. **Mark:** 'gH' and 'Sheffield'.

HORTON, SCOT,
PO Box 451, Buhl, ID 83316, Phone: 208-543-4222
Specialties: Traditional working stiff knives and folders. **Patterns:** Hunters, skinners, utility and show knives. **Technical:** Grinds ATS-34. Uses exotic woods and Micarta. **Prices:** $350 to $2500. **Remarks:** First knife sold in 1990. **Mark:** Full name in arch underlined with arrow, city, state.

HOSSOM, JERRY,
3585 Schilling Ridge, Duluth, GA 30096, Phone: 770-449-7809, jerry@hossom.com; Web: www.hossom.com
Specialties: Working straight knives of his own design. **Patterns:** Fighters, combat knives, modern Bowies and daggers, modern swords, concealment knives for military and LE uses. **Technical:** Grinds 154CM, S30V, CPM-3V, CPM-154 and stainless Damascus. Uses natural and synthetic handle materials. **Prices:** $350-1500, some higher. **Remarks:** Full-time maker since 1997. First knife sold in 1983. **Mark:** First initial and last name, includes city and state since 2002.

HOUSE, GARY,
2851 Pierce Rd, Ephrata, WA 98823, Phone: 509-754-3272, spindry101@aol.com
Specialties: Mosaic Damascus bar stock. Forged blades. **Patterns:** Unlimited, SW Indian designs, geometric patterns, using 1084, 15N20 and some nickel. Bowies, hunters and daggers. **Technical:** Forge mosaic Damascus. **Prices:** $500 & up. **Remarks:** Some of the finest and most unique patterns available. ABS Journeyman Smith. **Marks:** Initials GTH, G hanging T, H.

HOWARD, DURVYN M,
4220 McLain St S, Hokes Bluff, AL 35903, Phone: 256-492-5720
Specialties: Collectible upscale folders; one-of-a-kind, gentlemen's folders. Multiple patents. **Patterns:** Conceptual designs; each unique and different. **Technical:** Uses natural and exotic materials and precious metals. **Prices:** $5000 to $25,000. **Remarks:** Full-time maker; by commission or available work. Work displayed at select shows, K.G. Show etc. **Mark:** Howard: new for 2000; Howard in Garamond Narrow "etched."

HOWE, TORI,
30020 N Stampede Rd, Athol, ID 83801, Phone: 208-449-1509, wapiti@knifescales.com; Web:www.knifescales.com
Specialties Custom knives, knife scales & Damascus blades. **Remarks:** Carry James Luman polymer clay knife scales.

HOWELL, JASON G,
1112 Sycamore, Lake Jackson, TX 77566, Phone: 979-297-9454, tinyknives@yahoo.com; Web:www.howellbladesmith.com
Specialties: Fixed blades and LinerLock® folders. Makes own Damascus. **Patterns:** Clip and drop point. **Prices:** $150 to $750. **Remarks:** Likes making Mosaic Damascus out of the ordinary stuff. Member of TX Knifemakers and Collectors Association; apprentice in ABS; working towards Journeyman Stamp. **Mark:** Name, city, state.

HOWELL, LEN,
550 Lee Rd 169, Opelika, AL 36804, Phone: 334-749-1942
Specialties: Traditional and working knives of his design and to customer specs. **Patterns:** Buckskinner, hunters and utility/camp knives. **Technical:** Forges cable Damascus, 1085 and 5160; makes own Damascus. **Mark:** Engraved last name.

HOWELL, TED,
1294 Wilson Rd, Wetumpka, AL 36092, Phone: 205-569-2281, Fax: 205-569-1764
Specialties: Working/using straight knives and folders of his design;

period pieces. **Patterns:** Bowies, fighters, hunters. **Technical:** Forges 5160, 1085 and cable. Offers light engraving and scrimshaw; filework. **Prices:** $75 to $250; some to $450. **Remarks:** Part-time maker; first knife sold in 1991. Doing business as Howell Co. **Mark:** Last name, Slapout AL.

HOWSER, JOHN C,
54 Bell Ln, Frankfort, KY 40601, Phone: 502-875-3678
Specialties: Slip joint folders (old patterns-multi blades). **Patterns:** Traditional slip joint folders, lockbacks, hunters and fillet knives. **Technical:** Steel S30V, CPM154, ATS-34 and D2. **Prices:** $200 to $600 some to $800. **Remarks:** Full-time maker; first knife sold in 1974. **Mark:** Signature or stamp.

HOY, KEN,
54744 Pinchot Dr, North Fork, CA 93643, Phone: 209-877-7805

HRISOULAS, JIM,
SALAMANDER ARMOURY, 284-C Lake Mead Pkwy #157, Henderson, NV 89105, Phone: 702-566-8551
Specialties: Working straight knives; period pieces. **Patterns:** Swords, daggers and sgian dubhs. **Technical:** Double-edged differential heat treating. **Prices:** $85 to $175; some to $600 and higher. **Remarks:** Full-time maker; first knife sold in 1973. Author of *The Complete Bladesmith, The Pattern Welded Blade* and *The Master Bladesmith*. Doing business as Salamander Armory. **Mark:** 8R logo and sword and salamander.

HUCKABEE, DALE,
254 Hwy 260, Maylene, AL 35114, Phone: 205-664-2544, dalehuckabee@hotmail.com
Specialties: Fixed blade hunter and Bowies of his design. **Technical:** Steel used: 5160, 1095, 1084 and some Damascus. **Prices:** Starting at $150 and up, depending on materials used. **Remarks:** Hand forged. Journeyman Smith. Part-time maker. **Mark:** Stamped Huckabee J.S.

HUCKS, JERRY,
KNIVES BY HUCKS, 1807 Perch Road, Moncks Corner, SC 29461, Phone: 843-761-6481, knivesbyhucks@nitrockets.com
Specialties: Oyster knives, hunters, Bowies, fillets, Bowies being makers favorite with stag & ivory. **Patterns:** Yours and his. **Technical:** ATS-34, BG-42, makers cable Damascus also 1084 & 15N20. **Prices:** $95 and up. **Remarks:** Full-time maker, retired as a machinist in 1990. **Mark:** Robin Hood hat with moncke corner, S.C. in oval.

HUDSON, ANTHONY B,
PO Box 368, Amanda, OH 43102, Phone: 740-969-4200, jjahudson@wmconnect.com
Specialties: Hunting knives, fighters, survival. **Remarks:** ABS Journeyman Smith. **Mark:** A.B. HUDSON.

HUDSON, C ROBBIN,
497 Groton Hollow Rd, Rummney, NH 03266, Phone: 603-786-9944
Specialties: High-art working knives. **Patterns:** Hunters, Bowies, fighters and kitchen knives. **Technical:** Forges W2, nickel steel, pure nickel steel, composite and mosaic Damascus; makes knives one-at-a-time. **Prices:** 500 to $1200; some to $5000. **Remarks:** Full-time maker; first knife sold in 1970. **Mark:** Last name and MS.

HUDSON, ROB,
340 Roush Rd, Northumberland, PA 17857, Phone: 570-473-9588, robscustknives@aol.com Web:www.robscustomknives.com
Specialties: Presentation hunters and Bowies. **Technical:** Grinds ATS-34, stainless, CPM 154 Damascus hollow grinds or flat. Filework finger grooves. Engraving and scrimshaw available. **Prices:** $400 to $2000. **Remarks:** Full-time maker. Does business as Rob's Custom Knives. **Mark:** Capital R, Capital H in script.

HUDSON, ROBERT,
3802 Black Cricket Ct, Humble, TX 77396, Phone: 713-454-7207
Specialties: Working straight knives of his design. **Patterns:** Bowies, hunters, skinners, fighters and utility knives. **Technical:** Grinds D2, 440C, 154CM and commercial Damascus. **Prices:** $85 to $350; some to $1500. **Remarks:** Part-time maker; first knife sold in 1980. **Mark:** Full name, handmade, city and state.

HUGHES, BILL,
110 Royale Dr, Texarkana, TX 75503, Phone: 903-838-0134, chughes@tc.cc.tx.us

HUGHES, DAN,
301 Grandview Bluff Rd, Spencer, TN 38585, Phone: 931-946-3044
Specialties: Working straight knives to customer specs. **Patterns:** Hunters, fighters, fillet knives. **Technical:** Grinds 440C and ATS-34. **Prices:** $55 to $175; some to $300. **Remarks:** Part-time maker; first knife sold in 1984. **Mark:** Initials.

HUGHES, DARYLE,
10979 Leonard, Nunica, MI 49448, Phone: 616-837-6623, hughes.builders@verizon.net
Specialties: Working knives. Patterns: Buckskinners, hunters, camp knives, kitchen and fishing knives. **Technical:** Forges and grinds 52100 and Damascus. **Prices:** $125 to $1000. **Remarks:** Part-time maker; first knife sold in 1979. **Mark:** Name and city in logo.

HUGHES, ED,
280 1/2 Holly Lane, Grand Junction, CO 81503, Phone: 970-243-8547, edhughes26@msn.com
Specialties: Working and art folders. **Patterns:** Buys Damascus. **Technical:** Grinds stainless steels. Engraves. **Prices:** $300 and up. **Remarks:** Full-time maker; first knife sold in 1978. **Mark:** Name or initials.

HUGHES, LAWRENCE,
207 W Crestway, Plainview, TX 79072, Phone: 806-293-5406
Specialties: Working and display knives. **Patterns:** Bowies, daggers, hunters, buckskinners. **Technical:** Grinds D2, 440C and 154CM. **Prices:** $125 to $300; some to $2000. **Remarks:** Full-time maker; first knife sold in 1979. **Mark:** Name with buffalo skull in center.

HULETT, STEVE,
115 Yellowstone Ave, West Yellowstone, MT 59758-0131, Phone: 406-646-4116, Web: www.seldomseenknives.com
Specialties: Classic, working/using knives, straight knives, folders. Your design, custom specs. **Patterns:** Utility/camp knives, hunters, and LinerLock® folders. **Technical:** Grinds 440C stainless steel, O1 Carbon, 1095. Shop is retail and knife shop; people watch their knives being made. We do everything in house: "all but smelt the ore, or tan the hide." **Prices:** Strarting $250 to $7000. **Remarks:** Full-time maker; first knife sold in 1994. **Mark:** Seldom seen knives/West Yellowstone Montana.

HULL, MICHAEL J,
1330 S Hermits Circle, Cottonwood, AZ 86326, Phone: 928-634-2871, mjwhull@earthlink.net
Specialties: Period pieces and working knives. **Patterns:** Hunters, fighters, Bowies, camp and Mediterranean knives, etc. **Technical:** Grinds 440C, ATS-34 and BG42 and S30V. **Prices:** $125 to $750; some to $1000. **Remarks:** Full-time maker; first knife sold in 1983. **Mark:** Name, city, state.

HULSEY, HOYT,
379 Shiloh, Attalla, AL 35954, Phone: 256-538-6765
Specialties: Traditional working straight knives and folders of his design. **Patterns:** Hunters and utility/camp knives. **Technical:** Grinds 440C, ATS-34, O1 and A2. **Prices:** $75 to $250. **Remarks:** Part-time maker; first knife sold in 1989. **Mark:** Hoyt Hulsey Attalla AL.

HUME, DON,
2731 Tramway Circle NE, Albuquerque, NM 87122, Phone: 505-796-9451

HUMENICK, ROY,
PO Box 55, Rescue, CA 95672
Specialties: Multiblade folders. **Patterns:** Original folder and fixed blade designs, also traditional patterns. **Technical:** Grinds premium steels and Damascus. **Prices:** $350 and up; some to $1500. **Remarks:** First knife sold in 1984. **Mark:** Last name in ARC.

HUMPHREYS, JOEL,
90 Boots Rd, Lake Placid, FL 33852, Phone: 863-773-0439
Specialties: Traditional working/using straight knives and folders of his design and in standard patterns. **Patterns:** Hunters, folders and utility/camp knives. **Technical:** Grinds ATS-34, D2, 440C. All knives have tapered tangs, mitered bolster/handle joints, handles of horn or bone fitted sheaths. **Prices:** $135 to $225; some to $350. **Remarks:** Part-time maker; first knife sold in 1990. Doing business as Sovereign Knives. **Mark:** First name or "H" pierced by arrow.

HUNT, MAURICE,
10510 N CR 650 E, Winter: 2925 Argyle Rd. Venice FL 34293, Brownsburg, IN 46112, Phone: 317-892-2982/Winter: 941-493-4027, mdhuntknives@juno.com
Patterns: Bowies, hunters, fighters. **Prices:** $200 to $800. **Remarks:** Part-time maker. Journeyman Smith.

HUNTER, HYRUM,
285 N 300 W, PO Box 179, Aurora, UT 84620, Phone: 435-529-7244
Specialties: Working straight knives of his design or to customer specs. **Patterns:** Drop and clip, fighters dagger, some folders. **Technical:** Forged from two-piece Damascus. **Prices:** Prices are adjusted according to size, complexity and material used. **Remarks:** Will consider any design you have. Part-time maker; first knife sold in 1990. **Mark:** Initials encircled with first initial and last name and city, then state. Some patterns are numbered.

HUNTER, RICHARD D,
7230 NW 200th Ter, Alachua, FL 32615, Phone: 386-462-3150
Specialties: Traditional working/using knives of his design or customer suggestions; filework. **Patterns:** Folders of various types, Bowies, hunters, daggers. **Technical:** Traditional blacksmith; hand forges high-carbon steel (5160, 1084, 52100) and makes own Damascus; grinds 440C and ATS-34. **Prices:** $200 and up. **Remarks:** Part-time maker; first knife sold in 1992. **Mark:** Last name in capital letters.

HURST, COLE,
1583 Tedford, E. Wenatchee, WA 98802, Phone: 509-884-9206
Specialties: Fantasy, high-art and traditional straight knives. Patterns: Bowies, daggers and hunters. **Technical:** Blades are made of stone; handles are made of stone, wood or ivory and embellished with fancy woods, ivory or antlers. **Prices:** $100 to $300; some to $2000. **Remarks:** Spare-time maker; first knife sold in 1985. **Mark:** Name and year.

HURST, JEFF,
PO Box 247, Rutledge, TN 37861, Phone: 865-828-5729, jhurst@esper.com
Specialties: Working straight knives and folders of his design. **Patterns:** Tomahawks, hunters, boots, folders and fighters. **Technical:** Forges W2, O1 and his own Damascus. Makes mokume. **Prices:** $250 to $600. **Remarks:** Full-time maker; first knife sold in 1984. Doing business as Buzzard's Knob Forge. **Mark:** Last name; partnered knives are marked with Newman L. Smith, handle artisan, and SH in script.

HURT, WILLIAM R,
9222 Oak Tree Cir, Frederick, MD 21701, Phone: 301-898-7143
Specialties: Traditional and working/using straight knives. **Patterns:** Bowies, hunters, fighters and utility knives. **Technical:** Forges 5160, O1 and O6; makes own Damascus. Offers silver wire inlay. **Prices:** $200 to $600; some higher. **Remarks:** Full-time maker; first knife sold in 1989. **Mark:** First and middle initials, last name.

HUSIAK, MYRON,
PO Box 238, Altona 3018, Victoria, AUSTRALIA, Phone: 03-315-6752
Specialties: Straight knives and folders of his design or to customer specs. **Patterns:** Hunters, fighters, lock-back folders, skinners and boots. **Technical:** Forges and grinds his own Damascus, 440C and ATS-34. **Prices:** $200 to $900. **Remarks:** Part-time maker; first knife sold in 1974. **Mark:** First initial, last name in logo and serial number.

HUTCHESON, JOHN,
SURSUM KNIFE WORKS, 1237 Brown's Ferry Rd., Chattanooga, TN 37419, Phone: 423-667-6193, sursum5071@aol.com; Web: www.sursumknife.com
Specialties: Straight working knives, hunters. **Patterns:** Customer designs, hunting, speciality working knives. **Technical:** Grinds D2, S7, O1 and 5160, ATS-34 on request. **Prices:** $100 to $300, some to $600. **Remarks:** First knife sold 1985, also produces a mid-tech line. Doing business as Sursum Knife Works. **Mark:** Family crest boar's head over 3 arrows.

HYTOVICK, JOE "HY",
14872 SW 111th St, Dunnellon, FL 34432, Phone: 800-749-5339, Fax: 352-489-3732, hyclassknives@aol.com
Specialties: Straight, folder and miniature. **Technical:** Blades from Wootz, Damascus and Alloy steel. **Prices:** To $5000. **Mark:** HY.

I

IAMES, GARY,
PO Box 8493, South Lake, Tahoe, CA 96158, Phone: 530-541-2250, iames@charter.net
Specialties: Working and fancy straight knives and folders. **Patterns:** Bowies, hunters, wedding sets and liner locking folders. **Technical:** Grinds 440C, ATS-34, forges 5160 and 1080, makes Damascus. **Prices:** $300 and up. **Mark:** Initials and last name, city or last name.

IMBODEN II, HOWARD L.,
620 Deauville Dr, Dayton, OH 45429, Phone: 513-439-1536
Specialties: One-of-a-kind hunting, flint, steel and art knives. **Technical:** Forges and grinds stainless, high-carbon and Damascus. Uses obsidian, cast sterling silver, 14K and 18K gold guards. Carves ivory animals and more. **Prices:** $65 to $25,000. **Remarks:** Full-time maker; first knife sold in 1986. Doing business as Hill Originals. **Mark:** First and last initials, II.

IMEL, BILLY MACE,
1616 Bundy Ave, New Castle, IN 47362, Phone: 765-529-1651
Specialties: High-art working knives, period pieces and personal cutlery. **Patterns:** Daggers, fighters, hunters; locking folders and slip-joints with interframes. **Technical:** Grinds D2, 440C and 154CM. **Prices:** $300 to $2000; some to $6000. **Remarks:** Part-time maker; first knife sold in 1973. **Mark:** Name in monogram.

IRIE, MICHAEL L,
MIKE IRIE HANDCRAFT, 1606 Auburn Dr., Colorado Springs, CO 80909, Phone: 719-572-5330, mikeirie@aol.com
Specialties: Working fixed blade knives and handcrafted blades for the do-it-yourselfer. **Patterns:** Twenty standard designs along with custom. **Technical:** Blades are ATS-34, BG-43, 440C with some outside Damascus. **Prices:** Fixed blades $95 and up, blade work $45 and up. **Remarks:** Formerly dba Wood, Irie and Co. with Barry Wood. Full-time maker since 1991. **Mark:** Name.

IRON WOLF FORGE, SEE NELSON KEN,

ISAO, OHBUCHI,
, 702-1 Nouso Yame-City, Fukuoka, JAPAN, Phone: 0943-23-4439, www.5d.biglobe.ne.jp/~ohisao/

ISGRO, JEFFERY,
1516 First St, West Babylon, NY 11704, Phone: 631-235-1896
Specialties: File work, glass beading, kydex, leather. **Patterns:** Tactical use knives, skinners, capers, Bowies, camp, hunters. **Technical:** ATS-34, 440C and D2. **Price:** $120 to $600. **Remarks:** Part-time maker. **Mark:** First name, last name, Long Island, NY.

ISHIHARA, HANK,
86-18 Motomachi, Sakura City, Chiba Pref., JAPAN, Phone: 043-485-3208, Fax: 043-485-3208
Specialties: Fantasy working straight knives and folders of his design. **Patterns:** Boots, Bowies, daggers, fighters, hunters, fishing, locking folders and utility camp knives. **Technical:** Grinds ATS-34, 440C, D2, 440V, CV-134, COS25 and Damascus. Engraves. **Prices:** $250 to $1000; some to $10,000. **Remarks:** Full-time maker; first knife sold in 1987. **Mark:** HANK.

J

JACKS, JIM,
344 S. Hollenbeck Ave, Covina, CA 91723-2513, Phone: 626-331-5665
Specialties: Working straight knives in standard patterns. **Patterns:** Bowies, hunters, fighters, fishing and camp knives, miniatures. **Technical:** Grinds Stellite 6K, 440C and ATS-34. **Prices:** Start at $100. **Remarks:** Spare-time maker; first knife sold in 1980. **Mark:** Initials in diamond logo.

JACKSON, CHARLTON R,
6811 Leyland Dr, San Antonio, TX 78239, Phone: 210-601-5112

JACKSON, DAVID,
214 Oleander Ave, Lemoore, CA 93245, Phone: 559-925-8547, jnbcrea@lemoorenet.com
Specialties: Forged steel. **Patterns:** Hunters, camp knives, Bowies. **Prices:** $150 and up. **Mark:** G.D. Jackson -Maker -Lemoore CA.

JACKSON, JIM,
7 Donnington Close, Chapel Row Bucklebury RG7 6PU, ENGLAND, Phone: 011-89-712743, Fax: 011-89-710495, jlandsejackson@aol.com
Specialties: Large Bowies, concentrating on form and balance; collector quality Damascus daggers. **Patterns:** With fancy filework and engraving available. **Technical:** Forges O1, 5160 and CS70 and 15N20 Damascus. **Prices:** From $1000. **Remarks:** Part-time maker. All knives come with a custom tooled leather swivel sheath of exotic material. **Mark:** Jackson England with in a circle M.S.

JAKSIK JR., MICHAEL,
427 Marschall Creek Rd, Fredericksburg, TX 78624, Phone: 830-997-1119
Mark: MJ or M. Jaksik.

JANIGA, MATTHEW A,
2090 Church Rd, Hummelstown, PA 17036-9796, Phone: 717-533-5916
Specialties: Period pieces, swords, daggers. **Patterns:** Daggers, fighters and swords. **Technical:** Forges and Damascus. Does own heat treating. Forges own pattern-welded steel. **Prices:** $100 to $1000; some to $5000. **Remarks:** Spare-time maker; first knife sold in 1991. **Mark:** Interwoven initials.

JARVIS, PAUL M,
30 Chalk St, Cambridge, MA 02139, Phone: 617-547-4355 or 617-666-9090
Specialties: High-art knives and period pieces of his design. **Patterns:** Japanese and Mid-Eastern knives. **Technical:** Grinds Myer Damascus, ATS-34, D2 and O1. Specializes in height-relief Japanese-style carving. Works with silver, gold and gems. **Prices:** $200 to $17,000. **Remarks:** Part-time maker; first knife sold in 1978.

JEAN, GERRY,
25B Cliffside Dr, Manchester, CT 06040, Phone: 860-649-6449
Specialties: Historic replicas. **Patterns:** Survival and camp knives. **Technical:** Grinds A2, 440C and 154CM. Handle slabs applied in unique tongue-and-groove method. **Prices:** $125 to $250; some to $1000. **Remarks:** Spare-time maker; first knife sold in 1973. **Mark:** Initials and serial number.

JEFFRIES, ROBERT W,
Route 2 Box 227, Red House, WV 25168, Phone: 304-586-9780, wvknifeman@hotmail.com; Web: www.jeffriesknives wv.tripod.com
Specialties: Hunters, Bowies, daggers, lockback folders and LinerLock push buttons. **Patterns:** Skinning types, drop points, typical working hunters, folders one-of-a-kind. **Technical:** Grinds all types of steel. Makes his own Damascus. **Prices:** $125 to $600. Private collector pieces to $3000. **Remarks:** Starting engraving. Custom folders of his design. Part-time maker since 1988. **Mark:** Name etched or on plate pinned to blade.

JENSEN, JOHN LEWIS,
JENSEN KNIVES, PO Box 50041, Pasadena, CA 91116, Phone: 323-559-7454, Fax: 626-449-1148, john@jensenknives.com; Web: www.jensenknives.com
Specialties: Designer and fabricator of modern, original one-of-a-kind, hand crafted, custom ornamental edged weaponry. Combines skill, precision, distinction and the finest materials, geared toward the discriminating art collector. **Patterns:** Folding knives and fixed blades, daggers, fighters and swords. **Technical:** High embellishment, BFA 96 Rhode Island School of Design: jewelry and metalsmithing. Grinds 440C, ATS-34, Damascus. Works with custom made Damascus to his specs. Uses gold, silver, gemstones, pearl, titanium, fossil mastodon and walrus ivories. Carving, file work, soldering, deep etches Damascus,

engraving, layers, bevels, blood grooves. Also forges his own Damascus. **Prices:** Start at $10,000. **Remarks:** Available on a first come basis and via commission based on his designs. Knifemakers Guild voting member and ABS apprenticesmith and member of the Society of North American Goldsmiths. **Mark:** Maltese cross/butterfly shield.

JOBIN, JACQUES,
46 St Dominique, Levis Quebec, CANADA G6V 2M7, Phone: 418-833-0283, Fax: 418-833-8378
Specialties: Fancy and working straight knives and folders; miniatures. **Patterns:** Minis, fantasy knives, fighters and some hunters. **Technical:** ATS-34, some Damascus and titanium. Likes native snake wood. Heat-treats. **Prices:** Start at $250. **Remarks:** Full-time maker; first knife sold in 1986. **Mark:** Signature on blade.

JOEHNK, BERND,
Posadowskystrasse 22, 24148 Kiel, GERMANY, Phone: 0431-7297705, Fax: 0431-7297705
Specialties: One-of-a-kind fancy/embellished and traditional straight knives of his design and from customer drawing. **Patterns:** Daggers, fighters, hunters and letter openers. **Technical:** Grinds and file 440C, ATS-34, powder metal orgical, commercial Damascus and various stainless and corrosion-resistant steels. **Prices:** Upscale. **Remarks:** Likes filework. Leather sheaths. Offers engraving. Part-time maker; first knife sold in1990. Doing business as metal design kiel. All knives made by hand. **Mark:** From 2005 full name and city, with certificate.

JOHANNING CUSTOM KNIVES, TOM,
1735 Apex Rd, Sarasota, FL 34240 9386, Phone: 941-371-2104, Fax: 941-378-9427, Web: www.survivalknives.com
Specialties: Survival knives. **Prices:** $375 to $775.

JOHANSSON, ANDERS,
Konstvartarevagen 9, S-772 40 Grangesberg, SWEDEN, Phone: 46 240 23204, Fax: +46 21 358778, www.scrimart.u.se
Specialties: Scandinavian traditional and modern straight knives. **Patterns:** Hunters, fighters and fantasy knives. **Technical:** Grinds stainless steel and makes own Damascus. Prefers water buffalo and mammoth for handle material. **Prices:** Start at $100. **Remarks:** Spare-time maker; first knife sold in 1994. Works together with scrimshander Viveca Sahlin. **Mark:** Stylized initials.

JOHNS, ROB,
1423 S. Second, Enid, OK 73701, Phone: 405-242-2707
Specialties: Classic and fantasy straight knives of his design or to customer specs; fighters for use at Medieval fairs. **Patterns:** Bowies, daggers and swords. **Technical:** Forges and grinds 440C, D2 and 5160. Handles of nylon, walnut or wire-wrap. **Prices:** $150 to $350; some to $2500. **Remarks:** Full-time maker; first knife sold in 1980. **Mark:** Medieval Customs, initials.

JOHNSON, C E GENE,
1240 Coan Street, Chesterton, IN 46304, Phone: 219-787-8324, ddjlady55@aol.com
Specialties: Lock-back folders and springers of his design or to customer specs. **Patterns:** Hunters, Bowies, survival lock-back folders. **Technical:** Grinds D2, 440C, A18, O1, Damascus; likes filework. **Prices:** $100 to $2000. **Remarks:** Full-time maker; first knife sold in 1975. **Mark:** Gene.

JOHNSON, DAVID A,
1791 Defeated Creek Rd, Pleasant Shade, TN 37145, Phone: 615-774-3596, artsmith@mwsi.net

JOHNSON, DURRELL CARMON,
PO Box 594, Sparr, FL 32192, Phone: 352-622-5498
Specialties: Old-fashioned working straight knives and folders of his design or to customer specs. **Patterns:** Bowies, hunters, fighters, daggers, camp knives and Damascus miniatures. **Technical:** Forges 5160, his own Damascus, W2, wrought iron, nickel and horseshoe rasps. Offers filework. **Prices:** $100 to $2000. **Remarks:** Full-time maker and blacksmith; first knife sold in 1957. **Mark:** Middle name.

JOHNSON, GORDEN W,
5426 Sweetbriar, Houston, TX 77017, Phone: 713-645-8990
Specialties: Working knives and period pieces. **Patterns:** Hunters, boots and Bowies. **Technical:** Flat-grinds 440C; most knives have narrow tang. **Prices:** $90 to $450. **Remarks:** Full-time maker; first knife sold in 1974. **Mark:** Name, city, state.

JOHNSON, GORDON A.,
981 New Hope Rd, Choudrant, LA 71227, Phone: 318-768-2613
Specialties: Using straight knives and folders of my design, or customers. Offering filework and hand stitched sheaths. **Patterns:** Hunters, bowies, folders and miniatures. **Technical:** Forges 5160, 1084, 52100 and my own Damascus. Some stock removal on working knives and miniatures. **Prices:** Mid range. **Remarks:** First knife sold in 1990. ABS apprentice smith. **Mark:** Interlocking initials G.J. or G. A. J.

JOHNSON, JOHN R,
5535 Bob Smith Ave, Plant City, FL 33565, Phone: 813-986-4478, rottyjohn@msn.com
Specialties: Hand forged and stock removal. **Technical:** High tech. Folders. **Mark:** J.R. Johnson Plant City, FL.

JOHNSON, JOHN R,
PO Box 246, New Buffalo, PA 17069, Phone: 717-834-6265, jrj@jrjknives.com; Web: www.jrjknives.com
Specialties: Working hunting and tactical fixed blade sheath knives. **Patterns:** Hunters, tacticals, Bowies, daggers, neck knives and primitives. **Technical:** Flat, convex and hollow grinds. ATS-34, CPM154CM, L6, O1, D2, 5160, 1095 and Damascus. **Prices:** $60 to $700. **Remarks:** Full-time maker, first knife sold in 1996. Doing business as JRJ Knives. Custom sheath made by maker for every knife, **Mark:** Initials connected.

JOHNSON, MIKE,
38200 Main Rd, Orient, NY 11957, Phone: 631-323-3509, mjohnsoncustomknives@hotmail.com
Specialties: Large Bowie knives and cutters, fighters and working knives to customer specs. **Technical:** Forges 5160, O1. **Prices:** $325 to $1200. **Remarks:** Full-time bladesmith. **Mark:** Johnson.

JOHNSON, R B,
Box 11, Clearwater, MN 55320, Phone: 320-558-6128, Fax: 320-558-6128
Specialties: Liner locks with titanium, mosaic Damascus. **Patterns:** LinerLock® folders, skeleton hunters, frontier Bowies. **Technical:** Damascus, mosaic Damascus, A-2, O1, 1095. **Prices:** $200 and up. **Remarks:** Full-time maker since 1973. Not accepting orders. **Mark:** R B Johnson (signature).

JOHNSON, RANDY,
2575 E Canal Dr, Turlock, CA 95380, Phone: 209-632-5401
Specialties: Folders. **Patterns:** Locking folders. **Technical:** Grinds Damascus. **Prices:** $200 to $400. **Remarks:** Spare-time maker; first knife sold in 1989. Doing business as Puedo Knifeworks. **Mark:** PUEDO.

JOHNSON, RICHARD,
W165 N10196 Wagon Trail, Germantown, WI 53022, Phone: 262-251-5772, rlj@execpc.com; Web:http://www.execpc.com/~rlj/index.html
Specialties: Custom knives and knife repair.

JOHNSON, RUFFIN,
215 LaFonda Dr, Houston, TX 77060, Phone: 281-448-4407
Specialties: Working straight knives and folders. **Patterns:** Hunters, fighters and locking folders. **Technical:** Grinds 440C and 154CM; hidden tangs and fancy handles. **Prices:** $450 to $650; some to $1350. **Remarks:** Full-time maker; first knife sold in 1972. **Mark:** Wolf head logo and signature.

JOHNSON, RYAN M,
7320 Foster Hixson Cemetery Rd, Hixson, TN 37343, Phone: 615-842-9323
Specialties: Working and using straight knives of his design and to customer specs. **Patterns:** Bowies, hunters and utility/camp knives. **Technical:** Forges 5160, Damascus and files. Prices; $70 to $400; some to $800. **Remarks:** Full-time maker; first knife sold in 1986. **Mark:** Sledge-hammer with halo.

JOHNSON, STEVEN R,
202 E 200 N, PO Box 5, Manti, UT 84642, Phone: 435-835-7941, Fax: 435-835-7941, srj@mail.manti.com; Web: www.srjknives.com
Specialties: Investor-class working knives. **Patterns:** Hunters, fighters, boots. **Technical:** Grinds 154CM, ATS-34, CPM 154CM. **Prices:** $800 to $5000. **Remarks:** Full-time maker; first knife sold in 1972. **Mark:** Name, city, state and optional signature mark.

JOHNSTON, DR. ROBT,
PO Box 9887 1 Lomb Mem Dr, Rochester, NY 14623

JOKERST, CHARLES,
9312 Spaulding, Omaha, NE 68134, Phone: 402-571-2536
Specialties: Working knives in standard patterns. **Patterns:** Hunters, fighters and pocketknives. **Technical:** Grinds 440C, ATS-34. **Prices:** $90 to $170. **Remarks:** Spare-time maker; first knife sold in 1984. **Mark:** Early work marked RCJ; current work marked with last name and city.

JONES, BARRY M AND PHILLIP G,
221 North Ave, Danville, VA 24540, Phone: 804-793-5282
Specialties: Working and using straight knives and folders of their design and to customer specs; combat and self-defense knives. **Patterns:** Bowies, fighters, daggers, swords, hunters and LinerLock® folders. **Technical:** Grinds 440C, ATS-34 and D2; flat-grinds only. All blades hand polished. **Prices:** $100 to $1000, some higher. **Remarks:** Part-time makers; first knife sold in 1989. **Mark:** Jones Knives, city, state.

JONES, CHARLES ANTHONY,
36 Broadgate Close, Bellaire Barnstaple, No. Devon E31 4AL, ENGLAND, Phone: 0271-75328
Specialties: Working straight knives. **Patterns:** Simple hunters, fighters and utility knives. **Technical:** Grinds 440C, O1 and D2; filework offered. Engraves. **Prices:** $100 to $500; engraving higher. **Remarks:** Spare-time maker; first knife sold in 1987. **Mark:** Tony engraved.

JONES, CURTIS J,
210 Springfield Ave, Washington, PA 15301-5244, Phone: 724-225-8829
Specialties: Big Bowies, daggers, his own style of hunters. **Patterns:** Bowies, daggers, hunters, swords, boots and miniatures. **Technical:** Grinds 440C, ATS-34 and D2. Fitted guards only; does not solder. Heat-treats. Custom sheaths: hand-tooled and stitched. **Prices:** $125

to $1500; some to $3000. **Remarks:** Full-time maker; first knife sold in 1975. Mail orders accepted. **Mark:** Stylized initials on either side of three triangles interconnected.

JONES, ENOCH,
7278 Moss Ln, Warrenton, VA 20187, Phone: 540-341-0292
Specialties: Fancy working straight knives. **Patterns:** Hunters, fighters, boots and Bowies. **Technical:** Forges and grinds O1, W2, 440C and Damascus. **Prices:** $100 to $350; some to $1000. **Remarks:** Part-time maker; first knife sold in 1982. **Mark:** First name.

JONES, FRANKLIN (FRANK) W,
6030 Old Dominion Rd, Columbus, GA 31909, Phone: 706-563-6051, frankscuba@bellsouth.net
Specialties: Traditional/working/tactical/period straight knives of his or your design. **Patterns:** Hunters, skinners, utility/camp, Bowies, fighters, kitchen, neck knives, Harley chains. **Technical:** Forges using 5160, O1, 52100, 1084 1095 and Damascus. Also stock removal of stainless steel. **Prices:** $150 to $1000. **Remarks:** Full-time, American Bladesmith Society Journeyman Smith. **Mark:** F.W. Jones, Columbus, GA.

JONES, JOHN,
62 Sandy Creek Rd, Gympie, Queensland 4570, AUSTRALIA, Phone: 07-54838731, jaj36@bigpond.com
Specialties: Straight knives, gents folders and folders. **Patterns:** Hunters, Bowies, and art knives. **Technical:** Grinds 440C, AT34, Damasteel. **Prices:** $250 to $2000. **Remarks:** Using knives and collectibles. Prefer natural materials. Full-time maker. **Mark:** Jones in script and year of manufacture.

JONES, JOHN A,
779 SW 131 Hwy, Holden, MO 64040, Phone: 816-850-4318
Specialties: Working, using knives. Hunters, skinners and fighters. **Technical:** Grinds D2, O1, 440C, 1095. Prefers forging; creates own Damascus. File working on most blades. **Prices:** $50 to $500. **Remarks:** Part-time maker; first knife sold in 1996. Doing business as Old John Knives. **Mark:** OLD JOHN and serial number.

JONES, ROGER MUDBONE,
GREENMAN WORKSHOP, 320 Prussia Rd, Waverly, OH 45690, Phone: 740-739-4562, greenmanworkshop@yahoo.com
Specialties: Working in cutlery to suit working woodsman and fine collector. **Patterns:** Bowies, hunters, folders, hatchets in both period and modern style, scale miniatures a specialty. **Technical:** All cutlery hand forged to shape with traditional methods; multiple quench and draws, limited Damascus production hand carves wildlife and historic themes in stag/antler/ivory, full line of functional and high art leather. All work sole authorship. **Prices:** $50 to $5000 **Remarks:** Full-time maker/first knife sold in 1979. **Mark:** Stamped R. Jones hand made or hand engraved sig. W/Bowie knife mark.

JUSTICE, SHANE,
425 South Brooks St, Sheridan, WY 82801, Phone: 307-673-4432, justicecustomknives@yahoo.com
Specialties: Fixed blade working knives. **Patterns:** Hunters, skinners and camp knives. Other designs produced on a limited basis. **Technical:** Hand forged 5160 and 52100. **Remarks:** Part-time maker. Sole author. **Mark:** Last name.

K

K B S, KNIVES,
RSD 181, North Castlemaine, Vic 3450, AUSTRALIA, Phone: 0011 61 3 54 705864, Fax: 0011 61 3 54 706233
Specialties: Bowies, daggers and miniatures. **Patterns:** Art daggers, traditional Bowies, fancy folders and miniatures. **Technical:** Hollow or flat grind, most steels. **Prices:** $200 to $600+. **Remarks:** Full-time maker; first knife sold in 1983. **Mark:** Initials and address in Southern Cross motif.

KACZOR, TOM,
375 Wharncliffe Rd N, Upper London, Ont., CANADA N6G 1E4, Phone: 519-645-7640

KAGAWA, KOICHI,
1556 Horiyamashita, Hatano-Shi, Kanagawa, JAPAN
Specialties: Fancy high-tech straight knives and folders to customer specs. **Patterns:** Hunters, locking folders and slip-joints. **Technical:** Uses 440C and ATS-34. **Prices:** $500 to $2000; some to $20,000. **Remarks:** Part-time maker; first knife sold in 1986. **Mark:** First initial, last name-YOKOHAMA.

KAIN, CHARLES,
KAIN DESIGNS, 38 South Main St, Indianapolis, IN 46227, Phone: 317-781-8556, Fax: 317-781-8521, charles@kaincustomknives.com; Web: www.kaincustomknives.com
Specialties: Unique Damascus art folders. Patterns: Any. **Technical:** Specialized & patented mechanisms. **Remarks:** Unique knife & knife mechanism design. **Mark:** Kain and Signet stamp for unique pieces.

KAJIN, AL,
PO Box 1047, 342 South 6th Ave, Forsyth, MT 59327, Phone: 406-346-2442, kajinknives@cablemt.net
Specialties: Utility/working knives, hunters, kitchen cutlery. Produces own Damascus steel from 15N20 and 1084 and cable. Forges 52100, 5160, 1084, 15N20 and O1. Stock removal ATS-34, D2, O1, and L6. Patterns: All types, especially like to work with customer on their designs. **Technical:** Maker since 1989. ABS member since 1995. Does own differential heat treating, cryogenic soaking when appropriate. Does all leather work. **Prices:** Stock removal starts at $250. Forged blades and Damascus starts at $300. Kitchen cutlery starts at $100. **Remarks:** Likes to use exotic woods. **Mark:** Interlocked AK on forged blades, etched stylized Kajin in outline of Montana on stock removal knives.

KANDA, MICHIO,
7-32-5 Shinzutumi-cho, Shunan-shi, Yamaguchi 7460033, JAPAN, Phone: 0834-62-1910, Fax: 011-81-83462-1910
Specialties: Fantasy knives of his design. **Patterns:** Animal knives. **Technical:** Grinds ATS-34. **Prices:** $300 to $3000. **Remarks:** Full-time maker; first knife sold in 1985. Doing business as Shusui Kanda. **Mark:** Last name inside "M."

KANKI, IWAO,
14-25 3-Chome Fukui Miki, Hydugo, JAPAN 673-0433, Phone: 07948-3-2555
Specialties: Plane, knife. **Prices:** Not determined yet. **Remarks:** Masters of traditional crafts designated by the Minister of International Trade and Industry (Japan). **Mark:** Chiyozuru Sadahide.

KANSEI, MATSUNO,
109-8 Uenomachi Nishikaiden, Gitu-city, JAPAN 501-1168, Phone: 81-58-234-8643
Specialties: Folders of original design. **Patterns:** LinerLock® folder. **Technical:** Grinds VG-10, Damascus. **Prices:** $350 to $2000. **Remarks:** Full-time maker. First knife sold in 1993. **Mark:** Name.

KANTER, MICHAEL,
ADAM MICHAEL KNIVES, 14550 West Honey Ln., New Berlin, WI 53151, Phone: 262-860-1136, mike@adammichaelknives.com; Web: www.adammichaelknives.com
Specialties: Fixed blades and folders. **Patterns:** Drop point hunters, Bowies and fighters. **Technical:** Jerry Rados Damascus, BG42, CPM, S60V and S30V. **Prices:** $375 and up. **Remarls:** Ivory, mammoth ivory, stabilized woods, and pearl handles. **Mark:** Engraved Adam Michael.

KARP, BOB,
PO Box 47304, Phoenix, AZ 85068, Phone: 602 870-1234
602 870-1234, Fax: 602-331-0283
Remarks: Bob Karp "Master of the Blade."

KATO, SHINICHI,
Rainbow Amalke 402, Ohoragnchi, Nakashidami, Moriyama-ku Nagoya, JAPAN 463-0002, Phone: 81-52-736-6032, skato-402@u0l.gate01.com
Specialties: Flat grind and hand finish. **Patterns:** Bowie, fighter. Hunting and folding knives. **Technical:** Hand forged,flat grind. **Prices:** $100 to $2000. **Remarks:** Part-time maker. **Mark:** Name.

KATSUMARO, SHISHIDO,
, 2-6-11 Kamiseno Aki-ku, Hiroshima, JAPAN, Phone: 090-3634-9054, Fax: 082-227-4438, shishido@d8.dion.ne.jp

KAUFFMAN, DAVE,
4 Clark Creek Loop, Montana City, MT 59634, Phone: 406-442-9328
Specialties: Field grade and exhibition grade hunting knives and ultra light folders. **Patterns:** Fighters, Bowies and drop-point hunters. **Technical:** S30V and SS Damascus. **Prices:** $155 to $1200. **Remarks:** Full-time maker; first knife sold in 1989. On the cover of *Knives '94*. **Mark:** First and last name, city and state.

KAWASAKI, AKIHISA,
11-8-9 Chome Minamiamachi, Suzurandai Kita-Ku, Kobe, JAPAN, Phone: 078-593-0418, Fax: 078-593-0418
Specialties: Working/using knives of his design. **Patterns:** Hunters, kit camp knives. **Technical:** Forges and grinds Molybdenum Panadium. Grinds ATS-34 and stainless steel. Uses Chinese Quince wood, desert ironwood and cow leather. **Prices:** $300 to $800; some to $1000. **Remarks:** Full-time maker. **Mark:** A.K.

KAY, J WALLACE,
332 Slab Bridge Rd, Liberty, SC 29657

KAZSUK, DAVID,
PO Box 39, Perris, CA 92572-0039, Phone: 909-780-2288, ddkaz@hotmail.com
Specialties: Hand forged. **Prices:** $150+. **Mark:** Last name.

KEARNEY, JAROD,
10 Park St Hamlet, Bordentown, NJ 08505, Phone: 336-656-4617, jarodk@mindspring.com; Web: www.jarodsworkshop.com

KEESLAR, JOSEPH F,
391 Radio Rd, Almo, KY 42020, Phone: 270-753-7919, Fax: 270-753-7919, sjkees@apex.net
Specialties: Classic and contemporary Bowies, combat, hunters,

daggers and folders. **Patterns:** Decorative filework, engraving and custom leather sheaths available. **Technical:** Forges 5160, 52100 and his own Damascus steel. **Prices:** $300 to $3000. **Remarks:** Full-time maker; first knife sold in 1976. ABS Master Smith. **Mark:** First and middle initials, last name in hammer, knife and anvil logo, M.S.

KEESLAR, STEVEN C,
115 Lane 216 Hamilton Lake, Hamilton, IN 46742, Phone: 260-488-3161, sskeeslar@hotmail.com
Specialties: Traditional working/using straight knives of his design and to customer specs. **Patterns:** Bowies, hunters, utility/camp knives. **Technical:** Forges 5160, files 52100 Damascus. **Prices:** $100 to $600; some to $1500. **Remarks:** Part-time maker; first knife sold in 1976. ABS member. **Mark:** Fox head in flames over Steven C. Keeslar.

KEETON, WILLIAM L,
6095 Rehobeth Rd SE, Laconia, IN 47135-9550, Phone: 812-969-2836, wkeeton@epowerc.net; Web: www.keetoncustomknives.com
Specialties: Plain and fancy working knives. **Patterns:** Hunters and fighters; locking folders and slip-joints. Names patterns after Kentucky Derby winners. **Technical:** Grinds D2, ATS-34, 440C, 440V and 154CM; mirror and satin finishes. **Prices:** $135 to $2500. **Remarks:** Full-time maker; first knife sold in 1971. **Mark:** Logo of key.

KEHIAYAN, ALFREDO,
Cuzco 1455 Ing. Maschwitz, CP B1623GXU Buenos Aires, ARGENTINA, Phone: 54-03488-442212, Fax: 54-077-75-4493-5359, alfredo@kehiayan.com.ar; Web: www.kehiayan.com.ar
Specialties: Functional straight knives. **Patterns:** Utility knives, skinners, hunters and boots. **Technical:** Forges and grinds SAE 52.100, SAE 6180, SAE 9260, SAE 5160, 440C and ATS-34, titanium with nitride. All blades mirror-polished; makes leather sheath and wood cases. **Prices:** $70 to $800; some to $6000. **Remarks:** Full-time maker; first knife sold in 1983. Some knives are satin finish (utility knives). **Mark:** Name.

KEISUKE, GOTOH,
105 Cosumo-City, Otozu 202 Ohita-city, Ohita, JAPAN, Phone: 097-523-0750, k-u-an@ki.rim.or.jp

KELLER, BILL,
12211 Las Nubes, San Antonio, TX 78233, Phone: 210-653-6609
Specialties: Primarily folders, some fixed blades. **Patterns:** Autos, liner locks and hunters. **Technical:** Grinds stainless and Damascus. **Prices:** $400 to $1000, some to $4000. **Remarks:** Part-time maker, first knife sold 1995. **Mark:** Last name inside outline of Alamo.

KELLEY, GARY,
17485 SW Pheasant Lane, Aloha, OR 97006, Phone: 503-649-7867, Web: www.reproductionblades.com
Specialties: Primitive knives and blades. **Patterns:** Fur trade era rifleman's knives, fur trade, cowboy action, hunting knives. **Technical:** Hand-forges and precision investment casts. **Prices:** $35 to $125. **Remarks:** Family business, reproduction blades. Doing business as Reproduction Blades. **Mark:** Fir tree logo.

KELLY, LANCE,
1723 Willow Oak Dr, Edgewater, FL 32132, Phone: 904-423-4933
Specialties: Investor-class straight knives and folders. **Patterns:** Kelly-style in contemporary outlines. **Technical:** Grinds O1, D2 and 440C; engraves; inlays gold and silver. **Prices:** $600 to $3500. **Remarks:** Full-time engraver and knifemaker; first knife sold in 1975. **Mark:** Last name.

KELSEY, NATE,
3401 Cherry St, Anchorage, AK 99504, Phone: 907-360-4469, nkelsey@cox.net
Specialties: Hand forges or stock removal traditional working knives of own or customer design. Forges own Damascus, makes custom leather sheaths, does fine engraving and scrimshaw. **Technical:** Forges 52100, 1084/15N20, 5160. Grinds ATS-34, 154CM. Prefers natural handle materials. Prices $175 to $750. **Remarks:** Part-time maker since 1990. Member ABS, Arkansas Knifemakers Assoc. **Mark:** Name and city.

KELSO, JIM,
577 Collar Hill Rd, Worcester, VT 05682, Phone: 802-229-4254, Fax: 802-229-0595, kelsonmaker@gmail.com; Web:www.jimkelso.com
Specialties: Fancy high-art straight knives and folders that mix Eastern and Western influences. Only uses own designs. **Patterns:** Daggers, swords and locking folders. **Technical:** Grinds only custom Damascus. Works with top Damascus bladesmiths. **Prices:** $6000 to $20,000. **Remarks:** Full-time maker; first knife sold in 1980. **Mark:** Stylized initials.

KEMP, LAWRENCE,
8503 Water Tower Rd, Ooletwah, TN 37363, Phone: 423-344-2357, larry@kempknives.com
Specialties: Bowies, hunters and working knives. **Patterns:** Bowies, camp knives, hunters and skinners. **Technical:** Forges carbon steel, and his own Damascus. **Prices:** $150 to $1500. **Remarks:** Part-time maker, first knife sold in 1991. **Mark:** L.A. Kemp.

KENNEDY JR., BILL,
PO Box 850431, Yukon, OK 73085, Phone: 405-354-9150
Specialties: Working straight knives. **Patterns:** Hunters, fighters, minis and fishing knives. **Technical:** Grinds D2, 440C, ATS-34, BG42. **Prices:** $110 and up. **Remarks:** Part-time maker; first knife sold in 1980. **Mark:** Last name and year made.

KERANEN, PAUL,
1208 E Dirck St, Haysville, KS 67060, Phone: 316-640-7462, pkknives@gmail.com; Web:www.pkknives.blogspot.com
Specialties: Specializes in Japanese style knives and swords. Most clay tempered with hamon. **Patterns:** Does bowies, fighters and hunters. **Technical:** Forges and grinds carbons steel only. Make my own Damascus. **Prices:** $75 to $800. **Mark:** KERANEN etched.

KERN, R W,
20824 Texas Trail W, San Antonio, TX 78257-1602, Phone: 210-698-2549, rkern@ev1.net
Specialties: Damascus, straight and folders. **Patterns:** Hunters, Bowies and folders. **Technical:** Grinds ATS-34, 440C and BG42. Forges own Damascus. **Prices:** $200 and up. **Remarks:** First knives 1980; retired; work as time permits. Member ABS, Texas Knifemaker and Collectors Association. **Mark:** Outline of Alamo with kern over outline.

KEYES, DAN,
6688 King St, Chino, CA 91710, Phone: 909-628-8329

KHALSA, JOT SINGH,
368 Village St, Millis, MA 02054, Phone: 508-376-8162, Fax: 508-532-0517, jotkhalsa@comcast.net; Web: www.khalsakirpans.com and www.lifeknives.com
Specialties: Liner locks, one-of-a-kind daggers, swords, and kirpans (Sikh daggers) all original designs. **Technical:** Forges own Damascus, uses others high quality Damascus including stainless, and grinds stainless steels. Uses natural handle materials frequently unusual minerals. Pieces are frequently engraved and more recently carved. **Prices:** Start at $700.

KHARLAMOV, YURI,
Oboronnay 46, 2, Tula, 300007, RUSSIA
Specialties: Classic, fancy and traditional knives of his design. **Patterns:** Daggers and hunters. **Technical:** Forges only Damascus with nickel. Uses natural handle materials; engraves on metal, carves on nut-tree; silver and pearl inlays. **Prices:** $600 to $2380; some to $4000. **Remarks:** Full-time maker; first knife sold in 1988. **Mark:** Initials.

KI, SHIVA,
5222 Ritterman Ave, Baton Rouge, LA 70805, Phone: 225-356-7274, shivakicustomknives@netzero.net; Web: www.shivakicustomknives.com
Specialties: Working straight knives and folders. **Patterns:** Emphasis on personal defense knives, martial arts weapons. **Technical:** Forges and grinds; makes own Damascus; prefers natural handle materials. **Prices:** $135 to $850; some to $1800. **Remarks:** Full-time maker; first knife sold in 1981. **Mark:** Name with logo.

KIEFER, TONY,
112 Chateaugay Dr, Pataskala, OH 43062, Phone: 740-927-6910
Specialties: Traditional working and using straight knives in standard patterns. **Patterns:** Bowies, fighters and hunters. **Technical:** Grinds 440C and D2; forges D2. Flat-grinds Bowies; hollow-grinds drop-point and trailing-point hunters. **Prices:** $110 to $300; some to $200. **Remarks:** Spare-time maker; first knife sold in 1988. **Mark:** Last name.

KILBY, KEITH,
1902 29th St, Cody, WY 82414, Phone: 307-587-2732
Specialties: Works with all designs. **Patterns:** Mostly Bowies, camp knives and hunters of his design. **Technical:** Forges 52100, 5160, 1095, Damascus and mosaic Damascus. **Prices:** $250 to $3500. **Remarks:** Part-time maker; first knife sold in 1974. Doing business as Foxwood Forge. **Mark:** Name.

KILEY, MIKE AND JANDY,
ROCKING K KNIVES, 1325 Florida, Chino Valley, AZ 86323, Phone: 928-910-2647
Specialties: Period knives for cowboy action shooters and mountain men. **Patterns:** Bowies, drop-point hunters, skinners, sheepsfoot blades and spear points. **Technical:** Steels are 0-1, D2, 1095, ATS 34, 440C and others upon request. Handles include all types of wood, with cocobolo, ironwood, rosewood, maple and bacote being favorites as well as buffalo horn, stag, elk antler, mammoth ivory, giraffe boon, sheep horn and camel bone. **Prices:** $100 to $500 depending on style and materials. Hand-tooled leather sheaths by Jan and Mike.

KILPATRICK, CHRISTIAN A,
6925 Mitchell Ct, Citrus Hieghts, CA 95610, Phone: 916-729-0733, crimsonkil@gmail.com; Web:www.crimsonknives.com
Specialties: All forged weapons (no firearms) from ancient to modern. All blades produced are first and foremost useable tools, and secondly but no less importantly, artistic expressions. Patterns: Hunters, bowies, daggers, swords, axes, spears, boot knives, bird knives, ethnic blades and historical reproductions. Customer designs welcome. **Technical:** Forges and grinds, makes own Damascus. Does file work. **Prices:** $125 to $3200. **Remarks:** 26 year part time maker. First knife sold in 2002.

KIMBERLEY, RICHARD L.,
86-B Arroyo Hondo Rd, Santa Fe, NM 87508, Phone: 505-820-2727
Specialties: Fixed-blade and period knives. **Technical:** O1, 52100, 9260 steels. **Remarks:** Member ABS. Marketed under "Kimberleys of Santa Fe." **Mark:** "By D. KIMBERLEY SANTA FE NM."

KIMSEY, KEVIN,
198 Cass White Rd. NW, Cartersville, GA 30121, Phone: 770-387-0779 and 770-655-8879
Specialties: Tactical fixed blades and folders. **Patterns:** Fighters, folders, hunters and utility knives. **Technical:** Grinds 440C, ATS-34 and D2 carbon. **Prices:** $100 to $400; some to $600. **Remarks:** Three-time *Blade* magazine award winner, knifemaker since 1983. **Mark:** Rafter and stylized KK.

KING, BILL,
14830 Shaw Rd, Tampa, FL 33625, Phone: 813-961-3455
Specialties: Folders, lockbacks, liner locks, automatics and stud openers. **Patterns:** Wide varieties; folders. **Technical:** ATS-34 and some Damascus; single and double grinds. Offers filework and jewel embellishment; nickel-silver Damascus and mokume bolsters. **Prices:** $150 to $475; some to $850. **Remarks:** Full-time maker; first knife sold in 1976. All titanium fitting on liner-locks; screw or rivet construction on lock-backs. **Mark:** Last name in crown.

KING, FRED,
430 Grassdale Rd, Cartersville, GA 30120, Phone: 770-382-8478, Web: http://www.fking83264@aol.com
Specialties: Fancy and embellished working straight knives and folders. **Patterns:** Hunters, Bowies and fighters. **Technical:** Grinds ATS-34 and D2: forges 5160 and Damascus. Offers filework. **Prices:** $100 to $3500. **Remarks:** Spare-time maker; first knife sold in 1984. **Mark:** Kings Edge.

KING, JASON M,
5170 Rockenham Rd, St. George, KS 66423, Phone: 785-494-8377, Web: www.jasonmkingknives.com
Specialties: Working and using straight knives of his design and sometimes to customer specs. Some slip joint and lockback folders. **Patterns:** Hunters, Bowies, tacticals, fighters; some miniatures. **Technical:** Grinds D2, 440C and other Damascus. **Prices:** $75 to $200; some up to $500. **Remarks:** First knife sold in 1998. Likes to use height quality stabilized wood. **Mark:** JMK.

KING JR., HARVEY G,
32266 Hwy K4, Alta Vista, KS 66834, Phone: 785-499-5207, Web: www.harveykingknives.com
Specialties: Traditional working and using straight knives of his design and to customer specs. **Patterns:** Hunters, Bowies and fillet knives. **Technical:** Grinds O1, A2 and D2. Prefers natural handle materials; offers leatherwork. **Prices:** Start at $70. **Remarks:** Part-time maker; first knife sold in 1988. **Mark:** Name and serial number based on steel used, year made and number of knives made that year.

KINKER, MIKE,
8755 E County Rd 50 N, Greensburg, IN 47240, Phone: 812-663-5277, Fax: 812-662-8131, mokinker@hsonline.net
Specialties: Working/using knives, straight knives. Starting to make folders. Your design. **Patterns:** Boots, daggers, hunters, skinners, hatchets. **Technical:** Grind 440C and ATS-34, others if required. Damascus, dovetail bolsters, jeweled blade. **Prices:** $125 to 375; some to $1000. **Remarks:** Part-time maker; first knife sold in 1991. Doing business as Kinker Knives. **Mark:** Kinker and Kinker plus year.

KINNIKIN, TODD,
EUREKA FORGE, 8356 John McKeever Rd., House Springs, MO 63051, Phone: 314-938-6248
Specialties: Mosaic Damascus. **Patterns:** Hunters, fighters, folders and automatics. **Technical:** Forges own mosaic Damascus with tool steel Damascus edge. Prefers natural, fossil and artifact handle materials. **Prices:** $400 to $2400. **Remarks:** Full-time maker; first knife sold in 1994. **Mark:** Initials connected.

KIOUS, JOE,
1015 Ridge Pointe Rd, Kerrville, TX 78028, Phone: 830-367-2277, Fax: 830-367-2286, kious@ktc.com
Specialties: Investment-quality interframe and bolstered folders. **Patterns:** Folder specialist, all types. **Technical:** Both stainless and non-stainless Damascus. **Prices:** $650 to $3000; some to $10,000. **Remarks:** Full-time maker; first knife sold in 1969. **Mark:** Last name, city and state or last name only.

KIRK, RAY,
PO Box 1445, Tahlequah, OK 74465, Phone: 918-456-1519, ray@rakerknives.com; Web: www.rakerknives.com
Specialties: Folders, skinners fighters, and Bowies. Patterns: Neck knives and small hunters and skinners. **Technical:** Forges all knives from 52100 and own Damascus. **Prices:** $65 to $3000. **Remarks:** Started forging in 1989; makes own Damascus. Does custom steel rolling. Has some 52100 and Damascus in custom flat bar 512E3 for sale **Mark:** Stamped "Raker" on blade.

KITSMILLER, JERRY,
67277 Las Vegas Dr, Montrose, CO 81401, Phone: 970-249-4290
Specialties: Working straight knives in standard patterns. **Patterns:** Hunters, boots. **Technical:** Grinds ATS-34 and 440C only. **Prices:** $75 to $200; some to $300. **Remarks:** Spare-time maker; first knife sold in 1984. **Mark:** JandS Knives.

KLAASEE, TINUS,
PO Box 10221, George 6530, SOUTH AFRICA
Specialties: Hunters, skinners and utility knives. **Patterns:** Uses own designs and client specs. **Technical:** N690 stainless steel 440C Damascus. **Prices:** $700 and up. **Remarks:** Use only indigenous materials. Hardwood, horns and ivory. Makes his own sheaths and boxes. **Mark:** Initials and sur name over warthog.

KNAPP, RON,
The Cutting Edge, 1971 Fox Ave, Fairbanks, AK 99701, Phone: 907-452-7477, cuttingedge@gci.net
Specialties: Mosaic handles of exotic natural materials from Alaska and around the world. Folders, fixed blades, full and hidden tangs. **Patterns:** Folders, hunters, skinners and camp knives. **Technical:** Forges own Damascus, uses both forging and stock removal with ATS-34, 154CM, stainless Damascus, carbon steel and carbon Damascus. **Prices:** $800-$2000. **Remarks:** Full time maker, sold first knife in 2000. **Mark:** Mark Knapp Custom Knives Fairbanks, AK.

KNICKMEYER, HANK,
6300 Crosscreek, Cedar Hill, MO 63016, Phone: 314-285-3210
Specialties: Complex mosaic Damascus constructions. **Patterns:** Fixed blades, swords, folders and automatics. **Technical:** Mosaic Damascus with all tool steel Damascus edges. **Prices:** $500 to $2000; some $3000 and higher. **Remarks:** Part-time maker; first knife sold in 1989. Doing business as Dutch Creek Forge and Foundry. **Mark:** Initials connected.

KNICKMEYER, KURT,
6344 Crosscreek, Cedar Hill, MO 63016, Phone: 314-274-0481

KNIGHT, JASON,
110 Paradise Pond Ln, Harleyville, SC 29448, Phone: 843-452-1163, jasonknightknives.com
Specialties: Bowies. **Patterns:** Bowies and anything from history or his own design. **Technical:** 1084, 5160, O1, 52102, Damascus/forged blades. **Prices:** $200 and up. **Remarks:** Bladesmith. **Mark:** KNIGHT.

KNIPSCHIELD, TERRY,
808 12th Ave NE, Rochester, MN 55906, Phone: 507-288-7829, terry@knipknives.com; Web: www.knipknives.com
Specialties: Folders and fixed blades and woodcarving knives. **Patterns:** Variations of traditional patterns and his own new designs. **Technical:** Stock removal. Grinds ATS-34, stainless Damascus, O1 on woodcarvers. **Prices:** $60 to $1200 and higher for upscale folders. **Mark:** Etchd logo on blade, KNIP with shield image.

KNIPSTEIN, R C (JOE),
731 N Fielder, Arlington, TX 76012, Phone: 817-265-0573;817-265-2021, Fax: 817-265-3410
Specialties: Traditional pattern folders along with custom designs. **Patterns:** Hunters, Bowies, folders, fighters, utility knives. **Technical:** Grinds 440C, D2, 154CM and ATS-34. Natural handle materials and full tangs are standard. **Prices:** Start at $300. **Remarks:** Part-time maker; first knife sold in 1989. **Mark:** Last name.

KNOTT, STEVE,
KNOTT KNIVES, 203 Wild Rose, Guyton, GA 31312, Phone: 912-772-7655
Technical: Uses ATS-34/440C and some commercial Damascus, single and double grinds with mirror or satin finishes. **Patters:** Hunters, boot knives, Bowies, and tantos, slip joint and lock-back folders. Uses a wide variety of handle materials to include ironwood, coca-bola and colored stabilized wood, also horn, bone and ivory upon customer request. **Remarks:** First knife sold in 1991. Part-time maker.

KNUTH, JOSEPH E,
3307 Lookout Dr, Rockford, IL 61109, Phone: 815-874-9597
Specialties: High-art working straight knives of his design or to customer specs. **Patterns:** Daggers, fighters and swords. **Technical:** Grinds 440C, ATS-34 and D2. **Prices:** $150 to $1500; some to $15,000. **Remarks:** Full-time maker; first knife sold in 1989. **Mark:** Initials on bolster face.

KOHLS, JERRY,
N4725 Oak Rd, Princeton, WI 54968, Phone: 920-295-3648
Specialties: Working knives and period pieces. **Patterns:** Hunters-boots and Bowies, your designs or his. **Technical:** Grinds, ATS-34 440c 154CM and 1095 and commercial Damascus. **Remarks:** Part-time maker. **Mark:** Last name.

KOJETIN, W,
20 Bapaume Rd Delville, Germiston 1401, SOUTH AFRICA, Phone: 27118733305/mobile 27836256208
Specialties: High-art and working straight knives of all designs. Patterns: Daggers, hunters and his own Man hunter Bowie. **Technical:** Grinds D2 and ATS-34; forges and grinds 440B/C. Offers "wrap-around" pava and abalone handles, scrolled wood or ivory, stacked filework and setting of faceted semi-precious stones. **Prices:** $185 to $600; some to $11,000. **Remarks:** Spare-time maker; first knife sold in 1962. **Mark:** Billy K.

KOLITZ, ROBERT,
W9342 Canary Rd, Beaver Dam, WI 53916, Phone: 920-887-1287
Specialties: Working straight knives to customer specs. **Patterns:** Bowies, hunters, bird and trout knives, boots. **Technical:** Grinds O1, 440C; commercial Damascus. **Prices:** $50 to $100; some to $500. **Remarks:** Spare-time maker; first knife sold in 1979. **Mark:** Last initial.

KOMMER, RUSS,
4609 35th Ave N, Fargo, NC 58102, Phone: 907-346-3339
Specialties: Working straight knives with the outdoorsman in mind. **Patterns:** Hunters, semi-skinners, fighters, folders and utility knives, art knives. **Technical:** Hollow-grinds ATS-34, 440C and 440V. **Prices:** $125 to $850; some to $3000. **Remarks:** Full-time maker; first knife sold in 1995. **Mark:** Bear paw—full name, city and state or full name and state.

KOPP, TODD M,
PO Box 3474, Apache Jct., AZ 85217, Phone: 480-983-6143, tmkopp@msn.com
Specialties: Classic and traditional straight knives. Fluted handled daggers. **Patterns:** Bowies, boots, daggers, fighters, hunters, swords and folders. **Technical:** Grinds 5160, 440C, ATS-34. All Damascus steels, or customers choice. Some engraving and filework. **Prices:** $200 to $1200; some to $4000. **Remarks:** Part-time maker; first knife sold in 1989. **Mark:** Last name in Old English, some others name, city and state.

KOSTER, STEVEN C,
16261 Gentry Ln, Huntington Beach, CA 92647, Phone: 714-840-8621, hbkosters@verizon.net
Specialties: Bowies, daggers, skinners, camp knives. **Technical:** Use 5160, 52100, 1084, 1095 steels. **Prices:** $200 to $1000. **Remarks:** Wood and leather sheaths with silver furniture. ABS Journeyman 2003. **Mark:** Koster squeezed between lines.

KOVACIK, ROBERT,
Erenburgova 23, Lucenec 98407, SLOVAKIA, Phone: 00421474332566 Mobil:00421470907644800, Fax: 00421470907644800, robert.kovacik@post.sk Web: www.robertkovacik.com
Specialties: Engraved hunting knives, guns engraved; Knifemakers. **Technical:** Fixed blades, folder knives, miniatures. **Prices:** $350 to $20,000 U.S. **Mark:** R.

KOVAR, EUGENE,
2626 W 98th St., Evergreen Park, IL 60642, Phone: 708-636-3724/708-790-4115, baldemaster333@aol.com
Specialties: One-of-a-kind miniature knives only. **Patterns:** Fancy to fantasy miniature knives; knife pendants and tie tacks. **Technical:** Files and grinds nails, nickel-silver and sterling silver. **Prices:** $5 to $35; some to $100. **Mark:** GK.

KOYAMA, CAPTAIN BUNSHICHI,
3-23 Shirako-cho, Nakamura-ku, Nagoya City 453-0817, JAPAN, Phone: 052-461-7070, Fax: 052-461-7070
Specialties: Innovative folding knife. **Patterns:** General purpose one hand. **Technical:** Grinds ATS-34 and Damascus. **Prices:** $400 to $900; some to $1500. **Remarks:** Part-time maker; first knife sold in 1994. **Mark:** Captain B. Koyama and the shoulder straps of CAPTAIN.

KRAFT, STEVE,
408 NE 11th St, Abilene, KS 67410, Phone: 785-263-1411
Specialties: Folders, lockbacks, scale release auto, push button auto. **Patterns:** Hunters, boot knives and fighters. **Technical:** Grinds ATS-34, Damascus; uses titanium, pearl, ivory etc. **Prices:** $500 to $2500. **Remarks:** Part-time maker; first knife sold in 1984. **Mark:** Kraft.

KRAPP, DENNY,
1826 Windsor Oak Dr, Apopka, FL 32703, Phone: 407-880-7115
Specialties: Fantasy and working straight knives of his design. **Patterns:** Hunters, fighters and utility/camp knives. **Technical:** Grinds ATS-34 and 440C. **Prices:** $85 to $300; some to $800. **Remarks:** Spare-time maker; first knife sold in 1988. **Mark:** Last name.

KRAUSE, ROY W,
22412 Corteville, St. Clair Shores, MI 48081, Phone: 810-296-3995, Fax: 810-296-2663
Specialties: Military and law enforcement/Japanese-style knives and swords. **Patterns:** Combat and back-up, Bowies, fighters, boot knives, daggers, tantos, wakazashis and katanas. **Technical:** Grinds ATS-34, A2, D2, 1045, O1 and commercial Damascus; differentially hardened Japanese-style blades. **Prices:** Moderate to upscale. **Remarks:** Full-time maker. **Mark:** Last name on traditional knives; initials in Japanese characters on Japanese-style knives.

KREH, LEFTY,
210 Wichersham Way, "Cockeysville", MD 21030

KREIBICH, DONALD L.,
1638 Commonwealth Circle, Reno, NV 89503, Phone: 775-746-0533, dmkreno@sbcglobal.net
Specialties: Working straight knives in standard patterns. Patterns: Bowies, boots and daggers; camp and fishing knives. **Technical:** Grinds 440C, 154CM and ATS-34; likes integrals. **Prices:** $100 to $200; some to $500. **Remarks:** Part-time maker; first knife sold in 1980. **Mark:** First and middle initials, last name.

KRESSLER, D F,
Bruennenweg 1 D-28832, Schlossberg 1-85235, Achim 28832 DE, GERMANY, Phone: 49-420276574
Specialties: High-tech integral and interframe knives. **Patterns:** Hunters, fighters, daggers. **Technical:** Grinds new state-of-the-art steels; prefers natural handle materials. **Prices:** Upscale. **Mark:** Name in logo.

KRETSINGER JR., PHILIP W,
17536 Bakersville Rd, Boonsboro, MD 21713, Phone: 301-432-6771
Specialties: Fancy and traditional period pieces. **Patterns:** Hunters, Bowies, camp knives, daggers, carvers, fighters. **Technical:** Forges W2, 5160 and his own Damascus. **Prices:** Start at $200. **Remarks:** Full-time knifemaker. **Mark:** Name.

KUBASEK, JOHN A,
74 Northhampton St, Easthampton, MA 01027, Phone: 413-527-7917, jaknife01@verizon.net
Specialties: Left-and right-handed LinerLock® folders of his design or to customer specs. Also new knives made with Ripcord patent. **Patterns:** Fighters, tantos, drop points, survival knives, neck knives and belt buckle knives. **Technical:** Grinds 154CM, S30 and Damascus. **Prices:** $395 to $1500. **Remarks:** Part-time maker; first knife sold in 1985. **Mark:** Name and address etched.

L

LADD, JIM S,
1120 Helen, Deer Park, TX 77536, Phone: 713-479-7286
Specialties: Working knives and period pieces. **Patterns:** Hunters, boots and Bowies plus other straight knives. **Technical:** Grinds D2, 440C and 154CM. **Prices:** $125 to $225; some to $550. **Remarks:** Part-time maker; first knife sold in 1965. Doing business as The Tinker. **Mark:** First and middle initials, last name.

LADD, JIMMIE LEE,
1120 Helen, Deer Park, TX 77536, Phone: 713-479-7186
Specialties: Working straight knives. **Patterns:** Hunters, skinners and utility knives. **Technical:** Grinds 440C and D2. **Prices:** $75 to $225. **Remarks:** First knife sold in 1979. **Mark:** First and middle initials, last name.

LAGRANGE, FANIE,
12 Canary Crescent, Table View 7441, SOUTH AFRICA, Phone: 27 21 55 76 805
Specialties: African-influenced styles in folders and fixed blades. **Patterns:** All original patterns with many one-of-a-kind. **Technical:** Mostly stock removal in 12C27, ATS-34, stainless Damascus. **Prices:** $350 to $3000. **Remarks:** Professional maker. SA Guild member. **Mark:** Name over spear.

LAINSON, TONY,
114 Park Ave, Council Bluffs, IA 51503, Phone: 712-322-5222
Specialties: Working straight knives, liner locking folders. **Technical:** Grinds 154CM, ATS-34, 440C buys Damascus. Handle materials include Micarta, carbon fiber G-10 ivory pearl and bone. **Prices:** $95 to $600. **Remarks:** Part-time maker; first knife sold in 1987. **Mark:** Name and state.

LAIRSON SR., JERRY,
H C 68 Box 970, Ringold, OK 74754, Phone: 580-876-3426, bladesmt@brightok.net; Web: www.lairson-custom-knives.net
Specialties: Damascus collector grade knives & high performance field grade hunters & cutting competition knives. **Patterns:** Damascus, random, raindrop, ladder, twist and others. **Technical:** All knives hammer forged. Mar Tempering**Prices:** Field grade knives $300. Collector grade $400 & up. **Mark:** Lairson. **Remarks:** Makes any style knife but prefer fighters and hunters. ABS Mastersmith, AKA member, KGA member. Cutting competition competitor.

LAKE, RON,
3360 Bendix Ave, Eugene, OR 97401, Phone: 541-484-2683
Specialties: High-tech working knives; inventor of the modern interframe folder. **Patterns:** Hunters, boots, etc.; locking folders. **Technical:** Grinds 154CM and ATS-34. Patented interframe with special lock release tab. **Prices:** $2200 to $3000; some higher. **Remarks:** Full-time maker; first knife sold in 1966. **Mark:** Last name.

LALA, PAULO RICARDO P AND LALA, ROBERTO P.,
R Daniel Martins 636, Centro, Presidente Prudente, SP-19031-260, BRAZIL, Phone: 0182-210125, Web: http://www.orbita.starmedia/~korth
Specialties: Straight knives and folders of all designs to customer specs. **Patterns:** Bowies, daggers fighters, hunters and utility knives. **Technical:** Grinds and forges D6, 440C, high-carbon steels and Damascus. **Prices:** $60 to $400; some higher. **Remarks:** Full-time makers; first knife sold in 1991. All stainless steel blades are ultra sub-zero quenched. **Mark:** Sword carved on top of anvil under KORTH.

LAMB, CURTIS J,
3336 Louisiana Ter, Ottawa, KS 66067-8996, Phone: 785-242-6657

LAMBERT, JARRELL D,
2321 FM 2982, Granado, TX 77962, Phone: 512-771-3744
Specialties: Traditional working and using straight knives of his design

and to customer specs. **Patterns:** Bowies, hunters, tantos and utility/camp knives. **Technical:** Grinds ATS-34; forges W2 and his own Damascus. Makes own sheaths. **Prices:** $80 to $600; some to $1000. **Remarks:** Part-time maker; first knife sold in 1982. **Mark:** Etched first and middle initials, last name; or stamped last name.

LAMBERT, KIRBY,
536 College Ave, Regina Saskatchewan S4N X3, CANADA, kirby@lambertknives.com; Web: www.lambertknives.com
Specialties: Tactical/utility folders. Tactical/utility Japanese style fixed blades. **Prices:** $200 to $1500 U.S. **Remarks:** Full-time maker since 2002. **Mark:** Black widow spider and last name Lambert.

LAMEY, ROBERT M,
15800 Lamey Dr, Biloxi, MS 39532, Phone: 228-396-9066, Fax: 228-396-9022, rmlamey@ametro.net; Web: www.lameyknives.com
Specialties: Bowies, fighters, hard use knives. **Patterns:** Bowies, fighters, hunters and camp knives. **Technical:** Forged and stock removal. **Prices:** $125 to $350. **Remarks:** Lifetime reconditioning; will build to customer designs, specializing in hard use, affordable knives. **Mark:** LAMEY.

LAMPSON, FRANK G,
3215 Saddle Bag Circle, Rimrock, AZ 86335, Phone: 928-567-7395, fglampson@yahoo.com
Specialties: Working folders; one-of-a-kinds. **Patterns:** Folders, hunters, utility knives, fillet knives and Bowies. **Technical:** Grinds ATS-34, 440C and 154CM. **Prices:** $100 to $750; some to $3500. **Remarks:** Full-time maker; first knife sold in 1971. **Mark:** Name in fish logo.

LANCASTER, C G,
No 2 Schoonwinkel St, Parys, Free State, SOUTH AFRICA, Phone: 0568112090
Specialties: High-tech working and using knives of his design and to customer specs. **Patterns:** Hunters, locking folders and utility/camp knives. **Technical:** Grinds Sandvik 12C27, 440C and D2. Offers anodized titanium bolsters. **Prices:** $450 to $750; some to $1500. **Remarks:** Part-time maker; first knife sold in 1990. **Mark:** Etched logo.

LANCE, BILL,
PO Box 4427, Eagle River, AK 99577, Phone: 907-694-1487
Specialties: Ooloos and working straight knives; limited issue sets. **Patterns:** Several ulu patterns, drop-point skinners. **Technical:** Uses ATS-34, Vascomax 350; ivory, horn and high-class wood handles. **Prices:** $85 to $300; art sets to $3000. **Remarks:** First knife sold in 1981. **Mark:** Last name over a lance.

LANDERS, JOHN,
758 Welcome Rd, Newnan, GA 30263, Phone: 404-253-5719
Specialties: High-art working straight knives and folders of his design. **Patterns:** Hunters, fighters and slip-joint folders. **Technical:** Grinds 440C, ATS-34, 154CM and commercial Damascus. **Prices:** $85 to $250; some to $500. **Remarks:** Part-time maker; first knife sold in 1989. **Mark:** Last name.

LANE, BEN,
4802 Massie St, North Little Rock, AR 72218, Phone: 501-753-8238
Specialties: Fancy straight knives of his design and to customer specs; period pieces. **Patterns:** Bowies, hunters, utility/camp knives. **Technical:** Grinds D2 and 154CM; forges and grinds 1095. Offers intricate handle work including inlays and spacers. **Prices:** $120 to $450; some to $5000. **Remarks:** Part-time maker; first knife sold in 1989. **Mark:** Full name, city, state.

LANER, DEAN,
1480 Fourth St, Susanville, CA 96130, Phone: 530-310-1917, laner54knives@yahoo.com
Specialties: Fancy working fixed blades, of his design, will do custom orders. **Patterns:** Hunters, fighters, combat, fishing, Bowies, utility, and kitchen knives. **Technical:** Grinds 154CM, ATS-34, D2, buys Damascus. Does mostly hallow grinding, some flat grinds. Uses Micarta, mastodon ivory, hippo ivory, exotic woods. Loves doing spacer work on stick tang knives. A leather or kydes sheath comes with every knife. Lifetime warrantee and free sharpening also. **Remarks:** Part-time maker, first knife sold in 1993. **Prices:** $150 to $1000. **Mark:** LANER CUSTOM KNIVES over D next to a tree.

LANGLEY, GENE H,
1022 N. Price Rd, Florence, SC 29506, Phone: 843-669-3150
Specialties: Working knives in standard patterns. **Patterns:** Hunters, boots, fighters, locking folders and slip-joints. **Technical:** Grinds 440C, 154CM and ATS-34. **Prices:** $125 to $450; some to $1000. **Remarks:** Part-time maker; first knife sold in 1979. **Mark:** Name.

LANGLEY, MICK,
1015 Centre Crescent, Qualicum Beach, B.C., CANADA V9K 2G6, Phone: 250-752-4261
Specialties: Period pieces and working knives. Patterns: Bowies, push daggers, fighters, boots. Some folding lockers. **Technical:** Forges 5160, 1084, W2 and his own Damascus. **Prices:** $250 to $2500; some to $4500. **Remarks:** Full-time maker, first knife sold in 1977. **Mark:** Langley with M.S. (for ABS Master Smith)

LANKTON, SCOTT,
8065 Jackson Rd. R-11, Ann Arbor, MI 48103, Phone: 313-426-3735
Specialties: Pattern welded swords, krisses and Viking period pieces. **Patterns:** One-of-a-kind. **Technical:** Forges W2, L6 nickel and other steels. **Prices:** $600 to $12,000. **Remarks:** Part-time bladesmith, full-time smith; first knife sold in 1976. **Mark:** Last name logo.

LAOISLAV, SANTA-LASKY,
Tatranska 32 97401 Banska, Bystrica, SLOVAKIA, santa.ladislav@pobox.sk; Web: www.lasky.sk
Specialties: Damascus hunters, daggers and swords. **Patterns:** Carious Damascus patterns. **Prices:** $300 to 6000 U.S. **Mark:** L or Lasky.

LAPEN, CHARLES,
Box 529, W. Brookfield, MA 01585
Specialties: Chef's knives for the culinary artist. **Patterns:** Camp knives, Japanese-style swords and wood working tools, hunters. **Technical:** Forges 1075, car spring and his own Damascus. Favors narrow and Japanese tangs. **Prices:** $200 to $400; some to $2000. **Remarks:** Part-time maker; first knife sold in 1972. **Mark:** Last name.

LAPLANTE, BRETT,
4545 CR412, McKinney, TX 75071, Phone: 972-838-9191, blap007@aol.com
Specialties: Working straight knives and folders to customer specs. **Patterns:** Survival knives, Bowies, skinners, hunters. **Technical:** Grinds D2 and 440C. Heat-treats. **Prices:** $200 to $800. **Remarks:** Part-time maker; first knife sold in 1987. **Mark:** Last name in Canadian maple leaf logo.

LARAMIE, MARK,
301 McCain St., Raeford, NC 28376, Phone: 978-502-2726, mark@malknives.com; Web: www.malknives.com
Specialties: Traditional fancy & art knives. **Patterns:** Slips, back-lock L/ L, automatics, single and multi blades. **Technical:** Free hand ground blades of D2, 440, and Damascus. **Mark:** M.A.L. Knives w/fish logo.

LARGIN,
KELGIN KNIVES, 104 Knife Works Ln, Sevierville, TN 37876, Phone: 765-969-5012, kelginfinecutlery@hotmail.com; Web: wwwkelgin.com
Specialties: Retired from general knife making. Only take limited orders in meteroite Damascus or solid meterorite blades. **Patterns:** Any. **Technical:** Stock removal or forged. **Prices:** $500 & up. **Remarks:** Run the Kelgin Knife Makers Co-op at Smoky Mtn. Knife Works. **Mark:** K.C. Largin -Kelgin mark retired in 2004.

LARSON, RICHARD,
549 E Hawkeye Ave, Turlock, CA 95380, Phone: 209-668-1615, lebatardknives@aol.com
Specialties: Sound working knives, lightweight folders, practical tactical knives. **Patterns:** Hunters, trout and bird knives, fish fillet knives, Bowies, tactical sheath knives, one-and two-blade folders. **Technical:** Grinds ATS-34, A2, D2, CPM 3V and commercial. Damascus; forges and grinds 52100, O1 and 1095. Machines folder frames from aircraft aluminum. **Prices:** $40 to $650. **Remarks:** Full-time maker. First knife made in 1974. Offers knife repair, restoration and sharpening. All knives are serial numbered and registered in the name of original purchaser. **Mark:** Stamped last name or etched logo of last name, city, and state.

LARY, ED,
651 Rangeline Rd, Mosinee, WI 54476, Phone: 715-693-3940, laryblades@hotmail.com
Specialties: Upscale hunters and art knives with display presentations. **Patterns:** Hunters, period pieces. **Technical:** Grinds all steels, heat treats, fancy file work and engraving. **Prices:** Upscale. **Remarks:** Full-time maker since 1974. **Mark:** Hand engraved "Ed Lary" in script.

LAURENT, KERMIT,
1812 Acadia Dr, LaPlace, LA 70068, Phone: 504-652-5629
Specialties: Traditional and working straight knives and folders of his design. **Patterns:** Bowies, hunters, utilities and folders. **Technical:** Forges own Damascus, plus uses most tool steels and stainless. Specializes in altering cable patterns. Uses stabilized handle materials, especially select exotic woods. **Prices:** $100 to $2500; some to $50,000. **Remarks:** Full-time maker; first knife sold in 1982. Doing business as Kermit's Knife Works. Favorite material is meteorite Damascus. **Mark:** First name.

LAWRENCE, ALTON,
201 W Stillwell, De Queen, AR 71832, Phone: 870-642-7643, Fax: 870-642-4023, uncle21@riversidemachine.net; Web: riversidemachine.net
Specialties: Classic straight knives and folders to customer specs. **Patterns:** Bowies, hunters, folders and utility/camp knives. **Technical:** Forges 5160, 1095, 1084, Damascus and railroad spikes. **Prices:** Start at $100. **Remarks:** Part-time maker; first knife sold in 1988. **Mark:** Last name inside fish symbol.

LAY, L J,
602 Mimosa Dr, Burkburnett, TX 76354, Phone: 940-569-1329
Specialties: Working straight knives in standard patterns; some period pieces. Patterns: Drop-point hunters, Bowies and fighters. **Technical:** Grinds ATS-34 to mirror finish; likes Micarta handles. **Prices:** Moderate. **Remarks:** Full-time maker; first knife sold in 1985. **Mark:** Name or name with ram head and city or stamp L J Lay.

LAY, R J (BOB),
Box 1225, Logan Lake, B.C., CANADA V0K 1W0, Phone: 250-523-9923, Fax: SAME, rjlay@telus.net
Specialties: Traditional-styled, fancy straight knifes of his design. Specializing in hunters. **Patterns:** Bowies, fighters and hunters. **Technical:** Grinds 440C, ATS-34, S30V. Uses exotic handle and spacer material. File cut, prefers narrow tang. Sheaths available. **Price:** $200 to $500, some to $5000. **Remarks:** Full-time maker, first knife sold in 1976. Doing business as Lay's Custom Knives. **Mark:** Signature acid etched.

LEACH, MIKE J,
5377 W Grand Blanc Rd., Swartz Creek, MI 48473, Phone: 810-655-4850
Specialties: Fancy working knives. **Patterns:** Hunters, fighters, Bowies and heavy-duty knives; slip-joint folders and integral straight patterns. **Technical:** Grinds D2, 440C and 154CM; buys Damascus. **Prices:** Start at $300. **Remarks:** Full-time maker; first knife sold in 1952. **Mark:** First initial, last name.

LEAVITT JR., EARL F,
Pleasant Cove Rd Box 306, E. Boothbay, ME 04544, Phone: 207-633-3210
Specialties: 1500-1870 working straight knives and fighters; pole arms. **Patterns:** Historically significant knives, classic/modern custom designs. **Technical:** Flat-grinds O1; heat-treats. Filework available. **Prices:** $90 to $350; some to $1000. **Remarks:** Full-time maker; first knife sold in 1981. Doing business as Old Colony Manufactory. **Mark:** Initials in oval.

LEBATARD, PAUL M,
14700 Old River Rd, Vancleave, MS 39565, Phone: 228-826-4137, Fax: 228-826-2933, lebatardknives@aol.com
Specialties: Sound working hunting and fillet knives, lightweight folders, practical tactical knives. **Patterns:** Hunters, trout and bird knives, fish fillet knives, kitchen knives, Bowies, tactical sheath knives, lock back folders, one-and two-blade slip joint folders. **Remarks:** Full-time maker, first knife made in 1974. Offers knife repair, restoration and sharpening.

LEBER, HEINZ,
Box 446, Hudson's Hope, B.C., CANADA V0C 1V0, Phone: 250-783-5304
Specialties: Working straight knives of his design. **Patterns:** 20 models, from capers to Bowies. **Technical:** Hollow-grinds D2 and M2 steel; mirror-finishes and full tang only. Likes moose, elk, stone sheep for handles. **Prices:** $175 to $1000. **Remarks:** Full-time maker; first knife sold in 1975. **Mark:** Initials connected.

LECK, DAL,
Box 1054, Hayden, CO 81639, Phone: 970-276-3663
Specialties: Classic, traditional and working knives of his design and in standard patterns; period pieces. **Patterns:** Boots, daggers, fighters, hunters and push daggers. **Technical:** Forges O1 and 5160; makes his own Damascus. **Prices:** $175 to $700; some to $1500. **Remarks:** Part-time maker; first knife sold in 1990. Doing business as The Moonlight Smithy. **Mark:** Stamped: hammer and anvil with initials.

LEE, RANDY,
PO Box 1873, St. Johns, AZ 85936, Phone: 928-337-2594, Fax: 928-337-5002, info@randyleeknives.com; Web.www.randyleeknives.com
Specialties: Traditional working and using straight knives of his design. **Patterns:** Bowies, fighters, hunters, daggers and professional throwing knives. **Technical:** Grinds ATS-34, 440C and D2. Offers sheaths. **Prices:** $235 to $1500. **Remarks:** Part-time maker; first knife sold in 1979. **Mark:** Full name, city, state.

LEGGETT, PETE,
3995 Seeber Rd Canastota, New York 13032, Phone-315-697-2767, E-mail Skullmount2@yahoo.com
Specialties: Unique, hand-knapped by percussion or flake-over-grind blades. Functional artistic designs. **Patterns:** Hunter, skinner, dagger, tanto, fantasy or traditional point style knives. **Technical:** Blades of jasper, agate, flint or chert. Handles of antler (deer, moose or elk), bone, jaws (bear, deer coyote), stone, marble, wood, or combinations. Some knives include handmade sheaths. **Prices:** Material/design dependent. **Remarks:** Part time stone knife maker since 1999. Gives attention to detail, only the finest material used. **Mark:** Initials

LELAND, STEVE,
2300 Sir Francis Drake Blvd, Fairfax, CA 94930-1118, Phone: 415-457-0318, Fax: 415-457-0995, Web: www.stephenleland@comcast.net
Specialties: Traditional and working straight knives and folders of his design. **Patterns:** Hunters, fighters, Bowies, chefs. **Technical:** Grinds O1, ATS-34 and 440C. Does own heat treat. Makes nickel silver sheaths. **Prices:** $150 to $750; some to $1500. **Remarks:** Part-time maker; first knife sold in 1987. Doing business as Leland Handmade Knives. **Mark:** Last name.

LEMCKE, JIM L,
10649 Haddington Ste 180, Houston, TX 77043, Phone: 888-461-8632, Fax: 713-461-8221, jiml@hal-pc.org; Web: www.texasknife.com
Specialties: Large supply of custom ground and factory finished blades; knife kits; leather sheaths; in-house heat treating and cryogenic tempering; exotic handle material (wood, ivory, oosik, horn, stabilized woods); machines and supplies for knifemaking; polishing and finishing supplies; heat treat ovens; etching equipment; bar, sheet and rod material (brass, stainless steel, nickel silver); titanium sheet material. Catalog. $4.

LENNON, DALE,
459 County Rd 1554, Alba, TX 75410, Phone: 903-765-2392, devildaddy1@netzero.net
Specialties: Working/using knives. Patterns: Hunters, fighters and Bowies. **Technical:** Grinds high carbon steels, ATS-34, forges some. **Prices:** Starts at $120. **Remarks:** Part-time maker, first knife sold in 2000. **Mark:** Last name.

LEONARD, RANDY JOE,
188 Newton Rd, Sarepta, LA 71071, Phone: 318-994-2712

LEONE, NICK,
9 Georgetown, Pontoon Beach, IL 62040, Phone: 618-797-1179, nickleone@sbcglobal.net
Specialties: 18th century period straight knives. **Patterns:** Skinners, hunters, neck, leg and friction folders. **Technical:** Forges 5160, W2, O1, 1098, 52100 and his own Damascus. **Prices:** $100 to $1000; some to $3500. **Remarks:** Full-time maker; first knife sold in 1987. Doing business as Anvil Head Forge. **Mark:** Last name, NL, AHF.

LEPORE, MICHAEL J,
66 Woodcutters Dr, Bethany, CT 06524, Phone: 203-393-3823
Specialties: One-of-a-kind designs to customer specs; mostly handmade. **Patterns:** Fancy working straight knives and folders. **Technical:** Forges and grinds W2, W1 and O1; prefers natural handle materials. **Prices:** Start at $350. **Remarks:** Spare-time maker; first knife sold in 1984. **Mark:** Last name.

LERCH, MATTHEW,
N88 W23462 North Lisbon Rd, Sussex, WI 53089, Phone: 262-246-6362, Web: www.lerchcustomknives.com
Specialties: Folders and folders with special mechanisms. **Patterns:** Interframe and integral folders; lock backs, assisted openers, side locks, button locks and liner locks. **Technical:** Grinds ATS-34, 1095, 440 and Damascus. Offers filework and embellished bolsters. **Prices:** $900 and up. **Remarks:** Part-time maker; first knife sold in 1995. **Mark:** Last name.

LEVENGOOD, BILL,
15011 Otto Rd, Tampa, FL 33624, Phone: 813-961-5688, bill.levengood@verison.net
Specialties: Working straight knives and folders. **Patterns:** Hunters, Bowies, folders and collector pieces. **Technical:** Grinds ATS-34, 530V and Damascus. **Prices:** $175 to $1500. **Remarks:** Full time maker; first knife sold in 1983. **Mark:** Last name, city, state.

LEVIN, JACK,
7216 Bay Pkwy, Brooklyn, NY 11204, Phone: 718-232-8574
Specialties: Folders with mechanisms.

LEVINE, BOB,
101 Westwood Dr, Tullahoma, TN 37388, Phone: 931-454-9943, levineknives@msn.com
Specialties: Working left-and right-handed LinerLock® folders. **Patterns:** Hunters and folders. **Technical:** Grinds ATS-34, 440C, D2, O1 and some Damascus; hollow and some flat grinds. Uses sheep horn, fossil ivory, Micarta and exotic woods. Provides custom leather sheath with each fixed knife. **Prices:** $125 to $500; some higher. **Remarks:** Full-time maker; first knife sold in 1984. Voting member Knifemakers Guild, German Messermaker Guild. **Mark:** Name and logo.

LEWIS, BILL,
PO Box 63, Riverside, IA 52327, Phone: 319-629-5574, wildbill37@geticonnect.com
Specialties: Folders of all kinds including those made from one-piece of white tail antler with or without the crown. **Patterns:** Hunters, folding hunters, fillet, Bowies, push daggers, etc. **Prices:** $20 to $200. **Remarks:** Full-time maker; first knife sold in 1978. **Mark:** W.E.L.

LEWIS, MIKE,
21 Pleasant Hill Dr, DeBary, FL 32713, Phone: 386-753-0936, dragonsteel@prodigy.net
Specialties: Traditional straight knives. **Patterns:** Swords and daggers. **Technical:** Grinds 440C, ATS-34 and 5160. Frequently uses cast bronze and cast nickel guards and pommels. **Prices:** $100 to $750. **Remarks:** Part-time maker; first knife sold in 1988. **Mark:** Dragon Steel and serial number.

LEWIS, TOM R,
1613 Standpipe Rd, Carlsbad, NM 88220, Phone: 505-885-3616, lewisknives@carlsbadnm.com; Web: www.cavemen.net/ lewisknives/
Specialties: Traditional working straight knives. **Patterns:** Outdoor knives, hunting knives and Bowies. **Technical:** Grinds ATS-34 forges 5168 and O1. Makes wire, pattern welded and chainsaw Damascus. **Prices:** $130 to $1200. **Remarks:** Part-time maker; first knife sold in 1980. Doing business as TR Lewis Handmade Knives. **Mark:** Lewis family crest.

LICATA, STEVEN,
LICATA CUSTOM KNIVES, 844 Boonton Ave., Boonton, NJ 07005, Phone: 973-588-4909, steven.licata@att.net; Web: steven.licata.home.att.net
Specialties: Fantasy swords and knives. One-of-a-kind sculptures in steel. **Prices:** $200 to $25,000.

LIEBENBERG, ANDRE,
8 Hilma Rd, Bordeauxrandburg 2196, SOUTH AFRICA, Phone: 011-787-2303
Specialties: High-art straight knives of his design. Patterns: Daggers, fighters and swords. **Technical:** Grinds 440C and 12C27. **Prices:** $250 to $500; some $4000 and higher. Giraffe bone handles with semi-precious stones. **Remarks:** Spare-time maker; first knife sold in 1990. **Mark:** Initials.

LIEGEY, KENNETH R,
132 Carney Dr, Millwood, WV 25262, Phone: 304-273-9545
Specialties: Traditional working/using straight knives of his design and to customer specs. **Patterns:** Hunters, utility/camp knives, miniatures. **Technical:** Grinds 440C. **Prices:** $75 to $150; some to $300. **Remarks:** Spare-time maker; first knife sold in 1977. **Mark:** First and middle initials, last name.

LIGHTFOOT, GREG,
RR #2, Kitscoty, AB, CANADA T0B 2P0, Phone: 780-846-2812, Pitbull@lightfootknives.com; Web: www.lightfootknives.com
Specialties: Stainless steel and Damascus. **Patterns:** Boots, fighters and locking folders. **Technical:** Grinds BG-42, 440C, D2, CPM steels, Stellite 6K. Offers engraving. **Prices:** $500 to $2000. **Remarks:** Full-time maker; first knife sold in 1988. Doing business as Lightfoot Knives. **Mark:** Shark with Lightfoot Knives below.

LIKARICH, STEVE,
PO Box 961, Colfax, CA 95713, Phone: 530-346-8480
Specialties: Fancy working knives; art knives of his design. **Patterns:** Hunters, fighters and art knives of his design. **Technical:** Grinds ATS-34, 154CM and 440C; likes high polishes and filework. **Prices:** $200 to $2000; some higher. **Remarks:** Full-time maker; first knife sold in 1987. **Mark:** Name.

LINKLATER, STEVE,
8 Cossar Dr, Aurora, Ont., CANADA L4G 3N8, Phone: 905-727-8929, knifman@sympatico.ca
Specialties: Traditional working/using straight knives and folders of his design. **Patterns:** Fighters, hunters and locking folders. **Technical:** Grinds ATS-34, 440V and D2. **Prices:** $125 to $350; some to $600. **Remarks:** Part-time maker; first knife sold in 1987. Doing business as Links Knives. **Mark:** LINKS.

LISTER JR., WELDON E,
9140 Sailfish Dr, Boerne, TX 78006, Phone: 210-981-2210
Specialties: One-of-a-kind fancy and embellished folders. **Patterns:** Locking and slip-joint folders. **Technical:** Commercial Damascus and O1. All knives embellished. Engraves, inlays, carves and scrimshaws. **Prices:** Upscale. **Remarks:** Spare-time maker; first knife sold in 1991. **Mark:** Last name.

LITTLE, GARY M,
HC84 Box 10301, PO Box 156, Broadbent, OR 97414, Phone: 503-572-2656
Specialties: Fancy working knives. **Patterns:** Hunters, tantos, Bowies, axes and buckskinners; locking folders and interframes. **Technical:** Forges and grinds O1, L6, 1095; makes his own Damascus; bronze fittings. **Prices:** $85 to $300; some to $2500. **Remarks:** Full-time maker; first knife sold in 1979. Doing business as Conklin Meadows Forge. **Mark:** Name, city and state.

LITTLE, LARRY,
1A Cranberry Ln, Spencer, MA 01562, Phone: 508-885-2301
Specialties: Working straight knives of his design or to customer specs. Likes Scagel-style. **Patterns:** Hunters, fighters, Bowies, folders. **Technical:** Grinds and forges L6, O1, 5160, 1095, 1080. Prefers natural handle material especially antler. Uses nickel silver. Makes own heavy duty leather sheath. **Prices:** Start at $125. **Remarks:** Part-time maker. First knife sold in 1985. Offers knife repairs. **Mark:** Little on one side, LL brand on the other.

LIVELY, TIM AND MARIAN,
PO Box 1172, Marble Falls, TX 78654, Web: www.livelyknives.com
Specialties: Multi-cultural primitive knives of their design on speculation. **Patterns:** Old world designs. **Technical:** Hand forges using ancient techniques without electricity; hammer finish. **Prices:** High. **Remarks:** Full-time makers; first knife sold in 1974. Offers knifemaking DVD online. **Mark:** Last name.

LIVESAY, NEWT,
3306 S. Dogwood St, Siloam Springs, AR 72761, Phone: 479-549-3356, Fax: 479-549-3357, newt@newtlivesay.com; Web:www.newtlivesay.com
Specialties: Combat utility knives, hunting knives, titanium knives, swords, axes, KYDWX sheaths for knives and pistols, custom orders.

LIVINGSTON, ROBERT C,
PO Box 6, Murphy, NC 28906, Phone: 704-837-4155
Specialties: Art letter openers to working straight knives. **Patterns:** Minis to machetes. **Technical:** Forges and grinds most steels. **Prices:** Start at $20. **Remarks:** Full-time maker; first knife sold in 1988. Doing business as Mystik Knifeworks. **Mark:** MYSTIK.

LOCKETT, STERLING,
527 E Amherst Dr, Burbank, CA 91504, Phone: 818-846-5799
Specialties: Working straight knives and folders to customer specs. **Patterns:** Hunters and fighters. **Technical:** Grinds. **Prices:** Moderate. **Remarks:** Spare-time maker. **Mark:** Name, city with hearts.

LOERCHNER, WOLFGANG,
WOLFE FINE KNIVES, PO Box 255, Bayfield, Ont., CANADA N0M 1G0, Phone: 519-565-2196
Specialties: Traditional straight knives, mostly ornate. **Patterns:** Small swords, daggers and stilettos; locking folders and miniatures. **Technical:** Grinds D2, 440C and 154CM; all knives hand-filed and flat-ground. **Prices:** $300 to $5000; some to $10,000. **Remarks:** Part-time maker; first knife sold in 1983. Doing business as Wolfe Fine Knives. **Mark:** WOLFE.

LONEWOLF, J AGUIRRE,
481 Hwy 105, Demorest, GA 30535, Phone: 706-754-4660, Fax: 706-754-8470, Web: http://hemc.net/~lonewolf
Specialties: High-art working and using straight knives of his design. **Patterns:** Bowies, hunters, utility/camp knives and fine steel blades. **Technical:** Forges Damascus and high-carbon steel. Most knives have hand-carved moose antler handles. **Prices:** $55 to $500; some to $2000. **Remarks:** Full-time maker; first knife sold in 1980. Doing business as Lonewolf Trading Post. **Mark:** Stamp.

LONG, GLENN A,
10090 SW 186th Ave, Dunnellon, FL 34432, Phone: 352-489-4272
Specialties: Classic working and using straight knives of his design and to customer specs. **Patterns:** Hunters, Bowies, utility. **Technical:** Grinds 440C D2 and 440V. **Prices:** $85 to $300; some to $800. **Remarks:** Part-time maker; first knife sold in 1990. **Mark:** Last name inside diamond.

LONGWORTH, DAVE,
PO Box 222, Neville, OH 45156, Phone: 513-876-2372
Specialties: High-tech working knives. **Patterns:** Locking folders, hunters, fighters and elaborate daggers. **Technical:** Grinds O1, ATS-34, 440C; buys Damascus. **Prices:** $125 to $600; some higher. **Remarks:** Part-time maker; first knife sold in 1980. **Mark:** Last name.

LOOS, HENRY C,
210 Ingraham, New Hyde Park, NY 11040, Phone: 516-354-1943, hcloos@optonline.net
Specialties: Miniature fancy knives and period pieces of his design. **Patterns:** Bowies, daggers and swords. **Technical:** Grinds O1 and 440C. Uses sterling, 18K, rubies and emeralds. All knives come with handmade hardwood cases. **Prices:** $90 to $195; some to $250. **Remarks:** Spare-time maker; first knife sold in 1990. **Mark:** Script last initial.

LORO, GENE,
2457 State Route 93 NE, Crooksville, OH 43731, Phone: 740-982-4521, Fax: 740-982-1249, geney@aol.com
Specialties: Hand forged knives. **Patterns:** Damascus, Random, Ladder, Twist, etc. **Technical:** ABS Journeyman Smith. **Prices:** $200 and up. **Remarks:** Loro and hand forged by Gene Loro. **Mark:** Loro. Retired engineer.

LOTT, SHERRY,
1100 Legion Park Rd, Greensburg, KY 42743, Phone: 270-932-2212, sherrylott@alltel.net
Specialties: One-of-a-kind, usually carved handles. **Patterns:** Art. **Technical:** Carbon steel, stock removal. **Prices:** Moderate. **Mark:** Sherry Lott. **Remarks:** First knife sold in 1994.

LOVE, ED,
19443 Mill Oak, San Antonio, TX 78258, Phone: 210-497-1021, Fax: 210-497-1021, annaedlove@sbcglobal.net
Specialties: Hunting, working knives and some art pieces. **Technical:** Grinds ATS-34, and 440C. **Prices:** $150 and up. **Remarks:** Part-time maker. First knife sold in 1980. **Mark:** Name in a weeping heart.

LOVELESS, R W,
PO Box 7836, Riverside, CA 92503, Phone: 951-689-7800
Specialties: Working knives, fighters and hunters of his design. **Patterns:** Contemporary hunters, fighters and boots. **Technical:** Grinds 154CM and ATS-34. **Prices:** $850 to $4950. **Remarks:** Full-time maker since 1969. **Mark:** Name in logo.

LOVESTRAND, SCHUYLER,
1136 19th St SW, Vero Beach, FL 32962, Phone: 772-778-0282, Fax: 772-466-1126, lovestranded@aol.com
Specialties: Fancy working straight knives of his design and to customer specs; unusual fossil ivories. **Patterns:** Hunters, fighters, Bowies and fishing knives. **Technical:** Grinds stainless steel. **Prices:** $275 and up. **Remarks:** Part-time maker; first knife sold in 1982. **Mark:** Name in logo.

LOVETT, MICHAEL,
PO Box 691551, Killeen, TX 76549, Phone: 254-554-0956, michaellovett@earthlink.net; Web: wwwlovettknives.com
Specialties: Maker of the authorized Loveless Connection Knives. **Patterns:** Over 40 original R. W. Loveless patterns. **Technical:** ATS-34 ground to Loveless specs. **Prices:** $500 to several thousand. **Remarks:** R. W. Loveless -mentor; Jim Merritt -mentor; exact Loveless designs. These rendentions of the Loveless Knives are closest money can buy. The intent is for more people to be able to enjoy a true Loveless design.

LOZIER, DON,
5394 SE 168th Ave, Ocklawaha, FL 32179, Phone: 352-625-3576
Specialties: Fancy and working straight knives of his design and in standard patterns. Patterns: Daggers, fighters, boot knives, and hunters. **Technical:** Grinds ATS-34, 440C and Damascus. Most pieces are highly embellished by notable artisans. Taking limited number of orders per annum. **Prices:** Start at $250; most are $1250 to $3000; some to $12,000. **Remarks:** Full-time maker. **Mark:** Name.

LUCHAK, BOB,
15705 Woodforest Blvd, Channelview, TX 77530, Phone: 281-452-1779
Specialties: Presentation knives; start of The Survivor series. **Patterns:** Skinners, Bowies, camp axes, steak knife sets and fillet knives. **Technical:**

Grinds 440C. Offers electronic etching; filework. **Prices:** $50 to $1500. **Remarks:** Full-time maker; first knife sold in 1983. Doing business as Teddybear Knives. **Mark:** Full name, city and state with Teddybear logo.

LUCHINI, BOB,
1220 Dana Ave, Palo Alto, CA 94301, Phone: 650-321-8095, rwluchin@bechtel.com

LUCIE, JAMES R,
4191 E. Fruitport R, Fruitport, MI 49415, Phone: 231-865-6390, Fax: 231-865-3170, scagel@netonecom.net
Specialties: Hand-forges William Scagel-style knives. **Patterns:** Authentic scagel-style knives and miniatures. **Technical:** Forges 5160, 52100 and 1084 and forges his own pattern welded Damascus steel. **Prices:** Start at $750. **Remarks:** Full-time maker; first knife sold in 1975. Believes in sole authorship of his work. ABS Journeyman Smith. **Mark:** Scagel Kris with maker's name and address.

LUCKETT, BILL,
108 Amantes Ln, Weatherford, TX 76088, Phone: 817-594-9288, bill_luckett@hotmail.com
Specialties: Uniquely patterned robust straight knives. **Patterns:** Fighters, Bowies, hunters. **Technical:** 154CM stainless.**Prices:** $550 to $1500. **Remarks:** Part-time maker; first knife sold in 1975. **Mark:** Last name over Bowie logo.

LUDWIG, RICHARD O,
57-63 65 St, Maspeth, NY 11378, Phone: 718-497-5969
Specialties: Traditional working/using knives. **Patterns:** Boots, hunters and utility/camp knives folders. **Technical:** Grinds 440C, ATS-34 and BG42. File work on guards and handles; silver spacers. Offers scrimshaw. **Prices:** $325 to $400; some to $2000. **Remarks:** Full-time maker. **Mark:** Stamped first initial, last name, state.

LUI, RONALD M,
4042 Harding Ave, Honolulu, HI 96816, Phone: 808-734-7746
Specialties: Working straight knives and folders in standard patterns. **Patterns:** Hunters, boots and liner locks. **Technical:** Grinds 440C and ATS-34. **Prices:** $100 to $700. **Remarks:** Spare-time maker; first knife sold in 1988. **Mark:** Initials connected.

LUM, MITCH,
4616 25th Ave NE #563, Seattle, WA 98105, Phone: 206-356-6813, mitch@mitchlum.com; Web:www.mitchlum.com

LUM, ROBERT W,
901 Travis Ave, Eugene, OR 97404, Phone: 541-688-2737
Specialties: High-art working knives of his design. **Patterns:** Hunters, fighters, tantos and folders. **Technical:** Grinds 440C, 154CM and ATS-34; plans to forge soon. **Prices:** $175 to $500; some to $800. **Remarks:** Full-time maker; first knife sold in 1976. **Mark:** Chop with last name underneath.

LUMAN, JAMES R,
Clear Creek Trail, Anaconda, MT 59711, Phone: 406-560-1461
Specialties: San Mai and composite end patterns. **Patterns:** Pool and eye Spirograph southwest composite patterns. **Technical:** All patterns with blued steel; all made by him. **Prices:** $200 to $800. **Mark:** Stock blade removal. Pattern welded steel. Bottom ricasso JRL.

LUNDSTROM, JAN-AKE,
Mastmostigen 8, 66010 Dals-Langed, SWEDEN, Phone: 0531-40270
Specialties: Viking swords, axes and knives in cooperation with handle makers. **Patterns:** All traditional-styles, especially swords and inlaid blades. **Technical:** Forges his own Damascus and laminated steel. **Prices:** $200 to $1000. **Remarks:** Full-time maker; first knife sold in 1985; collaborates with museums. **Mark:** Runic.

LUNN, GAIL,
434 CR 1422, Mountain Home, AR 72653, Phone: 870-424-2662, gail@lunnknives.com; Web: www.lunnknives.com
Specialties: Fancy folders and double action autos, some straight blades. **Patterns:** One-of-a-kind, all types. **Technical:** Stock removal, hand made. **Prices:** $300 and up. **Remarks:** Fancy file work, exotic materials, inlays, stone etc. **Mark:** Name in script.

LUNN, LARRY A,
434 CR 1422, Mountain Home, AR 72653, Phone: 870-424-2662, larry@lunnknives.com; Web: www.lunnknives.com
Specialties: Fancy folders and double action autos; some straight blades. **Patterns:** All types; his own designs. **Technical:** Stock removal; commercial Damascus. **Prices:** $125 and up. **Remarks:** File work inlays and exotic materials. **Mark:** Name in script.

LUPOLE, JAMIE G,
KUMA KNIVES, 285 Main St., Kirkwood, NY 13795, Phone: 607-775-9368, jlupole@stny.rr.com
Specialties: Working and collector grade fixed blades, ethnic-styled blades. **Patterns:** Fighters, Bowies, tacticals, hunters, camp, utility, personal carry knives, some swords. **Technical:** Forges and grinds 10XX series and other high-carbon steels, grinds ATS-34 and 440C, will use just about every handle material available. **Prices:** $80 to $500 and up. **Remarks:** Part-time maker since 1999. **Marks:** "KUMA" hot stamped, name, city and state-etched, or "Daiguma saku" in kanji.

LUTZ, GREG,
127 Crescent Rd, Greenwood, SC 29646, Phone: 864-229-7340
Specialties: Working and using knives and period pieces of his design and to customer specs. **Patterns:** Fighters, hunters and swords. **Technical:** Forges 1095 and O1; grinds ATS-34. Differentially heat-treats forged blades; uses cryogenic treatment on ATS-34. **Prices:** $50 to $350; some to $1200. **Remarks:** Part-time maker; first knife sold in 1986. Doing business as Scorpion Forge. **Mark:** First initial, last name.

LYLE III, ERNEST L,
LYLE KNIVES, PO Box 1755, Chiefland, FL 32644, Phone: 352-490-6693, ernestlyle@msn.com
Specialties: Fancy period pieces; one-of-a-kind and limited editions. **Patterns:** Arabian/Persian influenced fighters, military knives, Bowies and Roman short swords; several styles of hunters. **Technical:** Grinds 440C, D2 and 154 CM. Engraves. **Prices:** Upscale. **Remarks:** Full-time maker; first knife sold in 1972. **Mark:** Last name in capital letters -LYLE over a much smaller Chief land.

LYNN, ARTHUR,
29 Camino San Cristobal, Galisteo, NM 87540, Phone: 505-466-3541, lynnknives@aol.com
Specialties: Handforged straight knives. **Patterns:** Hunters, Bowies, fighters, kitchen. **Technical:** Forges own Damascus. **Prices:** Moderate.

LYTTLE, BRIAN,
Box 5697, High River, AB, CANADA T1V 1M7, Phone: 403-558-3638, brian@lyttleknives.com; Web: www.lyttleknives.com
Specialties: Fancy working straight knives and folders; art knives. **Patterns:** Bowies, daggers, dirks, sgian dubhs, folders, dress knives, tantos, short swords. **Technical:** Forges Damascus steel; engraving; scrimshaw; heat-treating; classes. **Prices:** $450 to $15,000. **Remarks:** Full-time maker; first knife sold in 1983. **Mark:** Last name, country.

M

MACDONALD, DAVID,
2824 Hwy 47, Los Lunas, NM 87031, Phone: 505-866-5866

MACDONALD, JOHN,
9 David Dr, Raymond, NH 03077, Phone: 603-895-0918
Specialties: Working/using straight knives of his design and to customer specs. **Patterns:** Japanese cutlery, Bowies, hunters and working knives. **Technical:** Grinds O1, L6 and ATS-34. Swords have matching handles and scabbards with Japanese flair. **Prices:** $70 to $250; some to $500. **Remarks:** Part-time maker; first knife sold in 1988. Wood/glass-topped custom cases. Doing business as Mac the Knife. **Mark:** Initials.

MACKIE, JOHN,
13653 Lanning, Whittier, CA 90605, Phone: 562-945-6104
Specialties: Forged. **Patterns:** Bowie and camp knives. **Technical:** Attended ABS Bladesmith School. **Prices:** $75 to $500. **Mark:** JSM in a triangle.

MACKRILL, STEPHEN,
PO Box 1580, Pinegowrie 2123, Johannesburg, SOUTH AFRICA, Phone: 27-11-886-2893, Fax: 27-11-334-6230, info@mackrill.co.za; Web: www.mackrill.net
Specialties: Art fancy, historical, collectors and corporate gifts cutlery. **Patterns:** Fighters, hunters, camp, custom lock back and LinerLock® folders. **Technical:** N690, 12C27, ATS-34, silver and gold inlay on handles; wooden and silver sheaths. **Prices:** $330 and upwards. **Remarks:** First knife sold in 1978. **Mark:** Oval with first initial, last name, "Maker" country of origin.

MADRULLI, MME JOELLE,
Residence Ste Catherine B1, Salon De Provence, FRANCE 13330

MAE, TAKAO,
1-119 1-4 Uenohigashi, Toyonaka, Osaka, JAPAN 560-0013, Phone: 81-6-6852-2758, Fax: 81-6-6481-1649, takamae@nifty.com
Remarks: Distinction stylish in art-forged blades, with lacquered ergonomic handles.

MAESTRI, PETER A,
S11251 Fairview Rd, Spring Green, WI 53588, Phone: 608-546-4481
Specialties: Working straight knives in standard patterns. **Patterns:** Camp and fishing knives, utility green-river-styled. **Technical:** Grinds 440C, 154CM and 440A. **Prices:** $15 to $45; some to $150. **Remarks:** Full-time maker; first knife sold in 1981. Provides professional cutler service to professional cutters. **Mark:** CARISOLO, MAESTRI BROS., or signature.

MAGEE, JIM,
748 S Front #3, Salina, KS 67401, Phone: 785-820-6928, jimmagee@cox.net
Specialties: Working and fancy folding knives. **Patterns:** Liner locking folders, favorite is his Persian. **Technical:** Grinds ATS-34, Devin Thomas & Eggerling Damascus, titanium. Liners Prefer mother-of-pearl handles. **Prices:** Start at $225 to $1200. **Remarks:** Part-time maker, first knife sold in 2001. Purveyor since 1982. Past president of the Professional

Knifemakers Association **Mark:** Last name.

MAGRUDER, JASON,
10W Saint Elmo Ave, Colorado Springs, CO 80906, Phone: 719-210-1579, belstain@hotmail.com
Specialties: Fancy/embellished and working/using knives of his own design or to customer specs. Fancy filework and carving. **Patterns:** Tactical straight knives, hunters, Bowies and lockback folders. **Technical:** Flats grinds S30V, CPM3V, and 1080. Forges own Damascus. **Prices:** $150 and up. **Remarks:** Part-time maker; first knife sold in 2000. **Mark:** Magruder, or initials J M.

MAHOMEDY, A R,
PO Box 76280, Marble Ray KZN, 4035, SOUTH AFRICA, Phone: +27 31 577 1451, arm-koknives@mweb.co.za; Web: www.arm-koknives.co.za
Specialties: Daggers, elegant folders, hunters & utilities. Prefers to work to commissions, collections & presentations. With handles of mother-of-pearl, fossil & local ivories. Exotic dyed/stablized burls, giraffe bone and horns. **Technical:** Via stock removal grinds Damasteel, carbon and mosaic Damascus, ATS-34, N690, 440A, 440B, 12 C 27 and RWL 34. **Prices:** $500 and up. **Remarks:** Part-time maker. First knife sold in 1995. Member knifemakers guild of SA. **Mark:** Logo of initials A R M crowned with a "Minaret."

MAIENKNECHT, STANLEY,
38648 S R 800, Sardis, OH 43946

MAINES, JAY,
SUNRISE RIVER CUSTOM KNIVES, 5584 266th St., Wyoming, MN 55092, Phone: 651-462-5301, jaymaines@fronternet.net; Web: http://www.sunrisecustomknives.com
Specialties: Heavy duty working, classic and traditional fixed blades. Some high-tech and fancy embellished knives available. **Patterns:** Hunters, skinners, fillet, bowies tantos, boot daggers etc. etc. **Technical:** Hollow ground, stock removal blades of 440C, ATS-34 and CPM S-90V. Prefers natural handle materials, exotic hard woods, and stag, rams and buffalo horns. Offers dovetailed bolsters in brass, stainless steel and nickel silver. Custom sheaths from matching wood or hand-stitched from heavy duty water buffalo hide. **Prices:** Moderate to up-scale. **Remarks:** Part-time maker; first knife sold in 1992. Doing business as Sunrise River Custom Knives. Offers fixed blade knives repair and handle conversions. **Mark:** Full name under a Rising Sun logo.

MAISEY, ALAN,
PO Box 197, Vincentia 2540, NSW, AUSTRALIA, Phone: 2-4443 7829, tosanaji@excite.com
Specialties: Daggers, especially krisses; period pieces. **Technical:** Offers knives and finished blades in Damascus and nickel Damascus. **Prices:** $75 to $2000; some higher. **Remarks:** Part-time maker; provides complete restoration service for krisses. Trained by a Japanese Kris smith. **Mark:** None, triangle in a box, or three peaks.

MAJER, MIKE,
50 Palmetto Bay Rd, Hilton Head, SC 29928, Phone: 843-681-3483

MAKOTO, KUNITOMO,
3-3-18 Imazu-cho, Fukuyama-city, Hiroshima, JAPAN, Phone: 084-933-5874, kunitomo@po.iijnet.or.jp

MALABY, RAYMOND J,
835 Calhoun Ave, Juneau, AK 99801, Phone: 907-586-6981, Fax: 907-523-8031, malaby@gci.net
Specialties: Straight working knives. **Patterns:** Hunters, skiners, Bowies, and camp knives. **Technical:** Hand forged 1084, 5160, O1 and grinds ATS-34 stainless. **Prices:** $195 to $400. **Remarks:** First knife sold in 1994. **Mark:** First initial, last name, city, and state.

MALLOY, JOE,
1039 Schwabe St, Freeland, PA 18224, Phone: 570-636-2781, jdmalloy@msn.com
Specialties: Working straight knives and lock back folders—plain and fancy—of his design. **Patterns:** Hunters, utility, Bowie, survival knives, folders. **Technical:** Grinds ATS-34, 440C, D2 and A2 and Damascus. Makes own leather and kydex sheaths. **Prices:** $100 to $1800. **Remarks:** Part-time maker; first knife sold in 1982. **Mark:** First and middle initials, last name, city and state.

MANEKER, KENNETH,
RR 2, Galiano Island, B.C., CANADA V0N 1P0, Phone: 604-539-2084
Specialties: Working straight knives; period pieces. **Patterns:** Camp knives and hunters; French chef knives. **Technical:** Grinds 440C, 154CM and Vascowear. **Prices:** $50 to $200; some to $300. **Remarks:** Part-time maker; first knife sold in 1981. Doing business as Water Mountain Knives. **Mark:** Japanese Kanji of initials, plus glyph.

MANKEL, KENNETH,
7836 Cannonsburg Rd, PO Box 35, Cannonsburg, MI 49317, Phone: 616-874-6955, Fax: 616-8744-4053

MANLEY, DAVID W,
3270 Six Mile Hwy, Central, SC 29630, Phone: 864-654-1125, dmanleyknives@wmconnect.com
Specialties: Working straight knives of his design or to custom specs. **Patterns:** Hunters, boot and fighters. **Technical:** Grinds 440C and ATS-34. **Prices:** $60 to $250. **Remarks:** Part-time maker; first knife sold in 1994. **Mark:** First initial, last name, year and serial number.

MANN, MICHAEL L,
IDAHO KNIFE WORKS, PO Box 144, Spirit Lake, ID 83869, Phone: 509 994-9394, Web: www.idahoknifeworks.com
Specialties: Good working blades-historical reproduction, modern or custom design. **Patterns:** Cowboy Bowies, Mountain Man period blades, old-style folders, designer and maker of "The Cliff Knife", hunter knives, hand ax and fish fillet. **Technical:** High-carbon steel blades-hand forged 5160. Stock removed 15N20 steel. Also Damascus. **Prices:** $130 to $670+. **Remarks:** Made first knife in 1965. Full-time making knives as Idaho Knife Works since 1986. Functional as well as collectible. Each knife truly unique! **Mark:** Four mountain peaks are his initials MM.

MANN, TIM,
BLADEWORKS, PO Box 1196, Honokaa, HI 96727, Phone: 808-775-0949, Fax: 808-775-0949, birdman@shaka.com
Specialties: Hand-forged knives and swords. **Patterns:** Bowies, tantos, pesh kabz, daggers. **Technical:** Use 5160, 1050, 1075, 1095 and ATS-34 steels, cable Damascus. **Prices:** $200 to $800. **Remarks:** Just learning to forge Damascus. **Mark:** None yet.

MARAGNI, DAN,
RD 1 Box 106, Georgetown, NY 13072, Phone: 315-662-7490
Specialties: Heavy-duty working knives, some investor class. **Patterns:** Hunters, fighters and camp knives, some Scottish types. **Technical:** Forges W2 and his own Damascus; toughness and edge-holding a high priority. **Prices:** $125 to $500; some to $1000. **Remarks:** Full-time maker; first knife sold in 1975. **Mark:** Celtic initials in circle.

MARKLEY, KEN,
7651 Cabin Creek Lane, Sparta, IL 62286, Phone: 618-443-5284
Specialties: Traditional working and using knives of his design and to customer specs. **Patterns:** Fighters, hunters and utility/camp knives. **Technical:** Forges 5160, 1095 and L6; makes his own Damascus; does file work. **Prices:** $150 to $800; some to $2000. **Remarks:** Part-time maker; first knife sold in 1991. Doing business as Cabin Creek Forge. **Mark:** Last name, JS.

MARLOWE, CHARLES,
10822 Poppleton Ave, Omaha, NE 68144, Phone: 402-933-5065, cmarlowe1@cox.net; Web: www.marloweknives.com
Specialties: Folding knives and balisong. **Patterns:** Tactical pattern folders. **Technical:** Grind ATS-34, S30V, others on request. Forges/grinds 1095 on occasion. **Prices:** Start at $350. **Remarks:** First knife sold in 1993. Full-time since 1999. **Mark:** MARLOWE.

MARLOWE, DONALD,
2554 Oakland Rd, Dover, PA 17315, Phone: 717-764-6055
Specialties: Working straight knives in standard patterns. **Patterns:** Bowies, fighters, boots and utility knives. **Technical:** Grinds D2 and 440C. Integral design hunter models. **Prices:** $130 to $850. **Remarks:** Spare-time maker; first knife sold in 1977. **Mark:** Last name.

MARSHALL, GLENN,
PO Box 1099, 1117 Hofmann St., Mason, TX 76856, Phone: 325-347-6207
Specialties: Working knives and period pieces. **Patterns:** Straight and folding hunters, fighters and camp knives. **Technical:** Steel used 440C, D2, CPM and 440V. **Prices:** $200 and up according to options. **Remarks:** Full-time maker; first knife sold in 1930. Sold #1 in 1932. **Mark:** First initial, last name, city and state with anvil logo.

MARSHALL, STEPHEN R,
975 Harkreader Rd, Mt. Juliet, TN 37122

MARTIN, BRUCE E,
Rt. 6, Box 164-B, Prescott, AR 71857, Phone: 501-887-2023
Specialties: Fancy working straight knives of his design. **Patterns:** Bowies, camp knives, skinners and fighters. **Technical:** Forges 5160, 1095 and his own Damascus. Uses natural handle materials; filework available. **Prices:** $75 to $350; some to $500. **Remarks:** Full-time maker; first knife sold in 1979. **Mark:** Name in arch.

MARTIN, GENE,
PO Box 396, Williams, OR 97544, Phone: 541-846-6755, bladesmith@customknife.com
Specialties: Straight knives and folders. **Patterns:** Fighters, hunters, skinners, boot knives, spring back and lock back folders. **Technical:** Grinds ATS-34, 440C, Damascus and 154CM. Forges; makes own Damascus; scrimshaws. **Prices:** $150 to $2500. **Remarks:** Full-time maker; first knife sold in 1993. Doing business as Provision Forge. **Mark:** Name and/or crossed staff and sword.

MARTIN, HAL W,
781 Hwy 95, Morrilton, AR 72110, Phone: 501-354-1682, hal.martin@sbcglobal.net
Specialties: Hunters, Bowies and fighters. **Prices:** $250 and up. **Mark:** MARTIN.

MARTIN, HERB,
2500 Starwood Dr, Richmond, VA 23229, Phone: 804-747-1675, hamjlm@earthlink.net
Specialties: Working straight knives. **Patterns:** Skinners, hunters and

utility. **Technical:** Hollow grinds ATS-34, and Micarta handles. **Prices:** $85 to $125. **Remarks:** Part-time Maker. First knife sold in 2001. **Mark:** HA MARTIN.

MARTIN, MICHAEL W,
Box 572, Jefferson St, Beckville, TX 75631, Phone: 903-678-2161
Specialties: Classic working/using straight knives of his design and in standard patterns. **Patterns:** Hunters. **Technical:** Grinds ATS-34, 440C, O1 and A2. Bead blasted, Parkerized, high polish and satin finishes. Sheaths are handmade. Also hand forges cable Damascus. **Prices:** $185 to $280 some higher. **Remarks:** Part-time maker; first knife sold in 1995. Doing business as Michael W. Martin Knives. **Mark:** Name and city, state in arch.

MARTIN, PETER,
28220 N. Lake Dr, Waterford, WI 53185, Phone: 262-706-3076, Web: www.petermartinknives.com
Specialties: Fancy, fantasy and working straight knives and folders of his design and in standard patterns. **Patterns:** Bowies, fighters, hunters, locking folders and liner locks. **Technical:** Forges own Mosaic Damascus, powdered steel and his own Damascus. Prefers natural handle material; offers file work and carved handles. **Prices:** Moderate. **Remarks:** Full-time maker; first knife sold in 1988. Doing business as Martin Custom Products. Uses only natural handle materials. **Mark:** Martin Knives.

MARTIN, RANDALL J,
51 Bramblewood St, Bridgewater, MA 02324, Phone: 508-279-0682
Specialties: High tech folding and fixed blade tactical knives employing the latest blade steels and exotic materials. Employs a unique combination of 3d-CNC machining and hand work on both blades and handles. All knives are designed for hard use. Clean, radical grinds and ergonomic handles are hallmarks of RJ's work, as is his reputation for producing "Scary Sharp" knives. **Technical:** Grinds CPM30V, CPM 3V, CPM154CM, A2 and stainless Damascus. Other CPM alloys used on request. Performs all heat treating and cryogenic processing in-house. **Remarks:** Full-time maker since 2001 and materials engineer. Former helicopter designer. First knife sold in 1976.

MARTIN, TONY,
108 S. Main St., PO Box 324, Arcadia, MO 63621, Phone: 573-546-2254, arcadian@charter.net; Web: www.arcadianforge.com
Specialties: Specializes in historical designs, esp. puukko, skean dhu. **Remarks:** Premium quality blades, exotic wood handles, unmatched fit and finish. **Mark:** AF.

MARTIN, WALTER E,
570 Cedar Flat Rd, Williams, OR 97544, Phone: 541-846-6755

MARZITELLI, PETER,
19929 35A Ave, Langley, B.C., CANADA V3A 2R1, Phone: 604-532-8899, marzitelli@shaw.ca
Specialties: Specializes in unique functional knife shapes and designs using natural and synthetic handle materials. **Patterns:** Mostly folders, some daggers and art knives. **Technical:** Grinds ATS-34, S/S Damascus and others. **Prices:** $220 to $1000 (average $375). **Remarks:** Full-time maker; first knife sold in 1984. **Mark:** Stylized logo reads "Marz."

MASON, BILL,
1114 St Louis #33, Excelsior Springs, MO 64024, Phone: 816-637-7335
Specialties: Combat knives; some folders. **Patterns:** Fighters to match knife types in book *Cold Steel.* **Technical:** Grinds O1, 440C and ATS-34. **Prices:** $115 to $250; some to $350. **Remarks:** Spare-time maker; first knife sold in 1979. **Mark:** Initials connected.

MASSEY, AL,
Box 14 Site 15 RR#2, Mount Uniacke, Nova Scotia, CANADA B0N 1Z0, Phone: 902-866-4754, armjan@attcanada.ca
Specialties: Working knives and period pieces. **Patterns:** Swords and daggers of Celtic to medieval design, Bowies. **Technical:** Forges 5160, 1084 and 1095. Makes own Damascus. **Prices:** $100 to $400, some to $900. **Remarks:** Part-time maker, first blade sold in 1988. **Mark:** Initials and JS on Ricasso.

MASSEY, ROGER,
4928 Union Rd, Texarkana, AR 71854, Phone: 870-779-1018
Specialties: Traditional and working straight knives and folders of his design and to customer specs. **Patterns:** Bowies, hunters, daggers and utility knives. **Technical:** Forges 1084 and 52100, makes his own Damascus. Offers filework and silver wire inlay in handles. **Prices:** $200 to $1500; some to $2500. **Remarks:** Part-time maker; first knife sold in 1991. **Mark:** Last name, M.S.

MASSEY, RON,
61638 El Reposo St., Joshua Tree, CA 92252, Phone: 760-366-9239 after 5 p.m., Fax: 763-366-4620
Specialties: Classic, traditional, fancy/embellished, high art, period pieces, working/using knives, straight knives, folders, and automatics. Your design, customer specs, about 175 standard patterns. **Patterns:** Automatics, hunters and fighters. All folders are side-locking folders. Unless requested as lock books slip joint he specializes or custom designs. **Technical:** ATS-34, 440C, D-2 upon request. Engraving, filework, scrimshaw, most of the exotic handle materials. All aspects are performed by him: inlay work in pearls or stone, handmade Pem' work. **Prices:** $110 to $2500; some to $6000. **Remarks:** Part-time maker; first knife sold in 1976.

MATA, LEONARD,
3583 Arruza St, San Diego, CA 92154, Phone: 619-690-6935

MATHEWS, CHARLIE AND HARRY,
TWIN BLADES, 121 Mt Pisgah Church Rd., Statesboro, GA 30458, Phone: 912-865-9098, twinblades@bulloch.net; Web: www.twinxblades.com
Specialties: Working straight knives. **Patterns:** Hunters, fighters, Bowies and period pieces. **Technical:** Grinds D2, BG42, CPMS30V, CPM3V, ATS-34 and commercial Damascus; handmade sheaths some with exotic leather, file work. **Prices:** Starting at $125. **Remarks:** Twin brothers making knives full-time under the label of Twin Blades. Charter members Georgia Custom Knifemakers Guild. **Mark:** Twin Blades over crossed knives, reverse side steel type.

MATSUNO, KANSEI,
109-8 Uenomachi Nishikaiden, Gifu-City 501-1168, JAPAN, Phone: 81 58 234 8643

MATSUOKA, SCOT,
94-415 Ukalialii Place, Mililani, HI 96789, Phone: 808-625-6658, Fax: 808-625-6658, scottym@hawaii.rr.com; Web: www.matsuokaknives.com
Specialties: Folders, fixed blades with custom hand-stitched sheaths. **Patterns:** Gentleman's knives, hunters, tactical folders. **Technical:** CPM 154CM, 440C, 154, BG42, bolsters, file work, and engraving. **Prices:** Starting price $350. **Remarks:** Part-time maker, first knife sold in 2002. **Mark:** Logo, name and state.

MATSUSAKI, TAKESHI,
MATSUSAKI KNIVES, 151 Ono-Cho Sasebo-shi, Nagasaki, JAPAN, Phone: 0956-47-2938, Fax: 0956-47-2938
Specialties: Working and collector grade front look and slip joint. **Patterns:** Sheffierd type folders. **Technical:** Grinds ATS-34 k-120. **Price:** $250 to $1000, some to $8000. **Remarks:** Part-time maker, first knife sold in 1990. **Mark:** Name and initials.

MAXEN, MICK,
2 Huggins Welham Green, "Hatfield, Herts", UNITED KINGDOM AL97LR, Phone: 01707 261213, mmaxen@aol.com
Specialties: Damascus and Mosaic. **Patterns:** Medieval-style daggers and Bowies. **Technical:** Forges CS75 and 15N20 / nickel Damascus. **Mark:** Last name with axe above.

MAXFIELD, LYNN,
382 Colonial Ave, Layton, UT 84041, Phone: 801-544-4176, maxfieldknives@q.com
Specialties: Sporting knives, some fancy. **Patterns:** Hunters, fishing, fillet, special purpose: some locking folders. **Technical:** Grinds 440-C, 154-CM, ATS-34, D2, CPM S30V, T and Damascus. **Prices:** $125 to $400; some to $900. **Remarks:** Part-time maker; first knife sold in 1979. **Mark:** Name, city and state.

MAXWELL, DON,
1484 Celeste Ave, Clovis, CA 93611, Phone: 559-299-2197, maxwellknives@aol.com; Web: maxwellknives.com
Specialties: Fancy folding knives and fixed blades of his design. **Patterns:** Hunters, fighters, utility/camp knives, LinerLock® folders, flippers and fantasy knives. **Technical:** Grinds 440C, ATS-34, D2, CPM 154, and commercial Damascus. **Prices:** $250 to $1000; some to $2500. **Remarks:** Full-time maker; first knife sold in 1987. **Mark:** Last name only.

MAYNARD, LARRY JOE,
PO Box 493, Crab Orchard, WV 25827
Specialties: Fancy and fantasy straight knives. **Patterns:** Big knives; a Bowie with a full false edge; fighting knives. **Technical:** Grinds standard steels. **Prices:** $350 to $500; some to $1000. **Remarks:** Full-time maker; first knife sold in 1986. **Mark:** Middle and last initials.

MAYNARD, WILLIAM N.,
2677 John Smith Rd, Fayetteville, NC 28306, Phone: 910-425-1615
Specialties: Traditional and working straight knives of all designs. **Patterns:** Combat, Bowies, fighters, hunters and utility knives. **Technical:** Grinds 440C, ATS-34 and commercial Damascus. Offers fancy filework; handmade sheaths. **Prices:** $100 to $300; some to $750. **Remarks:** Full-time maker; first knife sold in 1988. **Mark:** Last name.

MAYO, ALTON, Jr.,
18036 Three Rivers Rd., Biloxi, MS 39532, Phone: 228-326-8298
Specialties: Traditional working straight knives, folders and tactical. Patterns: Hunters, fighters, tactical, bird, Bowies, fish fillet knives and lightweight folders. **Technical:** Grinds 440C, ATS-34, D-2, Damascus, forges and grinds 52100 and custom makes sheaths. **Prices:** $100 to $1000. **Remarks:** Part-time maker **Mark:** All knives are serial number and registered in the name of the original purchaser, stamped last name or etched.

MAYO JR., TOM,
67 412 Alahaka St, Waialua, HI 96791, Phone: 808-637-6560, mayot001@hawaii.rr.com; Web: www.mayoknives.com
Specialties: Framelocks/tactical knives. **Patterns:** Combat knives,

hunters, Bowies and folders. **Technical:** Titanium/stellite/S30V. **Prices:** $500 to $1000. **Remarks:** Full-time maker; first knife sold in 1982. **Mark:** Volcano logo with name and state.

MAYVILLE, OSCAR L,
2130 E. County Rd 910S, Marengo, IN 47140, Phone: 812-338-4159
Specialties: Working straight knives; period pieces. **Patterns:** Kitchen cutlery, Bowies, camp knives and hunters. **Technical:** Grinds A2, O1 and 440C. **Prices:** $50 to $350; some to $500. **Remarks:** Full-time maker; first knife sold in 1984. **Mark:** Initials over knife logo.

MCABEE, WILLIAM,
27275 Norton Grade, Colfax, CA 95713, Phone: 530-389-8163
Specialties: Working/using knives. **Patterns:** Fighters, Bowies, Hunters. **Technical:** Grinds ATS-34. **Prices:** $75 to $200; some to $350. **Remarks:** Part-time maker; first knife sold in 1990. **Mark:** Stylized WM stamped.

MCCALLEN JR., HOWARD H,
110 Anchor Dr, So Seaside Park, NJ 08752

MCCARLEY, JOHN,
4165 Harney Rd, Taneytown, MD 21787
Specialties: Working straight knives; period pieces. **Patterns:** Hunters, Bowies, camp knives, miniatures, throwing knives. **Technical:** Forges W2, O1 and his own Damascus. **Prices:** $150 to $300; some to $1000. **Remarks:** Part-time maker; first knife sold in 1977. **Mark:** Initials in script.

MCCARTY, HARRY,
1479 Indian Ridge Rd, Blaine, TN 37709
Specialties: Period pieces. **Patterns:** Trade knives, Bowies, 18th and 19th century folders and hunting swords. **Technical:** Forges and grinds high-carbon steel. **Prices:** $75 to $1300. **Remarks:** Full-time maker; first knife sold in 1977. Doing business as Indian Ridge Forge.**Mark:** Stylized initials inside a shamrock.

MCCLURE, JERRY,
3052 Isim Rd, Norman, OK 73026, Phone: 405-321-3614, jerry@mcclure.net; Web: www.jmcclureknives.net
Specialties: Gentleman's folder, linerlock with my jeweled pivot system of 10 rubies, forged one-of-a kind Damascus Bowies, and a line of hunting/camp knives. **Patterns:** Folders, Bowie, and hunting/camp **Technical** Forges own Damascus, also uses Damasteel and does own heat treating. **Prices** $500 to $3,000 and up **Remarks** Full-time maker, made first knife in 1965. **Mark** J.MCCLURE

MCCLURE, MICHAEL,
803 17th Ave, Menlo Park, CA 94025, Phone: 650-323-2596, mikesknives@comcast.net
Specialties: Working/using straight knives of his design and to customer specs. **Patterns:** Bowies, hunters, skinners, utility/camp, tantos, fillets and boot knives. **Technical:** Forges high-carbon and Damascus; also grinds stainless, all grades. **Prices:** Start at $200. **Remarks:** Part-time maker; first knife sold in 1991. ABS Journeyman Smith. **Mark:** Mike McClure.

MCCONNELL, CHARLES R,
158 Genteel Ridge, Wellsburg, WV 26070, Phone: 304-737-2015
Specialties: Working straight knives. **Patterns:** Hunters, Bowies, daggers, minis and push knives. **Technical:** Grinds 440C and 154CM; likes full tangs. **Prices:** $65 to $325; some to $800. **Remarks:** Part-time maker; first knife sold in 1977. **Mark:** Name.

MCCONNELL JR., LOYD A,
1710 Rosewood, Odessa, TX 79761, Phone: 915-363-8344, ccknives@ccknives.com; Web: www.ccknives.com
Specialties: Working straight knives and folders, some fancy. **Patterns:** Hunters, boots, Bowies, locking folders and slip-joints. **Technical:** Grinds CPM Steels, ATS-34 and BG-42 and commercial Damascus. **Prices:** $175 to $900; some to $10,000. **Remarks:** Full-time maker; first knife sold in 1975. Doing business as Cactus Custom Knives. Markets product knives under name: Lone Star Knives. **Mark:** Name, city and state in cactus logo.

MCCORNOCK, CRAIG,
MCC MTN OUTFITTERS, 4775 Rt. 212/PO 162, Willow, NY 12495, Phone: 845-679-9758, Mccmtn@aol.com; Web: www.mccmtn.com
Specialties: Carry, utility, hunters, defense type knives and functional swords. **Patterns:** Drop points, hawkbills, tantos, waklzashis, katanas **Technical:** Stock removal, forged and Damascus, (yes, he still flints knap). **Prices:** $200 to $2000. **Mark:** McM.

MCCOUN, MARK,
14212 Pine Dr, DeWitt, VA 23840, Phone: 804-469-7631, markmccoun@aol.com
Specialties: Working/using straight knives of his design and in standard patterns; custom miniatures. **Patterns:** Locking liners, integrals. **Technical:** Grinds Damascus, ATS-34 and 440C. **Prices:** $150 to $500. **Remarks:** Part-time maker; first knife sold in 1989. **Mark:** Name, city and state.

MCCRACKIN, KEVIN,
3720 Hess Rd, House Spings, MO 63051, Phone: 636-677-6066

MCCRACKIN AND SON, V J,
3720 Hess Rd, House Springs, MO 63051, Phone: 636-677-6066
Specialties: Working straight knives in standard patterns. **Patterns:** Hunters, Bowies and camp knives. **Technical:** Forges L6, 5160, his own Damascus, cable Damascus. **Prices:** $125 to $700; some to $1500. **Remarks:** Part-time maker; first knife sold in 1983. Son Kevin helps make the knives. **Mark:** Last name, M.S.

MCCULLOUGH, JERRY,
274 West Pettibone Rd, Georgiana, AL 36033, Phone: 334-382-7644, ke4er@alaweb.com
Specialties: Standard patterns or custom designs. **Technical:** Forge and grind scrap-tool and Damascus steels. Use natural handle materials and turquoise trim on some. Filework on others. **Prices:** $65 to $250 and up. **Remarks:** Part-time maker. **Mark:** Initials (JM) combined.

MCDONALD, RICH,
4590 Kirk Rd, Columbiana, OH 44408, Phone: 330-482-0007, Fax: 330-482-0007
Specialties: Traditional working/using and art knives of his design. **Patterns:** Bowies, hunters, folders, primitives and tomahawks. **Technical:** Forges 5160, 1084, 1095, 52100 and his own Damascus. Fancy filework. **Prices:** $200 to $1500. **Remarks:** Full-time maker; first knife sold in 1994. **Mark:** First and last initials connected.

MCDONALD, ROBERT J,
14730 61 Court N, Loxahatchee, FL 33470, Phone: 561-790-1470
Specialties: Traditional working straight knives to customer specs. **Patterns:** Fighters, swords and folders. **Technical:** Grinds 440C, ATS-34 and forges own Damascus. **Prices:** $150 to $1000. **Remarks:** Part-time maker; first knife sold in 1988. **Mark:** Electro-etched name.

MCDONALD, ROBIN J,
7300 Tolleson Ave NW, Albuquerque, NM 87114-3546
Specialties: Working knives of maker's design. **Patterns:** Bowies, hunters, camp knives and fighters. **Technical:** Forges primarily 5160. **Prices:** $100 to $500. **Remarks:** Part-time maker; first knife sold in 1999. **Mark:** Initials RJM.

MCDONALD, W J "JERRY",
7173 Wickshire Cove E, Germantown, TN 38138, Phone: 901-756-9924, wjmcdonaldknives@email.msn.com; Web: www.mcdonaldknives.com
Specialties: Classic and working/using straight knives of his design and in standard patterns. **Patterns:** Bowies, hunters kitchen and traditional spring back pocket knives. **Technical:** Grinds ATS-34, 154CM, D2, 440V, BG42 and 440C. **Prices:** $125 to $1000. **Remarks:** Full-time maker; first knife sold in 1989. **Mark:** First and middle initials, last name, maker, city and state. Some of his knives are stamped McDonald in script.

MCFALL, KEN,
PO Box 458, Lakeside, AZ 85929, Phone: 928-537-2026, Fax: 928-537-8066, knives@citlink.net
Specialties: Fancy working straight knives and some folders. **Patterns:** Daggers, boots, tantos, Bowies; some miniatures. **Technical:** Grinds D2, ATS-34 and 440C. Forges his own Damascus. **Prices:** $200 to $1200. **Remarks:** Part-time maker; first knife sold in 1984. **Mark:** Name, city and state.

MCFARLIN, ERIC E,
PO Box 2188, Kodiak, AK 99615, Phone: 907-486-4799
Specialties: Working knives of his design. **Patterns:** Bowies, skinners, camp knives and hunters. **Technical:** Flat and convex grinds 440C, A2 and AEB-L. **Prices:** Start at $200. **Remarks:** Part-time maker; first knife sold in 1989. **Mark:** Name and city in rectangular logo.

MCFARLIN, J W,
3331 Pocohantas Dr, Lake Havasu City, AZ 86404, Phone: 928-453-7612, Fax: 928-453-7612, aztheedge@NPGcable.com
Technical: Flat grinds, D2, ATS-34, 440C, Thomas and Peterson Damascus. **Remarks:** From working knives to investment. Customer designs always welcome. 100 percent handmade. Made first knife in 1972. **Prices:** $150 to $3000. **Mark:** Hand written in the blade.

MCGILL, JOHN,
PO Box 302, Blairsville, GA 30512, Phone: 404-745-4686
Specialties: Working knives. **Patterns:** Traditional patterns; camp knives. **Technical:** Forges L6 and 9260; makes Damascus. **Prices:** $50 to $250; some to $500. **Remarks:** Full-time maker; first knife sold in 1982. **Mark:** XYLO.

MCGOWAN, FRANK E,
2023 Robin Ct, Winter address, Sebring, FL 33870, Phone: 443-285-3815, fmcgowan1@comcast.net
Specialties: Fancy working knives and folders to customer specs. Patterns: Survivor knives, fighters, fishing knives, folders and hunters. **Technical:** Grinds and forges O1, 440C, 5160, ATS-34, 52100 or customer choice. **Prices:** $100 to $1000, some more. **Remarks:** Full-time maker. First knife sold in 1986. **Mark:** Last name.

MCGOWAN, FRANK E,
12629 Howard Lodge Dr, Summer address, Sykesvile, MD 21784, Phone: 443-285-3815, fmcgowan1@comcast.net
Specialties: Fancy working knives and folders to customer specs. **Patterns:** Survivor knives, fighters, fishing knives, folders and hunters. **Technical:** Grinds and forges O1, 440C, 5160, ATS-34, 52100, or customer choice. **Prices:** $100 to $1000; some more. **Remarks:** Full-time maker; first knife sold in 1986. **Mark:** Last name.

MCGRATH, PATRICK T,
8343 Kenyon Ave, Westchester, CA 90045, Phone: 310-338-8764, hidinginLA@excite.com

MCGRODER, PATRICK J,
5725 Chapin Rd, Madison, OH 44057, Phone: 216-298-3405, Fax: 216-298-3405
Specialties: Traditional working/using knives of his design. **Patterns:** Bowies, hunters and utility/camp knives. **Technical:** Grinds ATS-34, D2 and customer requests. Does reverse etching; heat-treats; prefers natural handle materials; custom made sheath with each knife. **Prices:** $125 to $250. **Remarks:** Part-time maker. **Mark:** First and middle initials, last name, maker, city and state.

MCGUANE IV, THOMAS F,
410 South 3rd Ave, Bozeman, MT 59715, Phone: 406-586-0248, Web: http://www.thomasmcguane.com
Specialties: Multi metal inlaid knives of handmade steel. **Patterns:** Lock back and LinerLock® folders, fancy straight knives. **Technical:** 1084/1SN20 Damascus and Mosaic steel by maker. **Prices:** $1000 and up. **Mark:** Surname or name and city, state.

MCHENRY, WILLIAM JAMES,
Box 67, Wyoming, RI 02898, Phone: 401-539-8353
Specialties: Fancy high-tech folders of his design. **Patterns:** Locking folders with various mechanisms. **Technical:** One-of-a-kind only, no duplicates. Inventor of the Axis Lock. Most pieces disassemble and feature top-shelf materials including gold, silver and gems. **Prices:** Upscale. **Remarks:** Full-time maker; first knife sold in 1988. Former goldsmith. **Mark:** Last name or first and last initials.

MCINTYRE, SHAWN,
71 Leura Grove, Hawthorn East Victoria, AUSTRALIA 3123, Phone: 61 3 9813 2049/Cell 61 412 041 062, macpower@netspace.net.au; Web: www.mcintyreknives.com
Specialties: Damascus & CS fixed blades and art knives. **Patterns:** Bowies, hunters, fighters, kukris, integrals. **Technical:** Forges, makes own Damascus including pattern weld, mosaic, and composite multi-bars form O1 & 15N20 Also uses 1084, W2, and 52100. **Prices:** $275 to $2000. **Remarks:** Full-time maker since 1999. **Mark:** Mcintyre in script.

MCKENZIE, DAVID BRIAN,
2311 B Ida Rd, Campbell River B, CANADA V9W-4V7

MCKIERNAN, STAN,
11751 300th St, Lamoni, IA 50140, Phone: 641-784-6873/641-781-0368, slmck@hotmailc.om
Specialties: Self-sheathed knives and miniatures. **Patterns:** Daggers, ethnic designs and individual styles. **Technical:** Grinds Damascus and 440C. **Prices:** $200 to $500, some to $1500. **Mark:** "River's Bend" inside two concentric circles.

MCLENDON, HUBERT W,
125 Thomas Rd, Waco, GA 30182, Phone: 770-574-9796
Specialties: Using knives; his design or customer's. **Patterns:** Bowies and hunters. **Technical:** Hand ground or forged ATS-34, 440C and D2. **Prices:** $100 to $300. **Remarks:** First knife sold in 1978. **Mark:** McLendon or Mc.

MCLUIN, TOM,
36 Fourth St, Dracut, MA 01826, Phone: 978-957-4899, tmcluin@comcast.net; Web: www.mcluinknives.com
Specialties: Working straight knives and folders of his design. **Patterns:** Boots, hunters and folders. **Technical:** Grinds ATS-34, 440C, O1 and Damascus; makes his own mokume. **Prices:** $100 to $400; some to $700. **Remarks:** Part-time maker; first knife sold in 1991. **Mark:** Last name.

MCLURKIN, ANDREW,
2112 Windy Woods Dr, Raleigh, NC 27607, Phone: 919-834-4693, mclurkincustomknives.com
Specialties: Collector grade folders, working folders, fixed blades, and miniatures. Knives made to order and to his design. **Patterns:** Locking liner and lock back folders, hunter, working and tactical designs. **Technical:** Using patterned Damascus, Mosaic Damascus, ATS-34, BG-42, and CPM steels. Prefers natural handle materials such as pearl, ancient ivory and stabilized wood. Also using synthetic materials such as carbon fiber, titanium, and G10. **Prices:** $250 and up. **Mark:** Last name. Mark is often on inside of folders.

MCMANUS, DANNY,
413 Fairhaven Drive, Taylors, SC 29687, Phone: 864-268-9849, Fax: 864-268-9699, DannyMcManus@bigfoot.com
Specialties: High-tech and traditional working/using straight knives of his design, to customer specs and in standard patterns. **Patterns:** Boots, Bowies, fighters, hunters and utility/camp knives. **Technical:** Forges stainless steel Damascus; grinds ATS-34. Offers engraving and scrimshaw. **Prices:** $300 to $2000; some to $3000. **Remarks:** Full-time maker; first knife sold in 1997. Doing business as Stamascus KnifeWorks Corp. **Mark:** Stamascus.

MCNABB, TOMMY,
CAROLINA CUSTOM KNIVES, PO Box 327, Bethania, NC 27010, Phone: 336-924-6053, Fax: 336-924-4854, tommy@tmcnabb.com; Web: carolinaknives.com
Specialties: Classic and working knives of his own design or to customer's specs. **Patterns:** Traditional bowies. Tomahawks, hunters and customer designs. **Technical:** Forges his own Damascus steel, hand forges or grinds ATS-34 and other hi-tech steels. Prefers mirror finish or satin finish on working knives. Uses exotic or natural handle material and stabilized woods. **Price:** $300-$3500. **Remarks:** Full time maker. Made first knife in 1982. **Mark**""Carolina Custom Knives" on stock removal blades "T. McNabb" on custom orders and Damascus knives.

MCRAE, J MICHAEL,
6100 Lake Rd, Mint Hill, NC 28227, Phone: 704-545-2929, scotia@carolina.rr.com; Web: www.scotiametalwork.com
Specialties: Scottish dirks and sgian dubhs. **Patterns:** Traditional blade styles with traditional and slightly non-traditional handle treatments. **Technical:** Forges 5160 and his own Damascus. Prefers stag and exotic hardwoods for handles, many intricately carved. **Prices:** Starting at $125, some to $3500. **Remarks:** Journeyman Smith in ABS, member of North Carolina Custom Knifemakers Guild and ABANA. Full-time maker, first knife sold in 1982. Doing business as Scotia Metalwork. **Mark:** Last name underlined with a claymore.

MEERDINK, KURT,
120 Split Rock Dr, Barryville, NY 12719, Phone: 845-557-0783
Specialties: Working straight knives. **Patterns:** Hunters, Bowies, tactical and neck knives. **Technical:** Grinds ATS-34, 440C, D2, Damascus. **Prices:** $95 to $1100. **Remarks:** Full-time maker, first knife sold in 1994. **Mark:** Meerdink Maker, Rio NY.

MEIER, DARYL,
75 Forge Rd, Carbondale, IL 62901, Phone: 618-549-3234
Specialties: One-of-a-kind knives and swords. **Patterns:** Collaborates on blades. **Technical:** Forges his own Damascus, W1 and A203E, 440C, 431, nickel 200 and clad steel. **Prices:** $250 to $450; some to $6000. **Remarks:** Full-time smith and researcher since 1974; first knife sold in 1974. **Mark:** Name or circle/arrow symbol or SHAWNEE.

MELIN, GORDON C,
14207 Coolbank Dr, La Mirada, CA 90638, Phone: 562-946-5753

MELLARD, J R,
17006 Highland Canyon Dr., Houston, TX 77095, Phone: 281-550-9464

MELOY, SEAN,
7148 Rosemary Lane, Lemon Grove, CA 91945-2105, Phone: 619-465-7173
Specialties: Traditional working straight knives of his design. **Patterns:** Bowies, fighters and utility/camp knives. **Technical:** Grinds 440C, ATS-34 and D2. **Prices:** $125 to $300. **Remarks:** Part-time maker; first knife sold in 1985. **Mark:** Broz Knives.

MENEFEE, RICKY BOB,
2440 County Road 1322, Blawchard, OK 73010, rmenefee@pldi.net
Specialties: Working straight knives and pocket knives. **Patterns:** Hunters, fighters, minis & Bowies. **Technical:** Grinds ATS-34, 440C, D2, BG42 and S30V. **Price:** $130 to $1000. **Remarks:** Part-time maker, first knife sold in 2001. Member of KGA of Oklahoma, also Knifemakers Guild. **Mark:** Menefee made or Menefee stamped in blade.

MENSCH, LARRY C,
Larry's Knife Shop, 578 Madison Ave, Milton, PA 17847, Phone: 570-742-9554
Specialties: Custom orders. **Patterns:** Bowies, daggers, hunters, tantos, short swords and miniatures. **Technical:** Grinds ATS-34, stainless steel Damascus; blade grinds hollow, flat and slack. Filework; bending guards and fluting handles with finger grooves. Offers engraving and scrimshaw. **Prices:** $200 and up. **Remarks:** Full-time maker; first knife sold in 1993. Doing business as Larry's Knife Shop. **Mark:** Connected capital "L" and small "m" in script.

MERCER, MIKE,
149 N. Waynesville Rd, Lebanon, OH 45036, Phone: 513-932-2837, mmercer08445@roadrunner.com
Specialties: Miniatures and autos. **Patterns:** All folder patterns. **Technical:** Diamonds and gold, one-of-a-kind, Damascus, O1, stainless steel blades. **Prices:** $500 to $5000. **Remarks:** Carved wax -lost wax casting. **Mark:** Stamp -Mercer.

MERCHANT, TED,
7 Old Garrett Ct, White Hall, MD 21161, Phone: 410-343-0380
Specialties: Traditional and classic working knives. Patterns: Bowies, hunters, camp knives, fighters, daggers and skinners. **Technical:** Forges W2 and 5160; makes own Damascus. Makes handles with wood, stag, horn, silver and gem stone inlay; fancy filework. **Prices:** $125 to $600; some to $1500. **Remarks:** Full-time maker; first knife sold in 1985. **Mark:** Last name.

MERZ III, ROBERT L,
1447 Winding Canyon, Katy, TX 77493, Phone: 281-391-2897, bobmerz@consolidated.net
Specialties: Folders. **Prices:** $250 to $700. **Remarks:** Full time maker; first knife sold in 1974. **Mark:** MERZ.

MESHEJIAN, MARDI,
5 Bisbee Court 109 PMB 230, Santa Fe, NM 87508, Phone: 505-310-7441, toothandnail13@yahoo.com
Specialties: One-of-a-kind fantasy and high art straight knives & folders. **Patterns:** Swords, daggers, folders and other weapons. **Technical:** Forged steel Damascus and titanium Damascus. **Prices:** $300 to $5000 some to $7000. **Mark:** Stamped stylized "M."

MESSER, DAVID T,
134 S Torrence St, Dayton, OH 45403-2044, Phone: 513-228-6561
Specialties: Fantasy period pieces, straight and folding, of his design. **Patterns:** Bowies, daggers and swords. **Technical:** Grinds 440C, O1, 06 and commercial Damascus. Likes fancy guards and exotic handle materials. **Prices:** $100 to $225; some to $375. **Remarks:** Spare-time maker; first knife sold in 1991. **Mark:** Name stamp.

METHENY, H A "WHITEY",
7750 Waterford Dr, Spotsylvania, VA 22553, Phone: 540-582-3095, Fax: 540-582-3095, hametheny@aol.com; Web: www methenyknives.com
Specialties: Working and using straight knives of his design and to customer specs. **Patterns:** Hunters and kitchen knives. **Technical:** Grinds 440C and ATS-34. Offers filework; tooled custom sheaths. **Prices:** $200 to $350. **Remarks:** Spare-time maker; first knife sold in 1990. **Mark:** Initials/full name football logo.

METZ, GREG T,
c/o James Ranch HC 83, Cascade, ID 83611, Phone: 208-382-4336, metzenterprise@yahoo.com
Specialties: Hunting and utility knives. **Prices:** $350 and up. **Remarks:** Natural handle materials; hand forged blades; 1084 and 1095. **Mark:** METZ (last name).

MEYER, CHRISTOPHER J,
737 Shenipsit Lake Rd, Tolland, CT 06084, Phone: 860-875-1826, shenipsitforge.cjm@gmail.com
Specialties: Hand forged tool steels. **Patterns:** Bowies, fighters, hunters, and camp knives. **Technical:** Forges O1, 1084, W2, Grinds ATS-34, O1, D2, CPM154CM. **Remarks:** Spare-time maker, sold first knife in 2003. **Mark:** "Meyer" or "Shenipsit forge, Meyer" "on ricasso".

MICHINAKA, TOSHIAKI,
I-679 Koyamacho-nishi Tottori-shi, Tottori 680-0947, JAPAN, Phone: 0857-28-5911
Specialties: Art miniature knives. **Patterns:** Bowies, hunters, fishing, camp knives & miniatures. **Technical:** Grinds ATS-34 and 440C. **Prices:** $300 to $900 some higher. **Remarks:** Part-time maker. First knife sold in 1982. **Mark:** First initial, last name.

MICHO, KANDA,
7-32-5 Shinzutsumi-cho, Shinnanyo-city, Yamaguchi, JAPAN, Phone: 0834-62-1910

MICKLEY, TRACY,
42112 Kerns Dr, North Mankato, MN 56003, Phone: 507-947-3760, tracy@mickleyknives.com; Web: www.mickleyknives.com
Specialties: Working and collectable straight knives using mammoth ivory or burl woods, LinerLock® folders. **Patterns:** Custom and classic hunters, utility, fighters and Bowies. **Technical:** Grinding 154-CM, BG-42 forging O1 and 52100. **Prices:** Starting at $325 **Remarks:** Part-time since 1999. **Mark:** Last name.

MILES JR., C R "IRON DOCTOR",
1541 Porter Crossroad, Lugoff, SC 29078, Phone: 803-438-5816
Specialties: Traditional working straight knives of his design or made to custom specs. **Patterns:** Hunters, fighters, utility camp knives and hatches. **Technical:** Grinds O1, D2, ATS-34, 440C, and 1095. Forges 18th century style cutlery of high carbon steels. Custom leather sheaths. **Prices:** $100 and up. **Remarks:** Part-time maker, first knife sold in 1997. Member of South Carolina Association of Knifemakers since 1997.

MILITANO, TOM,
CUSTOM KNIVES, 77 Jason Rd., Jacksonville, AL 36265-6655, Phone: 256-435-7132, jeffkin57@aol.com
Specialties: Fixed blade, one-of-a-kind knives. **Patterns:** Bowies, fighters, hunters and tactical knives. **Technical:** Grinds 440C, ATS-34, A2, and Damascus. Hollow grinds, flat grinds, and decorative filework. **Prices:** $150 plus. **Remarks:** Part-time maker. Sold first knives in the mid to late 1980s. Memberships: Founding member of New England Custom Knife Association. **Mark:** Name engraved in ricasso area -type of steel on reverse side.

MILLARD, FRED G,
27627 Kopezyk Ln, Richland Center, WI 53581, Phone: 608-647-5376
Specialties: Working/using straight knives of his design or to customer specs. Patterns: Bowies, hunters, utility/camp knives, kitchen/steak knives. **Technical:** Grinds ATS-34, O1, D2 and 440C. Makes sheaths. **Prices:** $110 to $300. **Remarks:** Full-time maker; first knife sold in 1993. Doing business as Millard Knives. **Mark:** Mallard duck in flight with serial number.

MILLER, BOB,
7659 Fine Oaks Pl, Oakville, MO 63129, Phone: 314-846-8934
Specialties: Mosaic Damascus; collector using straight knives and folders. **Patterns:** Hunters, Bowies, utility/camp knives, daggers. **Technical:** Forges own Damascus, mosaic-Damascus and 52100. **Prices:** $125 to $500. **Remarks:** Part-time maker; first knife sold in 1983. **Mark:** First and middle initials and last name, or initials.

MILLER, DON,
1604 Harrodsburg Rd, Lexington, KY 40503, Phone: 606-276-3299

MILLER, HANFORD J,
Box 97, Cowdrey, CO 80434, Phone: 970-723-4708
Specialties: Working knives in Moran styles, Bowie, period pieces, Cinquedea. **Patterns:** Daggers, Bowies, working knives. **Technical:** All work forged: W2, 1095, 5160 and Damascus. ABS methods; offers fine silver repousse, scabboard mountings and wire inlay, oak presentation cases. **Prices:** $400 to $1000; some to $3000 and up. **Remarks:** Full-time maker; first knife sold in 1968. **Mark:** Initials or name within Bowie logo.

MILLER, JAMES P,
9024 Goeller Rd, RR 2, Box 28, Fairbank, IA 50629, Phone: 319-635-2294, Web: www.damascusknives.biz
Specialties: All tool steel Damascus; working knives and period pieces. **Patterns:** Hunters, Bowies, camp knives and daggers. **Technical:** Forges and grinds 1095, 52100, 440C and his own Damascus. **Prices:** $175 to $500; some to $1500. **Remarks:** Full-time maker; first knife sold in 1970. **Mark:** First and middle initials, last name with knife logo.

MILLER, M A,
11625 Community Center Dr, Unit #1531, Northglenn, CO 80233, Phone: 303-280-3816
Specialties: Using knives for hunting. 3-1/2"-4" Loveless drop-point. Made to customer specs. **Patterns:** Skinners and camp knives. **Technical:** Grinds 440C, D2, O1 and ATS-34 Damascus miniatures. **Prices:** $225 to $350; miniatures $75 to $150. **Remarks:** Part-time maker; first knife sold in 1988. **Mark:** Last name stamped in block letters or first and middle initials, last name, maker, city and state with triangles on either side etched.

MILLER, MICHAEL,
3030 E Calle Cedral, Kingman, AZ 86401, Phone: 928-757-1359, mike@mmilleroriginals.com
Specialties: Hunters, Bowies, and skinners with exotic burl wood, stag, ivory and gemstone handles. **Patterns:** O1 and L6 Damascus 1084 and 1095 and O1 steel knives. **Technical:** L6 and O1 patterned Damascus. **Prices:** $185 to $1850. **Remarks:** Full-time maker since 2002, first knife sold 2000; doing business as M Miller Originals. **Mark:** First initial and last name with 'handmade' underneath.

MILLER, MICHAEL E,
1400 Skyview Dr, El Reno, OK 73036, Phone: 405-422-3602
Specialties: Traditional working/using knives of his design. **Patterns:** Bowies, hunters and kitchen knives. **Technical:** Grinds ATS-34, CPM 440V; forges Damascus and cable Damascus and 52100. Prefers scrimshaw, fancy pins, basket weave and embellished sheaths. **Prices:** $80 to $300; some to $500. **Remarks:** Part-time maker; first knife sold in 1984. Doing business as Miller Custom Knives. Member of KGA of Oklahoma and Salt Fork Blacksmith Association. **Mark:** First and middle initials, last name, maker.

MILLER, MICHAEL K,
28510 Santiam Hwy, Sweet Home, OR 97386, Phone: 541-367-4927, miller@ptlnet.net
Specialties: Specializes in kitchen cutlery of his design or made to customer specs. **Patterns:** Hunters, utility/camp knives and kitchen cutlery. **Technical:** Grinds ATS-34, AEBL and 440-C. Wife does scrimshaw as well. Makes custom sheaths and holsters. **Prices:** $200. **Remarks:** Full-time maker; first knife sold in 1989. **Mark:** MandM Kustom Krafts.

MILLER, NATE,
Sportsman's Edge, 1075 Old Steese Hwy N, Fairbanks, AK 99712, sportsmansedge@gci.net
Specialties: Fixed blade knives for hunting, fishing, kitchen and collector pieces. **Patterns:** Hunters, skinners, utility, tactical, fishing, camp knives-your pattern or mine. **Technical:** Stock removal maker, ATS-34, 154CM, D2, 1095, other steels on request. Handle material includes micarta, horn, antler, fossilized ivory and bone, wide selection of woods. **Prices:** $225-$800. **Remarks:** Full time maker since 2002. **Mark:** Nate Miller, Fairbanks, AK.

MILLER, R D,
10526 Estate Lane, Dallas, TX 75238, Phone: 214-348-3496
Specialties: One-of-a-kind collector-grade knives. Patterns: Boots, hunters, Bowies, camp and utility knives, fishing and bird knives, miniatures. **Technical:** Grinds a variety of steels to include O1, D2, 440C, 154CM and 1095. **Prices:** $65 to $300; some to $900. **Remarks:** Full-time maker; first knife sold in 1984. **Mark:** R.D. Custom Knives with date or bow and arrow logo.

MILLER, RICK,
516 Kanaul Rd, Rockwood, PA 15557, Phone: 814-926-2059
Specialties: Working/using straight knives of his design and in standard patterns. **Patterns:** Bowies, daggers, hunters and friction folders. **Technical:** Grinds L6. Forges 5160, L6 and Damascus. Patterns for Damascus are random, twist, rose or ladder. **Prices:** $75 to $250; some to $400. **Remarks:** Part-time maker; first knife sold in 1982. **Mark:** Script stamp "R.D.M."

MILLER, RON,
NORTH POLE KNIVES, PO BOX 55301, NORTH POLE, AK 99705, Phone: 907-488-5902, JTMRON@NESCAPE.NET
Specialties: Custom handmade hunting knives built for the extreme conditions of Alaska. Custom fillet blades, tactical fighting knives, custom kitchen knives. Handles are made from mammoth ivory, musk ox, fossilized walrus tusk. Hunters have micarta handles. **Patterns:** Hunters, skinners, fillets, fighters. **Technical:** Stock removal for D2, ATS-34, 109HR, 154CM, and Damascus. **Prices:** $180 and up. **Remarks:** Makes custom sheaths for the above knives. **Mark:** Ron Miller, circle with North Pole Knives with bowie style blade through circle.

MILLER, RONALD T,
12922 127th Ave N, Largo, FL 34644, Phone: 813-595-0378 (after 5 p.m.)
Specialties: Working straight knives in standard patterns. **Patterns:** Combat knives, camp knives, kitchen cutlery, fillet knives, locking folders and butterflies. **Technical:** Grinds D2, 440C and ATS-34; offers brass inlays and scrimshaw. **Prices:** $45 to $325; some to $750. **Remarks:** Part-time maker; first knife sold in 1984. **Mark:** Name, city and state in palm tree logo.

MILLS, LOUIS G,
9450 Waters Rd, Ann Arbor, MI 48103, Phone: 734-668-1839
Specialties: High-art Japanese-style period pieces. **Patterns:** Traditional tantos, daggers and swords. **Technical:** Makes steel from iron; makes his own Damascus by traditional Japanese techniques. **Prices:** $900 to $2000; some to $8000. **Remarks:** Spare-time maker. **Mark:** Yasutomo in Japanese Kanji.

MILLS, MICHAEL,
151 Blackwell Rd, Colonial Beach, VA 22443-5054, Phone: 804-224-0265
Specialties: Working knives, hunters, skinners, utility and Bowies. **Technical:** Forge 5160 differential heat-treats. **Prices:** $300 and up. **Remarks:** Part-time maker, ABS Journeyman. **Mark:** Last name in script.

MINK, DAN,
PO Box 861, 196 Sage Circle, Crystal Beach, FL 34681, Phone: 727-786-5408, blademkr@gmail.com
Specialties: Traditional and working knives of his design. **Patterns:** Bowies, fighters, folders and hunters. **Technical:** Grinds ATS-34, 440C and D2. Blades and tanges embellished with fancy filework. Uses natural and rare handle materials. **Prices:** $125 to $450. **Remarks:** Part-time maker; first knife sold in 1985. **Mark:** Name and star encircled by custom made, city, state.

MINNICK, JIM,
144 North 7th St, Middletown, IN 47356, Phone: 765-354-4108
Specialties: Lever-lock folding art knives, liner-locks. **Patterns:** Stilettos, Persian and one-of-a-kind folders. **Technical:** Grinds and carves Damascus, stainless, and high-carbon. **Prices:** $950 to $7000. **Remarks:** Part-time maker; first knife sold in 1976. Husband and wife team. **Mark:** Minnick and JMJ.

MIRABILE, DAVID,
1715 Glacier Ave, Juneau, AK 99801, Phone: 907-463-3404
Specialties: Elegant edged weapons. **Patterns:** Fighters, Bowies, claws, tklinget daggers, executive desk knives. **Technical:** Forged high-carbon steels, his own Damascus; uses ancient walrus ivory and prehistoric bone extensively, very rarely uses wood. **Prices:** $350 to $7000. **Remarks:** Full-time maker. Knives sold through art gallery in Juneau, AK. **Mark:** Last name etched or engraved.

MITCHELL, JAMES A,
PO Box 4646, Columbus, GA 31904, Phone: 404-322-8582
Specialties: Fancy working knives. **Patterns:** Hunters, fighters, Bowies and locking folders. **Technical:** Grinds D2, 440C and commercial Damascus. **Prices:** $100 to $400; some to $900. **Remarks:** Part-time maker; first knife sold in 1976. Sells knives in sets. **Mark:** Signature and city.

MITCHELL, MAX DEAN AND BEN,
3803 VFW Rd, Leesville, LA 71440, Phone: 318-239-6416
Specialties: Hatchet and knife sets with folder and belt and holster all match. **Patterns:** Hunters, 200 L6 steel. **Technical:** L6 steel; soft back, hand edge. **Prices:** $300 to $500. **Remarks:** Part-time makers; first knife sold in 1965. Custom orders only; no stock. **Mark:** First names.

MITCHELL, WM DEAN,
PO Box 2, Warren, TX 77664, Phone: 409-547-2213
Specialties: Functional and collectable cutlery. Patterns:Personal and collector's designs. **Technical:**Forges own Damascus and carbon steels. **Prices:** Determined by the buyer. **Remarks:**Gentleman knifemaker. ABS Master Smith 1994.**Mark:** Full name with anvil and MS or WDM and MS.

MITSUYUKI, ROSS,
PO Box 29577, Honolulu, HI 96820, Phone: 808-671-3335, Fax: 808-671-3335, rossman@hawaii.rr.com; Web:www.picturetrail.com/homepage/mrbing
Specialties: Working straight knives and folders/engraving titanium & 416 S.S. **Patterns:** Hunting, fighters, utility knives and boot knives. **Technical:** 440C, BG42, ATS-34, 530V, and Damascus. **Prices:** $100 and up. **Remarks:** Spare-time maker, first knife sold in 1998. **Mark:** (Honu) Hawaiian sea turtle.

MIVILLE-DESCHENES, ALAIN,
1952 Charles A Parent, Quebec, CANADA G2B 4B2, Phone: 418-845-0950, Fax: 418-845-0950, amd@miville-deschenes.com; Web: www.miville-deschenes.com
Specialties: Working knives of his design or to customer specs and art knives. **Patterns:** Bowies, skinner, hunter, utility, camp knives, fighters, art knives. **Technical:** Grinds ATS-34, CPMS30V, 0-1, D2, and sometime forge carbon steel. **Prices:** $250 to $700; some higher. **Remarks:** Part-time maker; first knife sold in 2001. **Mark:** Logo (small hand) and initials (AMD).

MIZE, RICHARD,
FOX CREEK FORGE, 2038 Fox Creek Rd., Lawrenceburg, KY 40342, Phone: 502-859-0602, foxcreek@kih.net; Web: www.foxcreekforge.com
Specialties: Forges spring steel, 5160, 10xx steels, natural handle materials. **Patterns:** Traditional working knives, period flavor Bowies, rifle knives. **Technical:** Does own heat treating, differential temper. **Prices:** $100 to $400. **Remarks:** Strongly advocates sole authorship. **Mark:** Initial M hot stamped.

MOJZIS, JULIUS,
B S Timravy 6, 98511 Halic, SLOVAKIA, mojzisj@stoneline.sk; Web: www.juliusmojzis.com
Specialties: Art Knives. **Prices:** USD $2000. **Mark:** MOJZIS.

MONCUS, MICHAEL STEVEN,
1803 US 19 N, Smithville, GA 31787, Phone: 912-846-2408

MONTANO, GUS A,
11217 Westonhill Dr, San Diego, CA 92126-1447, Phone: 619-273-5357
Specialties: Traditional working/using straight knives of his design. **Patterns:** Boots, Bowies and fighters. **Technical:** Grinds 1095 and 5160; grinds and forges cable. Double or triple hardened and triple drawn; hand-rubbed finish. Prefers natural handle materials. **Prices:** $200 to $400; some to $600. **Remarks:** Spare-time maker; first knife sold in 1997. **Mark:** First initial and last name.

MONTEIRO, VICTOR,
31 Rue D'Opprebais, 1360 Maleves Ste Marie, BELGIUM, Phone: 010 88 0441, victor.monteiro@skynet.be
Specialties: Working and fancy straight knives, folders and integrals of his design. **Patterns:** Fighters, hunters and kitchen knives. **Technical:** Grinds ATS-34, 440C, D2, Damasteel and other commercial Damascus, embellishment, filework and domed pins. **Prices:** $300 to $1000, some higher. **Remarks:** Part-time maker; first knife sold in 1989. **Mark:** Logo with initials connected.

MONTJOY, CLAUDE,
706 Indian Creek Rd, Clinton, SC 29325, Phone: 864-697-6160
Specialties: Folders, slip joint, lock, lock liner and interframe. **Patterns:** Hunters, boots, fighters, some art knives and folders. **Technical:** Grinds ATS-34 and Damascus. Offers inlaid handle scales. **Prices:** $100 to $500. **Remarks:** Full-time maker; first knife sold in 1982. Custom orders, no catalog. **Mark:** Montjoy.

MOONEY, MIKE,
19432 E Cloud Rd, Queen Creek, AZ 85242, Phone: 480-987-3576, mike@moonblades.com; Web: www.moonblades.com
Specialties: Fancy working straight knives of his design or customers. **Patterns:** Fighters, Bowies, daggers, hunters, kitchen, camp. **Technical:** Flat-grind, hand-rubbed finish, 530V, commercial Damascus, CPM154. **Prices:** $250 to $2000. **Remarks:** Doing business as moonblades.com. **Mark:** M. Mooney followed by crescent moon.

MOORE, JAMES B,
1707 N Gillis, Ft. Stockton, TX 79735, Phone: 915-336-2113
Specialties: Classic working straight knives and folders of his design. **Patterns:** Hunters, Bowies, daggers, fighters, boots, utility/camp knives, locking folders and slip-joint folders. **Technical:** Grinds 440C, ATS-34, D2, L6, CPM and commercial Damascus. **Prices:** $85 to $700; exceptional knives to $1500. **Remarks:** Full-time maker; first knife sold in 1972. **Mark:** Name, city and state.

MOORE, JON P,
304 South N Rd, Aurora, NE 68818, Phone: 402-849-2616, Web: www.sharpdecisionknives.com
Specialties: Working and fancy straight knives using antler, exotic bone, wood and Micarta. Will use customers antlers on request. Patterns: Hunters, skinners, camp Bowies. **Technical:** Hand forged high carbon steel. Makes his own Damascus. **Remarks:** Part-time maker, sold first knife in 2003, member of ABS -apprentice. Does on location knife forging

demonstrations. **Mark:** Signature.

MOORE, MARVE,
HC 89 Box 393, Willow, AK 99688, Phone: 907-232-0478, marvemoore@aol.com
Specialties: Fixed blades forged and stock removal. **Patterns:** Hunter, skinners, fighter, short swords. **Technical:** 100 percent of his work is done by hand. **Prices:** $100 to $500. **Remarks:** Also makes his own sheaths. **Mark:** -MM-.

MOORE, MICHAEL ROBERT,
70 Beauliew St, Lowell, MA 01850, Phone: 978-479-0589, Fax: 978-441-1819

MOORE, TED,
340 E Willow St, Elizabethtown, PA 17022, Phone: 717-367-3939, tedmoore@supernet.com; Web: www.tedmooreknives.com
Specialties: Damascus folders, cigar cutters. **Patterns:** Locking folders and slip joint. **Technical:** Grinds Damascus, high-carbon and stainless; also ATS-34 and D2. **Prices:** $250 to $1500. **Remarks:** Part-time maker; first knife sold 1993. Knife and gun leather also. **Mark:** Moore U.S.A.

MORETT, DONALD,
116 Woodcrest Dr, Lancaster, PA 17602-1300, Phone: 717-746-4888

MORGAN, JEFF,
9200 Arnaz Way, Santee, CA 92071, Phone: 619-448-8430
Specialties: Fancy working straight knives. **Patterns:** Hunters, fighters, boots, old west designs. **Technical:** Grinds D2, 440C, ATS-34, 5160 and 1095; likes exotic handles. **Prices:** $60 to $300; some to $800. **Remarks:** Full-time maker; first knife sold in 1977, Knifemakers Guild Member since 1984. **Mark:** Initials connected.

MORGAN, TOM,
14689 Ellett Rd, Beloit, OH 44609, Phone: 330-537-2023
Specialties: Working straight knives and period pieces. **Patterns:** Hunters, boots and presentation tomahawks. **Technical:** Grinds O1, 440C and 154CM. **Prices:** Knives, $65 to $200; tomahawks, $100 to $325. **Remarks:** Full-time maker; first knife sold in 1977. **Mark:** Last name and type of steel used.

MORRIS, C H,
1590 Old Salem Rd, Frisco City, AL 36445, Phone: 334-575-7425
Specialties: LinerLock® folders. **Patterns:** Interframe liner locks. **Technical:** Grinds 440C and ATS-34. **Prices:** Start at $350. **Remarks:** Full-time maker; first knife sold in 1973. Doing business as Custom Knives. **Mark:** First and middle initials, last name.

MORRIS, DARRELL PRICE,
92 Union, St. Plymouth, Devon, ENGLAND PL1 3EZ, Phone: 0752 223546
Specialties: Traditional Japanese knives, Bowies and high-art knives. **Technical:** Nickel Damascus and mokume. **Prices:** $1000 to $4000. **Remarks:** Part-time maker; first knife sold in 1990. **Mark:** Initials and Japanese name—Kuni Shigae.

MORRIS, ERIC,
306 Ewart Ave, Beckley, WV 25801, Phone: 304-255-3951

MORTENSON, ED,
2742 Hwy 93 N, Darby, MT 59829, Phone: 406-821-3146, Fax: 406-821-3146
Specialties: Period pieces and working/using straight knives of his design, to customer specs and in standard patterns. **Patterns:** Bowies, hunters and kitchen knives. **Technical:** Grinds ATS-34, 5160 and 1095. Sheath combinations: flashlight/knife, hatchet/knife, etc. **Prices:** $60 to $140; some to $300. **Remarks:** Full-time maker; first knife sold in 1993. Doing business as The Blade Lair. **Mark:** M with attached O.

MOSES, STEVEN,
1610 W Hemlock Way, Santa Ana, CA 92704

MOSIER, JOSHUA J,
SPRING CREEK KNIFE WORKS, PO Box 476/ 608 7th St, Deshler, NE 68340, Phone: 402-365-4386, joshm@sl-kw.com; Web:www.sc-kw.com
Specialties: Working straight and folding knives of his designs with customer specs. **Patterns:** Hunter/utility LinerLock® folders. **Technical:** Forges 5160, L6 and own Damascus. **Prices:** $55 and up. **Remarks:** Part-time maker, sold first knife in 1986. **Mark:** SCKW.

MOULTON, DUSTY,
135 Hillview Lane, Loudon, TN 37774, Phone: 865-408-9779, Web: www.moultonknives.com
Specialties: Fancy and working straight knives. **Patterns:** Hunters, fighters, fantasy and miniatures. **Technical:** Grinds ATS-34 and Damascus. **Prices:** $300 to $2000. **Remarks:** Full-time maker; first knife sold in 1991. Now doing engraving on own knives as well as other makers. **Mark:** Last name.

MOUNT, DON,
4574 Little Finch Ln, Las Vegas, NV 89115, Phone: 702-531-2925
Specialties: High-tech working and using straight knives of his design. Patterns: Bowies, fighters and utility/camp knives. **Technical:** Uses 440C and ATS-34. **Prices:** $150 to $300; some to $1000. **Remarks:** Part-time maker; first knife sold in 1985. **Mark:** Name below a woodpecker.

MOUNTAIN HOME KNIVES,
PO Box 167, Jamul, CA 91935, Phone: 619-669-0833
Specialties: High-quality working straight knives. **Patterns:** Hunters, fighters, skinners, tantos, utility and fillet knives, Bowies and *san-mai* Damascus Bowies. **Technical:** Hollow-grind 440C by hand. Feature linen Micarta handles, nickel-silver handle bolts and handmade sheaths. **Prices:** $65 to $270. **Remarks:** Company owned by Jim English. **Mark:** Mountain Home Knives.

MOYER, RUSS,
1266 RD 425 So, Havre, MT 59501, Phone: 406-395-4423
Specialties: Working knives to customer specs. **Patterns:** Hunters, Bowies and survival knives. **Technical:** Forges W2 & 5160. **Prices:** $150 to $350. **Remarks:** Part-time maker; first knife sold in 1976. **Mark:** Initials in logo.

MULKEY, GARY,
533 Breckenridge Rd, Branson, MO 65616, Phone: 417-335-0123, gary@mulkeyknives.com; Web: www.mulkeyknives.com
Specialties: Working and fancy fixed blades and folders of his design and to customer's specs. **Patterns:** Hunters, Bowies, fighters and folders. Lock back and single action autos. **Technical:** Prefers 1095 or D2 with Damascus, filework, inlets or clay coated blades available on order. **Prices:** $200 to $1000 plus. **Remarks:** Full-time maker since 1997. Shop/showroom open to public. **Mark:** MUL above skeleton key.

MULLER, JODY,
3359 S. 225th Rd., Goodson, MO 65663, Phone: 417-852-4306/417-752-3260, mullerforge2@hotmail.com; Web: www.mullerforge.com
Specialties: Hand engraving, carving and inlays, fancy folders and oriental styles. **Patterns:** One-of-a-kind fixed blades and folders in all styles. **Technical:** Forges own Damascus and high carbon steel. **Prices:** $300 and up. **Remarks:** Full-time Journeyman Smith, knifemaker, does hand engraving, carving and inlay. All work done by maker. **Mark:** Muller J.S.

MUNROE, DERYK C,
PO Box 3454, Bozeman, MT 59772

MURSKI, RAY,
12129 Captiva Ct, Reston, VA 22091-1204, Phone: 703-264-1102, murski@vtisp.com
Specialties: Fancy working/using folders of his design. **Patterns:** Hunters, slip-joint folders and utility/camp knives. **Technical:** Grinds CPM-3V **Prices:** $125 to $500. **Remarks:** Spare-time maker; first knife sold in 1996. **Mark:** Engraved name with serial number under name.

MYERS, PAUL,
644 Maurice St, Wood River, IL 62095, Phone: 618-258-1707
Specialties: Fancy working straight knives and folders. **Patterns:** Full range of folders, straight hunters and Bowies; tie tacks; knife and fork sets. **Technical:** Grinds D2, 440C, ATS-34 and 154CM. **Prices:** $100 to $350; some to $3000. **Remarks:** Full-time maker; first knife sold in 1974. **Mark:** Initials with setting sun on front; name and number on back.

MYERS, STEVE,
903 Hickory Rd., Virginia, IL 62691-8716, Phone: 217-452-3157
Specialties: Working Straight Knives and Integrals **Patterns:**Camp Knives, Hunters, Skinners, Bowies, and Boot Knives.**Technical:** Grinds high carbon and Damascus **Prices:** $250 to $1,000 **Remarks:** Full-time maker; First knife sold in 1985 **Mark** Last name in logo

N

NATEN, GREG,
1804 Shamrock Way, Bakersfield, CA 93304-3921
Specialties: Fancy and working/using folders of his design. **Patterns:** Fighters, hunters and locking folders. **Technical:** Grinds 440C, ATS-34 and CPM440V. Heat-treats; prefers desert ironwood, stag and mother-of-pearl. Designs and sews leather sheaths for straight knives. **Prices:** $175 to $600; some to $950. **Remarks:** Spare-time maker; first knife sold in 1992. **Mark:** Last name above battle-ax, handmade.

NEALY, BUD,
RR1, Box 1439, Stroudsburg, PA 18360, Phone: 570-402-1018, Fax: 570-402-1019, budnealy@ptd.net; Web: www.budnealyknifemaker.com
Specialties: Original design concealment knives with designer multi-concealment sheath system. **Patterns:** Concealment knives, boots, combat and collector pieces. **Technical:** Grinds CPM 154, S30V & Damascus. **Prices:** $200 to $2500. **Remarks:** Full-time maker; first knife sold in 1980. **Mark:** Name, city, state or signature.

NEDVED, DAN,
206 Park Dr, Kalispell, MT 59901, Phone: 406-752-5060
Specialties: Slip joint folders, liner locks, straight knives. Patterns: Mostly traditional or modern blend with traditional lines. **Technical:** Grinds ATS-34, 440C, 1095 and uses other makers Damascus. **Prices:** $95 and up. Mostly in the $150 to $200 range. **Remarks:** Part-time maker, averages 2 a month. **Mark:** Dan Nedved or Nedved with serial # on opposite side.

NEELY, GREG,
5419 Pine St, Bellaire, TX 77401, Phone: 713-991-2677, ediiorio@houston.rr.com
Specialties: Traditional patterns and his own patterns for work and/or

collecting. **Patterns:** Hunters, Bowies and utility/camp knives. **Technical:** Forges own Damascus, 1084, 5160 and some tool steels. Differentially tempers. **Prices:** $225 to $5000. **Remarks:** Part-time maker; first knife sold in 1987. **Mark:** Last name or interlocked initials, MS.

NEILSON, J,
RR 2 Box 16, Wyalusing, PA 18853, Phone: 570-746-4944, mountainhollow@epix.net; Web: www.mountainhollow.net
Specialties: Working and collectable fixed blade knives. **Patterns:** Hunter/fighters, Bowies, neck knives and daggers. **Technical:** 1084, 5160, maker's own Damascus. **Prices:** $200 to $2000. **Remarks:** ABS Journeyman Smith, full-time maker, first knife sold in 2000, doing business as Neilson's Mountain Hollow. Each knife comes with a sheath by Tess. **Mark:** J. Neilson, JS.

NELSON, DR CARL,
2500 N Robison Rd, Texarkana, TX 75501

NELSON, KEN,
11059 Hwy 73, Pittsville, WI 54466, Phone: 715-323-0538 or 715-884-6448, Email:dwarveniron@yahoo.com
Specialties: Working straight knives, period pieces. **Patterns:** Utility, hunters, dirks, daggers, throwers, hawks, axes, swords, pole arms and blade blanks as well. **Technical:** Forges 5160, 52100, W2, 10xx, L6, carbon steels and own Damascus. Does his own heat treating. **Prices:** $50 to $350, some to $3000. **Remarks:** Part-time maker. First knife sold in 1995. Doing business as Iron Wolf Forge. **Mark:** Stylized wolf paw print.

NELSON, TOM,
PO Box 2298, Wilropark 1731, Gauteng, SOUTH AFRICA, Phone: 27 11 7663991, Fax: 27 11 7687161, tom.nelson@telkomsa.net
Specialties: Own Damascus (Hosaic etc.) **Patterns:** One-of-a-kind art knives, swords and axes. **Prices:** $500 to $1000.

NETO JR., NELSON AND DE CARVALHO, HENRIQUE M.,
R. Joao Margarido No 20-V, Guerra, Braganca Paulista, SP-12900-000, BRAZIL, Phone: 011-7843-6889, Fax: 011-7843-6889
Specialties: Straight knives and folders. **Patterns:** Bowies, katanas, jambyias and others. **Technical:** Forges high-carbon steels. **Prices:** $70 to $3000. **Remarks:** Full-time makers; first knife sold in 1990. **Mark:** HandN.

NEUHAEUSLER, ERWIN,
Heiligenangerstrasse 15, 86179 Augsburg, GERMANY, Phone: 0821/81 49 97, ERWIN@AUASBURGKNIVES.DE
Specialties: Using straight knives of his design. **Patterns:** Hunters, boots, Bowies and folders. **Technical:** Grinds ATS-34, RWL-34 and Damascus. **Prices:** $200 to $750. **Remarks:** Spare-time maker; first knife sold in 1991. **Mark:** Etched logo, last name and city.

NEVLING, MARK,
BURR OAK KNIVES, PO Box 9, Hume, IL 61932, Phone: 217-887-2522
Specialties: Straight knives and folders of his own design. **Patterns:** Hunters, fighters, Bowies, folders, and small executive knives. **Technical:** Convex grinds, Forges, uses only high-carbon and Damascus. **Prices:** $200 to $2000. **Remarks:** Full-time maker, first knife sold 1988. Apprentice Damascus smith to George Werth.

NEWCOMB, CORBIN,
628 Woodland Ave, Moberly, MO 65270, Phone: 660-263-4639
Specialties: Working straight knives and folders; period pieces. **Patterns:** Hunters, axes, Bowies, folders, buckskinned blades and boots. **Technical:** Hollow-grinds D2, 440C and 154CM; prefers natural handle materials. Makes own Damascus; offers cable Damascus. **Prices:** $100 to $500. **Remarks:** Full-time maker; first knife sold in 1982. Doing business as Corbin Knives. **Mark:** First name and serial number.

NEWHALL, TOM,
3602 E 42nd Stravenue, Tucson, AZ 85713, Phone: 520-721-0562, gggaz@aol.com

NEWTON, LARRY,
1758 Pronghorn Ct, Jacksonville, FL 32225, Phone: 904-221-2340, Fax: 904-220-4098, CNewton1234@aol.com
Specialties: Traditional and slender high-grade gentlemen's automatic folders, locking liner type tactical, and working straight knives. **Patterns:** Front release locking folders, interframes, hunters, and skinners. **Technical:** Grinds Damascus, ATS-34, 440C and D2. **Prices:** Folders start at $350, straights start at $150. **Remarks:** Retired teacher. Full-time maker. First knife sold in 1989. **Mark:** Last name.

NEWTON, RON,
223 Ridge Ln, London, AR 72847, Phone: 479-293-3001, rnewton@cei.net
Specialties: Mosaic Damascus folders with accelerated actions. **Patterns:** One-of-a-kind. **Technical:** 1084-15N20 steels used in his mosaic Damascus steels. **Prices:** $1000 to $5000. **Remarks:** Also making antique Bowie repros and various fixed blades. **Mark:** All capital letters in NEWTON "Western Invitation" font.

NICHOLSON, R. KENT,
PO Box 204, Phoenix, MD 21131, Phone: 410-323-6925
Specialties: Large using knives. Patterns: Bowies and camp knives in the Moran-style. **Technical:** Forges W2, 9260, 5160; makes Damascus. **Prices:** $150 to $995. **Remarks:** Part-time maker; first knife sold in 1984. **Mark:** Name.

NIELSON, JEFF V,
1060 S Jones Rd, Monroe, UT 84754, Phone: 435-527-4242, jvn1u205@hotmail.com
Specialties: Classic knives of his design and to customer specs. **Patterns:** Fighters, hunters; miniatures. **Technical:** Grinds 440C stainless and Damascus. **Prices:** $100 to $1200. **Remarks:** Part-time maker; first knife sold in 1991. **Mark:** Name, location.

NIEMUTH, TROY,
3143 North Ave, Sheboygan, WI 53083, Phone: 414-452-2927
Specialties: Period pieces and working/using straight knives of his design and to customer specs. **Patterns:** Hunters and utility/camp knives. **Technical:** Grinds 440C, 1095 and A2. **Prices:** $85 to $350; some to $500. **Remarks:** Full-time maker; first knife sold in 1995. **Mark:** Etched last name.

NILSSON, JONNY WALKER,
Tingsstigen 11, SE-933 33 Arvidsjaur, SWEDEN, Phone: (46) 960-13048, 0960.1304@telia.com; Web: www.jwnknives.com
Specialties: High-end collectible Nordic hunters, engraved reindeer antler. World class freehand engravings. Matching engraved sheaths in leather, bone and Arctic wood with inlays. Combines traditional techniques and design with his own innovations. Master Bladesmith who specializes in forging mosaic Damascus. Sells unique mosaic Damascus bar stock to folder makers. **Patterns:** Own designs and traditional Sami designs. **Technical:** Mosaic Damascus of UHB 20 C 15N20 with pure nickel, hardness HRC 58-60. **Prices:** $1500 to $6000. **Remarks:** Full-time maker since 1988. Nordic Champion (5 countries) numerous times, 50 first prizes in Scandinavian shows. Yearly award in his name in Nordic Championship. Knives inspired by 10,000 year old indigenous Sami culture. **Mark:** JN on sheath, handle, custom wood box. JWN on blade.

NISHIUCHI, MELVIN S,
6121 Forest Park Dr, Las Vegas, NV 89156, Phone: 702-438-2327
Specialties: Collectable quality using/working knives. **Patterns:** Locking liner folders, fighters, hunters and fancy personal knives. **Technical:** Grinds ATS-34 and Devin Thomas Damascus; prefers semi-precious stone and exotic natural handle materials. **Prices:** $375 to $2000. **Remarks:** Part-time maker; first knife sold in 1985. **Mark:** Circle with a line above it.

NOLEN, R D AND STEVE,
105 Flowingwells Rd, Pottsboro, TX 75076, Phone: 903-786-2454, blademaster@nolenkinves.com; Web: www.nolenknives.com
Specialties: Working knives; display pieces. **Patterns:** Wide variety of straight knives, butterflies and buckles. **Technical:** Grind D2, 440C and 154CM. Offer filework; make exotic handles. **Prices:** $150 to $800; some higher. **Remarks:** Full-time makers; first knife sold in1958. Steve is third generation maker. **Mark:** NK in oval logo.

NORDELL, INGEMAR,
Skarpå 2103, 82041 Färila, SWEDEN, Phone: 0651-23347
Specialties: Classic working and using straight knives. **Patterns:** Hunters, Bowies and fighters. **Technical:** Forges and grinds ATS-34, D2 and Sandvik. **Prices:** $120 to $1500. **Remarks:** Part-time maker; first knife sold in 1985. **Mark:** Initials or name.

NOREN, DOUGLAS E,
14676 Boom Rd, Springlake, MI 49456, Phone: 616-842-4247, gnoren@icsdata.com
Specialties: Hand forged blades, custom built and made to order. Hand file work, carving and casting. Stag and stacked handles. Replicas of Scagel and Joseph Rogers. Hand tooled custom made sheaths. **Technical:** Master smith, 5160, 52100 and 1084 steel. **Prices:** Start at $250. **Remarks:** Sole authorship, works in all mediums, ABS Mastersmith, all knives come with a custom hand-tooled sheath. Also makes anvils. Enjoys the challenge and meeting people.

NORFLEET, ROSS W,
4110 N Courthouse Rd, Providence Forge, VA 23140-3420, Phone: 804-966-2596, rossknife@aol.com
Specialties: Classic, traditional and working/using knives of his design or in standard patterns. **Patterns:** Hunters and folders. **Technical:** Hollow-grinds 440C and ATS-34. **Prices:** $150 to $550. **Remarks:** Part-time maker; first knife sold in 1992. **Mark:** Last name.

NORRIS, DON,
8710 N Hollybrook, Tucson, AZ 85742, Phone: 520-744-2494, Fax: 520-744-2544
Specialties: Classic and traditional working/using straight knives and folders of his design, or to customer specs, etc. **Patterns:** Bowies, daggers, fighters, hunters and utility/camp knives. **Technical:** Grinds and forges Damascus; grinds ATS-34 and 440C. Cast sterling guards and bolsters on Bowies. **Prices:** $350 to $5000, some to $10,000. **Remarks:** Full-time maker; first knife sold in 1990. Doing business as Norris Custom Knives. **Mark:** Last name.

NORTON, DON,
95N Wilkison Ave, Port Townsend, WA 98368-2534, Phone: 306-385-1978
Specialties: Fancy and plain straight knives. **Patterns:** Hunters, small

Bowies, tantos, boot knives, fillets. **Technical:** Prefers 440C, Micarta, exotic woods and other natural handle materials. Hollow-grinds all knives except fillet knives. **Prices:** $185 to $2800; average is $200. **Remarks:** Full-time maker; first knife sold in 1980. **Mark:** Full name, Hsi Shuai, city, state.

NOTT, RON P,
PO Box 281, Summerdale, PA 17093, Phone: 717-732-2763, neitznott@aol.com
Specialties: High-art folders and some straight knives. **Patterns:** Scale release folders. **Technical:** Grinds ATS-34, 416 and nickel-silver. Engraves, inlays gold. **Prices:** $250 to $3000. **Remarks:** Full-time maker; first knife sold in 1993. Doing business as Knives By Nott, customer engraving. **Mark:** First initial, last name and serial number.

NOWLAND, RICK,
3677 E Bonnie Rd, Waltonville, IL 62894, Phone: 618-279-3170, ricknowland@frontiernet.net
Specialties: Slip joint folders in traditional patterns. **Patterns:** Trapper, whittler, sowbelly, toothpick and copperhead. **Technical:** Uses ATS-34, bolsters and liners have integral construction. **Prices:** $225 to $1000. **Remarks:** Part-time maker. **Mark:** Last name.

NUNN, GREGORY,
HC64 Box 2107, Castle Valley, UT 84532, Phone: 435-259-8607
Specialties: High-art working and using knives of his design; new edition knife with handle made from anatomized dinosaur bone, first ever made. **Patterns:** Flaked stone knives. **Technical:** Uses gem-quality agates, jaspers and obsidians for blades. **Prices:** $250 to $2300. **Remarks:** Full-time maker; first knife sold in 1989. **Mark:** Name, knife and edition numbers, year made.

O

OCHS, CHARLES F,
124 Emerald Lane, Largo, FL 33771, Phone: 727-536-3827, Fax: 727-536-3827, chuckandbelle@juno.com
Specialties: Working knives; period pieces. **Patterns:** Hunters, fighters, Bowies, buck skinners and folders. **Technical:** Forges 52100, 5160 and his own Damascus. **Prices:** $150 to $1800; some to $2500. **Remarks:** Full-time maker; first knife sold in 1978. **Mark:** OX Forge.

O'DELL, CLYDE,
176 Ouachita 404, Camden, AR 71701, Phone: 870-574-2754, abcodell@arkansas.net
Specialties: Working knives. **Patterns:** Hunters, camp knives, Bowies, daggers, tomahawks. **Technical:** Forges 5160 and 1084. **Prices:** Starting at $125. **Remarks:** Spare-time maker. **Mark:** Last name.

ODGEN, RANDY W,
10822 Sage Orchard, Houston, TX 77089, Phone: 713-481-3601

ODOM JR., VICTOR L.,
PO Box 572, North, SC 29112, Phone: 803-247-5614, vlodom@joimail.com
Specialties: Forged knives and tomahawks; stock removal knives. **Patterns:** Hunters, Bowies and folders. **Technical:** Use 1095, 5160, 52100 high carbon and alloy steels, ATS-34, and 55. **Prices:** Straight knives $60 and up. Folders @$250 and up. **Remarks:** Student of Mr. George Henron. SCAK.ORG. **Mark:** Steel stamp "ODOM" and etched "Odom Forge North, SC" plus a serial number.

OGDEN, BILL,
OGDEN KNIVES, PO Box 52, Avis
AVIS, PA 17721, Phone: 570-974-9114
Specialties: One-of-a-kind, liner-lock folders, hunters, skinners, minis. **Technical:** Grinds ATS-34, 440-C, D2, 52100, Damascus, natural and unnatural handle materials, hand-stitched custom sheaths. **Prices:** $50 and up. **Remarks:** Part-time maker since 1992. **Marks:** Last name or "OK" stamp (Ogden Knives).

OGLETREE JR., BEN R,
2815 Israel Rd, Livingston, TX 77351, Phone: 409-327-8315
Specialties: Working/using straight knives of his design. **Patterns:** Hunters, kitchen and utility/camp knives. **Technical:** Grinds ATS-34, W1 and 1075; heat-treats. **Prices:** $200 to $400. **Remarks:** Part-time maker; first knife sold in 1955. **Mark:** Last name, city and state in oval with a tree on either side.

O'HARE, SEAN,
PO Box 374, Fort Simpson, NT, CANADA X0E 0N0, Phone: 867-695-2619, sean@ohareknives.com; Web: www.ohareknives.com
Specialties: Fixed blade hunters and tactical knives. **Patterns:** Neck knives to larger hunter and tactical knives. **Technical:** Stock removal, full and hidden tang knives. **Prices:** $125 USD to $800 USD. **Remarks:** Strives to balance aesthetics, functionality and durability. **Mark:** 1st is "OHARE KNIVES", 2nd is "NWT CANADA."

OLIVE, MICHAEL E,
6388 Angora Mt Rd, Leslie, AR 72645, Phone: 870-363-4668
Specialties: Fixed blades. Patterns: Bowies, camp knives, fighters and hunters. **Technical:** Forged blades of 1084, W2, 5160, Damascus of 1084, and1572. **Prices:** $250 and up. **Remarks:** Received J.S. stamp in 2005. **Mark:** Olive.

OLIVER, TODD D,
894 Beaver Hollow, Spencer, IN 47460, Phone: 812-829-1762
Specialties: Damascus hunters and daggers. High-carbon as well. **Patterns:** Ladder, twist random. **Technical:** Sole author of all his blades. **Prices:** $350 and up. **Remarks:** Learned bladesmithing from Jim Batson at the ABS school and Damascus from Billy Merritt in Indiana. **Mark:** T.D. Oliver Spencer IN. Two crossed swords and a battle ax.

OLOFSON, CHRIS,
29 KNIVES, 1 Kendall SQ Bldg. 600, Cambridge, MA 02139, Phone: 617-492-0451, artistacie@earthlink.net

OLSON, DARROLD E,
PO Box 1539, Springfield, OR 97477, Phone: 541-285-1412
Specialties: Straight knives and folders of his design and to customer specs. **Patterns:** Hunters, liner locks and locking folders. **Technical:** Grinds 440C, ATS-34 and 154CM. Uses anodized titanium; sheaths wet-molded. **Prices:** $250 to $550. **Remarks:** Part-time maker; first knife sold in 1989. **Mark:** Etched logo, year, type of steel and name.

OLSON, ROD,
Box 5973, High River, AB, CANADA T1V 1P6, Phone: 403-652-2744, Fax: 403-646-5838
Specialties: Lockback folders with gold toothpicks. **Patterns:** Locking folders. **Technical:** Grinds ATS-34 blades and spring, filework-14kt bolsters and liners. **Prices:** Mid range. **Remarks:** Part-time maker; first knife sold in 1979. **Mark:** Last name on blade.

OLSON, WAYNE C,
890 Royal Ridge Dr, Bailey, CO 80421, Phone: 303-816-9486
Specialties: High-tech working knives. **Patterns:** Hunters to folding lockers; some integral designs. **Technical:** Grinds 440C, 154CM and ATS-34; likes hand-finishes; precision-fits stainless steel fittings—no solder, no nickel silver. **Prices:** $275 to $600; some to $3000. **Remarks:** Part-time maker; first knife sold in 1979. **Mark:** Name, maker.

OLSZEWSKI, STEPHEN,
1820 Harkney Hill Rd, Coventry, RI 02816, Phone: 401-397-4774, blade5377@yahoo.com; Web: www.olszewskiknives.com
Specialties: Lock back, liner locks, automatics (art knives). **Patterns:** One-of-a-kind art knives specializing in figurals. **Technical:** Damascus steel, titanium file worked liners, fossil ivory and pearl. Double actions. **Prices:** $1750 to $20,000. **Remarks:** Will custom build to your specifications. Quality work with guarantee. **Mark:** SCO inside fish symbol. Also "Olszewski."

O'MALLEY, DANIEL,
4338 Evanston Ave N, Seattle, WA 98103, Phone: 206-527-0315
Specialties: Custom chef's knives. **Remarks:** Making knives since 1997.

ONION, KENNETH J,
47-501 Hui Kelu St, Kaneohe, HI 96744, Phone: 808-239-1300, Fax: 808-289-1301, shopjunky@aol.com; Web: www.kenonionknives.com
Specialties: Folders featuring speed safe as well as other invention gadgets. **Patterns:** Hybrid, art, fighter, utility. **Technical:** S30V, CPM 154V, Cowry Y, SQ-2 and Damascus. **Prices:** $500 to $20,000. **Remarks:** Full-time maker; designer and inventor. First knife sold in 1991. **Mark:** Name and state.

ORTEGA, BEN M,
165 Dug Rd, Wyoming, PA 18644, Phone: 717-696-3234

ORTON, RICH,
3625 Fleming St, Riverside, CA 92509, Phone: 951-685-3019, ortonknifeworks@earthlink.net
Specialties: Straight knives only. **Patterns:** Bird, trout and bowies. **Technical:** Grinds ATS-34, CPM154. Heat treats by Paul Bos. **Prices:** $100 to $1000. **Remarks:** Full-time maker; first knife sold in 1992. Doing business as Orton Knife Works. Now making folders. **Mark:** Last name, city state (maker)

OSBORNE, DONALD H,
5840 N McCall, Clovis, CA 93611, Phone: 559-299-9483, Fax: 559-298-1751, oforge@sbcglobal.net
Specialties: Traditional working using straight knives and folder of his design. **Patterns:** Working straight knives, Bowies, hunters, camp knives and folders. **Technical:** Forges carbon steels and makes Damascus. Grinds ATS-34, 154CM, and 440C. **Prices:** $150 and up. **Remarks:** Part-time maker. **Mark:** Last name logo and J.S.

OSBORNE, WARREN,
#2-412 Alysa Ln, Waxahachie, TX 75167, Phone: 972-935-0899, Fax: 972-937-9004, ossie1@worldnet.att.net; Web: www.osborneknives.com
Specialties: Investment grade collectible, interframes, one-of-a-kinds; unique locking mechanisms and cutting competition knives. Patterns: Folders; bolstered and interframes; conventional lockers, front lockers and back lockers; some slip-joints; some high-art pieces. **Technical:** Grinds CPM M4, BG42, CPM S30V, Damascus -some forged and stock removed cutting competition knives. **Prices:** $1200 to $3500; some to $5000. Interframes $1250 to $3000. **Remarks:** Full-time maker; first knife sold in 1980. **Mark:** Last name in boomerang logo.

OTT, FRED,
1257 Rancho Durango Rd, Durango, CO 81303, Phone: 970-375-9669
Patterns: Bowies, hunters tantos and daggers. **Technical:** Forges 1086M, W2 and Damascus. **Prices:** $250 to $1000. **Remarks:** Full-time maker. **Mark:** Last name.

OUYE, KEITH,
PO Box 25307, Honolulu, HI 96825, Phone: 808-395-7000, keithouyeknives@yahoo.com
Specialties: Folders with 1/8 blades and titanium handles. **Patterns:** Tactical design with liner lock and flipper. **Technical:** Blades are stainless steel ATS 34, CPM154 stainless steel and S30V. Titanium liners (.071) and scales 3/16 pivots and stop pin, titanium pocket clip. Heat treat by Paul Bos.**Prices:** $450-$600 with engraved knives starting at $995 and up. **Remarks:** Engraving done by C.J. Cal (www.caiengraving.com) and Bruce Shaw Retired, so basically a full time knifemaker. Sold first fixed blade in 2004 and first folder in 2005. **Mark:** Ouye/Hawaii with steel type on back side **Other:** Selected by Blade Magazine (March 2006 issue) as one of five makers to watch in 2006.

OVEREYNDER, T R,
1800 S. Davis Dr, Arlington, TX 76013, Phone: 817-277-4812, Fax: 817-277-4812, trovereynderknives@sbcglobal.net; Web: www.overeynderknives.com
Specialties: Highly finished collector-grade knives. Multi-blades. **Patterns:** Fighters, Bowies, daggers, locking folders, 70 percent collector-grade multi blade slip joints, 25 percent interframe, 5 percent fixed blade **Technical:** Grinds CPM-D2, BG-42, S60V, S30V, CPM154, CPM M4, RWL-34 vendor supplied Damascus. Has been making titanium-frame folders since 1977. **Prices:** $500 to $1500; some to $7000. **Remarks:** Full-time maker; first knife sold in 1977. Doing business as TRO Knives. **Mark:** T.R. OVEREYNDER KNIVES, city and state.

OWENS, DONALD,
2274 Lucille Ln, Melbourne, FL 32935, Phone: 321-254-9765

OWENS, JOHN,
14500 CR 270, Nathrop, CO 81236, Phone: 719-395-0870
Specialties: Hunters. **Prices:** $200 to $375 some to $650. **Remarks:** Spare-time maker. **Mark:** Last name.

OWNBY, JOHN C,
3316 Springbridge Ln, Plano, TX 75025, john@johnownby.com; Web: www.johnownby.com
Specialties: Hunters, utility/camp knives. **Patterns:** Hunters, locking folders and utility/camp knives. **Technical:** 440C, D2 and ATS-34. All blades are flat ground. Prefers natural materials for handles—exotic woods, horn and antler. **Prices:** $150 to $350; some to $500. **Remarks:** Part-time maker; first knife sold in 1993. Doing business as John C. Ownby Handmade Knives. **Mark:** Name, city, state.

OYSTER, LOWELL R,
543 Grant Rd, Corinth, ME 04427, Phone: 207-884-8663
Specialties: Traditional and original designed multi-blade slip-joint folders. **Patterns:** Hunters, minis, camp and fishing knives. **Technical:** Grinds O1; heat-treats. **Prices:** $55 to $450; some to $750. **Remarks:** Full-time maker; first knife sold in 1981. **Mark:** A scallop shell.

P

PACHI, FRANCESCO,
Via Pometta 1, 17046 Sassello (SV), ITALY, Phone: 019 720086, Fax: 019 720086, Web: www.pachi-knives.com
Specialties: Folders and straight knives of his design. **Patterns:** Utility, hunters and skinners. **Technical:** Grinds RWL-34, CPM S30V and Damascus. **Prices:** $800 to $3500. **Remarks:** Full-time maker; first knife sold in 1991. **Mark:** Logo with last name.

PACKARD, BOB,
PO Box 311, Elverta, CA 95626, Phone: 916-991-5218
Specialties: Traditional working/using straight knives of his design and to customer specs. **Patterns:** Hunters, fishing knives, utility/camp knives. **Technical:** Grinds ATS-34, 440C; Forges 52100, 5168 and cable Damascus. **Prices:** $75 to $225. **Mark:** Engraved name and year.

PADGETT JR., EDWIN L,
340 Vauxhall St, New London, CT 06320-3838, Phone: 860-443-2938
Specialties: Skinners and working knives of any design. **Patterns:** Straight and folding knives. **Technical:** Grinds ATS-34 or any tool steel upon request. **Prices:** $50 to $300. **Mark:** Name.

PADILLA, GARY,
PO Box 4706, Bellingham, WA 98227, Phone: 360-756-7573, gkpadilla@yahoo.com
Specialties: Unique knives of all designs and uses. **Patterns:** Hunters, kitchen knives, utility/camp knives and obsidian ceremonial knives. **Technical:** Grinds 440C, ATS-34, O1 and Damascus. **Prices:** Generally $100 to $200. **Remarks:** Part-time maker; first knife sold in 1977. **Mark:** Stylized name.

PAGE, LARRY,
1200 Mackey Scott Rd, Aiken, SC 29801-7620, Phone: 803-648-0001
Specialties: Working knives of his design. **Patterns:** Hunters, boots and fighters. **Technical:** Grinds ATS-34. **Prices:** Start at $85. **Remarks:** Part-time maker; first knife sold in 1983. **Mark:** Name, city and state in oval.

PAGE, REGINALD,
6587 Groveland Hill Rd, Groveland, NY 14462, Phone: 716-243-1643
Specialties: High-art straight knives and one-of-a-kind folders of his design. **Patterns:** Hunters, locking folders and slip-joint folders. **Technical:** Forges O1, 5160 and his own Damascus. Prefers natural handle materials but will work with Micarta. **Remarks:** Spare-time maker; first knife sold in 1985. **Mark:** First initial, last name.

PAINTER, TONY,
87 Fireweed Dr, Whitehorse Yukon, CANADA Y1A 5T8, Phone: 867-633-3323, jimmies@klondiker.com; Web: www.tonypainterdesigns.com
Specialties: One-of-a-kind using knives, some fancy, fixed and folders. **Patterns:** No fixed patterns. **Technical:** Grinds ATS-34, D2, O1, S30V, Damascus satin finish. Prefers to use exotic woods and other natural materials. Micarta and G10 on working knives. **Prices:** Starting at $200. **Remarks:** Full-time knifemaker and carver. First knife sold in 1996. **Mark:** Two stamps used: initials TP in a circle and painter.

PALM, RIK,
10901 Scripps Ranch Blvd, San Diego, CA 92131, Phone: 858-530-0407, rikpalm@knifesmith.com; Web: www.knifesmith.com
Specialties: Sole authorship of one-of-a-kind unique art pieces, working/using knives and sheaths. **Patterns:** Carved nature themed knives, camp, hunters, friction folders, tomahawks, and small special pocket knives. **Technical:** Makes own Damascus, forges 5160H, 1084, 1095, W2, O1. Does his own heat treating including clay hardening. **Prices:** $80 and up. **Remarks:** American Bladesmith Society Journeyman Smith. First blade sold in 2000. **Mark:** Stamped, hand signed, etched last name signature.

PALMER, TAYLOR,
TAYLOR-MADE SCENIC KNIVES INC., Box 97, Blanding, UT 84511, Phone: 435-678-2523, taylormadewoodeu@citlink.net
Specialties: Bronze carvings inside of blade area. **Prices:** $250 and up. **Mark:** Taylor Palmer Utah.

PANAK, PAUL S,
9128 Stanhope-Kellogsville Rd, Kinsman, OH 44428, Phone: 330-876-2210, burn@burnknives.com; Web: www.burnknives.com
Specialties: Italian-styled knives. DA OTF's, Italian style stilettos. **Patterns:** Vintage-styled Italians, fighting folders and high art gothic-styles all with various mechanisms. **Technical:** Grinds ATS-34, 154 CM, 440C and Damascus. **Prices:** $800 to $3000. **Remarks:** Full-time maker, first knife sold in 1998. **Mark:** "Burn."

PARDUE, JOE,
PO Box 693, Spurger, TX 77660, Phone: 409-429-7074, Fax: 409-429-5657

PARDUE, MELVIN M,
4461 Jerkins, Repton, AL 36475, Phone: 251-248-2447, mpardue@frontiernet.net; Web: www.melpardueknives.com
Specialties: Folders, collectable, combat, utility and tactical. **Patterns:** Lockback, liner lock, push button; all blade and handle patterns. **Technical:** Grinds 154CM, 440C, 12C27. Forges mokume and Damascus. Uses titanium. **Prices:** $400 to $1600. **Remarks:** Full-time maker; Guild member, ABS member, AFC member. First knife made in 1957; first knife sold professionally in 1974. **Mark:** Mel Pardue.

PARKER, CLIFF,
6350 Tulip Dr, Zephyrhills, FL 33544, Phone: 813-973-1682
Specialties: Damascus gent knives. **Patterns:** Locking liners, some straight knives. **Technical:** Mostly use 1095, 1084, 15N20, 203E and powdered steel. **Prices:** $700 to $1800. **Remarks:** Making own Damascus and specializing in mosaics; first knife sold in 1996. Full-time beginning in 2000. **Mark:** CP.

PARKER, J E,
11 Domenica Cir, Clarion, PA 16214, Phone: 814-226-4837, jimparkerknives@hotmail.com Web: www.jimparkerknives.com
Specialties: Fancy/embellished, traditional and working straight knives of his design and to customer specs. Engraving and scrimshaw by the best in the business. **Patterns:** Bowies, hunters and LinerLock® folders. **Technical:** Grinds 440C, 440V, ATS-34 and nickel Damascus. Prefers mastodon, oosik, amber and malachite handle material. **Prices:** $75 to $5200. **Remarks:** Full-time maker; first knife sold in 1991. Doing business as Custom Knife. **Mark:** J E Parker and Clarion PA stamped or etched in blade.

PARKER, ROBERT NELSON,
1527 E Fourth St, Royal Oak, MI 48067, Phone: 248-545-8211, rnparkerknives@wowway.com; Web: classicknifedesign@wowway.com
Specialties: Traditional working and using straight knives of his design. Patterns: Chutes, subhilts, hunters, and fighters. **Technical:** Grinds ATS-34; GB-42, S-30V, BG-42, ATS, 34-D-Z, no forging, hollow and flat grinds, full and hidden tangs. Hand-stitched leather sheaths. **Prices:** $400 to $1400; some to $2000. **Remarks:** Full-time maker; first knife sold in 1986. **Mark:** Full name.

PARKS, BLANE C,
15908 Crest Dr, Woodbridge, VA 22191, Phone: 703-221-4680
Specialties: Knives of his design. **Patterns:** Boots, Bowies, daggers, fighters, hunters, kitchen knives, locking and slip-joint folders, utility/camp knives, letter openers and friction folders. **Technical:** Grinds ATS-34, 440C, D2 and other carbon steels. Offers filework, silver wire inlay and wooden sheaths. **Prices:** Start at $250 to $650; some to $1000. **Remarks:** Part-time maker; first knife sold in 1993. Doing business as B.C. Parks Knives. **Mark:** First and middle initials, last name.

PARKS, JOHN,
3539 Galilee Church Rd, Jefferson, GA 30549, Phone: 706-367-4916
Specialties: Traditional working and using straight knives of his design. **Patterns:** Trout knives, hunters and integral bolsters. **Technical:** Forges 1095 and 5168. **Prices:** $275 to $600; some to $800. **Remarks:** Part-time maker; first knife sold in 1989. **Mark:** Initials.

PARLER, THOMAS O,
11 Franklin St, Charleston, SC 29401, Phone: 803-723-9433

PARRISH, ROBERT,
271 Allman Hill Rd, Weaverville, NC 28787, Phone: 828-645-2864
Specialties: Heavy-duty working knives of his design or to customer specs. **Patterns:** Survival and duty knives; hunters and fighters. **Technical:** Grinds 440C, D2, O1 and commercial Damascus. **Prices:** $200 to $300; some to $6000. **Remarks:** Part-time maker; first knife sold in 1970. **Mark:** Initials connected, sometimes with city and state.

PARRISH III, GORDON A,
940 Lakloey Dr, North Pole, AK 99705, Phone: 907-488-0357, ga-parrish@gci.net
Specialties: Classic and high-art straight knives of his design and to customer specs; working and using knives. **Patterns:** Bowies and hunters. **Technical:** Grinds tool steel and ATS-34. Uses mostly Alaskan handle materials. **Prices:** $200 to $1000. **Remarks:** Spare-time maker; first knife sold in 1980. **Mark:** Last name, state.

PARSONS, LARRY,
1038 W Kyle Way, Mustang, OK 73064, Phone: 405-376-9408, s.m.parsons@sbcglobal.net
Specialties: Variety of sheaths from plain leather, geometric stamped, also inlays of various types. **Prices:** Starting at $35 and up

PARSONS, MICHAEL R,
MCKEE KNIVES, 7042 McFarland Rd., Indianapolis, IN 46227, Phone: 317-784-7943, mparsons@comcast.net
Specialties: Hand-forged fixed-blade knives, all fancy but all are useable knives. **Patterns:** Engraves, carves, wire inlay, and leather work. All knives one-of-a-kind. **Technical:** Blades forged from files, all work hand done. **Prices:** $350 to $2000. **Mark:** McKee.

PASSMORE, JIMMY D,
316 SE Elm, Hoxie, AR 72433, Phone: 870-886-1922

PATRICK, BOB,
12642 24A Ave, S. Surrey, B.C., CANADA V4A 8H9, Phone: 604-538-6214, Fax: 604-888-2683, bob@knivesonnet.com; Web: www.knivesonnet.com
Specialties: Maker's designs only, No orders. **Patterns:** Bowies, hunters, daggers, throwing knives. **Technical:** D2, 5160, Damascus. **Prices:** Good value for the money. **Remarks:** Full-time maker; first knife sold in 1987. Doing business as Crescent Knife Works. **Mark:** Logo with name and province or Crescent Knife Works.

PATRICK, CHUCK,
PO Box 127, Brasstown, NC 28902, Phone: 828-837-7627
Specialties: Period pieces. **Patterns:** Hunters, daggers, tomahawks, pre-Civil War folders. **Technical:** Forges hardware, his own cable and Damascus, available in fancy pattern and mosaic. **Prices:** $150 to $1000; some higher. **Remarks:** Full-time maker. **Mark:** Hand-engraved name or flying owl.

PATRICK, PEGGY,
PO Box 127, Brasstown, NC 28902, Phone: 828-837-7627
Specialties: Authentic period and Indian sheaths, braintan, rawhide, beads and quill work. **Technical:** Does own braintan, rawhide; uses only natural dyes for quills, old color beads.

PATRICK, WILLARD C,
PO Box 5716, Helena, MT 59604, Phone: 406-458-6552, Fax: 406-458-7068, wkamar2@onewest.net
Specialties: Working straight knives and one-of-a-kind art knives of his design or to customer specs. **Patterns:** Hunters, Bowies, fish, patch and kitchen knives. **Technical:** Grinds ATS-34, 1095, O1, A2 and Damascus. **Prices:** $100 to $2000. **Remarks:** Full-time maker; first knife sold in 1989. Doing business as Wil-A-Mar Cutlery. **Mark:** Shield with last name and a dagger.

PATTAY, RUDY,
510 E. Harrison St, Long Beach, NY 11561, Phone: 516-431-0847, dolphinp@optonline.net
Specialties: Fancy and working straight knives of his design. **Patterns:** Bowies, hunters, utility/camp knives. **Technical:** Hollow-grinds ATS-34, 440C, O1. Offers commercial Damascus, stainless steel soldered guards; fabricates guard and butt cap on lathe and milling machine. Heat-treats. Prefers synthetic handle materials. Offers hand-sewn sheaths. **Prices:** $100 to $350; some to $500. **Remarks:** Part-time maker; first knife sold in 1990. **Mark:** First initial, last name in sorcerer logo.

PATTERSON, PAT,
Box 246, Barksdale, TX 78828, Phone: 830-234-3586, pat@pattersonknives.com
Specialties: Traditional fixed blades and LinerLock® folders. **Patterns:** Hunters and folders. **Technical:** Grinds 440C, ATS-34, D2, O1 and Damascus. **Prices:** $250 to $1000. **Remarks:** Full-time maker. First knife sold in 1991. **Mark:** Name and city.

PATTON, DICK AND ROB,
6803 View Ln, Nampa, ID 83687, Phone: 208-468-4123, grpatton@pattonknives.com; Web: www.pattonknives.com
Specialties: Custom Damascus, hand forged, fighting knives, Bowie and tactical. **Patterns:** Mini Bowie, Merlin Fighter, Mandrita Fighting Bowie. **Prices:** $100 to $2000.

PAULO, FERNANDES R,
Raposo Tavares No 213, Lencois Paulista, 18680, Sao Paulo, BRAZIL, Phone: 014-263-4281
Specialties: An apprentice of Jose Alberto Paschoarelli, his designs are heavily based on the later designs. **Technical:** Grinds tool steels and stainless steels. Part-time knifemaker. **Prices:** Start from $100. **Mark:** P.R.F.

PAWLOWSKI, JOHN R,
111 Herman Melville Ave, Newport News, VA 23606, Phone: 757-870-4284, Fax: 757-223-5935, www.virginiacustomcutlery.com
Specialties: Traditional working and using straight knives and folders. **Patterns:** Hunters, Bowies, fighters and camp knives. **Technical:** Stock removal, grinds 440C, ATS-34, 154CM and buys Damascus. **Prices:** $150 to $500; some higher. **Remarks:** Part-time maker, first knife sold in 1983, Knifemaker Guild Member. **Mark:** Name with attacking eagle.

PEAGLER, RUSS,
PO Box 1314, Moncks Corner, SC 29461, Phone: 803-761-1008
Specialties: Traditional working straight knives of his design and to customer specs. **Patterns:** Hunters, fighters, boots. **Technical:** Hollow-grinds 440C, ATS-34 and O1; uses Damascus steel. Prefers bone handles. **Prices:** $85 to $300; some to $500. **Remarks:** Spare-time maker; first knife sold in 1983. **Mark:** Initials.

PEASE, W D,
657 Cassidy Pike, Ewing, KY 41039, Phone: 606-845-0387, Web: www.wdpeaseknives.com
Specialties: Display-quality working folders. **Patterns:** Fighters, tantos and boots; locking folders and interframes. **Technical:** Grinds ATS-34 and commercial Damascus; has own side-release lock system. **Prices:** $500 to $1000; some to $3000. **Remarks:** Full-time maker; first knife sold in 1970. **Mark:** First and middle initials, last name and state. W. D. Pease Kentucky.

PEELE, BRYAN,
219 Ferry St, PO Box 1363, Thompson Falls, MT 59873, Phone: 406-827-4633, banana_peele@yahoo.com
Specialties: Fancy working and using knives of his design. **Patterns:** Hunters, Bowies and fighters. **Technical:** Grinds 440C, ATS-34, D2, O1 and commercial Damascus. **Prices:** $110 to $300; some to $900. **Remarks:** Part-time maker; first knife sold in 1985. **Mark:** The Elk Rack, full name, city, state.

PENDLETON, LLOYD,
24581 Shake Ridge Rd, Volcano, CA 95689, Phone: 209-296-3353, Fax: 209-296-3353
Specialties: Contemporary working knives in standard patterns. **Patterns:** Hunters, fighters and boots. **Technical:** Grinds and ATS-34; mirror finishes. **Prices:** $400 to $900 **Remarks:** Full-time maker; first knife sold in 1973. **Mark:** First initial, last name logo, city and state.

PENDRAY, ALFRED H,
13950 NE 20th St, Williston, FL 32696, Phone: 352-528-6124
Specialties: Working straight knives and folders; period pieces. **Patterns:** Fighters and hunters, axes, camp knives and tomahawks. **Technical:** Forges Wootz steel; makes his own Damascus; makes traditional knives from old files and rasps. **Prices:** $125 to $1000; some to $3500. **Remarks:** Part-time maker; first knife sold in 1954. **Mark:** Last initial in horseshoe logo.

PENFOLD, MICK,
PENFOLD KNIVES, 5 Highview Close, Tremar, Cornwall PL14 5SJ, ENGLAND, Phone: 01579-345783, Fax: 01579-345783, mickpenfold@btinternet.com; Web: www.penfoldknives.com
Specialties: Hunters, fighters, Bowies. **Technical:** Grinds 440C, ATS-34, and Damascus. **Prices:** $200 to $1800. **Remarks:** Part-time maker. First knives sold in 1999. **Mark:** Last name.

PENNINGTON, C A,
163 Kainga Rd, Kainga Christchurch 8009, NEW ZEALAND, Phone: 03-3237292, capennington@xtra.co.nz
Specialties: Classic working and collectors knives. Folders a specialty. **Patterns:** Classical styling for hunters and collectors. **Technical:** Forges

his own all tool steel Damascus. Grinds D2 when requested. **Prices:** $240 to $2000. **Remarks:** Full-time maker; first knife sold in 1988. Color brochure $3. **Mark:** Name, country.

PEPIOT, STEPHAN,
73 Cornwall Blvd, Winnipeg, Man., CANADA R3J-1E9, Phone: 204-888-1499
Specialties: Working straight knives in standard patterns. **Patterns:** Hunters and camp knives. **Technical:** Grinds 440C and industrial hack-saw blades. **Prices:** $75 to $125. **Remarks:** Spare-time maker; first knife sold in 1982. Not currently taking orders. **Mark:** PEP.

PERRY, CHRIS,
1654 W. Birch, Fresno, CA 93711, Phone: 209-498-2342
Specialties: Traditional working/using straight knives of his design. **Patterns:** Boots, hunters and utility/camp knives. **Technical:** Grinds ATS-34 and 416ss fittings. **Prices:** $190 to $225. **Remarks:** Spare-time maker. **Mark:** Name above city and state.

PERRY, JIM,
Hope Star PO Box 648, Hope, AR 71801, jenn@comfabinc.com

PERRY, JOHN,
9 South Harrell Rd, Mayflower, AR 72106, Phone: 501-470-3043
Specialties: Investment grade and working folders; Antique Bowies and slip joints. **Patterns:** Front and rear lock folders, liner locks, hunters and Bowies. **Technical:** Grinds CPM440V, D2 and making own Damascus. Offers filework. **Prices:** $375 to $1200; some to $3500. **Remarks:** Part-time maker; first knife sold in 1991. Doing business as Perry Custom Knives. **Mark:** Initials or last name in high relief set in a diamond shape.

PERRY, JOHNNY,
PO Box 4666, Spartanburg, SC 29305-4666, Phone: 803-578-3533, comfabinc@mindspring.com

PERSSON, CONNY,
PL 588, 820 50 Loos, SWEDEN, Phone: +46 657 10305, Fax: +46 657 413 435, connyknives@swipnet.se; Web: www.connyknives.com
Specialties: Mosaic Damascus. **Patterns:** Mosaic Damascus. **Technical:** Straight knives and folders. **Prices:** $1000 and up. **Mark:** C. Persson.

PETEAN, FRANCISCO AND MAURICIO,
R. Dr. Carlos de Carvalho Rosa 52, Centro, Birigui, SP-16200-000, BRAZIL, Phone: 0186-424786
Specialties: Classic knives to customer specs. **Patterns:** Bowies, boots, fighters, hunters and utility knives. **Technical:** Grinds D6, 440C and high-carbon steels. Prefers natural handle material. **Prices:** $70 to $500. **Remarks:** Full-time maker; first knife sold in 1985. **Mark:** Last name, hand made.

PETERSEN, DAN L,
10610 SW 81st, Auburn, KS 66402, Phone: 785-256-2640, dan.petersen@washburn.edu
Specialties: Period pieces and forged integral hilts on hunters and fighters. **Patterns:** Texas-style Bowies, boots and hunters in high-carbon and Damascus steel. **Technical:** Austempers forged high-carbon sword blades. Precision heat treating using salt tanks. **Prices:** $400 to $5000. **Remarks:** First knife sold in 1978. ABS Master Smith. **Mark:** Stylized initials, MS.

PETERSON, CHRIS,
Box 143, 2175 W Rockyford, Salina, UT 84654, Phone: 801-529-7194
Specialties: Working straight knives of his design. **Patterns:** Large fighters, boots, hunters and some display pieces. **Technical:** Forges O1 and meteor. Makes and sells his own Damascus. Engraves, scrimshaws and inlays. **Prices:** $150 to $600; some to $1500. **Remarks:** Full-time maker; first knife sold in 1986. **Mark:** A drop in a circle with a line through it.

PETERSON, ELDON G,
368 Antelope Trl, Whitefish, MT 59937, Phone: 406-862-2204, draino@digisys.net; Web: http://www.kmg.org/egpeterson
Specialties: Fancy and working folders, any size. **Patterns:** Lockback interframes, integral bolster folders, liner locks, and two-blades. **Technical:** Grinds 440C and ATS-34. Offers gold inlay work, gem stone inlays and engraving. **Prices:** $285 to $5000. **Remarks:** Full-time maker; first knife sold in 1974. **Mark:** Name, city and state.

PETERSON, KAREN,
THE PEN AND THE SWORD LTD., PO Box 290741, Brooklyn, NY 11229-0741, Phone: 718-382-4847, Fax: 718-376-5745, info@pensword.com; Web: www.pensword.com

PETERSON, LLOYD (PETE) C,
64 Halbrook Rd, Clinton, AR 72031, Phone: 501-893-0000, wmblade@cyberback.com
Specialties: Miniatures and mosaic folders. **Prices:** $250 and up. **Remarks:** Lead time is 6-8 months. **Mark:** Pete.

PFANENSTIEL, DAN,
1824 Lafayette Ave, Modesto, CA 95355, Phone: 209-575-5937, dpfan@sbcglobal.net
Specialties: Japanese tanto, swords. One-of-a-kind knives. **Technical:** Forges simple carbon steels, some Damascus. **Prices:** $200 to $1000. **Mark:** Circle with wave inside.

PHILIPPE, D A,
PO Box 306, Cornish, NH 03746, Phone: 603-543-0662
Specialties: Traditional working straight knives. **Patterns:** Hunters, trout and bird, camp knives etc. **Technical:** Grinds ATS-34, 440C, A-2, Damascus, flat and hollow ground. Exotic woods and antler handles. Brass, nickel silver and stainless components. **Prices:** $125 to $800. **Remarks:** Full-time maker, first knife sold in 1984. **Mark:** First initial, last name.

PHILLIPS, DENNIS,
16411 West Bennet Rd, Independence, LA 70443, Phone: 985-878-8275
Specialties: Specializes in fixed blade military combat tacticals.

PHILLIPS, JIM,
PO Box 168, Williamstown, NJ 08094, Phone: 609-567-0695

PHILLIPS, RANDY,
759 E. Francis St, Ontario, CA 91761, Phone: 909-923-4381
Specialties: Hunters, collector-grade liner locks and high-art daggers. **Technical:** Grinds D2, 440C and 154CM; embellishes. **Prices:** Start at $200. **Remarks:** Part-time maker; first knife sold in 1981. Not currently taking orders. **Mark:** Name, city and state in eagle head.

PHILLIPS, SCOTT C,
671 California Rd, Gouverneur, NY 13642, Phone: 315-287-1280, Web: www.manguskives.com
Specialties: Sheaths in leather. Fixed blade hunters, boot knives, Bowies, buck skinners (hand forged and stock removal). **Technical:** 440C, 5160, 1095 and 52100. **Prices:** Start at $125. **Remarks:** Part-time maker; first knife sold in 1993. **Mark:** Before "2000" as above after S Mangus.

PICKENS, SELBERT,
2295 Roxalana Rd, Dunbar, WV 25064, Phone: 304-744-4048
Specialties: Using knives. **Patterns:** Standard sporting knives. **Technical:** Stainless steels; stock removal method. **Prices:** Moderate. **Remarks:** Part-time maker. **Mark:** Name.

PICKETT, TERRELL,
66 Pickett Ln, Lumberton, MS 39455, Phone: 601-794-6125, pickettfence66@bellsouth.net
Specialties: Fix blades, camp knives, Bowies, hunters, & skinners. Forge and stock removal and some firework. **Technical:** 5160, 1095, 52100, 440C and ATS-34. **Prices:** Range from $150 to $550. **Mark:** Logo on stock removal T.W. Pickett and on forged knives Terrell Pickett's Forge.

PIENAAR, CONRAD,
19A Milner Rd, Bloemfontein 9300, SOUTH AFRICA, Phone: 027 514364180, Fax: 027 514364180
Specialties: Fancy working and using straight knives and folders of his design, to customer specs and in standard patterns. **Patterns:** Hunters, locking folders, cleavers, kitchen and utility/camp knives. **Technical:** Grinds 12C27, D2 and ATS-34. Uses some Damascus. Scrimshaws; inlays gold. Knives come with wooden box and custom-made leather sheath. **Prices:** $300 to $1000. **Remarks:** Part-time maker; first knife sold in 1981. Doing business as C.P. Knifemaker. Makes slip joint folders and liner locking folders. **Mark:** Initials and serial number.

PIERCE, HAROLD L,
106 Lyndon Lane, Louisville, KY 40222, Phone: 502-429-5136
Specialties: Working straight knives, some fancy. **Patterns:** Big fighters and Bowies. **Technical:** Grinds D2, 440C, 154CM; likes sub-hilts. **Prices:** $150 to $450; some to $1200. **Remarks:** Full-time maker; first knife sold in 1982. **Mark:** Last name with knife through the last initial.

PIERCE, RANDALL,
903 Wyndam, Arlington, TX 76017, Phone: 817-468-0138

PIERGALLINI, DANIEL E,
4011 N. Forbes Rd, Plant City, FL 33565, Phone: 813-754-3908, Fax: 8137543908, coolnifedad@earthlink.net
Specialties: Traditional and fancy straight knives and folders of his design or to customer's specs. **Patterns:** Hunters, fighters, skinners, working and camp knives. **Technical:** Grinds 440C, O1, D2, ATS-34, some Damascus; forges his own mokume. Uses natural handle material. **Prices:** $450 to $800; some to $1800. **Remarks:** Part-time maker; sold first knife in 1994. **Mark:** Last name, city, state or last name in script.

PIESNER, DEAN,
1786 Sawmill Rd, Conestogo, Ont., CANADA N0B 1N0, Phone: 519-664-3648, dean47@rogers.com
Specialties: Classic and period pieces of his design and to customer specs. **Patterns:** Bowies, skinners, fighters and swords. **Technical:** Forges 5160, 52100, steel Damascus and nickel-steel Damascus. Makes own mokume gane with copper, brass and nickel silver. Silver wire inlays in wood. **Prices:** Start at $150. **Remarks:** Full-time maker; first knife sold in 1990. **Mark:** First initial, last name, JS.

PITMAN, DAVID,
PO Drawer 2566, Williston, ND 58802, Phone: 701-572-3325

PITT, DAVID F,
6812 Digger Pine Ln, Anderson, CA 96007, Phone: 530-357-2393
Specialties: Fixed blade, hunters and hatchets. Flat ground mirror finish. Patterns: Hatchets with gut hook, small gut hooks, guards, bolsters or guard less. **Technical:** Grinds A2, 440C, 154CM, ATS-34, D2. **Prices:** $150 to $750. **Remarks:** Guild member since 1982. **Mark:** Bear paw with name David F. Pitt.

PLUNKETT, RICHARD,
29 Kirk Rd, West Cornwall, CT 06796, Phone: 860-672-3419; Toll free: 888-KNIVES-8
Specialties: Traditional, fancy folders and straight knives of his design. **Patterns:** Slip-joint folders and small straight knives. **Technical:** Grinds O1 and stainless steel. Offers many different file patterns. **Prices:** $150 to $450. **Remarks:** Full-time maker; first knife sold in 1994. **Mark:** Signature and date under handle scales.

POLK, CLIFTON,
4625 Webber Creek Rd, Van Buren, AR 72956, Phone: 479-474-3828, cliffpolkknives1@aol.com; Web: www.polkknives.com
Specialties: Fancy working folders. **Patterns:** One blades spring backs in five sizes, LinerLock®, automatics, double blades spring back folder with standard drop & clip blade or bird knife with drop and vent hook or cowboy's knives with drop and hoof pick and straight knives. **Technical:** Uses D2 & ATS-34. Makes all own Damascus using 1084, 1095, O1, 15N20, 5160. Using all kinds of exotic woods. Stag, pearls, ivory, mastodon ivory and other bone and horns. **Prices:** $200 to $3000. **Remarks:** Retired fire fighter, made knives since 1974. **Mark:** Polk.

POLK, RUSTY,
5900 Wildwood Dr, Van Buren, AR 72956, Phone: 479-410-3661, polkknives@aol.com; Web: www.polkknives.com
Specialties: Skinners, hunters, Bowies, fighters and forging working knives fancy Damascus, daggers, boot knives and survival knives. **Patterns:** Drop point, and forge to shape. **Technical:** ATS-34, 440C, Damascus, D2, 51/60, 1084, 15N20, does all his forging. **Prices:** $200 to $1500. **Mark:** R. Polk all hand made. RP on miniatures.

POLKOWSKI, AL,
8 Cathy Lane, Chester, NJ 07930, Phone: 908-879-6030, Web: polkowskiknives.com
Specialties: High-tech straight knives and folders for adventurers and professionals. **Patterns:** Fighters, side-lock folders, boots and concealment knives. **Technical:** Grinds 154CM and S30V, satin and beadblast finishes; Kydex sheaths. **Prices:** Start at $100. **Remarks:** Full-time maker; first knife sold in 1985. **Mark:** Last name with lightning bolts.

POLLOCK, WALLACE J,
806 Russet Vly Dr, Cedar Park, TX 78613, wally@pollocknives.com
Specialties: Using knives, skinner, hunter, fighting, camp knives. **Patterns:** Use his own patterns or yours. Traditional hunters, daggers, fighters, camp knives. **Technical:** Grinds ATS-34, D-2, BG-42, makes own Damascus, D-2, 0-1, ATS-34, prefer D-2, handles exotic wood, horn, bone, ivory. **Remarks:** Full-time maker, sold first knife 1973. **Prices:** $250 to $2500. **Mark:** Last name, maker, city/state.

POLZIEN, DON,
1912 Inler Suite-L, Lubbock, TX 79407, Phone: 806-791-0766, blindinglightknives.net
Specialties: Traditional Japanese-style blades; restores antique Japanese swords, scabbards and fittings. **Patterns:** Hunters, fighters, one-of-a-kind art knives. **Technical:** 1045-1050 carbon steels, 440C, D2, ATS-34, standard and cable Damascus. **Prices:** $150 to $2500. **Remarks:** Full-time maker. First knife sold in 1990. **Mark:** Oriental characters inside square border.

PONZIO, DOUG,
10219 W State Rd 81, Beloit, WI 53511, Phone: 608-313-3223, prfgdoug@hughes.net; Web: www.ponziodamascus.com
Specialties: Mosaic Damascus, stainless Damascus. **Mark:** P.F.

POOLE, MARVIN O,
PO Box 552, Commerce, GA 30529, Phone: 803-225-5970
Specialties: Traditional working/using straight knives and folders of his design and in standard patterns. **Patterns:** Bowies, fighters, hunters, locking folders, bird and trout knives. **Technical:** Grinds 440C, D2, ATS-34. **Prices:** $50 to $150; some to $750. **Remarks:** Part-time maker; first knife sold in 1980. **Mark:** First initial, last name, year, serial number.

POSKOCIL, HELMUT,
Oskar Czeijastrasse 2, A-3340 Waidhofen/Ybbs, AUSTRIA, Phone: 0043-7442-54519, Fax: 0043-7442-54519
Specialties: High-art and classic straight knives and folders of his design. **Patterns:** Bowies, daggers, hunters and locking folders. **Technical:** Grinds ATS-34 and stainless and carbon Damascus. Hardwoods, fossil ivory, horn and amber for handle material; silver wire and gold inlays; silver butt caps. Offers engraving and scrimshaw. **Prices:** $350 to $850; some to $3500. **Remarks:** Part-time maker; first knife sold in 1991. **Mark:** Name.

POSNER, BARRY E,
12501 Chandler Blvd Suite 104, N. Hollywood, CA 91607, Phone: 818-752-8005, Fax: 818-752-8006
Specialties: Working/using straight knives. Patterns: Hunters, kitchen and utility/camp knives. **Technical:** Grinds ATS-34; forges 1095 and nickel. **Prices:** $95 to $400. **Remarks:** Part-time maker; first knife sold in 1987. Doing business as Posner Knives. Supplier of finished mosaic handle pin stock. **Mark:** First and middle initials, last name.

POTIER, TIMOTHY F,
PO Box 711, Oberlin, LA 70655, Phone: 337-639-2229, tpotier@hotmail.com
Specialties: Classic working and using straight knives to customer specs; some collectible. **Patterns:** Hunters, Bowies, utility/camp knives and belt axes. **Technical:** Forges carbon steel and his own Damascus; offers filework. **Prices:** $300 to $1800; some to $4000. **Remarks:** Part-time maker; first knife sold in 1981. **Mark:** Last name, MS.

POTOCKI, ROGER,
Route 1 Box 333A, Goreville, IL 62939, Phone: 618-995-9502

POTTER, BILLY,
6323 Hyland Dr., Dublin, OH 43017, Phone: 614-766-6845, potterknives@yahoo.com; Web: www.potterknives.com
Specialties: Working straight knives; his design or to customers patterns. **Patterns:** Bowie, fighters, utilities, skinners, hunters, folding lock blade, miniatures and tomahawks. **Technical:** Grinds and forges, carbon steel, L6, 0-1, 1095, 5160, 1084 and 52000. Grinds 440C stainless. Forges own Damascus. Handles: prefers exotic hardwood, curly and birdseye maples. Bone, ivory, antler, pearl and horn. Some scrimshaw. **Prices:** Start at $100 up to $800. **Remarks:** Part-time maker; first knife sold 1996. **Mark:** First and last name Nashport OH.

POWELL, JAMES,
2500 North Robinson Rd, Texarkana, TX 75501

POWELL, ROBERT CLARK,
PO Box 321, 93 Gose Rd., Smarr, GA 31086, Phone: 478-994-5418
Specialties: Composite bar Damascus blades. **Patterns:** Art knives, hunters, combat, tomahawks. **Patterns:** Hand forges all blades. **Prices:** $300 and up. **Remarks:** ABS Journeyman Smith. **Mark:** Powell.

PRATER, MIKE,
PRATER AND COMPANY, 81 Sanford Ln., Flintstone, GA 30725, cmprater@aol.com; Web: www.casecustomknives.com
Specialties: Customizing factory knives. **Patterns:** Buck knives, case knives, hen and rooster knives. **Technical:** Manufacture of mica pearl. **Prices:** Varied. **Remarks:** First knife sold in 1980. **Mark:** Mica pearl.

PRESSBURGER, RAMON,
59 Driftway Rd, Howell, NJ 07731, Phone: 732-363-0816
Specialties: BG-42. Only knifemaker in U.S.A. that has complete line of affordable hunting knives made from BG-42. **Patterns:** All types hunting styles. **Technical:** Uses all steels; main steels are D-2 and BG-42. **Prices:** $75 to $500. **Remarks:** Full-time maker; has been making hunting knives for 30 years. Makes knives to your patterning. **Mark:** NA.

PRICE, TIMMY,
PO Box 906, Blairsville, GA 30514, Phone: 706-745-5111

PRIMOS, TERRY,
932 Francis Dr, Shreveport, LA 71118, Phone: 318-686-6625, tprimos@sport.rr.com or terry@primosknives.com; Web: www.primosknives.com
Specialties: Traditional forged straight knives. **Patterns:** Hunters, Bowies, camp knives, and fighters. **Technical:** Forges primarily 1084 and 5160; also forges Damascus. **Prices:** $250 to $600. **Remarks:** Full-time maker; first knife sold in 1993. **Mark:** Last name.

PRINSLOO, THEUNS,
PO Box 2263, Bethlehem, 9700, SOUTH AFRICA, Phone: 27824663885, theunmesa@telkomsa.net; Web: www.theunsprinsloo.com
Specialties: Fancy folders. **Technical:** Own Damascus and mokume. **Prices:** $450 to $1500.

PRITCHARD, RON,
613 Crawford Ave, Dixon, IL 61021, Phone: 815-284-6005
Specialties: Plain and fancy working knives. **Patterns:** Variety of straight knives, locking folders, interframes and miniatures. **Technical:** Grinds 440C, 154CM and commercial Damascus. **Prices:** $100 to $200; some to $1500. **Remarks:** Part-time maker; first knife sold in 1979. **Mark:** Name and city.

PROVENZANO, JOSEPH D,
39043 Dutch Lane, Ponchatoula, LA 70454, Phone: 225-615-4846
Specialties: Working straight knives and folders in standard patterns. **Patterns:** Hunters, Bowies, folders, camp and fishing knives. **Technical:** Grinds ATS-34, 440C, 154CM, CPM 4400V, CPM420V and Damascus. Hollow-grinds hunters. **Prices:** $110 to $300; some to $1000. **Remarks:** Part-time maker; first knife sold in 1980. **Mark:** Joe-Pro.

PRYOR, STEPHEN L,
HC Rt 1, Box 1445, Boss, MO 65440, Phone: 573-626-4838, Fax: same, Knives4U3@juno.com; Web: www.stevescutler.com
Specialties: Working and fancy straight knives, some to customer specs. **Patterns:** Bowies, hunting/fishing, utility/camp, fantasy/art. **Technical:** Grinds 440C, ATS-34, 1085, some Damascus, and does filework. Stag and exotic hardwood handles. **Prices:** $250 and up. **Remarks:** Full-time maker; first knife sold in 1991. **Mark:** Stylized first initial and last name over city and state.

PUGH, JIM,
PO Box 711, Azle, TX 76020, Phone: 817-444-2679, Fax: 817-444-5455
Specialties: Fancy/embellished limited editions by request. **Patterns:**

5-to 7-inch Bowies, wildlife art pieces, hunters, daggers and fighters; some commemoratives. **Technical:** Multi color transplanting in solid 18K gold, fine gems; grinds 440C and ATS-34. Offers engraving, fancy file etching and leather sheaths for wildlife art pieces. Ivory and coco bolo handle material on limited editions. Designs animal head butt caps and paws or bear claw guards; sterling silver heads and guards. **Prices:** $60,000 to $80,000 each in the Big Five 2000 edition. **Remarks:** Full-time maker; first knife sold in 1970. **Mark:** Pugh (Old English).

PULIS, VLADIMIR,
CSA 230-95, SL Republic, 96701 Kremnica, SLOVAKIA, Phone: 00421 903 340076, Fax: 00427 903 390076, vpulis@host.sk; Web: www.vpulis.host.sk
Specialties: Fancy and high-art straight knives of his design. **Patterns:** Daggers and hunters. **Technical:** Forges Damascus steel. All work done by hand. **Prices:** $250 to $3000; some to $10,000. **Remarks:** Full-time maker; first knife sold in 1990. **Mark:** Initials in sixtagon.

PULLIAM, MORRIS C,
560 Jeptha Knob Rd, Shelbyville, KY 40065, Phone: 502-633-2261, mcpulliam@fastballinternet.com
Specialties: Working knives; classic Bowies. Cherokee River pattern Damascus. **Patterns:** Bowies, hunters, and tomahawks. **Technical:** Forges L6, W2, 1095, Damascus and bar 320 layer Damascus. **Prices:** $165 to $1200. **Remarks:** Full-time maker; first knife sold in 1974. Makes knives for Native American festivals. Doing business as Knob Hill Forge. Member of Piqua Sept Shawnee of Ohio. Indian name Waapiti NI-Paw-1 Elk Standing. As a member of a state tribe, is an American Indian artist and craftsman by federal law. **Mark:** Small and large -Pulliam.

PURSLEY, AARON,
8885 Coal Mine Rd, Big Sandy, MT 59520, Phone: 406-378-3200
Specialties: Fancy working knives. **Patterns:** Locking folders, straight hunters and daggers, personal wedding knives and letter openers. **Technical:** Grinds O1 and 440C; engraves. **Prices:** $900 to $2500. **Remarks:** Full-time maker; first knife sold in 1975. **Mark:** Initials connected with year.

PURVIS, BOB AND ELLEN,
2416 N Loretta Dr, Tucson, AZ 85716, Phone: 520-795-8290, repknives2@cox.net
Specialties: Hunter, skinners, Bowies, using knives, gentlemen folders and collectible knives. **Technical:** Grinds ATS-34, 440C, Damascus, Dama steel, heat-treats and cryogenically quenches. We do gold-plating, salt bluing, scrimshawing, filework and fashion handmade leather sheaths. Materials used for handles include exotic woods, mammoth ivory, mother-of-pearl, G-10 and Micarta. **Prices:** $165 to $800. **Remarks:** Knifemaker since retirement in 1984. Selling them since 1993. **Mark:** Script or print R.E. Purvis ~ Tucson, AZ or last name only.

PUTNAM, DONALD S,
590 Wolcott Hill Rd, Wethersfield, CT 06109, Phone: 860-563-9718, Fax: 860-563-9718, dpknives@cox.net
Specialties: Working knives for the hunter and fisherman. **Patterns:** His design or to customer specs. **Technical:** Uses stock removal method, O1, W2, D2, ATS-34, 154CM, 440C and CPM REX 20; stainless steel Damascus on request. **Prices:** $250 and up. **Remarks:** Full-time maker; first knife sold in 1985. **Mark:** Last name with a knife outline.

Q

QUAKENBUSH, THOMAS C,
2426 Butler Rd, Ft Wayne, IN 46808, Phone: 219-483-0749

QUARTON, BARR,
PO Box 4335, McCall, ID 83638, Phone: 208-634-3641
Specialties: Plain and fancy working knives; period pieces. **Patterns:** Hunters, tantos and swords. **Technical:** Forges and grinds 154CM, ATS-34 and his own Damascus. **Prices:** $180 to $450; some to $4500. **Remarks:** Part-time maker; first knife sold in 1978. Doing business as Barr Custom Knives. **Mark:** First name with bear logo.

QUATTLEBAUM, CRAIG,
18855 Andreanof Lp, Eagle River, AK 99577, Phone: 907-622-3919, mustang376@gci.net
Specialties: Traditional straight knives and one-of-a-kind knives of his design; period pieces. **Patterns:** Bowies and fighters. **Technical:** Forges 5168, 1095 and own Damascus. **Prices:** $300 to $2000. **Remarks:** Part-time maker; first knife sold in 1988. **Mark:** Stylized initials.

R

R. BOYES KNIVES,
731 Jean Ct, Addison, WI 53002, Phone: 262-391-2172, t.boyes2172@charter.net
Specialties: Hunters, working knives. **Technical:** Grinds ATS-34, 440C, O1 tool steel and Damascus. **Prices:** $60 to $1000. **Remarks:** First knife sold in 1998. Tom Boyes changed to R. Boyes Knives.

RACHLIN, LESLIE S,
1200 W Church St, Elmira, NY 14905, Phone: 607-733-6889, lrachlin@stry.rr.com
Specialties: Classic and working/using straight knives and folders of his design. **Patterns:** Hunters and utility/camp knives. **Technical:** Grinds 440C. **Prices:** $50 to $700. **Remarks:** Spare-time maker; first knife sold in 1989. Doing business as Tinkermade Knives. **Mark:** LSR

RADER, MICHAEL,
P.O. Box 393, Wilkeson, WA 98396, Phone: 253-255-7064, michael@raderblade.com; Web: www.raderblade.com
Specialties: Swords, kitchen knives, integrals. **Patterns:** Non traditional designs. Inspired by various cultures. **Technical:** Most blades in forged 51200 + 200-600 layer Damascus in ISN-20 + 8660. **Prices:** $350 -$5,000 **Remarks:** ABS Journeyman Smith **Mark:** "Rader" on one side, "J.S." on other

RADOS, JERRY F,
7523 E 5000 N Rd, Grant Park, IL 60940, Phone: 815-472-3350, Fax: 815-472-3944
Specialties: Deluxe period pieces. **Patterns:** Hunters, fighters, locking folders, daggers and camp knives. **Technical:** Forges and grinds his own Damascus which he sells commercially; makes pattern-welded Turkish Damascus. **Prices:** Start at $900. **Remarks:** Full-time maker; first knife sold in 1981. **Mark:** Last name.

RAGSDALE, JAMES D,
3002 Arabian Woods Dr, Lithonia, GA 30038, Phone: 770-482-6739
Specialties: Fancy and embellished working knives of his design or to customer specs. **Patterns:** Hunters, folders and fighters. **Technical:** Grinds 440C, ATS-34 and A2. **Prices:** $150 and up. **Remarks:** Full-time maker; first knife sold in 1984. **Mark:** Fish symbol with name above, town below.

RAINVILLE, RICHARD,
126 Cockle Hill Rd, Salem, CT 06420, Phone: 860-859-2776, w1jo@snet.net
Specialties: Traditional working straight knives. **Patterns:** Outdoor knives, including fishing knives. **Technical:** L6, 400C, ATS-34. **Prices:** $100 to $800. **Remarks:** Full-time maker; first knife sold in 1982. **Mark:** Name, city, state in oval logo.

RALEY, R. WAYNE,
825 Poplar Acres Rd, Collierville, TN 38017, Phone: 901-853-2026

RALPH, DARREL,
BRIAR KNIVES, 4185 S St Rt 605, Galena, OH 43021, Phone: 740-965-9970, dr@darrelralph.com; Web: www.darrelralph.com
Specialties: Fancy, high-art, high-tech, collectible straight knives and folders of his design and to customer specs; unique mechanisms, some disassemble. **Patterns:** Daggers, fighters and swords. **Technical:** Forges his own Damascus, nickel and high-carbon. Uses mokume and Damascus; mosaics and special patterns. Engraves and heat-treats. Prefers pearl, ivory and abalone handle material; uses stones and jewels. **Prices:** $250 to six figures. **Remarks:** Full-time maker; first knife sold in 1987. Doing business as Briar Knives. **Mark:** DDR.

RAMEY, LARRY,
1315 Porter Morris Rd, Chapmansboro, TN 37035-5120, Phone: 615-307-4233, larryrameyknives@hotmail.com; Web: www.larryrameyknives.com
Specialties: Titanium knives. **Technical:** Pictures taken by Hawkinson Photography.

RAMONDETTI, SERGIO,
VIA MARCONI N 24, 12013 CHIUSA DI PESIO (CN), ITALY, Phone: 0171 734490, Fax: 0171 734490, s.ramon@tin.it
Specialties: Folders and straight knives of his design. **Patterns:** Utility, hunters and skinners. **Technical:** Grinds RWL-34 and Damascus. **Prices:** $500 to $2000. **Remarks:** Part-time maker; first knife sold in 1999. **Mark:** Logo (S.Ramon) with last name.

RAMSEY, RICHARD A,
8525 Trout Farm Rd, Neosho, MO 64850, Phone: 417-451-1493, rams@direcway.com; Web: www.ramseyknives.com
Specialties: Drop point hunters. **Patterns:** Various Damascus. **Prices:** $125 to $1500. **Mark:** RR double R also last name-RAMSEY.

RANDALL JR., JAMES W,
11606 Keith Hall Rd, Keithville, LA 71047, Phone: 318-925-6480, Fax: 318-925-1709, jw@jwrandall-knives.com
Specialties: Collectible and functional knives. **Patterns:** Bowies, hunters, daggers, swords, folders and combat knives. **Technical:** Forges 5160, 1084, O1 and his Damascus. **Prices:** $400 to $8000. **Remarks:** Part-time. First knife sold in 1998. **Mark:** J.W Randall M.S.

RANDALL MADE KNIVES,
4857 South Orange Blossom Trail, Orlando, FL 32839, Phone: 407-855-8075, Fax: 407-855-9054, Web: http:// www.randallknives.com
Specialties: Working straight knives. Patterns: Hunters, fighters and Bowies. **Technical:** Forges and grinds O1 and 440B. **Prices:** $170 to $550; some to $450. **Remarks:** Full-time maker; first knife sold in 1937. **Mark:** Randall made, city and state in scimitar logo.

RANDOW, RALPH,
4214 Blalock Rd, Pineville, LA 71360, Phone: 318-640-3369

RANKL, CHRISTIAN,
Possenhofenerstr 33, 81476 Munchen, GERMANY, Phone: 0049 01 71 3 66 26 79, Fax: 0049 8975967265, christian@crankl.de.
Specialties: Tail-lock knives. **Patterns:** Fighters, hunters and locking folders. **Technical:** Grinds ATS-34, D2, CPM1440V, RWL 34 also stainless Damascus. **Prices:** $450 to $950; some to $2000. **Remarks:** Full-time maker; first knife sold in 1989. **Mark:** Electrochemical etching on blade.

RAPP, STEVEN J,
8033 US Hwy 25-70, Marshall, NC 28753, Phone: 828-649-1092
Specialties: Gold quartz; mosaic handles. **Patterns:** Daggers, Bowies, fighters and San Francisco knives. **Technical:** Hollow-and flat-grinds 440C and Damascus. **Prices:** Start at $500. **Remarks:** Full-time maker; first knife sold in 1981. **Mark:** Name and state.

RAPPAZZO, RICHARD,
142 Dunsbach Ferry Rd, Cohoes, NY 12047, Phone: 518-783-6843
Specialties: Damascus locking folders and straight knives. **Patterns:** Folders, dirks, fighters and tantos in original and traditional designs. **Technical:** Hand-forges all blades; specializes in Damascus; uses only natural handle materials. **Prices:** $400 to $1500. **Remarks:** Part-time maker; first knife sold in 1985. **Mark:** Name, date, serial number.

RARDON, A D,
1589 SE Price Dr, Polo, MO 64671, Phone: 660-354-2544
Specialties: Folders, miniatures. **Patterns:** Hunters, buck skinners, Bowies, miniatures and daggers. **Technical:** Grinds O1, D2, 440C and ATS-34. **Prices:** $150 to $2000; some higher. **Remarks:** Full-time maker; first knife sold in 1954. **Mark:** Fox logo.

RARDON, ARCHIE F,
1589 SE Price Dr, Polo, MO 64671, Phone: 660-354-2330
Specialties: Working knives. **Patterns:** Hunters, Bowies and miniatures. **Technical:** Grinds O1, D2, 440C, ATS-34, cable and Damascus. **Prices:** $50 to $500. **Remarks:** Part-time maker. **Mark:** Boar hog.

RAY, ALAN W,
1287 FM 1280 E, Lovelady, TX 75851, Phone: 936-544-6611, Fax: 936-636-2931, awray@rayzblades.com; Web: www.rayzblades.com
Specialties: Working straight knives of his design. **Patterns:** Hunters. **Technical:** Forges 01, L6 and 5160 for straight knives. **Prices:** $200 to $1000. **Remarks:** Full-time maker; first knife sold in 1979. **Mark:** Stylized initials.

REBELLO, INDIAN GEORGE,
358 Elm St, New Bedford, MA 02740-3837, Phone: 508-951-2719, indgeo@juno.com; Web: www.indiangeorgesknives.com
Specialties: One-of-a-kind fighters and Bowies. **Patterns:** To customer's specs, hunters and utilities. **Technical:** Forges his own Damascus, 5160, 52100, 1084, 1095, cable and O1. Grinds S30V, ATS-34, 154CM, 440C, D2 and A2. **Prices:** Starting at $250. **Remarks:** Full-time maker, first knife sold in 1991. Doing business as Indian George's Knives. Founding father of the New England Knife Guild. Member of the N.C.C.A. and A.B.S. **Mark:** Indian George's Knives.

RED, VERNON,
2020 Benton Cove, Conway, AR 72034, Phone: 501-450-7284, knivesvr@conwaycorp.net
Specialties: Custom design straight knives or folders of your design or his. **Patterns:** Hunters, fighters, Bowies, fillet, folders and lock-blades. **Technical:** Hollow Grind, flat grind, stock removal and forged blades. Uses 440C, D-2, ATS-34 and Damascus. **Prices:** $180 and up. **Remarks:** Made first skinner in 1982, first lock blade folder in 1992. 75% of knives made are folders. Member of (AKA) Arkansas Knives Assoc., attend annual show in Feb. at Little Rock, AR. Custom Made Knives by Vernon Red. **Mark:** Last name.

REDDIEX, BILL,
27 Galway Ave, Palmerston North, NEW ZEALAND, Phone: 06-357-0383, Fax: 06-358-2910
Specialties: Collector-grade working straight knives. **Patterns:** Traditional-style Bowies and drop-point hunters. **Technical:** Grinds 440C, D2 and O1; offers variety of grinds and finishes. **Prices:** $130 to $750. **Remarks:** Full-time maker; first knife sold in 1980. **Mark:** Last name around kiwi bird logo.

REED, DAVE,
Box 132, Brimfield, MA 01010, Phone: 413-245-3661
Specialties: Traditional styles. Makes knives from chains, rasps, gears, etc. **Patterns:** Bush swords, hunters, working minis, camp and utility knives. **Technical:** Forges 1075 and his own Damascus. **Prices:** Start at $50. **Remarks:** Part-time maker; first knife sold in 1970. **Mark:** Initials.

REED, JOHN M,
257 Navajo Dr, Oak Hill, FL 32759, Phone: 386-345-4763
Specialties: Hunter, utility, some survival knives. Patterns: Trailing Point, and drop point sheath knives. **Technical:** ATS-34, Rockwell 60 exotic wood or natural material handles. **Prices:** $135 to $300. Depending on handle material. **Remarks:** Likes the stock removal method. "Old Fashioned trainling point blades." Handmade and sewn leather sheaths. **Mark:** "Reed" acid etched on left side of blade.

REEVE, CHRIS,
11624 W President Dr., Ste. B, Boise, ID 83713, Phone: 208-375-0367, Fax: 208-375-0368, crkinfo@chrisreeve.com
Specialties: Originator and designer of the One Piece range of fixed blade utility knives and of the Sebenza Integral Lock folding knives made by Chris Reeve Knives. Currently makes only one or two pieces per year himself. **Patterns:** Art folders and fixed blades; one-of-a-kind. **Technical:** Grinds specialty stainless steels, Damascus and other materials to his own design. **Prices:** $1000 and upwards. **Remarks:** Full-time in knife business; first knife sold in 1982. **Mark:** Signature and date.

REGGIO JR., SIDNEY J,
PO Box 851, Sun, LA 70463, Phone: 504-886-5886
Specialties: Miniature classic and fancy straight knives of his design or in standard patterns. **Patterns:** Fighters, hunters and utility/camp knives. **Technical:** Grinds 440C, ATS-34 and commercial Damascus. Engraves; scrimshaws; offers filework. Hollow grinds most blades. Prefers natural handle material. Offers handmade sheaths. **Prices:** $85 to $250; some to $500. **Remarks:** Part-time maker; first knife sold in 1988. Doing business as Sterling Workshop. **Mark:** Initials.

REPKE, MIKE,
4191 N. Euclid Ave., Bay City, MI 48706, Phone: 517-684-3111
Specialties: Traditional working and using straight knives of his design or to customer specs; classic knives; display knives. **Patterns:** Hunters, Bowies, skinners, fighters boots, axes and swords. **Technical:** Grind 440C. Offer variety of handle materials. **Prices:** $99 to $1500. **Remarks:** Full-time makers. Doing business as Black Forest Blades. **Mark:** Knife logo.

REVERDY, NICOLE AND PIERRE,
5 Rue de L'egalite', 26100 Romans, FRANCE, Phone: 334 75 05 10 15, Web: http://www.reverdy.com
Specialties: Art knives; legend pieces. Pierre and Nicole, his wife, are creating knives of art with combination of enamel on pure silver (Nicole) and poetic Damascus (Pierre) such as the "La dague a la licorne." **Patterns:** Daggers, folding knives Damascus and enamel, Bowies, hunters and other large patterns. **Technical:** Forges his Damascus and "poetic Damascus"; where animals such as unicorns, stags, dragons or star crystals appear, works with his own EDM machine to create any kind of pattern inside the steel with his own touch. **Prices:** $2000 and up. **Remarks:** Full-time maker since 1989; first knife sold in 1986. Nicole (wife) collaborates with enamels. **Mark:** Reverdy.

REVISHVILI, ZAZA,
2102 Linden Ave, Madison, WI 53704, Phone: 608-243-7927
Specialties: Fancy/embellished and high-art straight knives and folders of his design. **Patterns:** Daggers, swords and locking folders. **Technical:** Uses Damascus; silver filigree, silver inlay in wood; enameling. **Prices:** $1000 to $9000; some to $15,000. **Remarks:** Full-time maker; first knife sold in 1987. **Mark:** Initials, city.

REXROAT, KIRK,
527 Sweetwater Circle Box 224, Wright, WY 82732, Phone: 307-464-0166, rexknives@vcn.com; Web: www.rexroatknives.com
Specialties: Using and collectible straight knives and folders of his design or to customer specs. **Patterns:** Bowies, hunters, folders. **Technical:** Forges Damascus patterns, mosaic and 52100. **Prices:** $400 and up. **Remarks:** Part-time maker, Master Smith in the ABS; first knife sold in 1984. Doing business as Rexroat Knives. **Mark:** Last name.

REYNOLDS, DAVE,
Rt 2 Box 36, Harrisville, WV 26362, Phone: 304-643-2889, wvreynolds@zoomintevnet.net
Specialties: Working straight knives of his design. **Patterns:** Bowies, kitchen and utility knives. **Technical:** Grinds and forges L6, 1095 and 440C. Heat-treats. **Prices:** $50 to $85; some to $175. **Remarks:** Full-time maker; first knife sold in 1980. Doing business as Terra-Gladius Knives. **Mark:** Mark on special orders only; serial number on all knives.

REYNOLDS, JOHN C,
#2 Andover HC77, Gillette, WY 82716, Phone: 307-682-6076
Specialties: Working knives, some fancy. **Patterns:** Hunters, Bowies, tomahawks and buck skinners; some folders. **Technical:** Grinds D2, ATS-34, 440C and forges own Damascus and knives. Scrimshaws. **Prices:** $200 to $3000. **Remarks:** Spare-time maker; first knife sold in 1969. **Mark:** On ground blades JC Reynolds Gillette, WY, on forged blades, initials make the mark-JCR.

RHEA, LIN,
413 Grant 291020, Prattsville, AR 72129, Phone: 870-699-5095, lwrhea1@windstream.net; Web: www.rheaknives.com
Specialties: Traditional and early American styled Bowies in high carbon steel or Damascus. Patterns: Bowies, hunters and fighters. **Technical:** Filework wire inlay. Sole authorship of construction, Damascus and embellishment. **Prices:** $280 to $1500. **Remarks:** Serious part-time maker and rated as a Journeyman Bladesmith in the ABS.

RHO, NESTOR LORENZO,
Primera Junta 589, (6000) Junin, Buenos Aires, ARGENTINA, Phone: (02362) 15670686
Specialties: Classic and fancy straight knives of his design. **Patterns:** Bowies, fighters and hunters. **Technical:** Grinds 420C, 440C and 1050. Offers semi-precious stones on handles, acid etching on blades and blade engraving. **Prices:** $60 to $300 some to $1200. **Remarks:** Full-time maker; first knife sold in 1975. **Mark:** Name.

RIBONI, CLAUDIO,
Via L Da Vinci, Truccazzano (MI), ITALY, Phone: 02 95309010, Web: www.riboni-knives.com

RICARDO ROMANO, BERNARDES,
Ruai Coronel Rennò 1261, Itajuba MG, BRAZIL 37500, Phone: 0055-2135-622-5896
Specialties: Hunters, fighters, Bowies. **Technical:** Grinds blades of stainless and tools steels. **Patterns:** Hunters. **Prices:** $100 to $700. **Mark:** Romano.

RICHARDS, RALPH (BUD),
6413 Beech St, Bauxite, AK

RICHARDS, RALPH (BUD),
6413 Beech St, Bauxite, AR 72011, Phone: 501-602-5367, DoubleR042@aol.com; Web: SwampPoodleCreations.com
Specialties: Forges 55160, 1084, and 15N20 for Damascus. S30V, 440C, and others. Wood, mammoth, giraffe and mother of pearl handles.

RICHARDS JR., ALVIN (CHUCK),
2889 Shields Ln, Fortuna, CA 95540-3241, Phone: 707-725-2526/707-845-4434, Fax: 707-202-8287, bldsmith@cox.net; Web: www.woodchuckforge.com
Specialties: Fixed blade Damascus. One-of-a-kind. **Patterns:** Hunters, fighters. **Prices:** $200 to $1200. **Remarks:** Likes to work with customers on a truly custom knife. **Mark:** A C Richards or ACR.

RICHARDSON JR., PERCY,
212 Thornridge St, Bridge City, TX 77611, Phone: 936-288-1690, Web:www.richardsonhandmadeknives.com
Specialties: Working straight knives and folders. **Patterns:** Hunters, skinners, bowies, fighters and folders. **Technical:** Grinds 154CM, ATS-34, S90V and D2. **Prices:** $175 -$750 some bowies to $1200. **Remarks:** Part time maker, first knife sold in 1990. Doing business as Richardsons Handmade Knives. **Mark:** Texas star with last name across it.

RICHTER, JOHN C,
932 Bowling Green Trail, Chesapeake, VA 23320
Specialties: Hand-forged knives in original patterns. **Patterns:** Hunters, fighters, utility knives and other belt knives, folders, swords. **Technical:** Hand-forges high-carbon and his own Damascus; makes mokume gane. **Prices:** $75 to $1500. **Remarks:** Part-time maker. **Mark:** Richter Forge.

RICHTER, SCOTT,
516 E. 2nd St, S. Boston, MA 02127, Phone: 617-269-4855
Specialties: Traditional working/using folders. **Patterns:** Locking folders, swords and kitchen knives. **Technical:** Grinds ATS-34, 5160 and A2. High-tech materials. **Prices:** $150 to $650; some to $1500. **Remarks:** Full-time maker; first knife sold in 1991. Doing business as Richter Made. **Mark:** Last name, Made.

RICKE, DAVE,
1209 Adams St, West Bend, WI 53090, Phone: 262-334-5739, R.L5710@sbcglobal.net
Specialties: Working knives; period pieces. **Patterns:** Hunters, boots, Bowies; locking folders and slip joints. **Technical:** Grinds ATS-34, A2, 440C and 154CM. **Prices:** $125 to $1600. **Remarks:** Full-time maker; first knife sold in 1976. Knifemakers Guild voting member. **Mark:** Last name.

RIDEN, DOUG,
12 Weeks Rd, Box 945, Eastford, CT 06242, Phone: 860-974-0518, Web: www.darkwaterforge.com
Specialties: Hard working, high performance knives. **Patterns:** Hunters, fighters, choppers, kitchen knives. **Technical:** Forged 5160, 1084, W2, L6. **Prices:** $100 to $600. **Remarks:** Full-time maker, first knife sold 2006.

RIDER, DAVID M,
PO Box 5946, Eugene, OR 97405-0911, Phone: 541-343-8747

RIEPE, RICHARD A,
17604 E 296 St, Harrisonville, MO 64701

RIETVELD, BERTIE,
PO Box 53, Magaliesburg 1791, SOUTH AFRICA, Phone: 2783 232 8766, Fax: +2714 5771294, bertie@rietveldknives.com; Web: www.rietveldknives.com
Specialties: Art daggers, Bolster lock folders, Persian designs, embraces elegant designs. **Patterns:** Mostly one-of-a-kind. **Technical:** Sole authorship, work only in own Damascus, gold inlay, blued stainless fittings. **Prices:** $500 -$8,000 **Remarks:** First knife made in 1979. Annual shows attended: ECCKS, Blade Show, Guild Show, Milan Show, South African Guild Show. **Marks:** Logo is elephant in half circle with name, enclosed in Stanhope lens

RIGNEY JR., WILLIE,
191 Colson Dr, Bronston, KY 42518, Phone: 606-679-4227
Specialties: High-tech period pieces and fancy working knives. **Patterns:** Fighters, boots, daggers and push knives. **Technical:** Grinds 440C and 154CM; buys Damascus. Most knives are embellished. **Prices:** $150 to $1500; some to $10,000. **Remarks:** Full-time maker; first knife sold in 1978. **Mark:** First initial, last name.

RINKES, SIEGFRIED,
Am Sportpl 2, D 91459, Markterlbach, GERMANY

RIZZI, RUSSELL J,
37 March Rd, Ashfield, MA 01330, Phone: 413-625-2842
Specialties: Fancy working and using straight knives and folders of his design or to customer specs. **Patterns:** Hunters, locking folders and fighters. **Technical:** Grinds 440C, D2 and commercial Damascus. **Prices:** $150 to $750; some to $2500. **Remarks:** Part-time maker; first knife sold in 1990. **Mark:** Last name, Ashfield, MA.

ROBBINS, BILL,
299 Fairview St, Globe, AZ 85501, Phone: 928-402-0052, billrknifemaker@aol.com
Specialties: Plain and fancy working straight knives. Makes to his designs and most anything you can draw. **Patterns:** Hunting knives, utility knives, and Bowies. **Technical:** Grinds ATS-34, 440C, tool steel, high carbon, buys Damascus. **Prices:** $70 to $450. **Remarks:** Part-time maker, first knife sold in 2001. **Mark:** Last name or desert scene with name.

ROBBINS, HOWARD P,
1407 S 217th Ave, Elkhorn, NE 68022, Phone: 402-289-4121, ARobb1407@aol.com
Specialties: High-tech working knives with clean designs, some fancy. **Patterns:** Folders, hunters and camp knives. **Technical:** Grinds 440C. Heat-treats; likes mirror finishes. Offers leatherwork. **Prices:** $100 to $500; some to $1000. **Remarks:** Full-time maker; first knife sold in 1982. **Mark:** Name, city and state.

ROBERTS, CHUCK,
PO Box 7174, Golden, CO 80403, Phone: 303-642-2388, chuck@crobertsart.com; Web: www.crobertsart.com
Specialties: Price daggers, large Bowies, hand-rubbed satin finish. **Patterns:** Bowies and California knives. **Technical:** Grinds 440C, 5160 and ATS-34. Handles made of stag, ivory or mother-of-pearl. **Prices:** $1250. **Remarks:** Full-time maker. Company name is C. Roberts -Art that emulates the past. **Mark:** Last initial or last name.

ROBERTS, E RAY,
191 Nursery Rd, Monticello, FL 32344, Phone: 850-997-4403
Specialties: High-Carbon Damascus knives and tomahawks.

ROBERTS, GEORGE A,
PO Box 31228, 211 Main St., Whitehorse, YT, CANADA Y1A 5P7, Phone: 867-667-7099, Fax: 867-667-7099, Web: www.yuk-biz.com/bandit blades
Specialties: Mastadon ivory, fossil walrus ivory handled knives, scrimshawed or carved. **Patterns:** Side lockers, fancy bird and trout knives, hunters, fillet blades. **Technical:** Grinds stainless Damascus, all surgical steels. **Prices:** Up to $3500 U.S. **Remarks:** Full-time maker; first knives sold in 1986. Doing business as Bandit Blades. Most recent works have gold nuggets in fossilized Mastodon ivory. Something new using mosaic pins in mokume bolster and in mosaic Damascus, it creates a new look. **Mark:** Bandit Yukon with pick and shovel crossed.

ROBERTS, JACK,
10811 Sagebluff Dr, Houston, TX 77089, Phone: 281-481-1784, jroberts59@houston.rr.com
Specialties: Hunting knives and folders, offers scrimshaw by wife Barbara. **Patterns:** Drop point hunters and LinerLock® folders. **Technical:** Grinds 440-C, offers file work, texturing, natural handle materials and Micarta. **Prices:** $200 to $800 some higher. **Remarks:** Part-time maker, sold first knife in 1965. **Mark:** Name, city, state.

ROBERTS, MICHAEL,
601 Oakwood Dr, Clinton, MS 39056, Phone: 601-540-6222, Fax: 601-213-4891
Specialties: Working and using knives in standard patterns and to customer specs. **Patterns:** Hunters, Bowies, tomahawks and fighters. **Technical:** Forges 5160, O1, 1095 and his own Damascus. Uses only natural handle materials. **Prices:** $145 to $500; some to $1100. **Remarks:** Part-time maker; first knife sold in 1988. **Mark:** Last name or first and last name in Celtic script.

ROBERTSON, LEO D,
3728 Pleasant Lake Dr, Indianapolis, IN 46227, Phone: 317-882-9899, ldr52@juno.com
Specialties: Hunting and folders. Patterns: Hunting, fillet, Bowie, utility, folders and tantos. **Technical:** Uses ATS-34, 154CM, 440C, 1095, D2 and Damascus steels. **Prices:** Fixed knives $75 to $350, folders $350 to $600. **Remarks:** Handles made with stag, wildwoods, laminates, mother-of-pearl. Made first knife in 1990. Member of American Bladesmith Society. **Mark:** Logo with full name in oval around logo.

ROBINSON, CHARLES (DICKIE),
PO Box 221, Vega, TX 79092, Phone: 806-267-2629, dickie@amaonline.com; Web: www.robinsonknives.com
Specialties: Classic and working/using knives. Does his own engraving. **Patterns:** Bowies, daggers, fighters, hunters and camp knives. **Technical:** Forges O1, 5160, 52100 and his own Damascus. **Prices:** $350 to $850; some to $5000. **Remarks:** Part-time maker; first knife sold in 1988. Doing business as Robinson Knives. ABS Master Smith. **Mark:** Robinson MS.

ROBINSON, CHUCK,
SEA ROBIN FORGE, 1423 Third Ave., Picayune, MS 39466, Phone: 601-798-0060, robi5515@bellsouth.net
Specialties: Deluxe period pieces and working / using knives of his design and to customer specs. **Patterns:** Bowies, fighters, hunters, utility knives and original designs. **Technical:** Forges own Damascus, 52100, O1, L6 and 1070 thru 1095. **Prices:** Start at $225. **Remarks:** First knife 1958. **Mark:** Fish logo, anchor and initials C.R.

ROBINSON, ROBERT W,
1569 N. Finley Pt, Polson, MT 59860, Phone: 406-887-2259, Fax: 406-887-2259
Specialties: High-art straight knives, folders and automatics of his design. **Patterns:** Hunters and locking folders. **Technical:** Grinds ATS-34, 154CM and 440V. Inlays pearl and gold; engraves sheep horn and ivory. **Prices:** $150 to $500; some to $2000. **Remarks:** Full-time maker; first knife sold in 1983. Doing business as Robbie Knife. **Mark:** Name on left side of blade.

ROBINSON III, REX R,
10531 Poe St, Leesburg, FL 34788, Phone: 352-787-4587
Specialties: One-of-a-kind high-art automatics of his design. **Patterns:** Automatics, liner locks and lock back folders. **Technical:** Uses tool steel and stainless Damascus and mokume; flat grinds. Hand carves folders. **Prices:** $1800 to $7500. **Remarks:** First knife sold in 1988. **Mark:** First name inside oval.

ROCHFORD, MICHAEL R,
PO Box 577, Dresser, WI 54009, Phone: 715-755-3520, mrrochford@centurytel.net
Specialties: Working straight knives and folders. Classic Bowies and Moran traditional. **Patterns:** Bowies, fighters, hunters: slip-joint, locking and liner locking folders. **Technical:** Grinds ATS-34, 440C, 154CM and D-2; forges W2, 5160, and his own Damascus. Offers metal and metal and leather sheaths. Filework and wire inlay. **Prices:** $150 to $1000; some to $2000. **Remarks:** Part-time maker; first knife sold in 1984. **Mark:** Name.

RODEBAUGH, JAMES L,
9374 Joshua Rd, Oak Hills, CA 92345

RODEWALD, GARY,
447 Grouse Ct, Hamilton, MT 59840, Phone: 406-363-2192
Specialties: Bowies of his design as inspired from historical pieces. **Patterns:** Hunters, Bowies and camp/combat. Forges 5160 1084 and his own Damascus of 1084, 15N20, field grade hunters AT-34-440C, 440V, and BG42. **Prices:** $200 to $1500. **Remarks:** Sole author on knives, sheaths done by saddle maker. **Mark:** Rodewald.

RODKEY, DAN,
18336 Ozark Dr, Hudson, FL 34667, Phone: 727-863-8264
Specialties: Traditional straight knives of his design and in standard patterns. **Patterns:** Boots, fighters and hunters. **Technical:** Grinds 440C, D2 and ATS-34. **Prices:** Start at $200. **Remarks:** Full-time maker; first knife sold in 1985. Doing business as Rodkey Knives. **Mark:** Etched logo on blade.

ROE JR., FRED D,
4005 Granada Dr, Huntsville, AL 35802, Phone: 205-881-6847
Specialties: Highly finished working knives of his design; period pieces. **Patterns:** Hunters, fighters and survival knives; locking folders; specialty designs like diver's knives. **Technical:** Grinds 154CM, ATS-34 and Damascus. Field-tests all blades. **Prices:** $125 to $250; some to $2000. **Remarks:** Part-time maker; first knife sold in 1980. **Mark:** Last name.

ROGERS, CHARLES W,
Rt. 1 Box 1552, Douglas, TX 75943, Phone: 409-326-4496

ROGERS, RAY,
PO Box 126, Wauconda, WA 98859, Phone: 509-486-8069, knives @rayrogers.com; Web: www.rayrogers.com
Specialties: LinerLock® folders. Asian and European professional chef's knives. Patterns: Rayzor folders, chef's knives and cleavers of his own and traditional designs, drop point hunters and fillet knives. **Technical:** Stock removal S30V, 440, 1095, O1 Damascus and other steels. Does all own heat treating, clay tempering, some forging G-10, Micarta, carbon fiber on folders, stabilized burl woods on fixed blades. **Prices:** $200 to $450. **Remarks:** Knives are made one-at-a-time to the customer's order. Happy to consider customizing knife designs to suit your preferences and sometimes create entirely new knives when necessary. As a full-time knifemaker is willing to spend as much time as it takes (usually through email) discussing the options and refining details of a knife's design to insure that you get the knife you really want.

ROGERS, RICHARD,
PO Box 769, Magdalena, NM 87825, Phone: 575-838-7237, r.s.rogers@hotmail.com
Specialties: Sheffield-style folders and multi-blade folders. **Patterns:** Folders: various traditional patterns. One-of-a-kind fixed blades: Bowies, daggers, hunters, utility knives. **Technical:** Mainly uses ATS-34 and prefer natural handle materials. **Prices:** $400 and up. **Mark:** Last name.

ROGERS, RODNEY,
602 Osceola St, Wildwood, FL 34785, Phone: 352-748-6114
Specialties: Traditional straight knives and folders. **Patterns:** Fighters, hunters, skinners. **Technical:** Flat-grinds ATS-34 and Damascus. Prefers natural materials. **Prices:** $150 to $1400. **Remarks:** Full-time maker; first knife sold in 1986. **Mark:** Last name, Handmade.

ROGHMANS, MARK,
607 Virginia Ave, LaGrange, GA 30240, Phone: 706-885-1273
Specialties: Classic and traditional knives of his design. **Patterns:** Bowies, daggers and fighters. **Technical:** Grinds ATS-34, D2 and 440C. **Prices:** $250 to $500. **Remarks:** Part-time maker; first knife sold in 1984. Doing business as LaGrange Knife. **Mark:** Last name and/or LaGrange Knife.

ROHN, FRED,
7675 W Happy Hill Rd, Coeur d'Alene, ID 83814, Phone: 208-667-0774
Specialties: Hunters, boot knives, custom patterns. **Patterns:** Drop points, double edge, etc. **Technical:** Grinds 440 or 154CM. **Prices:** $85 and up. **Remarks:** Part-time maker. **Mark:** Logo on blade; serial numbered.

ROLLERT, STEVE,
PO Box 65, Keenesburg, CO 80643-0065, Phone: 303-732-4858, steve@doveknives.com; Web: www.doveknives.com
Specialties: Highly finished working knives. **Patterns:** Variety of straight knives; locking folders and slip-joints. **Technical:** Forges and grinds W2, 1095, ATS-34 and his pattern-welded, cable Damascus and nickel Damascus. **Prices:** $300 to $1000; some to $3000. **Remarks:** Full-time maker; first knife sold in 1980. Doing business as Dove Knives. **Mark:** Last name in script.

RONZIO, N. JACK,
PO Box 248, Fruita, CO 81521, Phone: 970-858-0921

ROOT, GARY,
644 East 14th St, Erie, PA 16503, Phone: 814-459-0196
Specialties: Damascus Bowies with hand carved eagles, hawks and snakes for handles. Few folders made. **Patterns:** Daggers, fighters, hunter/field knives. **Technical:** Using handforged Damascus from Ray Bybar Jr (M.S.) and Robert Eggerling. Grinds D2, 440C, 1095 and 5160. Some 5160 is hand forged. **Prices:** $80 to $300 some to $1000. **Remarks:** Full time maker, first knife sold in 1976. **Mark:** Name over Erie, PA.

ROSE, DEREK W,
14 Willow Wood Rd, Gallipolis, OH 45631, Phone: 740-446-4627

ROSE II, DOUN T,
Ltc US Special Operations Command (ret), 1795/96 W Sharon Rd SW, Fife Lake, MI 49633, Phone: 231-645-1369, Web: www.epicureanclassic.com
Specialties: Straight working, collector and presentation knives to a high level of fit and finish. Design in collaboration with customer. **Patterns:** Field knives, Scagel, Bowies, period pieces, axes and tomahawks, fishing and hunting spears. Fine cutlery under "Epicurean Classic" name. **Technical:** Forged and billet ground, high carbon and stainless steel appropriate to end use. Sourced from: Crucible, Frye, Admiral and Starret. Some period pieces from recovered stock. Makes own damascus and mokume gane. **Remarks:** Full-time maker, ABS since 2000, William Scagel Memorial Scholarship 2002, Bill Moran School of Blade Smithing 2003, Apprentice under Master Blacksmith Dan Nickels at Black Rock Forge current. **Mark:** Last name ROSE in block letters with five petal "wild rose" in place of O. Doing business as Rose Cutlery.

ROSENBAUGH, RON,
2806 Stonegate Dr, Crystal Lake, IL 60012, Phone: 815-477-0027, rgr@rosenbaughcustomknives.com; Web: www.rosenbaughcustomknives.com
Specialties: Fancy and plain working knives using own designs, collaborations, and traditional patterns. **Patterns:** Bird, trout, boots, hunters, fighters, some Bowies. **Technical:** Grinds ATS-34, 440C, 154CM, tool steels and Damascus. **Prices:** $150 to $1000. **Remarks:** Part-time maker, first knife sold in 1004. **Mark:** Last name, logo, city.

ROSENFELD, BOB,
955 Freeman Johnson Rd, Hoschton, GA 30548, Phone: 770-867-2647, www.1bladesmith@msn.com
Specialties: Fancy and embellished working/using straight knives of his design and in standard patterns. Patterns: Daggers, hunters and utility/camp knives. **Technical:** Forges 52100, A203E, 1095 and L6 Damascus. Offers engraving. **Prices:** $125 to $650; some to $1000. **Remarks:** Full-time maker; first knife sold in 1984. Also makes folders; ABS Journeyman. **Mark:** Last name or full name, Knifemaker.

ROSS, D L,
27 Kinsman St, Dunedin, NEW ZEALAND, Phone: 64 3 464 0239, Fax: 64 3 464 0239
Specialties: Working straight knives of his design. **Patterns:** Hunters, various others. **Technical:** Grinds 440C. **Prices:** $100 to $450; some to $700 NZ (not U.S. $). **Remarks:** Part-time maker; first knife sold in 1988. **Mark:** Dave Ross, Maker, city and country.

ROSS, GREGG,
4556 Wenhart Rd, Lake Worth, FL 33463, Phone: 407-439-4681
Specialties: Working/using straight knives. **Patterns:** Bowies, hunters and utility/camp knives. **Technical:** Forges and grinds ATS-34, Damascus and cable Damascus. Uses decorative pins. **Prices:** $125 to $250; some to $400. **Remarks:** Part-time maker; first knife sold in 1992. **Mark:** Name, city and state.

ROSS, STEPHEN,
534 Remington Dr, Evanston, WY 82930, Phone: 307-789-7104
Specialties: One-of-a-kind collector-grade classic and contemporary straight knives and folders of his design and to customer specs; some fantasy pieces. **Patterns:** Combat and survival knives, hunters, boots and folders. **Technical:** Grinds stainless; forges spring and tool steel. Engraves, scrimshaws. Makes leather sheaths. **Prices:** $160 to $3000. **Remarks:** Part-time-time maker; first knife sold in 1971. **Mark:** Last name in modified Roman; sometimes in script.

ROSS, TIM,
3239 Oliver Rd, Thunder Bay, Ont., CANADA P7G 1S9, Phone: 807-935-2667, Fax: 807-935-3179
Specialties: Fixed blades. **Patterns:** Hunting, fishing, collector. **Technical:** Uses D2, Stellite, 440C, Forges 52100, Damascus cable. **Prices:** $150 to $750 some to $5000. **Mark:** Tang stamps Ross custom knives.

ROSSDEUTSCHER, ROBERT N,
133 S Vail Ave, Arlington Heights, IL 60005, Phone: 847-577-0404, Web: www.rnrknives.com
Specialties: Frontier-style and historically inspired knives. **Patterns:** Trade knives, Bowies, camp knives and hunting knives, tomahawks and lances. **Technical:** Most knives are hand forged, a few are stock removal. **Prices:** $135 to $1500. **Remarks:** Journeyman Smith of the American Bladesmith Society. **Mark:** Back-to-back "R's", one upside down and backwards, one right side up and forward in an oval. Sometimes with name, town and state; depending on knife style.

ROTELLA, RICHARD A,
643 75th St, Niagara Falls, NY 14304
Specialties: Working knives of his design. **Patterns:** Various fishing, hunting and utility knives; folders. **Technical:** Grinds ATS-34. Prefers hand-rubbed finishes. **Prices:** $65 to $450; some to $900. **Remarks:** Spare-time maker; first knife sold in 1977. Not taking orders at this time; only sells locally. **Mark:** Name and city in stylized waterfall logo.

ROULIN, CHARLES,
113 B Rt. de Soral, 1233 Geneva, SWITZERLAND, Phone: 022-757-4479, Fax: 022-757-4479, coutelier@coutelier-Roulin.com; Web: www.coutelier-roulin.com
Specialties: Fancy high-art straight knives and folders of his design. **Patterns:** Bowies, locking folders, slip-joint folders and miniatures. **Technical:** Grinds 440C, ATS-34 and D2. Engraves; carves nature scenes and detailed animals in steel, ivory, on handles and blades. **Prices:** $500 to $3000; some to $10,000. **Remarks:** Full-time maker; first knife sold in 1988. **Mark:** Symbol of fish with name or name engraved.

ROWE, FRED,
BETHEL RIDGE FORGE, 3199 Roberts Rd, Amesville, OH 45711, Phone: 866-325-2164, fred.rowe@bethelridgeforge.com; Web: www.bethelridgeforge.com
Specialties: Damascus and carbon steel sheath knives. **Patterns:** Bowies, hunters, fillet small kokris. **Technical:** His own Damascus, 52100, O1, L6, 1095 carbon steels. **Prices:** $200 to $1000. **Remarks:** All blades are clay hardened. **Mark:** Bethel Ridge Forge.

ROZAS, CLARK D,
1436 W "G" St, Wilmington, CA 90744, Phone: 310-518-0488
Specialties: Hand forged blades. **Patterns:** Pig stickers, toad stabbers, whackers, choppers. **Technical:** Damascus, 52100, 1095, 1084, 5160. **Prices:** $200 to $600. **Remarks:** A.B.S. member; part-time maker since 1995. **Mark:** Name over dagger.

RUANA KNIFE WORKS,
Box 520, Bonner, MT 59823, Phone: 406-258-5368, Fax: 406-258-2895, info@ruanaknives.com; Web: www.ruanaknives.com
Specialties: Working knives and period pieces. Patterns: Variety of straight knives. **Technical:** Forges 5160 chrome alloy for Bowies and 1095. **Prices:** $200 and up. **Remarks:** Full-time maker; first knife sold in 1938. Brand new non catalog knives available on ebay under seller name ruanaknives. For free catalog email regular mailing address to info@ruanaknives.com **Mark:** Name.

RUPERT, BOB,
301 Harshaville Rd, Clinton, PA 15026, Phone: 724-573-4569, rbrupert@aol.com
Specialties: Wrought period pieces with natural elements. **Patterns:** Elegant straight blades, friction folders. **Technical:** Forges colonial 7; 1095; 5160; diffuse mokume-gane and Damascus. **Prices:** $150 to $1500; some higher. **Remarks:** Part-time maker; first knife sold in 1980. Evening hours studio since 1980. Likes simplicity that disassembles. **Mark:** R etched in Old English.

RUPLE, WILLIAM H,
PO Box 370, Charlotte, TX 78011, Phone: 830-277-1371
Specialties: Multi-blade folders, slip joints, some lock backs. **Patterns:** Like to reproduce old patterns. **Technical:** Grinds 440C, ATS-34, D2 and commercial Damascus. Offers filework on back springs and liners. **Prices:** $300 to $500; some to $1000. **Remarks:** Full-time maker; first knife sold in 1988. **Mark:** Ruple.

RUSS, RON,
5351 NE 160th Ave, Williston, FL 32696, Phone: 352-528-2603, RussRs@aol.com
Specialties: Damascus and mokume. **Patterns:** Ladder, rain drop and butterfly. **Technical:** Most knives, including Damascus, are forged from 52100-E. **Prices:** $65 to $2500. **Mark:** Russ.

RUSSELL, MICK,
4 Rossini Rd, Pari Park, Port Elizabeth 6070, SOUTH AFRICA
Specialties: Art knives. **Patterns:** Working and collectible bird, trout and hunting knives, defense knives and folders. **Technical:** Grinds D2, 440C, ATS-34 and Damascus. Offers mirror or satin finishes. **Prices:** Start at $100. **Remarks:** Full-time maker; first knife sold in 1986. **Mark:** Stylized rhino incorporating initials.

RUSSELL, TOM,
6500 New Liberty Rd, Jacksonville, AL 36265, Phone: 205-492-7866
Specialties: Straight working knives of his design or to customer specs. **Patterns:** Hunters, folders, fighters, skinners, Bowies and utility knives. **Technical:** Grinds D2, 440C and ATS-34; offers filework. **Prices:** $75 to $225. **Remarks:** Part-time maker; first knife sold in 1987. Full-time tool and die maker. **Mark:** Last name with tulip stamp.

RUTH, MICHAEL G,
3101 New Boston Rd, Texarkana, TX 75501, Phone: 903-832-7166/cell:903-277-3663, Fax: 903-832-4710, mike@ruthknives.com; Web: www.ruthknives.com
Specialties: Hunters, bowies & fighters. Damascus & carbon steel. **Prices:** $375 & up. **Mark:** Last name.

RYBAR JR., RAYMOND B,
726 W Lynwood St, Phoenix, AZ 85007, Phone: 602-523-0201, ray_heidi_rybar@hotmail.com
Specialties: Straight knives or folders with customers name, logo, etc. in mosaic pattern. **Patterns:** Common patterns plus mosaics of all types. **Technical:** Forges own Damascus. Primary forging of self smelted steel -smelting classes. **Prices:** $200 to $1200; Bible blades to $10,000. **Remarks:** Master Smith (A.B.S.) Primary focus toward Biblicaly themed blades **Mark:** Rybar or stone church forge or Rev. 1:3 or R.B.R. between diamonds.

RYBERG, GOTE,
Faltgatan 2, S-562 00 Norrahammar, SWEDEN, Phone: 4636-61678

RYDBOM, JEFF,
PO Box 548, Annandale, MN 55302, Phone: 320-274-9639, jry1890@hotmail.com
Specialties: Ring knives. **Patterns:** Hunters, fighters, Bowie and camp knives. **Technical:** Straight grinds O1, A2, 1566 and 5150 steels. **Prices:** $150 to $1000. **Remarks:** No pinning of guards or pommels. All silver brazed. **Mark:** Capital "C" with J R inside.

RYUICHI, KUKI,
504-7 Tokorozawa-Shinmachi, Tokorozawa-city, Saitama, JAPAN, Phone: 042-943-3451

RZEWNICKI, GERALD,
8833 S Massbach Rd, Elizabeth, IL 61028-9714, Phone: 815-598-3239

S

SAINDON, R BILL,
233 Rand Pond Rd, Goshen, NH 03752, Phone: 603-863-1874, dayskiev71@aol.com
Specialties: Collector-quality folders of his design or to customer specs. **Patterns:** Latch release, LinerLock® and lockback folders. **Technical:** Offers limited amount of own Damascus; also uses Damas makers steel. Prefers natural handle material, gold and gems. **Prices:** $500 to $4000. **Remarks:** Full-time maker; first knife sold in 1981. Doing business as Daynia Forge. **Mark:** Sun logo or engraved surname.

SAKAKIBARA, MASAKI,
20-8 Sakuragaoka, 2-Chome Setagaya-ku, Tokyo 156-0054, JAPAN, Phone: 81-3-3420-0375

SAKMAR, MIKE,
1451 Clovelly Ave, Rochester, MI 48307, Phone: 248-852-6775, Fax: 248-852-8544, mikesakmar@yahoo.com
Specialties: Mokume in various patterns and alloy combinations. **Patterns:** Bowies, fighters, hunters and integrals. **Technical:** Grinds ATS-34, Damascus and high-carbon tool steels. Uses mostly natural handle materials—elephant ivory, walrus ivory, stag, wildwood, oosic, etc. Makes mokume for resale. **Prices:** $250 to $2500; some to $4000. **Remarks:** Part-time maker; first knife sold in 1990. Supplier of mokume. **Mark:** Last name.

SALLEY, JOHN D,
3965 Frederick-Ginghamsburg Rd., Tipp City, OH 45371, Phone: 937-698-4588, Fax: 937-698-4131
Specialties: Fancy working knives and art pieces. **Patterns:** Hunters, fighters, daggers and some swords. **Technical:** Grinds ATS-34, 12C27 and W2; buys Damascus. **Prices:** $85 to $1000; some to $6000. **Remarks:** Part-time maker; first knife sold in 1979. **Mark:** First initial, last name.

SAMPSON, LYNN,
381 Deakins Rd, Jonesborough, TN 37659, Phone: 423-348-8373
Specialties: Highly finished working knives, mostly folders. **Patterns:** Locking folders, slip-joints, interframes and two-blades. **Technical:** Grinds D2, 440C and ATS-34; offers extensive filework. **Prices:** Start at $300. **Remarks:** Full-time maker; first knife sold in 1982. **Mark:** Name and city in logo.

SANDBERG, RONALD B,
24784 Shadowwood Ln, Browntown, MI 48134, Phone: 734-671-6866, msc@ili.net
Specialties: Good looking and functional hunting knives, filework, mixing of handle materials. **Patterns:** Hunters, skinners and Bowies. **Prices:** $120 and up. **Remarks:** Doing business as Mighty Sharp Cuts. **Mark:** R.B. Sandberg.

SANDERS, A.A.,
3850 72 Ave NE, Norman, OK 73071, Phone: 405-364-8660
Specialties: Working straight knives and folders. **Patterns:** Hunters, fighters, daggers and Bowies. **Technical:** Forges his own Damascus; offers stock removal with ATS-34, 440C, A2, D2, O1, 5160 and 1095. **Prices:** $85 to $1500. **Remarks:** Full-time maker; first knife sold in 1985. Formerly known as Athern Forge. **Mark:** Name.

SANDERS, BILL,
335 Bauer Ave, PO Box 957, Mancos, CO 81328, Phone: 970-533-7223, Fax: 970-533-7390, billsand@frontier.net; Web: www.billsandershandmadeknives.com
Specialties: Survival knives, working straight knives, some fancy and some fantasy, of his design. **Patterns:** Hunters, boots, utility knives, using belt knives. **Technical:** Grinds 440C, ATS-34 and commercial Damascus. Provides wide variety of handle materials. **Prices:** $170 to $800. **Remarks:** Full-time maker. Formerly of Timberline Knives. **Mark:** Name, city and state.

SANDERS, MICHAEL M,
PO Box 1106, Ponchatoula, LA 70454, Phone: 225-294-3601, sanders@bellsouth.net
Specialties: Working straight knives and folders, some deluxe. **Patterns:** Hunters, fighters, Bowies, daggers, large folders and deluxe Damascus miniatures. **Technical:** Grinds O1, D2, 440C, ATS-34 and Damascus. **Prices:** $75 to $650; some higher. **Remarks:** Full-time maker; first knife sold in 1967. **Mark:** Name and state.

SANDLIN, LARRY,
4580 Sunday Dr, Adamsville, AL 35005, Phone: 205-674-1816
Specialties: High-art straight knives of his design. **Patterns:** Boots, daggers, hunters and fighters. **Technical:** Forges 1095, L6, O1, carbon steel and Damascus. **Prices:** $200 to $1500; some to $5000. **Remarks:** Part-time maker; first knife sold in 1990. **Mark:** Chiseled last name in Japanese.

SANDOW, NORMAN E,
63 B Moore St, Howick, Auckland, NEW ZEALAND, Phone: 095328912, sanknife@ezysurf.co.nz
Specialties: Quality LinerLock® folders. Working and fancy straight knives. Some one-of-a-kind. Embellishments available. **Patterns:** Most patterns, hunters, boot, bird and trout, etc., and to customer's specs. **Technical:** Predominate knife steel ATS-34. Also in use 12C27, D2 and Damascus. High class handle material used on both folders and straight knives. All blades made via the stock removal method. **Prices:** $250 to $1500. **Remarks:** Full-time maker. **Mark:** Norman E Sandow in semi-circular design.

SANDS, SCOTT,
2 Lindis Ln, New Brighton, Christchurch 9, NEW ZEALAND
Specialties: Classic working and fantasy swords. Patterns: Fantasy, medieval, celtic, viking, katana, some daggers. **Technical:** Forges own Damascus; 1080 and L6; 5160 and L6; O1 and L6. All hand-polished, does own heat-treating, forges non-Damascus on request. **Prices:** $1500 to $15,000+. **Remarks:** Full-time maker; first blade sold in 1996. **Mark:** Stylized Moon.

SANTIAGO, ABUD,
Av Gaona 3676 PB A, Buenos Aires 1416, ARGENTINA, Phone: 5411 4612 8396, info@phi-sabud.com; Web: www.phi-sabud.com/blades.html

SARGANIS, PAUL,
2215 Upper Applegate Rd, Jacksonville, OR 97530, Phone: 541-899-2831
Specialties: Hunters, folders, Bowies. **Technical:** Forges 5160, 1084. Grinds ATS-34 and 440C. **Prices:** $120 to $500. **Remarks:** Spare-time maker, first knife sold in 1987. **Mark:** Last name.

SARVIS, RANDALL J,
110 West Park Ave, Fort Pierre, SD 57532, Phone: 605-223-2772, rsarvis@sdln.net

SASS, GARY N,
2048 Buckeye Dr, Sharpsville, PA 16150, Phone: 724-866-6165, gnsass@yahoo.com
Specialties: Working straight knives of his design or to customer specifications. **Patterns:** Hunters, fighters, utility knives, push daggers. **Technical:** Grinds 440C, ATS-34 and Damascus. Uses exotic wood, buffalo horn, warthog tusk and semi-precious stones. **Prices:** $50 to $250, some higher. **Remarks:** Part-time maker. First knife sold in 2003. **Mark:** Initials G.S. formed into a diamond shape.

SAWBY, SCOTT,
480 Snowberry Ln, Sandpoint, ID 83864, Phone: 208-263-4171, scotmar@imbris.net; Web: www.sawbycustomknives.com
Specialties: Folders, working and fancy. **Patterns:** Locking folders, patent locking systems and interframes. **Technical:** Grinds D2, 440C, 154CM, CPM-T-440V and ATS-34. **Prices:** $500 to $1500. **Remarks:** Full-time maker; first knife sold in 1974. Engraving by wife Marian. **Mark:** Last name, city and state.

SCARROW, WIL,
c/o LandW Mail Service, PO Box 1036, Gold Hill, OR 97525, Phone: 541-855-1236, willsknife@earthlink.net
Specialties: Carving knives, also working straight knives in standard patterns or to customer specs. **Patterns:** Carving, fishing, hunting, skinning, utility, swords and Bowies. **Technical:** Forges and grinds: A2, L6, W1, D2, 5160, 1095, 440C, AEB-L, ATS-34 and others on request. Offers some filework. **Prices:** $105 to $850; some higher. Prices include sheath (carver's $40 and up). **Remarks:** Spare-time maker; first knife sold in 1983. Two to eight month construction time on custom orders. Doing business as Scarrow's Custom Stuff and Gold Hill Knife works (in Oregon). Carving knives available at Raven Dog Enterprises. Contact at Ravedog@aol.com. Carving knives available at the 'Wild Duck' Woodcarvers Supply. Contact at duckstore@aol.com. **Mark:** SC with arrow and date/year made.

SCHALLER, ANTHONY BRETT,
5609 Flint Ct. NW, Albuquerque, NM 87120, Phone: 505-899-0155, brett@schallerknives.com; Web: www.schallerknives.com
Specialties: Straight knives and locking-liner folders of his design and in standard patterns. **Patterns:** Boots, fighters, utility knives and folders. **Technical:** Grinds CPM154, S30V, and stainless Damascus. Offers filework, hand-rubbed finishes and full and narrow tangs. Prefers exotic woods or Micarta for handle materials, G-10 and carbon fiber to handle materials. **Prices:** $100 to $350; some to $500. **Remarks:** Part-time maker; first knife sold in 1990. **Mark:** A.B. Schaller -Albuquerque NM -handmade.

SCHEID, MAGGIE,
124 Van Stallen St, Rochester, NY 14621-3557
Specialties: Simple working straight knives. **Patterns:** Kitchen and utility knives; some miniatures. **Technical:** Forges 5160 high-carbon steel. **Prices:** $100 to $200. **Remarks:** Part-time maker; first knife sold in 1986. **Mark:** Full name.

SCHEMPP, ED,
PO Box 1181, Ephrata, WA 98823, Phone: 509-754-2963, Fax: 509-754-3212
Specialties: Mosaic Damascus and unique folder designs. **Patterns:** Primarily folders. **Technical:** Grinds CPM440V; forges many patterns of mosaic using powdered steel. **Prices:** $100 to $400; some to $2000. **Remarks:** Part-time maker; first knife sold in 1991. Doing business as Ed Schempp Knives. **Mark:** Ed Schempp Knives over five heads of wheat, city and state.

SCHEMPP, MARTIN,
PO Box 1181, 5430 Baird Springs Rd NW, Ephrata, WA 98823, Phone: 509-754-2963, Fax: 509-754-3212
Specialties: Fantasy and traditional straight knives of his design, to customer specs and in standard patterns; Paleolithic-styles. **Patterns:** Fighters and Paleolithic designs. **Technical:** Uses opal, Mexican rainbow and obsidian. Offers scrimshaw. **Prices:** $15 to $100; some to $250. **Remarks:** Spare-time maker; first knife sold in 1995. **Mark:** Initials and date.

SCHEPERS, GEORGE B,
PO Box 395, Shelton, NE 68876-0395
Specialties: Fancy period pieces of his design. Patterns: Bowies, swords, tomahawks; locking folders and miniatures. **Technical:** Grinds W1, W2 and his own Damascus; etches. **Prices:** $125 to $600; some higher. **Remarks:** Full-time maker; first knife sold in 1981. **Mark:** Schep.

SCHEURER, ALFREDO E FAES,
Av Rincon de los Arcos 104, Col Bosque Res del Sur, C.P. 16010, MEXICO, Phone: 5676 47 63
Specialties: Fancy and fantasy knives of his design. **Patterns:** Daggers. **Technical:** Grinds stainless steel; casts and grinds silver. Sets stones in silver. **Prices:** $2000 to $3000. **Remarks:** Spare-time maker; first knife sold in 1989. **Mark:** Symbol.

SCHILLING, ELLEN,
95 Line Rd, Hamilton Square, NJ 08690, Phone: 609-448-0483

SCHIPPNICK, JIM,
PO Box 326, Sanborn, NY 14132, Phone: 716-731-3715, ragnar@ragweedforge.com; Web: www.ragweedforge.com
Specialties: Nordic, early American, rustic. **Mark:** Runic R. **Remarks:** Also imports Nordic knives from Norway, Sweden and Finland.

SCHIRMER, MIKE,
34 Highway HH, Cherryville, MO 65446-3062, Phone: 573-743-3407, schirmer@3rivers.net
Specialties: Working straight knives of his design or to customer specs; mostly hunters and personal knives. **Patterns:** Hunters, camp, kitchen, Bowies and fighters. **Technical:** Grinds O1, D2, A2 and Damascus and Talonoite. **Prices:** Start at $150. **Remarks:** Full-time maker; first knife sold in 1992. Doing business as Ruby Mountain Knives. **Mark:** Name or name and location.

SCHLUETER, DAVID,
1117 Willis Ave, Syracuse, NY 13204-1048, Phone: 315-488-9230, david@oddfrogforge.com; Web: http://www.oddfrogforge.com
Specialties: Japanese-style swords. **Patterns:** Larger blades. O-tanto to Tachi, with focus on less common shapes. **Technical:** Forges and grinds carbon steels, heat-treats and polishes own blades, makes all fittings, does own mounting and finishing. **Prices:** Start at $3000. **Remarks:** Sells fully mounted pieces only, doing business as Odd Frog Forge. **Mark:** Full name and date.

SCHMITZ, RAYMOND E,
PO Box 1787, Valley Center, CA 92082, Phone: 760-749-4318

SCHNEIDER, CRAIG M,
5380 N Amity Rd, Claremont, IL 62421, Phone: 618-869-2094/217-377-5715
Specialties: Straight knives of his own design. **Patterns:** Bowies, hunters, tactical, bird & trout. **Technical:** Forged high-carbon steel and Damascus. Flat grind and differential heat treatment use a wide selection of handle, guard and bolster material, also offers leather sheaths. **Prices:** $100 to $3000. **Remarks:** Part-time maker; first knife sold in 1985. **Mark:** Stylized initials.

SCHNEIDER, HERMAN,
14084 Apple Valley Rd, Apple Valley, CA 92307, Phone: 760-946-9096
Specialties: Presentation pieces, Fighters, Hunters. **Prices:** Starting at $900. **Mark:** H.J. Schneider-Maker.

SCHNEIDER, KARL A,
209 N. Brownleaf Rd, Newark, DE 19713, Phone: 302-737-0277, dmatj@msn.com
Specialties: Traditional working and using straight knives of his design. **Patterns:** Hunters, kitchen and fillet knives. **Technical:** Grinds ATS-34, CM154, 52100, AUS8 -AUS6. Shapes handles to fit hands; uses Micarta, Pakkawood and exotic woods. Makes hand-stitched leather cases. **Prices:** $100 to $300. **Remarks:** Part-time maker; first knife sold in 1974. **Mark:** Name, address; also name in shape of fish.

SCHOEMAN, CORRIE,
Box 28596, Danhof 9310, SOUTH AFRICA, Phone: 027 51 4363528 Cell: 027 82-3750789, corries@intekom.co.za
Specialties: High-tech folders of his design or to customer's specs. **Patterns:** Linerlock folders and automatics. **Technical:** ATS-34, Damascus or stainless Damascus with titanium frames; prefers exotic materials for handles. **Prices:** $650 to $2000. **Remarks:** Full-time maker; first knife sold in 1984. All folders come with filed liners and back and jeweled inserts. **Mark:** Logo in knife shape engraved on inside of back bar.

SCHOENFELD, MATTHEW A,
RR #1, Galiano Island, B.C., CANADA V0N 1P0, Phone: 250-539-2806
Specialties: Working knives of his design. **Patterns:** Kitchen cutlery, camp knives, hunters. **Technical:** Grinds 440C. **Prices:** $85 to $500. **Remarks:** Part-time maker; first knife sold in 1978. **Mark:** Signature, Galiano Is. B.C., and date.

SCHOENINGH, MIKE,
49850 Miller Rd, North Powder, OR 97867, Phone: 541-856-3239

SCHOLL, TIM,
1389 Langdon Rd, Angier, NC 27501, Phone: 910-897-2051, tscholl@charter.net
Specialties: Fancy and working/using straight knives and folders of his design and to customer specs. Patterns: Bowies, hunters, tomahawks, daggers & fantasy knives. **Technical:** Forges high carbon and tool steel makes Damascus, grinds ATS-34 and D2 on request. **Prices:** $150 to $6000. **Remarks:** Part-time maker; first knife sold in 1990. Doing business as Tim Scholl Custom Knives. **Mark:** S pierced by arrow.

SCHRADER, ROBERT,
55532 Gross De, Bend, OR 97707, Phone: 541-598-7301
Specialties: Hunting, utility, Bowie. **Patterns:** Fixed blade. **Prices:** $150 to $600.

SCHRAP, ROBERT G,
CUSTOM LEATHER KNIFE SHEATH CO., 7024 W Wells St, Wauwatosa, WI 53213-3717, Phone: 414-771-6472, Fax: 414-479-9765, knifesheaths@aol.com; Web: www.customsheaths.com
Specialties: Leatherwork. **Prices:** $35 to $100. **Mark:** Schrap in oval.

SCHROEN, KARL,
4042 Bones Rd, Sebastopol, CA 95472, Phone: 707-823-4057, Fax: 707-823-2914
Specialties: Using knives made to fit. **Patterns:** Sgian dubhs, carving sets, wood-carving knives, fishing knives, kitchen knives and new cleaver design. **Technical:** Forges A2, ATS-34, D2 and L6 cruwear S30V 590V. **Prices:** $150 to $6000. **Remarks:** Full-time maker; first knife sold in 1968. Author of *The Hand Forged Knife*. **Mark:** Last name.

SCHUCHMANN, RICK,
3975 Hamblen Dr, Cincinnati, OH 45255, Phone: 513-553-4316
Specialties: Replicas of antique and out-of-production Scagels and Randalls, primarily miniatures. **Patterns:** All sheath knives, mostly miniatures, hunting and fighting knives, some daggers and hatchets. **Technical:** Stock removal, 440C and O1 steel. Most knives are flat ground, some convex. **Prices:** $175 to $600 and custom to $4000. **Remarks:** Part-time maker, sold first knife in 1997. Knives on display in the Randall Museum. Sheaths are made exclusively at Sullivan's Holster Shop, Tampa, FL **Mark:** SCAR.

SCHULTZ, ROBERT W,
PO Box 70, Cocolalla, ID 83813-0070

SCHWARZER, STEPHEN,
119-2 Shoreside Trail, Crescent City, FL 32112, Phone: 386-698-2840, Fax: 386-649-8585, steveschwarzer@gbso.net; Web: www.steveschwarzer.com
Specialties: Mosaic Damascus and picture mosaic in folding knives. All Japanese blades are finished working with Wally Hostetter considered the top Japanese lacquer specialist in the U.S.A. Also produces a line of carbon steel skinning knives at $300. **Patterns:** Folders, axes and buckskinner knives. **Technical:** Specializes in picture mosaic Damascus and powder metal mosaic work. Sole authorship; all work including carving done in-house. Most knives have file work and carving. Hand carved steel and precious metal guards. **Prices:** $1500 to $5000, some higher; carbon steel and primitive knives much less. **Remarks:** Full-time maker; first knife sold in 1976, considered by many to be one of the top mosaic Damascus specialists in the world. Mosaic Master level work. **Mark:** Schwarzer + anvil.

SCIMIO, BILL,
HC 01 Box 24A, Spruce Creek, PA 16683, Phone: 814-632-3751, blackcrowforge@aol.com

SCOFIELD, EVERETT,
2873 Glass Mill Rd, Chickamauga, GA 30707, Phone: 706-375-2790
Specialties: Historic and fantasy miniatures. **Patterns:** All patterns. **Technical:** Uses only the finest tool steels and other materials. Uses only natural, precious and semi-precious materials. **Prices:** $100 to $1500. **Remarks:** Full-time maker; first knife sold in 1971. Doing business as Three Crowns Cutlery. **Mark:** Three Crowns logo.

SCORDIA, PAOLO,
Via Terralba 143, 00050 Torrimpietra, Roma, ITALY, Phone: 06-61697231, pands@mail.nexus.it; Web: www.scordia-knives.com
Specialties: Working and fantasy knives of his own design. **Patterns:** Any pattern. **Technical:** Forges own Damascus, welds own mokume and grinds ATS-34, etc. use hardwoods and Micarta for handles, brass and nickel-silver for fittings. Makes sheaths. **Prices:** $100 to $1000. **Remarks:** Part-time maker; first knife sold in 1988. **Mark:** Initials with sun and moon logo.

SCOTT, AL,
2245 Harper Valley Rd, Harper, TX 78631, Phone: 830-864-4182
Specialties: High-art straight knives of his design. **Patterns:** Daggers, swords, early European, Middle East and Japanese knives. **Technical:** Uses ATS-34, 440C and Damascus. Hand engraves; does file work; cuts filigree in the blade; offers ivory carving and precious metal inlay. **Remarks:** Full-time maker; first knife sold in 1994. Doing business as Al Scott Maker of Fine Blade Art. **Mark:** Name engraved in Old English, sometime inlaid in 24K gold.

SCROGGS, JAMES A,
108 Murray Hill Dr, Warrensburg, MO 64093, Phone: 660-747-2568, jscroggsknives@embarqmail.com
Specialties: Straight knives, prefers light weight. Patterns: Hunters, hideouts, and fighters. **Technical:** Grinds CMP3V, CMPS30V, plus experiments in steels. Prefers handles of walnut in English, bastonge, American black. Also uses myrtle, maple, Osage orange. **Prices:** $200 to $1000. **Remarks:** 1st knife sold in 1985. Part-time maker, no orders taken. **Mark:** SCROGGS in block or script.

SCULLEY, PETER E,
340 Sunset Dr, Rising Fawn, GA 30738, Phone: 706-398-0169

SEARS, MICK,
1697 Peach Orchard Rd #302, Sumter, SC 29154, Phone: 803-464-2265
Specialties: Scots and confederate reproductions; Bowies and fighters. **Patterns:** Bowies, fighters. **Technical:** Grinds 440C and 1095. **Prices:** $50 to $150; some to $300. **Remarks:** Part-time maker; first knife sold in 1975. Doing business as Mick's Custom Knives. **Mark:** First name.

SELENT, CHUCK,
PO Box 1207, Bonners Ferry, ID 83805-1207, Phone: 208-267-5807
Specialties: Period, art and fantasy miniatures; exotics; one-of-a-kinds. **Patterns:** Swords, daggers and others. **Technical:** Works in Damascus, meteorite, 440C and tool steel. Offers scrimshaw. Offers his own casting and leatherwork; uses jewelry techniques. Makes display cases for miniatures. **Prices:** $75 to $400. **Remarks:** Part-time maker; first knife sold in 1990. **Mark:** Last name and bear paw print logo scrimshawed on handles or leatherwork.

SELF, ERNIE,
950 O'Neill Ranch Rd, Dripping Springs, TX 78620-9760, Phone: 512-940-7134, ernieself@hillcountrytx.net
Specialties: Traditional and working straight knives and folders of his design and in standard patterns. **Patterns:** Hunters, locking folders and slip-joints. **Technical:** Grinds 440C, D2, 440V, ATS-34 and Damascus. Offers fancy filework. **Prices:** $250 to $1000; some to $2500. **Remarks:** Full-time maker; first knife sold in 1982. Also customizes Buck 110's and 112's folding hunters. **Mark:** In oval shape -Ernie Self Maker Dripping Springs TX.

SELLEVOLD, HARALD,
S Kleivesmau:2, PO Box 4134, N5835 Bergen, NORWAY, Phone: 47 55-310682, haraldsellevold@c2i.net; Web:knivmakeren.com
Specialties: Norwegian-styles; collaborates with other Norse craftsmen. **Patterns:** Distinctive ferrules and other mild modifications of traditional patterns; Bowies and friction folders. **Technical:** Buys Damascus blades; blacksmiths his own blades. Semi-gemstones used in handles; gemstone inlay. **Prices:** $350 to $2000. **Remarks:** Full-time maker; first knife sold in 1980. **Mark:** Name and country in logo.

SELZAM, FRANK,
Martin Reinhard Str 23 97631, Bad Koenigshofen, GERMANY, Phone: 09761-5980
Specialties: Hunters, working knives to customers specs, hand tooled and stitched leather sheaths large stock of wood and German stag horn. **Patterns:** Mostly own design. **Technical:** Forged blades, own Damascus, also stock removal stainless. **Prices:** $250 to $1500. **Remark:** First knife sold in 1978. **Mark:** Last name stamped.

SENTZ, MARK C,
4084 Baptist Rd, Taneytown, MD 21787, Phone: 410-756-2018
Specialties: Fancy straight working knives of his design. **Patterns:** Hunters, fighters, folders and utility/camp knives. **Technical:** Forges 1085, 1095, 5160, 5155 and his Damascus. Most knives come with wood-lined leather sheath or wooden presentation sheath. **Prices:** Start at $275. **Remarks:** Full-time maker; first knife sold in 1989. Doing business as M. Charles Sentz Gunsmithing, Inc. **Mark:** Last name.

SERAFEN, STEVEN E,
24 Genesee St, New Berlin, NY 13411, Phone: 607-847-6903
Specialties: Traditional working/using straight knives of his design and to customer specs. **Patterns:** Bowies, fighters, hunters. **Technical:** Grinds ATS-34, 440C, high-carbon steel. **Prices:** $175 to $600; some to $1200. **Remarks:** Part-time maker; first knife sold in 1990. **Mark:** First and middle initial, last name in script.

SERVEN, JIM,
PO Box 1, Fostoria, MI 48435, Phone: 517-795-2255
Specialties: Highly finished unique folders. **Patterns:** Fancy working folders, axes, miniatures and razors; some straight knives. **Technical:** Grinds 440C; forges his own Damascus. **Prices:** $150 to $800; some to $1500. **Remarks:** Full-time maker; first knife sold in 1971. **Mark:** Name in map logo.

SEVEY CUSTOM KNIFE,
94595 Chandler Rd, Gold Beach, OR 97444, Phone: 541-247-2649, sevey@charter.net; Web: www.seveyknives.com
Specialties: Fixed blade hunters. **Patterns:** Drop point, trailing paint, clip paint, full tang, hidden tang. **Technical:** D-2, and ATS-34 blades, stock removal. Heat treatment by Paul Bos. **Prices:** $225 and up depending on overall length and grip material. **Mark:** Sevey Custom Knife.

SFREDDO, RODRIGO MENEZES,
Rua 15 De Setembro 66, Centro Nova Petropolis RS, cep g5 150-000, BRAZIL 95150-000, Phone: 011-55-54-303-303-90, www.brazilianbladesmiths.com.br; www.sbccutelaria.org.br
Specialties: Integrals, Bowies, hunters, dirks & swords. Patterns: Forges his own Damascus and 52100 steel. **Technical:** Specialized in integral knives and Damascus. **Prices:** From $350 and up. Most around $750 to $1000. **Remarks:** Considered by many to be the Brazil's best bladesmith. ABS SBC Member. **Mark:** S. Sfreddo on the left side of the blade.

SHADLEY, EUGENE W,
26315 Norway Dr, Bovey, MN 55709, Phone: 218-245-1639, Fax: call first, bses@uslink.net
Specialties: Gold frames are available on some models. **Patterns:** Whittlers, stockman, sowbelly, congress, trapper, etc. **Technical:** Grinds ATS-34, 416 frames. **Prices:** Starts at $600. **Remarks:** Full-time maker; first knife sold in 1985. Doing business as Shadley Knives. **Mark:** Last name.

SHADMOT, BOAZ,
MOSHAV PARAN D N, Arava, ISRAEL 86835, srb@arava.co.il

SHARRIGAN, MUDD,
111 Bradford Rd, Wiscasset, ME 04578-4457, Phone: 207-882-9820, Fax: 207-882-9835
Specialties: Custom designs; repair straight knives, custom leather sheaths. **Patterns:** Daggers, fighters, hunters, buckskinner, Indian crooked knives and seamen working knives; traditional Scandinavian-styles. **Technical:** Forges 1095, 52100, 5160, W2, O1. Laminates 1095 and mild steel. **Prices:** $50 to $325; some to $1200. **Remarks:** Full-time maker; first knife sold in 1982. **Mark:** First name and swallow tail carving.

SHAVER II, JAMES R,
1529 Spider Ridge Rd, Parkersburg, WV 26104, Phone: 304-422-2692, admin@spiderridgeforge.net Web:www.spiderridgeforge.net
Specialties: Hunting and working straight knives in carbon and Damascus steel. **Patterns:** Bowies and daggers in Damascus and carbon steels. **Technical:** Forges 5160 carbon and Damascus in 01 pure nickel 1018. **Prices:** $85 to $125; some to $750. Some to $1000 **Remarks:** Part-time maker; sold first knife in 1998. Believes in sole authorship. **Mark:** Last name.

SHEEHY, THOMAS J,
4131 NE 24th Ave, Portland, OR 97211-6411, Phone: 503-493-2843
Specialties: Hunting knives and ulus. **Patterns:** Own or customer designs. **Technical:** 1095/O1 and ATS-34 steel. **Prices:** $35 to $200. **Remarks:** Do own heat treating; forged or ground blades. **Mark:** Name.

SHEETS, STEVEN WILLIAM,
6 Stonehouse Rd, Mendham, NJ 07945, Phone: 201-543-5882

SHIFFER, STEVE,
PO Box 582, Leakesville, MS 39451, Phone: 601-394-4425, aiifish2@yahoo.com; Web: wwwchoctawplantationforge.com
Specialties: Bowies, fighters, hard use knives. **Patterns:** Fighters, hunters, combat/utility knives. Walker pattern LinerLock® folders. Allen pattern scale and bolster release autos. **Technical:** Most work forged, stainless stock removal. Makes own Damascus. O1 and 5160 most used also 1084, 440c, 154cm, s30v. **Prices:** $125 to $1000. **Remarks:** First knife sold in 2000, all heat treatment done by maker. Doing business as Choctaw Plantation Forge. **Mark:** Hot mark sunrise over creek.

SHIKAYAMA, TOSHIAKI,
259-2 Suka Yoshikawa Machi, Kitakatsusaika Sitiama, JAPAN, Phone: 04-89-81-6605, Fax: 04-89-81-6605
Specialties: Folders in standard patterns. **Patterns:** Locking and multi-blade folders. **Technical:** Grinds ATS, carbon steel, high speed steel. **Prices:** $400 to $2500; $4500 with engraving. **Remarks:** Full-time maker; first knife sold in 1952. **Mark:** First initial, last name.

SHINOSKY, ANDY,
3117 Meanderwood Dr, Canfield, OH 44406, Phone: 330-702-0299, andrew@shinosky.com; Web: www.shinosky.com
Specialties: Collectable folders and interframes. **Patterns:** Drop point, spear point, trailing point, daggers. **Technical:** Grinds ATS-34 and Damascus. Prefers natural handle materials. Most knives are engraved by Andy himself. **Prices:** Start at $800. **Remarks:** Part-time maker/engraver. First knife sold in 1992. **Mark:** Name.

SHIPLEY, STEVEN A,
800 Campbell Rd Ste 137, Richardson, TX 75081, Phone: 972-644-7981, Fax: 972-644-7985, steve@shipleysphotography
Specialties: Hunters, skinners and traditional straight knives. **Technical:** Hand grinds ATS-34, 440C and Damascus steels. Each knife is custom sheathed by his son, Dan. **Prices:** $175 to $2000. **Remarks:** Part-time maker; like smooth lines and unusual handle materials. **Mark:** S A Shipley.

SHOEMAKER, CARROLL,
380 Yellowtown Rd, Northup, OH 45658, Phone: 740-446-6695
Specialties: Working/using straight knives of his design. **Patterns:** Hunters, utility/camp and early American backwoodsmen knives. **Technical:** Grinds ATS-34; forges old files, O1 and 1095. Uses some Damascus; offers scrimshaw and engraving. **Prices:** $100 to $175; some to $350. **Remarks:** Spare-time maker; first knife sold in 1977. **Mark:** Name and city or connected initials.

SHOEMAKER, SCOTT,
316 S Main St, Miamisburg, OH 45342, Phone: 513-859-1935
Specialties: Twisted, wire-wrapped handles on swords, fighters and fantasy blades; new line of seven models with quick-draw, multi-carry Kydex sheaths. **Patterns:** Bowies, boots and one-of-a-kinds in his design or to customer specs. **Technical:** Grinds A6 and ATS-34; buys

Damascus. Hand satin finish is standard. **Prices:** $100 to $1500; swords to $8000. **Remarks:** Part-time maker; first knife sold in 1984. **Mark:** Angel wings with last initial, or last name.

SHOGER, MARK O,
14780 SW Osprey Dr Suite 345, Beaverton, OR 97007, Phone: 503-579-2495, mosdds@msn.com

Specialties: Working and using straight knives and folders of his design; fancy and embellished knives. **Patterns:** Hunters, Bowies, daggers and folders. **Technical:** Forges O1, W2, 1084, 5160, 52100 and 1084/15n20 pattern weld. **Remarks:** Spare-time maker. **Mark:** Last name or stamped last initial over anvil.

SHORE, JOHN I,
ALASKA KNIFEMAKER, 53335 Lee Ave, Kenai, AK 99611, Phone: 907-272-2253, akknife@acsalaska.net; Web: www.akknife.com

Specialties: Working straight knives, hatchets, and folders. **Patterns:** Hunters, skinners, Bowies, fighters, working using knives. **Technical:** Prefer using exotic steels, grinds most CPM's, Damasteel, RWL34, BG42, D2 and some ATS-34. Prefers exotic hardwoods, stabilized materials, Micarta, and pearl. **Prices:** Comparable to other top makers. **Remarks:** Full-time maker; first knife sold in 1985. Voting member Knifemakers Guild & Dertche Messermacker Guild. **Mark:** Name in script, Kenai, AK.

SHULL, JAMES,
5146 N US 231 W, Rensselaer, IN 47978, Phone: 219-866-0436, nbjs@netnitco.net

Specialties: Working knives of hunting, fillet, Bowie patterns. **Technical:** Forges or uses 1095, 5160, 52100 & O1. **Prices:** $100 to $300. **Remarks:** DBA Shull Handforged Knives. **Mark:** Last name in arc.

SIBRIAN, AARON,
4308 Dean Dr, Ventura, CA 93003, Phone: 805-642-6950

Specialties: Tough working knives of his design and in standard patterns. **Patterns:** Makes a "Viper utility"—a kukri derivative and a variety of straight using knives. **Technical:** Grinds 440C and ATS-34. Offers traditional Japanese blades; soft backs, hard edges, temper lines. **Prices:** $60 to $100; some to $250. **Remarks:** Spare-time maker; first knife sold in 1989. **Mark:** Initials in diagonal line.

SIMMONS, H R,
1100 Bay City Rd, Aurora, NC 27806, Phone: 252-322-5969

Specialties: Working/using straight knives of his design. **Patterns:** Fighters, hunters and utility/camp knives. **Technical:** Forges and grinds Damascus and L6; grinds ATS-34. **Prices:** $150 to $250; some to $400. **Remarks:** Part-time maker; first knife sold in 1987. Doing business as HRS Custom Knives, Royal Forge and Trading Company. **Mark:** Initials.

SIMONELLA, GIANLUIGI,
Via Battiferri 33, 33085 Maniago, ITALY, Phone: 01139-427-730350

Specialties: Traditional and classic folding and working/using knives of his design and to customer specs. **Patterns:** Bowies, fighters, hunters, utility/camp knives. **Technical:** Forges ATS-34, D2, 440C. **Prices:** $250 to $400; some to $1000. **Remarks:** Full-time maker; first knife sold in 1988. **Mark:** Wilson.

SIMS, BOB,
PO Box 772, Meridian, TX 76665, Phone: 254-435-6240

Specialties: Traditional working straight knives and folders in standard patterns. **Patterns:** Locking folders, slip-joint folders and hunters. **Technical:** Grinds D2, ATS-34 and O1. Offers filework on some knives. **Prices:** $150 to $275; some to $600. **Remarks:** Full-time maker; first knife sold in 1975. **Mark:** The division sign.

SINCLAIR, J E,
520 Francis Rd, Pittsburgh, PA 15239, Phone: 412-793-5778

Specialties: Fancy hunters and fighters, liner locking folders. **Patterns:** Fighters, hunters and folders. **Technical:** Flat-grinds and hollow grind, prefers hand rubbed satin finish. Uses natural handle materials. **Prices:** $185 to $800. **Remarks:** Part-time maker; first knife sold in 1995. **Mark:** First and middle initials, last name and maker.

SINYARD, CLESTON S,
27522 Burkhardt Dr, Elberta, AL 36530, Phone: 334-987-1361, nimoforge1@gulftel.com; Web: www.knifemakersguild

Specialties: Working straight knives and folders of his design. **Patterns:** Hunters, buckskinners, Bowies, daggers, fighters and all-Damascus folders. **Technical:** Makes Damascus from 440C, stainless steel, D2 and regular high-carbon steel; forges "forefinger pad" into hunters and skinners. **Prices:** In Damascus $450 to $1500; some $2500. **Remarks:** Full-time maker; first knife sold in 1980. Doing business as Nimo Forge. **Mark:** Last name, U.S.A. in anvil.

SISEMORE, CHARLES RUSSEL,
RR 2 Box 329AL, Mena, AR 71953, Phone: 918-383-1360

SISKA, JIM,
48 South Maple St, Westfield, MA 01085, Phone: 413-642-3059, siskaknives@comcast.net

Specialties: Traditional working straight knives, no folders. Patterns: Hunters, fighters, Bowies and one-of-a-kinds; folders. **Technical:** Grinds D2, A2, 54CM and ATS-34; buys Damascus. Likes exotic woods. **Prices:** $300 and up. **Remarks:** Part-time. **Mark:** Siska in Old English.

SJOSTRAND, KEVIN,
1541 S Cain St, Visalia, CA 93292, Phone: 209-625-5254

Specialties: Traditional and working/using straight knives and folders of his design or to customer specs. **Patterns:** Bowies, hunters, utility/camp knives, lockback, springbuck and LinerLock® folders. **Technical:** Grinds ATS-34, 440C and 1095. Prefers high polished blades and full tang. Natural and stabilized hardwoods, Micarta and stag handle material. **Prices:** $75 to $300. **Remarks:** Part-time maker; first knife sold in 1992. Doing business as Black Oak Blades. **Mark:** Oak tree, Black Oak Blades, name, or just last name.

SKIFF, STEVEN,
SKIFF MADE BLADES, PO Box 537, Broadalbin, NY 12025, Phone: 518-883-4875, skiffmadeblades @hotmail.com; Web: www.skiffmadeblades.com

Specialties: Custom using/collector grade straight blades and LinerLock® folders of maker's design or customer specifications. **Patterns:** Hunters, utility/camp knives, tactical/fancy art folders. **Prices:** Straight blades $225 and up. Folders $450 and up. **Technical:** Stock removal hollow ground ATS-34, 154 CM, S30V, and tool steel. Damascus-Devon Thomas, Robert Eggerling, Mike Norris and Delbert Ealy. Nickel silver and stainless in-house heat treating. Handle materials: man made and natural woods (stablilized). Horn shells sheaths for straight blades, sews own leather and uses sheaths by "Tree-Stump Leather." **Remarks:** First knife sold 1997. Started making folders in 2000. **Mark:** SKIFF on blade of straight blades and in inside of backspacer on folders.

SKOW, H A "TEX",
TEX KNIVES, 3534 Gravel Springs Rd, Senatobia, MS 38668, Phone: 662-301-1568, texknives@bellsouth.net

Specialties: One-of-a-kind daggers, Bowies, boot knives and hunters. **Patterns:** Different Damascus patterns (by Bob Eggerling). **Technical:** 440C, 58, 60 Rockwell hardness. Engraving by Joe Mason. **Prices:** Negotiable. **Mark:** TEX.

SLEE, FRED,
9 John St, Morganville, NJ 07751, Phone: 732-591-9047

Specialties: Working straight knives, some fancy, to customer specs. **Patterns:** Hunters, fighters, fancy daggers and folders. **Technical:** Grinds D2, 440C and ATS-34. **Prices:** $285 to $1100. **Remarks:** Part-time maker; first knife sold in 1980. **Mark:** Letter "S" in Old English.

SLOAN, SHANE,
4226 FM 61, Newcastle, TX 76372, Phone: 940-846-3290

Specialties: Collector-grade straight knives and folders. **Patterns:** Uses stainless Damascus, ATS-34 and 12C27. Bowies, lockers, slip-joints, fancy folders, fighters and period pieces. **Technical:** Grinds D2 and ATS-34. Uses hand-rubbed satin finish. Prefers rare natural handle materials. **Prices:** $250 to $6500. **Remarks:** Full-time maker; first knife sold in 1985. **Mark:** Name and city.

SLOBODIAN, BARBARA,
4101 River Ridge Dr, P.O. Box 1498, San Andreas, CA 95249, Phone: 209-286-1980, Fax: 209-286-1982, BarbaraS@dancethetide.com

Specialites: Japanese style engraving **Prices:**$501 HR

SLOBODIAN, SCOTT,
4101 River Ridge Dr, PO Box 1498, San Andreas, CA 95249, Phone: 209-286-1980, Fax: 209-286-1982, scott@slobodianswords.com; Web: www.slobodianswords.com

Specialties: Japanese-style knives and swords, period pieces, fantasy pieces and miniatures. **Patterns:** Small kweikens, tantos, wakazashis, katanas, traditional samurai swords. **Technical:** Flat-grinds 1050, commercial Damascus. **Prices:** $800 to $3500; some to $7500. **Remarks:** Full-time maker; first knife sold in 1987. **Mark:** Blade signed in Japanese characters and various scripts.

SMALE, CHARLES J,
509 Grove Ave, Waukegan, IL 60085, Phone: 847-244-8013

SMALL, ED,
Rt 1 Box 178-A, Keyser, WV 26726, Phone: 304-298-4254

Specialties: Working knives of his design; period pieces. **Patterns:** Hunters, daggers, buckskinners and camp knives; likes one-of-a-kinds. **Technical:** Forges and grinds W2, L6 and his own Damascus. **Prices:** $150 to $1500. **Remarks:** Full-time maker; first knife sold in 1978. Doing business as Iron Mountain Forge Works. **Mark:** Script initials connected.

SMART, STEVE,
907 Park Row Cir, McKinney, TX 75070-3847, Phone: 214-837-4216, Fax: 214-837-4111

Specialties: Working/using straight knives and folders of his design, to customer specs and in standard patterns. Patterns: Bowies, hunters, kitchen knives, locking folders, utility/camp, fishing and bird knives. **Technical:** Grinds ATS-34, D2, 440C and O1. Prefers mirror polish or satin finish; hollow-grinds all blades. All knives come with sheath. Offers some filework. **Prices:** $95 to $225; some to $500. **Remarks:** Spare-time maker; first knife sold in 1983. **Mark:** Name, Custom, city and state in oval.

SMIT, GLENN,
627 Cindy Ct, Aberdeen, MD 21001, Phone: 410-272-2959, wolfsknives@comcast.net
Specialties: Working and using straight and folding knives of his design or to customer specs. Customizes and repairs all types of cutlery. Exclusive maker of Dave Murphy Style knives. **Patterns:** Hunters, Bowies, daggers, fighters, utility/camp, folders, kitchen knives and miniatures, Murphy combat, C.H.A.I.K., Little 88 and Tiny 90-styles. **Technical:** Grinds 440C, ATS-34, O1, A2 also grinds 6AL4V titanium allox for blades. Reforges commercial Damascus and makes own Damascus, cast aluminum handles. **Prices:** Miniatures start at $30; full-size knives start at $50. **Remarks:** Spare-time maker; first knife sold in 1986. Doing business as Wolf's Knives. **Mark:** G.P. SMIT, with year on reverse side, Wolf's Knives-Murphy's way with date.

SMITH, GREGORY H,
8607 Coddington Ct, Louisville, KY 40299, Phone: 502-491-7439
Specialties: Traditional working straight knives and fantasy knives to customer specs. **Patterns:** Fighters and modified Bowies; camp knives and swords. **Technical:** Grinds O1, 440C and commercial Damascus bars. **Prices:** $55 to $300. **Remarks:** Part-time maker; first knife sold in 1985. **Mark:** JAGED, plus signature.

SMITH, J D,
69 Highland, Roxbury, MA 02119, Phone: 617-989-0723, jdsmith02119@yahoo.com
Specialties: Fighters, Bowies, Persian, locking folders and swords. **Patterns:** Bowies, fighters and locking folders. **Technical:** Forges and grinds D2, his Damascus, O1, 52100 etc. and wootz-pattern hammer steel. **Prices:** $500 to $2000; some to $5000. **Remarks:** Full-time maker; first knife sold in 1987. Doing business as Hammersmith. **Mark:** Last initial alone or in cartouche.

SMITH, JOHN M,
3450 E Beguelin Rd, Centralia, IL 62801, Phone: 618-249-6444, jknife@frontiernet.net
Specialties: Folders. **Patterns:** Folders. **Prices:** $250 to $2500. **Remarks:** First knife sold in 1980. Not taking orders at this time on fixed blade knives. Part-time maker. **Mark:** Etched signature or logo.

SMITH, JOHN W,
1322 Cow Branch Rd, West Liberty, KY 41472, Phone: 606-743-3599, jwsknive@mrtc.com; Web: www.jwsmithknives.com
Specialties: Fancy and working locking folders of his design or to customer specs. **Patterns:** Interframes, traditional and daggers. **Technical:** Grinds 530V and his own Damascus. Offers gold inlay, engraving with gold inlay, hand-fitted mosaic pearl inlay and filework. Prefers hand-rubbed finish. Pearl and ivory available. **Prices:** Utility pieces $375 to $650. Art knives $1200 to $10,000. **Remarks:** Full-time maker. **Mark:** Initials engraved inside diamond.

SMITH, JOSH,
Box 753, Frenchtown, MT 59834, Phone: 406-626-5775, josh@joshsmithknives.com; Web: www.joshsmithknives.com
Specialties: Mosaic, Damascus, LinerLock® folders, automatics, Bowies, fighters, etc. **Patterns:** All kinds. **Technical:** Advanced Mosaic and Damascus. **Prices:** $450 and up. **Remarks:** A.B.S. Master Smith. **Mark:** JOSH.

SMITH, LENARD C,
PO Box D68, Valley Cottage, NY 10989, Phone: 914-268-7359

SMITH, MICHAEL J,
1418 Saddle Gold Ct, Brandon, FL 33511, Phone: 813-431-3790, smithknife@hotmail.com; Web: www.smithknife.com
Specialties: Fancy high art folders of his design. **Patterns:** Locking locks and automatics. **Technical:** Uses ATS-34, non-stainless and stainless Damascus; hand carves folders, prefers ivory and pearl. Hand-rubbed satin finish. Liners are 6AL4V titanium. **Prices:** $500 to $3000. **Remarks:** Full-time maker; first knife sold in 1989. **Mark:** Name, city, state.

SMITH, NEWMAN L.,
865 Glades Rd Shop #3, Gatlinburg, TN 37738, Phone: 423-436-3322, thesmithshop@aol.com; Web: www.thesmithsshop.com
Specialties: Collector-grade and working knives. **Patterns:** Hunters, slip-joint and lock-back folders, some miniatures. **Technical:** Grinds O1 and ATS-34; makes fancy sheaths. **Prices:** $165 to $750; some to $1000. **Remarks:** Full-time maker; first knife sold in 1984. Partners part-time to handle Damascus blades by Jeff Hurst; marks these with SH connected. **Mark:** First and middle initials, last name.

SMITH, RALPH L,
525 Groce Meadow Rd, Taylors, SC 29687, Phone: 864-444-0819, ralph_smith1@charter.net; Web: www.smithhandcraftedknives.com
Specialties: Working knives: straight and folding knives. Hunters, skinners, fighters, bird, boot, Bowie and kitchen knives. **Technical:** Concave Grind D2, ATS 34, 440C, steel hand finish or polished. **Prices:** $125 to $350 for standard models. **Remarks:** First knife sold in 1976. KMG member since 1981. SCAK founding member and past president. **Mark:** SMITH handcrafted knives in SC state outline.

SMITH, RAYMOND L,
217 Red Chalk Rd, Erin, NY 14838, Phone: 607-795-5257, Bladesmith@earthlink.net; Web: www.theanvilsedge.com
Specialties: Working/using straight knives and folders to customer specs and in standard patterns; period pieces. **Patterns:** Bowies, hunters, skip-joints. **Technical:** Forges 5160, 52100, 1018, 15N20, 1084 Damascus and wire cable Damascus. Filework. **Prices:** $100 to $1500; estimates for custom orders. **Remarks:** Full-time maker; first knife sold in 1991. ABS Master Smith. Doing business as The Anvils Edge. **Mark:** Ellipse with RL Smith, Erin NY MS in center.

SMITH, RICK,
BEAR BONE KNIVES, 1843 W Evans Creek Rd., Rogue River, OR 97537, Phone: 541-582-4144, BearBoneSmith@msn.com; Web: www.bearbone.com
Specialties: Classic, historical style Bowie knives, hunting knives and various contemporary knife styles. **Technical:** Blades are either forged or made by stock removal method depending on steel used. Also forge weld wire Damascus. Does own heat treating and tempering using digital even heat kiln. Stainless blades are sent out for cryogenic "freeze treat." Preferred steels are O1, tool, 5160, 1095, 1084, ATS-34, 154CM, 440C and various high carbon Damascus. **Prices:** $350 to $1500. Custom leather sheaths available for knives. **Remarks:** Full-time maker since 1997. Serial numbers no longer put on knives. Official business name is "Bear Bone Knives." **Mark:** Early maker's mark was "Bear Bone" over capital letters "RS" with downward arrow between letters and "Hand Made" underneath letters. Mark on small knives is 3/8 circle containing "RS" with downward arrow between letters. Current mark since 2003 is "R Bear Bone Smith" arching over image of coffin Bowie knife with two shooting stars and "Rogue River, Oregon" underneath.

SMITH, SHAWN,
2644 Gibson Ave, Clouis, CA 93611, Phone: 559-323-6234, kslc@sbcglobal.net
Specialties:<BN Working and fancy straight knives. Patterns: Hunting, trout, fighters, skinners. Technical:<BN Hollow grinds ATS-34, 154CM, A-2. Prices: $150.00 and up. Remarks: Part time maker. Mark: Shawn Smith handmade.

SMITH JR., JAMES B "RED",
Rt 2 Box 1525, Morven, GA 31638, Phone: 912-775-2844
Specialties: Folders. **Patterns:** Rotating rear-lock folders. **Technical:** Grinds ATS-34, D2 and Vascomax 350. **Prices:** Start at $350. **Remarks:** Full-time maker; first knife sold in 1985. **Mark:** GA RED in cowboy hat.

SMOCK, TIMOTHY E,
1105 N Sherwood Dr, Marion, IN 46952, Phone: 765-664-0123

SMOKER, RAY,
113 Church Rd, Searcy, AR 72143, Phone: 501-796-2712
Specialties: Rugged, no nonsense working knives of his design only. **Patterns:** Hunters, skinners, utility/camp and flat-ground knives. **Technical:** Forges his own Damascus and 52100; makes sheaths. Uses improved multiple edge quench he developed. **Prices:** $450 and up; price includes sheath. **Remarks:** Semi-retired; first knife sold in 1992. **Mark:** Last name.

SNARE, MICHAEL,
3352 E Mescal St, Phoenix, AZ 85028

SNELL, JERRY L,
539 Turkey Trl, Fortson, GA 31808, Phone: 706-324-4922
Specialties: Working straight knives of his design and in standard patterns. **Patterns:** Hunters, boots, fighters, daggers and a few folders. **Technical:** Grinds 440C, ATS-34; buys Damascus. **Prices:** $175 to $1000. **Remarks:** Part-time maker. **Mark:** Last name, or name, city and state.

SNODY, MIKE,
135 Triple Creek Rd, Fredericksburg, TX 78624, Phone: 361-443-0161, info@snodyknives.com; Web: www.snodyknives.com
Specialties: High performance straight knives in traditional and Japanese-styles. **Patterns:** Skinners, hunters, tactical, Kwaiken and tantos. **Technical:** Grinds BG42, ATS-34, 440C and A2. Offers full or tapered tangs, upgraded handle materials such as fossil ivory, coral and exotic woods. Traditional diamond wrap over stingray on Japanese-style knives. Sheaths available in leather or Kydex. **Prices:** $100 to $1000. **Remarks:** Part-time maker; first knife sold in 1999. **Mark:** Name over knife maker.

SNOW, BILL,
4824 18th Ave, Columbus, GA 31904, Phone: 706-576-4390, tipikw@knology.net
Specialties: Traditional working/using straight knives and folders of his design and to customer specs. Offers engraving and scrimshaw. Patterns: Bowies, fighters, hunters and folders. **Technical:** Grinds ATS-34, 440V, 440C, 420V, CPM350, BG42, A2, D2, 5160, 52100 and O1; forges if needed. Cryogenically quenches all steels; inlaid handles; some integrals; leather or Kydex sheaths. **Prices:** $125 to $700; some to $3500. **Remarks:** Now also have 530V, 10V and 3V steels in use. Full-time maker; first knife sold in 1958. Doing business as Tipi Knife works. **Mark:** Old English scroll "S" inside a tipi.

SNYDER, MICHAEL TOM,
PO Box 522, Zionsville, IN 46077-0522, Phone: 317-873-6807, wildcatcreek@indy.pr.com

SOLOMON, MARVIN,
23750 Cold Springs Rd, Paron, AR 72122, Phone: 501-821-3170, Fax: 501-821-6541, mardot@swbell.net; Web: www.coldspringsforge.com
Specialties: Traditional working and using straight knives of his design and to customer specs, also lock back 7 LinerLock® folders. **Patterns:** Single blade folders. **Technical:** Forges 5160, 1095, O1 and random Damascus. **Prices:** $125 to $1000. **Remarks:** Part-time maker; first knife sold in 1990. Doing business as Cold Springs Forge. **Mark:** Last name.

SONNTAG, DOUGLAS W,
902 N 39th St, Nixa, MO 65714, Phone: 417-693-1640, Fax: 417-582-1392, dougsonntag@gmail.com
Specialties: Working knives; art knives. **Patterns:** Hunters, boots, straight working knives; Bowies, some folders, camp/axe sets. **Technical:** Grinds D2, ATS-34, forges own Damascus; does own heat treating. **Prices:** $225 and up. **Remarks:** Part-time maker; first knife sold in 1986. **Mark:** Etched name in arch.

SONTHEIMER, G DOUGLAS,
12604 Bridgeton Dr, Potomac, MD 20854, Phone: 301-948-5227
Specialties: Fixed blade knives. **Patterns:** Whitetail deer, backpackers, camp, claws, fillet, fighters. **Technical:** Hollow Grinds. **Price:** $500 and up. **Remarks:** Spare-time maker; first knife sold in 1976. **Mark:** LORD.

SOPPERA, ARTHUR,
"Pilatusblick", Oberer Schmidberg, CH-9631 Ulisbach, SWITZERLAND, Phone: 71-988 23 27, Fax: 71-988 47 57, doublelock@hotmail.com; Web: www.sopperaknifeart.ch
Specialties: High-art, high-tech knives of his design. **Patterns:** Locking folders, and fixed blade knives. **Technical:** Grinds ATS-34 and commercial Damascus. Folders have button lock of his own design; some are fancy folders in jeweler's fashion. Also makes jewelry with integrated small knives. **Prices:** $300 to $1500, some $2500 and higher. **Remarks:** Full-time maker; first knife sold in 1986. **Mark:** Stylized initials, name, country.

SORNBERGER, JIM,
25126 Overland Dr, Volcano, CA 95689, Phone: 209-295-7819
Specialties: Classic San Francisco-style knives. Collectible straight knives. **Patterns:** Forges 1095-1084/15W2. Makes own Damascus and powder metal. Fighters, daggers, Bowies; miniatures; hunters, custom canes, liner locks folders. **Technical:** Grinds 440C, 154CM and ATS-34; engraves, carves and embellishes. **Prices:** $500 to $20,000 in gold with gold quartz inlays. **Remarks:** Full-time maker; first knife sold in 1970. **Mark:** First initial, last name, city and state.

SOWELL, BILL,
100 Loraine Forest Ct, Macon, GA 31210, Phone: 478-994-9863, billsowell@reynoldscable.net
Specialties: Antique reproduction Bowies, forging Bowies, hunters, fighters, and most others. Also folders. **Technical:** Makes own Damascus, using 1084/15N20, also making own designs in powder metals, forges 5160-1095-1084, and other carbon steels, grinds ATS-34. **Prices:** Starting at $150 and up. **Remarks:** Part-time maker. Sold first knife in 1998. Does own leather work. **Mark:** Iron Horse Knives; Iron Horse Forge.

SPARKS, BERNARD,
PO Box 73, Dingle, ID 83233, Phone: 208-847-1883, dogknifeii@juno.com; Web: www.sparksknives.com
Specialties: Maker engraved, working and art knives. Straight knives and folders of his own design. **Patterns:** Locking inner-frame folders, hunters, fighters, one-of-a-kind art knives. **Technical:** Grinds 530V steel, 440-C, 154CM, ATS-34, D-2 and forges by special order; triple temper, cryogenic soak. Mirror or hand finish. New Liquid metal steel. **Prices:** $300 to $2000. **Remarks:** Full-time maker, first knife sold in 1967. **Mark:** Last name over state with a knife logo on each end of name. Prior 1980, stamp of last name.

SPENCER, KEITH,
PO Box 149, Chidlow Western Australia, AUSTRALIA 6556, Phone: 61 8 95727255, Fax: 61 8 95727266, spencer@knivesaustralia.com.au
Specialties: Survival & bushcraft bladeware. **Patterns:** Best known for Kakadu Bushcraft knife (since 1989). Leilira mini survival knife (since 1993). **Prices:** $100 to $400 AV. **Mark:** Spencer Australia.

SPICKLER, GREGORY NOBLE,
5614 Mose Cir, Sharpsburg, MD 21782, Phone: 301-432-2746

SPINALE, RICHARD,
4021 Canterbury Ct, Lorain, OH 44053, Phone: 440-282-1565
Specialties: High-art working knives of his design. **Patterns:** Hunters, fighters, daggers and locking folders. **Technical:** Grinds 440C, ATS-34 and 07; engraves. Offers gold bolsters and other deluxe treatments. **Prices:** $300 to $1000; some to $3000. **Remarks:** Spare-time maker; first knife sold in 1976. **Mark:** Name, address, year and model number.

SPIVEY, JEFFERSON,
9244 W Wilshire, Yukon, OK 73099, Phone: 405-721-4442
Specialties: The Saber tooth: a combination hatchet, saw and knife. **Patterns:** Built for the wilderness, all are one-of-a-kind. **Technical:** Grinds chromemoly steel. The saw tooth spine curves with a double row of biangular teeth. **Prices:** Start at $275. **Remarks:** First knife sold in 1977. As of September 2006 Spivey knives has resumed production of the sabertooth knife. **Mark:** Name and serial number.

SPRAGG, WAYNE E,
252 Oregon Ave, Lovell, WY 82431, Phone: 307-548-7212
Specialties: Working straight knives, some fancy. **Patterns:** Folders. **Technical:** Forges carbon steel and makes Damascus. **Prices:** $200 and up. **Remarks:** All stainless heat-treated by Paul Bos. Carbon steel in shop heat treat. **Mark:** Last name front side w/s initials on reverse side.

SPROKHOLT, ROB,
GATHERWOOD, Burgerweg 5, Netherlands, EUROPE 1754 KB Burgerbrug, Phone: 0031 6 51230225, Fax: 0031 84 2238446, info@gatherwood.nl; Web: www.gatherwood.nl
Specialties: One-of-a-kind knives. Top materials collector grade, made to use. **Patterns:** Outdoor knives (hunting, sailing, hiking), Bowies, man's surviving companions MSC, big tantos, folding knives. **Technical:** Handles mostly stabilized or oiled wood, ivory, Micarta, carbon fibre, G10. Stiff knives are full tang. Characteristic one row of massive silver pins or tubes. Folding knives have a LinerLock® with titanium or Damascus powdersteel liner thumb can have any stone you like. Stock removal grinder: flat or convex. Steel 440-C, RWL-34, ATS-34, PM damascener steel. **Prices:** Start at 320 euro. **Remarks:** Writer of the first Dutch knifemaking book, supply shop for knife enthusiastic. First knife sold in 2000. **Mark:** Gatherwood in an eclipse etched blade or stamped in an intarsia of silver in the spine.

ST. AMOUR, MURRAY,
RR 3, 222 Dicks Rd, Pembroke ON, CANADA K8A 6W4, Phone: 613-735-1061, knives@webhart.net; Web: www.stamourknives.com
Specialties: Working fixed blades. **Patterns:** Hunters, fish, fighters, Bowies and utility knives. **Technical:** Grinds ATS-34, 154CM, CPM-S-30-Y-60-Y-904 and Damascus. **Prices:** $75 and up. **Remarks:** Full-time maker; sold first knife in 1992. **Mark:** Last name over Canada.

ST. CLAIR, THOMAS K,
12608 Fingerboard Rd, Monrovia, MD 21770, Phone: 301-482-0264

ST. CYR, H RED,
1218 N Cary Ave, Wilmington, CA 90744, Phone: 310-518-9525

STAFFORD, RICHARD,
104 Marcia Ct, Warner Robins, GA 31088, Phone: 912-923-6372
Specialties: High-tech straight knives and some folders. **Patterns:** Hunters in several patterns, fighters, boots, camp knives, combat knives and period pieces. **Technical:** Grinds ATS-34 and 440C; satin finish is standard. **Prices:** Starting at $75. **Remarks:** Part-time maker; first knife sold in 1983. **Mark:** Last name.

STALCUP, EDDIE,
PO Box 2200, Gallup, NM 87305, Phone: 505-863-3107, sstalcup@cnetco.com
Specialties: Working and fancy hunters, bird and trout. Special custom orders. **Patterns:** Drop point hunters, locking liner and multi blade folders. **Technical:** ATS-34, 154 CM, 440C, CPM 154 and S30V. **Prices:** $150 to $1500. **Remarks:** Scrimshaw, exotic handle material, wet formed sheaths. Membership Arizona Knife Collectors Association. Southern California blades collectors & professional knife makers assoc. **Mark:** E.F. Stalcup, Gallup, NM.

STANCER, CHUCK,
62 Hidden Ranch Rd NW, Calgary, AB, CANADA T3A 5S5, Phone: 403-295-7370, stancerc@telusplanet.net
Specialties: Traditional and working straight knives. **Patterns:** Bowies, hunters and utility knives. **Technical:** Forges and grinds most steels. **Prices:** $175 and up. **Remarks:** Part-time maker. **Mark:** Last name.

STANLEY, JOHN,
604 Elm St, Crossett, AR 71635, Phone: 970-304-3005
Specialties: Hand forged fixed blades with engraving and carving. **Patterns:** Scottish dirks, skeans and fantasy blades. **Technical:** Forge high-carbon steel, own Damascus. Prices $70 to $500. **Remarks:** All work is sole authorship. Offers engraving and carving services on other knives and handles. **Mark:** Varies.

STAPEL, CHUCK,
Box 1617, Glendale, CA 91209, Phone: 213-66-KNIFE, Fax: 213-669-1577, www.stapelknives.com
Specialties: Working knives of his design. **Patterns:** Variety of straight knives, tantos, hunters, folders and utility knives. **Technical:** Grinds D2, 440C and AEB-L. **Prices:** $185 to $12,000. **Remarks:** Full-time maker; first knife sold in 1974. **Mark:** Last name or last name, U.S.A.

STAPLETON, WILLIAM E,
BUFFALO 'B' FORGE, 5425 Country Ln, Merritt Island, FL 32953
Specialties: Classic and traditional knives of his design and customer spec. Patterns: Hunters and using knives. **Technical:** Forges, O1 and L6 Damascus, cable Damascus and 5160; stock removal on request. **Prices:** $150 to $1000. **Remarks:** Part-time maker, first knife sold 1990. Doing business as Buffalo "B" Forge. **Mark:** Anvil with S initial in center of anvil.

STECK, VAN R,
260 W Dogwood Ave, Orange City, FL 32763, Phone: 407-416-1723, Web: www.van@thudknives.com
Specialties: Framelock folders with his own lock design. Fighters, hunting & fillet, spike hawks and Asian influence on swords, sickles, spears, also traditional Bowies. **Technical:** Stock removal ATS-34, D2, forges 5160, 1095 & 1084. **Prices:** $75 to $750. **Remarks:** Free hand grinds, distal taper, hollow and chisel. Specialize in filework and Japanese handle wrapping. Voting member of the Knifemakers' Guild. **Mark:** GEISHA with sword & initials and T.H.U.D. knives.

STEFFEN, CHUCK,
504 Dogwood Ave NW, St. Michael, MN, Phone: 763-497-3615
Specialties: Custom hunting knives, fixed blades folders. Specializing in exotic materials. Damascus excellent fit form and finishes.

STEGALL, KEITH,
701 Outlet View Dr, Wasilla, AK 99654, Phone: 907-376-0703, kas5200@yahoo.com
Specialties: Traditional working straight knives. **Patterns:** Most patterns. **Technical:** Grinds 440C and 154CM. **Prices:** $100 to $300. **Remarks:** Spare-time maker; first knife sold in 1987. **Mark:** Name and state with anchor.

STEGNER, WILBUR G,
9242 173rd Ave SW, Rochester, WA 98579, Phone: 360-273-0937, stegner@myhome.net; Web: landru.myhome.net/ stegner/
Specialties: Working/using straight knives and folders of his design. **Patterns:** Hunters and locking folders. **Technical:** Grinds ATS-34 and other tool steels. Quenches, tempers and hardness tests each blade. **Prices:** $100 to $1000; some to $5000. **Remarks:** Full-time maker; first knife sold in 1979. Google search key words-"STEGNER KNIVES." **Mark:** First and middle initials, last name in bar over shield logo.

STEIGER, MONTE L,
Box 186, Genesee, ID 83832, Phone: 208-285-1769, montesharon@genesee-id.com
Specialties: Traditional working/using straight knives of all designs. **Patterns:** Hunters, utility/camp knives, fillet and chefs. Carving sets and steak knives. **Technical:** Grinds 1095, O1, 440C, ATS-34. Handles of stacked leather, natural wood, Micarta or pakkawood. Each knife comes with right-or left-handed sheath. **Prices:** $110 to $600. **Remarks:** Spare-time maker; first knife sold in 1988. Retired librarian **Mark:** First initial, last name, city and state.

STEIGERWALT, KEN,
507 Savagehill Rd, Orangeville, PA 17859, Phone: 570-683-5156, Web: www.steigerwaltknives.com
Specialties: Carving on bolsters and handle material. **Patterns:** Folders, button locks and rear locks. **Technical:** Grinds ATS-34, 440C and commercial Damascus. Experiments with unique filework. **Prices:** $500 to $5000. **Remarks:** Full-time maker; first knife sold in 1981. **Mark:** Kasteigerwalt

STEINAU, JURGEN,
Julius-Hart Strasse 44, Berlin 0-1162, GERMANY, Phone: 372-6452512, Fax: 372-645-2512
Specialties: Fantasy and high-art straight knives of his design. **Patterns:** Boots, daggers and switch-blade folders. **Technical:** Grinds 440B, 2379 and X90 Cr.Mo.V. 78. **Prices:** $1500 to $2500; some to $3500. **Remarks:** Full-time maker; first knife sold in 1984. **Mark:** Symbol, plus year, month day and serial number.

STEINBERG, AL,
5244 Duenas, Laguna Woods, CA 92653, Phone: 949-951-2889, lagknife@fea.net
Specialties: Fancy working straight knives to customer specs. **Patterns:** Hunters, Bowies, fishing, camp knives, push knives and high end kitchen knives. **Technical:** Grinds O1, 440C and 154CM. **Prices:** $60 to $2500. **Remarks:** Full-time maker; first knife sold in 1972. **Mark:** Signature, city and state.

STEINBRECHER, MARK W,
4725 Locust Ave, Glenview, IL 60025, Phone: 847-298-5721
Specialties: Working and fancy folders. **Patterns:** Daggers, pocket knives, fighters and gents of his own design or to customer specs. **Technical:** Hollow grinds ATS-34, O1 other makers Damascus. Uses natural handle materials: stag, ivories, mother-of-pearl. File work and some inlays. **Prices:** $500 to $1200, some to $2500. **Remarks:** Part-time maker, first folder sold in 1989. **Mark:** Name etched or handwritten on ATS-34; stamped on Damascus.

STEKETEE, CRAIG A,
871 N Hwy 60, Billings, MO 65610, Phone: 417-744-2770, stekknives@earthlink.net
Specialties: Classic and working straight knives and swords of his design. Patterns: Bowies, hunters, and Japanese-style swords. **Technical:** Forges his own Damascus; bronze, silver and Damascus fittings, offers filework. Prefers exotic and natural handle materials. **Prices:** $200 to $4000. **Remarks:** Full-time maker. **Mark:** STEK.

STEPHAN, DANIEL,
2201 S Miller Rd, Valrico, FL 33594, Phone: 727-580-8617, knifemaker@verizon.net
Specialties: Art knives, one-of-a-kind.

STERLING, MURRAY,
693 Round Peak Church Rd, Mount Airy, NC 27030, Phone: 336-352-5110, Fax:Fax:336-352-5105,sterck@surry.net;Web:www.sterlingcustomknives.com
Specialties: Single and dual blade folders. Interframes and integral dovetail frames. **Technical:** Grinds ATS-34 or Damascus by Mike Norris and/or Devin Thomas. **Prices:** $300 and up. **Remarks:** Full-time maker; first knife sold in 1991. **Mark:** Last name stamped.

STERLING, THOMAS J,
ART KNIVES BY, 120 N Pheasant Run, Coupeville, WA 98239, Phone: 360-678-9269, Fax: 360-678-9269, netsuke@comcast.net; Web: www.bladegallery.com Or www.sterlingsculptures.com
Specialties: Since 2003 Tom Sterling and Dr. J.P. Higgins have created a unique collaboration of one-of-a-kind, ultra-quality art knives with percussion or pressured flaked stone blades and creatively sculpted handles. Their knives are often highly influenced by the traditions of Japanese netsuke and unique fusions of cultures, reflecting stylistically integrated choices of exotic hardwoods, fossil ivories and semi-precious materials, contrasting inlays and polychromed and pyrographed details. **Prices:** $300 to $900. **Remarks:** Limited output ensures highest quality artwork and exceptional levels of craftsmanship. **Mark:** Signatures Sterling and Higgins.

STETTER, J. C.,
115 E College Blvd PMB 180, Roswell, NM 88201, Phone: 505-627-0978
Specialties: Fixed and folding. **Patterns:** Traditional and yours. **Technical:** Forged and ground of varied materials including his own pattern welded steel. **Prices:** Start at $250. **Remarks:** Full-time maker, first knife sold 1989. **Mark:** Currently "J.C. Stetter."

STEWART, EDWARD L,
4297 Audrain Rd 335, Mexico, MO 65265, Phone: 573-581-3883
Specialties: Fixed blades, working knives some art. **Patterns:** Hunters, Bowies, utility/camp knives. **Technical:** Forging 1095-W-2-I-6-52100 makes own Damascus. **Prices:** $85 to $500. **Remarks:** Part-time maker first knife sold in 1993. **Mark:** First and last initials-last name.

STEYN, PETER,
PO Box 76, Welkom 9460, Freestate, SOUTH AFRICA, Phone: 27573525201, Fax: 27573523566, Web:www.petersteynknives.com email:info@petersteynknives.com
Specialties: Fixed blade working knives of own design, tendency toward tactical creative & artistic styles all with hand stitched leather sheaths. **Patterns:**Hunters, skinners, fighters & wedge ground daggers. **Technical:**Grinds 12C27, D2, N690. Blades are bead-blasted in plain or camo patterns & own exclusive crator finish. Prefers synthetic handle materials also uses cocobolo & ironwood. **Prices:** $200-$600. **Remarks:** Full time maker, first knife sold 2005, member of South African Guild. **Mark:** Letter 'S' in shape of pyramid with full name above & 'Handcrafted' below.

STIMPS, JASON M,
374 S Shaffer St, Orange, CA 92866, Phone: 714-744-5866

STIPES, DWIGHT,
2651 SW Buena Vista Dr, Palm City, FL 34990, Phone: 772-597-0550, dwightstipes@adelphia.net
Specialties: Traditional and working straight knives in standard patterns. **Patterns:** Boots, Bowies, daggers, hunters and fighters. **Technical:** Grinds 440C, D2 and D3 tool steel. Handles of natural materials, animal, bone or horn. **Prices:** $75 to $150. **Remarks:** Full-time maker; first knife sold in 1972. **Mark:** Stipes.

STOCKWELL, WALTER,
368 San Carlos Ave, Redwood City, CA 94061, Phone: 650-363-6069, walter@stockwellknives.com; Web: www.stockwellknives.com
Specialties: Scottish dirks, sgian dubhs. **Patterns:** All knives one-of-a-kind. **Technical:** Grinds ATS-34, forges 5160, 52100, L6. **Prices:** $125 to $500. **Remarks:** Part-time maker since 1992; graduate of ABS bladesmithing school. **Mark:** Shooting star over "STOCKWELL." Pre-2000, "WKS."

STODDART, W B BILL,
2357 Mack Rd #105, Fairfield, OH 45014, Phone: 513-851-1543
Specialties: Sportsmen's working knives and multi-blade folders. **Patterns:** Hunters, camp and fish knives; multi-blade reproductions of old standards. **Technical:** Grinds A2, 440C and ATS-34; makes sheaths to match handle materials. **Prices:** $80 to $300; some to $850. **Remarks:** Part-time maker; first knife sold in 1976. **Mark:** Name, Cincinnati, state.

STOKES, ED,
22614 Cardinal Dr, Hockley, TX 77447, Phone: 713-351-1319
Specialties: Working straight knives and folders of all designs. **Patterns:** Boots, Bowies, daggers, fighters, hunters and miniatures. **Technical:** Grinds ATS-34, 440C and D2. Offers decorative butt caps, tapered spacers on handles and finger grooves, nickel-silver inlays, handmade

sheaths. **Prices:** $185 to $290; some to $350. **Remarks:** Full-time maker; first knife sold in 1973. **Mark:** First and last name, Custom Knives with Apache logo.

STONE, JERRY,
PO Box 1027, Lytle, TX 78052, Phone: 830-709-3042
Specialties: Traditional working and using folders of his design and to customer specs; fancy knives. **Patterns:** Fighters, hunters, locking folders and slip joints. Also make automatics. **Technical:** Grinds 440C and ATS-34. Offers filework. **Prices:** $175 to $1000. **Remarks:** Full-time maker; first knife sold in 1973. **Mark:** Name over Texas star/town and state underneath.

STORCH, ED,
RR 4 Mannville, Alberta T0B 2W0, CANADA, Phone: 780-763-2214, storchkn@agt.net; Web: www.storchknives.com
Specialties: Working knives, fancy fighting knives, kitchen cutlery and art knives. Knifemaking classes. **Patterns:** Working patterns, Bowies and folders. **Technical:** Forges his own Damascus. Grinds ATS-34. Builds friction folders. Salt heat treating. **Prices:** $45 to $750 (U.S). **Remarks:** Part-time maker; first knife sold in 1984. Hosts annual Northwest Canadian Knifemakers Symposium; 60 to 80 knifemakers and families. **Mark:** Last name.

STORMER, BOB,
10 Karabair Rd, St. Peters, MO 63376, Phone: 636-441-6807, bobstormer@sbcglobal.net
Specialties: Straight knives, using collector grade. **Patterns:** Bowies, skinners, hunters, camp knives. **Technical:** Forges 5160, 1095. **Prices:** $150 to $400. **Remarks:** Part-time maker, ABS Journeyman Smith 2001. **Mark:** Setting sun/fall trees/initials.

STOUT, CHARLES,
RT3 178 Stout Rd, Gillham, AR 71841, Phone: 870-386-5521

STOUT, JOHNNY,
1205 Forest Trail, New Braunfels, TX 78132, Phone: 830-606-4067, johnny@stoutknives.com; Web: www.stoutknives.com
Specialties: Folders, some fixed blades. Working knives, some fancy. **Patterns:** Hunters, tactical, Bowies, automatics, liner locks and slip-joints. **Technical:** Grinds stainless and carbon steels; forges own Damascus. **Prices:** $450 to $895; some to $3500. **Remarks:** Full-time maker; first knife sold in 1983. Hosts semi-annual Guadalupe Forge Hammer-in and Knifemakers Rendezvous. **Mark:** Name and city in logo with serial number.

STOVER, HOWARD,
100 Palmetto Dr Apt 7, Pasadena, CA 91105, Phone: 765-452-3928

STOVER, TERRY "LEE",
1809 N 300 E, Kokomo, IN 46901, Phone: 765-452-3928
Specialties: Damascus folders with filework; Damascus Bowies of his design or to customer specs. **Patterns:** Lockback folders and Sheffield-style Bowies. **Technical:** Forges 1095, Damascus using O2, 203E or O2, pure nickel. Makes mokume. Uses only natural handle material. **Prices:** $300 to $1700; some to $2000. **Remarks:** Part-time maker; first knife sold in 1984. **Mark:** First and middle initials, last name in knife logo; Damascus blades marked in Old English.

STRAIGHT, KENNETH J,
11311 103 Lane N, Largo, FL 33773, Phone: 813-397-9817

STRANDE, POUL,
Soster Svenstrup Byvej 16, Dastrup 4130 Viby Sj., DENMARK, Phone: 46 19 43 05, Fax: 46 19 53 19, Web: www.poulstrande.com
Specialties: Classic fantasy working knives; Damasceret blade, Nikkel Damasceret blade, Lamineret: Lamineret blade with Nikkel. **Patterns:** Bowies, daggers, fighters, hunters and swords. **Technical:** Uses carbon steel and 15C20 steel. **Prices:** NA. **Remarks:** Full-time maker; first knife sold in 1985. **Mark:** First and last initials.

STRICKLAND, DALE,
1440 E Thompson View, Monroe, UT 84754, Phone: 435-896-8362
Specialties: Traditional and working straight knives and folders of his design and to customer specs. **Patterns:** Hunters, folders, miniatures and utility knives. **Technical:** Grinds Damascus and 440C. **Prices:** $120 to $350; some to $500. **Remarks:** Part-time maker; first knife sold in 1991. **Mark:** Oval stamp of name, Maker.

STRIDER, MICK,
STRIDER KNIVES, 120 N Pacific Unit L-7, San Marcos, CA 92069, Phone: 760-471-8275, Fax: 503-218-7069, striderguys@striderknives.com; Web: www.striderknives.com

STRONG, SCOTT,
1599 Beaver Valley Rd, Beavercreek, OH 45434, Phone: 937-426-9290
Specialties: Working knives, some deluxe. **Patterns:** Hunters, fighters, survival and military-style knives, art knives. **Technical:** Forges and grinds O1, A2, D2, 440C and ATS-34. Uses no solder; most knives disassemble. **Prices:** $75 to $450; some to $1500. **Remarks:** Spare-time maker; first knife sold in 1983. **Mark:** Strong Knives.

STROYAN, ERIC,
Box 218, Dalton, PA 18414, Phone: 717-563-2603
Specialties: Classic and working/using straight knives and folders of his design. **Patterns:** Hunters, locking folders, slip-joints. **Technical:** Forges Damascus; grinds ATS-34, D2. **Prices:** $200 to $600; some to $2000. **Remarks:** Part-time maker; first knife sold in 1968. **Mark:** Signature or initials stamp.

STUART, STEVE,
Box 168, Gores Landing, Ont., CANADA K0K 2E0, Phone: 905-342-5617, stevestuart@sympatico.ca
Specialties: Straight knives. **Patterns:** Tantos, fighters, skinners, file and rasp knives. **Technical:** Uses 440C, files, Micarta and natural handle materials. **Prices:** $60 to $400. **Remarks:** Part-time maker. **Mark:** SS.

STYREFORS, MATTIAS,
Unbyn 23, SE-96193 Boden, SWEDEN, infor@styrefors.com
Specialties: Damascus and mosaic Damascus. Fixed blade Nordic hunters, folders and swords. **Technical:** Forges, shapes and grinds Damascus and mosaic Damascus from mostly UHB 15N20 and 20C with contrasts in nickel and 15N20. Hardness HR 58. **Prices:** $800 to $3000. **Remarks:** Full-time maker since 1999. International reputation for high end Damascus blades. Uses stabilized Arctic birch and willow burl, horn, fossils, exotic materials, and scrimshaw by Viveca Sahlin for knife handles. Hand tools and hand stitches leather sheaths in cow raw hide. Works in well equipped former military forgery in northern Sweden. **Mark:** MS.

SUEDMEIER, HARLAN,
762 N 60th Rd, Nebraska City, NE 68410, Phone: 402-873-4372
Patterns: Straight knives. **Technical:** Forging hi carbon Damascus. **Prices:** Starting at $175. **Mark:** First initials & last name.

SUGIHARA, KEIDOH,
4-16-1 Kamori-Cho, Kishiwada City, Osaka, F596-0042, JAPAN, Fax: 0724-44-2677
Specialties: High-tech working straight knives and folders of his design. **Patterns:** Bowies, hunters, fighters, fishing, boots, some pocket knives and liner-lock folders. **Technical:** Grinds ATS-34, COS-25, buys Damascus and high-carbon steels. Prices $60 to $4000. **Remarks:** Full-time maker, first knife sold in 1980. **Mark:** Initial logo with fish design.

SUGIYAMA, EDDY K,
2361 Nagayu, Naoirimachi Naoirigun, Ohita, JAPAN, Phone: 0974-75-2050
Specialties: One-of-a-kind, exotic-style knives. **Patterns:** Working, utility and miniatures. **Technical:** CT rind, ATS-34 and D2. **Prices:** $400 to $1200. **Remarks:** Full-time maker. **Mark:** Name or cedar mark.

SUMMERLIN, DANNY,
7058 Howe, Groves, TX 77619, Phone: 409-344-3190
Specialties: Hunters and skinners. **Patterns:** Makes only hunters and skinners full tang. **Technical:** Grinds ATS-34 & 154 CM. **Prices:**$125-$250

SUMMERS, ARTHUR L,
1310HessRd,Concord,NC28025,Phone:704-644-0018,arthursummers88@hotmail.com
Specialties: Collector-grade knives in drop points, clip points or straight blades. **Patterns:** Fighters, hunters, Bowies and personal knives. **Technical:** Grinds 440C, ATS-34, D2 and Damascus. **Prices:** $250 to $1000; some to $2000. **Remarks:** Full-time maker; first knife sold in 1987. **Mark:** Serial number is the date.

SUMMERS, DAN,
2675 NY Rt. 11, Whitney Pt., NY 13862, Phone: 607-692-2391, dansumm11@msn.com
Specialties: Period knives and tomahawks. **Technical:** All hand forging. **Prices:** Most $100 to $400.

SUMMERS, DENNIS K,
827 E. Cecil St, Springfield, OH 45503, Phone: 513-324-0624
Specialties: Working/using knives. **Patterns:** Fighters and personal knives. **Technical:** Grinds 440C, A2 and D2. Makes drop and clip point. **Prices:** $75 to $200. **Remarks:** Part-time maker; first knife sold in 1995. **Mark:** First and middle initials, last name, serial number.

SUNDERLAND, RICHARD,
Av Infraganti 23, Col Lazaro Cardenas, Puerto Escondido Oaxaca, MEXICO 71980, Phone: 011 52 94 582 1451, sunamerica@prodigy.net.mx7
Specialties: Personal and hunting knives with carved handles in oosic and ivory. **Patterns:** Hunters, Bowies, daggers, camp and personal knives. **Technical:** Grinds 440C, ATS-34 and O1. Handle materials of rosewoods, fossil mammoth ivory and oosic. **Prices:** $150 to $1000. **Remarks:** Part-time maker; first knife sold in 1983. Doing business as Sun Knife Co. **Mark:** SUN.

SUTTON, S RUSSELL,
4900 Cypress Shores Dr, New Bern, NC 28562, Phone: 252-637-3963, srsutton@suddenlink.net; Web: www.suttoncustomknives.com
Specialties: Straight knives and folders to customer specs and in standard patterns. Patterns: Boots, hunters, interframes, slip joints and locking liners. **Technical:** Grinds ATS-34, 440C and stainless Damascus. **Prices:** $220 to $950; some to $1250. **Remarks:** Full-time maker; first knife sold in 1992. **Mark:** Etched last name. Other: Engraved bolsters and guards available on some knives by maker.

SWEAZA, DENNIS,
4052 Hwy 321 E, Austin, AR 72007, Phone: 501-941-1886, knives4den@aol.com

SWEENEY, COLTIN D,
1216 S 3 St W, Missoula, MT 59801, Phone: 406-721-6782

SWYHART, ART,
509 Main St, PO Box 267, Klickitat, WA 98628, Phone: 509-369-3451, swyhart@gorge.net; Web: www.knifeoutlet.com/swyhart.htm
Specialties: Traditional working and using knives of his design. **Patterns:** Bowies, hunters and utility/camp knives. **Technical:** Forges 52100, 5160 and Damascus 1084 mixed with either 15N20 or O186. Blades differentially heat-treated with visible temper line. **Prices:** $75 to $250; some to $350. **Remarks:** Part-time maker; first knife sold in 1983. **Mark:** First name, last initial in script.

SYMONDS, ALBERTO E,
Rambla M Gandhi 485, Apt 901, Montevideo 11300, URUGUAY, Phone: 011 598 5608207, Fax: 011 598 2 7103201, albertosymonds@hotmail.com
Specialties: All kinds including puukos, nice sheaths, leather and wood. **Prices:** $160 to $600. **Mark:** AESH and current year.

SYSLO, CHUCK,
3418 South 116 Ave, Omaha, NE 68144, Phone: 402-333-0647, ciscoknives@cox.net
Specialties: Hunters, working knives, daggers & misc. **Patterns:** Hunters, daggers and survival knives; locking folders. **Technical:** Flat-grinds D2, 440C and 154CM; hand polishes only. **Prices:** $250 to $1000; some to $3000. **Remarks:** Part-time maker; first knife sold in 1978. Uses many natural materials. **Mark:** CISCO in logo.

SZAREK, MARK G,
94 Oakwood Ave, Revere, MA 02151, Phone: 781-289-7102
Specialties: Classic period working and using straight knives and tools. **Patterns:** Hunting knives, American and Japanese woodworking tools. **Technical:** Forges 5160, 1050, Damascus; differentially hardens blades with fireclay. **Prices:** $50 to $750. **Remarks:** Part-time maker; first knife sold in 1989. Produces Japanese alloys for sword fittings and accessories. Custom builds knife presentation boxes and cabinets. **Mark:** Last name.

SZILASKI, JOSEPH,
29 Carroll Dr, Wappingers Falls, NY 12590, Phone: 845-297-5397, Web: www.szilaski.com
Specialties: Straight knives, folders and tomahawks of his design, to customer specs and in standard patterns. Many pieces are one-of-a-kind. **Patterns:** Bowies, daggers, fighters, hunters, art knives and early American-styles. **Technical:** Forges A2, D2, O1 and Damascus. **Prices:** $450 to $4000; some to $10,000. **Remarks:** Full-time maker; first knife sold in 1990. ABS Master Smith and voting member KMG. **Mark:** Snake logo.

T

TABOR, TIM,
18925 Crooked Lane, Lutz, FL 33548, Phone: 813-948-6141, taborknives.com
Specialties: Fancy folders, Damascus Bowies and hunters. **Patterns:** My own design folders & customer requests. **Technical:** ATS-34, hand forged Damascus, 1084, 15N20 mosaic Damascus, 1095, 5160 high carbon blades, flat grind, file work & jewel embellishments. **Prices:** $175 to $1500. **Remarks:** Part-time maker, sold first knife in 2003. **Mark:** Last name

TAKAHASHI, MASAO,
39-3 Sekine-machi, Maebashi-shi, Gunma 371 0047, JAPAN, Phone: 81 27 234 2223, Fax: 81 27 234 2223
Specialties: Working straight knives. **Patterns:** Daggers, fighters, hunters, fishing knives, boots. **Technical:** Grinds ATS-34 and Damascus. **Prices:** $350 to $1000 and up. **Remarks:** Full-time maker; first knife sold in 1982. **Mark:** M. Takahashi.

TALLY, GRANT,
26961 James Ave, Flat Rock, MI 48134, Phone: 734-789-8961
Specialties: Straight knives and folders of his design. **Patterns:** Bowies, daggers, fighters. **Technical:** Grinds ATS-34, 440C and D2. Offers filework. **Prices:** $250 to $1000. **Remarks:** Part-time maker; first knife sold in 1985. Doing business as Tally Knives. **Mark:** Tally (last name).

TAMBOLI, MICHAEL,
12447 N 49 Ave, Glendale, AZ 85304, Phone: 602-978-4308, mnbtamboli@gmail.com
Specialties: Miniatures, some full size. **Patterns:** Miniature hunting knives to fantasy art knives. **Technical:** Grinds ATS-34 & Damascus. **Prices:** $75 to $500; some to $2000. **Remarks:** Full time maker; first knife sold in 1978. **Mark:** Initials or last name, city and state, also M.T. Custom Knives.

TASMAN, KERLEY,
9 Avignon Retreat, Pt Kennedy 6172, Western Australia, AUSTRALIA, Phone: 61 8 9593 0554, Fax: 61 8 9593 0554, taskerley@optusnet.com.au
Specialties: Knife/harness/sheath systems for elite military personnel and body guards. **Patterns:** Utility/tactical knives, hunters small game and presentation grade knives. **Technical:** ATS-34 and 440C, Damascus, flat and hollow grids. **Prices:** $200 to $1800 U.S. **Remarks:** Will take presentation grade commissions. Multi award winning maker and custom jeweler. **Mark:** Maker's initials.

TAYLOR, BILLY,
10 Temple Rd, Petal, MS 39465, Phone: 601-544-0041
Specialties: Straight knives of his design. **Patterns:** Bowies, skinners, hunters and utility knives. **Technical:** Flat-grinds 440C, ATS-34 and 154CM. **Prices:** $60 to $300. **Remarks:** Part-time maker; first knife sold in 1991. **Mark:** Full name, city and state.

TAYLOR, C GRAY,
560 Poteat Ln, Fall Branch, TN 37656, Phone: 423-348-8304, grayskknives@aol.com or grayskknives@hotmail.com; Web: www.cgraytaylor.net
Specialties: Traditonal multi-blade lobster folders, also art display Bowies and daggers. **Patterns:** Orange Blossom, sleeveboard and gunstocks. **Technical:** Grinds. **Prices:** Upscale. **Remarks:** Full-time maker; first knife sold in 1975. **Mark:** Name, city and state.

TAYLOR, DAVID,
113 Stewart Hill Dr, Rogersville, TN 37857, Phone: 423-921-0733, dtaylor0730@charter.net; Web: www.dtguitars.com
Patterns: Multi-blade folders, traditional patterns. **Technical:** Grinds ATS-34. **Prices:** $400 and up. **Remarks:** First sold knife in 1981 at age 14. Became a member of Knifemakers Guild at age 14. Made first folder in 1983. Full-time pastor of Baptist Church and part-time knifemaker.

TAYLOR, SHANE,
18 Broken Bow Ln, Miles City, MT 59301, Phone: 406-234-7175, shane@taylorknives.com; Web: www.taylorknives.com
Specialties: One-of-a-kind fancy Damascus straight knives and folders. **Patterns:** Bowies, folders and fighters. **Technical:** Forges own mosaic and pattern welded Damascus. **Prices:** $450 and up. **Remarks:** ABS Master Smith, full-time maker; first knife sold in 1982. **Mark:** First name.

TERAUCHI, TOSHIYUKI,
7649-13 219-11 Yoshida, Fujita-Cho Gobo-Shi, JAPAN

TERRILL, STEPHEN,
16357 Goat Ranch Rd, Springville, CA 93265, Phone: 559-539-3116, slterrill@yahoo.com
Specialties: Deluxe working straight knives and folders. **Patterns:** Fighters, tantos, boots, locking folders and axes; traditional oriental patterns. **Technical:** Forges 1095, 5160, Damascus, stock removal ATS-34. **Prices:** $300+. **Remarks:** Full-time maker; first knife sold in 1972. **Mark:** Name, city, state in logo.

TERZUOLA, ROBERT,
3933 Agua Fria St, Santa Fe, NM 87507, Phone: 505-473-1002, Fax: 505-438-8018
Specialties: Working folders of his design; period pieces. **Patterns:** High-tech utility, defense and gentleman's folders. **Technical:** Grinds 154CM and CPM S30V. Offers titanium, carbon fiber and G10 composite for side-lock folders and tactical folders. **Prices:** $400 to $1200. **Remarks:** Full-time maker; first knife sold in 1980. **Mark:** Mayan dragon head, name.

THAYER, DANNY O,
8908S 100W, Romney, IN 47981, Phone: 765-538-3105, dot61h@juno.com
Specialties: Hunters, fighters, Bowies. **Prices:** $250 and up.

THEIS, TERRY,
21452 FM 2093, Harper, TX 78631, Phone: 830-864-4438
Specialties: All European and American engraving styles. **Prices:** $200 to $2000. **Remarks:** Engraver only.

THEVENOT, JEAN-PAUL,
16 Rue De La Prefecture, Dijon, FRANCE 21000
Specialties: Traditional European knives and daggers. **Patterns:** Hunters, utility-camp knives, daggers, historical or modern style. **Technical:** Forges own Damascus, 5160, 1084. **Remarks:** Part-time maker. ABS Master Smith. **Mark:** Interlocked initials in square.

THIE, BRIAN,
13250 150th St, Burlington, IA 52601, Phone: 319-985-2276, bkthie@mepotelco.net; Web: www.mepotelco.net/web/tknives
Specialties: Working using knives from basic to fancy. **Patterns:** Hunters, fighters, camp and folders. **Technical:** Forges blades and own Damascus. **Prices:** $100 and up. **Remarks:** Member of ABS, part-time maker. Sole author of blades including forging, heat treat, engraving and sheath making. **Mark:** Last name hand engraved into the blade.

THILL, JIM,
10242 Bear Run, Missoula, MT 59803, Phone: 406-251-5475
Specialties: Traditional and working/using knives of his design. Patterns: Fighters, hunters and utility/camp knives. **Technical:** Grinds D2 and ATS-34; forges 10-95-85, 52100, 5160, 10 series, reg. Damascus-mosaic. Offers hand cut sheaths with rawhide lace. **Prices:** $145 to $350; some to $1250. **Remarks:** Full-time maker; first knife sold in 1962. **Mark:** Running bear in triangle.

THOMAS, BOB G,
RR 1 Box 121, Thebes, IL 62990-9718

THOMAS, DAVID E,
8502 Hwy 91, Lillian, AL 36549, Phone: 251-961-7574, redbluff@gulftel.com

Specialties: Bowies and hunters. **Technical:** Hand forged blades in 5160, 1095 and own Damascus. **Prices:** $400 and up. **Mark:** Stylized DT, maker's last name, serial number.

THOMAS, DEVIN,
PO Box 568, Panaca, NV 89042, Phone: 775-728-4363, hoss@devinthomas.com; Web: www.devinthomas.com

Specialties: Traditional straight knives and folders in standard patterns. **Patterns:** Bowies, fighters, hunters. **Technical:** Forges stainless Damascus, nickel and 1095. Uses, makes and sells mokume with brass, copper and nickel-silver. **Prices:** $300 to $1200. **Remarks:** Full-time maker; first knife sold in 1979. **Mark:** First and last name, city and state with anvil, or first name only.

THOMAS, KIM,
PO Box 531, Seville, OH 44273, Phone: 330-769-9906

Specialties: Fancy and traditional straight knives of his design and to customer specs; period pieces. **Patterns:** Boots, daggers, fighters, swords. **Technical:** Forges own Damascus from 5160, 1010 and nickel. **Prices:** $135 to $1500; some to $3000. **Remarks:** Part-time maker; first knife sold in 1986. Doing business as Thomas Iron Works. **Mark:** KT.

THOMAS, ROCKY,
1716 Waterside Blvd, Moncks Corner, SC 29461, Phone: 843-761-7761

Specialties: Traditional working knives in standard patterns. **Patterns:** Hunters and utility/camp knives. **Technical:** ATS-34 and commercial Damascus. **Prices:** $130 to $350. **Remarks:** Spare-time maker; first knife sold in 1986. **Mark:** First name in script and/or block.

THOMPSON, KENNETH,
4887 Glenwhite Dr, Duluth, GA 30136, Phone: 770-446-6730

Specialties: Traditional working and using knives of his design. **Patterns:** Hunters, Bowies and utility/camp knives. **Technical:** Forges 5168, O1, 1095 and 52100. **Prices:** $75 to $1500; some to $2500. **Remarks:** Part-time maker; first knife sold in 1990. **Mark:** P/W; or name, P/W, city and state.

THOMPSON, LEON,
45723 SW Saddleback Dr, Gaston, OR 97119, Phone: 503-357-2573

Specialties: Working knives. **Patterns:** Locking folders, slip-joints and liner locks. **Technical:** Grinds ATS-34, D2 and 440C. **Prices:** $200 to $600. **Remarks:** Full-time maker; first knife sold in 1976. **Mark:** First and middle initials, last name, city and state.

THOMPSON, LLOYD,
PO Box 1664, Pagosa Springs, CO 81147, Phone: 970-264-5837

Specialties: Working and collectible straight knives and folders of his design. **Patterns:** Straight blades, lock back folders and slip joint folders. **Technical:** Hollow-grinds ATS-34, D2 and O1. Uses sambar stag and exotic woods. **Prices:** $150 to upscale. **Remarks:** Full-time maker; first knife sold in 1985. Doing business as Trapper Creek Knife Co. **Remarks:** Offers three-day knife-making classes. **Mark:** Name.

THOMPSON, TOMMY,
4015 NE Hassalo, Portland, OR 97232-2607, Phone: 503-235-5762

Specialties: Fancy and working knives; mostly liner-lock folders. **Patterns:** Fighters, hunters and liner locks. **Technical:** Grinds D2, ATS-34, CPM440V and T15. Handles are either hardwood inlaid with wood banding and stone or shell, or made of agate, jasper, petrified woods, etc. **Prices:** $75 to $500; some to $1000. **Remarks:** Part-time maker; first knife sold in 1987. Doing business as Stone Birds. Knife making temporarily stopped due to family obligations. **Mark:** First and last name, city and state.

THOMSEN, LOYD W,
30173 Black Banks Rd, Oelrichs, SD 57763, Phone: 605-535-6162, loydt@yahoo.com; Web: horseheadcreekknives.com

Specialties: High-art and traditional working/using straight knives and presentation pieces of his design and to customer specs; period pieces. Hand carved animals in crown of stag on handles and carved display stands. **Patterns:** Bowies, hunters, daggers and utility/camp knives. **Technical:** Forges and grinds 1095HC, 1084, L6, 15N20, 440C stainless steel, nickel 200; special restoration process on period pieces. Makes sheaths. Uses natural materials for handles. **Prices:** $350 to $1000. **Remarks:** Full-time maker; first knife sold in 1995. Doing business as Horsehead Creek Knives. **Mark:** Initials and last name over a horse's head.

THOUROT, MICHAEL W,
T-814 Co Rd 11, Napoleon, OH 43545, Phone: 419-533-6832, Fax: 419-533-3516, mike2row@henry-net.com; Web: wwwsafariknives.com

Specialties: Working straight knives to customer specs. Designed two-handled skinning ax and limited edition engraved knife and art print set. Patterns: Fishing and fillet knives, Bowies, tantos and hunters. **Technical:** Grinds O1, D2, 440C and Damascus. **Prices:** $200 to $5000. **Remarks:** Part-time maker; first knife sold in 1968. **Mark:** Initials.

THUESEN, ED,
21211 Knolle Rd, Damon, TX 77430, Phone: 979-553-1211, Fax: 979-553-1211

Specialties: Working straight knives. **Patterns:** Hunters, fighters and survival knives. **Technical:** Grinds D2, 440C, ATS-34 and Vascowear. **Prices:** $150 to $275; some to $600. **Remarks:** Part-time maker; first knife sold in 1979. Runs knifemaker supply business. **Mark:** Last name in script.

TICHBOURNE, GEORGE,
7035 Maxwell Rd #5, Mississauga, Ont., CANADA L5S 1R5, Phone: 905-670-0200, sales @tichbourneknives.com; Web: www.tichbourneknives.com

Specialties: Traditional working and using knives as well as unique collectibles. **Patterns:** Bowies, hunters, outdoor, kitchen, integrals, art, military, Scottish dirks, folders, kosher knives. **Technical:** Stock removal 440C, Stellite 6K, stainless Damascus. Handle materials include mammoth, meterorite, mother-of-pearl, precious gems, mosiac, abalone, stag, Micarta, exotic high resin woods and corian scrimshawed by George. Leather sheaths are hand stitched and tooled by George as well as the silver adornments for the dirk sheaths. **Prices:** $60 up to $5000 U.S. **Remarks:** Full-time maker with his OWN STORE. First knife sold in 1990. **Mark:** Full name over maple leaf.

TIENSVOLD, ALAN L,
PO Box 355, Rushville, NE 69360, Phone: 308-327-2046

Specialties: Working knives, tomahawks and period pieces, high end Damascus knives. **Patterns:** Random, ladder, twist and many more. **Technical:** Hand forged blades, forges own Damascus. **Prices:** Working knives start at $300. **Remarks:** Received Journeyman rating with the ABS in 2002. Does own engraving and fine work. **Mark:** Tiensvold hand made U.S.A. on left side, JS on right.

TIENSVOLD, JASON,
PO Box 795, Rushville, NE 69360, Phone: 308-327-2046, ironprik@gpcom.net

Specialties: Working and using straight knives of his design; period pieces. Gentlemen folders, art folders. **Patterns:** Hunters, skinners, Bowies, fighters, daggers, liner locks. **Technical:** Forges own Damascus using 15N20 and 1084, 1095, nickel, custom file work. **Prices:** $200 to $4000. **Remarks:** Full-time maker, first knife sold in 1994; doing business under Tiensvold Custom Knives. **Mark:** Tiensvold USA Handmade in a circle.

TIGHE, BRIAN,
12-111 Fourth Ave, Suite 376 Ridley Square, St. Catharines, Ont., CANADA L0S 1M0, Phone: 905-892-2734, Fax: 905-892-2734, Web: www.tigheknives.com

Specialties: High tech tactical folders. **Patterns:** Boots, daggers, locking and slip-joint folders. **Technical:** CPM 440V and CPM 420V. Prefers natural handle material inlay; hand finishes. **Prices:** $450 to $2000. **Remarks:** Part-time maker; first knife sold in 1989. **Mark:** Etched signature.

TILL, CALVIN E AND RUTH,
211 Chaping, Chadron, NE 69337

Specialties: Straight knives, hunters, Bowies; no folders **Patterns:** Training point, drop point hunters, Bowies. **Technical:** ATS-34 sub zero quench RC59, 61. **Prices:** $700 to $1200. **Remarks:** Sells only the absolute best knives they can make. Manufactures every part in their knives. **Mark:** RC Till. The R is for Ruth.

TILTON, JOHN,
24041 Hwy 383, Iowa, LA 70647, Phone: 337-582-6785, john@jetknives.com

Specialties: Bowies, camp knives, skinners and folders. **Technical:** All forged blades. Makes own Damascus. **Prices:** $150 and up. **Remarks:** ABS Journeyman Smith. **Mark:** Initials J.E.T.

TINDERA, GEORGE,
BURNING RIVER FORGE, 751 Hadcock Rd, Brunswick, OH 44212-2648, Phone: 330-220-6212

Specialties: Straight knives; his designs. **Patterns:** Personal knives; classic Bowies and fighters. **Technical:** Hand-forged high-carbon; his own cable and pattern welded Damascus. **Prices:** $100 to $400. **Remarks:** Spare-time maker; sold first knife in 1995. Natural handle materials.

TINGLE, DENNIS P,
19390 E Clinton Rd, Jackson, CA 95642, Phone: 209-223-4586, dtknives@earthlink.net

Specialties: Swords, fixed blades: small to medium, tomahawks. **Technical:** All blades forged. **Remarks:** ABS, JS. **Mark:** D. Tingle over JS.

TIPPETTS, COLTEN,
4068 W Miners Farm Dr, Hidden Springs, ID 83714, Phone: 208-229-7772, colten@interstate-electric.com

Specialties: Fancy and working straight knives and fancy locking folders of his own design or to customer specifications. Patterns: Hunters and skinners, fighters and utility. **Technical:** Grinds BG-42, high-carbon 1095 and Damascus. **Prices:** $200 to $1000. **Remarks:** Part-time maker; first knife sold in 1996. **Mark:** Fused initials.

TKOMA, FLAVIO,
R Manoel Rainho Teixeira 108-Pres, Prudonte SP19031-220, BRAZIL, Phone: 0182-22-0115, fikoma@itelesonica.com.br
Specialties: Tactical fixed blade knives, LinerLock® folders and balisongs. **Patterns:** Utility and defense tactical knives built with hi-tech materials. **Technical:** Grinds S30V and Damasteel. **Prices:** $500 to $1000. **Mark:** Ikoma hand made beside Samurai

TODD, RICHARD C,
RR 1, Chambersburg, IL 62323, Phone: 217-327-4380, ktodd45@yahoo.com
Specialties: Multi blade folders and silver sheaths. **Patterns:** Blacksmithing and tool making. **Mark:** RT with letter R crossing the T.

TOICH, NEVIO,
Via Pisacane 9, Rettorgole di Caldogna, Vincenza, ITALY 36030, Phone: 0444-985065, Fax: 0444-301254
Specialties: Working/using straight knives of his design or to customer specs. **Patterns:** Bowies, hunters, skinners and utility/camp knives. **Technical:** Grinds 440C, D2 and ATS-34. Hollow-grinds all blades and uses mirror polish. Offers hand-sewn sheaths. Uses wood and horn. **Prices:** $120 to $300; some to $450. **Remarks:** Spare-time maker; first knife sold in 1989. Doing business as Custom Toich. **Mark:** Initials and model number punched.

TOKAR, DANIEL,
Box 1776, Shepherdstown, WV 25443
Specialties: Working knives; period pieces. **Patterns:** Hunters, camp knives, buckskinners, axes, swords and battle gear. **Technical:** Forges L6, 1095 and his Damascus; makes mokume, Japanese alloys and bronze daggers; restores old edged weapons. **Prices:** $25 to $800; some to $3000. **Remarks:** Part-time maker; first knife sold in 1979. Doing business as The Willow Forge. **Mark:** Arrow over rune and date.

TOLLEFSON, BARRY A,
104 Sutter Pl, PO Box 4198, Tubac, AZ 85646, Phone: 520-398-9327
Specialties: Working straight knives, some fancy. **Patterns:** Hunters, skinners, fighters and camp knives. **Technical:** Grinds 440C, ATS-34 and D2. Likes mirror-finishes; offers some fancy filework. Handles made from elk, deer and exotic hardwoods. **Prices:** $75 to $300; some higher. **Remarks:** Part-time maker; first knife sold in 1990. **Mark:** Stylized initials.

TOMBERLIN, BRION R,
ANVIL TOP CUSTOM KNIVES, 825 W Timberdell, Norman, OK 73072, Phone: 405-202-6832, anviltopp@aol.com
Specialties: Hand forged blades, working pieces, standard classic patterns, some swords, and customer designs. **Patterns:** Bowies, hunters, fighters, Persian and eastern-styles. Likes Japanese blades. **Technical:** Forge 1050, 1075, 1084, 1095, 5160, some forged stainless, also do some stock removal in stainless. **Prices:** Start at $150 up to $800 or higher for swords and custom pieces. **Remarks:** Part-time maker, member America Bladesmith Society, Journeyman Smith. Prefers natural handle materials, hand rubbed finishes. Likes temperlines. **Mark:** "BRION" on forged blades, "ATCK" on stock removal, stainless and early forged blades.

TOMES, P J,
594 High Peak Ln, Shipman, VA 22971, Phone: 434-263-8662, tomgsknives@juno.com; Web: www.tomesknives.com
Specialties: Scagel reproductions. **Patterns:** Front-lock folders. **Technical:** Forges 52100. **Prices:** $150 to $750. **Mark:** Last name, USA, MS, stamped in forged blades.

TOMEY, KATHLEEN,
146 Buford Pl, Macon, GA 31204, Phone: 478-746-8454, ktomey@tomeycustomknives.com; Web: www.tomeycustomknives.com
Specialties: Working hunters, skinners, daily users in fixed blades, plain and embellished. Tactical neck and belt carry. Japanese influenced. Bowies. **Technical:** Grinds O1, ATS-34, flat or hollow grind, filework, satin and mirror polish finishes. High quality leather sheaths with tooling. Kydex with tactical. **Prices:** $150 to $500. **Remarks:** Almost full-time maker. **Mark:** Last name in diamond.

TOMPKINS, DAN,
PO Box 398, Peotone, IL 60468, Phone: 708-258-3620
Specialties: Working knives, some deluxe, some folders. **Patterns:** Hunters, boots, daggers and push knives. **Technical:** Grinds D2, 440C, ATS-34 and 154CM. **Prices:** $85 to $150; some to $400. **Remarks:** Part-time maker; first knife sold in 1975. **Mark:** Last name, city, state.

TONER, ROGER,
531 Lightfoot Pl, Pickering, Ont., CANADA L1V 5Z8, Phone: 905-420-5555
Specialties: Exotic sword canes. Patterns: Bowies, daggers and fighters. **Technical:** Grinds 440C, D2 and Damascus. Scrimshaws and engraves. Silver cast pommels and guards in animal shapes; twisted silver wire inlays. Uses semi-precious stones. **Prices:** $200 to $2000; some to $3000. **Remarks:** Part-time maker; first knife sold in 1982. **Mark:** Last name.

TORGESON, SAMUEL L,
25 Alpine Ln, Sedona, AZ 86336-6809

TOSHIFUMI, KURAMOTO,
3435 Higashioda, Asakura-gun, Fukuoka, JAPAN, Phone: 0946-42-4470

TOWELL, DWIGHT L,
2375 Towell Rd, Midvale, ID 83645, Phone: 208-355-2419
Specialties: Solid, elegant working knives; art knives, high quality hand engraving and gold inlay. **Patterns:** Hunters, Bowies, daggers and folders. **Technical:** Grinds 154CM, ATS-34, 440C and other maker's Damascus. **Prices:** Upscale. **Remarks:** Full-time maker. First knife sold in 1970. Member of AKI. **Mark:** Towell, sometimes hand engraved.

TOWNSEND, ALLEN MARK,
6 Pine Trail, Texarkana, AR 71854, Phone: 870-772-8945

TRACE RINALDI CUSTOM BLADES,
28305 California Ave, Hemet, CA 92545, Phone: 951-926-5422, Trace@thrblades.com; Web: www.thrblades.com
Technical: Grinds S30V, 3V, A2 and talonite fixed blades. **Prices:** $300-$1000. **Remarks:** Tactical and utility for the most part. **Mark:** Diamond with THR inside.

TRACY, BUD,
495 Flanders Rd, Reno, NV 8951-4784

TREIBER, LEON,
PO Box 342, Ingram, TX 78025, Phone: 830-367-2246, treiberknives@hotmail.com; Web: www.treiberknives.com
Specialties: Folders of his design and to customer specs. **Patterns:** Fixed blades. **Technical:** Grinds CPM-T-440V, D2, 440C, Damascus, 420V and ATS-34. **Prices:** $350 to $3500. **Remarks:** Part-time maker; first knife sold in 1992. Doing business as Treiber Knives. **Mark:** First initial, last name, city, state.

TREML, GLENN,
RR #14 Site 12-10, Thunder Bay, Ont., CANADA P7B 5E5, Phone: 807-767-1977
Specialties: Working straight knives of his design and to customer specs. **Patterns:** Hunters, kitchen knives and double-edged survival knives. **Technical:** Grinds 440C, ATS-34 and O1; stock removal method. Uses various woods and Micarta for handle material. **Prices:** $150 and up. **Mark:** Stamped last name.

TRINDLE, BARRY,
1660 Ironwood Trail, Earlham, IA 50072-8611, Phone: 515-462-1237
Specialties: Engraved folders. **Patterns:** Mostly small folders, classical-styles and pocket knives. **Technical:** 440 only. Engraves. Handles of wood or mineral material. **Prices:** Start at $1000. **Mark:** Name on tang.

TRISLER, KENNETH W,
6256 Federal 80, Rayville, LA 71269, Phone: 318-728-5541

TRITZ, JEAN JOSE,
Schopstrasse 23, 20255 Hamburg, GERMANY, Phone: 040-49 78 21
Specialties: Scandinavian knives, Japanese kitchen knives, friction folders, swords. **Patterns:** Puukkos, Tollekniven, Hocho, friction folders, swords. **Technical:** Forges tool steels, carbon steels, 52100 Damascus, mokume, San Maj. **Prices:** $200 to $2000; some higher. **Remarks:** Full-time maker; first knife sold in 1989. Does own leatherwork, prefers natural materials. Sole authorship. Speaks French, German, English, Norwegian. **Mark:** Initials in monogram.

TRU-GRIT INC.,
760 E Francis St #N, Ontario, CA 91761, Phone: 800-532-3336/ 909-923-4116, Fax: 909-923-9932, trugrit1@aol.com; Web: www.trugrit.com
Specialties: Complete line of 3/M, Norton and Hermes belts for grinding and polishing 24-3000 grit; also hard core, Bader and Burr King grinders. Baldor motors and buffers. ATS-34, 440C, BG42 and 416-CPM-154 and S-30V stainless steel.

TRUJILLO, ADAM,
6366 Commerce Blvd, Rohnert Park, CA 94928
Specialties: Working/using straight knives of his design. **Patterns:** Hunters and utility/camp knives. **Technical:** Grinds 440C, ATS-34 and O1; ice tempers blades. Sheaths are dipped in wax and oil base. **Prices:** $200 to $500; some to $1000. **Remarks:** Spare-time maker; first knife sold in 1995. Doing business as Alaska Knife and Service Co. **Mark:** NA.

TRUJILLO, ALBERT M B,
2035 Wasmer Cir, Bosque Farms, NM 87068, Phone: 505-869-0428, cutups@surfmk.com
Specialties: Working/using straight knives of his design or to customer specs. **Patterns:** Hunters, skinners, fighters, working/using knives. File work offered. **Technical:** Grinds ATS-34, D2, 440C, S30V. Tapers tangs, all blades cryogenically treated. **Prices:** $75 to $500. **Remarks:** Part-time maker; first knife sold in 1997. **Mark:** First and last name under logo.

TRUJILLO, MIRANDA,
6366 Commerce Blvd, Rohnert Park, CA 94928
Specialties: Working/using straight knives of her design. **Patterns:** Hunters and utility/camp knives. **Technical:** Grinds ATS-34 and 440C. Sheaths are water resistant. **Prices:** $145 to $400; some to $600. **Remarks:** Spare-time maker; first knife sold in 1989. Doing business as

Alaska Knife and Service Co. **Mark:** NA.

TRUJILLO, THOMAS A,
PMB 183 6366 Commerce Blvd, Rohnert Park, CA 94928-2404
Specialties: High-end art knives. **Patterns:** Hunters, Bowies, daggers and locking folders. **Technical:** Grinds to customer choice, including rock and commercial Damascus. Inlays jewels and carves handles. **Prices:** $150 to $900; some to $6000. **Remarks:** Full-time maker; first knife sold in 1976. Doing business as Alaska Knife and Service Co. **Mark:** Alaska Knife and/or Thomas Anthony.

TRUNCALI CUSTOM KNIVES,
2914 Anatole Court, Garland, TX 75043, Phone: 214-763-7127, ptiii@truncaliknives.com Web:www.truncaliknives.com
Specialties: Lockback folders, locking liner folders, automatics and fixed blades.

TSCHAGER, REINHARD,
Piazza Parrocchia 7, I-39100 Bolzano, ITALY, Phone: 0471-970642, Fax: 0471-970642, goldtschager@dnet.it
Specialties: Classic, high-art, collector-grade straight knives of his design. **Patterns:** Jewel knife, daggers, and hunters. **Technical:** Grinds ATS-34, D2 and Damascus. Oval pins. Gold inlay. Offers engraving. **Prices:** $500 to $1200; some to $2000. **Remarks:** Spare-time maker; first knife sold in 1979. **Mark:** Gold inlay stamped with initials.

TURCOTTE, LARRY,
1707 Evergreen, Pampa, TX 79065, Phone: 806-665-9369, 806-669-0435
Specialties: Fancy and working/using knives of his design and to customer specs. **Patterns:** Hunters, kitchen knives, utility/camp knives. **Technical:** Grinds 440C, D2, ATS-34. Engraves, scrimshaws, silver inlays. **Prices:** $150 to $350; some to $1000. **Remarks:** Part-time maker; first knife sold in 1977. Doing business as Knives by Turcotte. **Mark:** Last name.

TURECEK, JIM,
12 Elliott Rd, Ansonia, CT 06401, Phone: 203-734-8406
Specialties: Exotic folders, art knives and some miniatures. **Patterns:** Trout and bird knives with split bamboo handles and one-of-a-kind folders. **Technical:** Grinds and forges stainless and carbon Damascus. **Prices:** $750 to $1500; some to $3000. **Remarks:** Full-time maker; first knife sold in 1983. **Mark:** Last initial in script, or last name.

TURNBULL, RALPH A,
14464 Linden Dr, Spring Hill, FL 34609, Phone: 352-688-7089, tbull2000@bellsouth.net; Web: www.turnbullknives.com
Specialties: Fancy folders. **Patterns:** Primarily gents pocket knives. **Technical:** Wire EDM work on bolsters. **Prices:** $300 and up. **Remarks:** Full-time maker; first knife sold in 1973. **Mark:** Signature or initials.

TURNER, KEVIN,
17 Hunt Ave, Montrose, NY 10548, Phone: 914-739-0535
Specialties: Working straight knives of his design and to customer specs; period pieces. **Patterns:** Daggers, fighters and utility knives. **Technical:** Forges 5160 and 52100. **Prices:** $90 to $500. **Remarks:** Part-time maker; first knife sold in 1991. **Mark:** Acid-etched signed last name and year.

TYCER, ART,
23820 N Cold Springs Rd, Paron, AR 72122, Phone: 501-821-4487, blades1@tycerknives.com; Web: www.tycerknives.com
Specialties: Fancy working/using straight knives of his design, to customer specs and standard patterns. **Patterns:** Boots, Bowies, daggers, fighters, hunters, kitchen and utility knives. **Technical:** Grinds ATS-34, 440C and a variety of carbon steels. Uses exotic woods with spacer material, stag and water buffalo. Offers filework. **Prices:** $175 and up depending on size and embellishments or Damascus. **Remarks:** Now making folders (liner locks). Making and using his own Damascus and other Damascus also. Full-time maker. **Mark:** Flying "T" over first initial inside an oval.

TYRE, MICHAEL A,
1219 Easy St, Wickenburg, AZ 85390, Phone: 928-684-9601/602-377-8432, michaeltyre@msn.com
Specialties: Quality folding knives upscale gents folders one-of-a-kind collectable models. **Patterns:** Working fixed blades for hunting, kitchen and fancy Bowies. **Technical:** Grinds prefer hand rubbed satin finishes and use natural handle materials. **Prices:** $250 to $1300.

TYSER, ROSS,
1015 Hardee Court, Spartanburg, SC 29303, Phone: 864-585-7616
Specialties: Traditional working and using straight knives and folders of his design and in standard patterns. Patterns: Bowies, hunters and slip-joint folders. **Technical:** Grinds 440C and commercial Damascus. Mosaic pins; stone inlay. Does filework and scrimshaw. Offers engraving and cut-work and some inlay on sheaths. **Prices:** $45 to $125; some to $400. **Remarks:** Part-time maker; first knife sold in 1995. Doing business as RT Custom Knives. **Mark:** Stylized initials.

U

UCHIDA, CHIMATA,
977-2 Oaza Naga Shisui Ki, Kumamoto, JAPAN 861-1204

UEKAMA, NOBUYUKI,
3-2-8-302 Ochiai, Tama City, Tokyo, JAPAN

V

VAGNINO, MICHAEL,
PO Box 67, Visalia, CA 93279, Phone: 559-528-2800, mvknives@lightspeed.net; Web: www.mvknives.com
Specialties: Working and fancy straight knives and folders of his design and to customer specs. **Patterns:** Hunters, Bowies, camp, kitchen and folders: locking liners, slip-joint, lock-back and double-action autos. **Technical:** Forges 52100, A2, 1084 and 15N20 Damascus and grinds stainless. **Prices:** $275 to $2000 plus. **Remarks:** Full-time maker, ABS Master Smith. **Mark:** Logo, last name.

VAIL, DAVE,
554 Sloop Point Rd, Hampstead, NC 28443, Phone: 910-270-4456
Specialties: Working/using straight knives of his own design or to the customer's specs. **Patterns:** Hunters/skinners, camp/utility, fillet, Bowies. **Technical:** Grinds ATS-34, 440c, 154 CM and 1095 carbon steel. **Prices:** $90 to $450. **Remarks:** Part-time maker. Member of NC Custom Knifemakers Guild. **Mark:** Etched oval with "Dave Vail Hampstead NC" inside.

VALLOTTON, BUTCH AND AREY,
621 Fawn Ridge Dr, Oakland, OR 97462, Phone: 541-459-2216, Fax: 541-459-7473
Specialties: Quick opening knives w/complicated mechanisms. **Patterns:** Tactical, fancy, working, and some art knives. **Technical:** Grinds all steels, uses others' Damascus. Uses Spectrum Metal. **Prices:** From $350 to $4500. **Remarks:** Full-time maker since 1984; first knife sold in 1981. Co/designer, Appelgate Fairbarn folding w/Bill Harsey. **Mark:** Name w/viper head in the "V."

VALLOTTON, RAINY D,
1295 Wolf Valley Dr, Umpqua, OR 97486, Phone: 541-459-0465
Specialties: Folders, one-handed openers and art pieces. **Patterns:** All patterns. **Technical:** Stock removal all steels; uses titanium liners and bolsters; uses all finishes. **Prices:** $350 to $3500. **Remarks:** Full-time maker. **Mark:** Name.

VALLOTTON, SHAWN,
621 Fawn Ridge Dr, Oakland, OR 97462, Phone: 503-459-2216
Specialties: Left-hand knives. **Patterns:** All styles. **Technical:** Grinds 440C, ATS-34 and Damascus. Uses titanium. Prefers bead-blasted or anodized finishes. **Prices:** $250 to $1400. **Remarks:** Full-time maker. **Mark:** Name and specialty.

VALLOTTON, THOMAS,
621 Fawn Ridge Dr, Oakland, OR 97462, Phone: 541-459-2216
Specialties: Custom autos. **Patterns:** Tactical, fancy. **Technical:** File work, uses Damascus, uses Spectrum Metal. **Prices:** From $350 to $700. **Remarks:** Full-time maker. Maker of Protégé 3 canoe. **Mark:** T and a V mingled.

VALOIS, A. DANIEL,
3552 W Lizard Ck Rd, Lehighton, PA 18235, Phone: 717-386-3636
Specialties: Big working knives; various sized lock-back folders with new safety releases. **Patterns:** Fighters in survival packs, sturdy working knives, belt buckle knives, military-style knives, swords. **Technical:** Forges and grinds A2, O1 and 440C; likes full tangs. **Prices:** $65 to $240; some to $600. **Remarks:** Full-time maker; first knife sold in 1969. **Mark:** Anvil logo with last name inside.

VAN CLEVE, STEVE,
Box 372, Sutton, AK 99674, Phone: 907-745-3038

VAN DE MANAKKER, THIJS,
Koolweg 34, 5759 px Helenaveen, HOLLAND, Phone: 0493539369
Specialties: Classic high-art knives. **Patterns:** Swords, utility/camp knives and period pieces. **Technical:** Forges soft iron, carbon steel and Bloomery Iron. Makes own Damascus, Bloomery Iron and patterns. **Prices:** $20 to $2000; some higher. **Remarks:** Full-time maker; first knife sold in 1969. **Mark:** Stylized "V."

VAN DEN ELSEN, GERT,
Purcelldreef 83, 5012 AJ Tilburg, NETHERLANDS, Phone: 013-4563200, gvdelsen@home.nl; Web: www.7knifedwarfs.com
Specialties: Fancy, working/using, miniatures and integral straight knives of the maker's design or to customer specs. **Patterns:** Bowies, fighters, hunters and Japanese-style blades. **Technical:** Grinds ATS-34 and 440C; forges Damascus. Offers filework, differentially tempered blades and some mokume-gane fittings. **Prices:** $350 to $1000; some to $4000. **Remarks:** Part-time maker; first knife sold in 1982. Doing business as G-E Knives. **Mark:** Initials GE in lozenge shape.

VAN DER WESTHUIZEN, PETER,
PO Box 1698, Mossel Bay 6500, SOUTH AFRICA, Phone: 27 446952388
Specialties: Working knives, folders, daggers and art knives. **Patterns:** Hunters, skinners, bird, trout and sidelock folders. **Technical:** Sandvik, 12627. Damascus indigenous wood and ivory. **Prices:** From $450 to $5500. **Remarks:** First knife sold in 1987. Full-time since 1996. **Mark:** Initial & surname. Handmade RSA.

VAN DIJK, RICHARD,
76 Stepney Ave Rd 2, Harwood Dunedin, NEW ZEALAND, Phone: 0064-3-4780401, Web: www.hoihoknives.com
Specialties: Damascus, Fantasy knives, sgiandubhs, dirks, swords, and hunting knives. **Patterns:** Mostly one-ofs, anything from bird and trout to swords, no folders. **Technical:** Forges mainly own Damascus, some 5160, O1, 1095, L6. Prefers natural handle materials, over 35 years experience as goldsmith, handle fittings are often made from sterling silver and sometimes gold, manufactured to cap the handle, use gemstones if required. Makes own sheaths. **Prices:** $300 and up. **Remarks:** Full-time maker, first knife sold in 1980. Doing business as HOIHO KNIVES. **Mark:** Stylized initials RvD in triangle.

VAN EIZENGA, JERRY W,
14281 Cleveland, Nunica, MI 49448, Phone: 616-638-2275
Specialties: Hand forged blades, Scagel patterns and other styles. **Patterns:** Camp, hunting, bird, trout, folders, axes, miniatures. **Technical:** 5160, 52100, 1084. **Prices:** Start at $250. **Remarks:** Part-time maker, sole author of knife and sheath. First knife made 1970s. ABS member who believes in the beauty of simplicity. **Mark:** J.S. stamp.

VAN ELDIK, FRANS,
Ho Flaan 3, 3632BT Loenen, NETHERLANDS, Phone: 0031 294 233 095, Fax: 0031 294 233 095
Specialties: Fancy collector-grade straight knives and folders of his design. **Patterns:** Hunters, fighters, boots and folders. **Technical:** Forges and grinds D2, 154CM, ATS-34 and stainless Damascus. **Prices:** Start at $225. **Remarks:** Spare-time maker; first knife sold in 1979. Knifemaker 25 years. **Mark:** Lion with name and Amsterdam.

VAN REENEN, IAN,
6003 Harvard St, Amarillo, TX 79109, Phone: 806-236-8333, ianvanreenen@suddenlink.net Web:www.ianvanreenenknives.com
Specialties: Safari pocketknife sold over 700 in Amarillo alone. **Patterns:** Folders and fixed blades. **Technical:** ATS-34 and 440C blade steels, or the maker forges 5160 and 1084 carbon steel.**Prices:**$330 for fixed blades to $600 for folders. **Remarks:**First knife sold in 1998. **Mark:** "IVR" with "Texas" underneath. Forged blades and slip joints marked with last name Van Reenen only.

VAN RIJSWIJK, AAD,
AVR KNIVES, Arij Koplaan 16B, 3132 AA Vlaardingen, NETHERLANDS, Phone: +31 10 2343227, Fax: +31 10 2343648, info@avrknives.com; Web: www.avrknives.com
Specialties: High-art interframe folders of his design and in shaving sets. **Patterns:** Hunters and locking folders. **Technical:** Uses semi-precious stones, mammoth, ivory, walrus ivory, iron wood. **Prices:** $550 to $3800. **Remarks:** Full-time maker; first knife sold in 1993. **Mark:** NA.

VAN RIPER, JAMES N,
PO Box 7045, Citrus Heights, CA 95621-7045, Phone: 916-721-0892

VANDERFORD, CARL G,
2290 Knob Creek Rd, Columbia, TN 38401, Phone: 931-381-1488
Specialties: Traditional working straight knives and folders of his design. **Patterns:** Hunters, Bowies and locking folders. **Technical:** Forges and grinds 440C, O1 and wire Damascus. **Prices:** $60 to $125. **Remarks:** Part-time maker; first knife sold in 1987. **Mark:** Last name.

VANDERKOLFF, STEPHEN,
5 Jonathan Crescent, Mildmay Ontario, CANADA N0g 2J0, Phone: 519-367-3401, steve@vanderkolffknives.com; Web: www.vanderkolffknives.com
Specialties: Fixed blades from gent's pocketknives and drop hunters to full sized Bowies and art knives. **Technical:** Primary blade steel 440C, Damasteel or custom made Damascus. All heat treat done by maker and all blades hardness tested. Handle material: stag, stabilized woods or MOP. **Prices:** $150 to $1200. **Remarks:** Started making knives in 1998 and sold first knife in 2000. Winner of the best of show art knife 2005 Wolverine Knife Show.

VANDEVENTER, TERRY L,
3274 Davis Rd, Terry, MS 39170-8719, Phone: 601-371-7414, tvandeventer@comcast.net
Specialties: Bowies, hunters, camp knives, friction folders. **Technical:** 1084, 1095, 15N20 and L6 steels. Damascus and mokume. Natural handle materials. **Prices:** $350 to $2500. **Remarks:** Sole author; makes everything here. First ABS MS from the state of Mississippi. **Mark:** T.L. Vandeventer (silhouette of snake underneath). MS on ricasso.

VANHOY, ED and TANYA,
24255 N Fork River Rd, Abingdon, VA 24210, Phone: 276-944-4885, vanhoyknives@hughes.net
Specialties: Traditional and working/using straight knives of his design, make folders. **Patterns:** Fighters, straight knives, folders, hunters and art knives. **Technical:** Grinds ATS-34 and 440V; forges D2. Offers filework, engraves, acid etching, mosaic pins, decorative bolsters and custom fitted English bridle leather sheaths. **Prices:** $250 to $3000. **Remarks:** Full-time maker; first knife sold in 1977. Wife also engraves. Doing business as Van Hoy Custom Knives. **Mark:** Acid etched last name.

VARDAMAN, ROBERT,
2406 Mimosa Lane, Hattiesburg, MS 39402, Phone: 601-268-3889, rv7x@comcast.net
Specialties: Working straight knives of his design or to customer specs. **Patterns:** Bowies, hunters, skinners, utility and camp knives. **Technical:** Forges 5160, 1084 and 1095. Filework. **Prices:** $100 to $500. **Remarks:** Part-time maker. First knife sold in 2004. **Mark:** Last name, last name with Mississippi state logo.

VASQUEZ, JOHNNY DAVID,
1552 7th St, Wyandotte, MI 48192, Phone: 734-281-2455

VAUGHAN, IAN,
351 Doe Run Rd, Manheim, PA 17545-9368, Phone: 717-665-6949

VECERA, J R,
213 Douglas, Thrall, TX 76578, Phone: 512-365-8627
Specialties: Own and customers designs. Fighters, folders, exotic skinners. **Technical:** Flat, hollow and convex grinds. As of now some forging with more in the future. O1, D2, 440C, ATS-34 steels. **Prices:** $125 to $1400. **Remarks:** Love to do unique & one-of-a-kind designs. **Mark:** Native TX Vecera in oval or Vecera

VEIT, MICHAEL,
3289 E Fifth Rd, LaSalle, IL 61301, Phone: 815-223-3538, whitebear@starband.net
Specialties: Damascus folders. **Technical:** Engraver, sole author. **Prices:** $2500 to $6500. **Remarks:** Part-time maker; first knife sold in 1985. **Mark:** Name in script.

VELARDE, RICARDO,
7240 N Greenfield Dr, Park City, UT 84098, Phone: 435-901-1773, velardeknives.com
Specialties: Investment grade integrals and interframs. **Patterns:** Boots, fighters and hunters; hollow grind. **Technical:** BG on Integrals. **Prices:** $950 to $4800. **Remarks:** First knife sold in 1992. **Mark:** First initial, last name on blade; city, state, U.S.A. at bottom of tang.

VELICK, SAMMY,
3457 Maplewood Ave, Los Angeles, CA 90066, Phone: 310-663-6170, metaltamer@gmail.com
Specialties: Working knives and art pieces. **Patterns:** Hunter, utility and fantasy. **Technical:** Stock removal and forges. **Prices:** $100 and up. **Mark:** Last name.

VENSILD, HENRIK,
GI Estrup, Randersvei 4, DK-8963 Auning, DENMARK, Phone: +45 86 48 44 48
Specialties: Classic and traditional working and using knives of his design; Scandinavian influence. **Patterns:** Hunters and using knives. **Technical:** Forges Damascus. Hand makes handles, sheaths and blades. **Prices:** $350 to $1000. **Remarks:** Part-time maker; first knife sold in 1967. **Mark:** Initials.

VEREYNDER MARTIN, JOHN ALEXANDER,
821 N Grand Ave, Okmulgee, OK 74447, Phone: 918-758-1099, jam@jamblades.com; Web: www.jamblades.com
Specialties: Inlaid and engraved handles. **Patterns:** Bowies, fighters, hunters and traditional patterns. Swords, fixed blade knives, folders and axes. **Technical:** Forges 5160, 1084, 10XX, O1, L6 and his own Damascus. **Prices:** Start at $300. **Remarks:** Part-time maker. **Mark:** Two initials with last name and MS or 5 pointed star.

VIALLON, HENRI,
Les Belins, 63300 Thiers, FRANCE, Phone: 04-73-80-24-03, Fax: 04 73-51-02-02
Specialties: Folders and complex Damascus **Patterns:** His draws. **Technical:** Forge. **Prices:** $1000 to $5000. **Mark:** H. Viallon.

VIELE, H J,
88 Lexington Ave, Westwood, NJ 07675, Phone: 201-666-2906, h.viele@verizon.net
Specialties: Folding knives of distinctive shapes. **Patterns:** High-tech folders and one-of-a-kind. **Technical:** Grinds ATS-34 and S30V. **Prices:** Start at $575. **Remarks:** Full-time maker; first knife sold in 1973. **Mark:** Japanese design for the god of war.

VIKING KNIVES (SEE JAMES THORLIEF ERIKSEN),

VILAR, RICARDO AUGUSTO FERREIRA,

Rua Alemada Dos Jasmins NO 243, Parque Petropolis, Mairipora Sao Paulo, BRAZIL 07600-000, Phone: 011-55-11-44-85-43-46, ricardovilar@ig.com.br.

Specialties: Traditional Brazilian-style working knives of the Sao Paulo state. **Patterns:** Fighters, hunters, utility, and camp knives, welcome customer design. Specialize in the "true" Brazilian camp knife "Soracabana." **Technical:** Forges only with sledge hammer to 100 percent shape in 5160 and 52100 and his own Damascus steels. Makes own sheaths in the "true" traditional "Paulista"-style of the state of Sao Paulo. **Remark:** Full-time maker. **Prices:** $250 to $600. Uses only natural handle materials. **Mark:** Special designed signature styled name R. Vilar.

VILLA, LUIZ,

R. Com. Miguel Calfat, 398 Itaim Bibi, Sao Paulo, SP-04537-081, BRAZIL, Phone: 011-8290649

Specialties: One-of-a-kind straight knives and jewel knives of all designs. **Patterns:** Bowies, hunters, utility/camp knives and jewel knives. **Technical:** Grinds D6, Damascus and 440C; forges 5160. Prefers natural handle material. **Prices:** $70 to $200. **Remarks:** Part-time maker; first knife sold in 1990. **Mark:** Last name and serial number.

VILLAR, RICARDO,

Al. dos Jasmins 243 Mairipora, S.P. 07600-000, BRAZIL, Phone: 011-4851649

Specialties: Straight working knives to customer specs. **Patterns:** Bowies, fighters and utility/camp knives. **Technical:** Grinds D6, ATS-34 and 440C stainless. **Prices:** $80 to $200. **Remarks:** Part-time maker; first knife sold in 1993. **Mark:** Percor over sword and circle.

VINING, BILL,

9 Penny Lane, Methuen, MA 01844, Phone: 978-688-4729, billv@medawebs.com; Web: www.medawebs.com/knives

Specialties Liner locking folders. Slip joints & lockbacks. **Patterns:** Likes to make patterns of his own design. **Technical:** S30V, 440C, ATS-34. Damascus from various makers. **Prices:** $450 and up. **Remarks:** Part-time maker. **Mark:** VINING or B. Vining.

VISTE, JAMES,

EDGE WISE FORGE, 13401 Mt Elliot, Detroit, MI 48212, Phone: 313-664-7455, grumblejunky@hotmail.com

Mark: EWF touch mark.

VISTNES, TOR,

N-6930 Svelgen, NORWAY, Phone: 047-57795572

Specialties: Traditional and working knives of his design. **Patterns:** Hunters and utility knives. **Technical:** Grinds Uddeholm Elmax. Handles made of rear burls of different Nordic stabilized woods. **Prices:** $300 to $1100. **Remarks:** Part-time maker; first knife sold in 1988. **Mark:** Etched name and deer head.

VITALE, MACE,

925 Rt 80, Guilford, CT 06437, Phone: 203-457-5591, Web: www.laurelrockforge.com

Specialties: Hand forged blades. **Patterns:** Hunters, utility, chef, Bowies and fighters. **Technical:** W2, 1095, 1084, L6. Hand forged and finished. **Prices:** $100 to $1000. **Remarks:** American Bladesmith Society, Journeyman Smith. Full-time maker; first knife sold 2001. **Mark:** MACE.

VOGT, DONALD J,

9007 Hogans Bend, Tampa, FL 33647, Phone: 813 973-3245, vogtknives@aol.com

Specialties: Art knives, folders, automatics, large fixed blades. **Technical:** Uses Damascus steels for blade and bolsters, filework, hand carving on blade bolsters and handles. Other materials used: jewels, gold, stainless steel, mokume. Prefers to use natural handle materials. **Prices:** $800 to $7000. **Remarks:** Part-time maker; first knife sold in 1997. **Mark:** Last name.

VOGT, PATRIK,

Kungsvagen 83, S-30270 Halmstad, SWEDEN, Phone: 46-35-30977

Specialties: Working straight knives. **Patterns:** Bowies, hunters and fighters. **Technical:** Forges carbon steel and own Damascus. **Prices:** From $100. **Remarks:** Not currently making knives. **Mark:** Initials or last name.

VOORHIES, LES,

14511 Lk Mazaska Tr, Faribault, MN 55021, Phone: 507-332-0736, lesvor@msn.com; Web: www.lesvoorhiesknives.com

Specialties: Steels. **Patterns:** Liner locks & autos. **Technical:** ATS-34 Damascus. **Prices:** $250 to $1200. **Mark:** L. Voorhies.

VOSS, BEN,

362 Clark St, Galesburg, IL 61401, Phone: 309-342-6994

Specialties: Fancy working knives of his design. **Patterns:** Bowies, fighters, hunters, boots and folders. **Technical:** Grinds 440C, ATS-34 and D2. **Prices:** $35 to $1200. **Remarks:** Part-time maker; first knife sold in 1986. **Mark:** Name, city and state.

VOTAW, DAVID P,

305 S State St, Pioneer, OH 43554, Phone: 419-737-2774

Specialties: Working knives; period pieces. **Patterns:** Hunters, Bowies, camp knives, buckskinners and tomahawks. **Technical:** Grinds O1 and D2. **Prices:** $100 to $200; some to $500. **Remarks:** Part-time maker; took over for the late W.K. Kneubuhler. Doing business as W-K Knives. **Mark:** WK with V inside anvil.

W

WADA, YASUTAKA,

2-6-22 Fujinokidai, Nara City, Nara prefect 631-0044, JAPAN, Phone: 0742 46-0689

Specialties: Fancy and embellished one-of-a-kind straight knives of his design. **Patterns:** Bowies, daggers and hunters. **Technical:** Grinds ATS-34. **Prices:** $400 to $2500; some higher. **Remarks:** Part-time maker; first knife sold in 1990. **Mark:** Owl eyes with initial and last name underneath or last name.

WAGAMAN, JOHN K,

107 E Railroad St, Selma, NC 27576, Phone: 919-965-9659, Fax: 919-965-9901

Specialties: Fancy working knives. **Patterns:** Bowies, miniatures, hunters, fighters and boots. **Technical:** Grinds D2, 440C, 154CM and commercial Damascus; inlays mother-of-pearl. **Prices:** $110 to $2000. **Remarks:** Part-time maker; first knife sold in 1975. **Mark:** Last name.

WAITES, RICHARD L,

PO Box 188, Broomfield, CO 80038, Phone: 303-465-9970, Fax: 303-465-9971, dick.waites@oneida.com

Specialties: Working fixed blade knives of all kinds including "paddle blade" skinners. Hand crafted sheaths, some upscale and unusual. **Technical:** Grinds 440C, ATS 34, D2. **Prices:** $100 to $500. **Remarks:** Part-time maker. First knife sold in 1998. Doing business as R.L. Waites Knives. **Mark:** Oval etch with first and middle initial and last name on top and city and state on bottom. Memberships; Professional Knifemakers Association and Rocky Mountain Blade Collectors Club.

WALKER, BILL,

431 Walker Rd, Stevensville, MD 21666, Phone: 410-643-5041

WALKER, DON,

2850 Halls Chapel Rd, Burnsville, NC 28714, Phone: 828-675-9716, dlwalkernc@aol.com

WALKER, JIM,

22 Walker Ln, Morrilton, AR 72110, Phone: 501-354-3175, jwalker46@att.net

Specialties: Period pieces and working/using knives of his design and to customer specs. **Patterns:** Bowies, fighters, hunters, camp knives. **Technical:** Forges 5160, O1, L6, 52100, 1084, 1095. **Prices:** Start at $450. **Remarks:** Full-time maker; first knife sold in 1993. **Mark:** Three arrows with last name/MS.

WALKER, JOHN W,

10620 Moss Branch Rd, Bon Aqua, TN 37025, Phone: 931-670-4754

Specialties: Straight knives, daggers and folders; sterling rings, 14K gold wire wrap; some stone setting. **Patterns:** Hunters, boot knives, others. **Technical:** Grinds 440C, ATS-34, L6, etc. Buys Damascus. **Prices:** $150 to $500 some to $1500. **Remarks:** Knifemakers Guild member, part-time maker; first knife sold in 1982. **Mark:** Hohenzollern Eagle with name, or last name.

WALKER, MICHAEL L,

925-A Paseo del, Pueblo Sur Taos, NM 87571, Phone: 505-751-3409, Fax: 505-751-3417, metalwerkr@msn.com

Specialties: Innovative knife designs and locking systems; titanium and SS furniture and art. **Patterns:** Folders from utility grade to museum quality art; others upon request. **Technical:** State-of-the-art materials: titanium, stainless Damascus, gold, etc. **Prices:** $3500 and above. **Remarks:** Designer/MetalCrafts; full-time professional knifemaker since 1980; four U.S. patents; invented LinerLock® and was awarded registered U.S. trademark no. 1,585,333. **Mark:** Early mark MW, Walker's Lockers by M.L. Walker; current M.L. Walker or Michael Walker.

WALKER III, JOHN WADE,
2595 Hwy 1647, Paintlick, KY 40461, Phone: 606-792-3498

WALLINGFORD JR., CHARLES W,
9024 Old Union Rd, Union, KY 41091, Phone: 859-384-4141, Web: www.cwknives.com

Specialties: 18th and 19th century styles, patch knives, rifleman knives. **Technical:** 1084 and 5160 forged blades. **Prices:** $125 to $300. **Mark:** CW.

WALTERS, A F,
PO Box 523, 275 Crawley Rd., TyTy, GA 31795, Phone: 229-528-6207

Specialties: Working knives, some to customer specs. Patterns: Locking folders, straight hunters, fishing and survival knives. **Technical:** Grinds D2, 154CM and 13C26. **Prices:** Start at $200. **Remarks:** Part-time maker. Label: "The jewel knife." **Mark:** "J" in diamond and knife logo.

WARD, CHUCK,
PO Box 2272, 1010 E North St, Benton, AR 72018-2272, Phone: 501-778-4329, chuckbop@aol.com

Specialties: Traditional working and using straight knives and folders of his design. **Technical:** Grinds 440C, D2, A2, ATS-34 and O1; uses natural and composite handle materials. **Prices:** $90 to $400, some higher. **Remarks:** Part-time maker; first knife sold in 1990. **Mark:** First initial, last name.

WARD, J J,
7501 S R 220, Waverly, OH 45690, Phone: 614-947-5328

Specialties: Traditional and working/using straight knives and folders of his design. **Patterns:** Hunters and locking folders. **Technical:** Grinds ATS-34, 440C and Damascus. Offers handmade sheaths. **Prices:** $125 to $250; some to $500. **Remarks:** Spare-time maker; first knife sold in 1980. **Mark:** Etched name.

WARD, KEN,
1125 Lee Roze Ln, Grants Pass, OR 97527, Phone: 541-956-8864

Specialties: Working knives, some to customer specs. **Patterns:** Straight, axes, Bowies, buckskinners and miniatures. **Technical:** Grinds ATS-34, Damascus. **Prices:** $100 to $700. **Remarks:** Part-time maker; first knife sold in 1977. **Mark:** Name.

WARD, RON,
1363 Nicholas Dr, Loveland, OH 45140, Phone: 513-722-0602

Specialties: Classic working and using straight knives, fantasy knives. **Patterns:** Bowies, hunter, fighters, and utility/camp knives. **Technical:** Grinds 440C, 154CM, ATS-34, uses composite and natural handle materials. **Prices:** $50 to $750. **Remarks:** Part-time maker, first knife sold in 1992. Doing business as Ron Ward Blades. **Mark:** Ron Ward Blades, Loveland OH.

WARD, W C,
817 Glenn St, Clinton, TN 37716, Phone: 615-457-3568

Specialties: Working straight knives; period pieces. **Patterns:** Hunters, Bowies, swords and kitchen cutlery. **Technical:** Grinds O1. **Prices:** $85 to $150; some to $500. **Remarks:** Part-time maker; first knife sold in 1969. He styled the Tennessee Knife Maker. **Mark:** TKM.

WARDELL, MICK,
20 Clovelly Rd, Bideford, N Devon EX39 3BU, ENGLAND, Phone: 01237 475312, wardellknives@hotmail.co.uk Web: www.wardellscustomknives.com

Specialties: Folders of his design. **Patterns:** Locking and slip-joint folders, Bowies. **Technical:** Grinds stainless Damascus, S30V and RWL34. Heat-treats. **Prices:** $300 to $2500. **Remarks:** Full-time maker; first knife sold in 1986. **Mark:** M. Wardell -England.

WARDEN, ROY A,
275 Tanglewood Rd, Union, MO 63084, Phone: 314-583-8813, rwarden@yhti.net

Specialties: Complex mosaic designs of "EDM wired figures" and "stack up" patterns and "lazer cut" and "torch cut" and "sawed" patterns combined. **Patterns:** Mostly "all mosaic" folders, automatics, fixed blades. **Technical:** Mosaic Damascus with all tool steel edges. **Prices:** $500 to $2000 and up. **Remarks:** Part-time maker; first knife sold in 1987. **Mark:** WARDEN stamped or initials connected.

WARE, TOMMY,
PO Box 488, Datil, NM 87821, Phone: 505-772-5817

Specialties: Traditional working and using straight knives, folders and automatics of his design and to customer specs. **Patterns:** Hunters, automatics and locking folders. **Technical:** Grinds ATS-34, 440C and D2. Offers engraving and scrimshaw. **Prices:** $425 to $650; some to $1500. **Remarks:** Full-time maker; first knife sold in 1990. Doing business as Wano Knives. **Mark:** Last name inside oval, business name above, city and state below, year on side.

WARREN, AL,
1423 Sante Fe Circle, Roseville, CA 95678, Phone: 916-784-3217/Cell phone 916-257-5904, Fax: 215-318-2945, al@warrenknives.com; Web: www.warrenknives.com

Specialties: Working straight knives and folders, some fancy. **Patterns:** Hunters, Bowies, fillets, lockback, folders & multi blade. **Technical:** Grinds ATS-34 and S30V.440V. **Prices:** $135 to $3200. **Remarks:** Part-time maker; first knife sold in 1978. **Mark:** First and middle initials, last name.

WARREN, DANIEL,
571 Lovejoy Rd, Canton, NC 28716, Phone: 828-648-7351

Specialties: Using knives. **Patterns:** Drop point hunters. **Prices:** $200 to $500. **Mark:** Warren-Bethel NC.

WARREN (SEE DELLANA), DELLANA,

WARTHER, DALE,
331 Karl Ave, Dover, OH 44622, Phone: 216-343-7513, dalew@warthers.com

Specialties: Working knives; period pieces. **Patterns:** Kitchen cutlery, daggers, hunters and some folders. **Technical:** Forges and grinds O1, D2 and 440C. **Prices:** $350 to $15,000. **Remarks:** Full-time maker; first knife sold in 1967. Takes orders only at shows or by personal interviews at his shop. **Mark:** Dale Warther.

WASHBURN, ARTHUR D,
ADW CUSTOM KNIVES, 10 Hinman St/POB 625, Pioche, NV 89043, Phone: 775-962-5463, awashburn@adwcustomknives.com; Web: www.adwcustomknives.com

Specialties: Locking liner folders. **Patterns:** Slip joint folders (single and multiplied), lock-back folders, some fixed blades. Do own heat-treating; Rockwell test each blade. **Technical:** Carbon and stainless Damascus, some 1084, 1095, ATS-34, 154CM and S30V. Makes own two color Mokum. **Prices:** $200 to $1000 and up. **Remarks:** Sold first knife in 1997. Part-time maker. **Mark:** ADW enclosed in an oval or ADW.

WASHBURN JR., ROBERT LEE,
1162 West Diamond Valley Drive, St George, UT 847700, Phone: 435-619-4432, Fax: 435-574-8554, rlwashburn@excite.com; Web:www.washburnknives.com

Specialties: Hand-forged period, Bowies, tactical, boot and hunters. **Patterns:** Bowies, tantos, loot hunters, tactical and folders. **Prices:** $100 to $2500. **Remarks:** All hand forged. 52100 being his favorite steel. **Mark:** Washburn Knives W.

WATANABE, WAYNE,
PO Box 3563, Montebello, CA 90640, wwknives@gmail.com; Web: www.geocities.com/ww-knives

Specialties: Straight knives in Japanese-styles. One-of-a-kind designs; welcomes customer designs. **Patterns:** Tantos to katanas, Bowies. **Technical:** Flat grinds A2, O1 and ATS-34. Offers hand-rubbed finishes and wrapped handles. **Prices:** Start at $200. **Remarks:** Part-time maker. **Mark:** Name in characters with flower.

WATERS, GLENN,
11 Shinakawa Machi, Hirosaki City 036-8183, JAPAN, Phone: 172-33-8881, gwaters@luck.ocn.ne.jp; Web: www.glennwaters.com

Specialties: One-of-a-kind collector-grade highly embellished art knives. Folders, fixed blades, and automatics. **Patterns:** Locking liner folders, automatics and fixed art knives. **Technical:** Grinds blades from Damasteel, and selected Damascus makers, mostly stainless. Does own engraving, gold inlaying and stone setting, filework, and carving. Gold and Japanese precious metal fabrication. Prefers exotic material, high karat gold, silver, Shyaku Dou, Shibu Ichi Gin, precious gemstones. **Prices:** Upscale. **Remarks:** Designs and makes some-of-a-kind highly embellished art knives often with fully engraved handles and blades. A jeweler by trade for 20 years before starting to make knives. Full-time since 1999, first knife sold in 1994. **Mark:** Glenn Waters maker Japan, G. Waters or Glen in Japanese writing.

WATERS, HERMAN HAROLD,
2516 Regency, Magnolia, AR 71753, Phone: 870-234-5409

WATERS, LU,
2516 Regency, Magnolia, AR 71753, Phone: 870-234-5409

WATSON, BERT,
PO Box 26, Westminster, CO 80036-0026, Phone: 303-426-7577, watsonlock@aol.com

Specialties: Working/using straight knives of his design and to customer specs. **Patterns:** Hunters, utility/camp knives. **Technical:** Grinds O1, ATS-34, 440C, D2, A2 and others. **Prices:** $150 to $800. **Remarks:** Part-time maker; first knife sold in 1974. Doing business as Game Trail Knives. **Mark:** GTK or Bert or Watson.

WATSON, BILLY,
440 Forge Rd, Deatsville, AL 36022, Phone: 334-365-1482, billy@watsonknives.com; Web: www.watsonknives.com
Specialties: Working and using straight knives and folders of his design; period pieces. **Patterns:** Hunters, Bowies and utility/camp knives. **Technical:** Forges and grinds his own Damascus, 1095, 5160 and 52100. **Prices:** $40 to $1500. **Remarks:** Full-time maker; first knife sold in 1970. Doing business as Billy's Blacksmith Shop. **Mark:** Last name.

WATSON, DANIEL,
350 Jennifer Ln, Driftwood, TX 78619, Phone: 512-847-9679, info@angelsword.com; Web: http://www.angelsword.com
Specialties: One-of-a-kind knives and swords. **Patterns:** Hunters, daggers, swords. **Technical:** Hand-purify and carbonize his own high-carbon steel, pattern-welded Damascus, cable and carbon-induced crystalline Damascus. Teehno-Wootz™ Damascus steel, heat treats including cryogenic processing. European and Japanese tempering. **Prices:** $125 to $25,000. **Remarks:** Full-time maker; first knife sold in 1979. **Mark:** "Angel Sword" on forged pieces; "Bright Knight" for stock removal. Avatar on Techno-Wootz™ Damascus. Bumon on traditional Japanese blades.

WATSON, PETER,
66 Kielblock St, La Hoff 2570, SOUTH AFRICA, Phone: 018-84942
Specialties: Traditional working and using straight knives and folders of his design. Patterns: Hunters, locking folders and utility/camp knives. **Technical:** Sandvik and 440C. **Prices:** $120 to $250; some to $1500. **Remarks:** Part-time maker; first knife sold in 1989. **Mark:** Buffalo head with name.

WATSON, TOM,
1103 Brenau Terrace, Panama City, FL 32405, Phone: 850-785-9209, tomwatsonknives@aol.com; Web: www.tomwatsonknives.com
Specialties: Linerlock folders. **Patterns:** Tactical, utility and art investment pieces. **Technical:** Flat grinds D2, ATS 34, and Damascus satin finished. **Prices:** Tactical start at $250, investment pieces $500 and up. **Remarks:** Full time maker. In business since 1978. **Mark:** Name and city.

WATTELET, MICHAEL A,
PO Box 649, 125 Front, Minocqua, WI 54548, Phone: 715-356-3069, redtroll@nnex.net
Specialties: Working and using straight knives of his design and to customer specs; fantasy knives. **Patterns:** Daggers, fighters and swords. **Technical:** Grinds 440C and L6; forges and grinds O1. Silversmith. **Prices:** $75 to $1000; some to $5000. **Remarks:** Full-time maker; first knife sold in 1966. Doing business as M and N Arts Ltd. **Mark:** First initial, last name.

WATTS, JOHNATHAN,
9560 S Hwy 36, Gatesville, TX 76528, Phone: 254-487-2866
Specialties: Traditional folders. **Patterns:** One and two blade folders in various blade shapes. **Technical:** Grinds ATS-34 and Damascus on request. **Prices:** $120 to $400. **Remarks:** Part-time maker; first knife sold in 1997. **Mark:** J Watts.

WATTS, WALLY,
9560 S Hwy 36, Gatesville, TX 76528, Phone: 254-487-2866
Specialties: Unique traditional folders of his design. **Patterns:** One- to five-blade folders and single-blade gents in various blade shapes. **Technical:** Grinds ATS-34; Damascus on request. **Prices:** $165 to $500. **Remarks:** Full-time maker; first knife sold in 1986. **Mark:** Last name.

WEBSTER, BILL,
58144 West Clear Lake Rd, Three Rivers, MI 49093, Phone: 269-244-2873, Web: www.websterknifeworks.com
Specialties: Working and using straight knives, especially for hunters. His patterns are custom designed. **Patterns:** Hunters, skinners, camp knives, Bowies and daggers. **Technical:** Hand-filed blades made of D2 steel only, unless other steel is requested. Preferred handle material is stabilized and exotic wood and stag. Sheaths are made by Green River Leather in Kentucky. Hand-sewn sheaths by Bill Dehn in Three Rivers, MI. **Prices:** $75 to $500. **Remarks:** Part-time maker, first knife sold in 1978. **Mark:** Originally WEB stamped on blade, at present, Webster Knifeworks Three Rivers, MI laser etched on blade.

WEDDLE JR., DEL,
2703 Green Valley Rd, St. Joseph, MO 64505, Phone: 816-364-1981
Specialties: Working knives; some period pieces. **Patterns:** Hunters, fighters, locking folders, push knives. **Technical:** Grinds D2 and 440C; can provide precious metals and set gems. Offers his own forged wire-cable Damascus in his finished knives. **Prices:** $80 to $250; some to $2000. **Remarks:** Full-time maker; first knife sold in 1972. **Mark:** Signature with last name and date.

WEHNER, RUDY,
297 William Warren Rd, Collins, MS 39428, Phone: 601-765-4997
Specialties: Reproduction antique Bowies and contemporary Bowies in full and miniature. **Patterns:** Skinners, camp knives, fighters, axes and Bowies. **Technical:** Grinds 440C, ATS-34, 154CM and Damascus. **Prices:** $100 to $500; some to $850. **Remarks:** Full-time maker; first knife sold in 1975. **Mark:** Last name on Bowies and antiques; full name, city and state on skinners.

WEILAND JR., J REESE,
PO Box 2337, Riverview, FL 33568, Phone: 813-671-0661, RWPHIL413@earthlink.net; Web: www.rwcustomknive.som
Specialties: Hawk bills; tactical to fancy folders. **Patterns:** Hunters, tantos, Bowies, fantasy knives, spears and some swords. **Technical:** Grinds ATS-34, 154CM, 440C, D2, O1, A2, Damascus. Titanium hardware on locking liners and button locks. **Prices:** $150 to $4000. **Remarks:** Full-time maker, first knife sold in 1978. Knifemakers Guild member since 1988.

WEILER, DONALD E,
PO Box 1576, Yuma, AZ 85366-9576, Phone: 928-782-1159
Specialties: Working straight knives; period pieces. **Patterns:** Strong springbuck folders, blade and spring ATS-34. **Technical:** Forges O1, W2, 5160, ATS-34, D2, 52100, L6 and cable Damascus. Makes his own high-carbon steel Damascus. **Prices:** $150 to $1000. **Remarks:** Full-time maker; first knife sold in 1952. **Mark:** Last name, city.

WEINAND, GEROME M,
14440 Harpers Bridge Rd, Missoula, MT 59808, Phone: 406-543-0845
Specialties: Working straight knives. Patterns: Bowies, fishing and camp knives, large special hunters. **Technical:** Grinds O1, 440C, ATS-34, 1084, L6, also stainless Damascus, Aebl and 304; makes all-tool steel Damascus; Dendritic D2 from powdered steel. Heat-treats. **Prices:** $30 to $100; some to $500. **Remarks:** Full-time maker; first knife sold in 1982. **Mark:** Last name.

WEINSTOCK, ROBERT,
PO Box 170028, San Francisco, CA 94117-0028, Phone: 415-731-5968, weinstock_r@msn.com
Specialties: Fancy and high-art straight knives of his design. **Patterns:** Daggers, folders, poignards and miniatures. **Technical:** Grinds A2, O1 and 440C. Chased and hand-carved blades and handles. Also using various Damascus steels from other makers. **Prices:** $3000 to 7000+. **Remarks:** Full-time maker; first knife sold in 1994. **Mark:** Last name carved.

WEISS, CHARLES L,
18847 N 13th Ave, Phoenix, AZ 85027, Phone: 623-582-6147, weissknife@juno.com; Web: www.weissknives.com
Specialties: High-art straight knives and folders; deluxe period pieces. **Patterns:** Daggers, fighters, boots, push knives and miniatures. **Technical:** Grinds 440C, 154CM and ATS-34. **Prices:** $300 to $1200; some to $2000. **Remarks:** Full-time maker; first knife sold in 1975. **Mark:** Name and city.

WELLING, RONALD L,
15446 Lake Ave, Grand Haven, MI 49417, Phone: 616-846-2274
Specialties: Scagel knives of his design or to customer specs. **Patterns:** Hunters, camp knives, miniatures, bird, trout, folders, double edged, hatchets, skinners and some art pieces. **Technical:** Forges Damascus 1084 and 1095. Antler, ivory and horn. **Prices:** $250 to $3000. **Remarks:** Full-time maker. ABS Journeyman maker. **Mark:** First initials and or name and last name. City and state. Various scagel kris (1or 2).

WERTH, GEORGE W,
5223 Woodstock Rd, Poplar Grove, IL 61065, Phone: 815-544-4408
Specialties: Period pieces, some fancy. **Patterns:** Straight fighters, daggers and Bowies. **Technical:** Forges and grinds O1, 1095 and his Damascus, including mosaic patterns. **Prices:** $200 to $650; some higher. **Remarks:** Full-time maker. Doing business as Fox Valley Forge. **Mark:** Name in logo or initials connected.

WESCOTT, CODY,
5330 White Wing Rd, Las Cruces, NM 88012, Phone: 505-382-5008
Specialties: Fancy and presentation grade working knives. **Patterns:** Hunters, locking folders and Bowies. **Technical:** Hollow-grinds D2 and ATS-34; all knives file worked. Offers some engraving. Makes sheaths. **Prices:** $80 to $300; some to $950. **Remarks:** Full-time maker; first knife sold in 1982. **Mark:** First initial, last name.

WEST, CHARLES A,
1315 S Pine St, Centralia, IL 62801, Phone: 618-532-2777
Specialties: Classic, fancy, high tech, period pieces, traditional and working/using straight knives and folders. **Patterns:** Bowies, fighters and locking folders. **Technical:** Grinds ATS-34, O1 and Damascus. Prefers hot blued finishes. **Prices:** $100 to $1000; some to $2000. **Remarks:** Full-time maker; first knife sold in 1963. Doing business as West Custom Knives. **Mark:** Name or name, city and state.

WEST, PAT,
PO Box 9, Charlotte, TX 78011, Phone: 830-277-1290
Specialties: Classic working and using straight knives and folders. **Patterns:** Hunters, slip-joint folders. **Technical:** Grinds ATS-34, D2. Offers filework and decorates liners on folders. **Prices:** $300 to $600. **Remarks:** Spare-time maker; first knife sold in 1984. **Mark:** Name.

WESTBERG, LARRY,
305 S Western Hills Dr, Algona, IA 50511, Phone: 515-295-9276
Specialties: Traditional and working straight knives of his design and in standard patterns. **Patterns:** Bowies, hunters, fillets and folders. **Technical:** Grinds 440C, D2 and 1095. Heat-treats. Uses natural handle materials. **Prices:** $85 to $600; some to $1000. **Remarks:** Part-time maker; first knife sold in 1987. **Mark:** Last name-town and state.

WHEELER, GARY,
351 Old Hwy 48, Clarksville, TN 37040, Phone: 931-552-3092, ir22shtr@charter.net
Specialties: Working to high end fixed blades. **Patterns:** Bowies, Hunters, combat knives, daggers and a few folders. **Technical:** Forges 5160, 1080, 52100 and his own Damascus, will use stainless steel on request. **Prices:** $125 to $2000. **Remarks:** Full-time maker since 2001, first knife sold in 1985 collaborates/works at B&W Blade Works. **Mark:** Stamped last name.

WHEELER, ROBERT,
289 S Jefferson, Bradley, IL 60915, Phone: 815-932-5854

WHETSELL, ALEX,
1600 Palmetto Tyrone Rd, Sharpsburg, GA 30277, Phone: 770-463-4881
Specialties: Knifekits.com, a source for fold locking liner type and straight knife kits. These kits are industry standard for folding knife kits. **Technical:** Many selections of colored G10 carbon fiber and wood handle material for kits, as well as bulk sizes for the custom knifemaker, heat treated folding knife pivots, screws, bushings, etc.

WHIPPLE, WESLEY A,
PO Box 3771, Kodiak, AK 99615, Phone: 907-486-6737
Specialties: Working straight knives, some fancy. **Patterns:** Hunters, Bowies, camp knives, fighters. **Technical:** Forges high-carbon steels, Damascus, offers relief carving and silver wire inlay checkering. **Prices:** $200 to $1400; some higher. **Remarks:** Part-time maker; first knife sold in 1989. A.K.A. Wilderness Knife and Forge. **Mark:** Last name/JS.

WHITE, BRYCE,
1415 W Col Glenn Rd, Little Rock, AR 72210, Phone: 501-821-2956
Specialties: Hunters, fighters, makes Damascus, file work, handmade only. **Technical:** L6, 1075, 1095, O1 steels used most. **Patterns:** Will do any pattern or use his own. **Prices:** $200 to $300. Sold first knife in 1995. **Mark:** White.

WHITE, DALE,
525 CR 212, Sweetwater, TX 79556, Phone: 325-798-4178, dalew@taylortel.net
Specialties: Working and using knives. **Patterns:** Hunters, skinners, utilities and Bowies. **Technical:** Grinds 440C, offers file work, fancy pins and scrimshaw by Sherry Sellers. **Prices:** From $45 to $300. **Remarks:** Sold first knife in 1975. **Mark:** Full name, city and state.

WHITE, GARRETT,
871 Sarijon Rd, Hartwell, GA 30643, Phone: 706-376-5944
Specialties: Gentlemen folders, fancy straight knives. **Patterns:** Locking liners and hunting fixed blades. **Technical:** Grinds 440C, S30V, and stainless Damascus. **Prices:** $150 to $1000. **Remarks:** Part-time maker. **Mark:** Name.

WHITE, GENE E,
9005 Ewing Dr, Bethesda, MD 20817-3357, Phone: 301-564-3164
Specialties: Small utility/gents knives. **Patterns:** Eight standard hunters; most other patterns on commission basis. Currently no swords, axes and fantasy knives. **Technical:** Stock removal 440C and D2; others on request. Mostly hollow grinds; some flat grinds. Prefers natural handle materials. Makes own sheaths. **Prices:** Start at $85. **Remarks:** Part-time maker; first knife sold in 1971. **Mark:** First and middle initials, last name.

WHITE, JOHN PAUL,
231 S Bayshore, Valparaiso, FL 32580, Phone: 850-729-9174
Specialties: Forged hunters, fighters, traditional Bowies and personal carry knives with handles of natural materials and fittings with detailed file work. **Technical:** Forges carbon steel and own Damascus. **Prices:** $400 to $2000. **Remarks:** Master Smith, American Bladesmith Society. **Mark:** First initial, last name.

WHITE, LOU,
7385 Red Bud Rd NE, Ranger, GA 30734, Phone: 706-334-2273

WHITE, RICHARD T,
359 Carver St, Grosse Pointe Farms, MI 48236, Phone: 313-881-4690

WHITE, ROBERT J,
RR 1 641 Knox Rd 900 N, Gilson, IL 61436, Phone: 309-289-4487
Specialties: Working knives, some deluxe. **Patterns:** Bird and trout knives, hunters, survival knives and locking folders. **Technical:** Grinds A2, D2 and 440C; commercial Damascus. Heat-treats. **Prices:** $125 to $250; some to $600. **Remarks:** Full-time maker; first knife sold in 1976. **Mark:** Last name in script.

WHITE JR., ROBERT J BUTCH,
RR 1, Gilson, IL 61436, Phone: 309-289-4487
Specialties: Folders of all sizes. **Patterns:** Hunters, fighters, boots and folders. **Technical:** Forges Damascus; grinds tool and stainless steel. **Prices:** $500 to $1800. **Remarks:** Spare-time maker; first knife sold in 1980. **Mark:** Last name in block letters.

WHITENECT, JODY,
Elderbank, Halifax County, Nova Scotia, CANADA B0N 1K0, Phone: 902-384-2511
Specialties: Fancy and embellished working/using straight knives of his design and to customer specs. **Patterns:** Bowies, fighters and hunters. **Technical:** Forges 1095 and O1; forges and grinds ATS-34. Various filework on blades and bolsters. **Prices:** $200 to $400; some to $800. **Remarks:** Part-time maker; first knife sold in 1996. **Mark:** Longhorn stamp or engraved.

WHITLEY, L WAYNE,
1675 Carrow Rd, Chocowinity, NC 27817-9495, Phone: 252-946-5648

WHITLEY, WELDON G,
4308 N Robin Ave, Odessa, TX 79764, Phone: 432-530-0448, Fax: 432-530-0048, wgwhitley@juno.com
Specialties: Working knives of his design or to customer specs. **Patterns:** Hunters, folders and various double-edged knives. **Technical:** Grinds 440C, 154CM and ATS-34. **Prices:** $150 to $1250. **Mark:** Name, address, road-runner logo.

WHITMAN, JIM,
21044 Salem St, Chugiak, AK 99567, Phone: 907-688-4575, Fax: 907-688-4278, Web: www.whitmanknives.com
Specialties: Working straight knives and folders; some art pieces. **Patterns:** Hunters, skinners, Bowies, camp knives, working fighters, swords and hatchets. **Technical:** Grinds AEB-L Swedish, 440C, 154CM, ATS-34, and Damascus in full convex. Prefers exotic hardwoods, natural and native handle materials: whale bone, antler, ivory and horn. **Prices:** Start at $150. **Remarks:** Full-time maker; first knife sold in 1983. **Mark:** Name, city, state.

WHITTAKER, ROBERT E,
PO Box 204, Mill Creek, PA 17060
Specialties: Using straight knives. Has a line of knives for buckskinners. **Patterns:** Hunters, skinners and Bowies. **Technical:** Grinds O1, A2 and D2. Offers filework. **Prices:** $35 to $100. **Remarks:** Part-time maker; first knife sold in 1980. **Mark:** Last initial or full initials.

WHITTAKER, WAYNE,
2900 Woodland Ct, Metamore, MI 48455, Phone: 810-797-5315, lindorwayne@yahoo.com
Specialties: Liner lock folders-lock backs-autos.**Patterns:** Bowies, daggers and hunters. **Technical:** Damascus **Prices:** $300 to $500; some to $2000. **Remarks:** Full-time maker; first knife sold in 1985. **Mark:** Initials on inside of backbar.

WHITTEMORE, RYAN A,
725 Alder St, Montomery, AL 36113-6123, ryan.whittemore@us.army.mil
Specialties: Working using straight knives of his design or to customer specs. Patterns: Hunters, fighters, and Bowies. **Technical:** Forges 5160, 1084, 52100, O1. Flat grinds D2, A2, 440C. **Prices:** $100 to $200. **Remarks:** Part-time maker, first knife sold in 1994. Active duty military, frequent moves and/or deployments may affect deliver times. Due to frequent moves, email is the best contact method. **Mark:** Last name.

WHITWORTH, KEN J,
41667 Tetley Ave, Sterling Heights, MI 48078, Phone: 313-739-5720
Specialties: Working straight knives and folders. **Patterns:** Locking folders, slip joints and boot knives. **Technical:** Grinds 440C, 154CM and D2. **Prices:** $100 to $225; some to $450. **Remarks:** Part-time maker; first knife sold in 1976. **Mark:** Last name.

WICKER, DONNIE R,
2544 E 40th Ct, Panama City, FL 32405, Phone: 904-785-9158
Specialties: Traditional working and using straight knives of his design or to customer specs. **Patterns:** Hunters, fighters and slip-joint folders. **Technical:** Grinds 440C, ATS-34, D2 and 154CM. Heat-treats and does hardness testing. **Prices:** $90 to $200; some to $400. **Remarks:** Part-time maker; first knife sold in 1975. **Mark:** First and middle initials, last name.

WIGGINS, HORACE,
203 Herndon Box 152, Mansfield, LA 71502, Phone: 318-872-4471
Specialties: Fancy working knives. **Patterns:** Straight and folding hunters. **Technical:** Grinds O1, D2 and 440C. **Prices:** $90 to $275. **Remarks:** Part-time maker; first knife sold in 1970. **Mark:** Name, city and state in diamond logo.

WILCHER, WENDELL L,
RR 6 Box 6573, Palestine, TX 75801, Phone: 903-549-2530
Specialties: Fantasy, miniatures and working/using straight knives and folders of his design and to customer specs. **Patterns:** Fighters, hunters, locking folders. **Technical:** Hand works (hand file and hand sand knives), not grind. **Prices:** $75 to $250; some to $600. **Remarks:** Part-time maker; first knife sold in 1987. **Mark:** Initials, year, serial number.

WILE, PETER,
RR 3, Bridgewater, Nova Scotia, CANADA B4V 2W2, Phone: 902-543-1373, peterwile@ns.sympatico.ca
Specialties: Collector-grade one-of-a-kind file-worked folders. **Patterns:** Folders or fixed blades of his design or to customers specs. **Technical:** Grinds ATS-34, carbon and stainless Damascus. Does intricate filework on blades, spines and liners. Carves. Prefers natural handle materials. Does own heat treating. **Prices:** $350 to $2000; some to $4000. **Remarks:** Part-time maker; sold first knife in 1985; doing business as Wile Knives. **Mark:** Wile.

WILKINS, MITCHELL,
15523 Rabon Chapel Rd, Montgomery, TX 77316, Phone: 936-588-2696, mwilkins@consolidated.net

WILLEY, WG,
14210 Sugar Hill Rd, Greenwood, DE 19950, Phone: 302-349-4070, Web: www.willeyknives.com
Specialties: Fancy working straight knives. **Patterns:** Small game knives, Bowies and throwing knives. **Technical:** Grinds 440C and 154CM. **Prices:** $350 to $600; some to $1500. **Remarks:** Part-time maker; first knife sold in 1975. Owns retail store. **Mark:** Last name inside map logo.

WILLIAMS, JASON L,
PO Box 67, Wyoming, RI 02898, Phone: 401-539-8353, Fax: 401-539-0252
Specialties: Fancy and high tech folders of his design, co-inventor of the Axis Lock. **Patterns:** Fighters, locking folders, automatics and fancy pocket knives. **Technical:** Forges Damascus and other steels by request. Uses exotic handle materials and precious metals. Offers inlaid spines and gemstone thumb knobs. **Prices:** $1000 and up. **Remarks:** Full-time maker; first knife sold in 1989. **Mark:** First and last initials on pivot.

WILLIAMS JR., RICHARD,
1440 Nancy Circle, Morristown, TN 37814, Phone: 615-581-0059
Specialties: Working and using straight knives of his design or to customer specs. **Patterns:** Hunters, dirks and utility/camp knives. **Technical:** Forges 5160 and uses file steel. Hand-finish is standard; offers filework. **Prices:** $80 to $180; some to $250. **Remarks:** Spare-time maker; first knife sold in 1985. **Mark:** Last initial or full initials.

WILLIAMSON, TONY,
Rt 3 Box 503, Siler City, NC 27344, Phone: 919-663-3551
Specialties: Flint knapping: knives made of obsidian flakes and flint with wood, antler or bone for handles. **Patterns:** Skinners, daggers and flake knives. **Technical:** Blades have width/thickness ratio of at least 4 to 1. Hafts with methods available to prehistoric man. **Prices:** $58 to $160. **Remarks:** Student of Errett Callahan. **Mark:** Initials and number code to identify year and number of knives made.

WILLIS, BILL,
RT 7 Box 7549, Ava, MO 65608, Phone: 417-683-4326
Specialties: Forged blades, Damascus and carbon steel. **Patterns:** Cable, random or ladder lamented. **Technical:** Professionally heat treated blades. **Prices:** $75 to $600. **Remarks:** Lifetime guarantee on all blades against breakage. All work done by maker; including leather work. **Mark:** WF.

WILSON, CURTIS M,
PO Box 383, Burleson, TX 76097, Phone: 817-295-3732, cwknifeman@peoplepc.com; Web: www.cwilsonknives.com
Specialties: Traditional working/using knives, fixed blade, folders, slip joint, LinerLock® and lock back knives. Art knives, presentation grade Bowies, folder repair, heat treating services. Sub-zero quench. **Patterns:** Hunters, camp knives, military combat, single and multi-blade folders. Dr's knives large or small or custom design knives. **Technical:** Grinds ATS-34, 440C 52100, D2, S30V, CPM 154, mokume gane, engraves, scrimshaw, sheaths leather of kykex heat treating and file work. **Prices:** $150-750. **Remarks:** Part-time maker since 1984. Sold first knife in 1993. **Mark:** Curtis Wilson in ribbon or Curtis Wilson with hand made in a half moon.

WILSON, JAMES G,
PO Box 4024, Estes Park, CO 80517, Phone: 303-586-3944
Specialties: Bronze Age knives; Medieval and Scottish-styles; tomahawks. Patterns: Bronze knives, daggers, swords, spears and battle axes; 12-inch steel Misericorde daggers, sgian dubhs, "his and her" skinners, bird and fish knives, capers, boots and daggers. **Technical:** Casts bronze; grinds D2, 440C and ATS-34. **Prices:** $49 to $400; some to $1300. **Remarks:** Part-time maker; first knife sold in 1975. **Mark:** WilsonHawk.

WILSON, JON J,
1826 Ruby St, Johnstown, PA 15902, Phone: 814-266-6410
Specialties: Miniatures and full size. **Patterns:** Bowies, daggers and hunters. **Technical:** Grinds Damascus, 440C and O1. Scrimshaws and carves. **Prices:** $75 to $500; some higher. **Remarks:** Full-time maker; first knife sold in 1988. **Mark:** First and middle initials, last name.

WILSON, MIKE,
1416 McDonald Rd, Hayesville, NC 28904, Phone: 828-389-8145
Specialties: Fancy working and using straight knives of his design or to customer specs, folders. **Patterns:** Hunters, Bowies, utility knives, gut hooks, skinners, fighters and miniatures. **Technical:** Hollow grinds 440C, L6, O1 and D2. Mirror finishes are standard. Offers filework. **Prices:** $50 to $600. **Remarks:** Full-time maker; first knife sold in 1985. **Mark:** Last name.

WILSON, PHILIP C,
SEAMOUNT KNIFEWORKS, PO Box 846, Mountain Ranch, CA 95246, Phone: 209-754-1990, seamount@bigplanet.com; Web: www.seamountknifeworks.com
Specialties: Working knives; emphasis on salt water fillet knives and utility hunters of his design. **Patterns:** Fishing knives, hunters, kitchen knives. **Technical:** Grinds CPM S-30V, CPM10V, S-90V and CPM154. Heat-treats and Rockwell tests all blades. **Prices:** Start at $320. **Remarks:** First knife sold in 1985. Doing business as Sea-Mount Knife Works. **Mark:** Signature.

WILSON, RON,
2639 Greenwood Ave, Morro Bay, CA 93442, Phone: 805-772-3381
Specialties: Classic and fantasy straight knives of his design. **Patterns:** Daggers, fighters, swords and axes, mostly all miniatures. **Technical:** Forges and grinds Damascus and various tool steels; grinds meteorite. Uses gold, precious stones and exotic wood. **Prices:** Vary. **Remarks:** Part-time maker; first knives sold in 1995. **Mark:** Stamped first and last initials.

WILSON, RW,
PO Box 2012, Weirton, WV 26062, Phone: 304-723-2771
Specialties: Working straight knives; period pieces. Patterns: Bowies, tomahawks and patch knives. **Technical:** Grinds 440C; scrimshaws. **Prices:** $85 to $175; some to $1000. **Remarks:** Part-time maker; first knife sold in 1966. Knifemaker supplier. Offers free knife-making lessons. **Mark:** Name in tomahawk.

WILSON, STAN,
1908 Souvenir Dr, Clearwater, FL 33755, Phone: 727-461-1992, swilson@stanwilsonknives.com; Web: www.stanwilsonknives.com
Specialties: Fancy folders and automatics of his own design. **Patterns:** Locking liner folders, single and dual action autos, daggers. **Technical:** Stock removal, uses Damascus, stainless and high carbon steels, prefers ivory and pearl, Damascus with blued finishes and filework. **Prices:** $400 and up. **Remarks:** Member of Knifemakers Guild and Florida Knifemakers Association. Full-time maker will do custom orders. **Mark:** Name in script.

WILSON (SEE SIMONELLA, GIANLUIGI),

WINGO, GARY,
240 Ogeechee, Ramona, OK 74061, Phone: 918-536-1067, wingg_2000@yahoo.com; Web: www.geocities.com/wingg_2000/ gary.html
Specialties: Folder specialist. Steel 44OC, D2, others on request. Handle bone-stag, others on request. **Patterns:** Trapper three-blade stockman, four-blade congress, single-and two-blade barlows. **Prices:** 150 to $400. **Mark:** First knife sold 1994. Steer head with Wingo Knives or Straight line Wingo Knives.

WINGO, PERRY,
22 55th St, Gulfport, MS 39507, Phone: 228-863-3193
Specialties: Traditional working straight knives. **Patterns:** Hunters, skinners, Bowies and fishing knives. **Technical:** Grinds 440C. **Prices:** $75 to $1000. **Remarks:** Full-time maker; first knife sold in 1988. **Mark:** Last name.

WINKLER, DANIEL,
PO Box 2166, Blowing Rock, NC 28605, Phone: 828-295-9156, daniel@winklerknives.com; Web: www.winklerknives.com
Specialties: Forged cutlery styled in the tradition of an era past. **Patterns:** Fixed blades, friction folders, axes/tomahawks and war clubs. **Technical:** Forges and grinds carbon steels and his own Damascus. **Prices:** $200 to $4000. **Remarks:** Full-time maker since 1988. Exclusively offers leatherwork by Karen Shook. ABS Master Smith; Knifemakers Guild voting member. **Mark:** Initials connected.

WINN, TRAVIS A.,
558 E 3065 S, Salt Lake City, UT 84106, Phone: 801-467-5957
Specialties: Fancy working knives and knives to customer specs. **Patterns:** Hunters, fighters, boots, Bowies and fancy daggers, some miniatures, tantos and fantasy knives. **Technical:** Grinds D2 and 440C. Embellishes. **Prices:** $125 to $500; some higher. **Remarks:** Part-time maker; first knife sold in 1976. **Mark:** TRAV stylized.

WINSTON, DAVID,
1671 Red Holly St, Starkville, MS 39759, Phone: 601-323-1028
Specialties: Fancy and traditional knives of his design and to customer specs. **Patterns:** Bowies, daggers, hunters, boot knives and folders. **Technical:** Grinds 440C, ATS-34 and D2. Offers filework; heat-treats. **Prices:** $40 to $750; some higher. **Remarks:** Part-time maker; first knife sold in 1984. Offers lifetime sharpening for original owner. **Mark:** Last name.

WINTER, GEORGE,
5940 Martin Hwy, Union City, TN 38261

WIRTZ, ACHIM,
Mittelstrasse 58, Wuerselen, D-52146, GERMANY, Phone: 0049-2405-462-486, wootz@web.de; Web: www.7knifedwarfs.com
Specialties: Medieval, Scandinavian and Middle East-style knives. **Technical:** Forged blades only, Damascus steel, Woots, Mokume. **Prices:** Start at $200. **Remarks:** Part-time maker. First knife sold in 1997. **Mark:** Stylized initials.

WISE, DONALD,
304 Bexhill Rd, St Leonardo-On-Sea, East Sussex, TN3 8AL, ENGLAND
Specialties: Fancy and embellished working straight knives to customer specs. **Patterns:** Hunters, Bowies and daggers. **Technical:** Grinds Sandvik 12C27, D2 D3 and O1. Scrimshaws. **Prices:** $110 to $300; some to $500. **Remarks:** Full-time maker; first knife sold in 1983. **Mark:** KNIFECRAFT.

WITSAMAN, EARL,
3957 Redwing Circle, Stow, OH 44224, Phone: 330-688-4208, eawits@aol.com; Web: http://hometown.aol.com//eawits/ index.html
Specialties: Straight and fantasy miniatures. **Patterns:** Wide variety—Randalls to D-guard Bowies. **Technical:** Grinds O1, 440C and 300 stainless; buys Damascus; highly detailed work. **Prices:** $85 to $300. **Remarks:** Part-time maker; first knife sold in1974. **Mark:** Initials.

WOLF, BILL,
4618 N 79th Ave, Phoenix, AZ 85033, Phone: 623-846-3585, Fax: 623-846-3585, wolfknives@yahoo.com
Specialties: Investor-grade folders and straight knives. Patterns: Lockback, slip joint and side lock interframes. **Technical:** Grinds ATS-34 and 440C. **Prices:** $400 to $10,000. **Remarks:** Full-time maker; first knife sold in 1989. **Mark:** Name.

WOLF JR., WILLIAM LYNN,
4006 Frank Rd, Lagrange, TX 78945, Phone: 409-247-4626

WOOD, ALAN,
Greenfield Villa, Greenhead, Brampton CA8 7HH, ENGLAND, a.wood@knivesfreeserve.co.uk; Web: www.alanwoodknives.co.uk
Specialties: High-tech working straight knives of his design. **Patterns:** Hunters, utility/camp and bushcraft knives. **Technical:** Grinds 12027, RWL-34, stainless Damascus and O1. Blades are cryogenic treated. **Prices:** $200 to $800; some to $750. **Remarks:** Full-time maker; first knife sold in 1979. Not currently taking orders. **Mark:** Full name with stag tree logo.

WOOD, LARRY B,
6945 Fishburg Rd, Huber Heights, OH 45424, Phone: 513-233-6751
Specialties: Fancy working knives of his design. **Patterns:** Hunters, buckskinners, Bowies, tomahawks, locking folders and Damascus miniatures. **Technical:** Forges 1095, file steel and his own Damascus. **Prices:** $125 to $500; some to $2000. **Remarks:** Full-time maker; first knife sold in 1974. Doing business as Wood's Metal Studios. **Mark:** Variations of last name, sometimes with blacksmith logo.

WOOD, OWEN DALE,
6492 Garrison St, Arvada, CO 80004-3157, Phone: 303-456-2748, wood.owen@gmail.com; Web: www.owenwoodcustomknives.com
Specialties: Folding knives and daggers. **Patterns:** Own Damascus, specialties in 456 composite blades. **Technical:** Materials: Damascus stainless steel, exotic metals, gold, rare handle materials. **Prices:** $1000 to $9000. **Remarks:** Folding knives in art deco and art noveau themes. Full-time maker from 1981. **Mark:** OWEN WOOD.

WOOD, WEBSTER,
22041 Shelton Trail, Atlanta, MI 49709, Phone: 989-785-2996, littlewolf@racc2000.com
Specialties: Works mainly in stainless; art knives, Bowies, hunters and folders. **Remarks:** Full-time maker; first knife sold in 1980. Guild member since 1984. All engraving done by maker. **Mark:** Initials inside shield and name.

WRIGHT, KEVIN,
671 Leland Valley Rd W, Quilcene, WA 98376-9517, Phone: 360-765-3589, kevinw@ptpc.com
Specialties: Fancy working or collector knives to customer specs. **Patterns:** Hunters, boots, buckskinners, miniatures. **Technical:** Forges and grinds L6, 1095, 440C and his own Damascus. **Prices:** $75 to $500; some to $2000. **Remarks:** Part-time maker; first knife sold in 1978. **Mark:** Last initial in anvil.

WRIGHT, L T,
1523 Pershing Ave, Steubenville, OH 43952, Phone: 740-282-4947, knifemkr@sbcglobal.net; Web: www.ltwrightknives.com
Specialties: Hunting and tactical knives. **Patterns:** Drop point hunters, bird, trout and tactical. **Technical:** Grinds D2, 440C and O1. **Remarks:** Full-time maker.

WRIGHT, RICHARD S,
PO Box 201, 111 Hilltop Dr, Carolina, RI 02812, Phone: 401-364-3579, rswswitchblades@hotmail.com; Web: www.richardswright.com
Specialties: Bolster release switchblades. **Patterns:** Folding fighters, gents pocket knives, one-of-a-kind high-grade automatics. **Technical:** Reforges and grinds various makers Damascus. Uses a variety of tool steels. Uses natural handle material such as ivory and pearl, extensive file-work on most knives. **Prices:** $2000 and up. **Remarks:** Part-time knifemaker with background as a gunsmith. Made first folder in 1991. **Mark:** RSW on blade, all folders are serial numbered.

WRIGHT, TIMOTHY,
PO Box 3746, Sedona, AZ 86340, Phone: 928-282-4180
Specialties: High-tech folders and working knives. **Patterns:** Interframe locking folders, non-inlaid folders, straight hunters and kitchen knives. **Technical:** Grinds BG-42, AEB-L, K190 and Cowry X; works with new steels. All folders can disassemble and are furnished with tools. **Prices:** $150 to $1800; some to $3000. **Remarks:** Full-time maker; first knife sold in 1975. **Mark:** Last name and type of steel used.

WUERTZ, TRAVIS,
2487 E Hwy 287, Casa Grande, AZ 85222, Phone: 520-723-4432

WYATT, WILLIAM R,
Box 237, Rainelle, WV 25962, Phone: 304-438-5494
Specialties: Classic and working knives of all designs. Patterns: Hunters and utility knives. **Technical:** Forges and grinds saw blades, files and rasps. Prefers stag handles. **Prices:** $45 to $95; some to $350. **Remarks:** Part-time maker; first knife sold in 1990. **Mark:** Last name in star with knife logo.

Y

YASHINSKI, JOHN L,
207 N Platt, PO Box 1284, Red Lodge, MT 59068, Phone: 406-446-3916
Specialties: Native American Beaded sheathes. **Prices:** Vary.

YEATES, JOE A,
730 Saddlewood Circle, Spring, TX 77381, Phone: 281-367-2765, joeyeates291@cs.com; Web: www.yeatesBowies.com
Specialties: Bowies and period pieces. Patterns: Bowies, toothpicks and combat knives. **Technical:** Grinds 440C, D2 and ATS-34. **Prices:** $600 to $2500. **Remarks:** Full-time maker; first knife sold in 1975. **Mark:** Last initial within outline of Texas; or last initial.

YESKOO, RICHARD C,
76 Beekman Rd, Summit, NJ 07901

YORK, DAVID C,
PO Box 3166, Chino Valley, AZ 86323, Phone: 928-636-1709
Specialties: Working straight knives and folders. **Patterns:** Prefers small hunters and skinners; locking folders. **Technical:** Grinds D2 and 440C; buys Damascus. **Prices:** $75 to $300; some to $600. **Remarks:** Part-time maker; first knife sold in 1975. **Mark:** Last name.

YOSHIHARA, YOSHINDO,
8-17-11 Takasago Katsushi, Tokyo, JAPAN

YOSHIKAZU, KAMADA,
, 540-3 Kaisaki Niuta-cho, Tokushima, JAPAN, Phone: 0886-44-2319

YOSHIO, MAEDA,
, 3-12-11 Chuo-cho tamashima Kurashiki-city, Okayama, JAPAN, Phone: 086-525-2375

YOUNG, BUD,
Box 336, Port Hardy, BC, CANADA V0N 2P0, Phone: 250-949-6478
Specialties: Fixed blade, working knives, some fancy. **Patterns:** Drop-points to skinners. **Technical:** Hollow or flat grind, 5160, 440C, mostly ATS-34, satin finish. **Prices:** $150 to $500 CDN. **Remarks:** Spare-time maker; making knives since 1962; first knife sold in 1985. Not taking orders at this time, sell as produced. **Mark:** Name.

YOUNG, CLIFF,
Fuente De La Cibeles No 5, Atascadero, San Miguel De Allende, GTO., MEXICO, Phone: 37700, Fax: 011-52-415-2-57-11
Specialties: Working knives. **Patterns:** Hunters, fighters and fishing knives. **Technical:** Grinds all; offers D2, 440C and 154CM. **Prices:** Start at $250. **Remarks:** Part-time maker; first knife sold in 1980. **Mark:** Name.

YOUNG, ERROL,
4826 Storey Land, Alton, IL 62002, Phone: 618-466-4707
Specialties: Traditional working straight knives and folders. **Patterns:** Wide range, including tantos, Bowies, miniatures and multi-blade folders. **Technical:** Grinds D2, 440C and ATS-34. **Prices:** $75 to $650; some to $800. **Remarks:** Part-time maker; first knife sold in 1987. **Mark:** Last name with arrow.

YOUNG, GEORGE,
713 Pinoak Dr, Kokomo, IN 46901, Phone: 765-457-8893
Specialties: Fancy/embellished and traditional straight knives and folders of his design and to customer specs. **Patterns:** Hunters, fillet/camp knives and locking folders. **Technical:** Grinds 440C, CPM440V, and stellite 6K. Fancy ivory, black pearl and stag for handles. Filework: all stellite construction (6K and 25 alloys). Offers engraving. **Prices:** $350 to $750; some $1500 to $3000. **Remarks:** Full-time maker; first knife sold in 1954. Doing business as Young's Knives. **Mark:** Last name integral inside Bowie.

YOUNG, RAYMOND L,
CUTLER/BLADESMITH, 2922 Hwy 188E, Mt. Ida, AR 71957, Phone: 870-867-3947
Specialties: Cutler-Bladesmith, sharpening service. **Patterns:** Hunter, skinners, fighters, no guard, no ricasso, chef tools. **Technical:** Edge tempered 1095, 516C, mosiac handles, water buffalo and exotic woods. **Prices:** $100 and up. **Remarks:** Federal contractor since 1995. Surgical steel sharpening. **Mark:** R.

YURCO, MIKE,
PO Box 712, Canfield, OH 44406, Phone: 330-533-4928, shorinki@aol.com
Specialties: Working straight knives. **Patterns:** Hunters, utility knives, Bowies and fighters, push knives, claws and other hideouts. **Technical:** Grinds 440C, ATS-34 and 154CM; likes mirror and satin finishes. **Prices:** $20 to $500. **Remarks:** Part-time maker; first knife sold in 1983. **Mark:** Name, steel, serial number.

Z

ZACCAGNINO JR., DON,
2256 Bacom Point Rd, Pahokee, FL 33476-2622, Phone: 561-924-7032, zackknife@aol.com
Specialties: Working knives and some period pieces of their designs. Patterns: Heavy-duty hunters, axes and Bowies; a line of light-weight hunters, fillets and personal knives. **Technical:** Grinds 440C and 17-4 PH; highly finished in complex handle and blade treatments. **Prices:** $165 to $500; some to $2500. **Remarks:** Part-time maker; first knife sold in 1969 by Don Zaccagnino Sr. **Mark:** ZACK, city and state inside oval.

ZAHM, KURT,
488 Rio Casa, Indialantic, FL 32903, Phone: 407-777-4860
Specialties: Working straight knives of his design or to customer specs. **Patterns:** Daggers, fancy fighters, Bowies, hunters and utility knives. **Technical:** Grinds D2, 440C; likes filework. **Prices:** $75 to $1000. **Remarks:** Part-time maker; first knife sold in 1985. **Mark:** Last name.

ZAKABI, CARL S,
PO Box 893161, Mililani Town, HI 96789-0161, Phone: 808-626-2181
Specialties: Working and using straight knives of his design. **Patterns:** Fighters, hunters and utility/camp knives. **Technical:** Grinds 440C and ATS-34. **Prices:** $90 to $400. **Remarks:** Spare-time maker; first knife sold in 1988. Doing business as Zakabi's Knifeworks LLC. **Mark:** Last name and state inside a Hawaiian sharktooth dagger.

ZAKHAROV, GLADISTON,
Bairro Rio Comprido, Rio Comprido Jacarei, Jacaret SP, BRAZIL 12302-070, Phone: 55 12 3958 4021, Fax: 55 12 3958 4103, arkhip@terra.com.br; Web: www.arkhip.com.br
Specialties: Using straight knives of his design. **Patterns:** Hunters, kitchen, utility/camp and barbecue knives. **Technical:** Grinds his own "secret steel." **Prices:** $30 to $200. **Remarks:** Full-time maker. **Mark:** Arkhip Special Knives.

ZBORIL, TERRY,
5320 CR 130, Caldwell, TX 77836, Phone: 979-535-4157, terry.zboril@worldnet.att.net
Specialties: ABS Journeyman Smith.

ZEMBKO III, JOHN,
140 Wilks Pond Rd, Berlin, CT 06037, Phone: 860-828-3503, johnzembko@hotmail.com
Specialties: Working knives of his design or to customer specs. **Patterns:** Likes to use stabilized high-figured woods. **Technical:** Grinds ATS-34, A2, D2; forges O1, 1095; grinds Damasteel. **Prices:** $50 to $400; some higher. **Remarks:** First knife sold in 1987. **Mark:** Name.

ZEMITIS, JOE,
14 Currawong Rd, Cardiff Hts, 2285 Newcastle, AUSTRALIA, Phone: 0249549907, jjvzem@networksmm.com.au
Specialties: Traditional working straight knives. **Patterns:** Hunters, Bowies, tantos, fighters and camp knives. **Technical:** Grinds O1, D2, W2 and 440C; makes his own Damascus. Embellishes; offers engraving and scrimshaw. **Prices:** $150 to $3000. **Remarks:** Full-time maker; first knife sold in 1983. **Mark:** First initial, last name and country, or last name.

ZIMA, MICHAEL F,
732 State St, Ft. Morgan, CO 80701, Phone: 970-867-6078, Web: http://www.zimaknives.com
Specialties: Working and collector quality straight knives and folders. **Patterns:** Hunters, lock backs, LinerLock®, slip joint and automatic folders. **Technical:** Grinds Damascus, 440C, ATS-34 and 154CM. **Prices:** $200 and up. **Remarks:** Full-time maker; first knife sold in 1982. **Mark:** Last name.

ZINKER, BRAD,
BZ KNIVES, 1591 NW 17 St, Homestead, FL 33030, Phone: 305-216-0404, bzknives@aol.com
Specialties: Fillets, folders and hunters. **Technical:** Uses ATS-34 and stainless Damascus. **Prices:** $200 to $600. **Remarks:** Voting member of Knifemakers Guild and Florida Knifemakers Association. **Mark:** Offset connected initials BZ.

ZIRBES, RICHARD,
Neustrasse 15, D-54526 Niederkail, GERMANY, Phone: 0049 6575 1371
Specialties: Fancy embellished knives with engraving and self-made scrimshaw (scrimshaw made by maker). High-tech working knives and high-tech hunters, boots, fighters and folders. All knives made by hand. **Patterns:** Boots, fighters, folders, hunters. **Technical:** Uses only the best steels for blade material like CPM-T 440V, CPM-T 420V, ATS-34, D2, C440, stainless Damascus or steel according to customer's desire. **Prices:** Working knives and hunters: $200 to $600. Fancy embellished knives with engraving and/or scrimshaw: $800 to $3000. **Remarks:** Part-time maker; first knife sold in 1991. Member of the German Knifemaker Guild. **Mark:** Zirbes or R. Zirbes.

ZOWADA, TIM,
4509 E Bear River Rd, Boyne Falls, MI 49713, Phone: 231-348-5446, knifeguy@nmo.net
Specialties: Working knives, some fancy. **Patterns:** Hunters, camp knives, boots, swords, fighters, tantos and locking folders. **Technical:** Forges O2, L6, W2 and his own Damascus. **Prices:** $150 to $1000; some to $5000. **Remarks:** Full-time maker; first knife sold in 1980.

ZSCHERNY, MICHAEL,
1840 Rock Island Dr, Ely, IA 52227, Phone: 319-848-3629, zschernyknives@aol.com
Specialties: Quality folding knives. **Patterns:** Liner-lock and lock-back folders in titanium, working straight knives. **Technical:** Grinds ATS-34 and commercial Damascus, prefers natural materials such as pearls and ivory. **Prices:** Starting at $500. **Remarks:** Full-time maker, first knife sold in 1978. **Mark:** Last name, city and state; folders, last name with stars inside folding knife.

AK

Barlow, Jana Poirier — Anchorage
Brennan, Judson — Delta Junction
Breuer, Lonnie — Wasilla
Broome, Thomas A — Kenai
Cannon, Raymond W — Homer
Cawthorne, Christopher A — Wrangell
Chamberlin, John A — Anchorage
Cutting Edge, The, Mark — Fairbanks
Dempsey, Gordon S — N. Kenai
Dufour, Arthur J — Anchorage
England, Virgil — Anchorage
Flint, Robert — Anchorage
Gouker, Gary B — Sitka
Grebe, Gordon S — Anchor Point
Hibben, Westley G — Anchorage
Hook, Bob — North Pole
Hook, Bob — North Pole
Kelsey, Nate — Anchorage
Knapp, Ron — Fairbanks
Lance, Bill — Eagle River
Malaby, Raymond J — Juneau
Mcfarlin, Eric E — Kodiak
Miller, Nate — Fairbanks
Miller, Ron — NORTH POLE
Mirabile, David — Juneau
Moore, Marve — Willow
Parrish Iii, Gordon A — North Pole
Quattlebaum, Craig — Eagle River
Richards, Ralph (Bud) — Bauxite
Shore, John I — Kenai
Stegall, Keith — Wasilla
Van Cleve, Steve — Sutton
Whipple, Wesley A — Kodiak
Whitman, Jim — Chugiak

AL

Andress, Ronnie — Satsuma
Batson, James — Madison
Baxter, Dale — Trinity
Bell, Tony — Woodland
Bowles, Chris — Reform
Brend, Walter — Vinemont
Bullard, Bill — Andalusia
Coffman, Danny — Jacksonville
Conn Jr., C T — Attalla
Daniels, Alex — Town Creek
Dark, Robert — Oxford
Di Marzo, Richard — Birmingham
Durham, Kenneth — Cherokee
Elrod, Roger R — Enterprise
Fikes, Jimmy L — Jasper
Fogg, Don — Jasper
Fowler, Ricky And Susan — Robertsdale
Gilbreath, Randall — Dora
Golden, Randy — Montgomery
Hammond, Jim — Arab
Howard, Durvyn M — Hokes Bluff
Howell, Len — Opelika
Howell, Ted — Wetumpka
Huckabee, Dale — Maylene
Hulsey, Hoyt — Attalla
Mccullough, Jerry — Georgiana
Militano, Tom — Jacksonville
Morris, C H — Frisco City
Pardue, Melvin M — Repton
Roe Jr., Fred D — Huntsville
Russell, Tom — Jacksonville
Sandlin, Larry — Adamsville
Sinyard, Cleston S — Elberta
Thomas, David E — Lillian
Watson, Billy — Deatsville
Whittemore, Ryan A — Montomery

AR

Anders, David — Center Ridge
Ardwin, Corey — North Little Rock
Barnes Jr., Cecil C. — Center Ridge
Brown, Jim — Little Rock
Browning, Steven W — Benton
Bullard, Tom — Flippin
Cabe, Jerry (Buddy) — Hattieville
Cook, James R — Nashville
Copeland, Thom — Nashville
Crawford, Pat And Wes — West Memphis
Crowell, James L — Mtn. View
Dozier, Bob — Springdale
Duvall, Fred — Benton
Echols, Roger — Nashville
Edge, Tommy — Cash
Ferguson, Lee — Hindsville
Ferguson, Linda — Hindsville
Fisk, Jerry — Nashville
Fitch, John S — Clinton
Flournoy, Joe — El Dorado
Foster, Ronnie E — Morrilton
Foster, Timothy L — El Dorado
Frizzell, Ted — West Fork
Gadberry, Emmet — Hattieville
Greenaway, Don — Fayetteville
Herring, Morris — Dyer
Lane, Ben — North Little Rock
Lawrence, Alton — De Queen
Livesay, Newt — Siloam Springs
Lunn, Gail — Mountain Home
Lunn, Larry A — Mountain Home
Martin, Bruce E — Prescott
Martin, Hal W — Morrilton
Massey, Roger — Texarkana
Newton, Ron — London
O'Dell, Clyde — Camden
Olive, Michael E — Leslie
Passmore, Jimmy D — Hoxie
Perry, Jim — Hope
Perry, John — Mayflower
Peterson, Lloyd (Pete) C — Clinton
Polk, Clifton — Van Buren
Polk, Rusty — Van Buren
Red, Vernon — Conway
Rhea, Lin — Prattsville
Richards, Ralph (Bud) — Bauxite
Sisemore, Charles Russel — Mena
Smoker, Ray — Searcy
Solomon, Marvin — Paron
Stanley, John — Crossett
Stout, Charles — Gillham
Sweaza, Dennis — Austin
Townsend, Allen Mark — Texarkana
Tycer, Art — Paron
Walker, Jim — Morrilton
Ward, Chuck — Benton
Waters, Herman Harold — Magnolia
Waters, Lu — Magnolia
White, Bryce — Little Rock
Young, Raymond L — Mt. Ida

ARGENTINA

Ayarragaray, Cristian L. — (3100) Parana-Entre Rios
Bertolami, Juan Carlos — Neuquen
Gibert, Pedro — San Rafael Mendoza
Kehiayan, Alfredo — CP B1623GXU Buenos Aires
Rho, Nestor Lorenzo — Buenos Aires
Santiago, Abud — Buenos Aires 1416

AUSTRALIA

Bennett, Peter — Engadine N.S.W. 2233
Brodziak, David — Albany
Crawley, Bruce R — Croydon 3136 Victoria
Cross, Robert — Tamworth 2340, NSW
Del Raso, Peter — Mt. Waverly, Victoria, 3149
Gerner, Thomas — Western Australia
Giljevic, Branko — N.S.W.
Green, William (Bill) — View Bank Vic.
Harvey, Max — Perth 6155, Western Australia
Husiak, Myron — Victoria
Jones, John — Gympie, Queensland 4570
K B S, Knives — Vic 3450
Maisey, Alan — Vincentia 2540, NSW
Mcintyre, Shawn — Hawthorn East Victoria
Spencer, Keith — Chidlow Western Australia
Tasman, Kerley — Western Australia
Zemitis, Joe — 2285 Newcastle

AUSTRIA

Poskocil, Helmut — A-3340 Waidhofen/Ybbs

AZ

Ammons, David C — Tucson
Bennett, Glen C — Tucson
Birdwell, Ira Lee — Bagdad
Boye, David — Dolan Springs
Bryan, Tom — Gilbert
Cheatham, Bill — Laveen
Choate, Milton — Somerton
Dawson, Lynn — Prescott Valley
Dodd, Robert F — Camp Verde
Fuegen, Larry — Prescott
Goo, Tai — Tucson
Hancock, Tim — Scottsdale
Hankins, R — Tempe
Hoel, Steve — Pine
Holder, D'Alton — Peoria
Hull, Michael J — Cottonwood
Karp, Bob — Phoenix
Kiley, Mike And Jandy — Chino Valley
Kopp, Todd M — Apache Jct.
Lampson, Frank G — Rimrock
Lee, Randy — St. Johns
Mcfall, Ken — Lakeside
Mcfarlin, J W — Lake Havasu City
Miller, Michael — Kingman
Mooney, Mike — Queen Creek
Newhall, Tom — Tucson
Norris, Don — Tucson
Purvis, Bob And Ellen — Tucson
Robbins, Bill — Globe
Rybar Jr., Raymond B — Phoenix
Snare, Michael — Phoenix
Tamboli, Michael — Glendale
Tollefson, Barry A — Tubac
Torgeson, Samuel L — Sedona
Tyre, Michael A — Wickenburg
Weiler, Donald E — Yuma
Weiss, Charles L — Phoenix
Wolf, Bill — Phoenix
Wright, Timothy — Sedona
Wuertz, Travis — Casa Grande
York, David C — Chino Valley

BELGIUM

Dox, Jan — B 2900 Schoten
Monteiro, Victor — 1360 Maleves Ste Marie

BRAZIL

Bodolay, Antal
Belo Horizonte MG-31730-700
Bossaerts, Carl
14051-110, Ribeirao Preto, S.P.
Campos, Ivan — Tatui, SP
Dorneles, Luciano Oliverira
Nova Petropolis, RS
Gaeta, Angelo — SP-17201-310
Gaeta, Roberto — Sao Paulo
Garcia, Mario Eiras
Sao Paulo SP-05516-070
Lala, Paulo Ricardo P And Lala, Roberto P. — SP- 19031-260
Neto Jr., Nelson And De Carvalho, Henrique M. — SP-12900-000
Paulo, Fernandes R — Sao Paulo
Petean, Francisco And Mauricio
SP-16200-000
Ricardo Romano, Bernardes Itajuba MG
Sfreddo, Rodrigo Menezes
cep g5 150-000
Tkoma, Flavio — Prudonte SP19031-220
Vilar, Ricardo Augusto Ferreira Mairipora Sao Paulo
Villa, Luiz — Sao Paulo, SP-04537-081
Villar, Ricardo — S.P. 07600-000
Zakharov, Gladiston — Jacaret SP

CA

Abegg, Arnie — Huntington Beach
Abernathy, Paul J — Eureka
Adkins, Richard L — Mission Viejo
Aldrete, Bob — Lomita
Athey, Steve — Riverside
Barnes, Gregory — Altadena
Barron, Brian — San Mateo
Benson, Don — Escalon
Berger, Max A. — Carmichael
Biggers, Gary — Ventura
Blum, Chuck — Brea
Bost, Roger E — Palos Verdes
Boyd, Francis — Berkeley
Brack, Douglas D — Ventura
Breshears, Clint — Manhattan Beach
Brooks, Buzz — Los Angles
Browne, Rick — Upland
Brunetta, David — Laguna Beach
Butler, Bart — Ramona
Cabrera, Sergio B — Wilmington
Cantrell, Kitty D — Ramona
Caston, Darriel — Sacramento
Caswell, Joe — Newbury
Clark, R W — Corona
Coffey, Bill — Clovis
Cohen, Terry A — Laytonville
Coleman, John A — Citrus Heightss
Connolly, James — Oroville
Davis, Charlie — Santee
De Maria Jr., Angelo — Carmel Valley
Dion, Greg — Oxnard
Dixon Jr., Ira E — Ventura
Doolittle, Mike — Novato
Driscoll, Mark — La Mesa
Ellis, Dave/Abs Mastersmith — Vista
Ellis, William Dean — Sanger
Emerson, Ernest R — Torrance
English, Jim — Jamul
Ernest, Phil — Wittier
Ernest, Phil (Pj) — Whittier
Essegian, Richard — Fresno
Felix, Alexander — Torrance
Ferguson, Jim — Temecula
Fisher, Theo (Ted) — Montague
Forrest, Brian — Descanso
Fraley, D B — Dixon
Fraley, D B — Dixon
Francis, Vance — Alpine
Fred, Reed Wyle — Sacramento
Freer, Ralph — Seal Beach
Fulton, Mickey — Willows
Girtner, Joe — Brea
Gofourth, Jim — Santa Paula
Guarnera, Anthony R — Quartzhill
Guidry, Bruce — Murrieta
Hall, Jeff — Los Alamitos
Hardy, Scott — Placerville
Harris, Jay — Redwood City
Harris, John — Riverside
Hartsfield, Phill — Newport Beach
Hayes, Dolores — Los Angeles
Helton, Roy — San Diego
Herndon, Wm R "Bill" — Acton
Hink Iii, Les — Stockton
Hoy, Ken — North Fork
Humenick, Roy — Rescue
Iames, Gary — Tahoe
Jacks, Jim — Covina
Jackson, David — Lemoore
Jensen, John Lewis — Pasadena
Johnson, Randy — Turlock
Kazsuk, David — Perris
Keyes, Dan — Chino
Kilpatrick, Christian A — Citrus Hieghts
Koster, Steven C — Huntington Beach
Laner, Dean — Susanville
Larson, Richard — Turlock
Leland, Steve — Fairfax
Likarich, Steve — Colfax
Lockett, Sterling — Burbank
Loveless, R W — Riverside
Luchini, Bob — Palo Alto
Mackie, John — Whittier
Massey, Ron — Joshua Tree
Mata, Leonard — San Diego
Maxwell, Don — Clovis
Mcabee, William — Colfax
Mcclure, Michael — Menlo Park
Mcgrath, Patrick T — Westchester
Melin, Gordon C — La Mirada
Meloy, Sean — Lemon Grove
Montano, Gus A — San Diego
Morgan, Jeff — Santee
Moses, Steven — Santa Ana
Mountain Home Knives, — Jamul
Naten, Greg — Bakersfield
Orton, Rich — Riverside
Osborne, Donald H — Clovis
Packard, Bob — Elverta
Palm, Rik — San Diego
Pendleton, Lloyd — Volcano
Perry, Chris — Fresno
Pfanenstiel, Dan — Modesto
Phillips, Randy — Ontario
Pitt, David F — Anderson
Posner, Barry E — N. Hollywood
Richards Jr., Alvin (Chuck) — Fortuna
Rodebaugh, James L — Oak Hills
Rozas, Clark D — Wilmington
Schmitz, Raymond E — Valley Center
Schneider, Herman — Apple Valley
Schroen, Karl — Sebastopol
Sibrian, Aaron — Ventura
Sjostrand, Kevin — Visalia
Slobodian, Barbara — San Andreas
Slobodian, Scott — San Andreas
Smith, Shawn — Clouis
Sornberger, Jim — Volcano
St. Cyr, H Red — Wilmington
Stapel, Chuck — Glendale
Steinberg, Al — Laguna Woods
Stimps, Jason M — Orange
Stockwell, Walter — Redwood City
Stover, Howard — Pasadena
Strider, Mick — San Marcos
Terrill, Stephen — Springville
Tingle, Dennis P — Jackson
Trace Rinaldi Custom Blades, — Hemet
Tru-Grit Inc., — Ontario
Trujillo, Adam — Rohnert Park
Trujillo, Miranda — Rohnert Park
Trujillo, Thomas A — Rohnert Park
Vagnino, Michael — Visalia
Van Riper, James N — Citrus Heights
Velick, Sammy — Los Angeles
Warren, Al — Roseville
Watanabe, Wayne — Montebello
Weinstock, Robert — San Francisco
Wilson, Philip C — Mountain Ranch
Wilson, Ron — Morro Bay

CANADA

Arnold, Joe — London, Ont.
Beauchamp, Gaetan — Stoneham, PQ
Beets, Marty — Williams Lake, BC
Bell, Donald — Bedford, Nova Scotia
Berg, Lothar — Kitchener ON
Beshara, Brent (Besh) — Stayner, Ont.
Boos, Ralph — Edmonton, Alberta
Bourbeau, Jean Yves — Ile Perrot, Quebec
Bradford, Garrick — Kitchener ON
Dallyn, Kelly — Calgary, AB
Debraga, Jose C — Aux Lievres, Quebec
Debraga, Jovan — Quebec
Deringer, Christoph — Cookshire, Quebec
Diotte, Jeff — LaSalle Ontario
Doiron, Donald — Messines, PQ
Doucette, R — Brantford, Ont.
Doussot, Laurent — Montreal, Quebec
Downie, James T — Port Franks, Ont.
Dublin, Dennis — Enderby, B.C.
Freeman, John — Cambridge, Ont.
Frigault, Rick — Niagara Falls, Ont.
Garvock, Mark W — Balderson, Ont.
Gilbert, Chantal — Quebec City Quebec
Haslinger, Thomas — Calgary, AB
Hayes, Wally — Orleans, Ont.
Hindmarch, G — Carlyle SK S0C 0R0
Hofer, Louis — Rose Prairie, B.C.
Jobin, Jacques — Levis Quebec
Kaczor, Tom — Upper London, Ont.
Lambert, Kirby — Regina Saskatchewan S4N X3
Langley, Mick — Qualicum Beach, B.C.
Lay, R J (Bob) — Logan Lake, B.C.
Leber, Heinz — Hudson's Hope, B.C.
Lightfoot, Greg — Kitscoty, AB
Linklater, Steve — Aurora, Ont.
Loerchner, Wolfgang — Bayfield, Ont.
Lyttle, Brian — High River, AB
Maneker, Kenneth — Galiano Island, B.C.
Marzitelli, Peter — Langley, B.C.
Massey, Al — Mount Uniacke, Nova Scotia
Mckenzie, David Brian — Campbell River B
Miville-Deschenes, Alain — Quebec
O'Hare, Sean — Fort Simpson, NT
Olson, Rod — High River, AB
Painter, Tony — Whitehorse Yukon
Patrick, Bob — S. Surrey, B.C.

Pepiot, Stephan Winnipeg, Man.
Piesner, Dean Conestogo, Ont.
Roberts, George A Whitehorse, YT
Ross, Tim Thunder Bay, Ont.
Schoenfeld, Matthew A Galiano Island, B.C.
St. Amour, Murray Pembroke ON
Stancer, Chuck Calgary, AB
Storch, Ed Alberta T0B 2W0
Stuart, Steve Gores Landing, Ont.
Tichbourne, George Mississauga, Ont.
Tighe, Brian St. Catharines, Ont.
Toner, Roger Pickering, Ont.
Treml, Glenn Thunder Bay, Ont.
Vanderkolff, Stephen Mildmay Ontario
Whitenect, Jody Nova Scotia
Wile, Peter Bridgewater, Nova Scotia
Young, Bud Port Hardy, BC

CO

Anderson, Mark Alan Denver
Anderson, Mel Hotchkiss
Barrett, Cecil Terry Colorado Springs
Booco, Gordon Hayden
Brandon, Matthew Denver
Brock, Kenneth L Allenspark
Burrows, Chuck Durango
Dannemann, Randy Hotchkiss
Davis, Don Loveland
Dawson, Barry Durango
Delong, Dick Aurora
Dennehy, Dan Del Norte
Dennehy, John D Wellington
Dill, Robert Loveland
Fronefield, Daniel Peyton
High, Tom Alamosa
Hughes, Ed Grand Junction
Irie, Michael L Colorado Springs
Kitsmiller, Jerry Montrose
Leck, Dal Hayden
Magruder, Jason Colorado Springs
Miller, Hanford J Cowdrey
Miller, M A Northglenn
Olson, Wayne C Bailey
Ott, Fred Durango
Owens, John Nathrop
Roberts, Chuck Golden
Rollert, Steve Keenesburg
Ronzio, N. Jack Fruita
Sanders, Bill Mancos
Thompson, Lloyd Pagosa Springs
Waites, Richard L Broomfield
Watson, Bert Westminster
Wilson, James G Estes Park
Wood, Owen Dale Arvada
Zima, Michael F Ft. Morgan

CT

Barnes, William Wallingford
Buebendorf, Robert E Monroe
Chapo, William G Wilton
Framski, Walter P Prospect
Jean, Gerry Manchester
Lepore, Michael J Bethany
Meyer, Christopher J Tolland
Padgett Jr., Edwin L New London
Plunkett, Richard West Cornwall
Putnam, Donald S Wethersfield
Rainville, Richard Salem
Riden, Doug Eastford
Turecek, Jim Ansonia
Vitale, Mace Guilford
Zembko Iii, John Berlin

DE

Antonio Jr., William J Newark
Schneider, Karl A Newark
Willey, Wg Greenwood

DENMARK

Andersen, Henrik Lefolii 3480, Fredensborg
Anso, Jens 116, 8472 Sporup
Bentzen, Leif
Dyrnoe, Per DK 3400 Hilleroed
Henriksen, Hans J DK 3200 Helsinge
Strande, Poul Dastrup 4130 Viby Sj.
Vensild, Henrik DK-8963 Auning

ENGLAND

Boden, Harry Derbyshire DE4 2AJ
Farid R, Mehr Kent
Harrington, Roger East Sussex
Jackson, Jim Chapel Row Bucklebury RG7 6PU
Jones, Charles Anthony No. Devon E31 4AL
Morris, Darrell Price Devon
Penfold, MickTremar, Cornwall PL14 5SJ
Wardell, Mick N Devon EX39 3BU
Wise, Donald East Sussex, TN3 8AL
Wood, Alan Brampton CA8 7HH

EUROPE

Sprokholt, Rob Netherlands

FL

Adams, Les Hialeah
Anders, Jerome Miramar
Angell, Jon Hawthorne
Atkinson, Dick Wausau
Bacon, David R. Bradenton
Barry Iii, James J. West Palm Beach
Bartrug, Hugh E. St. Petersburg
Beckett, Norman L. Satsuma
Beers, Ray Lake Wales
Benjamin Jr., George Kissimmee
Birnbaum, Edwin Miami
Blackwood, Neil Lakeland
Bosworth, Dean Key Largo
Bradley, John Pomona Park
Bray Jr., W Lowell New Port Richey
Brown, Harold E Arcadia
Burris, Patrick R Jacksonville
Butler, John Havana
Chase, Alex DeLand
Cole, Dave Satellite Beach
D'Andrea, John Citrus Springs
Davis Jr., Jim Zephyrhills
Dietzel, Bill Middleburg
Doggett, Bob Brandon
Dotson, Tracy Baker
Ellerbe, W B Geneva
Ellis, Willy B Palm Harbor
Enos Iii, Thomas M Orlando
Fagan, James A Lake Worth
Ferrara, Thomas Naples
Ferris, Bill Palm Beach Garden
Fowler, Charles R Ft McCoy
Gamble, Roger St. Petersburg
Garner Jr., William O Pensacola
Gibson Sr., James Hoot Bunnell
Goers, Bruce Lakeland
Griffin Jr., Howard A Davie
Grospitch, Ernie Orlando
Harris, Ralph Dewey Brandon
Heaney, John D Haines City
Heitler, Henry Tampa
Hodge Iii, John Palatka
Holland, John H Titusville
Humphreys, Joel Lake Placid
Hunter, Richard D Alachua
Hytovick, Joe "Hy" Dunnellon
Johanning Custom Knives, TomSarasota
Johnson, Durrell Carmon Sparr
Johnson, John R Plant City
Kelly, Lance Edgewater
King, Bill Tampa
Krapp, Denny Apopka
Levengood, Bill Tampa
Lewis, Mike DeBary
Long, Glenn A Dunnellon
Lovestrand, Schuyler Vero Beach
Lozier, Don Ocklawaha
Lyle Iii, Ernest L Chiefland
Mcdonald, Robert J Loxahatchee
Mcgowan, Frank E Sebring
Miller, Ronald T Largo
Mink, Dan Crystal Beach
Newton, Larry Jacksonville
Ochs, Charles F Largo
Owens, Donald Melbourne
Parker, Cliff Zephyrhills
Pendray, Alfred H Williston
Piergallini, Daniel E Plant City
Randall Made Knives, Orlando
Reed, John M Oak Hill
Roberts, E Ray Monticello
Robinson Iii, Rex R Leesburg
Rodkey, Dan Hudson
Rogers, Rodney Wildwood
Ross, Gregg Lake Worth
Russ, Ron Williston
Schwarzer, Stephen Crescent City
Smith, Michael J Brandon
Stapleton, William E Merritt Island
Steck, Van R Orange City
Stephan, Daniel Valrico
Stipes, Dwight Palm City
Straight, Kenneth J Largo
Tabor, Tim Lutz
Turnbull, Ralph A Spring Hill
Vogt, Donald J Tampa
Watson, Tom Panama City
Weiland Jr., J Reese Riverview
White, John Paul Valparaiso
Wicker, Donnie R Panama City
Wilson, Stan Clearwater
Zaccagnino Jr., Don Pahokee
Zahm, Kurt Indialantic
Zinker, Brad Homestead

FRANCE

Bennica, Charles 34190 Moules et Baucels
Chauzy, Alain 21140 Seur-en-Auxios
Doursin, Gerard Pernes les Fontaines
Ganster, Jean-PierreF-67000 Strasbourg
Graveline, Pascal And Isabelle 29350 Moelan- sur-Mer
Headrick, Gary Juane Les Pins
Madrulli, Mme Joelle Salon De Provence
Reverdy, Nicole And Pierre
Thevenot, Jean-Paul Dijon
Viallon, Henri

GA

Arrowood, Dale	Sharpsburg
Ashworth, Boyd	Powder Springs
Barker, Robert G.	Bishop
Bentley, C L	Albany
Bish, Hal	Jonesboro
Black, Scott	Covington
Bradley, Dennis	Blairsville
Buckner, Jimmie H	Putney
Chamblin, Joel	Concord
Cole, Welborn I	Athens
Crockford, Jack	Chamblee
Davis, Steve	Powder Springs
Dempsey, David	Macon
Dunn, Charles K	Shiloh
Frost, Dewayne	Barnesville
Gaines, Buddy	Commerce
Glover, Warren D	Cleveland
Granger, Paul J	Kennesaw
Greene, David	Covington
Halligan, Ed	Sharpsburg
Hammond, Hank	Leesburg
Hardy, Douglas E	Franklin
Hawkins, Rade	Fayetteville
Hensley, Wayne	Conyers
Hinson And Son, R	Columbus
Hoffman, Kevin L	Savannah
Hossom, Jerry	Duluth
Jones, Franklin (Frank) W	Columbus
Kimsey, Kevin	Cartersville
King, Fred	Cartersville
Knott, Steve	Guyton
Landers, John	Newnan
Lonewolf, J Aguirre	Demorest
Mathews, Charlie And Harry	Statesboro
Mcgill, John	Blairsville
Mclendon, Hubert W	Waco
Mitchell, James A	Columbus
Moncus, Michael Steven	Smithville
Parks, John	Jefferson
Poole, Marvin O	Commerce
Powell, Robert Clark	Smarr
Prater, Mike	Flintstone
Price, Timmy	Blairsville
Ragsdale, James D	Lithonia
Roghmans, Mark	LaGrange
Rosenfeld, Bob	Hoschton
Scofield, Everett	Chickamauga
Sculley, Peter E	Rising Fawn
Smith Jr., James B "Red"	Morven
Snell, Jerry L	Fortson
Snow, Bill	Columbus
Sowell, Bill	Macon
Stafford, Richard	Warner Robins
Thompson, Kenneth	Duluth
Tomey, Kathleen	Macon
Walters, A F	TyTy
Whetsell, Alex	Sharpsburg
White, Garrett	Hartwell
White, Lou	Ranger

GERMANY

Balbach, Markus	35789 Weilmunster-Laubuseschbach/Ts.
Becker, Franz	84533, Marktl/Inn
Boehlke, Guenter	56412 Grossholbach
Borger, Wolf	76676 Graben-Neudorf
Dell, Wolfgang	D-73277 Owen-Teck
Faust, Joachim	95497 Goldkronach
Fruhmann, Ludwig	84489 Burghausen
Greiss, Jockl	D 77773 Schenkenzell
Hehn, Richard Karl	55444 Dorrebach
Herbst, Peter	91207 Lauf a.d. Pegn.
Joehnk, Bernd	24148 Kiel
Kressler, D F	Achim 28832 DE
Neuhaeusler, Erwin	86179 Augsburg
Rankl, Christian	81476 Munchen
Rinkes, Siegfried	Markterlbach
Selzam, Frank	Bad Koenigshofen
Steinau, Jurgen	Berlin 0-1162
Tritz, Jean Jose	20255 Hamburg
Wirtz, Achim	D-52146
Zirbes, Richard	D-54526 Niederkail

GREECE

Filippou, Ioannis-Minas	Athens 17122

HI

Bucholz, Mark A	Holualoa
Dolan, Robert L.	Kula
Fujisaka, Stanley	Kaneohe
George, Les	Kaneohe
Gibo, George	Hilo
Lui, Ronald M	Honolulu
Mann, Tim	Honokaa
Matsuoka, Scot	Mililani
Mayo Jr., Tom	Waialua
Mitsuyuki, Ross	Honolulu
Onion, Kenneth J	Kaneohe
Ouye, Keith	Honolulu
Zakabi, Carl S	Mililani Town

HOLLAND

Van De Manakker, Thijs	5759 px Helenaveen

IA

Brooker, Dennis	Derby
Brower, Max	Boone
Clark, Howard F	Runnells
Cockerham, Lloyd	Denham Springs
Helscher, John W	Washington
Lainson, Tony	Council Bluffs
Lewis, Bill	Riverside
Mckiernan, Stan	Lamoni
Miller, James P	Fairbank
Thie, Brian	Burlington
Trindle, Barry	Earlham
Westberg, Larry	Algona
Zscherny, Michael	Ely

ID

Alderman, Robert	Sagle
Alverson, Tim (R.V.)	Moscow
Burke, Bill	Boise
Eddy, Hugh E	Caldwell
Hawk, Grant And Gavin	Idaho City
Hogan, Thomas R	Boise
Horton, Scot	Buhl
Howe, Tori	Athol
Mann, Michael L	Spirit Lake
Metz, Greg T	Cascade
Patton, Dick And Rob	Nampa
Quarton, Barr	McCall
Reeve, Chris	Boise
Rohn, Fred	Coeur d'Alene
Sawby, Scott	Sandpoint
Schultz, Robert W	Cocolalla
Selent, Chuck	Bonners Ferry
Sparks, Bernard	Dingle
Steiger, Monte L	Genesee
Tippetts, Colten	Hidden Springs
Towell, Dwight L	Midvale

IL

Bloomer, Alan T	Maquon
Camerer, Craig	Chesterfield
Cook, Louise	Ozark
Cook, Mike	Ozark
Detmer, Phillip	Breese
Dicristofano, Anthony P	Northlake
Eaker, Allen L	Paris
Hawes, Chuck	Weldon
Heath, William	Bondville
Hill, Rick	Maryville
Knuth, Joseph E	Rockford
Kovar, Eugene	Evergreen Park
Leone, Nick	Pontoon Beach
Markley, Ken	Sparta
Meier, Daryl	Carbondale
Myers, Paul	Wood River
Myers, Steve	Virginia
Nevling, Mark	Hume
Nowland, Rick	Waltonville
Potocki, Roger	Goreville
Pritchard, Ron	Dixon
Rados, Jerry F	Grant Park
Rosenbaugh, Ron	Crystal Lake
Rossdeutscher, Robert N	Arlington Heights
Rzewnicki, Gerald	Elizabeth
Schneider, Craig M	Claremont
Smale, Charles J	Waukegan
Smith, John M	Centralia
Steinbrecher, Mark W	Glenview
Thomas, Bob G	Thebes
Todd, Richard C	Chambersburg
Tompkins, Dan	Peotone
Veit, Michael	LaSalle
Voss, Ben	Galesburg
Werth, George W	Poplar Grove
West, Charles A	Centralia
Wheeler, Robert	Bradley
White, Robert J	Gilson
White Jr., Robert J Butch	Gilson
Young, Errol	Alton

IN

Adkins, Larry	Indianapolis
Ball, Ken	Mooresville
Barkes, Terry	Edinburgh
Barrett, Rick L. (Toshi Hisa)	Goshen
Bose, Reese	Shelburn
Bose, Tony	Shelburn
Chaffee, Jeff L	Morris
Claiborne, Jeff	Franklin
Damlovac, Sava	Indianapolis
Darby, Jed	Greensburg
Fitzgerald, Dennis M	Fort Wayne
Fraps, John R	Indianpolis
Hunt, Maurice	Brownsburg
Imel, Billy Mace	New Castle
Johnson, C E Gene	Chesterton
Kain, Charles	Indianapolis
Keeslar, Steven C	Hamilton
Keeton, William L	Laconia
Kinker, Mike	Greensburg
Mayville, Oscar L	Marengo
Minnick, Jim	Middletown
Oliver, Todd D	Spencer
Parsons, Michael R	Indianapolis
Quakenbush, Thomas C	Ft Wayne
Robertson, Leo D	Indianapolis
Shull, James	Rensselaer

Smock, Timothy E Marion
Snyder, Michael Tom Zionsville
Stover, Terry "Lee" Kokomo
Thayer, Danny O Romney
Young, George Kokomo

ISRAEL

Shadmot, Boaz Arava

ITALY

Albericci, Emilio 24100, Bergamo
Ameri, Mauro 16010 Genova
Ballestra, Santino 18039 Ventimiglia (IM)
Bertuzzi, Ettore24068 Seriate (Bergamo)
Bonassi, Franco Pordenone 33170
Fogarizzu, Boiteddu 07016 Pattada
Giagu, Salvatore And Deroma Maria Rosaria 07016 Pattada (SS)
Pachi, Francesco 17046 Sassello (SV)
Ramondetti, Sergio 12013 CHIUSA DI PESIO (CN)
Riboni, Claudio Truccazzano (MI)
Scordia, Paolo Roma
Simonella, Gianluigi 33085 Maniago
Toich, Nevio Vincenza
Tschager, Reinhard I-39100 Bolzano
Wilson (See Simonella, Gianluigi)

JAPAN

Aida, Yoshihito Itabashi-ku, Tokyo 175-0094
Ebisu, Hidesaku Hiroshima City
Fujikawa, Shun Osaka 597 0062
Fukuta, Tak Seki-City, Gifu-Pref
Hara, Kouji Gifu-Pref. 501-3922
Hirayama, Harumi Saitama Pref. 335-0001
Hiroto, Fujihara Hiroshima
Isao, Ohbuchi Fukuoka
Ishihara, Hank Chiba Pref.
Kagawa, Koichi Kanagawa
Kanda, Michio Yamaguchi 7460033
Kanki, Iwao Hydugo
Kansei, Matsuno Gitu-city
Kato, Shinichi Moriyama-ku Nagoya
Katsumaro, Shishido Hiroshima
Kawasaki, Akihisa Kobe
Keisuke, Gotoh Ohita
Koyama, Captain Bunshichi Nagoya City 453- 0817
Mae, Takao Toyonaka, Osaka
Makoto, Kunitomo Hiroshima
Matsuno, Kansei Gifu-City 501-1168
Matsusaki, Takeshi Nagasaki
Michinaka, Toshiaki Tottori 680-0947
Micho, Kanda Yamaguchi
Ryuichi, Kuki Saitama
Sakakibara, Masaki Tokyo 156-0054
Shikayama, Toshiaki Kitakatsusaika Sitiama
Sugihara, Keidoh Osaka, F596-0042
Sugiyama, Eddy K Ohita
Takahashi, Masao Gunma 371 0047
Terauchi, Toshiyuki Fujita-Cho Gobo-Shi
Toshifumi, Kuramoto Fukuoka
Uchida, Chimata Kumamoto
Uekama, Nobuyuki Tokyo
Wada, Yasutaka Nara prefect 631-0044
Waters, Glenn Hirosaki City 036-8183
Yoshihara, Yoshindo Tokyo
Yoshikazu, Kamada Tokushima
Yoshio, Maeda Okayama

KS

Bradburn, Gary Wichita
Burrows, Stephen R Humboldt
Chard, Gordon R Iola
Courtney, Eldon Wichita
Craig, Roger L Topeka
Culver, Steve Meriden
Darpinian, Dave Olathe
Dawkins, Dudley L Topeka
Dick, Dan Hutchinson
Dugger, Dave Westwood
Greene, Steve Rossville
Hegwald, J L Humboldt
Herman, Tim Overland Park
Keranen, Paul Haysville
King, Jason M St. George
King Jr., Harvey G Alta Vista
Kraft, Steve Abilene
Lamb, Curtis J Ottawa
Magee, Jim Salina
Petersen, Dan L Auburn

KY

Addison, Kyle A Murray
Barbara Baskett Custom Knives, Eastview
Barr, A.T. Nicholasville
Baskett, Barbara Eastview
Baumgardner, Ed Glendale
Bodner, Gerald "Jerry" Louisville
Bybee, Barry J Cadiz
Carson, Harold J "Kit" Vine Grove
Clay, J D Greenup
Coil, Jimmie J Owensboro
Downing, Larry Bremen
Dunn, Steve Smiths Grove
Edwards, Mitch Glasgow
Finch, Ricky D West Liberty
Fister, Jim Simpsonville
France, Dan Cawood
Frederick, Aaron West Liberty
Gevedon, Hanners (Hank) Crab Orchard
Greco, John Greensburg
Hibben, Daryl LaGrange
Hibben, Gil LaGrange
Hibben, Joleen LaGrange
Hoke, Thomas M LaGrange
Holbrook, H L Sandy Hook
Howser, John C Frankfort
Keeslar, Joseph F Almo
Lott, Sherry Greensburg
Miller, Don Lexington
Mize, Richard Lawrenceburg
Pease, W D Ewing
Pierce, Harold L Louisville
Pulliam, Morris C Shelbyville
Rigney Jr., Willie Bronston
Smith, Gregory H Louisville
Smith, John W West Liberty
Walker Iii, John Wade Paintlick
Wallingford Jr., Charles W Union

LA

Barker, Reggie Springhill
Blaum, Roy Covington
Caldwell, Bill West Monroe
Calvert Jr., Robert W (Bob) Rayville
Capdepon, Randy Carencro
Capdepon, Robert Carencro
Chauvin, John Scott
Culpepper, John Monroe
Dake, C M New Orleans
Dake, Mary H New Orleans
Diebel, Chuck Broussard
Durio, Fred Opelousas
Elkins, Van Bastrop
Faucheaux, Howard J Loreauville
Fontenot, Gerald J Mamou
Gorenflo, Gabe Baton Rouge
Gorenflo, James T (Jt) Baton Rouge
Johnson, Gordon A. Choudrant
Ki, Shiva Baton Rouge
Laurent, Kermit LaPlace
Leonard, Randy Joe Sarepta
Mitchell, Max Dean And Ben Leesville
Phillips, Dennis Independence
Potier, Timothy F Oberlin
Primos, Terry Shreveport
Provenzano, Joseph D Ponchatoula
Randall Jr., James W Keithville
Randow, Ralph Pineville
Reggio Jr., Sidney J Sun
Sanders, Michael M Ponchatoula
Tilton, John Iowa
Trisler, Kenneth W Rayville
Wiggins, Horace Mansfield

MA

Dailey, G E Seekonk
Entin, Robert Boston
Gaudette, Linden L Wilbraham
Gedraitis, Charles J Holden
Grossman, Stewart Clinton
Hinman, Ted Watertown
Jarvis, Paul M Cambridge
Khalsa, Jot Singh Millis
Kubasek, John A Easthampton
Lapen, Charles W. Brookfield
Little, Larry Spencer
Martin, Randall J Bridgewater
Mcluin, Tom Dracut
Moore, Michael Robert Lowell
Olofson, Chris Cambridge
Rebello, Indian George New Bedford
Reed, Dave Brimfield
Richter, Scott S. Boston
Rizzi, Russell J Ashfield
Siska, Jim Westfield
Smith, J D Roxbury
Szarek, Mark G Revere
Vining, Bill Methuen

MD

Bagley, R. Keith White Plains
Barnes, Aubrey G. Hagerstown
Barnes, Gary L. New Windsor
Beers, Ray Monkton
Bouse, D. Michael Waldorf
Cohen, N J (Norm) Baltimore
Dement, Larry Prince Fredrick
Freiling, Albert J Finksburg
Fuller, Jack A New Market
Gossman, Scott Forest Hill
Hart, Bill Pasadena
Hendrickson, E Jay Frederick
Hendrickson, Shawn Knoxville
Hurt, William R Frederick
Kreh, Lefty "Cockeysville"
Kretsinger Jr., Philip W Boonsboro
Mccarley, John Taneytown
Mcgowan, Frank E Sykesvile
Merchant, Ted White Hall
Nicholson, R. Kent Phoenix
Sentz, Mark C Taneytown

Smit, Glenn	Aberdeen
Sontheimer, G Douglas	Potomac
Spickler, Gregory Noble	Sharpsburg
St. Clair, Thomas K	Monrovia
Walker, Bill	Stevensville
White, Gene E	Bethesda

ME

Coombs Jr., Lamont	Bucksport
Courtois, Bryan	Saco
Gray, Daniel	Brownville
Hillman, Charles	Friendship
Leavitt Jr., Earl F	E. Boothbay
Oyster, Lowell R	Corinth
Sharrigan, Mudd	Wiscasset

MEXICO

Scheurer, Alfredo E Faes	C.P. 16010
Sunderland, Richard	Puerto Escondido Oaxaca
Young, Cliff	San Miguel De Allende, GTO.

MI

Ackerson, Robin E	Buchanan
Andrews, Eric	Grand Ledge
Arms, Eric	Tustin
Behnke, William	Kingsley
Bethke, Lora Sue	Grand Haven
Booth, Philip W	Ithaca
Buckbee, Donald M	Grayling
Canoy, Andrew B	Hubbard Lake
Carr, Tim	Muskegon
Carroll, Chad	Grant
Cashen, Kevin R	Hubbardston
Cook, Mike A	Portland
Cousino, George	Onsted
Cowles, Don	Royal Oak
Dilluvio, Frank J	Warren
Ealy, Delbert	Indian River
Erickson, Walter E.	Atlanta
Gordon, Larry B	Farmington Hills
Gottage, Dante	Clinton Twp.
Gottage, Judy	Clinton Twp.
Harm, Paul W	Attica
Harrison, Brian	Cedarville
Hartman, Arlan (Lanny)	Baldwin
Hughes, Daryle	Nunica
Krause, Roy W	St. Clair Shores
Lankton, Scott	Ann Arbor
Leach, Mike J	Swartz Creek
Lucie, James R	Fruitport
Mankel, Kenneth	Cannonsburg
Mills, Louis G	Ann Arbor
Noren, Douglas E	Springlake
Parker, Robert Nelson	Royal Oak
Repke, Mike	Bay City
Rose Ii, Doun T	Fife Lake
Sakmar, Mike	Rochester
Sandberg, Ronald B	Browntown
Serven, Jim	Fostoria
Tally, Grant	Flat Rock
Van Eizenga, Jerry W	Nunica
Vasquez, Johnny David	Wyandotte
Viste, James	Detroit
Webster, Bill	Three Rivers
Welling, Ronald L	Grand Haven
White, Richard T	Grosse Pointe Farms
Whittaker, Wayne	Metamore
Whitworth, Ken J	Sterling Heights
Wood, Webster	Atlanta
Zowada, Tim	Boyne Falls

MN

Davis, Joel	Albert Lea
Goltz, Warren L	Ada
Griffin, Thomas J	Windom
Hagen, Doc	Pelican Rapids
Hansen, Robert W	Cambridge
Johnson, R B	Clearwater
Knipschield, Terry	Rochester
Maines, Jay	Wyoming
Mickley, Tracy	North Mankato
Rydbom, Jeff	Annandale
Shadley, Eugene W	Bovey
Steffen, Chuck	St. Michael
Voorhies, Les	Faribault

MO

Adrews, Russ	Sugar Creek
Buxton, Bill	Kaiser
Cover, Raymond A	Festus
Cox, Colin J	Raymore
Davis, W C	El Dorado Springs
Dippold, Al	Perryville
Ehrenberger, Daniel Robert	Mexico
Engle, William	Boonville
Hanson Iii, Don L.	Success
Harris, Jeffery A	Chesterfield
Harrison, Jim (Seamus)	St. Louis
Jones, John A	Holden
Kinnikin, Todd	House Springs
Knickmeyer, Hank	Cedar Hill
Knickmeyer, Kurt	Cedar Hill
Martin, Tony	Arcadia
Mason, Bill	Excelsior Springs
Mccrackin, Kevin	House Spings
Mccrackin And Son, V J	House Springs
Miller, Bob	Oakville
Mulkey, Gary	Branson
Muller, Jody	Goodson
Newcomb, Corbin	Moberly
Pryor, Stephen L	Boss
Ramsey, Richard A	Neosho
Rardon, A D	Polo
Rardon, Archie F	Polo
Riepe, Richard A	Harrisonville
Schirmer, Mike	Cherryville
Scroggs, James A	Warrensburg
Sonntag, Douglas W	Nixa
Steketee, Craig A	Billings
Stewart, Edward L	Mexico
Stormer, Bob	St. Peters
Warden, Roy A	Union
Weddle Jr., Del	St. Joseph
Willis, Bill	Ava

MS

Black, Scott	Picayune
Boleware, David	Carson
Davis, Jesse W	Sarah
Dickerson, Gordon S	New Augusta
Evans, Bruce A	Booneville
Lamey, Robert M	Biloxi
Lebatard, Paul M	Vancleave
Mayo, Alton, Jr.	Biloxi
Pickett, Terrell	Lumberton
Roberts, Michael	Clinton
Robinson, Chuck	Picayune
Shiffer, Steve	Leakesville
Skow, H A "Tex"	Senatobia
Taylor, Billy	Petal
Vandeventer, Terry L	Terry
Vardaman, Robert	Hattiesburg
Wehner, Rudy	Collins
Wingo, Perry	Gulfport
Winston, David	Starkville

MT

Barnes, Jack	Whitefish
Barnes, Wendell	Clinton
Barth, J.D.	Alberton
Beam, John R.	Kalispell
Beaty, Robert B.	Missoula
Bell, Don	Lincoln
Bizzell, Robert	Butte
Boxer, Bo	Whitefish
Brooks, Steve R	Walkerville
Caffrey, Edward J	Great Falls
Carlisle, Jeff	Simms
Christensen, Jon P	Shepherd
Colter, Wade	Colstrip
Conklin, George L	Ft. Benton
Crowder, Robert	Thompson Falls
Curtiss, Steve L	Eureka
Dunkerley, Rick	Seeley Lake
Eaton, Rick	Broadview
Ellefson, Joel	Manhattan
Fassio, Melvin G	Lolo
Forthofer, Pete	Whitefish
Fritz, Erik L	Forsyth
Gallagher, Barry	Lewistown
Harkins, J A	Conner
Hill, Howard E	Polson
Hintz, Gerald M	Helena
Hulett, Steve	West Yellowstone
Kajin, Al	Forsyth
Kauffman, Dave	Montana City
Luman, James R	Anaconda
Mcguane Iv, Thomas F	Bozeman
Mortenson, Ed	Darby
Moyer, Russ	Havre
Munroe, Deryk C	Bozeman
Nedved, Dan	Kalispell
Patrick, Willard C	Helena
Peele, Bryan	Thompson Falls
Peterson, Eldon G	Whitefish
Pursley, Aaron	Big Sandy
Robinson, Robert W	Polson
Rodewald, Gary	Hamilton
Ruana Knife Works,	Bonner
Smith, Josh	Frenchtown
Sweeney, Coltin D	Missoula
Taylor, Shane	Miles City
Thill, Jim	Missoula
Weinand, Gerome M	Missoula
Yashinski, John L	Red Lodge

NC

Baker, Herb	Eden
Bauchop, Peter	Cary
Best, Ron	Stokes
Britton, Tim	Bethania
Carolina Custom Knives	See Tommy Mcnabb
Busfield, John	Roanoke Rapids
Coltrain, Larry D	Buxton
Daniel, Travis E	Chocowinity
Drew, Gerald	Mill Spring
Edwards, Fain E	Topton
Fox, Paul	Claremont
Gaddy, Gary Lee	Washington
Goguen, Scott	Newport
Goode, Brian	Shelby
Greene, Chris	Shelby
Gross, W W	Archdale
Gurganus, Carol	Colerain

Gurganus, Melvin H	Colerain
Guthrie, George B	Bassemer City
Hazen, Mark	Charlotte
Kommer, Russ	Fargo
Laramie, Mark	Raeford
Livingston, Robert C	Murphy
Maynard, William N.	Fayetteville
Mclurkin, Andrew	Raleigh
Mcnabb, Tommy	Bethania
Mcrae, J Michael	Mint Hill
Parrish, Robert	Weaverville
Patrick, Chuck	Brasstown
Patrick, Peggy	Brasstown
Rapp, Steven J	Marshall
Scholl, Tim	Angier
Simmons, H R	Aurora
Sterling, Murray	Mount Airy
Summers, Arthur L	Concord
Sutton, S Russell	New Bern
Vail, Dave	Hampstead
Wagaman, John K	Selma
Walker, Don	Burnsville
Warren, Daniel	Canton
Whitley, L Wayne	Chocowinity
Williamson, Tony	Siler City
Wilson, Mike	Hayesville
Winkler, Daniel	Blowing Rock

ND

Pitman, David	Williston

NE

Hockensmith, Dan	Morrill
Jokerst, Charles	Omaha
Marlowe, Charles	Omaha
Moore, Jon P	Aurora
Mosier, Joshua J	Deshler
Robbins, Howard P	Elkhorn
Schepers, George B	Shelton
Suedmeier, Harlan	Nebraska City
Syslo, Chuck	Omaha
Tiensvold, Alan L	Rushville
Tiensvold, Jason	Rushville
Till, Calvin E And Ruth	Chadron

NETHERLANDS

Van Den Elsen, Gert	5012 AJ Tilburg
Van Eldik, Frans	3632BT Loenen
Van Rijswijk, Aad	3132 AA Vlaardingen

NEW ZEALAND

Pennington, C A 8009	Kainga Christchurch
Reddiex, Bill	Palmerston North
Ross, D L	Dunedin
Sandow, Norman E	Howick, Auckland
Sands, Scott	Christchurch 9
Van Dijk, Richard	Harwood Dunedin

NH

Carlson, Kelly	Antrim
Hill, Steve E	Goshen
Hitchmough, Howard	Peterborough
Hudson, C Robbin	Rummney
Macdonald, John	Raymond
Philippe, D A	Cornish
Saindon, R Bill	Goshen

NJ

Eden, Thomas	Cranbury
Grussenmeyer, Paul G	Cherry Hill
Kearney, Jarod	Bordentown
Licata, Steven	Boonton
Mccallen Jr., Howard H	So Seaside Park
Phillips, Jim	Williamstown
Polkowski, Al	Chester
Pressburger, Ramon	Howell
Schilling, Ellen	Hamilton Square
Sheets, Steven William	Mendham
Slee, Fred	Morganville
Viele, H J	Westwood
Yeskoo, Richard C	Summit

NM

Black, Tom	Albuquerque
Cherry, Frank J	Albuquerque
Coleman, Keith E	Albuquerque
Cordova, Joseph G	Peralta
Cumming, Bob	Cedar Crest
Digangi, Joseph M	Santa Cruz
Duran, Jerry T	Albuquerque
Dyess, Eddie	Roswell
Fisher, Jay	Clovis
Goode, Bear	Navajo Dam
Gunter, Brad	Tijeras
Hartman, Tim	Albuquerque
Hethcoat, Don	Clovis
Hume, Don	Albuquerque
Kimberley, Richard L.	Santa Fe
Lewis, Tom R	Carlsbad
Lynn, Arthur	Galisteo
Macdonald, David	Los Lunas
Mcdonald, Robin J	Albuquerque
Meshejian, Mardi	Santa Fe
Rogers, Richard	Magdalena
Schaller, Anthony Brett	Albuquerque
Stalcup, Eddie	Gallup
Stetter, J. C.	Roswell
Terzuola, Robert	Santa Fe
Trujillo, Albert M B	Bosque Farms
Walker, Michael L	Pueblo Sur Taos
Ware, Tommy	Datil
Wescott, Cody	Las Cruces

NORWAY

Bache-Wiig, Tom	Eivindvik
Sellevold, Harald	N5835 Bergen
Vistnes, Tor	

NV

Barnett, Van	Reno
Beasley, Geneo	Wadsworth
Cameron, Ron G	Logandale
Dellana,	Reno
George, Tom	Henderson
Hrisoulas, Jim	Henderson
Johnson,Warren	(See Dellana), Dellana
Kreibich, Donald L.	Reno
Mount, Don	Las Vegas
Nishiuchi, Melvin S	Las Vegas
Thomas, Devin	Panaca
Tracy, Bud	Reno
Washburn, Arthur D	Pioche

NY

Baker, Wild Bill	Boiceville
Castellucio, Rich	Amsterdam
Cute, Thomas	Cortland
Davis, Barry L	Castleton
Farr, Dan	Rochester
Faust, Dick	Rochester
Hobart, Gene	Windsor
Isgro, Jeffery	West Babylon
Johnson, Mike	Orient
Johnston, Dr. Robt	Rochester
Levin, Jack	Brooklyn
Loos, Henry C	New Hyde Park
Ludwig, Richard O	Maspeth
Lupole, Jamie G	Kirkwood
Maragni, Dan	Georgetown
Mccornock, Craig	Willow
Meerdink, Kurt	Barryville
Page, Reginald	Groveland
Pattay, Rudy	Long Beach
Peterson, Karen	Brooklyn
Phillips, Scott C	Gouverneur
Rachlin, Leslie S	Elmira
Rappazzo, Richard	Cohoes
Rotella, Richard A	Niagara Falls
Scheid, Maggie	Rochester
Schippnick, Jim	Sanborn
Schlueter, David	Syracuse
Serafen, Steven E	New Berlin
Skiff, Steven	Broadalbin
Smith, Lenard C	Valley Cottage
Smith, Raymond L	Erin
Summers, Dan	Whitney Pt.
Szilaski, Joseph	Wappingers Falls
Turner, Kevin	Montrose

OH

Babcock, Raymond G.	Vincent
Bailey, Ryan	Galena
Bendik, John	Olmsted Falls
Busse, Jerry	Wauseon
Collins, Lynn M	Elyria
Coppins, Daniel	Cambridge
Cottrill, James I	Columbus
Downing, Tom	Cuyahoga Falls
Downs, James F	Powell
Etzler, John	Grafton
Foster, R L (Bob)	Mansfield
Francis, John D	Ft. Loramie
Franklin, Mike	Aberdeen
Geisler, Gary R	Clarksville
Gittinger, Raymond	Tiffin
Glover, Ron	Mason
Greiner, Richard	Green Springs
Guess, Raymond L	Mechanicstown
Hinderer, Rick	Wooster
Hudson, Anthony B	Amanda
Imboden Ii, Howard L.	Dayton
Jones, Roger Mudbone	Waverly
Kiefer, Tony	Pataskala
Longworth, Dave	Neville
Loro, Gene	Crooksville
Maienknecht, Stanley	Sardis
Mcdonald, Rich	Columbiana
Mcgroder, Patrick J	Madison
Mercer, Mike	Lebanon
Messer, David T	Dayton
Morgan, Tom	Beloit
Panak, Paul S	Kinsman
Potter, Billy	Dublin
Ralph, Darrel	Galena
Rose, Derek W	Gallipolis
Rowe, Fred	Amesville
Salley, John D	Tipp City
Schuchmann, Rick	Cincinnati
Shinosky, Andy	Canfield

Shoemaker, Carroll	Northup
Shoemaker, Scott	Miamisburg
Spinale, Richard	Lorain
Stoddart, W B Bill	Fairfield
Strong, Scott	Beavercreek
Summers, Dennis K	Springfield
Thomas, Kim	Seville
Thourot, Michael W	Napoleon
Tindera, George	Brunswick
Votaw, David P	Pioneer
Ward, J J	Waverly
Ward, Ron	Loveland
Warther, Dale	Dover
Witsaman, Earl	Stow
Wood, Larry B	Huber Heights
Wright, L T	Steubenville
Yurco, Mike	Canfield

OK

Baker, Ray	Sapulpa
Burke, Dan	Edmond
Carrillo, Dwaine	Moore
Crenshaw, Al	Eufaula
Damasteel Stainless Damascus,	Norman
Darby, David T	Cookson
Dill, Dave	Bethany
Duff, Bill	Poteau
Englebretson, George	Oklahoma City
Gepner, Don	Norman
Giraffebone Inc.,	Norman
Heimdale, J E	Tulsa
Johns, Rob	Enid
Kennedy Jr., Bill	Yukon
Kirk, Ray	Tahlequah
Lairson Sr., Jerry	Ringold
Mcclure, Jerry	Norman
Menefee, Ricky Bob	Blawchard
Miller, Michael E	El Reno
Parsons, Larry	Mustang
Sanders, A.A.	Norman
Spivey, Jefferson	Yukon
Tomberlin, Brion R	Norman
Vereynder	
Martin, John Alexander	Okmulgee
Wingo, Gary	Ramona

OR

Bell, Michael	Coquille
Bochman, Bruce	Grants Pass
Brandt, Martin W	Springfield
Buchanan, Thad	Prineville
Buchman, Bill	Bend
Buchner, Bill	Idleyld Park
Busch, Steve	Oakland
Cameron House,	Salem
Carter, Murray M	Vernonia
Clark, Nate	Yoncalla
Coon, Raymond C	Gresham
Davis, Terry	Sumpter
Dowell, T M	Bend
Frank, Heinrich H	Dallas
Gamble, Frank	Salem
Goddard, Wayne	Eugene
Harsey, William H	Creswell
Hilker, Thomas N	Williams
Horn, Jess	Eugene
Kelley, Gary	Aloha
Lake, Ron	Eugene
Little, Gary M	Broadbent
Lum, Robert W	Eugene
Martin, Gene	Williams
Martin, Walter E	Williams
Miller, Michael K	Sweet Home
Olson, Darrold E	Springfield
Rider, David M	Eugene
Sarganis, Paul	Jacksonville
Scarrow, Wil	Gold Hill
Schoeningh, Mike	North Powder
Schrader, Robert	Bend
Sevey Custom Knife,	Gold Beach
Sheehy, Thomas J	Portland
Shoger, Mark O	Beaverton
Smith, Rick	Rogue River
Thompson, Leon	Gaston
Thompson, Tommy	Portland
Vallotton, Butch And Arey	Oakland
Vallotton, Rainy D	Umpqua
Vallotton, Shawn	Oakland
Vallotton, Thomas	Oakland
Ward, Ken	Grants Pass

PA

Anderson, Gary D	Spring Grove
Anderson, Tom	Manchester
Appleby, Robert	Shickshinny
Besedick, Frank E	Ruffsdale
Candrella, Joe	Warminster
Chavar, Edward V	Bethlehem
Clark, D E (Lucky)	Johnstown
Corkum, Steve	Littlestown
Darby, Rick	Levittown
Evans, Ronald B	Middleton
Frey Jr., W Frederick	Milton
Goldberg, David	Ft Washington
Goodling, Rodney W	York Springs
Gottschalk, Gregory J	Carnegie
Heinz, John	Upper Black Eddy
Hudson, Rob	Northumberland
Janiga, Matthew A	Hummelstown
Johnson, John R	New Buffalo
Jones, Curtis J	Washington
Malloy, Joe	Freeland
Marlowe, Donald	Dover
Mensch, Larry C	Milton
Miller, Rick	Rockwood
Moore, Ted	Elizabethtown
Morett, Donald	Lancaster
Nealy, Bud	Stroudsburg
Neilson, J	Wyalusing
Nott, Ron P	Summerdale
Ogden, Bill	Avis
AVIS	
Ortega, Ben M	Wyoming
Parker, J E	Clarion
Root, Gary	Erie
Rupert, Bob	Clinton
Sass, Gary N	Sharpsville
Scimio, Bill	Spruce Creek
Sinclair, J E	Pittsburgh
Steigerwalt, Ken	Orangeville
Stroyan, Eric	Dalton
Valois, A. Daniel	Lehighton
Vaughan, Ian	Manheim
Whittaker, Robert E	Mill Creek
Wilson, Jon J	Johnstown

RI

Bardsley, Norman P.	Pawtucket
Dickison, Scott S	Portsmouth
Mchenry, William James	Wyoming
Olszewski, Stephen	Coventry
Williams, Jason L	Wyoming
Wright, Richard S	Carolina

RUSSIA

Kharlamov, Yuri	300007

SC

Barefoot, Joe W.	Liberty
Beatty, Gordon H.	Seneca
Branton, Robert	Awendaw
Campbell, Courtnay M	Columbia
Cannady, Daniel L	Allendale
Cox, Sam	Gaffney
Denning, Geno	Gaston
Easler Jr., Russell O	Woodruff
Fecas, Stephen J	Anderson
Gainey, Hal	Greenwood
George, Harry	Aiken
Gregory, Michael	Belton
Hendrix, Jerry	Clinton
Hendrix, Wayne	Allendale
Hucks, Jerry	Moncks Corner
Kay, J Wallace	Liberty
Knight, Jason	Harleyville
Langley, Gene H	Florence
Lutz, Greg	Greenwood
Majer, Mike	Hilton Head
Manley, David W	Central
Mcmanus, Danny	Taylors
Miles Jr., C R "Iron Doctor"	Lugoff
Montjoy, Claude	Clinton
Odom Jr., Victor L.	North
Page, Larry	Aiken
Parler, Thomas O	Charleston
Peagler, Russ	Moncks Corner
Perry, Johnny	Spartanburg
Sears, Mick	Sumter
Smith, Ralph L	Taylors
Thomas, Rocky	Moncks Corner
Tyser, Ross	Spartanburg

SD

Boley, Jamie	Parker
Boysen, Raymond A	Rapid Ciy
Ferrier, Gregory K	Rapid City
Sarvis, Randall J	Fort Pierre
Thomsen, Loyd W	Oelrichs

SLOVAK REPUBLIC

Albert, Stefan	Filakovo 98604

SLOVAKIA

Bojtos, Arpa D	98403 Lucenec
Kovacik, Robert	Lucenec 98407
Laoislav, Santa-Lasky	Bystrica
Mojzis, Julius	
Pulis, Vladimir	96701 Kremnica

SOUTH AFRICA

Arm-Ko Knives,	Marble Ray 4035 KZN
Baartman, George	Limpopo
Bauchop, Robert	Kwazulu-Natal 4278
Beukes, Tinus	Vereeniging 1939
Bezuidenhout, Buzz	Malvern, Queensburgh, Natal 4093
Boardman, Guy	New Germany 3619
Brown, Rob E	Port Elizabeth
Burger, Fred	Kwa-Zulu Natal
Dickerson, Gavin	Petit 1512
Fellows, Mike	Mosselbay 6500
Grey, Piet	Naboomspruit 0560
Harvey, Heather	Belfast 1100
Harvey, Kevin	Belfast 1100

South Africa

Herbst, Thinus Karenpark 0118, Akasia

SOUTH AFRICA

Horn, Des
Klaasee, Tinus George 6530
Kojetin, W Germiston 1401
Lagrange, Fanie Table View 7441
Lancaster, C G Free State
Liebenberg, Andre Bordeauxrandburg 2196
Mackrill, Stephen Johannesburg
Mahomedy, A R Marble Ray KZN, 4035
Nelson, Tom Gauteng
Pienaar, Conrad Bloemfontein 9300
Prinsloo, Theuns Bethlehem, 9700
Rietveld, Bertie Magaliesburg 1791
Russell, Mick Port Elizabeth 6070
Schoeman, Corrie Danhof 9310
Steyn, Peter Freestate
Van Der Westhuizen, Peter Mossel Bay 6500
Watson, Peter La Hoff 2570

SWEDEN

Bergh, Roger 91598 Bygdea
Billgren, Per
Eklund, Maihkel S-820 41 Farila
Embretsen, Kaj S-82821 Edsbyn
Hogstrom, Anders T
Johansson, Anders S-772 40 Grangesberg
Lundstrom, Jan-Ake 66010 Dals-Langed
Nilsson, Jonny Walker SE-933 33 Arvidsjaur
Nordell, Ingemar 82041 Färila
Persson, Conny 820 50 Loos
Ryberg, Gote S-562 00 Norrahammar
Styrefors, Mattias
Vogt, Patrik S-30270 Halmstad

SWITZERLAND

Roulin, Charles 1233 Geneva
Soppera, Arthur CH-9631 Ulisbach

TN

Accawi, Fuad Clinton
Bailey, Joseph D. Nashville
Baker, Vance Riceville
Blanchard, G R (Gary) Pigeon Forge
Breed, Kim Clarksville
Byrd, Wesley L Evensville
Canter, Ronald E Jackson
Casteel, Dianna Monteagle
Casteel, Douglas Monteagle
Centofante, Frank Madisonville
Claiborne, Ron Knox
Clay, Wayne Pelham
Conley, Bob Jonesboro
Coogan, Robert Smithville
Copeland, George Steve Alpine
Corby, Harold Johnson City
Elder Jr., Perry B Clarksville
Ewing, John H Clinton
Harley, Larry W Bristol
Harley, Richard Bristol
Heflin, Christopher M Nashville
Hughes, Dan Spencer
Hurst, Jeff Rutledge
Hutcheson, John Chattanooga
Johnson, David A Pleasant Shade
Johnson, Ryan M Hixson
Kemp, Lawrence Ooletwah
Largin, Sevierville
Levine, Bob Tullahoma
Marshall, Stephen R Mt. Juliet
Mccarty, Harry Blaine
Mcdonald, W J "Jerry" Germantown
Moulton, Dusty Loudon
Raley, R. Wayne Collierville
Ramey, Larry Chapmansboro
Sampson, Lynn Jonesborough
Smith, Newman L. Gatlinburg
Taylor, C Gray Fall Branch
Taylor, David Rogersville
Vanderford, Carl G Columbia
Walker, John W Bon Aqua
Ward, W C Clinton
Wheeler, Gary Clarksville
Williams Jr., Richard Morristown
Winter, George Union City

TX

Adams, William D Burton
Alexander, Eugene Ganado
Allen, Mike "Whiskers" Malakoff
Appleton, Ron Bluff Dale
Ashby, Douglas Dallas
Bailey, Kirby C. Lytle
Barnes, Marlen R. Atlanta
Barr, Judson C. Irving
Batts, Keith Hooks
Blasingame, Robert Kilgore
Blum, Kenneth Brenham
Bradshaw, Bailey Diana
Bratcher, Brett Plantersville
Broadwell, David Wichita Falls
Brooks, Michael Lubbock
Bullard, Randall Canyon
Burden, James Burkburnett
Cairnes Jr., Carroll B Palacios
Callahan, F Terry Boerne
Carpenter, Ronald W Jasper
Carter, Fred Wichita Falls
Champion, Robert Amarillo
Chase, John E Aledo
Chew, Larry Granbury
Churchman, T W (Tim) Bandera
Cole, James M Bartonville
Connor, John W Odessa
Connor, Michael Winters
Cosgrove, Charles G Arlington
Costa, Scott Spicewood
Crain, Jack W Granbury
Darcey, Chester L College Station
Davey, Kevin Boerne
Davidson, Jeff Haltom City
Davidson, Larry Cedar Hill
Davis, Vernon M Waco
Dean, Harvey J Rockdale
Dietz, Howard New Braunfels
Dominy, Chuck Colleyville
Dyer, David Granbury
Eldridge, Allan Ft. Worth
Elishewitz, Allen Canyon Lake
Epting, Richard College Station
Eriksen, James Thorlief Garland
Evans, Carlton Fort Davis
Fant Jr., George Atlanta
Ferguson, Jim San Angelo
Fortune Products, Inc., Marble Falls
Foster, Al Magnolia
Foster, Norvell C Marion
Fowler, Jerry Hutto
Fritz, Jesse Slaton
Fuller, Bruce A Baytown
Garner, Larry W Tyler
Gault, Clay Lexington
Goytia, Enrique El Paso
Graham, Gordon New Boston
Green, Bill Sachse
Griffin, Rendon And Mark Houston
Halfrich, Jerry San Marcos
Hamlet Jr., Johnny Clute
Hand, Bill Spearman
Hawkins, Buddy Texarkana
Hayes, Scotty Tesarkana
Haynes, Jerry Gunter
Hays, Mark Austin
Hemperley, Glen Willis
Hicks, Gary Tuscola
Howell, Jason G Lake Jackson
Hudson, Robert Humble
Hughes, Bill Texarkana
Hughes, Lawrence Plainview
Jackson, Charlton R San Antonio
Jaksik Jr., Michael Fredericksburg
Johnson, Gorden W Houston
Johnson, Ruffin Houston
Keller, Bill San Antonio
Kern, R W San Antonio
Kious, Joe Kerrville
Knipstein, R C (Joe) Arlington
Ladd, Jim S Deer Park
Ladd, Jimmie Lee Deer Park
Lambert, Jarrell D Granado
Laplante, Brett McKinney
Lay, L J Burkburnett
Lemcke, Jim L Houston
Lennon, Dale Alba
Lister Jr., Weldon E Boerne
Lively, Tim And Marian Marble Falls
Love, Ed San Antonio
Lovett, Michael Killeen
Luchak, Bob Channelview
Luckett, Bill Weatherford
Marshall, Glenn Mason
Martin, Michael W Beckville
Mcconnell Jr., Loyd A Odessa
Mellard, J R Houston
Merz Iii, Robert L Katy
Miller, R D Dallas
Mitchell, Wm Dean Warren
Moore, James B Ft. Stockton
Neely, Greg Bellaire
Nelson, Dr Carl Texarkana
Nolen, R D And Steve Pottsboro
Odgen, Randy W Houston
Ogletree Jr., Ben R Livingston
Osborne, Warren Waxahachie
Overeynder, T R Arlington
Ownby, John C Plano
Pardue, Joe Spurger
Patterson, Pat Barksdale
Pierce, Randall Arlington
Pollock, Wallace J Cedar Park
Polzien, Don Lubbock
Powell, James Texarkana
Pugh, Jim Azle
Ray, Alan W Lovelady
Richardson Jr., Percy Bridge City
Roberts, Jack Houston
Robinson, Charles (Dickie) Vega
Rogers, Charles W Douglas
Ruple, William H Charlotte
Ruth, Michael G Texarkana
Scott, Al Harper
Self, Ernie Dripping Springs
Shipley, Steven A Richardson

Sims, Bob Meridian
Sloan, Shane Newcastle
Smart, Steve McKinney
Snody, Mike Fredericksburg
Stokes, Ed Hockley
Stone, Jerry Lytle
Stout, Johnny New Braunfels
Summerlin, Danny Groves
Theis, Terry Harper
Thuesen, Ed Damon
Treiber, Leon Ingram
Truncali Custom Knives, Garland
Turcotte, Larry Pampa
Van Reenen, Ian Amarillo
Vecera, J R Thrall
Viking Knives (See James Thorlief Eriksen)
Watson, Daniel Driftwood
Watts, Johnathan Gatesville
Watts, Wally Gatesville
West, Pat Charlotte
White, Dale Sweetwater
Whitley, Weldon G Odessa
Wilcher, Wendell L Palestine
Wilkins, Mitchell Montgomery
Wilson, Curtis M Burleson
Wolf Jr., William Lynn Lagrange
Yeates, Joe A Spring
Zboril, Terry Caldwell

UK

Hague, Geoff Quarley, SP11 8PX

UNITED KINGDOM

Heasman, H G Llandudno, N. Wales
Horne, Grace Sheffield Britain
Maxen, Mick "Hatfield, Herts"

URUGUAY

Gonzalez, Leonardo Williams CP 20000
Symonds, Alberto E Montevideo 11300

UT

Allred, Bruce F Layton
Black, Earl Salt Lake City
Ence, Jim Richfield
Ennis, Ray Ogden
Erickson, L.M. Ogden
Hunter, Hyrum Aurora
Johnson, Steven R Manti
Maxfield, Lynn Layton
Nielson, Jeff V Monroe
Nunn, Gregory Castle Valley
Palmer, Taylor Blanding
Peterson, Chris Salina
Strickland, Dale Monroe
Velarde, Ricardo Park City
Washburn Jr., Robert Lee St George
Winn, Travis A. Salt Lake City

VA

Apelt, Stacy E Norfolk
Arbuckle, James M Yorktown
Ballew, Dale Bowling Green
Batley, Mark S. Wake
Batson, Richard G. Rixeyville
Beverly Ii, Larry H Spotsylvania
Callahan, Errett Lynchburg
Catoe, David R Norfolk
Chamberlain, Charles R Barren Springs
Davidson, Edmund Goshen
Douglas, John J Lynch Station
Eaton, Frank L Jr Stafford
Foster, Burt Bristol
Frazier, Ron Powhatan
Harris, Cass Bluemont
Hedrick, Don Newport News
Hendricks, Samuel J Maurertown
Herb, Martin Richmond
Holloway, Paul Norfolk
Jones, Barry M And Phillip G Danville
Jones, Enoch Warrenton
Martin, Herb Richmond
Mccoun, Mark DeWitt
Metheny, H A "Whitey" Spotsylvania
Mills, Michael Colonial Beach
Murski, Ray Reston
Norfleet, Ross W Providence Forge
Parks, Blane C Woodbridge
Pawlowski, John R Newport News
Richter, John C Chesapeake
Tomes, P J Shipman
Vanhoy, Ed And Tanya Abingdon

VT

Haggerty, George S Jacksonville
Kelso, Jim Worcester

WA

Amoureux, A W Northport
Begg, Todd M. Spanaway
Ber, Dave San Juan Island
Berglin, Bruce D Mount Vernon
Bloomquist, R Gordon Olympia
Boguszewski, Phil Lakewood
Boyer, Mark Bothell
Bromley, Peter Spokane
Brothers, Robert L Colville
Brown, Dennis G Shoreline
Brunckhorst, Lyle Bothell
Bump, Bruce D. Walla Walla
Butler, John R Shoreline
Campbell, Dick Colville
Chamberlain, Jon A E. Wenatchee
Conti, Jeffrey D Bonney Lake
Conway, John Kirkland
Crain, Frank Spokane
Crowthers, Mark F Rolling Bay
D'Angelo, Laurence Vancouver
Davis, John Selah
Diskin, Matt Freeland
Dole, Roger Buckley
Evans, Vincent K And Grace Cathlamet
Ferry, Tom Auburn
Frey, Steve Snohomish
Gray, Bob Spokane
Greenfield, G O Everett
Hansen, Lonnie Spanaway
House, Gary Ephrata
Hurst, Cole E. Wenatchee
Lum, Mitch Seattle
Norton, Don Port Townsend
O'Malley, Daniel Seattle
Padilla, Gary Bellingham
Rader, Michael Wilkeson
Rogers, Ray Wauconda
Schempp, Ed Ephrata
Schempp, Martin Ephrata
Stegner, Wilbur G Rochester
Sterling, Thomas J Coupeville
Swyhart, Art Klickitat
Wright, Kevin Quilcene

WI

Bostwick, Chris T Burlington
Brandsey, Edward P Janesville
Bruner Jr., Fred Bruner BladesFall Creek
Coats, Ken Stevens Point
Delarosa, Jim Janesville
Fiorini, Bill DeSoto
Genske, Jay Fond du Lac
Haines, Jeff Haines Custom Knives Wauzeka
Hembrook, Ron Neosho
Iron Wolf Forge, See Nelson Ken
Johnson, Richard Germantown
Kanter, Michael New Berlin
Kohls, Jerry Princeton
Kolitz, Robert Beaver Dam
Lary, Ed Mosinee
Lerch, Matthew Sussex
Maestri, Peter A Spring Green
Martin, Peter Waterford
Millard, Fred G Richland Center
Nelson, Ken Pittsville
Niemuth, Troy Sheboygan
Ponzio, Doug Beloit
R. Boyes Knives, Addison
Revishvili, Zaza Madison
Ricke, Dave West Bend
Rochford, Michael R Dresser
Schrap, Robert G Wauwatosa
Wattelet, Michael A Minocqua

WV

Bowen, Tilton Baker
Derr, Herbert St. Albans
Drost, Jason D French Creek
Drost, Michael B French Creek
Elliott, Jerry Charleston
Jeffries, Robert W Red House
Liegey, Kenneth R Millwood
Maynard, Larry Joe Crab Orchard
Mcconnell, Charles R Wellsburg
Morris, Eric Beckley
Pickens, Selbert Dunbar
Reynolds, Dave Harrisville
Shaver Ii, James R Parkersburg
Small, Ed Keyser
Tokar, Daniel Shepherdstown
Wilson, Rw Weirton
Wyatt, William R Rainelle

WY

Alexander, Darrel Ten Sleep
Ankrom, W.E. Cody
Archer, Ray And Terri Medicine Bow
Banks, David L. Riverton
Barry, Scott Laramie
Bartlow, John Sheridan
Bennett, Brett C Cheyenne
Draper, Audra Riverton
Draper, Mike Riverton
Fowler, Ed A. Riverton
Friedly, Dennis E Cody
Justice, Shane Sheridan
Kilby, Keith Cody
Rexroat, Kirk Wright
Reynolds, John C Gillette
Ross, Stephen Evanston
Spragg, Wayne E Lovell

ZIMBABWE

Burger, Pon Bulawayo

Not all knifemakers are organization-types, but those listed here are in good standing with these organizations.

the knifemakers' guild

2008 voting membership

a Les Adams, Douglas A. Alcorn, Mike "Whiskers" Allen, Tom Anderson, W. E. Ankrom, Santino e Arlete Ballestra

b Norman P. Bardsley, A. T. Barr, James J. Barry, III, John Bartlow, Gene Baskett, Donald I. Bell, Tom Black, Gary Blanchard, Arpad Bojtos, Philip W. Booth, Tony Bose, Dennis Bradley, Gordon Gayle Bradley, Edward Brandsey, W. Lowell Bray, Jr., George Clint Breshears, Rick Browne, Fred Bruner, Jr., Jimmie H. Buckner, R. D. "Dan" Burke, Patrick R. Burris, John Busfield, Robert K. Bagley

c Ron G. Cameron, Daniel Cannady, Robert Capdepon, Harold J. "Kit" Carson, Casteel Custom Knives, Frank Centofante, Joel Chamblin, William Chapo, Alex W. Chase, Edward V. Chavar, William Cheatham, Howard F. Clark, Wayne Clay, Vernon W. Coleman, Blackie Collins, Bob F. Conley, Gerald Corbit, George Cousino, Colin J. Cox, Pat Crawford, Dan Cruze, Roy D. Cutchin

d Charles Dake, Alex K. Daniels, Jack Davenport, Edmund Davidson, Jim Davis, Kenneth D. Davis, Terry A. Davis, Vernon M. Davis, William C. Davis, Dan Dennehy, Herbert K. Derr, Joseph R. DeWitt, William J. Dietzel, Frank Dilluvio, Dippold Forge, David Dodds, Bob Doggett, Tracy Dotson, T. M. Dowell, Larry Downing, Tom Downing, James F. Downs, William Duff, Richard J. Dunkerley, Fred Durio, Ralph . D'Elia, Jr

e Easler Knives, Allen Elishewitz, Jim Elliott, David Ellis, William B. Ellis, William E. Engle, Viking Knives - James T. Eriksen, Carlton R. Evans

f Howard Faucheaux, Stephen J. Fecas, Lee Ferguson, Linda Ferguson, Jay Fisher, Derek B. Fraley, Franklin Custom Knives, John R Fraps, Ronald A. Frazier, Aaron Frederick, Dennis E. Friedly, Lynx Mountain View Estates - Larry Fuegen, Shun Fujikawa, Stanley Fujisaka, Tak Fukuta, Bruce A. Fuller, Shiro Furukawa

g Frank Gamble, Roger Gamble, Clay Gault, Charles Gedraitis, James "Hoot" Gibson,Sr., Warren Glover, Stefan Gobec, Warren L. Goltz, Gregory J. Gottschalk, Jockl Greiss, Kenneth W. Guth

h Philip (Doc) L. Hagen, The Malt House - Geoff Hague, Gerald Halfrich, Jeff Hall, Jim Hammond, Koji Hara, Larry Harley, Ralph Dewey Harris, Rade Hawkins, Henry Heitler, Glenn Hemperley, Earl Jay Hendrickson, Wayne Hendrix, Wayne G. Hensley, Don D. Hethcoat, Gil Hibben, Steven E. Hill, Harumi Hirayama, Steven W. Hoel, Kevin Hoffman, Miles (Jerry) G. Hossom, Durvyn Howard, Rob Hudson, Roy Humenick, Joseph Hytovick

i Billy Mace Imel, Michael Irie

j James T. Jacks, Paul Jarvis, Steve Jernigan, Brad Johnson, Ronald B. Johnson, Steven R. Johnson, William "Bill" C. Johnson, Enoch D. Jones

k William L. Keeton, Bill Kennedy, Jr., Jot Singh Khalsa, Harvey King, Jr., Bill King, Joe Kious, Roy W. Krause, Dietmar Dietmar Kressler, John Kubasek

l Kermit Laurent, Gary E. Le Blanc, William L. Levengood, Bob Levine, Yakov Levin, Steve Linklater, Ken Linton, Wolfgang Loerchner, R. W. Loveless, Schuyler Lovestrand, Don Lozier, Gail Lunn, Larry Lunn, Ernest Lyle

m Stephen Mackrill, Joe Malloy, Jerry McClure, Loyd A. McConnell, Jr., Charles R. McConnell, Robert J. McDonald, W. J. McDonald, Frank McGowan, Mike Mercer, Ted Merchant, Robert L. Merz, III, Toshiaki Michinaka, Stephen C. Miller, Daniel J. Mink, Sidney "Pete" Moon, James B. Moore, Jeff Morgan

n Bud Nealy, Corbin Newcomb, Larry Newton, R. D. Nolen, Ingemar Nordell, Ross W Norfleet

o Charles F. Ochs, III, Ben R. Ogletree, Jr., Raymond Frank Oldham, Stephen C. Olszewski, Warren Osborne, T. R. Overeynder, John E. Owens, Jr.

p Larry Page, Joseph Pardue, Mel Pardue, Cliff Parker, Larry D. Patterson, John R. Pawlowski, W. D. Pease, Alfred Pendray, John W. Permar, John L. Perry, Daniel Piergallini, David F. Pitt, Leon M. Pittman, Otakar Pok, Alvin J. Polkowski, Joseph R. Prince, Theunis C. Prinsloo, Jim Pugh, Morris C. Pulliam

r James D. Ragsdale, Steven Rapp, John Reynolds, Ronald F. Richard, Dave Ricke, Michael Rochford, A. G. Russell

s Masaki Sakakibara, Michael A. Sakmar, Hiroyuki Sakurai, Scott W. Sawby, Juergen Schanz, Maurice & Alan Schrock, Steve Schwarzer, Mark C. Sentz, Yoshinori Seto, Eugene W. Shadley, James R. Shaver, II, Brad Shepherd, John I. Shore, Bill Simons, R. J. Sims, James E. Sinclair, Cleston S. Sinyard, Jim Siska, Scott Slobodian, J. D. Smith, John W. Smith, Ralph Smith, Marvin Solomon, James Sornberger, W. C. Sowell, David Steier, Kenneth A. Steigerwalt, Jurgen Steinau, Daniel L. Stephan, Murray Sterling, Johnny Stout, Keidoh Sugihara, Russ Sutton, Charles C. Syslo, Joseph Szilaski

t Grant Tally, Robert Terzuola, Leon Thompson, Dan Tompkins, John Toner, Bobby L. Toole, Dwight Towell, Leon Treiber, Reinhard Tschager, Ralph Turnbull, Arthur Tycer

v Louis Van De Walt, Frans Van Eldik, Aas van Rijswijk, Edward T. VanHoy, Ricardo Velarde, Donald Vogt

w George A. Walker, John W. Walker, Charles B. Ward, Dale E. Warther, Charles G. Weeber, John S. Weever, Weldon G. Whitley, Wayne Whittaker, Donnie R. Wicker, R. W. Wilson, Stan Wilson, Daniel Winkler, Richard S. Wright, Timothy Wright

y Yoshindo Yoshihara, George L. Young, John Young, Mike Yurco

z Brad Zinker, Michael Zschemy

abs mastersmith listing

a David Anders, Jerome Anders, Gary D. Anderson

b Bailey Bradshaw, Gary Barnes, Aubrey G. Barnes Sr., James L. Batson, Jimmie H. Buckner, Bruce Bump

c Ed Caffrey, Murray Carter, Kevin R. Cashen, Jon Christensen, Howard F. Clark, Wade Colter, Michael Connor, James R. Cook, Joseph G. Cordova, Jim Crowell

d Sava Damlovac, Harvey J. Dean, Christoph Deringer, Bill Dietzel, Audra L. Draper, Rick Dunkerley, Steve Dunn, Ken Durham

e Dave Ellise

f Robert Ferry, William Fiorini, Jerry Fisk, James O. Fister, John S. Fitch, Joe Flournoy, Don Fogg, Burt Foster, Ronnie Foster, Tim Foster, Ed Fowler, Larry Fuegen, Bruce A. Fuller, Jack A. Fuller

g Bert Gaston, Thomas Gerner, Wayne Goddard, Greg Gottschalk

h Ed Halligan, Timothy J. Hancock, Kevin Harvey, Heather Harvey, Wally Hayes, Charlie E. Haynes, E. Jay Hendrickson, Don Hethcoat, John Horrigan, C. Robbin Hudson

j Jim L. Jackson

k Joseph F. Keelsar, Keith Kilby, Ray Kirk, Hank Knickmeyer, Bob Kramer, Phil Kretsinger

l J.D. Lambert, Mick Langley, Jerry Lairson Sr.

m Dan Maragni, Chris J. Marks, John Martin, Roger D. Massey, Victor J. McCrackin, Hanford Miller, William Dean Mitchell

n Gregory T. Neely, Ron Newton, Doug Noren

o Charles F. Ochs III

p Alfred Pendray, John Perry, Dan L. Petersen, Timothy Potier

r James W. Randall Jr., Kirk Rexroat, Charles R. Robinson, James Rodebaugh, Raymond B. Rybar Jr.

s Stephen C. Schwarzer, Mark C. Sentz, J.D. Smith, Jousha J. Smith, Raymond L. Smith, H. Red St. Cry, Joseph Szilaski

t Shane Taylor, Jason Tiensvold, P.J. Tomes

v Michael V. Vagnino Jr., Terry Vandeventer

w James L. Walker, Michael L. Williams, Daniel Winkler

miniature knifemaker's society

Paul Abernathy, Gerald Bodner, Fred Cadwell, Barry Carithers, Kenneth Corey, Don Cowles, David J. Davis, Allen Eldridge, Linda Ferguson, Buddy Gaines, Larry Greenburg, Tom & Gwenn Guinn, Karl Hallberg, Bob Hergert, Laura Holmes, Brian Jacobson, Gary Kelley, R. F. Koebeman, Sterling Kopke, Gary E. Lack, Les Levinson, Henry C. Loos, Howard Maxwell, Mal Mele, Ray Mende, Toshiaki Michinaka, Paul Myer, Noriaki Narushima, Carol A. Olmsted, Allen R. Olsen, Charles Ostendorf, David Perkins, John Rakusan, Mark Rogers, Mary Ann Schultz, Jack Taylor, Valentin V. Timofeyev, Mike Viehman, Michael A. Wattelet, Kenneth P. Whitchard Jr., James D. Whitehead, Steve Williams, Carol A. Winold, Earl and Sue Witsaman, John Yashinski

professional knifemaker's association

Mike Allen, James Agnew, Usef Arie, Ray Archer, Eddie J. Baca, John Bartlow, Donald Bell, Brett C. Bennett, Tom Black, James E. Bliss, Philip Booth, Douglas Brack, Kenneth L. Brock, Ron Burke, Lucas Burnley, Ward Byrd, Craig Camerer, Tim S. Cameron, Ken Cardwell, Rod S. Carter, Del Corsi, Roger L. Craig, Joel Davis, John D. Dennehy, Dan Dennehy, Chester Deubel, Audra L. Draper, Mike J. Draper, Jim English, Ray W. Ennis, James T. Eriksen, Kirby Evers, Lee Ferguson, John Fraps, Scott Gere, Bob Glassman, Sal Glesser, Marge Hartman, Mike Henry, Don Hethcoat, Gary Hicks, Guy E. Hielscher, Alan Hodges, Mike L. Irie, David Johansen, Donald Jones, Jack Jones, Jot Singh Khalsa, Harvey King, Steve Kraft, Jim R. Largent, Ken Linton, Mike A. Lundemann, Jim Magee, Daniel May, Jerry & Sandy McClure, Clayton Miller, Skip Miller, Mark S. Molnar, Tyree L. Montell, Mike Mooney, Gary Moore, Steve Nolen, Rick Nowland, Fred A. Ott, Rob Patton, Dick Patton, James L. Poplin, Bill Redd, Dennis Riley, Terry Roberts, Steve Rollert, Charles R. Sauer, Jerry Schroeder, James Scroggs, Pete Semich, Eddie F. Stalcup, Craig Steketee, J.C. Stetter, Troy Taylor, Robert Terzuola, Roy Thompson, Loyd W. Thomsen, Jim D. Thrash, Ed Thuesen, Dick Waites, Mark Waites, Bill Waldrup, Tommy Ware, David Wattenberg, Hans Weinmueller, Dan Westlind, Harold J. Wheeler, RW Wilson, Denise Wolford, Michael C. Young, Monte Zavatta, Michael F. Zima, Daniel F. Zvonek

state/regional associations

alaska knifemakers association

A.W. Amoureux, John Arnold, Bud Aufdermauer, Robert Ball, J.D. Biggs, Lonnie Breuer, Tom Broome, Mark Bucholz, Irvin Campbell, Virgil Campbell, Raymond Cannon, Christopher Cawthorne, John Chamberlin, Bill Chatwood, George Cubic, Bob Cunningham, Gordon S. Dempsey, J.L. Devoll, James Dick, Art Dufour, Alan Eaker, Norm Grant, Gordon Grebe, Dave Highers, Alex Hunt, Dwight Jenkins, Hank Kubaiko, Bill Lance, Bob Levine, Michael Miller, John Palowski, Gordon Parrish, Mark W. Phillips, Frank Pratt, Guy Recknagle, Ron Robertson, Steve Robertson, Red Rowell, Dave Smith, Roger E. Smith, Gary R. Stafford, Keith Stegall, Wilbur Stegner, Norm Story, Robert D. Shaw, Thomas Trujillo, Ulys Whalen, Jim Whitman, Bob Willis

arizona knifemakers association

D. "Butch" Beaver, Bill Cheatham, Dan Dagget, Tom Edwards, Anthony Goddard, Steve Hoel, Ken McFall, Milford Oliver, Jerry Poletis, Merle Poteet, Mike Quinn, Elmer Sams, Jim Sornberger, Glen Stockton, Bruce Thompson, Sandy Tudor, Charles Weiss

arkansas knifemakers association

David Anders, Auston Baggs, Don Bailey, Reggie Barker, Marlen R. Barnes, Paul Charles Basch, Lora Sue Bethke, James Black, R.P. Black, Joel Bradford, Gary Braswell, Paul Brown, Shawn Brown, Troy L. Brown, Jim Butler, Buddy Cabe, Allen Conner, James Cook, Thom Copeland, Gary L. Crowder, Jim Crowell, David T. Darby, Fred Duvall, Rodger Echols, David Etchieson, Lee Ferguson, Jerry Fisk, John Fitch, Joe & Gwen Flournoy, Dewayne Forrester, John Fortenbury, Ronnie Foster, Tim Foster, Emmet Gadberry, Larry Garner, Ed Gentis, Paul Giller, James T. Gilmore, Terry Glassco, D.R. (Rick) Gregg, Lynn Griffith, Arthur J. Gunn, Jr., David Gunnell, Morris Herring, Don "Possum" Hicks, Jim Howington, B. R. Hughes, Ray Kirk, Douglas Knight, Lile Handmade Knives, Jerry Lairson Sr., Claude Lambert, Alton Lawrence, Jim Lemcke, Michael H. Lewis, Willard Long, Dr. Jim Lucie, Hal W. Martin, Tony Martin, Roger D. Massey, Douglas Mays, Howard McCallen Jr., Jerry McClure, John McKeehan, Joe McVay, Bart Messina, Thomas V. Militano, Jim Moore, Jody Muller, Greg Neely, Ron Newton, Douglas Noren, Keith Page, Jimmy Passmore, John Perry, Lloyd "Pete" Peterson, Cliff Polk, Terry Primos, Paul E. Pyle Jr., Ted Quandt, Vernon Red, Tim Richardson, Dennis Riley, Terry Roberts, Charles R. Robinson, Kenny Rowe, Mike Ruth, Ken Sharp, Terry Shurtleff, Roy Slaughter, Joe D. Smith, Marvin Solomon, Hoy Spear, Charles Stout, Arthur Tycer, Ross Tyser, James Walker, Chuck Ward, Herman Waters, Bryce White, Tillmon T. Whitley III, Mike Williams, Rick Wilson, Terry Wright, Ray Young

australian knifemakers guild inc.

Peter Bald, Col Barn, Wayne Barrett, Alistair Bastian, David Brodziak, Stuart Burdett, Terry Cox, John Creedy, Malcolm Day, John Deering, Peter Del Raso, Glen Drane, Michael Fechner, John Foxwell, Keith Fludder, Adam Fromholtz, Thomas Gerner, Peter Gordon, Stephen Gregory-Jones, Barry Gunston, Karim Haddad, Frank Heine, Glen Henke, Michael Hint, Douglas Jarrett, Dean Johnson, John Jones, Wolf Kahrau, Peter Kandavnieks, Peter Kenney, Tasman Kerley, John Kilby, Robert Klitscher, Greg Lyell, Maurice McCarthy, Shawn McIntyre, Alex Mead, Ray Mende, Richard Moase, Dave Myhill, Adam Parker, Mike Petersen, Murray Shanaughan, Gary Siemer, Peter Spann, Rod Stines, Jim Steele, David Strickland, Doug Timbs, Hardy Wangemann, Brendon Ware, Bob Wilhelm, Kwong Yeang, Ross Yeats

california knifemakers association

Arnie Abegg, George J. Antinarelli, Elmer Art, Gregory Barnes, Mary Michael Barnes, Hunter Baskins, Gary Biggers, Roger Bost, Clint Breshears, Buzz Brooks, Steven E. Bunyea, Peter Carey, Joe Caswell, Frank Clay, Richard Clow, T.C. Collins, Richard Corbaley, Stephanie Engnath, Alex Felix, Jim Ferguson, Dave Flowers, Logwood Gion, Peter Gion, Joseph Girtner, Tony Gonzales, Russ Green, Tony Guarnera, Bruce Guidry, Dolores Hayes, Bill Herndon, Neal A. Hodges, Richard Hull, Jim Jacks, Lawrence Johnson, David Kazsuk, James P. Kelley, Richard D. Keyes, Michael P. Klein, Steven Koster, John Kray, Bud Lang, Tomas N. Lewis, R.W. Loveless, John Mackie, Thomas Markey, James K. Mattis, Toni S. Mattis, Patrick T. McGrath, Larry McLean, Jim Merritt, Greg Miller, Walt Modest, Russ Moody, Emil Morgan, Gerald Morgan, Mike Murphy, Thomas Orth, Tom Paar, Daniel Pearlman, Mel Peters, Barry Evan Posner, John Radovich, James L. Rodebaugh, Clark D. Rozas, Ron Ruppe, Brian Saffran, Red St. Cyr, James Stankovich, Bill Stroman, Tony Swatton, Gary Tamms, James P. Tarozon, Scott Taylor, Tru-Grit Inc., Tommy Voss, Jessie C. Ward, Wayne Watanabe, Charles Weiss, Steven A. Williams, Harlan M. Willson, Steve Wolf, Barry B. Wood

canadian knifemakers guild

Gaetan Beauchamp, Shawn Belanger, Don Bell, Brent Beshara, Dave Bolton, Conrad Bondu, Darren Chard, Garry Churchill, Guillaume J. Cote, Christoph Deringer, Jeff Diotte, Randy Doucette, Jim Downie, John Dorrell, Eric Elson, Lloyd Fairbairn, Paul-Aime Fortier, Rick Frigault, John Freeman, Mark Garvock, Brian Gilbert, Murray Haday, Tom Hart, Thomas Haslinger, Ian Hubel, Paul Johnston (London, Ont.), Paul Johnston (Smith Falls, Ont.), Jason Kilcup, Kirby Lambert, Greg Lightfoot, Jodi Link, Wolfgang Loerchner, Mel Long, Brian Lyttle, David Macdonald, Michael Mason, Alan Massey, Leigh Maulson, James McGowan, Edward McRae, Mike Mossington, Sean O'Hare, Rod Olson, Neil Ostroff, Ron Post, George Roberts, Brian Russell, Murray St. Armour, Michael Sheppard, Corey Smith, David Smith, Jerry Smith, Walt Stockdale, Matt Stocker, Ed Storch, Steve Stuart, George Tichbourne, Brian Tighe, Robert Tremblay, Glenn Treml, Steve Vanderkloff, James Wade, Bud Weston, Peter Wile

florida knifemaker's association

Dick Atkinson, Barney Barnett, James J. Barry III, Dawayne Batten, Howard Bishop, Andy Blackton, Dennis Blaine, Dennis Blankenhem, Dr. Stephen A. Bloom, Dean Bosworth, John Boyce, Bill Brantley, W. Lowell Bray Jr., Patrick Burris, Norman J. Caesar, Steve Christian, Mark Clark, Lowell Cobb, William Cody, David Cole, Steve Corn, David Cross, Jack Davenport, Kevin Davey, J.D. Davis, Kenny Davis, Ralph D'Elia, Bob Doggett, Jim Elliot, William Ellis, Tom M. Enos, Jon Feazell, Mike Fisher, Todd Fisher, Roger Gamble, James "Hoot" Gibson, Pedro Gonzalez, Ernie Grospitch, Fred Harrington, Dewey Harris, Henry Heitler, Kevin Hoffman, Edward O. Holloway, Stewart Holloway, Joe Hytovick, Tom Johanning, Raymond C. Johnson II, Richard Johnson, Roy Kelleher, Paul S. Kent, Bill King, F.D. Kingery, John E. Klingensmith, William S. Letcher, Bill Levengood, Glenn Long, Gail Lunn, Larry Lunn, Ernie Lyle, Bob Mancuso, Joe Mandt, Kevin A. Manley, Michael Matthews, Jim McNeil, Faustina Mead, Steve Miller, Dan Mink, Steven Morefield, Martin L. "Les" Murphy, Gary Nelson, Larry Newton, Toby Nipper, Praddep Singh Parihar, Cliff Parker, Larry Patterson, Dan Piergallini, Martin Prudente, Bud Pruitt, John "Mickey" Reed, Terry Lee Renner, Roberto Sanchez, Rusty Sauls, Dennis J. Savage, David Semones, Ann Sheffield, Brad Shepherd, Bill Simons, Stephen J. Smith, Kent Swicegood, Tim Tabor, Michael Tison, Ralph Turnbull, Louis M. Vallet, Donald Vogt, Reese Weiland Jr., Travis Williamson, Stan Wilson, Denny & Maggie Young, Brad Zinker

georgia custom knifemakers' guild

Don Adams, Aaron Brewer, Henry Cambron, Frank Chikey, John Costa, Scott Davison, Steve Davis, Carroll Dutton, Emory Fennell, Brent Fisher, Dewayne Frost, Buddy Gaines, Dean Gates, Warren Glover, George Hancox, Wayne Hensley, Franklin Jones, Alvin Kinsey, Charlie Mathews, Harry Mathews, Leroy Mathews, Dan Mink, James Mitchell, Sandy Morrissey, Joan Poythress, Carey Quinn, Carl Rechsteiner, Joe Sangster, Jamey Saunders, Ken Simmons, Brad Singley, Jim Small, Bill Snow, Pat Steadman, Kathleen Tomey, Don Tommey, David Turner, Alex Whetsel, Garrett White, Gerald White, Ryan Whittemore, Richard Wittman

knife group association of oklahoma

David Anders, Rocky Anderson, Wally Armstrong, Jerry Barlow, Troy Brown, Tom Buchanan, Jayson H. Bucy, Tony Cable, Dawnavan Crawford, Gary Crowder, Steve Culver, David Darby, Lynn Drury, Bill Duff, David Etchieson, Harry Fentress, Lee Ferguson, Linda Ferguson, Randy Folks, Daniel Fulk, Michael Gibbons, Darren Gower, Paul Happy, Bob Hathaway, Billy Helton, Ed Hites, David Horton, Ed Jones, Les Jones, Jim Keen, Bill Kennedy, Barbara Kirk, Ray Kirk, Reese Lane, Jerry Lairson, Sr., Al Lawrence, Jerry Ligon, Aidan Martin, Barbara Martin, Duncan Martin, John Martin, Jerry McClure, Sandy McClure, Rick Menefee, Michael E. Miller, Ray Milligan, Duane Morganflash, Gary Mulkey, Jerald Nickels, Darrel Parent, Jerry Parkhurst, Chris Parson, Larry Parsons, Jerry Paul, Larry Paulen, Paul Piccola, Cliff Polk, Rusty Polk, Roland Quimby, Ron Reeves, Justin Reichert, Lin Rhea, Dan Schneringer, Terry Schreiner, Allen Shafer, Charlie Smith, Clifford Smith, Doug Sonntag, Mike Stegall, Gary Steinmetz, Bob Tidwell, Brian Tomberlin, Chuck Ward, Jesse Webb, Rob Weber, Joe Wheeler, Joe Wilkie, Larry Winegar, Gary Wingo

knifemakers' guild of southern africa

Jeff Angelo, John Arnold, George Baartman, Francois Basson, Rob Bauchop, George Beechey, Arno Bernard, Buzz Bezuidenhout, Harucus Blomerus, Chris Booysen, Thinus Bothma, Ian Bottomley, Peet Bronkhorst, Rob Brown, Fred Burger, Sharon Burger, Trevor Burger, William Burger, Brian Coetzee, Larry Connelly, Andre de Beer, André de Villiers, Melodie de Witt, Gavin Dickerson, Roy Dunseith, Mike Fellows, Leigh Fogarty, Werner Fourie, Andrew Frankland, Brian Geyer, Ettoré Gianferrari, Dale Goldschmidt, Stan Gordon, Nick Grabe, John Grey, Piet Gray, Heather Harvey, Kevin Harvey, Dries Hattingh, Gawie Herbst, Thinus Herbst, Greg Hesslewood, Des Horn, Nkosi Jubane, Billy Kojetin, Mark Kretschmer, Steven Lewis, Garry Lombard, Steve Lombard, Ken Madden, Abdur-Rasheed Mahomedy, Peter Mason, Edward Mitchell, George Muller, Günther Muller, Tom Nelson, Andries Olivier, Jan Olivier, Christo Oosthuizen, Cedric Pannell, Willie Paulsen, Nico Pelzer, Conrad Pienaar, David Pienaar, Jan Potgieter, Lourens Prinsloo, Theuns Prinsloo, Hilton Purvis, Derek Rausch, Chris Reeve, Bertie Rietveld, Melinda Rietveld, Dean Riley, John Robertson, Corrie Schoeman, Eddie Scott, Harvey Silk, Mike Skellern, Toi Skellern, Carel Smith, Ken Smythe, Graham Sparks, Peter Steyn, André Thorburn, Hennie Van Brakel, Fanie Van Der Linde, Johan van der Merwe, Van van der Merwe, Marius Van der Vyver, Louis Van der Walt, Cor Van Ellinckhuijzen, Andre van Heerden, Danie Van Wyk, Ben Venter, Willie Venter, Gert Vermaak, René Vermeulen, Erich Vosloo, Desmond, Waldeck, Albie Wantenaar, Henning Wilkinson, John Wilmot, Wollie Wolfaardt, Owen Wood

midwest knifemakers association

E.R. Andrews III, Frank Berlin, Charles Bolton, Tony Cates, Mike Chesterman, Ron Duncan, Larry Duvall, Bobby Eades, Jackie Emanuel, James Haynes, John Jones, Mickey Koval, Ron Lichlyter, George Martoncik, Gene Millard, William Miller, Corbin Newcomb, Chris Owen, A.D. Rardon, Archie Rardon, Max Smith, Ed Stewart, Charles Syslo, Melvin Williams

montana knifemaker's association

Peter C. Albert, Chet Allinson, Marvin Allinson, Tim & Sharyl Alverson, Bill Amoureux, Jan Anderson, Wendell Barnes, Jim & Kay Barth, Bob & Marian Beaty, Don Bell, Brett Bennett, Robert Bizzell, BladeGallery, Paul Bos, Daryl & Anna May Boyd, Chuck Bragg, Frederick Branch, Peter Bromley, Bruce Brown, Emil Bucharksky, Bruce & Kay Bump,

Bill Burke, Alpha Knife Supply Bybee, Ed Caffrey, Jim & Kate Carroll, Murray Carter, Jon & Brenda Christensen, Norm Cotterman, Seith Coughlin, Bob Crowder, Mike Dalimata, John Davis, Maria DesJardins, Rich & Jacque Duxbury, Dan Erickson, Mel & Darlene Fassio, E.V. Ford, Eric Fritz, Dana & Sandy Hackney, Doc & Lil Hagen, Gary & Betsy Hannon, Eli Hansen, J.A. Harkins, Tedd Harris, Sam & Joy Hensen, Loren Higgins, Mickey Hines, Gerald & Pamela Hintz, Gary House, Tori Howe, Kevin Hutchins, Al Inman, Frank & Shelley Jacobs, Karl Jermunson, Keith Johnson, Don Kaschmitter, Steven Kelly, Dan & Penny Kendrick, Monte Koppes, Donald Kreuger, David Lisch, James Luman, Robert Martin, Max McCarter, Neil McKee, Larry McLaughlin, Mac & Nancy McLaughlin, Phillip Moen, Gerald Morgan, Randy Morgan, Dan & Andrea Nedved, Daniel O'Malley, Joe Olson, Collin Paterson, Willard & Mark Patrick, Jeffrey & Tyler Pearson, Brian Pender, James Poling, Chance & Kerri Priest, Richard Prusz, Greg Rabatin, Jim Raymond, Jim Rayner, Darren Reeves, John Reynolds, Ryan Robison, Gary Rodewald, Buster Ross, Ruana Knifeworks, Charles Sauer, Dean Schroeder, Michael Sheperes, Mike Smith, Gordon St. Clair, Terry Steigers, George Stemple, Dan & Judy Stucky, Art & Linda Swyhart, Jim Thill, Cary Thomas, James & Tammy Venne, Bill & Lori Waldrup, Jonathan & Doris Walther, Kenneth Ward, Michael Wattelet, Darlene Weinand, Gerome & Darlene Weinand, Daniel & Donna Westlind, Matt & Michelle Whitmus, Dave Wilkes, Mike & Sean Young

national independent cutlery association

Ron & Patsy Beck, Bob Bennett, Dave Bishop, Steve Corn, Dave Harvey, C.J. McKay, Mike Murray, Gary Parker, Rachel Schindler, Joe Tarbell

new england bladesmiths guild

Phillip Baldwin, Gary Barnes, Paul Champagne, Jimmy Fikes, Don Fogg, Larry Fuegen, Rob Hudson, Midk Langley, Louis Mills, Dan Maragni, Jim Schmidt, Wayne Valachovic and Tim Zowada

north carolina custom knifemakers' guild

Douglas M. Bailey, Lester "Red" Banks, Robert E. Barber, Dr. James Batson, Wayne Bernauer, William M. Bisher, Tim Britton, Richard Brown, E. Gene Calloway, Joe Corbin, Gary W. Cunningham, Travis Daniel, Rob Davis, Jim A. Decoster, Geno Denning, David W. Diggs, Charles F. Fogarty, Alan Folts, Phillip L. Gaddy, Jim L. Gardner, Norman A. Gervais, Ed Halligan, Robert R. Ham, Koji Hara, Cap Hayes, John B. Hege, Mark Hazen, Mark R. Henry, Terrill Hoffman, Jesse Houser, Jr., B.R. Hughes, Dan Johnson, Tommy Johnson, Barry & Phillip Jones, Frank Joyce, Jacob Kelly, Tony Kelly, Robert Knight, Dr. Jim Lucie, Gerry McGinnis, Dave McKeithan, Andrew McLurkin, Tommy McNabb, Michael McRae, William T. Morris, Ron Newton, Calvin Nichols, Victor L. Odom Jr., Charles Ostendorf, Cory Owens, Avery Parker, Howard Peacock, James Poplin, Murphy G. Ragsdale, William B. Roberson, Henry Clay Runion, Bruce M. Ryan, Steve Sallee, Tim Scholl, Danks Seel, Andy D. Sharpe, J. Wayne Short, Harland & Karen Simmons, Ken Simmons, Richard M. Snelling, Johnnie Sorrell, Chuck Staples Jr., Murray Sterling, Russ Sutton, Kathleen Tomey, Bruce Turner, Dave Vail, Ed & Tanya VanHoy, Wayne Whitley, James A. Williams, L.E. Wilson, Daniel Winkler, Rob Wotzak

ohio knifemakers association

Raymond Babcock, Van Barnett, Harold A. Collins, Larry Detty, Tom Downing, Jim Downs, Patty Ferrier, Jeff Flannery, James Fray, Bob Foster, Raymond Guess, Scott Hamrie, Rick Hinderer, Curtis Hurley, Ed Kalfayan, Michael Koval, Judy Koval, Larry Lunn, Stanley Maienknecht, Dave Marlott, Mike Mercer, David Morton, Patrick McGroder, Charles Pratt, Darrel Ralph, Roy Roddy, Carroll Shoemaker, John Smith, Clifton Smith, Art Summers, Jan Summers, Donald Tess, Dale Warther, John Wallingford, Earl Witsaman, Joanne Yurco, Mike Yurco

saskatchewan knifemakers guild

Marty Beets, Art Benson, Doug Binns, Darren Breitkrenz, Clarence Broeksma, Irv Brunas, Emil Bucharsky, Ernie Cardinal, Raymond Caron, Faron Comaniuk, Murray Cook, Sanford Crickett, Jim Dahlin, Herb Davison, Kevin Donald, Brian Drayton, Dallas Dreger, Roger Eagles, Brian Easton, Marvin Engel, Ray Fehler, Rob Fehler, Ken Friedrick, Calvin Granshorn, Vernon Ganshorn, Dale Garling, Alan Goode, Dave Goertz, Darren Greenfield, Gary Greer, Jay Hale, Wayne Hamilton, Phil Haughian, Robert Hazell, Bryan Hebb, Daug Heuer, Garth Hindmarch, John R. Hopkins, Lavern Ilg, Clifford Kaufmann, Meryl Klassen, Bob Kowalke, Todd Kreics, Donald Krueger, Paul Laronge, Patricia Leahy, Ron Lockhart, Pat Macnamara, Bengamin Manton, Ed Mcrac, Len Meeres, Randy Merkley, Arnold Miller, Robert Minnes, Ron Nelson, Brian Obrigewitsch, Bryan Olafson, Blaine Parrry, Doug Peltier, Darryl Perlett, Dean Pickrell, Barry Popick, Jim Quickfall, Bob Robson, Gerry Rush, Geoff Rutledge, Carl Sali, Kim Senft, Eugene Schreiner, Curtis Silzer, Christopher Silzer, David Silzer, Kent Silzer, Don Spasoff, Bob Stewart, Dan Stinnen, Lorne Stadyk, Eugene R. Thompson, Ron Wall, Ken Watt, Trevor, Whitfield, David Wilkes, Merle Williams, Gerry Wozencroft, Ed Zelter, Al Zerr, Brian Zerr, Ronald Zinkhan

south carolina association of knifemakers

Douglas Bailey, Ken Black, Bobby Branton, Gordo Brooks, Daniel Cannaday, Thomas Clegg, John Conn, Allen Corbett, Bill Dauksch, Geno Denning, Charlie Douan, Perry B. Elder Jr. Eddy Elsmore, Robert D. "Robbie" Estabrook, Lewis A. Fowler, Jim Frazier, Meck Hartfield, Tracy L. Hartfield, Jerry G. Hendrix, Wayne Hendrix, George Herron, Jerry Hucks, Johnny Johnson, Lonnie L. Jones, John Keaton, Jason Knight, Thomas D. (Col.) Kreger, Gene Langley, Eddie Lee, David Maley, Willilam "Bill" Massey, David McFalls, Bill Metcalf, C.R. Miles, Claude Montjoy, Patrick H. Morgan, Barry L. Myers, Paul Nystrom, Lee O'Quinn, Victor Odom, Larry Page, James C. Rabb, Ralph Smith, Ricky Rankin, Rick Rockwood, Gene Scaffe, Mick Sears, S. David Stroud, Robert Stuckey, Rocky Thomas, Allen Timmons, Mickey Walker, Woodrow W. Walker, Charley Webb, H. Syd Willis Jr.

tennessee knifemakers association

John Bartlow, Doug Casteel, Harold Crisp, Larry Harley, John W. Walker, Harold Woodward, Harold Wright

texas knifemakers & collectors association

Dwyane A. Bandy, Ed Barker, Zane W. Blackwell, Robert Blassingame, Tim Bradberry, Gayle Bradley, Craig Brewer, Stanley G. Buzek, Daniel J. Cassidy, David Childers, Emil R. Colmenares, Stephen J. Conway, Ed Crater, Steward P. Crawford, Chester L. Darcey, Wesley W. Davis, Harvey J. Dean, James E. Drouillard II, Allen Elishewitz, Richard G. Eptin, Carlton R. Evans, Jesse H. Everett Jr., Jeffrey Feller, Christopher Flo, Bill Fotte, Norvell C. Foster, Theodore G. Freisenhahn, Emiliano Garcia, Mark Grimes, Don Halter, Johnny Hamlet, Bill Hand, Glenn Hemperley, Robert Hensarling, Roy Hinds, Jason Howell, Karl Jakubik, Jose Jalomo, Jr., Bill Keller, Greg Ledet, Jim Lemcke, Dale Lennon, Ken Linton, Charlie O. Majors, Glenn Marshall, Roger McBee, Jerry McClure, Sandy McClure, Larry A. Meyers, Bill Middlebrook, Perry W. Miller, Richard G. Morgan, Don Morrow, Guy W. Nelson, Mike O'Brien, Warren Osborne, Ed Osorio, Tom R. Overeynder, John Ownby, Glenn Parks, Pat Patterson, William P. Petersen III, Benjamin Paul, Piccola, Wallace J. Pollock, Rusty Presgon, Don Robinson, Michael J. Rudolph, Bill Ruple, Merle L. Rush, James A. Schiller, Richard Self, Scott K. Stevens, Johnny L. Stout, Gene Tedford, John Thompson, Jason C. Tippy, Turner E. Touchton Jr., Don Townsend, Leon Treiber, Larry Turcotte, Carlos R. Valenzuela, Ian Van Reenen, John Venier, Jeffery A. Vesley, Ray R. Villarreal, Bruce Voyles, Harold A. Waddle, Harold Wheeler, Weldon Whitley, Steve Woods, John Woody, Forrest M. Young

photo index

The firms listed here are special in the sense that they make or market special kinds of knives made in facilities they own or control either in the U.S. or overseas. Or they are special because they make knives of unique design or function. The second phone number listed is the fax number.

sporting cutlers

A.G. RUSSELL KNIVES INC
2900 S. 26th St
Rogers, AR 72758-8571
800-255-9034; 749-631-8493
ag@agrussell.com; www.agrussell.com
The oldest knife mail-order company, highest quality. Free catalog available. In these catalogs you will find the newest and the best. If you like knives, this catalog is a must

AL MAR KNIVES
PO Box 2295
Tualatin, OR 97062-2295
503-670-9080; 503-639-4789
www.almarknives.com
Featuring our Ultralight™ series of knives. Sere 2000™ Shrike, Sere™, Operator™, Nomad™ and Ultraligh series™

ALCAS CORPORATION
1116 E State St
Olean, NY 14760
716-372-3111; 716-373-6155
www.cutco.com
Household cutlery / sport knives

ANZA KNIVES
C Davis
Dept BL 12 PO Box 710806
Santee, CA 92072-0806
619-561-9445; 619-390-6283
sales@anzaknives.com;
www.anzaknives.com

B&D TRADING CO.
3935 Fair Hill Rd
Fair Oaks, CA 95628

BARTEAUX MACHETES, INC.
1916 SE 50th St
Portland, OR 97215
503-233-5880
barteaux@machete.com; www.machete.com
Manufacture of machetes, saws, garden tools

BEAR & SON CUTLERY (FORMERLY BEAR MGC CUTLERY)
PO Box 600
5111 Berwyn Rd Suite 110
College Park, MD 20740 USA
800-338-6799; 301-486-0901
www.knifecenter.com
Folding pocket knives, fixed blades, specialty products

BECK'S CUTLERY & SPECIALTIES
McGregor Village Center
107 Edinburgh South Dr
Cary, NC 27511
919-460-0203; 919-460-7772
beckscutlery@mindspring.com;
www.beckscutlery.com

BENCHMADE KNIFE CO. INC.
300 Beavercreek Rd
Oregon City, OR 97045
800-800-7427
info@benchmade.com;
www.benchmade.com
Sports, utility, law enforcement, military, gift and semi custom

BERETTA U.S.A. CORP.
17601 Beretta Dr
Accokeek, MD 20607
800-636-3420 Customer Service
www.berettausa.com
Full range of hunting & specialty knives

BEST KNIVES / GT KNIVES
PO Box 151048
Fort Myers, FL 33914
800-956-5696; Fax: 941-240-1756
info@bestknives.com;
www.bestknives.com/gtknives.com
Law enforcement & military automatic knives

BLACKJACK KNIVES
PO Box 3
Greenville, WV 24945
304-832-6878; Fax 304-832-6550
knifeware@verizon.net;
www.knifeware.com

BLUE GRASS CUTLERY CORP.
20 E Seventh St PO Box 156
Manchester, OH 45144
937-549-2602; 937-549-2709 or 2603
sales @bluegrasscutlery.com;
www.bluegrasscutlery.com
Manufacturer of Winchester Knives, John Primble Knives and many contract lines

BOB'S TRADING POST
308 N Main St
Hutchinson, KS 67501
620-669-9441
www.gunshopfinder.com
Tad custom knives with Reichert custom sheaths one at a time, one-of-a-kind

BOKER USA INC
1550 Balsam St
Lakewood, CO 80214-5917
303-462-0662; 303-462-0668
sales@bokerusa.com; www.bokerusa.com
Wide range of fixed blade and folding knives for hunting, military, tactical and general use

BROWNING
One Browning Place
Morgan, UT 84050
800-333-3504; Customer Service: 801-876-2711 or 800-333-3288
www.browning.com
Outdoor hunting & shooting products

BUCK KNIVES INC.
660 S Lochsa St
Post Falls, ID 83854-5200
800-326-2825; Fax: 208-262-0555
www.buckknives.com
Sports cutlery

BULLDOG BRAND KNIVES
6715 Heritage Business Ct
Chattanooga, TN 37421
423-894-5102; 423-892-9165
Fixed blade and folding knives for hunting and general use

BUSSE COMBAT KNIFE CO.
11651 Co Rd 12
Wauseon, OH 43567
419-923-6471; 419-923-2337
www.bussecombat.com
Simple & very strong straight knife designs for tactical & expedition use

CAMILLUS CUTLERY CO.
54 W Main St.
Camillus, NY 13031
315-672-8111; 315-672-8832
customerservice@camillusknives.com

CAS IBERIA INC.
650 Industrial Blvd
Sale Creek, TN 37373
423-332-4700
www.casiberia.com
Extensive variety of fixed-blade and folding knives for hunting, diving, camping, military and general use.

CASE CUTLERY
W R & Sons
PO Box 4000
Owens Way
Bradford, PA 16701
800-523-6350; Fax: 814-368-1736
consumer-relations@wrcase.com
www.wrcase.com
Folding pocket knives

CHICAGO CUTLERY CO.
5500 Pearl St.
Rosemont, IL 60018
847-678-8600
www.chicagocutlery.com
Sport & utility knives.

CHRIS REEVE KNIVES
11624 W President Dr. Suite B
Boise, ID 83713
208-375-0367; Fax: 208-375-0368
crknifo@chrisreeve.com;
www.chrisreeve.com
Makers of the award winning Yarborough/ Green Beret Knife; the One Piece Range; and the Sebenza and Mnandi folding knives

COAST CUTLERY CO
PO Box 5821
Portland, OR 97288
800-426-5858
www.coastcutlery.com
Variety of fixed-blade and folding knives and multi-tools for hunting, camping and general use

COLD STEEL INC
3036-A Seaborg Ave.
Ventura, CA 93003
800-255-4716 or 805-650-8481
customerservice@coldsteel.com;
www.coldsteel.com
Wide variety of folding lockbacks and fixed-blade hunting, fishing and neck knives, as well as bowies, kukris, tantos, throwing knives, kitchen knives and swords

COLONIAL KNIFE COMPANY DIVISION OF COLONIAL CUTLERY INTERNATIONAL
PO Box 960
North Scituate, RI 02857
866-421-6500; Fax: 401-737-0054
colonialcutlery@aol.com;
www.colonialcutlery@aol.com or
www.colonialknifecompany.com
Collectors edition specialty knives. Special promotions. Old cutler, barion, trappers, military knives. Industrial knives-electrician.

COLUMBIA RIVER KNIFE & TOOL
18348 SW 126th Place
Tualatin, OR 97026
800-891-3100; 503-685-5015
info@crkt.com; www.crkt.com
Complete line of sport, work and tactical knives

CONDOR™ TOOL & KNIFE
Rick Jones, Natl. Sales Manager
6309 Marina Dr
Orlando, FL 32819
407-876-0886
rtj@earthlink.net

CRAWFORD KNIVES, LLC
205 N Center Drive
West Memphis, AR 72301
870-732-2452
www.crawfordknives.com
Folding knives for tactical and general use

DAVID BOYE KNIVES
PO Box 1238
Dolan Springs, AZ 86441-1238
800-853-1617 or 928-767-4273
boye@ctaz.com; www.boyeknives.com
Boye Dendritic Cobalt boat knives

DUNN KNIVES
Steve Greene
PO Box 204; 5830 NW Carlson Rd
Rossville KS 66533
800-245-6483
steve.greene@dunnknives.com;
www.dunnknives.com
Custom knives

EMERSON KNIVES, INC.
PO Box 4180
Torrance, CA 90510-4180
310-212-7455; Fax: 310-212-7289
www.emersonknives.com
Hard use tactical knives; folding & fixed blades

EXTREMA RATIO SAS
Mauro Chiostri/Maurizio Castrati
Via Tourcoing 40/p
59100 Prato
ITALY
0039 0574 584639; Fax: 0039 0574 581312
info@extremaratio.com
Tactical/military knives and sheaths, blades and sheaths to customers specs

FALLKNIVEN AB
Havrevägen 10
S-961 42 Boden
SWEDEN
46-921 544 22; Fax: 46-921 544 33
info@fallkniven.se; www.fallkniven.com
High quality stainless knives

FROST CUTLERY CO
PO Box 22636
Chattanooga, Tn 37422
800-251-7768; Fax: 423-894-9576
www.frostcutleryco.com
Wide range of fixed-blade and folding knives with a multitude of handle materials

GATCO SHARPENERS
PO Box 600
Getzville, NY 14068
716-877-2200; Fax: 716-877-2591
gatco@buffnet.net;
www.gatcosharpeners.com
Precision sharpening systems, diamond sharpening systems, ceramic sharpening systems, carbide sharpening systems, natural Arkansas stones

GERBER LEGENDARY BLADES
14200 SW 72nd Ave
Portland, OR 97224
503-639-6161; Fax: 503-684-7008
www.gerberblades.com
Knives, multi-tools, axes, saws, outdoor products

GROHMANN KNIVES LTD.
PO Box 40
116 Water St
Pictou, Nova Scotia B0K 1H0
CANADA
888-756-4837; Fax: 902-485-5872
www.grohmannknives.com
Fixed-blade belt knives for hunting and fishing, folding pocketknives for hunting and general use

H&B FORGE CO.
235 Geisinger Rd
Shiloh, OH 44878
419-895-1856
hbforge@direcway.com; www.hbforge.com
Special order hawks, camp stoves, fireplace accessories, muzzleloading accroutements

HISTORIC EDGED WEAPONRY
1021 Saddlebrook Dr
Hendersonville, NC 28739
828-692-0323; 828-692-0600
histwpn@bellsouth.net
Antique knives from around the world; importer of puukko and other knives from Norway, Sweden, Finland and Lapland; also edged weaponry book "Travels for Daggers" by Eiler R. Cook

JOY ENTERPRISES-FURY CUTLERY
Port Commerce Center III
1862 M.L. King Jr. Blvd
Riviera Beach, FL 33404
800-500-3879; Fax: 561-863-3277
mail@joyenterprises.com;
www.joyenterprises.com;
www.furycutlery.com
Fury™ Mustang™ extensive variety of fixed-blade and folding knives for hunting, fishing, diving, camping, military and general use; novelty key-ring knives. Muela Sporting Knives

KA-BAR KNIVES INC
200 Homer St
Olean, NY 14760
800-282-0130; Fax: 716-790-7188
info@ka-bar.com; www.ka-bar.com

KATZ KNIVES, INC.
10924 Mukilteo Speedway #287
Mukilteo, WA 98275
480-786-9334; 480-786-9338
katzkn@aol.com; www.katzknives.com

KELLAM KNIVES CO.
902 S Dixie Hwy
Lantana, FL 33462
800-390-6918; Fax: 561-588-3186
info@kellamknives.com;
www.kellamknives.com
Largest selection of Finnish knives; handmade & production

KERSHAW/KAI CUTLERY CO.
7939 SW Burns Way
Wilsonville, OR 97070

KLOTZLI (MESSER KLOTZLI)
Hohengasse 3 CH 3400
Burgdorf
SWITZERLAND
(34) 422-23 78; Fax: (34) 422-76 93
info@klotzli.com; www.klotzli.com
High-tech folding knives for tactical and general use

KNIFEWARE INC
PO Box 3
Greenville, WV 24945
304-832-6878; Fax: 304-832-6550
knifeware@verizon.net; www.knifeware.com
Blackjack and Big Country Cross reference Big Country Knives see Knifeware Inc.

KNIGHTS EDGE LTD.
5696 N Northwest Highway
Chicago, IL 60646-6136
773-775-3888; Fax: 773-775-3339
sales@knightsedge.com;
www.knightsedge.com
Medieval weaponry, swords, suits of armor, katanas, daggers

KNIVES OF ALASKA, INC.
Charles or Jody Allen
3100 Airport Dr
Denison, TX 75020
800-572-0980; 903-786-7371
info@knivesofalaska.com;
www.knivesofalaska.com
High quality hunting & outdoorsmen's knives

KUTMASTER KNIVES
Div of Utica Cutlery Co
820 Noyes St
Utica, NY 13503
800-888-4223; Fax: 315-733-6602
www.kutmaster.com
Manufacturer and importer of pocket, lockback, tool knives and multi-purpose tools

LAKOTA (BRUNTON CO.)
620 E Monroe Ave
Riverton, WY 82501
307-856-6559
AUS 8-A high-carbon stainless steel blades

LEATHERMAN TOOL GROUP, INC.
PO Box 20595
Portland, OR 97294-059 0595 5
800-847-8665; Fax: 503-253-7830
mktg@leatherman.com;
www.leatherman.com
Multi-tools

LONE WOLF KNIVES
Doug Hutchens, Marketing Manager
9373 SW Barber Street, Suite A
Wilsonville, OR 97070
503-431-6777
customerservice@lonewolfknives.com;
www.lonewolfknives.com

MARBLE'S OUTDOORS
420 Industrial Park
Gladstone, MI 49837
906-428-3710; Fax: 906-428-3711
info@marblescutlery.com;
www.marblesoutdoors.com

MASTER CUTLERY INC
701 Penhorn Ave
Secaucus, NJ 07094
888-271-7229; Fax: 201-271-7666
www.mastercutlery.com
Largest variety in the knife industry

MASTERS OF DEFENSE KNIFE CO. (BLACKHAWK PRODUCTS GROUP)
4850 Brookside Court
Norfolk, VA 23502
800-694-5263; 888-830-2013
cs@blackhawk.com; www.modknives.com
Fixed-blade and folding knives for tactical and general use

MCCANN INDUSTRIES
132 S 162nd PO Box 641
Spanaway, WA 98387
253-537-6919; Fax: 253-537-6993
mccann.machine@worldnet.att.net;
www.mccannindustries.com

MEYERCO MANUFACTURING
4481 Exchange Service Dr
Dallas, TX 75236
214-467-8949; 214-467-9241
www.meyercousa.com
Folding tactical,rescue and speed-assisted pocketknives; fixed-blade hunting and fishing designs; multi-function camping tools and machetes

MICROTECH KNIVES
300 Chestnut Street Ext.
Bradford, PA 16701
814-363-9260; Fax: 814-363-9284
mssweeney@microtechknives.com;
www.microtechknives.com
Manufacturers of the highest quality production knives

MORTY THE KNIFE MAN, INC.
80 Smith St
Farmingdale, NY 11735
631-249-2072
clkiff@mtkm.com;
www.mortytheknifeman.com

MUSEUM REPLICAS LTD.
P.O. Box 840
2147 Gees Mill Rd
Conyers, GA 30012
800-883-8838; Fax: 770-388-0246
www.museumreplicas.com
Historically accurate & battle-ready swords & daggers

MYERCHIN, INC.
14765 Nova Scotia Dr
Fontana, CA 92336
909-463-6741; 909-463-6751
myerchin@myerchin.com;
www.myerchin.com
Rigging/ Police knives

NATIONAL KNIFE DISTRIBUTORS
125 Depot St
Forest City, NC 28043
800-447-4342; 828-245-5121
nkdi@nkdi.com; www.nkdi.com
Benchmark pocketknives from Solingen, Germany

NORMARK CORP.
10395 Yellow Circle Dr
Minnetonka, MN 55343-9101
800-874-4451; 612-933-0046
www.rapala.com
Hunting knives, game shears and skinning ax

ONTARIO KNIFE CO.
PO Box 145
Franklinville, NY 14737
800-222-5233; 800-299-2618
sales@ontarioknife.com;
www.ontarioknife.com
Fixed blades, tactical folders, military & hunting knives, machetes

OUTDOOR EDGE CUTLERY CORP.
4699 Nautilus Ct. S #503
Boulder, CO 80301
800-447-3343; 303-530-7667
info@outdooredge.com;
www.outdooredge.com

PILTDOWN PRODUCTIONS
Errett Callahan
2 Fredonia Ave
Lynchburg, VA 24503
434-528-3444
www.errettcallahan.com

QUEEN CUTLERY COMPANY
PO Box 500
Franklinville, NY 14737
800-222-5233; 800-299-2618
sales@ontarioknife.com;
www.queencutlery.com
Pocket knives, collectibles, Schatt & Morgan, Robeson, club knives

QUIKUT
118 East Douglas Road
Walnut Ridge, AR 72476
800-338-7012; Fax: 870-886-9162
www.quikut.com

RANDALL MADE KNIVES
4857 South Orange Blossom Trail
Orlando, FL 32839
407-855-8075; Fax: 407-855-9054
grandall@randallknives.com;
www.randallknives.com
Handmade fixed-blade knives for hunting, fishing, diving, military and general use

REMINGTON ARMS CO., INC.
PO Box 700
870 Remington Drive
Madison, NC 27025-0700
800-243-9700; Fax: 336-548-7801
www.remington.com

SANTA FE STONEWORKS
3790 Cerrillos Rd.
Santa Fe, NM 87507
800-257-7625; Fax: 505-471-0036
knives@rt66.com;
www.santafestoneworks.com
Gem stone handles

SARCO CUTLERY LLC
449 Lane Dr
Florence AL 35630
256-766-8099
www.sarcoknives.com
Etching and engraving services, club knives, etc. New knives, antique-collectible knives

SOG SPECIALTY KNIVES & TOOLS, INC.
6521 212th St SW
Lynnwood, WA 98036
425-771-6230; Fax: 425-771-7689
info@sogknives.com; www.sogknives.com
SOG assisted technology, Arc-Lock, folding knives, specialized fixed blades, multi-tools

SPYDERCO, INC.
820 Spyderco Way
Golden, CO 80403
800-525-7770; 303-278-2229
sales@spyderco.com;
www.spyderco.com
Knives and sharpeners

SWISS ARMY BRANDS INC.
Service Center
65 Trap Falls Road
Shelton, CT 06484
800-442-2706; Fax: 800-243-4006
www.swissarmy.com
Folding multi-blade designs and multi-tools for hunting, fishing, camping, hiking, golfing and general use. One of the original brands (Victorinox) of Swiss Army Knives

TAYLOR BRANDS LLC
1043 Fordtown Road
Kingsport, TN 37662-1638
800-251-0254; Fax: 423-247-5371
info@taylorbrandsllc.com;
www.taylorcutlery.com
Fixed-blade and folding knives for tactical, rescue, hunting and general use

TIGERSHARP TECHNOLOGIES
1002 N Central Expwy Suite 499
Richardson TX 75080
888-711-8437; Fax: 972-907-0716
www.tigersharp.com

TIMBERLINE KNIVES
PO Box 600
Getzville, NY 14068-0600
800-548-7427; Fax: 716-877-2591
www.timberlineknives.com
High technology production knives for professionals, sporting, tradesmen & kitchen use

TINIVES
1725 Smith Rd
Fortson, GA 31808
888-537-9991; 706-322-9892
info@tinives.com; www.tinives.com
High-tech folding knives for tactical, law enforcement and general use

TRU-BALANCE KNIFE CO.
6869 Lake Bluff Dr
Comstock Park, MI 49321
(616) 647-1215

TURNER, P.J., KNIFE MFG., INC.
P.O. Box 1549
164 Allred Rd
Afton, WY 83110
307-885-0611
pjtkm@silverstar.com;
www2.silverstar.com/turnermfg

UTICA CUTLERY CO
820 Noyes St
PO Box 10527
Utica, NY 13503-1527
800-879-2526; Fax: 315-733-6602
info@uticacutlery.com; www.uticacutlery.com
Wide range of folding and fixed-blade designs, multi-tools and steak knives

WARNER, KEN
PO Box 3
Greenville, WV 24945
304-832-6878; 304-832-6550
www.knifeware.com

WENGER NORTH AMERICA
15 Corporate Dr
Orangeburg, NY 10962
800-267-3577 or 800-447-7422
www.wengerna.com
One of the official makers of folding multi-blade Swiss Army knives

WILD BOAR BLADES / KOPROMED USA
1701 Broadway PMB 282
Vancouver, WA 98663
360-735-0570; Fax: 360-735-0390
info@wildboarblades.com;
wildboarblades@aol.com;
www.wildboarblade.com
Wild Boar Blades is pleased to carry a full line of Kopromed knives and kitchenware imported from Poland

WILLIAM HENRY FINE KNIVES
3200 NE Rivergate St
McMinnville, OR 97128
888-563-4500; Fax: 503-434-9704
www.williamhenryknives.com
Semi-custom folding knives for hunting and general use; some limited editions

WUU JAU CO. INC
2600 S Kelly Ave
Edmond, OK 73013
800-722-5760; Fax: 877-256-4337
mail@wuujau.com; www.wuujau.com
Wide variety of imported fixed-blade and folding knives for hunting, fishing, camping, and general use. Wholesale to knife dealers only

WYOMING KNIFE CORP.
101 Commerce Dr
Ft. Collins, CO 80524
970-224-3454; Fax: 970-226-0778
wyoknife@hotmail.com;
www.wyomingknife.com

XIKAR INC
PO Box 025757
Kansas City MO 64102
888-676-7380; 816-474-7555
info@xikar.com; www.xikar.com
Gentlemen's cutlery and accessories

importers

A.G. RUSSELL KNIVES INC
2900 S. 26th St
Rogers, AR 72758-8571
800-255-9034; 749-631-8493
ag@agrussell.com; www.agrussell.com
The oldest knife mail-order company, highest quality. Free catalog available. In these catalogs you will find the newest and the best. If you like knives, this catalog is a must. Celebrating 40 years in the industry

ADAMS INTERNATIONAL KNIFEWORKS
8710 Rosewood Hills
Edwardsville, IL 62025
Importers & foreign cutlers

AITOR-BERRIZARGO S.L.
P.I. Eitua PO Box 26
48240 Berriz Vizcaya
SPAIN
946826599; 94602250226
info@aitor.com; www.aitor.com
Sporting knives

ATLANTA CUTLERY CORP.
P.O.Box 839
Conyers, Ga 30012
800-883-0300; Fax: 770-388-0246
custserve@atlantacutlery.com;
www.atlantacutlery.com
Exotic knives from around the world

BAILEY'S
PO Box 550
Laytonville, CA 95454
800-322-4539; 707-984-8115
baileys@baileys-online.com;
www.baileys-online.com

BELTRAME, FRANCESCO
Fratelli Beltrame F&C snc Via dei Fabbri
15/B-33085 MANIAGO (PN)
ITALY
39 0427 701859
www.italianstiletto.com

BOKER USA, INC.
1550 Balsam St
Lakewood, CO 80214-5917
303-462-0662; 303-462-0668
sales@bokerusa.com; www.bokerusa.com
Ceramic blades

CAMPOS, IVAN DE ALMEIDA
R. Stelio M. Loureiro, 205
Centro, Tatui
BRAZIL
00-55-15-33056867
www.ivancampos.com

C.A.S. IBERIA, INC.
650 Industrial Blvd
Sale Creek, TN 37373
423-332-4700; 423-332-7248
info@casiberia.com; www.casiberia.com

CAS/HANWEI, MUELA
Catoctin Cutlery
PO Box 188
Smithsburg, MD 21783

CLASSIC INDUSTRIES
1325 Howard Ave, Suite 408
Burlingame, CA 94010

COAST CUTLERY CO.
8033 NE Holman St.
Portland, OR 97218
800-426-5858
staff@coastcutlery.com;
www.coastcutlery.com

COLUMBIA PRODUCTS CO.
PO Box 1333
Sialkot 51310
PAKISTAN

COLUMBIA PRODUCTS INT'L
PO Box 8243
New York, NY 10116-8243
201-854-3054; Fax: 201-854-7058
nycolumbia@aol.com;
http://www.columbiaproducts.homestead.com/cat.html
Pocket, hunting knives and swords of all kinds

COMPASS INDUSTRIES, INC.
104 E. 25th St
New York, NY 10010
800-221-9904; Fax: 212-353-0826
jeff@compassindustries.com;
www.compassindustries.com
Imported pocket knives

CONAZ COLTELLERIE
Dei F.Lli Consigli-Scarperia
Via G. Giordani, 20
50038 Scarperia (Firenze)
ITALY
36 55 846187; 39 55 846603
conaz@dada.it; www.consigliscarpeia.com
Handicraft workmanship of knives of the ancient Italian tradition. Historical and collection knives

CONSOLIDATED CUTLERY CO., INC.
696 NW Sharpe St
Port St. Lucie, FL 34983
772-878-6139

CRAZY CROW TRADING POST
PO Box 847
Pottsboro, TX 75076
800-786-6210; Fax: 903-786-9059
info@crazycrow.com; www.crazycrow.com
Solingen blades, knife making parts & supplies

DER FLEISSIGEN BEAVER
(The Busy Beaver)
Harvey Silk
PO Box 1166
64343 Griesheim
GERMANY
49 61552231; 49 6155 2433
Der.Biber@t-online.de
Retail custom knives. Knife shows in Germany & UK

EXTREMA RATIO SAS
Mauro Chiostri; Mavrizio Castrati
Via Tourcoing 40/p
59100 Prato (PO)
ITALY
0039 0574 58 4639; 0039 0574 581312
info@extremarazio.com; www.extremaratio.com
Tactical & military knives manufacturing

FALLKNIVEN AB
Havrevagen 10
S-96142 Boden
SWEDEN
46 92154422; 46 92154433
info@fallkniven.se
www.fallkniven.com
High quality knives

FREDIANI COLTELLI FINLANDESI
Via Lago Maggiore 41
I-21038 Leggiuno
ITALY

GIESSER MESSERFABRIK GMBH, JOHANNES
Raiffeisenstr 15
D-71349 Winnenden
GERMANY
49-7195-1808-29
info@giesser.de; www.giesser.de
Professional butchers and chef's knives

HIMALAYAN IMPORTS
3495 Lakeside Dr
Reno, NV 89509
775-825-2279
unclebill@himalayan-imports.com; www.himilayan-imports.com

IVAN DE ALMEIDA CAMPOS-KNIFE DEALER
R. Xi De Agosto
107, Centro, Tatui, Sp 18270
BRAZIL
55-15-251-8092; 55-15-251-4896
campos@bitweb.com.br
Custom knives from all Brazilian knifemakers

JOY ENTERPRISES
1862 M.L. King Blvd
Riviera Beach, FL 33404
800-500-3879; 561-863-3277
mail@joyenterprises.com; www.joyenterprises.com
Fury™, Mustang™, Hawg Knives, Muela

KELLAM KNIVES CO.
902 S Dixie Hwy
Lantana, FL 33462
800-390-6918; 561-588-3186
info@kellamknives.com; www.kellamknives.com
Knives from Finland; own line of knives

KNIFE IMPORTERS, INC.
11307 Conroy Ln
Manchaca, TX 78652
512-282-6860, Fax: 512-282-7504
Wholesale only

KNIGHTS EDGE
5696 N Northwest Hwy
Chicago, IL 60646
773-775-3888; 773-775-3339
www.knightsedge.com
Exclusive designers of our Rittersteel, Stagesteel and Valiant Arms and knightedge lines of weapon

LEISURE PRODUCTS CORP.
PO Box 1171
Sialkot-51310
PAKISTAN

L. C. RISTINEN
Suomi Shop
17533 Co Hwy 38
Frazee MN 56544
218-538-6633; 218-538-6633
icrist@wcta.net
Scandinavian cutlery custom antique, books and reindeer antler

LINDER, CARL NACHF.
Erholungstr. 10
D-42699 Solingen
GERMANY
212 33 0 856; Fax: 212 33 71 04
info@linder.de; www.linder.de

MARTTIINI KNIVES
PO Box 44 (Marttiinintie 3)
96101 Rovaniemi
FINLAND

MATTHEWS CUTLERY
4401 Sentry Dr, Suite K
Tucker, GA 30084-6561
770-939-6915

MESSER KLÖTZLI
PO Box 104
Hohengasse 3, Ch-3402 Burgdorf
SWITZERLAND
034 422 2378; 034 422 7693
info@klotzli.com; www.klotzli.com

MURAKAMI, ICHIRO
Knife Collectors Assn. Japan
Tokuda Nishi 4 Chome, 76 Banchi, Ginancho
Hashimagun, Gifu
JAPAN
81 58 274 1960; 81 58 273 7369
www.gix.orjp/~n-resin/

MUSEUM REPLICAS LIMITED
2147 Gees Mill Rd
Conyers, GA 30012
800-883-8838
www.museumreplicas.com

NICHOLS CO.
Pomfret Rd
South Pomfret, VT 05067
Import & distribute knives from EKA (Sweden), Helle (Norway), Brusletto (Norway), Roselli (Finland). Also market Zippo products, Snow, Nealley axes and hatchets and snow & Neally axes

NORMARK CORP.
Craig Weber
10395 Yellow Circle Dr
Minnetonka, MN 55343

PRODUCTORS AITOR, S.A.
Izelaieta 17
48260 Ermua
SPAIN
943-170850; 943-170001
info@aitor.com
Sporting knives

PROFESSIONAL CUTLERY SERVICES
9712 Washburn Rd
Downey, CA 90241
562-803-8778; 562-803-4261
Wholesale only. Full service distributor of domestic & imported brand name cutlery. Exclusive U.S. importer for both Marto Swords and Battle Ready Valiant Armory edged weapons

SCANDIA INTERNATIONAL INC.
5475 W Inscription Canyon Dr
Prescott, AZ 86305
928-442-0140; Fax: 928-442-0342
mora@cableone.net; www.frosts-scandia.com
Frosts Knives of Sweden

STAR SALES CO., INC.
1803 N. Central St
Knoxville, TN 37917
800-745-6433; Fax: 865-524-4889
www.starknives.com

SVORD KNIVES
Smith Rd., RD 2
Waiuku, South Auckland
NEW ZEALAND
64 9 2358846; Fax: 64 9 2356483
www.svord.com

SWISS ARMY BRANDS LTD.
The Forschner Group, Inc.
One Research Drive
Shelton, CT 06484
203-929-6391; 203-929-3786
www.swissarmy.com

TAYLOR CUTLERY
PO Box 1638
1736 N. Eastman Rd
Kingsport, TN 37662
Colman Knives along with Smith & Wesson, Cuttin Horse, John Deere, Zoland knives

UNITED CUTLERY CORP.
1425 United Blvd
Sevierville, TN 37876
865-428-2532; 865-428-2267
order@unitedcutlery.com; www.unitedcutlery.com
Harley-Davidson ® Colt ®, Stanley ®, U21 ®, Rigid Knives ®, Outdoor Life ®, Ford ®, hunting, camping, fishing, collectible & fantasy knives

UNIVERSAL AGENCIES INC
4690 S Old Peachtree Rd, Suite C
Norcross, GA 30071-1517
678-969-9147; Fax: 678-969-9169
info@knifecupplies.com;
www.knifesupplies.com;
www.thunderforged.com; www.uai.org
Serving the cutlery industry with the finest selection of India Stag, Buffalo Horn, Thurnderforged ™ Damascus. Mother of Pearl, Knife Kits and more

VALOR CORP.
1001 Sawgrass Corp Pkwy
Sunrise, FL 33323
800-899-8256; Fax: 954-377-4941
www.valorcorp.com
Wide variety of imported & domestic knives

WENGER N. A.
15 Corporate Dr
Orangeburg, NY 10962
800-431-2996
www.wengerna.com
Swiss Army ™ Knives

WILD BOAR BLADES
1701 Broadway, Suite 282
Vancouver, WA 98663
888-476-4400; 360-735-0390
usakopro@aol.com;
www.wildboarblades.com
Carries a full line of Kopromed knives and kitchenware imported from Poland

ZWILLING J.A. HENCKELS USA
171 Saw Mill River Rd
Hawthorne, NY 10532
800-777-4308; Fax: 914-747-1850
info@jahenckels.com;
www.jahenckels.com
Kitchen cutlery, scissors, gadgets, flatware and cookware

knife making supplies

AFRICAN IMPORT CO.
Alan Zanotti
22 Goodwin Rd
Plymouth, MA 02360
508-746-8552; 508-746-0404
africanimport@aol.com
Ivory

AMERICAN SIEPMANN CORP.
65 Pixley Industrial Parkway
Rochester, NY 14624
800-724-0919; Fax: 585-247-1883
www.siepmann.com
CNC blade grinding equipment, grinding wheels, production blade grinding services. Sharpening stones and sharpening equipment

ATLANTA CUTLERY CORP.
P.O.Box 839
Conyers, Ga 30012
800-883-0300; Fax: 770-388-0246
custserve@atlantacutlery.com;
www.atlantacutlery.com

BATAVIA ENGINEERING
PO Box 53
Magaliesburg, 1791
SOUTH AFRICA
27-14-5771294
bertie@batavia.co.za; www.batavia.co.za
Contact wheels for belt grinders and surface grinders; damascus and mokume

BLADEMAKER, THE
Gary Kelley
17485 SW Phesant Ln
Beaverton, OR 97006
503-649-7867
garykelly@theblademaker.com;
www.theblademaker.com
Period knife and hawk blades for hobbyists & re-enactors and in dendritic D2 steel. "Ferroulithic" steel-stone spear point, blades and arrowheads

BOONE TRADING CO., INC.
PO Box 669
562 Coyote Rd
Brinnon, WA 98320
800-423-1945; Fax: 360-796-4511
www.boonetrading.com
Ivory of all types, bone, horns

BORGER, WOLF
Benzstrasse 8
76676 Graben-Neudorf
GERMANY
wolf@messerschmied.de;
www.messerschmied.de

BOYE KNIVES
PO Box 1238
Dolan Springs, AZ 86441-1238
800-853-1617; 928-767-4273
info@boyeknives.com;
www.boyeknives.com
Dendritic steel and Dendritic cobalt

BRONK'S KNIFEWORKS
Lyle Brunckhorst
Country Village
23706 7th Ave SE, Suite B
Bothell, WA 98021
425-402-3484
bronks@bronksknifeworks.com;
www.bronksknifeworks.com
Damascus steel

CRAZY CROW TRADING POST
PO Box 847
Pottsboro, TX 75076
800-786-6210; Fax: 903-786-9059
info@crazycrow.com; www.crazycrow.com
Solingen blades, knife making parts & supplies

CUSTOM FURNACES
PO Box 353
Randvaal, 1873
SOUTH AFRICA
27 16 365-5723; 27 16 365-5738
johnlee@custom.co.za
Furnaces for hardening & tempering of knives

DAMASCUS-USA CHARLTON LTD.
149 Deans Farm Rd
Tyner, NC 27980-9607
252-221-2010
rcharlton@damascususa.com;
www.damascususa.com

DAN'S WHETSTONE CO., INC.
418 Hilltop Rd
Pearcy, AR 71964
501-767-1616; 501-767-9598
questions@danswhetstone.com;
www.danswhetstone.com
Natural abrasive Arkansas stone products

DIAMOND MACHINING TECHNOLOGY, INC. DMT
85 Hayes Memorial Dr
Marlborough, MA 01752
800-666-4DMT
dmtsharp@dmtsharp.com;
www.dmtsharp.com
Knife and tool sharpeners-diamond, ceramic and easy edge guided sharpening kits

DIGEM DIAMOND SUPPLIERS
7303 East Earll Drive
Scottsdale, Arizona 85251
602-620-3999
eglasser@cox.net
#1 international diamond tool provider. Every diamond tool you will ever need 1/16th of an inch to 11'x9'. BURRS, CORE DRILLS, SAW BLADES, MILLING SHAPES, AND WHEELS

DIXIE GUN WORKS, INC.
PO Box 130
Union City, TN 38281
800-238-6785; Fax: 731-885-0440
www.dixiegunworks.com
Knife and knifemaking supplies

EZE-LAP DIAMOND PRODUCTS
3572 Arrowhead Dr
Carson City, NV 89706
800-843-4815; Fax: 775-888-9555
sales@eze-lap.com; www.eze-lap.com
Diamond coated sharpening tools

FLITZ INTERNATIONAL, LTD.
821 Mohr Ave
Waterford, WI 53185
800-558-8611; Fax: 262-534-2991
info@flitz.com; www.flitz.com
Metal polish, buffing pads, wax

FORTUNE PRODUCTS, INC.
205 Hickory Creek Rd
Marble Falls, TX 78654-3357
830-693-6111; Fax: 830-693-6394
www.accusharp.com
AccuSharp knife sharpeners

GILMER WOOD CO.
2211 NW St Helens Rd
Portland, OR 97210
503-274-1271; Fax: 503-274-9839
www.gilmerwood.com

GRS CORP.
D.J. Glaser
PO Box 1153
Emporia, KS 66801
800-835-3519; Fax: 620-343-9640
glendo@glendo.com; www.glendo.com
Engraving, equipment, tool sharpener, books/ videos

HALPERN TITANIUM INC.
Les and Marianne Halpern
PO Box 214
4 Springfield St
Three Rivers, MA 01080
888-283-8627; Fax: 413-289-2372
info@halperntitanium.com;
www.halperntitanium.com
Titanium, carbon fiber, G-10, fasteners; CNC milling

HAWKINS KNIVE MAKING SUPPLIES
110 Buckeye Rd
Fayetteville, GA 30214
770-964-1177; Fax: 770-306-2877
Sales@hawkinsknifemakingsupplies.com
www.HawkinsKnifeMakingSupllies.com
All styles

HILTARY-USGRC
6060 East Thomas Road
Scottsdale, AZ 85251
Office: 480-945-0700
Fax: 480-945-3333
usgrc@cox.net
Gibeon Meteorite, Recon Gems, Diamond cutting tools, Exotic natural minerals, garaffe bone. Atomic absorbtion/ spectographic analyst, precisious metal

HOUSE OF TOOLS LTD.
#54-5329 72 Ave. S.E.
Calgary, Alberta
CANADA T2C 4X
403-640-4594; Fax: 403-451-7006

INDIAN JEWELERS SUPPLY CO.
Mail Order: 601 E Coal Ave
Gallup, NM 87301-6005
2105 San Mateo Blvd NE
Albuquerque, NM 87110-5148
505-722-4451; 505-265-3701
orders@ijsinc.com; www.ijsinc.com
Handle materials, tools, metals

INTERAMCO INC.
5210 Exchange Dr
Flint, MI 48507
810-732-8181; 810-732-6116
solutions@interamco.com
Knife grinding and polishing

JANTZ SUPPLY / KOVAL KNIVES
PO Box 584
309 West Main
Davis, OK 73030
800-351-8900; 580-369-2316
jantz@brightok.net; www.knifemaking.com
Pre shaped blades, kit knives, complete knifemaking supply line

JOHNSON, R.B.
I.B.S. Int'l. Folder Supplies
Box 11
Clearwater, MN 55320
320-558-6128; 320-558-6128
Threaded pivot pins, screws, taps, etc.

JOHNSON WOOD PRODUCTS
34897 Crystal Rd
Strawberry Point, IA 52076
563-933-6504

K&G FINISHING SUPPLIES
1972 Forest Ave
Lakeside, AZ 85929
800-972-1192; 928-537-8877
csinfo@knifeandgun.com;
www.knifeandgun.com
Full service supplies

KOWAK IVORY
Roland and Kathy Quimby
(April-Sept): PO Box 350
Ester, AK 99725
907-479-9335
(Oct-March)
PO Box 693
Bristow, OK 74010
918-367-2684
sales@kowakivory.com;
www.kowakivory.com
Fossil ivories

LITTLE GIANT POWER HAMMER
Harlan "Sid" Suedmeier
420 4th Corso
Nebraska City, NE 68410
402-873-6603

LIVESAY, NEWT
3306 S Dogwood St
Siloam Springs, AR 72761
479-549-3356; 479-549-3357
Combat utility knives, titanium knives, sportsmen knives, custom made orders taken on knives and after market Kydex© sheaths for commercial or custom cutlery

LOHMAN CO., FRED
3405 NE Broadway
Portland, OR 97232
503-282-4567; Fax: 503-287-2678
lohman@katana4u.com;
www.japanese-swords.com

M MILLER ORIGINALS
Michael Miller
2960 E Carver Ave
Kingman AZ 86401
928-757-1359
mike@milleroriginals.com;
www.mmilleroriginals.com
Supplies stabilized juniper burl blocks and scales

MARKING METHODS, INC.
Sales
301 S. Raymond Ave
Alhambra, CA 91803-1531
626-282-8823; Fax: 626-576-7564
experts@markingmethods.com;
www.markingmethods.com
Knife etching equipment & service

MASECRAFT SUPPLY CO.
254 Amity St
Meriden, CT 06450
800-682-5489; Fax: 203-238-2373
info@masecraftsupply.com;
www.masecraftsupply.com
Natural & specialty synthetic handle materials & more

MEIER STEEL
Daryl Meier
75 Forge Rd
Carbondale, IL 62903
618-549-3234; Fax: 618-549-6239
www.meiersteel.com

CULPEPPER & CO.
Joe Culpepper
P.O. Box 690
8285 Georgia Rd.
Otto, NC 28763
828-524-6842; Fax: 828-369-7809
culpepperandco@verizon.net
www.knifehandles.com http://www.knifehandles.com
www.stingrayproducts.com <http://www.stingrayproducts.com>
Mother of pearl, bone, abalone, stingray, dyed stag, blacklip, ram's horn, mammoth ivory, coral, scrimshaw

NICO, BERNARD
PO Box 5151
Nelspruit 1200
SOUTH AFRICA
011-2713-7440099; 011-2713-7440099
bernardn@iafrica.com

NORRIS, MIKE
Rt 2 Box 242A
Tollesboro, KY 41189
606-798-1217
Damascus steel

OSO FAMOSO
PO Box 654
Ben Lomond, CA 95005
831-336-2343
oso@osofamoso.com;
www.osofamoso.com
Mammoth ivory bark

OZARK KNIFE & GUN
3165 S Campbell Ave
Springfield, MO 65807
417-886-CUTT; 417-887-2635
danhoneycutt@sbcglobal.net
28 years in the cutlery business, Missouri's oldest cutlery firm

PARAGON INDUSTRIES, INC. L. P.
2011 South Town East Blvd
Mesquite, TX 75149-1122
800-876-4328; Fax: 972-222-0646
info@paragonweb.com;
www.paragonweb.com
Heat treating furnaces for knifemakers

POPLIN, JAMES / POP'S KNIVES & SUPPLIES
103 Oak St
Washington, GA 30673
706-678-5408; Fax: 706-678-5409
www.popsknifesupplies.com

PUGH, JIM
PO Box 711
917 Carpenter
Azle, TX 76020
817-444-2679; Fax: 817-444-5455
Rosewood and ebony Micarta blocks,rivets for Kydex sheaths, 0-80 screws for folders

RADOS, JERRY
7523E 5000 N. Rd
Grant Park, IL 60940
815-405-5061
jerry@radosknives.com;
www.radosknives.com
Damascus steel

REACTIVE METALS STUDIO, INC.
PO Box 890
Clarksdale, AZ 86324
800-876-3434; 928-634-3434; Fax: 928-634-6734
info@reactivemetals.com; www.reactivemetals.com

R. FIELDS ANCIENT IVORY
Donald Fields
790 Tamerlane St
Deltona, FL 32725
386-532-9070
donaldfields@aol.com
Selling ancient ivories; Mammoth, fossil & walrus

RICK FRIGAULT CUSTOM KNIVES
3584 Rapidsview Dr
Niagara Falls, Ontario
CANADA L2G 6C4
905-295-6695
zipcases@zipcases.com;
www.zipcases.com
Selling padded zippered knife pouches with an option to personalize the outside with the marker, purveyor, stores-address, phone number, email web-site or any other information needed. Available in black cordura, mossy oak camo in sizes 4"x2" to 20"x4.5"

RIVERSIDE MACHINE
201 W Stillwell
DeQueen, AR 71832
870-642-7643; Fax: 870-642-4023
uncleal@riversidemachine.net
www.riversidemachine.net

ROCKY MOUNTAIN KNIVES
George L. Conklin
PO Box 902, 615 Franklin
Ft. Benton, MT 59442
406-622-3268; Fax: 406-622-3410
bbgrus@ttc-cmc.net
Working knives

RUMMELL, HANK
10 Paradise Lane
Warwick, NY 10990
845-469-9172
hank@newyorkcustomknives.com;
www.newyorkcustomknives.com

SAKMAR, MIKE
1451 Clovelly Ave
Rochester, MI 48307
248-852-6775; Fax: 248-852-8544
mikesakmar@yahoo.com
Mokume bar stock. Retail & wholesale

SANDPAPER, INC. OF ILLINOIS
P.O. Box 2579
Glen Ellyn, IL 60138
630-629-3320; Fax: 630-629-3324
sandinc@aol.com; www.sandpaperinc.com
Abrasive belts, rolls, sheets & discs

SCHEP'S FORGE
PO Box 395
Shelton, NE 68876-0395

SENTRY SOLUTIONS LTD.
PO Box 214
Wilton, NH 03086
800-546-8049; Fax: 603-654-3003
info@sentrysolutions.com;
www.sentrysolutions.com
Knife care products

SHEFFIELD KNIFEMAKERS SUPPLY, INC.
PO Box 741107
Orange City, FL 32774
386-775-6453
email@sheffieldsupply.com;
www.sheffieldsupply.com

SHINING WAVE METALS
PO Box 563
Snohomish, WA 98291
425-334-5569
info@shiningwave.com;
www.shiningwave.com
A full line of mokume-gane in precious and non-precious metals for knifemakers, jewelers and other artists

SMITH ABRASIVES, INC. / SMITH WHETSTONE, INC.
1700 Sleepy Valley Rd
Hot Springs, AR 71901
www.smithabrasives.com

SMOLEN FORGE, INC.
Nick Smolen
S1735 Vang Rd
Westby, WI 54667
608-634-3569; Fax: 608-634-3869
smoforge@mwt.net;
www.smolenforge.com
Damascus billets & blanks, Mokume gane billets

SOSTER SVENSTRUP BYVEJ 16
Søster Svenstrup Byvej 16
4130 Viby Sjælland
Denmark
45 46 19 43 05; Fax: 45 46 19 53 19
www.poulstrande.com

STAMASCUS KNIFEWORKS INC.
Ed VanHoy
24255 N Fork River Rd
Abingdon, VA 24210
276-944-4885; Fax: 276-944-3187
stamascus@hughes.net;
www.stamascus-knive-works.com
Blade steels

STOVER, JEFF
PO Box 43
Torrance, CA 90507
310-532-2166
edgedealer1@yahoo.com;
www.edgedealer.com
Fine custom knives, top makers

TEXAS KNIFEMAKERS SUPPLY
10649 Haddington Suite 180
Houston TX 77043
713-461-8632; Fax: 713-461-8221
sales@texasknife.com;
www.texasknife.com
Working straight knives. Hunters including upswept skinners and custom walking sticks

TRU-GRIT, INC.
760 E Francis Unit N
Ontario, CA 91761
909-923-4116; Fax: 909-923-9932
www.trugrit.com
The latest in Norton and 3/M ceramic grinding belts. Also Super Flex, Trizact, Norax and Micron belts to 3000 grit. All of the popular belt grinders. Buffers and variable speed motors. ATS-34, 440C, BG-42, CPM S-30V, 416 and Damascus steel

UNIVERSAL AGENCIES INC
4690 S Old Peachtree Rd, Suite C
Norcross, GA 30071-1517
678-969-9147; Fax: 678-969-9169
info@knifecupplies.com;
www.knifesupplies.com;
www.thunderforged.com; www.uai.org
Serving the cutlery industry with the finest selection of India Stag, Buffalo Horn, Thurnderforged ™ Damascus. Mother of Pearl, Knife Kits and more

WASHITA MOUNTAIN WHETSTONE CO.
PO Box 20378
Hot Springs, AR 71903-0378
501-525-3914; Fax: 501-525-0816
wmw@hsnp

WEILAND, J. REESE
PO Box 2337
Riverview, FL 33568
813-671-0661; 727-595-0378
rwphil413@earthlink.net
Folders, straight knives, etc.

WILD WOODS
Jim Fray
9608 Monclova Rd
Monclova, OH 43542
419-866-0435

WILSON, R.W.
PO Box 2012
113 Kent Way
Weirton, WV 26062
304-723-2771

WOOD CARVERS SUPPLY, INC.
PO Box 7500-K
Englewood, FL 34223
800-284-6229; 941-460-0123
info@woodcarverssupply.com;
www.woodcarverssupply.com
Over 2,000 unique wood carving tools

WOOD STABILIZING SPECIALISTS INT'L. LLC
2940 Fayette Ave
Ionia, IA 50645
800-301-9774; 641-435-4746
mike@stabilizedwood.com;
www.stabilizedwood.com
Processor of acrylic impregnated materials

ZOWADA CUSTOM KNIVES
Tim Zowada
4509 E. Bear River Rd
Boyne Falls, MI 49713
231-348-5416
tim@tzknives.com; www.tzknives.com
Damascus, pocket knives, swords, Lower case gothic tz logo

mail order sales

A.G. RUSSELL KNIVES INC
2900 S. 26th St
Rogers, AR 72758-8571
800-255-9034; 749-631-8493
ag@agrussell.com; www.agrussell.com
The oldest knife mail-order company, highest quality. Free catalog available. In these catalogs you will find the newest and the best. If you like knives, this catalog is a must

ARIZONA CUSTOM KNIVES
Julie Hyman
35 Miruela Ave
St. Augustine, FL 32080
904-826-4178
sharptalk@arizonacustomknifes.com; www.arizonacustomknives.com
Color catalog $5 U.S. / $7 Foreign

ARTISAN KNIVES
Ty Young
575 Targhee Twn Rd
Alta, WY 83414
304-353-8111
ty@artisanknives.com; www.artisanknives.com
Feature master artisan knives and makers in a unique "coffee table book" style format

ATLANTA CUTLERY CORP.
P.O.Box 839
Conyers, Ga 30012
800-883-0300; Fax: 770-388-0246
custserve@atlantacutlery.com; www.atlantacutlery.com

ATLANTIC BLADESMITHS/PETER STEBBINS
50 Mill Rd
Littleton, MA 01460
978-952-6448
Sell, trade, buy; carefully selected handcrafted, benchmade and factory knives

BALLARD CUTLERY
1495 Brummel Ave.
Elk Grove Village, IL 60007
847-228-0070

BECK'S CUTLERY SPECIALTIES
107 S Edinburgh Dr
Cary, NC 27511
919-460-0203; Fax: 919-460-7772
beckscutlery@mindspring.com; www.beckscutlery.com
Knives

BLADEGALLERY, INC. / EPICUREAN EDGE, THE
107 Central Way
Kirkland, WA 98033
425-889-5980; Fax: 425-889-5981
info@bladegallery.com; www.bladegallery.com
Bladegallery.com specializes in hand-made one-of-a-kind knives from around the world. We have an emphasis on forged knives and high-end gentlemen's folders

BLUE RIDGE KNIVES
166 Adwolfe Rd
Marion, VA 24354
276-783-6143; 276-783-9298
onestop@blueridgeknives.com; www.blueridgeknives.com
Wholesale distributor of knives

BOB NEAL CUSTOM KNIVES
PO Box 20923
Atlanta, GA 30320
770-914-7794
bob@bobnealcustomknives.com; www.bobnealcustomknives.com
Exclusive limited edition custom knives-sets & single

BOB'S TRADING POST
308 N Main St
Hutchinson, KS 67501
620-669-9441
bobstradingpost@cox.net; www.gunshopfinder.com
Tad custom knives with reichert custom sheaths one at a time, one of a kind

BOONE TRADING CO., INC.
PO Box 669
562 Coyote Rd
Brinnon, WA 98320
800-423-1945; Fax: 360-796-4511
www.boonetrading.com
Ivory of all types, bone, horns

CARMEL CUTLERY
Dolores & 6th
PO Box 1346
Carmel, CA 93921
831-624-6699; 831-624-6780
ccutlery@ix.netcom.com; www.carmelcutlery.com
Quality custom and a variety of production pocket knives, swords; kitchen cutlery; personal grooming items

CUSTOM KNIFE CONSIGNMENT
PO Box 20923
Atlanta, GA 30320
770-914-7794; 770-914-7796
bob@customknifeconsignment.com; www.customknifeconsignment.com
We sell your knives

CUTLERY SHOPPE
3956 E Vantage Pointe Ln
Meridian, ID 83642-7268
800-231-1272; Fax: 208-884-4433
order@cutleryshoppe.com; www.cutleryshoppe.com
Discount pricing on top quality brands

CUTTING EDGE, THE
2900 South 26th St
Rogers, AR 72758-8571
800-255-9034; Fax: 479-631-8493
ce_info@cuttingedge.com; www.cuttingedge.com
After-market knives since 1968. They offer about 1,000 individual knives for sale each month. Subscription by first class mail, in U.S. $20 per year, Canada or Mexico by air mail, $25 per year. All overseas by air mail, $40 per year. The oldest and the most experienced in the business of buying and selling knives. They buy collections of any size, take knives on consignment. Every month there are 4-8 pages in color featuring the work of top makers

DENTON, J.W.
102 N. Main St
Hiawassee, GA 30546
706-896-2292
jwdenton@alltel.net
Loveless knives

DUNN KNIVES INC.
PO Box 204
5830 NW Carlson Rd
Rossville, KS 66533
800-245-6483
steve.greene@dunnknives.com; www.dunnknives.com

FAZALARE, ROY
PO Box 1335
Agoura Hills, CA 91376
818-879-6161 after 7pm
ourfaz@aol.com
Handmade multiblades; older case; Fight'n Rooster; Bulldog brand & Cripple Creek

FROST CUTLERY CO.
PO Box 22636
Chattanooga, TN 37422
800-251-7768; Fax: 423-894-9576
www.frostcutlery.com

GENUINE ISSUE INC.
949 Middle Country Rd
Selden, NY 11784
631-696-3802; 631-696-3803
gicutlery@aol.com
Antique knives, swords

GEORGE TICHBOURNE CUSTOM KNIVES
7035 Maxwell Rd #5
Mississauga, Ontario L5S 1R5
CANADA
905-670-0200
sales@tichbourneknives.com; www.tichbourneknives.com
Canadian custom knifemaker has full retail knife store

GODWIN, INC. G. GEDNEY
PO Box 100
Valley Forge, PA 19481
610-783-0670; Fax: 610-783-6083
sales@gggodwin.com; www.gggodwin.com
18th century reproductions

GUILD KNIVES
Donald Guild
320 Paani Place 1A
Paia, HI 96779
808-877-3109
don@guildknives.com; www.guildknives.com
Purveyor of custom art knives

HOUSE OF TOOLS LTD.
#136, 8228 Macleod Tr. SE
Calgary, Alberta, Canada
T2H 2B8

JENCO SALES, INC. / KNIFE IMPORTERS, INC. / WHITE

LIGHTNING
PO Box 1000
11307 Conroy Ln
Manchaca, TX 78652
303-444-2882
kris@finishlineusa.com
www.whitelightningco.com
Wholesale only

KELLAM KNIVES CO.
902 S Dixie Hwy
Lantana, FL 33462
800-390-6918; 561-588-3186
info@kellamknives.com;
www.kellamknives.com
Largest selection of Finnish knives; own line of folders and fixed blades

KNIFEART.COM
13301 Pompano Dr
Little Rock AR 72211
501-221-1319; Fax: 501-221-2695
www.knifeart.com
Large internet seller of custom knives & upscale production knives

KNIFEMASTERS CUSTOM KNIVES/J&S FEDER
PO Box 208
Westport, CT 06880
(203) 226-5211
Investment grade custom knives

KNIVES PLUS
2467 I 40 West
Amarillo, TX 79109
800-687-6202
salessupport@knivesplus.com; www.knivesplus.com
Retail cutlery and cutlery accessories since 1987

KRIS CUTLERY
2314 Monte Verde Dr
Pinole, CA 94564
510-758-9912 Fax: 510-223-8968
kriscutlery@aol.com; www.kriscutlery.com
Japanese, medieval, Chinese & Philippine

LONE STAR WHOLESALE
2407 W Interstate 40
Amarillo, TX 79109
806-356-9540
Wholesale only; major brands and accessories

MATTHEWS CUTLERY
4401 Sentry Dr
Tucker, GA 30084-6561
770-939-6915

MOORE CUTLERY
PO Box 633
Lockport, IL 60441
708-301-4201
www.knives.cx
Owned & operated by Gary Moore since 1991 (a full-time dealer). Purveyor of high quality custom & production knives

MORTY THE KNIFE MAN, INC.
4 Manorhaven Blvd
Pt Washington, NY 11050
516-767-2357; 516-767-7058

MUSEUM REPLICAS LIMITED
2147 Gees Mill Rd
Conyers, GA 30012
800-883-8838
www.museumreplicas.com
Historically accurate and battle ready swords & daggers

NORDIC KNIVES
1634-C Copenhagen Drive
Solvang, CA 93463
805-688-3612; Fax: 805-688-1635
info@nordicknives.com;
www.nordicknives.com
Custom and Randall knives

PARKERS' KNIFE COLLECTOR SERVICE
6715 Heritage Business Court
Chattanooga, TN 37422
615-892-0448; Fax: 615-892-9165

PLAZA CUTLERY, INC.
3333 S. Bristol St., Suite 2060
South Coast Plaza
Costa Mesa, CA 92626
866-827-5292; 714-549-3932
dan@plazacutlery.com;
www.plazacutlery.com
Largest selection of knives on the west coast. Custom makers from beginners to the best. All customs, William Henry, Strider, Reeves, Randalls & others available online by phone

RANDALL KNIFE SOCIETY
PO Box 158
Meadows of Dan, VA 24120
276-952-2500
payrks@gate.net;
www.randallknifesociety.com
Randall, Loveless, Scagel, moran, antique pocket knives

ROBERTSON'S CUSTOM CUTLERY
4960 Sussex Dr
Evans, GA 30809
706-650-0252; 706-860-1623
rccedge@csranet.com; www.robertsoncustomcutlery.com
World class custom knives, Vanguard knives-Limited exclusive design

SHADOW, JAY & KAREN
9719 N Hayden Rd
Scottsdale, AZ 85258
866-455-1344; 480-947-2136
service@mustlovepens.com;
www.jaykar.com
Diamonds imported direct from Belgium

SMOKY MOUNTAIN KNIFE WORKS, INC.
2320 Winfield Dunn Pkwy
PO Box 4430
Sevierville, TN 37864
800-251-9306; 865-453-5871
info@smkw.com; www.eknifeworks.com
The world's largest knife showplace, catalog and website

STODDARD'S, INC.
50 Temple Pl
Boston, MA 02116
617-426-4187
Cutlery (kitchen, pocket knives, Randall-made knives, custom knives, scissors & manicure tools) binoculars, Iwo vision aids, personal care items (hair brushes, manicure sets mirrors)

VOYLES, BRUCE
PO Box 22007
Chattanooga, TN 37422
423-238-6753; Fax: 423-238-3960
bruce@jbrucevoyles.com;
www.jbrucevoyles.com
Knives, knife auctions

appraisers

Levine, Bernard, P.O. Box 2404, Eugene, OR, 97402, 541-484-0294, brlevine@ix.netcom.com

Russell, A.G., Knives Inc, 2900 S. 26th St.,

knife services

Rogers, AR 72758-8571, 800-255-9034, 479-631-8493, ag@agrussell.com, www.agrussell.com
Vallini, Massimo, Via G. Bruno 7, 20154 Milano, ITALY, 02-33614751, massimo_vallini@yahoo.it, Knife expert

custom grinders

McGowan Manufacturing Company, 4854 N Shamrock Pl #100, Tucson, AZ, 85705, 800-342-4810, 520-219-0884, info@mcgowanmfg.com, www.mcgowanmfg.com, Knife sharpeners, hunting axes
Peele, Bryan, The Elk Rack, 215 Ferry St. P.O. Box 1363, Thompson Falls, MT, 59873
Schlott, Harald, Zingster Str. 26, 13051 Berlin, GERMANY, 049 030 9293346, harald.schlott@T-online.de, Custom grinder, custom handle artisan, display case/box maker, etcher, scrimshander
Wilson, R.W., P.O. Box 2012, Weirton, WV, 26062

custom handles

Cooper, Jim, 1221 Cook St, Ramona, CA, 92065-3214, 760-789-1097, (760) 788-7992, jamcooper@aol.com
Burrows, Chuck, dba Wild Rose Trading Co, 289 Laposta Canyon Rd, Durango, CO, 81303, 970-259-8396, chuck@wrtcleather.com, www.wrtcleather.com
Fields, Donald, 790 Tamerlane St, Deltona, FL, 32725, 386-532-9070, donaldfields@aol.com, Selling ancient ivories; mammoth & fossil walrus
Grussenmeyer, Paul G., 310 Kresson Rd, Cherry Hill, NJ, 08034, 856-428-1088, 856-428-8997, pgrussentne@comcast.net, www.pgcarvings.com
Holland, Dennis K., 4908-17th Pl., Lubbock, TX, 79416
Imboden II, Howard L., hi II Originals, 620 Deauville Dr., Dayton, OH, 45429
Kelso, Jim, 577 Collar Hill Rd, Worcester, VT, 05682, 802-229-4254, (802) 223-0595
Knack, Gary, 309 Wightman, Ashland, OR, 97520
Marlatt, David, 67622 Oldham Rd., Cambridge, OH, 43725, 740-432-7549
Mead, Dennis, 2250 E. Mercury St., Inverness, FL, 34453-0514
Myers, Ron, 6202 Marglenn Ave., Baltimore, MD, 21206, 410-866-6914
Saggio, Joe, 1450 Broadview Ave. #12, Columbus, OH, 43212, jvsag@webtv.net, www.j.v.saggio@worldnet.att.net, Handle Carver
Schlott, Harald, Zingster Str. 26, 13051 Berlin, GERMANY, 049 030 9293346, harald.schlott@T-online.de, Custom grinder, custom handle artisan, display case/box maker, etcher, scrimshander
Snell, Barry A., 4801 96th St. N., St. Petersburg, FL, 33708-3740
Vallotton, A., 621 Fawn Ridge Dr., Oakland, OR, 97462
Watson, Silvia, 350 Jennifer Lane, Driftwood, TX, 78619
Wilderness Forge, 315 North 100 East, Kanab, UT, 84741, 435-644-3674, bhatting@xpressweb.com
Williams, Gary, (GARBO), PO Box 210, Glendale, KY, 42740-2010

display cases and boxes

Bill's Custom Cases, P O Box 603, Montague, CA, 96064, 530-459-5968, billscustomcases@earthlink.net
Brooker, Dennis, Rt. 1, Box 12A, Derby, IA, 50068
Chas Clements' Custom Leathercraft, Chas, 1741 Dallas St., Aurora, CO, 80010-2018, 303-364-0403, GRYPHONS@HOME.NET, Display case/box maker, Leatherworker, Knife appraiser
Freund, Steve, Tomway LLC, 1646 Tichenor Court, Atlanta, GA, 30338, 770-393-8349, steve@tomway.com, www.tomway.com
Gimbert, Nelson, P.O. Box 787, Clemmons, NC, 27012
McLean, Lawrence, 12344 Meritage Ct, Rancho Cucamonga, CA, 91739, 714-848-5779, lmclean@charter.net
Miller, Michael K., M&M Kustom Krafts, 28510 Santiam Highway, Sweet Home, OR, 97386
Miller, Robert, P.O. Box 2722, Ormond Beach, FL, 32176
Retichek, Joseph L., W9377 Co. TK. D, Beaver Dam, WI, 53916
Robbins, Wayne, 11520 Inverway, Belvidere, IL, 61008
S&D Enterprises, 20 East Seventh St, Manchester, OH, 45144, 937-549-2602, 937-549-2602, sales@s-denterprises.com, www.s-denterprises.com, Display case/ box maker. Manufacturer of aluminum display, chipboard type displays, wood displays. Silk screening or acid etching for logos on product
Schlott, Harald, Zingster Str. 26, 13051 Berlin, GERMANY, 049 030 9293346, harald.schlott@T-online.de, Custom grinder, custom handle artisan, display case/box maker, etcher, scrimshander

engravers

Adlam, Tim, 1705 Witzel Ave., Oshkosh, WI, 54902, 920-235-4589, www.adlamngraving.com
Alfano, Sam, 36180 Henry Gaines Rd., Pearl River, LA, 70452
Allard, Gary, 2395 Battlefield Rd., Fishers Hill, VA, 22626
Alpen, Ralph, 7 Bentley Rd., West Grove, PA, 19390, 610-869-7141
Baron, David, Baron Technology Inc., 62 Spring Hill Rd., Trumbull, CT, 06611, 203-452-0515, bti@baronengraving.com, www.baronengraving.com, Polishing, plating, inlays, artwork
Bates, Billy, 2302 Winthrop Dr. SW, Decatur, AL, 35603, bbrn@aol.com, www.angelfire.com/al/billybates
Bettenhausen, Merle L., 17358 Ottawa, Tinley Park, IL, 60477
Blair, Jim, PO Box 64, 59 Mesa Verde, Glenrock, WY, 82637, 307-436-8115, jblairengrav@msn.com
Bonshire, Benita, 1121 Burlington, Muncie, IN, 47302
Boster, A.D., 3000 Clarks Bridge Rd Lot 42, Gainesville, GA, 30501, 770-532-0958
Brooker, Dennis B., Rt. 1 Box 12A, Derby, IA, 50068
Churchill, Winston G., RFD Box 29B, Proctorsville, VT, 05153
Collins, Michael, Rt. 3075, Batesville Rd., Woodstock, GA, 30188
Cupp, Alana, PO Box 207, Annabella, UT, 84711
Dashwood, Jim, 255 Barkham Rd., Wokingham, Berkshire RG11 4BY, ENGLAND
Dean, Bruce, 13 Tressider Ave., Haberfield, N.S.W. 2045, Sydney, AUSTRALIA, 02 97977608
DeLorge, Ed, 6734 W Main St, Houma, LA, 70360, 504-223-0206
Dickson, John W., PO Box 49914, Sarasota, FL, 34230
Dolbare, Elizabeth, PO Box 502, Dubois, WY, 82513-0502
Downing, Jim, PO Box 4224, Springfield, MO, 65808, 417-865-5953, www.thegunengraver.com, Scrimshander
Duarte, Carlos, 108 Church St., Rossville, CA, 95678
Dubben, Michael, 414 S. Fares Ave., Evansville, IN, 47714
Dubber, Michael W., 8205 Heather Pl, Evansville, IN, 47710-4919
Eklund, Maihkel, Föne 1111, S-82041 Färila, SWEDEN, www.art-knives.com
Eldridge, Allan, 1424 Kansas Lane, Gallatin, TN, 37066
Ellis, Willy B, Willy B's Customs by William B Ellis, 4941 Cardinal Trail, Palm Harbor, FL, 34683, 727-942-6420, www.willyb.com
Engel, Terry (Flowers), PO Box 96, Midland, OR, 97634
Flannery Engraving Co., Jeff, 11034 Riddles Run Rd., Union, KY, 41091, engraving@fuse.net, http://home.fuse.net/ engraving/
Foster, Norvell, Foster Enterprises, PO Box 200343, San Antonio, TX, 78220
Fountain Products, 492 Prospect Ave., West Springfield, MA,

01089
Gipe, Sandi, Rt. 2, Box 1090A, Kendrick, ID, 83537
Glimm, Jerome C., 19 S. Maryland, Conrad, MT, 59425
Gournet, Geoffroy, 820 Paxinosa Ave., Easton, PA, 18042, 610-559-0710, www.geoffroygournet.com
Halloran, Tim 316 Fence line Dr. Blue Grass, IA 52726 563-381-5202
Harrington, Fred A., Winter: 3725 Citrus, Summer: 2107 W Frances Rd Mt Morris MI 48458-8215, St. James City, FL, 33956, Winter: 239-283-0721 Summer: 810-686-3008
Henderson, Fred D., 569 Santa Barbara Dr., Forest Park, GA, 30297, 770-968-4866
Hendricks, Frank, 396 Bluff Trail, Dripping Springs, TX, 78620, 512-858-7828
Holder, Pat, 7148 W. Country Gables Dr., Peoria, AZ, 85381
Ingle, Ralph W., 151 Callan Dr., Rossville, GA, 30741, 706-858-0641, riengraver@aol.com, Photographer
Johns, Bill, 1716 8th St, Cody, WY, 82414, 307-587-5090
Kelly, Lance, 1723 Willow Oak Dr., Edgewater, FL, 32132
Kelso, Jim, 577 Coller Hill Rd, Worcester, VT, 05682
Koevenig, Eugene and Eve, Koevenig's Engraving Service, Rabbit Gulch, Box 55, Hill City, SD, 57745-0055
Kostelnik, Joe and Patty, RD #4, Box 323, Greensburg, PA, 15601
Kudlas, John M., 55280 Silverwolf Dr, Barnes, WI, 54873, 715-795-2031, jkudlas@cheqnet.net, Engraver, scrimshander
Limings Jr., Harry, 959 County Rd. 170, Marengo, OH, 43334-9625
Lindsay, Steve, 3714 West Cedar Hills Drive, Kearney, NE, 68847
Lyttle, Brian, Box 5697, High River AB CANADA, T1V 1M7
Lytton, Simon M., 19 Pinewood Gardens, Hemel Hempstead, Herts. HP1 1TN, ENGLAND
Mason, Joe, 146 Value Rd, Brandon, MS, 39042, 601-824-9867, www.joemasonengraving.com
McCombs, Leo, 1862 White Cemetery Rd., Patriot, OH, 45658
McDonald, Dennis, 8359 Brady St., Peosta, IA, 52068
McKenzie, Lynton, 6940 N Alvernon Way, Tucson, AZ, 85718
McLean, Lawrence, 12344 Meritage Ct, Rancho Cucamonga, CA, 91739, 714-848-5779, lmclean@charter.net
Meyer, Chris, 39 Bergen Ave., Wantage, NJ, 07461, 973-875-6299
Minnick, Joyce, 144 N. 7th St., Middletown, IN, 47356
Morgan, Tandie, P.O. Box 693, 30700 Hwy. 97, Nucla, CO, 81424
Morton, David A., 1110 W. 21st St., Lorain, OH, 44052
Moulton, Dusty, 135 Hillview Ln, Loudon, TN, 37774, 865-408-9779
Muller, Jody & Pat, PO Box 35, Pittsburg, MO, 65724, 417-852-4306/417-752-3260, mullerforge@hotmail.com, www.mullerforge.com
Nelida, Toniutti, via G. Pasconi 29/c, Maniago 33085 (PN), ITALY
Nilsson, Jonny Walker, Tingsstigen 11, SE-933 33 Arvidsjaur, SWEDEN, +(46) 960-13048, 0960.13048@telia.com, www.jwnknives.com
Nott, Ron, Box 281, Summerdale, PA, 17093
Parsons, Michael R., McKee Knives, 7042 McFarland Rd, Indianapolis, IN, 46227, 317-784-7943
Patterson, W.H., P.O. Drawer DK, College Station, TX, 77841
Peri, Valerio, Via Meucci 12, Gardone V.T. 25063, ITALY
Pilkington Jr., Scott, P.O. Box 97, Monteagle, TN, 37356, 931-924-3400, scott@pilkguns.com, www.pilkguns.com
Poag, James, RR1, Box 212A, Grayville, IL, 62844
Potts, Wayne, 1580 Meade St Apt A, Denver, CO, 80204
Rabeno, Martin, Spook Hollow Trading Co, 530 Eagle Pass, Durango, CO, 81301
Raftis, Andrew, 2743 N. Sheffield, Chicago, IL, 60614
Roberts, J.J., 7808 Lake Dr., Manassas, VA, 20111, 703-330-0448, jjrengraver@aol.com, www.angelfire.com/va2/ engraver
Robidoux, Roland J., DMR Fine Engraving, 25 N. Federal Hwy. Studio 5, Dania, FL, 33004
Rosser, Bob, Hand Engraving, 2809 Crescent Ave Ste 20, Homewood, AL, 35209-2526, www.hand-engravers.com
Rudolph, Gil, 20922 Oak Pass Ave, Tehachapi, CA, 93561, 661-822-4949, www.gtraks@csurfers.net
Rundell, Joe, 6198 W. Frances Rd., Clio, MI, 48420
Schickl, L., Ottingweg 497, A-5580 Tamsweg, AUSTRIA, 0043 6474 8583, Scrimshander
Schlott, Harald, Zingster Str. 26, 13051 Berlin, GERMANY, 049 030 9293346, 049 030 9293346, harald.schlott@T-online.de, www.gravur-kunst-atelier.de.vu, Custom grinder, custom handle artisan, display case/box maker, etcher, scrimshander
Schönert, Elke, 18 Lansdowne Pl., Central, Port Elizabeth, SOUTH AFRICA
Shaw, Bruce, P.O. Box 545, Pacific Grove, CA, 93950, 831-646-1937, 831-644-0941
Shostle, Ben, 1121 Burlington, Muncie, IN, 47302
Slobodian, Barbara 4101 River Ridge Dr. PO Box 1498 San Adreas, CA 95249 209-286-1980
Smith, Ron, 5869 Straley, Ft. Worth, TX, 76114
Smitty's Engraving, 21320 Pioneer Circle, Hurrah, OK, 73045, 405-454-6968, smittys.engraving@prodigy.net, www.smittys-engraving.us
Spode, Peter, Tresaith Newland, Malvern, Worcestershire WR13 5AY, ENGLAND
Swartley, Robert D., 2800 Pine St., Napa, CA, 94558
Takeuchi, Shigetoshi, 21-14-1-Chome kamimuneoka Shiki shi, 353 Saitama, JAPAN
Theis, Terry, 21452 FM 2093, Harper, TX, 78631, 830-864-4438
Valade, Robert B., 931 3rd Ave., Seaside, OR, 97138, 503-738-7672, (503) 738-7672
Waldrop, Mark, 14562 SE 1st Ave. Rd., Summerfield, FL, 34491
Warenski, Julie, 590 East 500 N., Richfield, UT, 84701, 435-896-5319, julie@warenskiknives.com, www.warenskiknives.com
Warren, Kenneth W., P.O. Box 2842, Wenatchee, WA, 98807-2842, 509-663-6123, (509) 663-6123
Whitehead, James 2175 South Willow Ave. Space 22 Fresno, CA 93725 559-412-4374 jdwmks@yahoo.com
Whitmore, Jerry, 1740 Churchill Dr., Oakland, OR, 97462
Winn, Travis A., 558 E. 3065 S., Salt Lake City, UT, 84106
Wood, Mel, P.O. Box 1255, Sierra Vista, AZ, 85636
Zietz, Dennis, 5906 40th Ave., Kenosha, WI, 53144

etchers

Baron Technology Inc., David Baron, 62 Spring Hill Rd., Trumbull, CT, 06611
Fountain Products, 492 Prospect Ave., West Springfield, MA, 01089
Hayes, Dolores, P.O. Box 41405, Los Angeles, CA, 90041
Holland, Dennis, 4908 17th Pl., Lubbock, TX, 79416
Kelso, Jim, 577 Collar Hill Rd, Worcester, VT, 05682
Larstein, Francine, FRANCINE ETCHINGS & ETCHED KNIVES, 368 White Rd, Watsonville, CA, 95076, 800-557-1525/831-426-6046, 831-684-1949, francine@francinetchings.com, www.boyeknivesgallery.com
Lefaucheux, Jean-Victor, Saint-Denis-Le-Ferment, 27140 Gisors, FRANCE
Mead, Faustina L., 2550 E. Mercury St., Inverness, FL, 34453-0514, 352-344-4751, scrimsha@infionline.net, www.scrimshaw-by-faustina.com
Myers, Ron, 6202 Marglenn Ave., Baltimore, MD, 21206, (acid) etcher
Nilsson, Jonny Walker, Tingsstigen 11, SE-933 33 Arvidsjaur, SWEDEN, +(46) 960-13048, 0960.13048@telia.com, www.jwnknives.com
Schlott, Harald, Zingster Str. 26, 13051 Berlin, GERMANY, 049 030 9293346, harald.schlott@T-online.de, Custom grinder, custom handle artisan, display case/box maker, etcher, scrimshander
Vallotton, A., Northwest Knife Supply, 621 Fawn Ridge Dr., Oakland, OR, 97462
Watson, Silvia, 350 Jennifer Lane, Driftwood, TX, 78619

heat treaters

Bay State Metal Treating Co., 6 Jefferson Ave., Woburn, MA, 01801
Bos Heat Treating, Paul, Shop: 1900 Weld Blvd., El Cajon, CA, 92020, 619-562-2370 / 619-445-4740 Home, PaulBos@BuckKnives.com
Holt, B.R., 1238 Birchwood Drive, Sunnyvale, CA, 94089
Kazou, Okaysu, 12-2 1 Chome Higashi, Ueno, Taito-Ku, Tokyo, JAPAN, 81-33834-2323, 81-33831-3012
Metal Treating Bodycote Inc., 710 Burns St., Cincinnati, OH, 45204
O&W Heat Treat Inc., One Bidwell Rd., South Windsor, CT, 06074, 860-528-9239, (860) 291-9939, owht1@aol.com
Progressive Heat Treating Co., 2802 Charles City Rd, Richmond, VA, 23231, 804-545-0010, 804-545-0012
Texas Heat Treating Inc., 303 Texas Ave., Round Rock, TX, 78664
Texas Knifemakers Supply, 10649 Haddington, Suite 180, Houston, TX, 77043
Tinker Shop, The, 1120 Helen, Deer Park, TX, 77536
Valley Metal Treating Inc., 355 S. East End Ave., Pomona, CA, 91766
Wilderness Forge, 315 North 100 East, Kanab, UT, 84741, 435-644-3674, bhatting@xpressweb.com
Wilson, R.W., P.O. Box 2012, Weirton, WV, 26062

leather workers

Abramson, David, 116 Baker Ave, Wharton, NJ, 07885, lifter4him1@aol.com, www.liftersleather.com
Bruner, Rick, 7756 Aster Lane, Jenison, MI, 49428, 616-457-0403
Burrows, Chuck, dba Wild Rose Trading Co, 289 Laposta Canyon Rd, Durango, CO, 81303, 970-259-8396, chuck@wrtcleather.com
Clements' Custom Leathercraft, Chas, 1741 Dallas St., Aurora, CO, 80010-2018
Cooper, Harold, 136 Winding Way, Frankfort, KY, 40601
Cooper, Jim, 1221 Cook St, Ramona, CA, 92065-3214, 760-789-1097, 760-788-7992, jamcooper@aol.com
Cow Catcher Leatherworks, 3006 Industrial Dr, Raleigh, NC, 27609
Cubic, George, GC Custom Leather Co., 10561 E. Deerfield Pl., Tucson, AZ, 85749, 520-760-0695, gcubic@aol.com
Dawkins, Dudley, 221 N. Broadmoor Ave, Topeka, KS, 66606-1254, 785-235-3871, dawkind@sbcglobal.net, ABS member/knifemaker forges straight knives
Evans, Scott V, Edge Works Mfg, 1171 Halltown Rd, Jacksonville, NC, 28546, 910-455-9834, (910) 346-5660, edgeworks@coastalnet.com, www.tacticalholsters.com
Genske, Jay, 283 Doty St, Fond du Lac, WI, 54935, 920-921-8019/Cell Phone 920-579-0144, jaygenske@hotmail.com, Custom Grinder, Custom Handle Artisan
Hawk, Ken, Rt. 1, Box 770, Ceres, VA, 24318-9630
Homyk, David N., 8047 Carriage Ln., Wichita Falls, TX, 76306
John's Custom Leather, John R. Stumpf, 523 S. Liberty St, Blairsville, PA, 15717, 724-459-6802, 724-459-5996
Kelley, Jo Ann, Watertown, WI 53094, 920-206-0807 jkelleyleathers@yahoo.com
Kravitt, Chris, HC 31 Box 6484, Rt 200, Ellsworth, ME, 04605-9805, 207-584-3000, 207-584-3000, sheathmkr@aol.com, www.treestumpleather.com, Reference: Tree Stump Leather
Larson, Richard, 549 E. Hawkeye, Turlock, CA, 95380
Layton, Jim, 2710 Gilbert Avenue, Portsmouth, OH, 45662
Lee, Randy, P.O. Box 1873, 270 N 9th West, St. Johns, AZ, 85936, 928-337-2594, 928-337-5002, randylee@randyleeknives.com, info@randyleeknives.com, Custom knifemaker; www.randyleeknives.com
Long, Paul, 108 Briarwood Ln W, Kerrville, TX, 78028, 830-367-5536, kgebauer@classicnet.net
Mason, Arne, 258 Wimer St., Ashland, OR, 97520, 541-482-2260, (541) 482-7785, www.arnemason.com
McGowan, Liz, 12629 Howard Lodge Dr., Winter Add-2023 Robin Ct Sebring FL 33870, Sykesville, MD, 21784, 410-489-4323
Metheny, H.A. "Whitey", 7750 Waterford Dr., Spotsylvania, VA, 22553, 540-582-3228 Cell 540-542-1440, 540-582-3095, nametheny@aol.com, www.methenyknives.com
Miller, Michael K., 28510 Santiam Highway, Sweet Home, OR, 97386
Mobley, Martha, 240 Alapaha River Road, Chula, GA, 31733
Morrissey, Martin, 4578 Stephens Rd., Blairsville, GA, 30512
Niedenthal, John Andre, Beadwork & Buckskin, Studio 3955 NW 103 Dr., Coral Springs, FL, 33065-1551, 954-345-0447, a_niedenthal@hotmail.com
Neilson, Tess, RR2 Box 16, Wyalusing, PA, 18853, 570-746-4944, www.mountainhollow.net, Doing business as Neilson's Mountain Hollow
Parsons, Larry, 1038 W. Kyle, Mustang, OK 73064 405-376-9408 s.m.parsons@sbcglobal.net
Parsons, Michael R., McKee Knives, 7042 McFarland Rd, Indianapolis, IN, 46227, 317-784-7943
Poag, James H., RR #1 Box 212A, Grayville, IL, 62844
Red's Custom Leather, Ed Todd, 9 Woodlawn Rd., Putnam Valley, NY, 10579, 845-528-3783
Rowe, Kenny, 3219 Hwy 29 South, Hope, AR, 71801, 870-777-8216, 870-777-0935, rowesleather@yahoo.com, www.knifeart.com or www.theedgeequipment.com
Schrap, Robert G., 7024 W. Wells St., Wauwatosa, WI, 53213-3717, 414-771-6472, (414) 479-9765, knifesheaths@aol.com, www.customsheaths.com
Strahin, Robert, 401 Center St., Elkins, WV, 26241, *Custom Knife Sheaths
Tierney, Mike, 447 Rivercrest Dr., Woodstock ON CANADA, N4S 5W5
Turner, Kevin, 17 Hunt Ave., Montrose, NY, 10548
Velasquez, Gil, 7120 Madera Dr., Goleta, CA, 93117
Walker, John, 17 Laber Circle, Little Rock, AR, 72210, 501-455-0239, john.walker@afbic.com
Watson, Bill, #1 Presidio, Wimberly, TX, 78676
Whinnery, Walt, 1947 Meadow Creek Dr., Louisville, KY, 40218
Williams, Sherman A., 1709 Wallace St., Simi Valley, CA, 93065

miscellaneous

Hendryx Design, Scott, 5997 Smokey Way, Boise, ID, 83714, 208-377-8044, www.shdsheaths@msn.com
Kydex Sheath Maker
Robertson, Kathy, Impress by Design, PO Box 1367, Evans, GA, 30809-1367, 706-650-0982, (706) 860-1623, impressbydesign@comcast.net, Advertising/graphic designer
Strahin, Robert, 401 Center St., Elkins, WV, 26241, 304-636-0128, rstrahin@copper.net, *Custom Knife Sheaths

photographers

Alfano, Sam, 36180 Henery Gaines Rd., Pearl River, LA, 70452
Allen, John, Studio One, 3823 Pleasant Valley Blvd., Rockford, IL, 61114
Bilal, Mustafa, Turk's Head Productions, 908 NW 50th St., Seattle, WA, 98107-3634, 206-782-4164, (206) 783-5677, mustafa@turkshead.com, www.turkshead.com, Graphic design, marketing & advertising
Bogaerts, Jan, Regenweg 14, 5757 Pl., Liessel, HOLLAND
Box Photography, Doug, 1804 W Main St, Brenham, TX, 77833-3420
Brown, Tom, 6048 Grants Ferry Rd., Brandon, MS, 39042-8136
Butman, Steve, P.O. Box 5106, Abilene, TX, 79608
Calidonna, Greg, 205 Helmwood Dr., Elizabethtown, KY, 42701
Campbell, Jim, 7935 Ranch Rd., Port Richey, FL, 34668
Cooper, Jim, Sharpbycoop.com photography, 9 Mathew Court,

Norwalk, CT, 06851, jcooper@sharpbycoop.com, www.sharpbycoop.com
Courtice, Bill, P.O. Box 1776, Duarte, CA, 91010-4776
Crosby, Doug, RFD 1, Box 1111, Stockton Springs, ME, 04981
Danko, Michael, 3030 Jane Street, Pittsburgh, PA, 15203
Davis, Marshall B., P.O. Box 3048, Austin, TX, 78764
Earley, Don, 1241 Ft. Bragg Rd., Fayetteville, NC, 28305
Ehrlich, Linn M., 1850 N Clark St #1008, Chicago, IL, 60614, 312-209-2107
Etzler, John, 11200 N. Island Rd., Grafton, OH, 44044
Fahrner, Dave, 1623 Arnold St., Pittsburgh, PA, 15205
Faul, Jan W., 903 Girard St. NE, Rr. Washington, DC, 20017
Fedorak, Allan, 28 W. Nicola St., Amloops BC CANADA, V2C 1J6
Fox, Daniel, Lumina Studios, 6773 Industrial Parkway, Cleveland, OH, 44070, 440-734-2118, (440) 734-3542, lumina@en.com
Freiberg, Charley, PO Box 42, Elkins, NH, 03233, 603-526-2767, charleyfreiberg@tos.net
Gardner, Chuck, 116 Quincy Ave., Oak Ridge, TN, 37830
Gawryla, Don, 1105 Greenlawn Dr., Pittsburgh, PA, 15220
Goffe Photographic Associates, 3108 Monte Vista Blvd., NE, Albuquerque, NM, 87106
Graham, James, 7434 E Northwest Hwy, Dallas, TX, 75231, 214-341-5138, jamie@jamiephoto.com, www.jamiephoto.com, Product photographer
Graley, Gary W., RR2 Box 556, Gillett, PA, 16925
Griggs, Dennis, 118 Pleasant Pt Rd, Topsham, ME, 04086, 207-725-5689
Hanusin, John, Reames-Hanusin Studio, PO Box 931, Northbrook, IL, 60065 0931
Hardy, Scott, 639 Myrtle Ave., Placerville, CA, 95667
Hodge, Tom, 7175 S US Hwy 1 Lot 36, Titusville, FL, 32780-8172, 321-267-7989, egdoht@hotmail.com
Holter, Wayne V., 125 Lakin Ave., Boonsboro, MD, 21713, 301-416-2855, mackwayne@hotmail.com
Hopkins, David W, Hopkins Photography inc, 201 S Jefferson, Iola, KS, 66749, 620-365-7443, nhoppy@netks.net
Kerns, Bob, 18723 Birdseye Dr., Germantown, MD, 20874
LaFleur, Gordon, 111 Hirst, Box 1209, Parksville BC CANADA, V0R 270
Lear, Dale, 6544 Cora Mill Rd, Gallipolis, OH, 45631, 740-245-5482, dalelear@yahoo.com, Ebay Sales
LeBlanc, Paul, No. 3 Meadowbrook Cir., Melissa, TX, 75454
Lester, Dean, 2801 Junipero Ave Suite 212, Long Beach, CA, 90806-2140
Leviton, David A., A Studio on the Move, P.O. Box 2871, Silverdale, WA, 98383, 360-697-3452
Long, Gary W., 3556 Miller's Crossroad Rd., Hillsboro, TN, 37342
Long, Jerry, 402 E. Gladden Dr., Farmington, NM, 87401
Lum, Billy, 16307 Evening Star Ct., Crosby, TX, 77532
Lum, Mitch 4616 25th Ave. NE #563 Seattle, WA 98105 www.mitchlum.com mitch@mitchlum.com 206-356-6813
McCollum, Tom, P.O. Box 933, Lilburn, GA, 30226
Mitch Lum Website and Photography, 4616 25th Ave NE #563, Seattle, WA, 98105, mitch@mitchlum.com, www.mitchlum.com
Moake, Jim, 18 Council Ave., Aurora, IL, 60504
Moya Inc., 4212 S. Dixie Hwy., West Palm Beach, FL, 33405
Norman's Studio, 322 S. 2nd St., Vivian, LA, 71082
Owens, William T., Box 99, Williamsburg, WV, 24991
Palmer Studio, 2008 Airport Blvd., Mobile, AL, 36606
Payne, Robert G., P.O. Box 141471, Austin, TX, 78714
Pigott, John, 9095 Woodprint LN, Mason, OH, 45040
Point Seven, 810 Seneca St., Toledo, OH, 43608, 419-243-8880, www.pointsevenstudios.com
Rasmussen, Eric L., 1121 Eliason, Brigham City, UT, 84302
Rhoades, Cynthia J., Box 195, Clearmont, WY, 82835
Rice, Tim, PO Box 663, Whitefish, MT, 59937
Richardson, Kerry, 2520 Mimosa St., Santa Rosa, CA, 95405, 707-575-1875, kerry@sonic.net, www.sonic.net/~kerry
Ross, Bill, 28364 S. Western Ave. Suite 464, Rancho Palos Verdes, CA, 90275
Rubicam, Stephen, 14 Atlantic Ave., Boothbay Harbor, ME, 04538-1202
Rush, John D., 2313 Maysel, Bloomington, IL, 61701
Schreiber, Roger, 429 Boren Ave. N., Seattle, WA, 98109
Semmer, Charles, 7885 Cyd Dr., Denver, CO, 80221
Silver Images Photography, 2412 N Keystone, Flagstaff, AZ, 86004
Slobodian, Scott, 4101 River Ridge Dr., P.O. Box 1498, San Andreas, CA, 95249, 209-286-1980, (209) 286-1982, www.slobodianswords.com
Smith, Earl W., 5121 Southminster Rd., Columbus, OH, 43221
Smith, Randall, 1720 Oneco Ave., Winter Park, FL, 32789
Storm Photo, 334 Wall St., Kingston, NY, 12401
Surles, Mark, P.O. Box 147, Falcon, NC, 28342
Third Eye Photos, 140 E. Sixth Ave., Helena, MT, 59601
Thurber, David, P.O. Box 1006, Visalia, CA, 93279
Tighe, Brian, RR 1, Ridgeville ON CANADA, L0S 1M0, 905-892-2734, www.tigheknives.com
Towell, Steven L., 3720 N.W. 32nd Ave., Camas, WA, 98607, 360-834-9049, sltowell@netscape.net
Valley Photo, 2100 Arizona Ave., Yuma, AZ, 85364
Verno Studio, Jay, 3030 Jane Street, Pittsburgh, PA, 15203
Ward, Chuck, 1010 E North St, PO Box 2272, Benton, AR, 72018, 501-778-4329, chuckbop@aol.com
Weyer International, 2740 Nebraska Ave., Toledo, OH, 43607, 800-448-8424, (419) 534-2697, law-weyerinternational@msn.com, Books
Wise, Harriet, 242 Dill Ave., Frederick, MD, 21701
Worley, Holly, Worley Photography, 6360 W David Dr, Littleton, CO, 80128-5708, 303-257-8091, 720-981-2800, hsworley@aol.com, Products, Digital & Film

scrimshanders

Adlam, Tim, 1705 Witzel Ave., Oshkosh, WI, 54902, 920-235-4589, www.adlamngraving.com
Alpen, Ralph, 7 Bentley Rd., West Grove, PA, 19390, 610-869-7141
Anderson, Terry Jack, 10076 Birnamwoods Way, Riverton, UT, 84065-9073
Bailey, Mary W., 3213 Jonesboro Dr., Nashville, TN, 37214, mbscrim@aol.com, www.members.aol.com/mbscrim/ scrim.html
Baker, Duane, 2145 Alum Creek Dr., Cambridge Park Apt. #10, Columbus, OH, 43207
Barrows, Miles, 524 Parsons Ave., Chillicothe, OH, 45601
Brady, Sandra, P.O. Box 104, Monclova, OH, 43542, 419-866-0435, (419) 867-0656, sandyscrim@hotmail.com, www.knifeshows.com
Beauchamp, Gaetan, 125 de la Riviere, Stoneham, PQ, G0A 4P0, CANADA, 418-848-1914, (418) 848-6859, knives@gbeauchamp.ca, www.beauchamp.cjb.net
Bellet, Connie, PO Box 151, Palermo, ME, 04354 0151, 207-993-2327, phwhitehawk@gwl.net
Benade, Lynn, 2610 Buckhurst Dr, Beachwood, OH, 44122, 216-464-0777, llbnc17@aol.com
Bonshire, Benita, 1121 Burlington Dr., Muncie, IN, 47302
Boone Trading Co. Inc., P.O. Box 669, Brinnon, WA, 98320, 800-423-1945, ww.boonetrading.com
Bryan, Bob, 1120 Oak Hill Rd., Carthage, MO, 64836
Byrne, Mary Gregg, 1018 15th St., Bellingham, WA, 98225-6604
Cable, Jerry, 332 Main St., Mt. Pleasant, PA, 15666
Caudill, Lyle, 7626 Lyons Rd., Georgetown, OH, 45121
Cole, Gary, PO Box 668, Naalehu, HI, 96772, 808-929-9775, 808-929-7371, www.community.webshots.com/album/11836830uqyeejirsz

Collins, Michael, Rt. 3075, Batesville Rd., Woodstock, GA, 30188
Conover, Juanita Rae, P.O. Box 70442, Eugene, OR, 97401, 541-747-1726 or 543-4851, juanitaraeconover@yahoo.com
Courtnage, Elaine, Box 473, Big Sandy, MT, 59520
Cover Jr., Raymond A., Rt. 1, Box 194, Mineral Point, MO, 63660
Cox, J. Andy, 116 Robin Hood Lane, Gaffney, SC, 29340
Dietrich, Roni, Wild Horse Studio, 1257 Cottage Dr, Harrisburg, PA, 17112, 717-469-0587, ronimd@aol
DiMarzo, Richard, 2357 Center Place, Birmingham, AL, 35205
Dolbare, Elizabeth, PO Box 502, Dubois, WY, 82513-0502
Eklund, Maihkel, Föne 1111, S-82041 Färila, SWEDEN, +46 6512 4192, maihkel.eklund@swipnet.se, www.art-knives.com
Eldridge, Allan, 1424 Kansas Lane, Gallatin, TN, 37066
Ellis, Willy b, Willy B's Customs by William B Ellis, 4941 Cardinal Trail, Palm Harbor, FL, 34683, 727-942-6420, www.willyb.com
Fisk, Dale, Box 252, Council, ID, 83612, dafisk@ctcweb.net
Foster Enterprises, Norvell Foster, P.O. Box 200343, San Antonio, TX, 78220
Fountain Products, 492 Prospect Ave., West Springfield, MA, 01089
Gill, Scott, 925 N. Armstrong St., Kokomo, IN, 46901
Halligan, Ed, 14 Meadow Way, Sharpsburg, GA, 30277, ehkiss@bellsouth.net
Hands, Barry Lee, 26192 East Shore Route, Bigfork, MT, 59911
Hargraves Sr., Charles, RR 3 Bancroft, Ontario CANADA, K0L 1C0
Harless, Star, c/o Arrow Forge, P.O. Box 845, Stoneville, NC, 27048-0845
Harrington, Fred A., Summer: 2107 W Frances Rd, Mt Morris MI 48458 8215, Winter: 3725 Citrus, St. James City, FL, 33956, Winter 239-283-0721, Summer 810-686-3008
Hergert, Bob, 12 Geer Circle, Port Orford, OR, 97465, 541-332-3010, hergert@harborside.com, www.scrimshander.com
Hielscher, Vickie, 6550 Otoe Rd, P.O. Box 992, Alliance, NE, 69301, 308-762-4318, hielscher@premaonline.com
High, Tom, 5474 S. 112.8 Rd., Alamosa, CO, 81101, 719-589-2108, scrimshaw@vanion.com, www.rockymountainscrimshaw.com, Wildlife Artist
Himmelheber, David R., 11289 40th St. N., Royal Palm Beach, FL, 33411
Holland, Dennis K., 4908-17th Place, Lubbock, TX, 79416
Hutchings, Rick "Hutch", 3007 Coffe Tree Ct, Crestwood, KY, 40014, 502-241-2871, baron1@bellsouth.net
Imboden II, Howard L., 620 Deauville Dr., Dayton, OH, 45429, 937-439-1536, Guards by the "Last Wax Technic"
Johnson, Corinne, W3565 Lockington, Mindora, WI, 54644
Johnston, Kathy, W. 1134 Providence, Spokane, WA, 99205
Karst Stone, Linda, 903 Tanglewood Ln, Kerrville, TX, 78028-2945, 830-896-4678, 830-257-6117, karstone@ktc.com
Kelso, Jim, 577 Coller Hill Rd, Worcester, VT, 05682
Kirk, Susan B., 1340 Freeland Rd., Merrill, MI, 48637
Koevenig, Eugene and Eve, Koevenig's Engraving Service, Rabbit Gulch, Box 55, Hill City, SD, 57745-0055
Kostelnik, Joe and Patty, RD #4, Box 323, Greensburg, PA, 15601
Lemen, Pam, 3434 N. Iroquois Ave., Tucson, AZ, 85705
Martin, Diane, 28220 N. Lake Dr., Waterford, WI, 53185
McDonald, René Cosimini-, 14730 61 Court N., Loxahatchee, FL, 33470
McFadden, Berni, 2547 E Dalton Ave, Dalton Gardens, ID, 83815-9631
McGowan, Frank, 12629 Howard Lodge Dr., Winter Add-2023 Robin Ct Sebring FL 33870, Sykesville, MD, 21784, 863-385-1296
McGrath, Gayle, PMB 232 15201 N Cleveland Ave, N Ft Myers, FL, 33903
McLaran, Lou, 603 Powers St., Waco, TX, 76705
McWilliams, Carole, P.O. Box 693, Bayfield, CO, 81122
Mead, Faustina L., 2550 E. Mercury St., Inverness, FL, 34453-0514, 352-344-4751, scrimsha@infionline.net, www.scrimshaw-by-faustina.com
Mitchell, James, 1026 7th Ave., Columbus, GA, 31901
Moore, James B., 1707 N. Gillis, Stockton, TX, 79735
Ochonicky, Michelle "Mike", Stone Hollow Studio, 31 High Trail, Eureka, MO, 63025, 636-938-9570, www.bestofmissourihands.com
Ochs, Belle, 124 Emerald Lane, Largo, FL, 33771, 727-530-3826, chuckandbelle@juno.com, www.oxforge.com
Pachi, Mirella, Via Pometta 1, 17046 Sassello (SV), ITALY, 019 720086, WWW.PACHI-KNIVES.COM
Parish, Vaughn, 103 Cross St., Monaca, PA, 15061
Peterson, Lou, 514 S. Jackson St., Gardner, IL, 60424
Poag, James H., RR #1 Box 212A, Grayville, IL, 62844
Polk, Trena, 4625 Webber Creek Rd., Van Buren, AR, 72956
Purvis, Hilton, P.O. Box 371, Noordhoek, 7979, SOUTH AFFRIC, 27 21 789 1114, hiltonp@telkomsa.net, www.kgsa.co.za/member/hiltonpurvis
Ramsey, Richard, 8525 Trout Farm Rd, Neosho, MO, 64850
Ristinen, Lori, 14256 County Hwy 45, Menahga, MN, 56464, 218-538-6608, lori@loriristinen.com, www.loriristinen.com
Roberts, J.J., 7808 Lake Dr., Manassas, VA, 22111, 703-330-0448, jjrengraver@aol.com, www.angelfire.com/va2/ engraver
Rudolph, Gil, 20922 Oak Pass Ave, Tehachapi, CA, 93561, 661-822-4949, www.gtraks@csurfers.net
Rundell, Joe, 6198 W. Frances Rd., Clio, MI, 48420
Saggio, Joe, 1450 Broadview Ave. #12, Columbus, OH, 43212, 614-481-1967, jvsaggio@earthlink.net, www.j.v.saggio@worldnet.att.net
Sahlin, Viveca, Konstvaktarevagem 9, S-772 40 Grangesberg, SWEDEN, 46 240 23204, www.scrimart.use
Satre, Robert, 518 3rd Ave. NW, Weyburn SK CANADA, S4H 1R1
Schlott, Harald, Zingster Str. 26, 13051 Berlin, 929 33 46, GERMANY, 049 030 9293346, 049 030 9293346, harald.schlott@t-online.de, www.gravur-kunst-atelier.de.vu
Schulenburg, E.W., 25 North Hill St., Carrollton, GA, 30117
Schwallie, Patricia, 4614 Old Spartanburg Rd. Apt. 47, Taylors, SC, 29687
Selent, Chuck, P.O. Box 1207, Bonners Ferry, ID, 83805
Semich, Alice, 10037 Roanoke Dr., Murfreesboro, TN, 37129
Shostle, Ben, 1121 Burlington, Muncie, IN, 47302
Smith, Peggy, 676 Glades Rd., #3, Gatlinburg, TN, 37738
Smith, Ron, 5869 Straley, Ft. Worth, TX, 76114
Stahl, John, Images In Ivory, 2049 Windsor Rd., Baldwin, NY, 11510, 516-223-5007, imivory@msn.com, www.imagesinivory.org
Steigerwalt, Jim, RD#3, Sunbury, PA, 17801
Stuart, Stephen, 15815 Acorn Circle, Tavares, FL, 32778, 352-343-8423, (352) 343-8916, inkscratch@aol.com
Talley, Mary Austin, 2499 Countrywood Parkway, Memphis, TN, 38016, matalley@midsouth.rr.com
Thompson, Larry D., 23040 Ave. 197, Strathmore, CA, 93267
Toniutti, Nelida, Via G. Pascoli, 33085 Maniago-PN, ITALY
Trout, Lauria Lovestrand, 1555 Delaney Dr, No. 1723, Talahassee, FL, 32309, 850-893-8836, mayalaurie@aol.com
Tucker, Steve, 3518 W. Linwood, Turlock, CA, 95380
Tyser, Ross, 1015 Hardee Court, Spartanburg, SC, 29303
Velasquez, Gil, Art of Scrimshaw, 7120 Madera Dr., Goleta, CA, 93117
Wilderness Forge, 475 NE Smith Rock Way, Terrebonne, OR, 97760, bhatting@xpressweb.com
Williams, Gary, PO Box 210, Glendale, KY, 42740, 270-369-6752,

organizations

garywilliam@alltel.net
Winn, Travis A., 558 E. 3065 S., Salt Lake City, UT, 84106
Young, Mary, 4826 Storeyland Dr., Alton, IL, 62002

AMERICAN BLADESMITH SOCIETY
c/o Jan DuBois; PO Box 1481; Cypress, TX 77410-1481; 281-225-9159; Web: www.americanbladesmith.com

AMERICAN KNIFE & TOOL INSTITUTE***
David Kowalski, Comm. Coordinator, AKTI; DEPT BL2, PO Box 432, Iola, WI 54945-0432;715-445-3781; Web: communications@akti.org; www. akti.org

AMERICAN KNIFE THROWERS ALLIANCE
c/o Bobby Branton; 4976 Seewee Rd; Awendaw, SC 29429; www.AKTA-USA.com

ARIZONA KNIFE COLLECTOR'S ASSOCIATION
c/o D'Alton Holder, President, 7148 W. Country Gables Dr., Peoria, AZ 85381; Web: www.akca.net

ART KNIFE COLLECTOR'S ASSOCIATION
c/o Mitch Weiss, Pres.; 2211 Lee Road, Suite 104; Winter Park, FL 32789

BAY AREA KNIFE COLLECTOR'S ASSOCIATION
Doug Isaacson, B.A.K.C.A. Membership, 36774 Magnolia, Newark, CA 94560; Web: www.bakca.org

ARKANSAS KNIFEMAKERS ASSOCIATION
David Etchieson, 60 Wendy Cove, Conway, AR 72032; Web: www.arkansasknifemakers.com

AUSTRALASIAN KNIFE COLLECTORS
PO BOX 149 CHIDLOW 6556 WESTERN AUSTRALIA TEL: (08) 9572 7255; FAX: (08) 9572 7266. International Inquiries: TEL: + 61 8 9572 7255; FAX: + 61 8 9572 7266; akc@knivesaustralia.com.au

CALIFORNIA KNIFEMAKERS ASSOCIATION
c/o Clint Breshears, Membership Chairman; 1261 Keats St; Manhattan Beach CA 90266; 310-372-0739; breshears@mindspring.com
Dedicated to teaching and improving knifemaking

CANADIAN KNIFEMAKERS GUILD
c/o Peter Wile; RR # 3; Bridgewater N.S. CANADA B4V 2W2; 902-543-1373; www.ckg.org

CUTTING EDGE, THE
1920 N 26th St; Lowell AR 72745; 479-631-0055; 479-636-4618; ce-info@cuttingedge.com
After-market knives since 1968. We offer about 1,000 individual knives each month. The oldest and the most experienced in the business of buying and selling knives. We buy collections of any size, take knives on consignment or we will trade. Web: www.cuttingedge.com

FLORIDA KNIFEMAKERS ASSOCIATION
c/o President, Dan Mink, PO Box 861, Crystal beach, Florida, 34681 (727) 786 5408; Web: www.floridaknifemakers.org

JAPANESE SWORD SOCIETY OF THE U.S.
PO Box 712; Breckenridge, TX 76424

KNIFE COLLECTORS CLUB INC, THE
1920 N 26th St; Lowell AR 72745; 479-631-0130; 479-631-8493; ag@agrussell.com; Web:www.club@k-c-c.com
The oldest and largest association of knife collectors. Issues limited edition knives, both handmade and highest quality production, in very limited numbers. The very earliest was the CM-1, Kentucky Rifle

KNIFE WORLD
PO Box 3395; Knoxville, TN 37927; 800-828-7751; 865-397-1955; 865-397-1969; knifepub@knifeworld.com
Publisher of monthly magazine for knife enthusiasts and world's largest knife/cutlery bookseller. Web: www.knifeworld.com

KNIFEMAKERS GUILD
c/o Beverly Imel, Knifemakers Guild, Box 922, New Castle, IN 47362; (765) 529-1651; Web: www.knifemakersguild.com

KNIFEMAKERS GUILD OF SOUTHERN AFRICA, THE
c/o Carel Smith; PO Box 1744; Delmars 2210; SOUTH AFRICA; carelsmith@therugby.co.za; Web:www.kgsa.co.za

KNIVES ILLUSTRATED
265 S. Anita Dr., Ste. 120; Orange, CA 92868; 714-939-9991; 714-939-9909; knivesillustrated@yahoo.com; Web:www.knivesillustrated.com
All encompassing publication focusing on factory knives, new handmades, shows and industry news, plus knifemaker features, new products, and travel pieces

MONTANA KNIFEMAKERS' ASSOCIATION, THE
14440 Harpers Bridge Rd; Missoula, MT 59808; 406-543-0845
Annual book of custom knife makers' works and directory of knife making supplies; $19.99

NATIONAL KNIFE COLLECTORS ASSOCIATION
PO Box 21070; Chattanooga, TN 37424; 423-892-5007; 423-899-9456; info@nationalknife.org; Web: www.nationalknife.org

NEO-TRIBAL METALSMITHS
PO Box 44095; Tucson, AZ 85773-4095; Web: www.neo-tribalmetalsmiths.com

NEW ENGLAND CUSTOM KNIFE ASSOCIATION
George R. Rebello, President; 686 Main Rd; Brownville, ME 04414; Web: www.knivesby.com/necka.html

NORTH CAROLINA CUSTOM KNIFEMAKERS GUILD
c/o 2112 Windy Woods Drive, Raleigh, NC 27607 (919) 834-4693; Web: www.ncknifeguild.org

NORTH STAR BLADE COLLECTORS
PO Box 20523, Bloomington, MN 55420

OHIO KNIFEMAKERS ASSOCIATION
c/o Jerry Smith, Anvils and Ink Studios, P.O. Box 7887, Columbus, Ohio 43229-7887; Web: www.geocities.com/ohioknives/

OREGON KNIFE COLLECTORS ASSOCIATION
Web: www.oregonknifeclub.org

RANDALL KNIFE SOCIETY
PO Box 158, Meadows of Dan, VA 24120 email: payrks@gate.net; Web: www.randallknifesociety.com

ROCKY MOUNTAIN BLADE COLLECTORS ASSOCIATION
Mike Moss. Pres., P.O. Box 324, Westminster, CO 80036

RESOURCE GUIDE AND NEWSLETTER / AUTOMATIC KNIVES
2269 Chestnut St., Suite 212; San Francisco, CA 94123; 415-731-0210; Web: www.thenewsletter.com

SOUTH CAROLINA ASSOCIATION OF KNIFEMAKERS
c/o Victor Odom, Jr., Post Office Box 572, North, SC 29112
(803) 247-5614; Web: www.scak.org

SOUTHERN CALIFORNIA BLADES
SC Blades, PO Box 1140, Lomita, CA 90717; Web: www.scblades.com

TEXAS KNIFEMAKERS & COLLECTORS ASSOCIATION
2254 Fritz Allen Street, Fort Worth, Texas 76114; Web: www.tkca.org

TACTICAL KNIVES
Harris Publications; 1115 Broadway; New York, NY 10010; Web: www.tacticalknives.com

TRIBAL NOW!
Neo-Tribal Metalsmiths; PO Box 44095; Tucson, AZ 85733-4095; Web: www.neo-tribalmetalsmiths.com

WEYER INTERNATIONAL BOOK DIVISION
2740 Nebraska Ave; Toledo, OH 43607-3245; Web: www.weyerinternational.com

publications

BLADE
700 E. State St., Iola, WI 54990-0001; 715-445-2214; Web: www.blademag.com
The world's No. 1 knife magazine.

KNIFE WORLD
PO Box 3395, Knoxville, TN 37927; www.knifeworld.com

KNIVES ILLUSTRATED
265 S. Anita Dr., Ste. 120, Orange, CA 92868; 714-939-9991; knivesillustrated@yahoo.com; Web: www.knivesillustrated.com
All encompassing publication focusing on factory knives, new handmades, shows and industry news

RESOURCE GUIDE AND NEWSLETTER / AUTOMATIC KNIVES
2269 Chestnut St., Suite 212, San Francisco, CA 94123; 415-731-0210; Web: www.thenewsletter.com

TACTICAL KNIVES
Harris Publications, 1115 Broadway, New York, NY 10010; Web: www.tacticalknives.com

WEYER INTERNATIONAL BOOK DIVISION
2740 Nebraska Ave., Toledo, OH 43607-3245